BATTLESPACE

OF
MIND

MICHAEL J. MCCARRON

Published by:
Trine Day LLC
PO Box 577
Walterville, OR 97489
1-800-556-2012
www.TrineDay.com
TrineDay@icloud.com

Library of Congress Control Number: 2023952279
McCarron, Michael J.
–1st ed.
p. cm.
Epub (ISBN-13) 978-1-63424-425-1
Trade Paperback (ISBN-13) 978-1-63424-424-4
1. Decision making. 2.Cyberterrorism. 3. Weapons of Mass Disruption. 4. Social media Political aspects. 5. Asymmetric warfare Moral and ethical aspects. 6.Terrorism Prevention Moral and ethical aspects. 7. Information warfare I.McCarron, Michael J. II. Title

First Edition
10 9 8 7 6 5 4 3 2 1

Printed in the USA
Distribution to the Trade by:
Independent Publishers Group (IPG)
814 North Franklin Street
Chicago, Illinois 60610
312.337.0747
www.ipgbook.com

Publisher's Foreword

Sticks and stones may break my bones,
But words shall never hurt me.

– English-language children's rhyme

Big Daddy: *What's that smell in this room? Didn't you notice it, Brick? Didn't you notice a powerful and obnoxious odor of mendacity in this room? There ain't nothin' more powerful than the odor of mendacity. You can smell it. It smells like death.* Brick: *Mendacity is a system that we live in. Liquor is one way out an' death's the other."*

– Tennessee Williams, *Cat on a Hot Tin Roof* (1958)

You have meddled with the primal forces of nature, Mr. Beale, and I won't have it! … You are an old man who thinks in terms of nations and peoples. There are no nations. There are no peoples. There are no Russians. There are no Arabs. There are no third worlds. There is no West. There is only one holistic system of systems, one vast and inane, interwoven, interacting, multivariate, multinational dominion of dollars. Petro-dollars, electro-dollars, multi-dollars, reichmarks, rins, rubles, pounds, and shekels. It is the international system of currency which determines the totality of life on this planet. That is the natural order of things today.… There is no America. There is no democracy. There is only IBM, and ITT, and AT&T, and DuPont, Dow, Union Carbide, and Exxon. Those are the nations of the world today. What do you think the Russians talk about in their councils of state, Karl Marx? They get out their linear programming charts, statistical decision theories, minimax solutions, and compute the price-cost probabilities of their transactions and investments, just like we do. We no longer live in a world of nations and ideologies, Mr. Beale. The world is a college of corporations, inexorably determined by the immutable bylaws of business. The world is a business, Mr. Beale. It has been since man crawled out of the slime. And our children will live, Mr. Beale, to see that... perfect world... in which there's no war or famine, oppression or brutality. One vast and ecumenical holding company, for whom all men will work to serve a common profit, in which all men will hold a share of stock. All necessities provided, all anxieties tranquilized, all boredom amused. And I have chosen you, Mr. Beale, to preach this evangel.

Paddy Chayefsky, *Network* (1976)

We are born, go to schools, get educated and edified … and then thrown to the wolves. Michael J. McCarron's timely research gives us heads-up about the "Sirens" that are singing to befuddle us. *BattleSpace of the Mind: AI, Cybernetics and Information Warfare* is a book of immense importance in helping us understand our contentious contemporaneous experiences. Covering many different intellectual disciplines, Michael leads the reader into the arcane realms of quantam physics, propaganda, persuasion and meme warfare. Delving into many new techniques that have been and are being developed to divide us, dominate our conversations and infect our *Zeitgeist* with calculated contentions.

This book is so important that the book is available for free via PDF. The book and extra appendices are available at the author's web archive: https://github.com/autonomous019/Battlespace-of-Mind.

Onward to the Utmost of Futures,
Peace,
RA "Kris" Millegan
Publisher
TrineDay
January 11, 2024

All this was inspired by the principle – which is quite true within itself – that in the big lie there is always a certain force of credibility; because the broad masses of a nation are always more easily corrupted in the deeper strata of their emotional nature than consciously or voluntarily; and thus in the primitive simplicity of their minds they more readily fall victims to the big lie than the small lie, since they themselves often tell small lies in little matters but would be ashamed to resort to large-scale falsehoods.

It would never come into their heads to fabricate colossal untruths, and they would not believe others could have the impudence to distort the truth so infamously. Even though the facts which prove this to be so may be brought clearly to their minds, they will still doubt and waver and will continue to think there may be some other explanation. For the grossly impudent lie always leaves traces behind it, even after it has been nailed down, a fact which is known to all expert liars in this world and to all who conspire together in the art of lying.

– Adolf Hitler, *Mein Kampf*, vol. I, ch. X

Dr. Ramani Durvasula: Repetition is important, because the Big Lie works through indoctrination. The Big Lie then becomes its own evidence base – if it is repeated enough, people believe it, and the very repetition almost tautologically becomes the support for the Lie. ... Hear something enough it becomes truth. People assume there is an evidence base when the lie is big (it's like a blind spot). ... [People also fail to realize] that there are people in our midst that lack empathy, have no care for the common good, are grandiose, arrogant, and willing to exploit and manipulate people for solely their own egocentric needs. ... [Instead] a sort of halo effect imbues leaders with presumed expertise and power – when that is not at all the case (most if not all megalomaniacal leaders, despots, tyrants, oligarchs share narcissism/psychopathy as a trait)....

It was easier to dislodge untruths before social media. In social media, people tend to take public positions. When that position turns out to be wrong, it's embarrassing. And backing down is typically seen as weakness. So they double-down on untrue claims to save face and personal credibility. ... We are way too emotionally attached to being right. It would be better for our culture as a whole to value uncertainty and intellectual humility and curiosity. Those values help us ask questions without the expectation of permanent answe

– Rozsa, Matthew (February 3, 2021)
"The psychological reason that so many fall for the 'Big Lie,'" *Salon*

TABLE OF CONTENTS

INTRODUCTION

This book is an investigation into cybernetics, automation, AI, cognitive science and physics for the purposes of Information Warfare. Specifically, focusing on the particular area of using neurocognitive science for the purposes of conducting warfare in the battlespace of the mind, information warfare targeting the psyche known as neuroweapons, a biological weapon.

It is a part of cybersecurity studies as it relates to the cybernetics-- the control of both machine and animals, in the case of animals using computer based algorithms to influence biological objects. The primary target is the human brain, using scientific technology to alter human organisms and functionality, which is to say human behavior.

This book is intended as a technical reference to help researchers, engineers, physicists, software engineers, doctors and others interested in the use of technology in the pursuit of Information Warfare, it is also of interest to those that are part of the Targeted Individuals community in an effort to understand the exact nature of the technology that may be affecting common citizens that have no role in the Military or Intelligence Communities. Each chapter of this work can be read independently or in succession, each chapter addresses a particular technological aspect of Information Warfare. This work is not intended as a general overview of 'Mind Control' as others have already provided such high level discussions of remote influencing in Information Warfare, such as Krishnan.

In the pages that follow the reader will find general information regarding the subjects of Cybersecurity and Information Warfare along with more specific and very technical discussions of how this technology functions and the scientific theories behind this technology. I begin with a brief on the sociology of far-right German society with particular focus on Nazi Germany and it's successor the Black International. Then move into a discussion of Information Warfare, followed by defining what Neuroweapons are and how they function and the progression through both Soviet and Nazi science of altering human biology to achieve political goals. These first three chapters are lessons in the history of science on human modification. Chapter 4 jumps from the distant past to technology developed by an American engineer, Dr. John Norseen, during the 1990s to early 2000s which introduces the key concepts that are addressed in the remaining chapter, most of which are technical discussions of the subjects addressed in Norseen's work. Following up on the topic of Cybernetics from Norseen's work the next chapter goes into the use of computers in control systems, which is what cybernetics is, remote influencing and cybernetics are dual sciences with regard to Information Warfare. This is followed by a discussion of the physics behind neuroweapons with an emphasis on the use of Gravitational based technology to induce Electromagnetic effects in the human body, the use of gravitational tech is a major distinction in this work from the works of others and answers some of the criticisms of the ideal of Remote Influencing which is usually related to EM waves (such as microwaves), the use of Gravitational Waves shows how those criticisms can be discarded. This is followed by a stand-alone chapter on the history of Radar, and addresses how radar is used in remote influencing. The next chapter is a technical discussion of Quantum Physics and Consciousness with special attention to the science cited by Dr. John Norseen. Chapter 9 goes into this technology as it relates to Havana Syndrome and provides insights into countermeasures against this technology and the science behind those countermeasures which are attributed to the research of Dr. Michael Persinger. Chapter 10 delves into the use of Hypnosis in Warfare paying attention to physiology in hypnosis and the brain centers impacted by hypnosis. The final chapter goes into the development of this technology by the US and UK including the use of computer automation in pursuit of Information Warfare.

THREAT ANALYSIS:

Since the end of World War I, the study of EM and Gravitational Waves for the purpose of information warfare has been pursued by global strategic players such as the Nazi Regime in Germany, the USSR, and NATO alliance, while also pursued by the Peoples Republic of China (PRC), while keeping in mind the only country not to ratify treaties banning biological weapons with the technical resources to do it, is Israel (ACA, 2018), which also has a history of conducting espionage against allies like the United States and has recruited many ex-Soviet engineers and is a society based in ethno-religious supremacy (HRW, 2021). State actors are not the only ones that could have this capability as it is available on the black market, as well as any small technically outfitted terrorist group could also accomplish this technology. Indeed, the roots of political deception are found in the intoxication tactics of the authoritarian 4th Reich inspired Black International.

The threat of using EM and Gravitoelectromagnetic weapons, of which Aharonov-Bohm (A-B) effect is a party to, was encountered primarily in the 1980s in the USSR. Soviet military-industrial research focused on 'remote biological effects' or remote (non-local, entanglement) influencing using A-B generators designed initially by Akimov (Kernbach, 2017) from at least around 1986. Later his research associate AV Bobrov experimented with using LEDs (lasers) with modulated pulsed rhythms for the same purpose. Previous to this Soviet research also focused on using gravitational waves for the purposes of non-local influence, possibly also involving the proposed Gravitational Aharonov-Bohm effect. After the fall of the Soviet Union Soviet researchers were brought to the west to be debriefed, for instance one remote influencing researcher Dr. Okhtarin was interviewed by the CIA regarding his research into remote influencing using the Aharonov-Bohm effect. In western parlance remote influencing is known as "remote action." When the Russians came west they were employed by Lockheed-Martin to collaborate with their engineers, such as Dr. John Norseen who invented 'Bio-Fusion' and 'Thought-Injection' technology based on previous Soviet inventions. It is also worth noting that this technology is available on the black market according to Dr. Kernbach. Incidents in the Soviet Union targeting the US Embassy using this technology are well documented. And recently the Havana US Embassy incident implicated the use of remote influencing technology as the source of the medical problems encountered by embassy staff (Verma et al, 2019) .

This work is organized into the following chapters:

CHAPTER 1 – THE BLACK INTERNATIONAL

This chapter covers the history of Military Intelligence in Weimar Germany leading to the founding of the Nazi State through the use of military intelligence of the far-right military leaders of Germany, such as Luddendorf and von Luttwitz, from which Hitler was recruited as a military intelligence agent before joining the NSDAP ("Nazis"). There is a historical development in Germanic society of powerful merchants influencing the overall society. I trace out the history of the Hanseatic League and how powerful trade guilds have always influenced German society, including the founding of the Nazi state through the Keppler Circle and Harzburg front. The history of the German far-right leadership in the military (Reichswehr) is addressed and the relationship between powerful Generals such as Baron Von Luttwitz and Luddendorf and that of the attempts to overthrow by armed insurrection of the Weimar Republic such as the Kapp Putsch and Beer Hall Putsch is reviewed as well as the significance of a far-right militia the Black Reichswehr in these attempted putsches and the eventual founding of the Nazi state. The Reichswehr also engineered the infiltration and intoxication of the German far-right parties, with special attention to the role of Adolf Hitler in these infiltrations.

After these initial explorations of the development leading to the Nazi State the concept of the 4th Reich is addressed under the leadership of the chief of the Nazi SS, Himmler, who planned on rebuilding the Nazi movement after it's military defeat. A discussion hearkening back to the background of the Hanseatic Leagues is the role of rich German industrialists in this scheme as well as the role of the banking interests of the City of London-Hamburg axis which were also seen in the Harzburg Front.

A side journey is taken to understand the relationship of far-right military organizations on the international scene with the discussion of the attempted overthrow of FDR by rich Anglo-Saxon supremacists of the United States, the financiers of international fascism, such as J.P. Morgan and others. This is followed on by a discussion of the founding of the CIA through far-right intermediaries such as Bill Donovan and the role of British intelligence in this founding with special attention to the influence of a Nazi spy within British intelligence that advised fellow fascist Bill Donovan on how to conduct a secret intelligence organization.

All of this concludes with the discussion of what is known as the Black International, a 4th Reich experiment at creating fascist states to replace fascist Germany. This fascist terrorist network was headed up by SS officer Otto

Skorzeny, who was appointed by Himmler to develop this network. The main techniques of the Black International is discussed such as Action Psychologie, which included such concepts of intoxication-- conducting mind poisoning operations, infiltration, false flag ops, military deception and the very important 'strategy of tension'-- the promotion of conflict between different social groups.

CHAPTER 2 – INFORMATION WARFARE, PSYOPS, AND INFORMATION OPERATIONS

This chapter provides a definition of what Information Operations (IO) are in Information Warfare (IW). There are specific definitions and elements as defined by the US DoD Joint Chiefs of Staff that are considered part of IO. There are 6 major elements of IW covered in this chapter:

I. Information Operations (IO)
II. Electronic Warfare (EW)
III. Computer Network Operations (CNO)
IV. Psychological Operations (PSYOPS)
V. Military Deception (MILDEC)
VI. Operational Security (OPSEC)

I pay special attention to PSYOPS in this chapter it is important to understand the history of PSYOPS or what is contemporarily known as Military Support Information Operations (MISO) in current military documentation. The history of the development of the theories behind PSYOPS was first made in America after the first world war, with the works of Lasswell and Lippman. From these early theoretical contributions came later in the 1990s the military theorist Col. Richard Szafranski's concept of 'Neo-cortical Warfare' which presaged the ideals of Neuroweapons. Col. John Boyd's work in expanding on Szafranski's work is also addressed, where expeditious action is introduced into neo-cortical warfare, the battle for ever faster decision processes that lead to using machines for that purpose. Also covered is the technique of using Neuro-Linguistic Programming inspired Narrative Networks, using narratives to influence cognition. The speed needed to effectively conduct Neo-cortical Warfare is addressed in the Brain Computer Interface section where we start to see how the joining of computers with minds in IW is a critical part of effective IW.

CHAPTER 3 – NEUROWEAPONS

This chapter reviews the terminology associated with Neuroweapons and it's history of development. Neuroweapons development begins in the early Soviet Union just after WWI with the early work of Bekhterov, Vasiliev and Kazhinsky, all working in Russia. While at the same time early work was also begun in post-war Wiemar Germany by Von Ardenne. To understand the developments in Neuroweapons one has to understand the beginnings of authoritarian psychology in Germany began and the influence of German psychology and the influence of Nazi ideology on early German psychological researchers. Hence I trace out the development from Wundt centered on the University of Leipzig and his students, who later became attached and engaged with the Nazi movement such as Krueger, who led Wundt's experimental center after Wundt retired, also covered are psychologists Sanders and parapsychologist Hans Bender. We also study another medical aspect of Nazi Germany that involving the use of Genetic Engineering to achieve political goals, aiming to re-invent the supreme race using technology to mold human biology into an obedient state citizenship under central control. I detail the work of such early genetic engineering in Germany in the works of Butenandt, Von Verschuer, Mengele and Magnusson where perverse experiments in human biological manipulation were carried out showing the extent of the use of biological modification to create the perfect Nazi regime.

Another part of this chapter covers the development of molecular biology at the Kaiser Wilhelm Institute Berlin Brain Institute, involving the early founders of molecular biology, which is also directly related to genetic and biological modification of the citizenry. The KWI Brain Institute was notably the place where the greats of molecular biology worked together: Delbruck, Zimmer, Timofeeff-Ressovsky, and Pascual Jordan, the physicist. A timeline of Zimmer's involvment is reviewed as he was taken with other leading molecular biologists and Nazi Nuclear Program veterans to the Soviet Union as prison-labor to work on the Soviet nuclear program after WWII.

Another key aspect of Nazi weapons development was the creation of what was an early prototypical Remote Viewing program, the ability to use telepathy to gather information on remote targets. The creation of the Nazi remote viewing program is reviewed focusing on the contribution of Reichskreig (Navy) Submarine Captain Roader, with the collaboration of a famous German astrologer and psychic Straniak headquartered at a secret Reichskrieg lab in Berlin.

CHAPTER 4 – LESSONS FROM AN AMERICAN WEAPONS DEVELOPERS

Chapter 4 leap frogs early remote influencing operations of the United States such as Project Monarch and MK-Ultra, which have been extensively written about by others, see Krishnan (2017). Skipping ahead to the technological driven methods of the 1990s. This chapter does a dive into the work of Lockheed-Martin weapons developer Dr. John Norseen (Lt. US Navy, retired). Dr. Norseen developed American copies of Soviet Psychological Warfare programs using the same methodologies and technological approaches, this chapter studies those methodologies for altering human consciousness and physiology using technology.

I cover some of the key concepts used by Dr. Norseen to develop his 'anti-terrorism' thought injection. Semiotics, the science of signs, covers the topics of Biofusion, semiotics is a linguistic term borrowed here to refer to the images of the mind. A discussion of some of the brain areas affected by 'thought injection': TC-22 (Temporal Cortex) and Broadmann's Area 44, the Broca Area and it's connection to the Wernicke area, the Inferior Frontal Gyrus (IFG), these are further developed in Chapter 9. The use of reflexive control (RC) is brought up by Norseen in relation to his weaponization of neurotechnology, the use of RC is directly tied to neuroweapons by Soviet scientists and is carried on here by Norseen. A fuller discussion of Reflexive Control is in Chapter 5. A discussion of Semiotics and Quantum Consciousness as discussed by Norseen in his correpondences and publications is reviewed, a detailed discussion of Quantum Consciousness is provided in Chapter 8. The discussion in this chapter focuses on the use of Norseen of the ideals of Nobel Laureate Sir Dr. Roger Penrose and Dr. Stuart Hameroff of the University of Arizona related to the gravitational collapse of the quantum state believed to be used in the brain giving the formation of 'consciousness' through the brain's network of microtubules (MTs).

Cyber Semiotics is then discussed which relates the use of Cybernetics, the study of controllers, and using semiotics as a means of control. A further elucidation in cyber semiotics is brought up in a discussion of semiotic diplomatic cybernetics, using this technology and RC with automated processes in cybernetics to develop RC in international, national and local politics.

The final discussion relates to the utilization of hormones, neurotransmitters, found in the human body, which are used to 'control' a human. The use of Tetrahydroisoquinoline THIQ is also addressed as brought forward by Dr. Norseen. A brief mention is made of the apocalyptic world view of Dr. Norseen brings this chapter to a close.

CHAPTER 5 – COMPUTATION, CYBERNETICS AND CONTROL

Few who use hand held devices today would recognize their origin in warfare, that is, that the development of computer technology is directly related to the efforts of both the Allies and Axis powers to develop more efficient killing systems. Later, the development of efficient machines to run weapons systems merges with operations research leading to cybernetics. Which form a trinity of specializations from the Soviets of Reflexive Control, Computation and Cybernetics. This chapter covers the development of the modern computer as well as it's corollary of Cybernetics, the study of control in machines and animals with an eye toward it's utilization in Reflexive Control.

The first discussion is that of the History of Computers by tracing the contributions of the two chief developers of computers one in the UK, one in Germany, for the UK Alan Turing working at Blechley for the precursor to GCHQ, Britian's NSA. The other for Germany a wiz kid who started his own computing company after being called up to service by the German state and funded by the Deutsche Versuchsanstalt für Luftfahrt (DVL; German Research Institute for Aviation). One developing further the "Bombe" to crack German codes, the other developing the 'Z2' used to calculate wing spans for German missiles. A further discussion is brought forth involving the post-war relationship of UKUSA and German computer engineers, with special mention of the contributions of German Heinz Billing.

Our journey into the combination of intelligence with computation takes us to the most developed Intelligence Force on earth in the mid-20th century, that of the British Empire. The next discussion topic is that of the history of computing in the war against the various factions of the "Irish Republican Army." For which some in the Irish Republican community have charged the British with using automated psyops against them during the Troubles, intoxication and infiltration operations. The use of machines in policing or occupying Ireland is studied and it's development into full automation is discussed.

Development of Operations Research led to what we know as Cybernetics, which is further elucidated in the British Operations Researcher Stafford Beers and his theories on cybernetics and automated systems to achieve homeostasis in socio-economic terms. A discussion of 'cybersyn' designed by Beers to run the state of Chile is discussed, which came to an end in the hands of the fascist dictatorship of Pinochet.

An extensive discussion of Reflexive Control is brought forward with special awareness toward Cybernetics and RC. The beginning of RC comes from the Soviets with the advent of a Soviet military computer engineer. Col. V. Lefebvre creating a computerized version of Reflexive Control. Later, after the fall of the Soviets, Lefebvre came to America and taught the US Intelligence Community the methodologies of RC as developed by the Soviets. A discussion of the computational rules of RC are gone over, as well as such topics as: situational awareness and management; AI Decision Aides and automated decision making; fast reflexion- hijacking the amygdala for automated control; RC Games-- the use of game theoretic systems for RC by researcher Novikov. Cognitive RC-- the use of cognitive mapping of adversaries in conflict; Novikov's Mob control using RC; Tarasenko's Reflexive Robots-- use of robots in networks of humans to influence humans.

CHAPTER 6 – PHYSICS OF NEUROWEAPONS

This chapter addresses the physics behind remote influencing technology focusing on the use of Gravitational Waves (GW) and Gravitoelectromagnetics (GEM). One of the contentious areas of claims regarding remote influencing is that it is usually explained via Electromagnetics (EM) alone, usually associating the tech with microwaves. However, according to my research as presented in this chapter the real basis of this technology is GW which cannot be blocked by anything aside from another gravitational field, see Chapter 9. This association of remote influencing or monitoring technology with GW is seen by the Soviet attempts to use GW to control animals. In Gravitational Basis of Neuroweapons, focuses on the development in Russia of gravitational wave based technology for control of animals by Bunin in 1972, further goes into the history of ideals of Soviet researcher Dubrov, who advocated for a gravitational basis of remote influencing. In Modern Theories of Gravity and Remote Sensing, the research of Dr. Michael Persinger who researches the effect of gravitation on the brain among other effects is covered and later elaborated on in Chapter 9.

The history of the development of theories regarding gravitation in Germany is not complete without the contributions of Nazi Physicist Dr. Pascual Jordan, a founder of Quantum Mechanics, who is believed to be the theoretician that gravitational basis of this technology originated from via intermediaries taken as prisoners to the Soviet Union post WW-II, such as the members of the Berlin Brain Institute where he collaborated. Also in Germany we have the gravitational theories of Burkhard Heim, who was a young scientist during the Nazi Regime, developed another gravitational theory for this technology, that Jordan collaborated on, he also worked with Hans Bender on a physical solution to Psi, which was also of interest to Capt. Hans Roader of the Remote Sensing project.

A further historical narrative is presented regarding the development of the detection of GW. The Rocky Road to Gravitational Wave Detection, this covers the history of trying to detect GW and the many hurdles encountered to their final confirmed discovery in 2015, also covered is interferometry -- a technique which uses the interference of superimposed waves to extract information, the brain is an interferometer. We take a more theoretical journey in Gravitational Waves and Surveillance, covering the work of Dr. Bob Baker, formerly an engineer at Lockheed, who proposed using GW for military applications such as surveillance in the early 2000s. Dr. Baker and his team faced many oppositions to their ideals in Suppression of HFGW, covers the US government funded report to debunk High Frequency Gravitational Waves (HFGW) after being interested in the technology, Dr. Baker relates this as a suppression effort.

Finally, in A Timeline of Gravitational Technology a succinct account in the historical development of GW based technology is presented.

CHAPTER 7 – RADAR IN NEUROWEAPONS

In many histories of neuroweapons you will read of how 'mind control' developed out of Radar, which was a direct result of the military needs of World War II. In this chapter a technical overview of how radar works and how it relates to intelligence and surveillance is provided. I begin with a discussion of the EM Spectrum and how it related to the Radar Bands. It is important to understand that radar is a transmitter that sends out a signal to a target or object, and the signal returns to the transmitter now acting as a receiver, so it is clear that also using remote influencing is a form of radar, whether line-of-sight (LOS) such as radar vs over-the-horizon (OTH) of which remote influencing is a sub-part of. A discussion of the History of Radar is presented to understand the development and involvement of British and German militaries in radar. The concept of illumination, lighting up a target with EM energy is discussed, you have to illuminate an object to read the object, as described by Dr. John Norseen. For the engineers reading this a brief discussion of the Radar equations are mentioned, the most important points being regarding signal loss and signal-to-noise ratio.

The use of Radar in Intelligence and Surveillance is discussed with reference to the use of Radar in covert surveillance via the account of former British agent Carl Clark where use of a 3 point radar system to surveille targets is discussed The use of Radar illumination by the NSA of hardware installed on subject computers to retrieve information and images is also discussed. Dr. John Norseen describes how reading the neurons in the brain relate to radar.

To transmit a voice to someone's auditory cortex could be done using Time Reversed Waves (TR) as related by former US Air Force Lt. Col. Tom Bearden in his discussion of TR.

Finally, the discussion of the Eyes as Radar and Antenna systems is discussed in the research work of Singh et al, that relates the eyes as fractal antennas with high quality (High-Q) rating. The eyes are mentioned, see Chapter 9, as being a primary instrument in "Thought Injection."

CHAPTER 8 – QUANTUM CONSCIOUSNESS

This chapter covers the work of Hameroff and Penrose in greater detail as far as explaining the quantum physics of consciousness and how it is used in Neuroweapons, it also traces out the possible origination of these ideals in both Nazi Germany and the Soviet Union. The ideal of consciousness being affected by outside signals is primarily concerned with the microtubules in the neuronal networks of the brain. The work of Penrose and Hameroff is gone into in detail to give a better understanding how this process of altering cognition is accomplished with technology.

The first concept discussed is that of the Objective Reduction of the Quantum state and how that affects consciousness according to Hameroff. The process by which EM is used by Microtubulin (MT) is also studied in the section Electromagnetic (EM) Resonance of Microtubules, goes into the resonance of brain MT as studied by Indian scientist, Dr. Anibar Badhyapadhyay. An important scientific principle involved in this is the use of the Casimir Effect. Dr. Michael Persinger relates Casimir to Consciousness this is discussed in some detail here with elaborations from other researchers, an important ideal is that of the relationship of fluid viscosity and thixotropy which affects density of fluids and brain matter. The history of Soviet developments in this area is discussed which covers the contributions of Russian scientists to the study of quantum consciousness: Akimov, Sokolov, Bobrov, as well as German researcher Barron Manfred von Ardenne (Istok Institute), and the Russian researcher, Devyatkov, reverse engineering of Nazi Microwave generators suspected of being used as Neuroweaponry. Finally, reviewing the work of in terms of remote biological influencing.

The next topic covered is a review of the Puthoff Generators which parts of which are used in experiments of Dr. Michael Persinger, Dr. Hal Puthoff reverse engineered Soviet "Torsion" Generators which use spin-entanglement and the Aharonov-Bohm effect . Then we discuss the original ideal of P. Jordan, the Nazi physicist, and it's development in the Soviet Union of Molecular Resonance. Molecular Resonance developed in Soviet science to influence remote biological objects, referencing the work of former communist Yugoslavian scientist Irene Cosic's Resonant Recognition Model as advocated by Persinger. This model is important in that it provides an alternative signaling pathway to influence proteins in the brain, such as MT, presenting an alternative signal propogation in the brain to the traditional JAK-STAT signalling pathway-- a chain of interactions between proteins in a cell .

CHAPTER 9 – COUNTERMEASURES

This chapter addresses this question: Are changing angular momentum velocities a countermeasure to Aharonov-Bohm based neuroweapons as exemplified in the Havana Syndrome. Which is to say enveloping a biological object, like the brain, in a shielding gravitational field impenetrable by unsynched gravitational waves and EM waves. Throughout the cold war and currently there are many reports of EM manipulation of US State Department personnel on assignment in foreign lands, which is known by the term Havana Syndrome. Those suffering from these attacks have physical changes in their brains. This was studied by Dr. Verma and their team by examining the physical properties of brain matter. This chapter is divided into 3 sections:

I. Profiling a Directed Energy Attack Medically Speaking, looks into the study of Verma and Persinger into non-local attacks on the brains of victims.

II. Technological Briefing, drills down into the physics theories that explain non-local targeting by reviewing such theories as the Aharonov-Bohm effect, spin entanglement, Casimir Effect and GEM Equations.

III. Brain Profile, a look at EEG studies on Havana Syndrome, non-local targeting and the waves produced by victims brains during attacks or interactions with non-local attack vectors.

In the first section we look at creating a profile of an attacked persons brain referencing Verma and Persinger's work in this area. I review the specific areas of the Brain, known as Broadmann areas, and how they are affected by EM waves.

In the second section, we look at the technological theories underpinning the use of Aharonov-Bohm effect to induce these changes with a discussion of quantum entanglement of which Dr. Norseen mentioned is the basis of Thought Injection. We look at the role of angular momentum in the process of entanglement, the coupling of gravity and electromagnetics in gravitoelectromagnetics (GEM) as discussed by renowned physicist Dr. Raymond Chiao of the University of California. We also look at the Casimir Effect as it relates to gravitation and entanglement. We then study the Poynting Vector-- the directional energy flux of an EM field (EMF) produced by generators studied by Russian-German researcher Dr. Serge Kernbach of the University of Stuttgart. A brief discussion of the skin as medium of transmission is discussed with special attention paid to how lasers are used to affect brain waves through lasers aimed at the skin of a patient and how genetic differences in skin pigmentation affect this process. A technical discussion of remote monitoring and mapping of biological objects is presented via the research of Dr. Kernbach. Then we bring up the discussion of countermeasures to remote influencing through the work of Dr. Michael Persinger and his team in Canada. The mechanics of the countermeasures are discussed including the use of rhythmic point durations of EM potentials in the A-B coil generator of Persinger and how it was derived from the reverse engineering by Dr. Hal Puthoff, an intelligence linked physicist in America. We conclude this section with a discussion of the medical use case for A-B Generators as Transcerebral Magnetic Stimulation devices and it's relationship to Transcranial Magenetic Stimulation (TMS).

In the third section we review the Brain Profile of an attacked brain and also compare it to epilepsy. We reference the use of EEG for measuring brain activity to localize areas in the brain affected by outside manipulation. In this section we also offer explanations to detractors regarding this technology. We discuss the brain waves (alpha, beta, theta…) produced by the human brain and how this is altered by these devices. Dr. Persinger's Harribance Configuration, which was a series of experiments with a psychic named Harribance and how that relates to areas of the brain and malformation of brain matter. Then we explain the exact areas of the brain that are affected and how one can provide a profile to show a person is being attacked.

CHAPTER 10 – HYPNOSIS IN WARFARE

This chapter looks at the use of Hypnosis in warfare and espionage and how they are related to neuroweapons. This chapter drills down into specific brain organelles that control hypnotic influence, with a differentiation between Highly Hypnotizables and Low Hypnotizables, the use of suggestion, brain differentiation that explains political differentiation as informed by brain physiological differences between categories of left and right and how that relates to hypnosis. This chapter begins with an introduction into hypnosis and defines high, medium and low hypnotizables and the physiological differences between the different susceptibilities to hypnotic control. Parasitic

Consciousness, studies the work of Michael Persinger in studying non-local technology and Epilepsy studies, with a common element found with partial epileptic conditions and the brain profile of those under non-local influence, with reference to an invasive consciousness known as "parasitic." Then we discuss the physiological differences between Left and right (red vs blue) political tendencies and the brain centers involved, where leftists tend to have a different anterior cingulate complex, like less suggestibles-hypnotizables and righties have a different amygdala, which is also found in high hypnotizables, and is used for the purposes of fast reflexion in RC. The amygdala is studied in more detail in the next section and finally we discuss the relationship of obesity and hypnosis as well as voting patterns that can be traced by obesity prevalence in a geographical area.

CHAPTER 11 – UKUSA DECEPTION MANAGEMENT AND CYBERNETICS

This chapter covers the use by western powers, the American and British (UKUSA) military alliance, of 'remote action' and the automation of remote action via cybernetics. In this chapter the topics of US Security and Intelligence methods of Effects Based Operations, Reflexive Management, Cost of Actions and Effects and their integration into deceptive games. In the subsequent section we study the engineering of an Information Warfare Engine, which covers the research of Lockheed-Martin researchers Backus and Glass in the development of automated programs for remote action. Next, we cover the use of Psychological Profiling for Computation which is related to the earlier work of Tarasenko in that it uses neurocognitive science in computation of groups and changing group membership by influencing members of groups. Analytics is then studied, the metrics of measuring effectiveness of the remote action methodologies. Then we see how it was intended to control soldiers in military operations through simulated soldiering, which covers the automation of troop management focusing on the work of Lockheed-Martin scientist Behzadan, which also uses cybernetics to foment instability in groups and societies. Finally, we review the programs UMBRA and SCREAM – an analysis of the cybernetic programs used to manage groups and societies, as well as armed formations. This section focuses on the work of Lockheed-Martin scientist Xavier, also looks into the Dante Scenario Manager that allows for a text based data input that a computer program (algorithm) uses to make the world look like it's instructions.

Appendix and on-line supplement

All appendices are at the on-line supplement to this book at:

https://github.com/autonomous019/Battlespace-of-Mind-Supplement

Appendix A: General Timelines of Book, timelines of neuroweapons developments

Appendix B: Timeline of the Wiemar Republic

Appendix C: Case Study of Targeted Individuals, case study of internet user group dedicated to people claiming to be targeted by neuroweapons, popularly known as 'Targeted Individuals'

Appendix D: Play AI: Machine Learning and Video Games

a. AI, includes topics on Linear Regression, Problems of Statistical Methods, Machine Bias and Algorithmic Complexity

b. Serious Games (Simulations), Game AI and Military Intelligence. Covers Reflexive Rewards and Gaming, AI in Simulation Design, the Game World, Agents, Elements of an AI Game, Kinematics in Simulated Worlds.

c. Decision Making, covers the use of AI in making decisions in simulations with Behavior Trees and Goal Oriented Action Planning (GOAP).

d. Dialogue and Chatbots in AI Agents

e. Emotions in Simulations, the use of emotions in Agents, focusing on the Russian Researcher Tarasenko PAD model.

f. Diplomacy

g. Real Time Strategy Simulations including the use of Neuroevolution- when computers write their own game programs.

Appendix E: Timeline on Development of Computation and Computer Hardware.

CHAPTER 1

THE BLACK INTERNATIONAL: THE HISTORICAL AND POLITICAL BACKGROUND TO THE CREATION OF NEUROWEAPONS

INTRO

It is 1933; the United States of America is an independent and free country living in a world that is increasingly being threatened by totalitarianism, not from despotic Kings and Queens but from a political philosophy known as Fascism. The first country to fall was Italy in 1922 when Mussolini took control. From the roots in neo-Roman Imperialism would grow the greatest threat to humanity ever encountered. Within eleven years Germany would fall too to this Fascist philosophy, but the Fascists main prize and actual root of its origins lie in the United States, which in 1933 saw an attempted Fascist coup of the Roosevelt administration from wealthy Bankers, who also financed the Italian Fascists and German Fascists with the USA being the main target all along. However, before we can learn about the English and Anglo-American roots of Fascism, we need to examine the time after the First World War when Prussian militarists, deeply allied with Anglo Supremacy, sought to resurrect Germany out of defeat, in a Third Reich. Now we see, these militarist interests would use a new weapon to create a Fourth Reich, using the principles of infiltration and control gained from years of Military Intelligence work, that have been applied to other nations. Indeed, we see this repeated pattern in Imperialism; for instance the British Secret Intelligence and Military Intelligence developed an algebra, or in computer terms, algorithm, for invading and conquering others which was most brought out during the 1950s and 1960s when the British empire fought to hold onto its last remains. In fact, the largest and most capable intelligence network of the First World War era was run by England, so that even Himmler based his intelligence and security on the British model.

As we shall read, many of the key players in what would eventually lead to the founding of the Nazi State in Germany can be traced back to a long line of historical developments influencing politics and social relations as well as militarism in Germany stretching back to the founding of the Holy Roman Empire.

One nexus of interest to Nazism in terms of a Fourth Reich and international finance was that of Hamburg, which became a center of Fourth Reich activism after WWII. Hamburg styles itself as a Hanseatic City. It is important to realize that German interests in America stretch back to the 18th and 19th centuries, where Germans of Philadelphia established the Democratic-Republican clubs, later German immigrants such as Orestes Brownson, anglicized from Braun, a philosopher who claimed that as a young man he was recruited by Bismarck's forces to infiltrate America with the goal of taking it over.

This is seen in earlier German society with the goals and methods of the medieval Hanseatic League headed by Germans. The League was an association for the purposes of trade in Northern Europe of independent cities and their states-within-states which had an assembly of tradespersons called a Diet, which is somewhat reminiscent of the Anglo-Saxon Witan, an assembly of landed Anglo-Saxons in England of the same period. Indeed, the areas making up the Hanseatic League overlap with those of Anglo-Saxony in Europe. The Hansa developed from the 14th century and existed at some level up to the 19th century, although never officially disbanded, hence we have cities like Hamburg still claiming to be Hansa. The Hansa as a trading bloc, but without larger states, resembles more a corporate body as envisioned by Fascism than by the later liberal creation of Adam Smith's capitalism. When any power threatened its trading routes or economic dominance they would collectively draw up an Army or Navy as needed to put down such threats.

As the Hansa developed it also became more monopolistic. From the 14th century onward, the need was to defend old markets against growing competition. The whole strength of the league was mustered to organize economic, political, and military resistance against the forces of change, against all opposition to Hanseatic monopoly. The weapons of the German merchants in that struggle varied. They retained of course their initial advantages of geographical position and their ability to call up a large merchant navy. They made increasing use of large gifts and loans to political leaders to secure their privileges and stifle opposition. When such means proved inadequate, the withdrawal of Hanseatic trade was threatened and coupled with an economic embargo and blockade that broke most forms of resistance, the same as using economic sanctions today. Only in extreme cases, when vital interests had to be defended against enemies undeterred by less stringent methods, did the league engage in organized warfare. It's primary means of defense being economic, through the tools of siege mechanisms, although one could argue any monopoly is a kind of siege method.

As its institutions matured so too did it's control and influence. It was a decentralized minimalist state, much akin to modern Right Libertarian ideals, it had no standing army or navy, no central taxes, it simply governed itself, it had no central treasury and no central court. It was "governed" by a diet that met generally at Lübeck and theoretically every three years, but the meetings were in fact held irregularly, and their frequency declined after 1400 as divergences between the various members grew and as the conduct of routine affairs was gradually transferred to the town council of Lübeck. The diets were assemblies of delegates from the various towns, and their decisions (Recesse) were determined by a majority vote of the towns represented.

One instrument of the Hansa that should be noted is that of the Kontore, which were trading entities that were established as Hansa Merchant-German colonies in other non-German areas, there were four of these, with an important one established in London; their operation and structure is much akin to that of the trading blocs of the City of London. The four Kontore of London, Bruges, Novgorod, and Bergen colonies that enjoyed exemption from the jurisdiction of the land in which they were established, administering their own (German) law and subject to the directives of the Hanseatic diet. Their members corporately owned a large complex of houses, halls, warehouses, and other buildings where they lived a severely disciplined life and carried on their trade with the natives. It is not with surprise that we will read how powerful Banking families of the City of London and Hamburg would later create the Nazi state through their financing, and indeed even lead the negotiations that could lead to a Fourth Reich with Himmler after it was apparent the Nazis would not win a military victory, one could argue that after that point the Nazi campaign became a financial one under Himmler's influence.

GERMAN SECRET SOCIETIES AND THE THULE SOCIETY

One can imagine a young Heinrich Himmler sitting and watching attentively to every little detail at the meetings of the Thule Society he and his father attended, taking assiduous notes and entering them into his dairy at the end of each day as was his custom. The Nazi's are said to have grown out of this secret mystical society that had seances and other "meditative" practices. Many early Nazis were members, including nobles such as Countess Heila von Westarp, and Prince Gustav of Thurn and Taxis. Also, major arms manufacturer and early investor in what would become Neuroweapons research, Fritz Thyssen, was instrumental in the Harzburg Front which helped create the Nazi state. It is no coincidence that Himmler would later be interested in using psychics for war and security purposes as Reich leader of the Nazi SS and started research into psychic phenomena, neuroweapons, in the Ahbernebe research division of the SS [see Chapters 3, 6 and 8 for more information on the development of neuroweapons by the Nazi State.] Another group around this time doing the same research and interested in psychic phenomena was founded by the leadership of the Soviet Secret Police [see Soviet research section, Ch. 3]. The use of secret societies to steer public policy is nothing new in German speaking lands.

Secret Societies in Germany were initially student associations, but when the King banned such associations they went underground. Orders first appeared among students in the 1750s in Germany. The Illuminati (1776), Amizisten, Constantisten, Unitisten, Harmonisten were some early associations. They were in conflict with the Landsmannschaften. The above orders were multi-ethnic, the Landsmannschaften were "nationalist" and "regionalist." Landmannschaften practiced an extreme form of bullying (hazing, pennalism) on freshmen, which we also see in the notion of "fagging" at Anglo-Saxon elite schools in Britain such as Eton. On the other hand, we have another form of student association based in German nationalism, the Burschenschaften, which were not secret. Quite often Burschenschaften decided to stress extreme nationalist or sometimes liberal ideals, leading in time to the exclusion of Jews, who were considered un-German. In a loose sense we have Orders that are left-wing and Orders that are right-wing, but even out of the "liberal" orders some of whose members went on to such vocations as revolutionaries in France, could tend to reactionary sentiments such as the Eudomonists, former Illuminati, that were against liberal trajectories, creating a reactionary Illuminati subgroup. Previously to these groups the Landesmannschaften existed, founded in 1717 in Halle, comprised of seniors and sub-seniors, which is mirrored today in Yale's Skull and Bones, WolfsHead and other fraternities at Yale and other schools associated with the Boston Brahmin, or traditional upper-class of America. According to Von Raumer these associations were immediately outlawed (Von Raumer, 52). Being outlawed, to continue their activities they became absolutely covert using absolute secrecy:

> ...the statute of one of the Landesmannschaften, for example, provide that a new member, at his entrance, shall give his word of honor 'that he will never reveal what happens at any time within the society, that he will always be diligently watchful against renouncers (students belonging to no society), and will never reveal that such a society exists and will even endeavor to cause the contrary to be believed. But in case he shall be seriously questioned on the subject by the police or the rector, he must lie stoutly, and be willing to give up his existence at the university for the sake of the society." (Von Raumer, 52)

As one can see, the secret nature of their activities was of utmost importance, but why would a student association mean so much to young men of the noble classes? It was a matter of beliefs – beliefs based in part if not totally on the Prussian Military culture of their day, which was absolutist militarism. There was no united Germany at this time, rather Prussia tended to dictate to others in either financial or military terms what it wanted. Prussia in the east of Germany, and now with some parts in Poland, was the seat of the House of Hohenzollern. The Prussian Militarist believed in an absolutist monarch, but not an ostentatious king, with gold-coated delicacies; rather the King of a "Sparta of the North" (warrior-citizens). It was ruled with the assistance of the Junkers – aristocratic nobles with land rights. These Junkers ruled over the serfs in council with the king and served in the Military. They had a non-representative assembly, more like a House of Lords which could tax by fiat. They did encourage education of the masses in a certain sense, as they sought to instill in their subjects their values and needs through mass conditioning. To what extent different houses sought to overthrow the King's line and establish their own is not clear. However, for whatever reasons the King viewed the Landesmannschaften as a threat.

Take the Illuminati for instance. Weishaupt is credited as its founder, but it also had the membership of other royals in Germanic lands such as Duke Ferdinand of Brunswick-Wuffenbuttel, who was a Prussian Field Marshal, member of the Masonic Lodge of the Three Globes in Berlin. Prince Charles of Hesse-Kassel, son of Frederick II, Landgrave of Hesse-Kassel who created cameralist plans for central control of the economy and, hawkish on foreign policy, was responsible for overseeing the famous Hessians hired as mercenaries to suppress the American revolution for the German holders of the British Crown. The Dukes of Gotha, the future House of Windsor, were also involved, as well as Duke of Weimar Franz Xavier von Zwack, whose nickname was "Cato." What did they espouse? They espoused that the dominant men in society should have totalitarian rule:

> Men originally led a patriarchal life ... but they suffered themselves to be oppressed – gave themselves up to civil societies, and formed states.... To get out of this state ... there is no other means than the use of Pure Reason by which general morality will be established, which will ... dispense with all political supports, and potentiary rulers. This can be done in no other way but by secret associations, which will by degrees and in silence [hidden], possess themselves of the government of the states.... We shall restore the rights of man [patriarchy], original liberty and independence. (Source: N. Bonneville, *Illuminati Manifesto of World Revolution*, p.p. 53-54)

It is important to keep in mind that when they speak of original liberty and independence it is for only one class or group in society: dominant militaristic men. Of course, all this reminds us of Nazism. It is important to see how secret student associations were used to cultivate this belief over generations, eventually leading to the National "Socialist" government in 1933. The eventual creation in 1919 of the Deutsch Gildenschaft which was extremely nationalist and racist, then the creation of the NS-Deutscher Studentbund, which also engaged in paramilitary training of college students and ideological conditioning.

In an interesting connection to America, of which we see even more later, out of these student associations also grew the notion of infiltration of the young American republic. As was seen later in the 19th century, as Germany had not been founded as a unified country, they fell behind in the colonial imperialistic conquests of other people's resources for self-enrichment. What better prize then taking over the independent American state, still finding its legs as a new nation.

It was through German immigrant John Peter Gabriel Muhlenberg who studied at Halle, where the Landes-mannschaft were a heavy presence, that the Democratic-Republican societies were started in Germantown, Pennsylvania, eventually leading to unforeseen development of partisan politics which was never part of the American founders' reasoning behind the Constitution and Representative Democracy. George Washington himself believed they were trying to divide America and connected them to the Illuminati.

The Democratic Republicans argued against strong Federalism, as noted in the Federalist Papers, of Madison. It is also interesting that in 1832 an American student, W. H. Russell, returning to Yale from his German university studies, founded the Skull and Bones Senior fraternity, which was also mirrored in other fraternities, and like German Nationalist secret fraternities forbade Jewish membership until the 20th century. The membership of the fraternity is heavily connected with the Boston Brahmin, and the term "spook" in reference to being in the CIA derives from the nickname of membership of that fraternity, who comprised a large number of early CIA agents and leaders. An additional interesting note is found in the transcendentalist notebooks of Orestes Brownson, a German immigrant, who accounts how he was recruited into a secret German order to take over America as he says: "by secret societies under the direction of Bismark and his Italian allies (Brownson 2017)."

In many conspiracy theories there is a blanket condemnation of "Masons" as running the world, which was also echoed by the Nazi leadership, at least that leadership faction associated with Hitler, the Austro-Bavarian faction or South German faction, which formally banned many Masonic Lodges after rising to power. So, it is important to look more closely at these connections. German Masonry started in Hamburg in 1737 and then spread from there; eventually, the royal Prussian King became a Mason, although leaving it at a later date. It became associated with the Junker classes as it developed and by the 1930s had developed into a "Humanitarian" Internationalist faction, that was multi-cultural ethnic and religious.

Juxtaposed to this was the Prussian Nationalist faction, that was headquartered at the Three Globes Lodge in Prussian Berlin. This Prussian Nationalist faction was allowed to exist in the early years of the Nazi regime, although with neo-Germanic religion supplanting all forms of worship by the Nazis, it also was eventually disbanded. The important point is that in the secret orders of the Masons we again have a liberal tendency vs. a nationalist tendency identified with anti-semitism and a natural ally of Nazi beliefs.

Indeed, during World War II the Nazi regime did form a temporary alliance with the Three Globes Masonic Lodge of Berlin in Prussia, which represented the nationalist tendency in Freemasonry whereas the Internationalist tendency was officially banned by the Nazi Regime, because the Internationalists allowed Jews to be members. Returning to earlier history we also see the use of nationalism in the propaganda generated against the Illuminati by rival secret organizations such as the Prussian Rosicrucians, under Johann Christoph von Wöllner, which allegedly took over control of the Three Globes in the 18th Century. It was the Three Globes that convinced Frederick the Great in 1783 that the Illuminati had anti-government anti-religious tracts; the evidence being from the reactionary right-wing Masonic lodges, perhaps an early form of secret disinformation.

The Masons are part of esoteric teachings that are common to many lodge-like organizations, partly carried out in secret. As such, their secrecy is fertile ground for secret plans and hidden relationships. For instance the founder of the Ulster Volunteer Force in Northern Ireland, Gusty Spence, was previously a member of the Orange Order before being initiated into a secret organization. Of course, juxtaposed to Protestant Orders are Catholic ones. The esoteric teachings also can attract an "imaginative" group of people that believe in supernatural powers; one such group was the Thule Gesselschaft (Society), which does indicate a certain vulnerability to hypnotic suggestibility (see Hitler's post WWI medical treatment).

In 1919, Germany lay in military and economic ruin after signing the Armistice which created a heavy burden on the German Nation. In these circumstances many returning veterans and citizens of Germany begin to look for answers to their problems. One such German was Anton Drexler, who founded the predecessor to the Nazi party, the Deutsche Arbeiterpartei (DAP; German Workers' Party) on January 5, 1919, with the Thule Society's Karl Harrer, changing their name in 1920 to the Nationalsozialistische Deutsche Arbeiterpartei (NSDAP; National Socialist German Workers Party, eventually the "Nazis").

An early creator of the Thule Society, Sebottendorff, left before the Nazi involvement in the group. Some members of the Thule Society, Dietrich Eckart (Hitler's speaking coach and political consultant), Erik Jan Hanussen, Gottfried Feder, Hans Frank, Hermann Goring (also connected to Swedish Royalty, Leader of the Luftwaffe), Karl Haushofer, Rudolf Hess (Minister of Propaganda) and Alfred Rosenberg. Wilhelm Laforce and Max Sesselmann (staff on the Münchener Beobachter) were Thule members who later joined the NSDAP; the Beobachter being the propaganda newspaper of the Nazis. Another member and part of the Nazi propaganda influence machine was Julius Friedrich Lehmann, the publisher and brother of bacteriologist Karl Bernhard Lehmann. In 1900 Lehmann left Switzerland and moved to Germany, where he bought the medical journal Münchener Medizinische Wochenschrift (i.e. Munich Medical Weekly Magazine), which he soon managed to make the most widely circulated journal of its kind in Germany, which advocated for instance "Eugenics." He established the Deutsche Volksverlag, which he handed over to Ernst Boepple. Lehmann also published the journal Deutschlands Erneuerung (Germany's Renewal), which was edited by the Pan-German League. Lehmann's publishing house was an important connection between the German Nationalist Protection and Defiance Federation, the Marinebrigade Ehrhardt, then the Organisation Consul and the German National People's Party. In 1923 Lehmann took part in the Beer Hall Putsch. He joined the Militant League for German Culture in 1928 and became a member of the NSDAP in 1931.

WEIMAR REPUBLIC (POST-WWI) GERMAN MILITARY INTELLIGENCE CREATION OF FAR-RIGHT POLITICAL FORMATIONS

Before the Nazi Party existed, key members of what would become the Nazi hierachy were members of what was known as the "Freikorps." The Freikorp was an unofficial wing of the German Reichswehr, organized as the "Black Reichswehr." A brief account of the history of the Freikorps after WWI gives us valuable insight into the founding of the Nazi Party. After World War I, in a war that the victors continue to claim was fabricated by the German Royal family, although there is not convincing evidence of this. Other than certain financial interests being served by a mass war, the German nation lay in ruins. With only a hollowed out, anemic military known as the Reichswehr (Government Military) led by conservative leaders drawn from the historical militarist Prussian population in the East, which today is split between eastern Germany and modern-day Poland. The Reichswehr leadership, most notably under Gen. Von Seeckt, began a secret covert program to fight various threats to their nation, such is in the Ruhr valley, and extending all the way to the Baltics, where minority German populations lived. The Reichswehr termed this underground army the Black Reichswehr; it also became known as the Freikorps (a free army).

In 1918, Wilhelm Groener, Quartermaster General of the German Army, had assured the government of the military's loyalty. But most military leaders refused to accept the democratic Weimar Republic as legitimate and instead the Reichswehr under the leadership of Hans von Seeckt became a state within the state that operated largely outside of the control of the politicians. Reflecting this position as a "state within the state," the Reichswehr created the Ministeramt or Office of the Ministerial Affairs in 1928 under Kurt von Schleicher to lobby the politicians. The German historian Eberhard Kolb (2005) wrote that "...from the mid-1920s onwards the Army leaders had developed and propagated new social conceptions of a militarist kind, tending towards a fusion of the military and civilian sectors and ultimately a totalitarian military state (Wehrstaat)."

The biggest influence on the development of the Reichswehr was Hans von Seeckt (1866-1936), who served from 1920 to 1926 as Chef der Heeresleitung (Chief of the Army Command), succeeding Walther Reinhardt.

After the Kapp Putsch, Hans von Seeckt took over this post. After Seeckt was forced to resign in 1926, Wilhelm Heye took the post. Heye was succeeded in 1930 by Kurt Freiherr von Hammerstein-Equord, who submitted his resignation on 27 December 1933.

Many future prominent members of the Nazi movement were drawn from their membership in the Black Reichswehr:

Heinrich Himmler – Freikorps Landshot, Beer Hall Putsch

Adolf Hitler – German Military Intelligence

Capt. Ernst Roehm – Chief of Staff under Gen. Ritter von Epp, in autonomous Bavarian Reichswehr, friend of Himmler

Martin Bormann – Freikorp Rossbach Brigade, involved in covert ops pre-WWII and post-WWII

Hermann Goering – Freikorps, and related to Swedish Royal family members that founded the Swedish Fascist party.

Kurt Blome – Freikorps, Nazi scientist, part of Project Paperclip

Konstantin Hierl – Freikorps member, oversaw Hitler in Mil-Intel

Kehr, Seisser – Lossow mil conspirators in Munich Putsch (1923)

von Mohl – 1920 Putsch

Ehrhardt – Freikorp leader, brigade associated with Junkers, later formed Organization Consul (financed by Pan-German League), lived with Princess Hohenlohe, fell out with Hitler's Nazis later.

Sepp Dietrich – General in Waffen SS

Rudolf Hess

Karl Wolff – SS Ubergruppenfuhrer, Chief of Himmler's Staff

Werner Lorenz – SS Ubergruppenfuhrer, Chief Resettlement Staff

Kurt Jahnke – Black Reichswehr Intelligence agent, involved in Ruhr resistance in 1920s. Previously in charge of sabotage in the United States during World War I. Leader in SS Intelligence.

A normative historical interpretation based on sociological analysis might try to explain the Nazi rise through angst at economic questions imposed on the German people by outside forces. However, a deeper investigation beyond sociological and anthropological understandings and based on military membership and connections shows that the Nazi movement was a direct outgrowth of extreme right wing German nationalism in the Reichswehr. For instance, if we take the case of Adolf Hitler it comes as a surprise to many that he was a low level German Military Intelligence agent (Verbindungsmann) sent into the political movements of his day, not just the NSDAP, but he looked into or reconned many different right wing groups before being dispatched to the party that eventually became the Nazis by German Military command.

Hitler's military career may have publicly ended upon being mustered out of the military in 1920, however, it seems this is just a cover story. As Prof. Eric Weitz explains how Hitler became involved in Military Intelligence:

> After experiencing the November Revolution and the "Councils Republic" [Räterepublik], the Bavarian Reichswehr Group Commando No. 4, which was established on May 11, 1919, decided to keep an eye on political groups and to carry out "educational work" (i.e., indoctrination) in order to combat revolutionary activities among the troops. Led by Karl Mayr, the Reichswehr's "Information Department" (Ib/P) was commissioned for this purpose. Adolf Hitler, who had previously belonged to the demobilization unit, joined the "Information Department" as a propaganda writer and informant [Vertrauensmann], and participated in education courses organized by the department. Hitler's contributions to group discussions caught the attention of one course lecturer, historian Karl Alexander von Müller, who knew Mayr from their school days. Müller informed Mayr of Hitler's rhetorical gifts. Soon thereafter, Hitler was appointed as a lecturer for an educational course in Lechfeld (August 20-25, 1919). (Weitz 2019)

As later related after World War 2 by Hitler's direct superior in German Military Intelligence, Maj. Karl Mayr, who later became Hitler's opponent, and wrote in his memoirs that General Erich Ludendorff had personally ordered him to have Hitler join the German Workers' Party (DAP) and build it up. In 1919 the DAP (soon to become the NSDAP) had a membership of around 100 people. In his capacity as head of the intelligence department, Mayr recruited Adolf Hitler as an undercover agent in early June 1919. Hitler's role involved informing on soldiers suspected of communist sympathies. After this training Mayr issued Hitler the order to become "anti-Bolshevik educational speaker" to the soldiers at the Munich barracks. Furthermore, Hitler was sent as an observer to the numerous meetings of the various newly formed political parties in Munich. Hitler spent much time at the meetings and wrote reports on the political ideas, goals and methods of the groups. This included studying the activities of the DAP (German Workers' Party). Hitler became impressed with founder Anton Drexler's anti-semitic, nationalist, anti-capitalist and anti-Marxist ideas. This anti-capitalist sentiment would later be a driving wedge between Nazi factions, the North Ger-

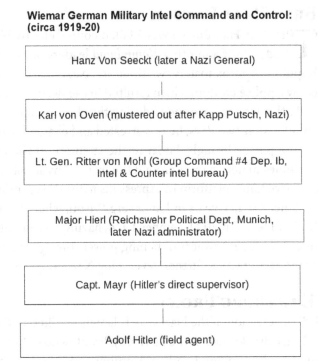

Wiemar German Military Intel Command and Control:
(circa 1919-20)

> Hanz Von Seeckt (later a Nazi General)

> Karl von Oven (mustered out after Kapp Putsch, Nazi)

> Lt. Gen. Ritter von Mohl (Group Command #4 Dep. Ib, Intel & Counter intel bureau)

> Major Hierl (Reichswehr Political Dept, Munich, later Nazi administrator)

> Capt. Mayr (Hitler's direct supervisor)

> Adolf Hitler (field agent)

mans and Bavarian-Austrian Nazis. Drexler was impressed with Hitler's oratorical skills and invited him to join the DAP, which Hitler accepted on 12 September 1919. After attending a further meeting on 3 October, Hitler stated to Mayr in his report "…must join this club or party, as these were the thoughts of the soldiers from the front-line."

In March 1920, Mayr sent Hitler, Dietrich Eckart and Ritter von Greim to Berlin to observe, recon, at close range the events of the Kapp Putsch. On 8 July 1920, Mayr was released from military service as a major of the General Staff of the military district command VII, but reappeared in September 1920 as commander of Section I b/P of army intelligence. Mayr in 1921 was a Nazi Party supporter, but later became a critic (Wikipedia, "Karl Mayr," https://en.wikipedia.org/wiki/Karl_Mayr)

In an interesting episode from young Adolph Hitler's life, it should be noted that, while hospitalized in Pasewalk for treatment of combat wounds consisting of a hysterical blindness that was treated through hypnosis, he heard voices and had visionary dreams related to being Germany's savior. It has been alleged that his doctor at the time had placed him under hypnotic influence and even used trauma programming on the young man. (Horstmann, 2017)

KAPP–LÜTTWITZ PUTSCH

The reconnaissance of the Kapp Putsch by Adolf Hitler is not well known. In early 1920 the leader of the Reichswehr grew weary of the stipulations to disband the German military and re-organize, including the disbandment of Marinebrigade Ehrhardt of the Black Reicshwehr. The Kapp–Lüttwitz Putsch, named after its leaders Wolfgang Kapp and Walther von Lüttwitz, was an attempted coup against the German national government in Berlin on 13 March 1920. Its goal was to undo the German Revolution of 1918-1919, overthrow the Weimar Republic, and establish a Prussian inspired military centered government in its place. It was supported by parts of the Reichswehr, as well as nationalist and monarchist factions.

Though the legitimate German government was forced to flee the city, the coup failed after a few days, when large sections of the German population followed a call by the government to join a general strike. Most civil servants refused to cooperate with Kapp and his allies, low government officials staging a civil resistance labor strike. Despite its failure, the Putsch had significant consequences for the future of the Weimar Republic. It was one of the direct causes of the Ruhr uprising a few weeks later, which the government suppressed by military force, after having dealt leniently with leaders of the Putsch.

BEER HALL PUTSCH

The Beer Hall Putsch was a failed coup d'état by Nazi Party leader Adolf Hitler, *Generalquartiermeister* Erich Ludendorff and other *Kampfbund* leaders in Munich, Bavaria, on 8–9 November 1923, during the Weimar Republic. Approximately two thousand Nazis marched on the *Feldherrnhalle*, in the city center, but were confronted by a police cordon, which resulted in the deaths of 16 Nazi Party members and four police officers.

Hitler, who was wounded during the clash, escaped immediate arrest and was spirited off to safety in the countryside. After two days, he was arrested and charged with treason.

The putsch brought Hitler to the attention of the German nation for the first time and generated front-page headlines in newspapers around the world. His arrest was followed by a 24-day trial, which was widely publicized and gave him a platform to express his nationalist sentiments to the nation. Hitler was found guilty of treason and sentenced to five years in Landsberg Prison, where he dictated *Mein Kampf* to fellow prisoners Emil Maurice and Rudolf Hess. On 20 December 1924, having served only nine months, Hitler was released. Once free, Hitler redirected his focus towards obtaining power through legal means rather than by revolution or force, and accordingly changed his tactics, further developing Nazi propaganda. (Wikipedia, "Beer Hall Putsch," 2021)

HARZBURG FRONT

The creation of the Nazi state is largely credited to the group of politicians, military leaders, bankers and industrialists known as the Harzburg Front, who held a secret meeting on Sunday, 11 October 1931. Chief among these is the banking family of Hamburg and the City of London, Schroeder Bank, who also financed the South during the American Civil War, including arms supplies. It is not without coincidence that plans for the rebirth of Germany after World War II would center on controlling banking and industries under the plans developed by the Nazi SS for a Fourth Reich. The Harzburg Front was a short-lived radical right-wing, anti-democratic political alliance in Weimar Germany, formed in 1931 as an attempt to present a unified opposition to the government of Chancellor Heinrich Brüning. It was a coalition of the national conservative German National People's Party (DNVP), under millionaire press-baron Alfred Hugenberg with Adolf Hitler's NSDAP, the leadership of the Stahlhelm paramilitary veterans' association, the Agricultural League and the Pan-German League organizations.

In addition to the leaderships of the DNVP and NSDAP, the SA chief Ernst Röhm, Reichsführer–SS Heinrich Himmler and Reichstag MP Hermann Göring, the meeting was attended by numerous representatives on the right of German politics including the Hohenzollern princes Eitel Friedrich of Prussia and his brother August Wilhelm (sons of the exiled Emperor Wilhelm II) and further prominent members of the Prussian aristocracy, the Stahlhelm leaders Franz Seldte and Theodor Duesterberg, former general Walther von Lüttwitz, former Reichswehr Chief of Staff Hans von Seeckt (then Reichstag MP of the national liberal German People's Party, today's People's Party of the EU), the Pan-German League chairman Heinrich Class, State Minister Klagges as well as some representatives of the business party such as steel magnate Fritz Thyssen and the Vereinigten vaterländischen Verbände Deutschlands ("United Patriotic Associations of Germany") under Rüdiger von der Goltz. The non-partisan Hjalmar Schacht, as a highly respected fiscal expert who had resigned as Reichsbank president the year before in protest against the Young Plan, vehemently spoke against Brüning's economic and financial policy, which caused a great stir. However, most leaders of industry and big business who had been invited to attend were notably absent. Only Ernst Brandi attended. (Wikipedia, "Harzburg Front," 2021)

Schroeder was implicated through his own testimony after the war during the Nuremberg legal proceedings. In Schröder's famous affidavit in the Nuremberg IG Farben trial of 1947, it says about this meeting:

> Before I took this step, I discussed with a number of gentlemen in business and found out in general how the business world felt about cooperation between the two. The general aspiration of the men of business was to see a strong leader come to power in Germany who would form a government that would remain in power for a long time. When the NSDAP suffered its first setback on November 6, 1932 and thus passed its climax, support from German business was particularly urgent. A common interest of business was the fear of Bolshevism and the hope that the National Socialists – once in power – would establish a stable political and economic basis in Germany. (Eberhard Czichon, 1967 *Who Helped Hitler to Power?* Cologne, p. 78)

Industrielleneingabe

The Industrielleneingabe (Industrial petition) signed by 19 representatives of industry, finance, and agriculture on November 19, 1932 requested German President Paul von Hindenburg to make Adolf Hitler the German Chancellor. The idea for the Industrielleneingabe had emerged at the end of October 1932 in the Freundeskreis der Wirtschaft ("Keppler circle"; Keppler-Kreis) and was supported by Heinrich Himmler, who worked as a liaison to the Brown House, Nazi Party Headquarters until it was bombed in 1943. The drafting of the letter was aided especially by Hjalmar Schacht, the banking figure, who was the only member of the Keppler-Kreis with any significant political experience.

The following banking and defense interests were represented by signing the letter:

- Hjalmar Schacht, former president of the Reichsbank, member of the Keppler circle.

- Kurt Baron von Schröder, ITT Corporation executive and private banker from Cologne, member of the Keppler circle and the Deutscher Herrenklub (de), a social club for rich capitalists in Germany. Several weeks later in his house, the decisive negotiations took place before Hitler's appointment as German Chancellor.

- Fritz Beindorff, owner of the Pelikan AG, in the supervisory board of Deutsche Bank.

- Emil Helfferich, member on the board of the German-American Petroleum Company [American Koch family built a refinery for this group], Chairman of the Supervisory Board of HAPAG, member of the Keppler circle

- Franz Heinrich Witthoefft, Chairman on the Board of Commerzbank and Privat-Bank, president of the Hamburg Chamber of Commerce, member of the Keppler circle.

- Carl Vincent Krogmann, co-owner of the Hamburg Bank, shipping company and trading house Wachsmuth and Krogmann, board member of the Hamburg National Club, mayor of Hamburg from 1933 to 1945, member of the Hamburg Chamber of Commerce and a member of the Keppler circle.

- Kurt von Eichborn, co-owner of a private bank in Breslau.

- Erwin Merck, supervisor of H. J. Merck & Co., a Hamburg commercial bank.

- Fritz Thyssen, chairman of the Supervisory Board of the Vereinigte Stahlwerke.

The Keppler Circle's group secretary Fritz Kranefuß, was a member of Himmler's personal staff. Its group financial manager was Kurt Baron von Schröder.

Another interesting connection to the defense sector is that of Gustav Krupp von Bohlen und Halbach attending the 1933 fundraising meeting of Goering to raise money for the Nazi political campaign by rich industrialists, of which many donated, showing industrial support for the Nazi movement. The Deutsche HerrenKlub of rich conservative industrialists fashioned after City of London elite social clubs had an influence on the Harzburg Front, the Keppler Circle, and the 1933 Goering fundraiser. All leading to financial support of major economic forces in Germany being behind the rise of the Nazi state, later Fourth Reich plans developed by Himmler were no different, as he was already familiar with the process of getting economic interests behind the Nazi state from the 1930s, which also influenced his founding of Economic Intelligence offices within the Nazi SS.

Post-War Fourth Reich Plans

"If we must die, then let the whole [German] people die."

– Gen. Schellenberg

After it became apparent that the Nazi's would not win the war, mainly due to lack of resources such as oil, many covert feelers were sent out to British sympathizers with the Nazi cause to form a detente. What may not be apparent to the obvious Ally in the British against Nazi Germany during World War II was that British society was divided on its participation in the war, with of course the "Peace in Our Time" of Chamberlain, whose main political allies were sympathizers to the Nazi cause, such as Lord Londonderry, Lord Hamilton. Yet, deeper and more lasting socio-cultural ties lay in the Banking families centered around Hamburg and the City of London: Schroeder, Kleinwort, etc., previous members of the Harzburg front in Germany while also having deep banking ties in the United Kingdom. It was through this channel that Nazi post-war plans began to come into view, just as after World War I these same interests had previously planned to raise the German Nation out of the ashes of defeat and create a Third Reich, albeit one with a financial empire at its core rather than a state.

The negotiations between German Nazis and British Fascist sympathizers centered in the neutral country of Sweden starting in 1943, with the main parties involved that of Himmler and the British banking interests, ultimately tied to Tiarks banking family. Himmler was a sort of anglophile, often talking of how he appreciated the English way of dealing with colonial subjects; he was attracted to tales of the round table of Arthur as a child, later he even wanted to base his Intel organization on that of the British:

> Himmler, however, was said to have stated once that, after Victory, he intended to build up a German Intelligence Service, on the pattern of the British. (MI5, 2011, From: PF.601.833, pg 54)

Liddell notes the anglophile nature of Himmler as well as a component of "revenge":

> Zech talked a certain amount of Heinrich Himmler, and he regards him as a sadist and slightly mad. He is not intelligent and can easily be bowled out in argument, but he has a great deal of peasant cunning. His father was the principal of some school and he himself received a very good education. Zech has heard him talk about the English and their colonial policy. He paints the English as a people who walk about cracking whips and referred to an incident in India where it was alleged that an Indian had struck a British subject. All local inhabitants had apparently been made to crawl on their hands and knees through the village. These incidents are held up to the Germans as something to be learned from the British as the correct method for the Herrenvolk to treat an insubordinate nation.
>
> Zech said that he hoped that we would not think that he was merely concerned with giving us amusing and interesting details regarding his experiences. His mind was running on much bigger things. He had gone through an appalling time, both physically and mentally. He had taken the decision to act as he had and hoped that we would make the best possible use of him. He said that most people in Germany deplored the atrocities but that very few of them were prepared to do anything. He referred to his circle of friends at home, some of whom listened to the British wireless and longed for the overthrow of the Nazis, but always said "Well, we must wait and see what happens. One day it will all come to an end." He was convinced, however, that if we treated Germany too leniently all those people and also the army would make preparation for a war of revenge. The whole country needed reeducating from top to bottom, otherwise the glorification of war and prowess on the battlefield would once more recreate a German Army or movements which would be as bad as that which had been experienced during the last ten years." (Lidell, 2005, 116)

HIMMLER'S FOURTH REICH PLANS

In 2011 the United Kingdom declassified several "top secret" MI-5 reports from 1944 to 1949 that regarded the establishment of a Fourth Reich centered in the leadership of SS-1 Heinrich Himmler.

This set of reports contains various indications that the German Intelligence Service (G.I.S) had plans for continued activity despite defeat, after the end of World War II. The file includes reports and assessments of the Sicherheitsdienst (SD) attempts to install a "stay-behind" organization in Europe for use behind Allied lines (led by Skorzeny), after the cessation of hostilities, to build a Fourth Reich. One would wonder how they would manage to build a Fourth Reich; according to the interrogations of captured SS agents, this plan involved creating confusion for the Allies, by mainly turning the United States against Russia. Thereby allying themselves with the United States against Russia. Other plans, which would be later echoed in the Black International terrorism campaigns of the 1960s and 1970s, called for fomenting "civil war" in France.

According to the interrogation of Julius Hagemann, who was part of a secret organization, the Friedensorganisation set up by the Abwehr, German Military Intelligence, not the SS, an organization like the Black Reichswehr before, was to foment civil unrest, including false flag tactics.

They were planning the rebirth of Germany and were already beginning to work "usefully."

The main purpose was to "make the allies post-war task as hard as possible," and to "ferment distrust between Americans and Russians." (MI5, 2011)

It is revealed in MI-5 Director, Guy Liddell's, notebooks that the other Nazis viewed Himmler as the Commander:

> It is for this reason that Heinrich Himmler is gradually extending his control. He is further to say that defeat, although not yet a fait accompli, must be regarded as a possibility, and that it is, therefore, important that his followers should take no overt action which would spoil their chances of reforming and playing their part in the preparation for the next war. (West 2005, pg. 220 10 July 1944).

Further evidence of Himmler being the leader of a Fourth Reich plan is that of Eastern Front Intelligence chief Major General von Gehlen's discussion with Himmler's assistant, Dir. Amt. IV, Gen. Schellenberg (Chief of SS Intel, worked with Jahnke). Later, Gehlen would go on to organize former SS agents into anti-communist West German agents also working with the CIA.

> Major General von Gehlen in March 1945 asked Schellenberg for a quiet talk in private. One evening he spent three hours with Schellenberg. In the course of this talk Gehlen estimated that militarily a resistance would last another two months. Then the end had to be counted with. Gehlen said that preparations had to be made for this case. The only man with the necessary imagination and energy to undertake this task was Himmler. Himmler should as Commander of the home Army, authorize Schellenberg to build up, together with Gehlen and the best general staff officers, a resistance movement and army on the lines of the Polish resistance…. The evening ended with Schellenberg's assurance that he would think it all over thoroughly and then secure the decision of Himmler (MI5, 2011, Schellenberg Interrogation).

The German Intelligence Service was already planning to regroup under different covers. As the secret report relates:

> 1. Survivors of the GIS are regrouping, reorganizing their service and recruiting new agents. They have great hopes in the rebirth of Germany and are already beginning to work "usefully."

> 2. They are counting on differences of opinion between the Allies and foresee an automatic reaction for the peoples of Europe to the "intense Bolshevik propoganda," and the successes that this might eventually have. By intelligently exploiting the upheavals in this sphere of adversity, they are reckoning on Germany becoming powerful once again, regardless of the ways and means of achieving this. The new GIS is especially relying on the reaction of the big industrial firms to the "communist menace," and on the support from abroad (Spain, the Hearst Press in the USA) to help with the reconstruction [Marshall Plan] of Germany. (MI5, 2011)

The important issue from the above is that they were planning on using German industrial firms in their plans. This is also echoed in other ways.

> [Otto] Skorzeny (from Austria) brought the subject up again by telling Schellenberg in rather condescending manner that the SS Jagdverbande [fighting organization] (north, east, south and west) were all being concentrated in the Alps and were fighting there as commandos. All who could join would have to place themselves under his orders, everything else was rubbish. He and Kaltenbrunner (Austrian SS) were absolutely agreed on that. (MI5, 2011, Schellenberg Interrogation)

> The progressive break-up of the Reich showed that a disappearance into civilian clothes and corresponding civilian professions, if necessary even in an extreme way (clergymen, monks, etc), was the only thing one could advice others to do. It amounted to an endeavor to save "human substance." (MI5, 2011, Schellenberg interrogation)

It is worth noting that the Ratlines out of Germany through Italy were in part run through reactionary Catholic orders, not with Papal permission, but it does show the cultural strength of reactionary tendencies throughout different parts of society that could be harnessed to support the building up of a Fourth Reich. It is also worth noting the main resistance was comprised of the Bavarian-Austrian alliance within the Nazi Party, while a North German faction of Nazism was negotiating with Swedish and British financial society. Skorzeny is of interest in Irish politics as he tried to settle in Ireland and was involved in connections to Fianna Fail politicians.

The pre-planning and logistics associated with post-war efforts on behalf of a Nazi Reich (Administration) are given in the following interrogation regarding SS AMT IIIB RSHA, "Spheres of German Life" or the Inland-SD, headed by SS-Gruppenführer Otto Ohlendorf, was the SS information gathering service for inside Germany:

> When Source attended the conference at DEISENHOFEN, near MUNICH, in mid Apr 45, it was presided over by an Obergruppenfuehrer in full SS uniform...
>
> The agents were to lie low for a certain period after the end of the war in Europe and at a given time were to start organizing "national" movements which would be thoroughly in keeping with the traditions of each country but which would all preach anti-Bolshevism and stir up unrest culminating in civil war. If the cult of anti-Bolshevism were not particularly popular, then any other sore point, such as the burden of supporting an Army of Occupation or of having to cede territory, might be seized on. The main purpose was to make the Allies' post-war task as hard as possible, so that the Nazi Party could, in time, reappear in a suitable disguise and build up the Fourth Reich.
>
> In going to work, no movement was to make mention of its pro-Nazi sentiments or to indulge in anti-Semitic propaganda. This was stressed as a cardinal rule.
>
> Each movement should also strive to create different slogans, methods of approach to the public, initiation ceremonies [such as used in the creation of C company in Belfast, Ulster Volunteer Force (UVF)], ranks, etc., in order to lessen the risk of the affinity between movements being suspected. (MI5, 2011)

It is not a coincidence that many former Nazis became Christian Union activists and politicians after the war, thus in keeping with the "cover" of just being pro-German, not Nazi.

The use of information management is key to the success of such a project. Like the lodge structures of secret societies, here we are dealing with a secret society but based in extremist ideals of German Nationalism, so that we see the same structures employed:

> The Nazi intended to form a "three-layer" [compartmentalized] organization to control the various movements. The first layer would concentrate on forming a German Schultzinschaft [brain trust] out of Europe and so would direct the high policy. The second layer would be that which had to model the policy of the first layer to suit the various countries. Unlike the first two layers, the third layer might (in carrying out its general propaganda work) become known to the various movements. (MI5, 2011, P.F.602,431, pg. 43)

It is important to note that this is a layer above those of public front groups, say for instance the Christian Democratic Union in Germany, three Layers among insiders, with an uninitiated layer or layers below that, with its first two layers completely covert and only an interface layer with the convenient idiot orgs. Lodge structures are used throughout European societies; for instance we could look at the Lodges of the Orange and Black Orders associated with British Unionism, not to mention the well-known Masonic Orders, some internationalist, some xenophobic nationalist, like Three Globes in Berlin, which cooperated with the Nazi state.

Interrogations further elucidated how this covert network was supposed to operate, with main emphasis on intelligence gathering:

> The most important espionage function required of these agents is the collection of political intelligence especially relating to anti-Allied underground movements and the position of pro-Fascist and pro-German elements ... it is easy to discern Skorzeny's [sent to Ireland, among other places] overriding anxiety to keep his finger on the pulse of political movements or quarrels which could be used for his purposes. (MI5, 2011)

The main vehicle for intelligence gathering and general hidden administrative and research work was the use of front companies, both before and after the war, not just in Germany but also in England. MI-5 notes:

> These points taken separately are admittedly not very convincing, but taken together it seems that it must be more than mere coincidence that so many of these names should have come to light in connection with suspicious commercial undertakings working in this country and on the continent before the war and later in connections with the stay behind organization working in Western Europe.... Such phoney firms could equally

well have been used to finance pro-German (or even more sinister) activities in England … by doing business with genuine firms. (MI5, 2011)

Hamburg Fourth Reich Nexus

As previously noted above, the Saxon area of Hamburg was a center of Anglo-Saxon-German Banking families. According to Lord Hugh Thomas, a respected British historian, in his work on the death of Heinrich Himmler, he has linked Hamburg with post-war Nazi plans:

> German Communists unmasked concealed Nazi assets and tracked down Nazi war criminals – activities that were often inextricably linked. Disturbingly often, they also uncovered links to Allied interests. They studied individual Länder (states) to see whether there was any substantial difference in the post-war concentration of such Nazi power and influence and discovered the state of Hamburg was unique, not only for its remarkable post-war prosperity. Several Nazi war criminals listed by the Nuremberg trial remained at large in Hamburg, many more than in any other Lander. They were left unmolested by German authorities, and the selective indifference and inertia of the British military government ensured that most remained undisturbed. Their position was doubly secure thanks to the very rightwing Hamburg justice and police departments. In the 1950s the police alone contained thirty-one former SS men, many of them officially named as war criminals. They were employed as chief inspectors, chief superintendents, and one was even chief commissioner in charge of police training. Their appointments were made so soon after the end of hostilities that the East German investigators came to believe they had been prearranged in wartime. This view was supported by the fact that at the end of the war, most senior SS men and members of the Nazi hierarchy had gravitated to Hamburg. (Thomas, 2002, 118)

These East German Intelligence findings were confirmed by the United States Military as early as 1948:

> Confirmation of this East German finding came independently from the American Secret Service in Germany who, in the immediate aftermath of war, concluded that Hamburg was the kernel and headquarters of a well-established SS network. They found that within two years of the end of the war a conference had been arranged in Dortmund to teach the methodology evolved after May 1945 by senior SS personnel in Hamburg. The new organization was structured following the same sub-groups as the original SS. Hamburg was also the first German city to benefit from Himmler's carefully laid financial plans. Herman Abs, one of twelve directors of the Deutsche Bank, was appointed to the Hamburg branch after the Maison Rouge [red house] meeting as a guardian to thwart hostile Allied intentions and keep control of SS funds. However, the intentions of some of the British finance houses and merchant banks were to prove anything but hostile, even to a bank with such a tainted reputation. Worse still, a remarkably complacent British Military Governor failed to enforce American General Clay's orders that Abs be physically barred from entering any Deutsche Bank. Despite heated representations, the British did not put into effect any of the banking controls they had agreed with the Americans, which were essential to prevent the Deutsche Bank from resuming its all-powerful position. (Thomas, 2002, 119)

Hamburg is no stranger to the SS. As the SS had placed their economic and financial analysis divisions in Hamburg, as well as nearby Kiel:

> … two research institutes within his own SS organization. The first, Gruppe VI WI, studied world economics under Amt VI in a large, scientifically run institute in Hamburg, and the second, based in Kiel, focused on world markets and trade. Gruppe VI WI was created to train hand-picked SS men in finance according to strictly agreed requirements of individual businesses and industrial firms. (Thomas, 2002, 75)

Dr. Marcus, formerly of Jahnke's J-Buro Intel part of the SS, also located in Hamburg, was protected by the British authorities. During this time, he seems pre-occupied with infiltrating Hamburg banks and identifying Nazis working to build a Fourth Reich. Dr. Marcus was a member of J-buro which was responsible for initiating contacts with the British during the war to arrange a detente. J-buro was also staffed by a member of the Schroeder banking family.

In a further example of the centrality of Hamburg to Fourth Reich plans we have this report:

So he [Ljundgreen in Denmark] under the present war conditions for instance go to England and work there. The Intelligence Service might be partly military and partly business. Ljunggreen need not fear any German organizations, as neither SD, Sipo, Abwehr or similar organizations could do him any harm, as the "Doctor's" Intelligence Service was above all of it.

When Ljunggreen still declined, the "Doctor" told him that when he had thought it all over, he would get a telephone No. in Kopenhagen which he could call, after this the matter would be settled. It did not matter that the war would soon be finished as they were working far ahead, and the "Doctor" mentioned that an occupation of Germany in a way would cause some disorder, but the very first thing which would be organized would be the Secret Intelligence Service

The Head Quarter of this Intelligence Service was situated in Hamburg, and they had a transmitter in Halle. (Thomas, 2001)

Collusion and Blocking Investigations:

The question of Allied collusion with the Nazi Germans during the post-war is not really open to debate, as such former Nazis as Reinhard Gehlen headed West German Intelligence after the war with the aim of using former Nazis' professional skills in hunting Communists during the war to having them do it during the "Cold War." Throughout our research we have seen many Nazis escape under questionable circumstances: Mengele, Skorzeny, and Himmler allegedly never died. We could also point out that such important men of science involved in Nazi Research were never even put before the Nuremburg process, such as Von Verschuer and the public disinformation campaign blaming a subservient Mengele as somehow being the leader of these experiments rather than Von Verschuer.

Another aspect of collusion is that of thwarting investigations. During the end of the war, the Nazis started moving their funds around to plan a revival after their military defeat. The overwhelming negotiation points with Himmler and friendly British interests was primarily a financial affair.

In 1944 the Allies started to worry and investigate that the Nazi State would move its assets and begin the Fourth Reich organizing in South America:

> In response to the Red House report, British and American investigators started working in concert from the end of 1944. As they delved deeper into Himmler's financial maze, they discovered a multiplicity of complex yet expertly concealed transfers of much of Germany's wealth. The sheer magnitude of Himmler's enterprise and its breathtaking purpose astonished them. As they mined for information, they were also perplexed by the extent of personal wealth that he had stashed away, minor in comparison with the business ventures, yet disturbing evidence of compulsive personal greed. But Himmler's ambition for the transfer of Germany's wealth was the main focus of the British and American governments' anxiety. They responded in very different ways. In America, the FBI and OSS were the main investigators, backed up by the US Treasury Department and US State Department. They threw massive resources into a top-priority operation in the United States and Latin America, reporting their progress to the Sub-committee on War Mobilization for the Committee on Military Affairs. (Thomas, 2002, 78)

The money began moving to South America:

> Mordrelle told his handlers that he had attended a conference in Deisenhofen near Munich in April 1945. He said that the meeting was presided over by an Obergruppenfuehrer in full SS uniform, comprising 15 representatives from countries west of Germany. Mordrelle said that plans to promote post-war unrest were discussed. At the meeting it was said that ample funds had been planted in South America (mainly Argentina) and trustworthy bankers had been sent to live in Spain and Switzerland. (Thomas, 2002)

It is noted that an investigation into tracking Nazi assets was set up by the United States with the following threats highlighted:

> The fear was that the German political and economic leadership, sensing, defeat, would act to transfer secretly blocs of industrial and fiscal capital to neutral countries, thereby escaping confiscation and the reparations bill. If this happened, German economic and industrial power would be largely intact and would act as a power base

from which an unrepentant German leadership could build a resurgent Fourth Reich in 20 years. The military defeat of Germany thus would again be meaningless. (MI5, 2011)

One investigation by the US to track Nazi gold was foiled from within; Alan Dulles was part of investigating Nazi financial transactions in Switzerland. Earlier the State Department had been in charge of investigations and intelligence, creating a one-man bottleneck as far as intelligence information and sharing went, while FDR did have his own Intelligence sources to inform him, such as the Astor led network, working for the Naval Reserves. Officially a 16-page article from the Summer 2000 issue of the CIA journal, "Studies in Intelligence" titled, "The OSS and Project SAFEHAVEN, Tracking Nazi Gold" was written by Donald P. Steury, who at the time was a CIA Officer in Residence at the University of Southern California. The article recounts the OSS role (SI–Secret Intelligence and X-2–Counterintelligence) in support of US policy to track, locate, and prevent Nazi postwar control of Germany's gold and other valuable assets in neutral countries as an Allied victory approached. The overriding goal of SAFEHAVEN was to make it impossible for Germany to start another war. (MI5, 2011)

SAFEHAVEN brought out these differences in a form in which they were incapable of resolution. Jockeying for position reached a peak in August, when Foreign Economic Administration (FEA) official Samuel Klaus [Special Assistant to the General Counsel of the Treasury Department] set out on a factfinding tour of Allied and neutral capitals accompanied only by State Department official Herbert J. Cummings, with the Treasury Department deliberately excluded from participation. It found out anyway, and two Treasury officials set out in hot pursuit of the Klaus mission, catching up with it in London. Klaus grudgingly allowed them to accompany him to Stockholm, but he refused to permit them to continue further with his delegation. Undeterred, the two Treasury Department officials followed Klaus to Spain. This was too much for Klaus, who canceled the remainder of his trip and returned to Washington.

The situation was worse in Spain, where US Ambassador Carlton J. Hayes was accused of actively blocking implementation of SAFEHAVEN. It should be noted that in Switzerland, Dulles was supposed to track down German financial interests as head of the OSS in Switzerland, the financial capital of Europe.

Aside from deliberate interference there is also bureaucratic interference as noted in the conflicts between Head of British Military Intelligence Guy Liddell and other government agencies:

Liddell's second continuing anxiety was his deteriorating co-operation with Section V [MI-5] whose inflexible head, Felix Cowgill, had spent most of his career studying Communist infiltration in India and had a highly-developed sense of tight compartmentalisation. Cowgill recognised that ISOS [Intelligence Service Oliver Strachey] with its derivatives was the holy grail, a source that had to be protected at all costs. Liddell, on the other hand, while acknowledging the value of signals intelligence, wanted to exploit the opportunities it offered. As Liddell documented, the two opposing cultures frequently came into long and bitter conflict, and threatened to compromise numerous other areas of mutual interest (Liddel, 2005, 1).

USA Fascist Plot to Overthrow FDR

In 1933 there was a plot to overthrow FDR, which was revealed by retired Marine Corps General Smedley Butler to the House Un-American Activities Committee. The tracing back of the plot leads to Wall Street Investment interests, such as J.P. Morgan, who also financed Nikola Tesla. In the 1930s as Fascism swept Germany it too had its adherents here in America, not usually associated with the American Bund, but from homegrown Anglo-Saxon Supremacy. For instance, in one law firm associated with far-right tendencies, Sullivan & Cromwell, Sullivan (Ulster Scots Protestant background) backed neo-Confederate racist social clubs in New York City. Others involved in funding far right groups such as the American Liberty League, the Crusaders and Sentinels, included the DuPont's, W.S. Farish, Howard Heinz (Mellon Bank), J. Howard Pew, John L. Pratt, Alfred Sloan, E.T. Wier, to name a few.

Evidence of continued efforts by powerful U.S. fascists to regain control of the White House is illustrated by a 1936 statement by William Dodd, the U.S. Ambassador to Germany. In a letter to Roosevelt, he stated:

A clique of U.S. industrialists is hell-bent to bring a fascist state to supplant our democratic government and is working closely with the fascist regime in Germany and Italy. I have had plenty of opportunity in my post in Berlin to witness how close some of our American ruling families are to the Nazi regime .... A prominent executive of one of the largest corporations, told me point blank that he would be ready to take definite action to bring fascism into America if President Roosevelt continued his progressive policies. Certain American industrialists had a great deal to do with bringing fascist regimes into being in both Germany and Italy. They extended aid to help Fascism occupy the seat of power, and they are helping to keep it there. Propagandists for fascist groups try to dismiss the fascist scare. We should be aware of the symptoms. When industrialists ignore laws designed for social and economic progress they will seek recourse to a fascist state when the institutions of our government compel them to comply with the provisions. (COAT, 2004)

Mind you this is during the period when the Securities and Exchange Commission (SEC) is being formulated and finally established in 1934 in defiance of J.P. Morgan, with Joseph Kennedy as its head, a close ally of FDR, and one of the first Irish-Americans to break through into the political elite, dominated by Boston Brahmin, WASP Americans.

American Intelligence, at least in the beginning and probably framing its history for good, is heavily influenced by Wall Street Law firms, such as the founder of the CIA and OSS Bill Donovan, descended from Scottish Unionists. In the coup planning, although Donovan does not appear, his friends and associates do, for instance you can look at the law firm Sullivan and Cromwell, where Donovan worked, as did the Dulles brothers, and its involvement with far-right reactionary tendencies as previously noted. One friend of Donovan's who served with him in the military is Robert Sterling Clark, who was a grandson of the opium trading Boston Brahmin Cabot family, Edward Cabot Clark, and also heir to the Singer Sewing Co. fortune. Robert served in China during the Boxer Rebellion, was mainly involved with supporting the American Liberty League and the Committee for a Sound Dollar and Sound Currency (CSDSC), which was a Morgan Front group lobbying for the gold standard, rather than floating currency. Included among its members were several Morgan partners and Walter E. Frew, of the Corn Exchange Bank, which was controlled through National City Bank after a 1929 deal engineered by Morgan and exposed by the Pecora congressional investigation. One of the initial meetings between the coup plotters and General Butler was organized by Gerald MacGuire, associate of Clark and a member of the same organization, (CSDSC). Frew personally gave MacGuire $30,000 for the project under discussion with General Butler.

One family that spans the Atlantic with both American and English houses, like many Boston Brahmin intermarrying with British nobility for prestige and to spread their power, is the Mallet family. One of the conspirators to overthrow fellow blue blood, though from New York, FDR, was Grayson Mallet-Prevost Murphy, who ran a stock trading company that employed MacGuire. MacGuire, working with Donovan on behalf of J.P. Morgan, had previously visited fascist Italy and Germany to observe veteran organizations which promoted the Fascist dictatorships, such as those associated with the Black Reichswehr and the Croix de Fue (Fire Cross) which assisted a failed coup attempt in France on Feb 6, 1934. Donovan also gained access to behind the scenes troop movements in Italy and Germany, declaring himself a fascist to Mussolini to gain such insider information.

> In November 1935 Donovan traveled to Italy, where he met Benito Mussolini; convincing the dictator he was sympathetic to the Fascist Cause, Donovan received permission to visit the Italian lines in Abyssinia, which Italy had invaded the previous month. Donovan spent two weeks touring facilities and interviewing Italian officers. Upon his return to the United States, Donovan – who had traveled at his law firm's expense – briefed an excited War Department, which had been unable to place spies among the Italian invaders. Continuing to travel as a private citizen and making use of his network of contacts, he visited Germany in 1937 and observed German Army maneuvers; in 1938 he toured the Czechoslovak defenses in Sudetenland, witnessed the fighting in Spain, and again observed maneuvers in Germany. (Linderman, 2016)

Grayson Mallet-Prevost Murphy is a relative of the Dulles brothers, was senior vice president of Guaranty Trust Company which financed Mussolini; and is connected to the British Kleinwort Bank that financed Franco's fascist coup in Spain. Though named Murphy he is not Irish Catholic, but again of Protestant Scottish Unionist descent. He fought in the Spanish-American War and World War I, he had a metal plate in his head and probably suffered from a traumatic brain disorder. Murphy was on J.P. Morgan's "preferred client list," was a director of Morgan's Guaranty Trust bank and several Morgan-connected corporations. He and his banking house played an important role in syndicating Morgan loans to fascist Italy, for which he was decorated by Mussolini with the Order of the Crown of Italy, Commander class. Researcher, L. Wolfe, notes regarding Murphy:

> As early as 1903, President Theodore Roosevelt [advocate of Anglo-Saxon supremacy, cousin of FDR] selected him for secret assignments, including planning U.S. military interventions in the Americas. After WWI, Murphy headed the American Red Cross in Europe, which he used to develop a network of informants in European governments. In the 1920s, he made several "fact-finding'" trips to Europe, with "Wild Bill" Donovan who was later director, Office of Strategic Services. These missions, including meetings with Mussolini prior to his coup, were done at the behest of Morgan and London interests.
>
> In 1919, Murphy was one of 20 elite U.S. officers who met in Paris with the guidance of J.P. Morgan & Co. operatives to found the American Legion [based on the model of the Croix de Feu]. Murphy personally underwrote that operation to the tune of $125,000 and solicited additional funds from allies of Morgan in the industrial and financial community. Murphy was "kingmaker" for the legion's "Royal Family" because the legion still owed him and his friends a great deal of money. (COAT, 2004)

The British Mallets are well respected as statesman and military people. The Mallet name pops up in negotiations with Himmler; and is also connected with the German Kleinwort Banking family, which also was located in the City of London, again showing the importance of the City of London financial empire. Lord Thomas writes regarding this connection:

> The atmosphere [in the British Legation in Stockholm] was petty, childish and demeaning, confessed undercover SOE officer Sir Peter Tennant, the Legation's press attaché, and he was partly to blame. The problems had started when he noticed that Sir Victor Mallet, Chief of the British Legation, had been holding secret meetings with his friend Marcus Wallenberg, the Swedish financier, and Himmler's envoy Dr Karl Gördeler. (Mallet also came from a family of bankers that had ties with the German Kleinwort family who owned the merchant bank of that name.) Gördeler was a constant visitor to Sweden, making some ten trips during 1940 alone, when he was known to have met with Thoma and Calissendorf, wealthy ex-diplomats and prominent members of the Swedish establishment who were involved in peace manoeuvres. According to Tennant, Schellenberg first met with Mallet in March or early April 1943. Before then, on several occasions in January Mallet had met with Himmler's envoy, the lawyer Dr Schmidt, always in the company of Marcus Wallenberg, and Georg Conrad van der Golz, who left Sweden to work at the Deutsche Bank later that year. Tennant immediately sent a strongly worded report to London, which was … six weeks went by before Tennant first suspected from Mallet's manner that he knew what Tennant had done. It was not until much later that autumn that Tennant was approached by Robert Turnbull, head of the SOE in Stockholm, with a confidential message from Sir Charles Hambro to "festina lente." They wanted him to take it easy because Mallet was representing banking interests. By that time relations between the two men were decidedly frosty. Tennant, with some relish, made Mallet a prime intelligence target, while Mallet struggled to maintain his dignity and make life as unpleasant as possible for Tennant.
>
> Tennant thought his position had strengthened considerably when on 23 December 1943 the Soviet government demanded Sir Victor Mallet's recall on the grounds that he had been supplying the German High Command with details of the Soviet Army. But the Soviet request was ignored. (Thomas, 2002, Ch.6)

The Mallet connection to the Kleinwort Bank of England shows a continuity of interest between this family and Fascism, the Kleinwort Bank financed fascist Spain. The firm helped finance Francisco Franco's coup d'état in Spain by approving a credit of 800,000 pounds at 4% interest on 15 September 1937. A month later Kleinworts agreed another loan of 1,500,000 pounds sterling at 3%. (Torrus, 2016).

The planning for a Fourth Reich entailed, according to Himmler, the rebuilding of German Industry after the war, one final connection with American fascist activists is that of William Lockhart Clayton who was on the American Liberty League executive committee. Son of a plantation slave-owning southern family with holdings in the cotton industry, he was the author of the Marshall Plan, which financed the re-building of German Industry after World War II, which whether done in concert with German Fascists to rebuild Germany as per Himmler's plan, or just a coincidence that a far-right American designed the Marshall Plan, the relationship is something to be aware of: that the designers of the re-building of Germany, even after the military defeat of Nazism, were American far-right big business interests.

One other intriguing parallel between the American far-right Anglo-Saxon Nationalists and Nazi Germany is that of the issue of using a formal process in tracking its enemies. The IBM tabulator machines the Nazi's used to organize the Holocaust and the Prison systems was foreshadowed in the United States in 1926, with one far right group, the Sentinels, boasting that it had "card-indexed more than 2000 radical propagandists making it comparatively easy to check their movements and counteract their activities" (COAT, 2008). In this way the card-indexing used by the Sentinels is eerily presaging a full decade earlier the same card-indexing IBM machines the Nazis used. Some leading industrialists involved in the Sentinels were Raymond Pitcairn, billionaire son of PPG Industries founder, John Pitcairn, Jr., who served as the Sentinels' national chairman for several years, also the group's primary benefactor: in early 1935 he single-handedly revitalized the Sentinels with a donation of $85,000 (more than $1.25 million in 2008 dollars). To a group which had raised exactly $15,378.74 since 1931, this was a massive injection of capital. Board members included Edward T. Stotesbury, a prominent investment banker and partner of J.P. Morgan & Co. and Drexel & Co.; Horatio Lloyd, also a partner of J.P. Morgan & Co.; J. Howard Pew, the President of Sun Oil; and Bernard Kroger, founder of the Kroger chain of supermarkets.

In 1936 the J. Henry Schroeder Bank of New York had entered into a partnership with the Rockefellers. Schroeder, Rockefeller and Company, Investment Bankers, was formed as part of an overall company that *Time* magazine exposed as being "the economic booster of the Rome-Berlin Axis." The partners in Schroeder, Rockefeller and Company included Avery Rockefeller, nephew of John D., Baron Bruno von Schroeder in London, and Kurt von Schroeder of the BIS and the Gestapo in Cologne founding member of the Harzburg Front. Avery Rockefeller owned 42 percent of Schroeder; Rockefeller, and Baron Bruno and his Nazi cousin 47 percent. Their lawyers were John Foster Dulles and Allen Dulles of Sullivan and Cromwell. Allen Dulles (later of the Office of Strategic Services) was on the board of Schroeder. Further connections linked the Paris branch of Chase to Schroeder as well as the pro-Nazi Worms Bank and Standard Oil of New Jersey in France. Standard Oil's Paris representatives were directors of the Banque de Paris et des Pays-Bas, which had intricate connections to the Nazis and to Chase. (Higham, 2007)

The complicity of the Dulles brothers is noted by US lawmakers and jurisprudents – it's alleged that former US Supreme Court Justice Goldberg called the Dulles brothers traitors; he was a WWII OSS operative himself. As one senator noted about the Dulles brothers' involvement through Sullivan and Cromwell:

> Senator Claude Pepper criticized John Foster Dulles, Gov. Dewey's foreign relations advisor for his connection with the law firm of Sullivan and Cromwell and having aided Hitler financially in 1933. Pepper described the January 4, 1933 meeting of Franz von Papen and Hitler in Baron Schroeder's home in Cologne, and from that time on the Nazis were able to continue their march to power. (*New York Times*, Oct. 11, 1944)

Later, after the war, both Dulles brothers would serve in the Government, with Alan going on to become head of the CIA and John becoming Secretary of State under Eisenhower. Their friend Bill Donovan would play a role in the creation of the CIA after the war as the OSS became a permanent body governing American Intelligence.

ENGLAND, A NAZI SPY AND THE FOUNDING OF THE CIA

The founding of the CIA is largely owed to a relationship with secret British Intelligence just before and during the war. It is interesting to note that the US was under pressure from British Intelligence in America to join the war on the Allies side, including covert operations by Britain on American soil. These ops were headed up by a British agent, William Stephenson, a Canadian, heading the British intelligence efforts in America as British Security Coordination (BSC). As one can imagine the intertwining of Anglo-Americans and English is not that surprising. Often professionals were in social circles with common elements of both antagonistic and beneficial relationships depending on these persons of substance's interests. The state of Intelligence was not just limited to the state, but often involved the use of Private Intelligence, this was common to both Britain, America and Germany, for instance in Germany Jahnke's J-Buro provided private intel to the SS. In the UK "The Room" club, "The Walrus" club were common names for private intel gatherings of upper social elites. In America, "The Room; the Club – President Roosevelt's personal intelligence service of upper-class anglophile New Yorkers, led by FDR's friend and kinsman Vincent Astor. Astor was a conduit for information from British intelligence to FDR." (Mahl, 1998, 199)

In Germany with the Jahnkeburo (J-Buro) which provided private intelligence to the SS Amt IV (SS Intelligence), and Jahnke was known as being in charge of Amt IV along with Schellenberg. One example of the intertwining interests, an associate of FDR and a friend of Allen Dulles, was the WWI enemy agent for Germany against America Frederico Stallforth, from a German-Mexican banking family (Dulles, 1958). Though an enemy agent during the war, Stallforth was from the proper social class and continued his life as though nothing happened; he was a back channel conduit to the Nazi regime for FDR's administration.

Differently, Stephenson was not of an upper social class, but had success in the business world, before becoming head of BSC in the US. He eventually became the point man for interface between British and American power including intelligence; a friend of FDR, he was asked to mentor Bill Donovan as the newly minted Coordinator of Intelligence (COI). He went to Britain under Stephenson's tutelage and Stephenson's aide, Ellis, to learn the ways of secret intelligence, though Donovan himself had plenty of experience between the wars for the Morgan organization. Stephenson is an interesting person, he was the founder of the "Dirty War" of British Intelligence used during the decolonization of the British Empire, such as that in Ireland. While also found to be somewhat absent minded at times: "Stephenson's occasional inability to recall things that struck me as ordinarily memorable." (Troy, 1996, 7)

Stephenson was soon a close adviser to Roosevelt and suggested that he put Stephenson's good friend William J. "Wild Bill" Donovan in charge of all U.S. intelligence services. Donovan founded the U.S. Office of Strategic Services (OSS), which in 1947 would become the Central Intelligence Agency (CIA). As senior representative of British intelligence in the western hemisphere, Stephenson was one of the few persons in the Americas who were authorized to view raw Ultra transcripts of German Enigma ciphers that had been decrypted at Britain's Bletchley Park facility. He was trusted by Churchill to decide what Ultra information to pass along to various branches of the U.S. and Canadian governments.

On 2 May 2000, CIA Executive Director David W. Carey, representing Director of Central Intelligence George Tenet and Deputy Director John A. Gordon, accepted from the Intrepid Society of Winnipeg, Manitoba, a bronze statuette of Stephenson. In his remarks, Carey said:

> Sir William Stephenson played a key role in the creation of the CIA. He realized early on that America needed a strong intelligence organization and lobbied contacts close to President Roosevelt to appoint a U.S. "coordinator" to oversee FBI and military intelligence. He urged that the job be given to William J. "Wild Bill" Donovan, who had recently toured British defences and gained the confidence of Prime Minister Winston Churchill. Although Roosevelt didn't establish exactly what Sir William had in mind, the organization created represented a revolutionary step in the history of American intelligence. Donovan's Office of Strategic Services was the first "central" U.S. intelligence service. (https://www.ikn.army.mil/apps/MIHOF/biographies/Stephenson%20William.pdf)

OSS worked closely with and learned from Sir William and other Canadian and British officials during the war. A little later, these OSS officers formed the core of the CIA. Intrepid may not have technically been the father of CIA, but he's certainly in our lineage someplace. One scholar that has reviewed this history, specifically looking into the origins of the CIA, has noted about Stephenson and Donovan's relationship and how it developed:

> "For us, in the United States," Declared William J Casey in 1974, "it all began with a New York lawyer who saw his country facing a deadly menace and knew that it was unprepared and uninformed. It's hard for us to realize today that there was a time in 1940 and 1941, When William J. Donovan was a one-man CIA for President Roosevelt." (Troy, 1996, 3)

> "...British dimension to the story of the CIA's origin. What intrigued me was the oh so subtle suggestion that, at least initially, Donovan, our CIA hero, had been London's "man in Washington" (Troy, 1996, 5)

> Then Stephenson had on that Donovan trip to London, had the royal red carpet rolled out for him, and helped arrange for the second trip, wherein Donovan received an introductory course in British intelligence and unconventional warfare. Then Stephenson, under his SIS cover as director of British Security Coordination (BSC), convinced both Donovan and FDR of the need for establishing COI. maneuvered Donovan into heading the new agency, and thereafter played intelligence schoolmaster to him and his fledgling organization. (Troy, 1996, 5)

It was not necessarily a desire of the CIA for its origins and reliance on William Stephenson to be publicly known. Indeed, it does not appear in any early versions of its origin story:

> Thus, it never appeared in the US War Department's two-volume top secret history of OSS, which was completed as close to events as 1946-47. Nor did it appear in Arthur B. Darling's CIA history, which was written in 1953, still not too long after the events, but which was shortly thereafter deep-sixed because of official displeasure with it. (Troy, 1996, 5)

Even internal historians to the CIA had problems accessing the materials and knowledge, Whitney H. Shepardson, tried to look into the origins of the CIA but: "…Shepardson never moved past the research stage before reported frustration over limited access to documents caused him to throw in the sponge. Hence, Stephenson's name was still lost to CIA history. (Troy, 1996, 6)

One of the sticky points with this knowledge is that of Dick Ellis, Stephenson's confidant and aide, who rather dramatically was revealed to be a Nazi spy, who was responsible for taking Donovan in hand to show the ropes of the Secret Intelligence world in Britain; Donovan who previously confessed to being a fascist. Charles H. ("Dick") Ellis, deputy to Stephenson, Nazi spy: "Ellis, said Stephenson, was the tradecraft expert, the organization man, the one who furnished Bill Donovan with charts and memoranda on running an intelligence organization." (Troy, 1996, 7)

> Now, understand what? Stephenson told me, on my return trip, that "they" – presumably men from MI-5 or MI-6 (British Military Intelligence, Section Five or the Security Service) had questioned him about Ellis's loyalty. There had been some 'fuss', they said, about Ellis having allegedly worked for the Germans before the war. Suffice it to say that by 1966 it had become a very contentious issue within MI-5 and MI-6 and led to what the experts call a "hostile" interrogation of Ellis. Out of that came, reportedly his admission of Nazi, but denial of Soviet, espionage. (Troy, 1996, 14)

> Nor has anyone speculated on the possible damage done by Ellis to SIS, COI and OSS. Likewise, no trace of Ellis is found in Pavel and Anatoli Sudaplatov's account of Soviet espionage in the United States during the war years. Still, one must wonder what seismic secrets, such as Ellis's actual confession, are locked up in British and American intelligence vaults. (Troy, 1996, 15)

Thus, we see that the creation of the CIA was a result of WWII operations in terms of the OSS, being based on British models of secret intelligence work, though the main organizers are obviously implicated in being allied with Fascism. Later, Allen Dulles became head of the CIA; it was known that the OSS and CIA were both largely comprised of Boston Brahmin White Anglo-Saxon Protestant aristocracy. As we shall read, the development of the CIA was a contentious issue.

"On Nov. 18, 1944, Col. William Donovan had submitted a long and detailed report to President Roosevelt which called for the creation of a permanent central authority for intelligence within the Executive Office of the President." (Carter 2016, 107) The creation of a civilian intelligence agency was a critical issue to be overcome in DC at this time, as it would directly impinge on traditional military oversight of intelligence by transferring that from the military to a civilian entity which would not be comprised of Academy grads but rather Ivy League grads.

> Army G-2 head General Clayton Bissell authored the most direct challenge to Donovan's blueprint for a postwar intelligence system. Bissell asserted that the director of this new central intelligence organization would hold too much control over the flow of information and analysis reaching the president, with the inevitable result that the commander-in-chief would be denied a diversity of perspectives and analysis. For their part, the Joint Chiefs of Staff (JCS) preferred a model in which an intelligence coordinator would report to a council of agency heads who would be comprised of the secretaries of State, War, and Navy as well as the members of the JCS. In follow-up memoranda to key actors, Donovan strongly asserted the advantage for the president of an intelligence community that would speak with one authoritative voice and the need for a director of intelligence who could act autonomously as a general manager of the whole intelligence community. (Carter 2016, 108)

Nonetheless, plans for creating a central organ for Intelligence moved forward. In June 1946, General Hoyt Vandenberg [first CIA director] succeeded Admiral Souers of CIG. "During his eleven-month tenure Vandenberg was able to convince the NIA directors to return to him all of the old OSS clandestine intelligence collection units that had been transferred to Army Intelligence when the OSS had been disbanded. Vandenberg merged these espionage and counterintelligence units into an Office of Special Operations." (Carter 2016, 114) He was consolidating all intel into a central organization, which would soon lead to the act of Congress that founded the CIA in 1947:

> With the enactment of the 1947 National Security Act, the CIG essentially became a congressionally chartered and therefore more permanent CIA. The CIA was afforded a clearly articulated chain of command reaching through the newly created National Security Council to the president himself. By the time Vandenberg resigned as DCI in May 1947 his intelligence agency had grown from an organization of about four hundred to over four thousand employees. By that time Vandenberg had also managed to acquire the FBI's former intelligence jurisdiction over Latin America [where the Nazis now regrouped] and had taken over the Army's espionage and counterintelligence operations [no countermeasures independently deployed]. By the summer of 1947 the CIA had already emerged as an all-purpose intelligence bureaucracy, but its emphases were on espionage, counter-espionage, and intelligence analysis, not covert action, and no CIA non-ambiguous authority to conduct covert operations, and although the agency was already engaged in some such actions by mid-1947, it was not until NSC Directive 10/2 was issued in 1948 that the CIA was officially authorized to conduct covert political and paramilitary operations. At that point onward the CIA was very nearly the organization which Colonel Donovan had originally proposed as the successor to the OSS. (Carter 2016, 115)

At first information warfare was not part of the CIA; this changed in 1948:

> On June 18, 1948, the National Security Council created the new Office of Policy Coordination (OPC) specifically to carry out covert political, psychological, economic, and paramilitary operations. The OPC was a hybrid agency that operated as independent service alongside and sometimes in competition with the CIA's Operations Directorate from September 1948 until it was finally merged into the CIA in August of 1952. The OPC's director was a State Department appointee, but the agency operated under the joint supervision of the departments of State and Defense. However, the OPC received its operational directions from the DCI. OSS veteran Frank Wisner was appointed to direct the OPC. (Carter 2016, 119)

Wisner played a role in creating the Gehlen organization in Germany, which was led by the former Nazi SS General. (Carter 2016, 124-5). Wisner was a University of Virginia graduate and member of the Seven Society secret club, he was involved with the start of the influential Georgetown Club within the world of secret intelligence, primarily comprised of Brahmin Blue bloods working for the government or its direct correlates. He later went insane, which may be an example of psyops directed against him.

> Once Congress had chartered the creation of the CIA, Truman signed National Security Directive 4-A in December 1947. This directive explicitly authorized the Director of Central Intelligence to conduct covert psychological operations. President Truman followed this in early 1948 with NSC Directive 10/2, which formally authorized the CIA to undertake covert political and paramilitary operations as directed by the NSC. (Carter 2016, 120)

With this we have the CIA entering the work of psychological operations, information warfare and research into this battle space begins with some of the Operation Paperclip Nazi scientists brought to America also alleged to begin psychological experiments building on their Nazi war research.

THE "BLACK" TERRORIST INTERNATIONAL: NEO-FASCIST PARAMILITARY NETWORKS

A lasting legacy of the Nazi interest in subversion and information warfare is that which became known in the fascist terrorist campaigns of the 1960s-80s as that of the use of "intoxication," a direct output of research by Nazis on turning resistance fighters into informants. It is explained by Bale as:

> The French term intoxication, which in general means "poisoning," is used by Leroy and other guerre revolutionnaire proponents to refer to the "poisoning" of the mind. Specifically, it signifies the manipulation of the political environment by means of the systematic dissemination of false or misleading information to a targeted group (or groups), the purpose of which is to paralyze or otherwise influence that group's subsequent actions. The targeted group can be relatively small or encompass an entire society. (Bale 1994, 227-8)

This was used by the Black International which sought to foment civil wars in France, Italy and elsewhere through false flag operations. For instance, Skorzeny who had been appointed in charge of the continuing fight of the SS at the end of the war, was now leading this movement after escaping Dortmund prison under suspicious – in terms of Allied collusion – circumstances, as noted: "that Skorzeny escaped from Darmstadt prison on 27 July 1948 with the help of a relatively extensive Nazi support network that operated both inside and outside of various prisons and detention centers." (Bale 1994) He was alleged to have trained Americans in commando arts, then later he was noted as training Arab forces against Israel. He even made an attempt at establishing a residence in Ireland but was rejected by "pressure" from the Irish government, so he was not successful in gaining residence in Ireland. He was later outed in a false flag operation of his in France where he tried to infiltrate Communist groups but was outed by a journalist's photo. This is not an isolated case; as Bale points out other operatives had the same fate:

> Leroy collaborated with Guillou at Aginter until his left-wing cover was "burned" by various journalists and he lost his ability to continue conducting "infiltration and intoxication" operations. Others who formed the core group of the action-oriented Ordre et Tradition were Jay S. Sablonsky (alias "Castor," "Jay Salby," "Hugh Franklin," and several other pseudonyms) of Philadelphia, who apparently was affiliated in some way with American intelligence (Bale, 1994, 135) (Kruger et al, 2015)

One of the other methodologies taught by Skorzeny and other SS agents working for a Fourth Reich is that of the "strategy of tension":

> The following passages have particular relevance in connection with the types of terrorist actions that characterized the *"strategy of tension"*: Subversion acts with appropriate means upon the minds and wills in order to induce them to act outside of all logic, against all rules, against all laws: in this way it conditions individuals and enables one to make use of them as one wishes.* *Action psychologique [is] a non-violent weapon [used] to condition public opinion through the use of the press, the radio, conferences, demonstrations, etc…with the goal of uniting the masses against the authorities.* (Bale, 1994, 138) [emphasis added]

As we shall read later, this is the equivalent of the Soviet creation of Reflexive Control. These methods of Information Warfare do not originate with the Soviets but have been practiced for a long time by all colonizing powers, for instance.

Bibliography:

Bale, J. (1994) *The "Black" Terrorist International: Neo-Fascist Paramilitary Networks and the Strategy of Tension" in Italy*, 1968-1974 Ph.D. Dissertation UC Berkeley

Bonneville, N. (1792) *Illuminati Manifesto of World Revolution*. Booksurge Publishing, 2011

Brownson, O. (2017) *The Works of Orestes A. Brownson "Politics."* BiblioLife 2017

Campani G. (2016) *Neo-fascism from the Twentieth Century to the Third Millennium: The Case of Italy*. In: Lazaridis G., Campani G., Benveniste A. (eds) *The Rise of the Far Right in Europe*. Palgrave Macmillan, London. https://doi.org/10.1057/978-1-137-55679-0_2

Carter, J. (2016) *The Development of the American Surveillance State, 1900-1960*. Edwin Mellen Press 2016

COAT- Coalition to Oppose the Arms Trade (2004) *Wall Street's Plot to Seize the White House: Facing the Corporate Roots of American Fascism* in Press for Conversion! (issue #53) http://coat.ncf.ca/our_magazine/links/53/53-index.html

Dulles, A. (1958) *LETTER TO FEDERICO STALLFORTH FROM ALLEN W. DULLES* 18 March 1958 https://www.cia.gov/readingroom/docs/CIA-RDP80B01676R003900010091-1.pdf

Higham, C. (2007) *Trading with the Enemy: The Nazi-American Money Plot 1933-1949*. iUniverse 2007

Horstmann, B. (2017) *Hitler in Pasewalk: Die Hypnose und ihre Folgen*. Droste Verlag 2017

Kolb, E (2005). *The Weimar Republic*. London: Routledge. 2005 p. 172.

Kruger, H., Meldon, J., Scott, P.D. (2015) *Great Heroin Coup: Drugs, Intelligence & International Fascism* Trine-Day 2015

Linderman, A. (2016) *Rediscovering Irregular Warfare.* University of Oklahoma Press (February 19, 2016) Pg. 134-5

Thomas, Lord Hugh, (2002) *SS-1: The Unlikely Death of Heinrich Himmler.* William Collins (March 31, 2016)

Mahl, T. (1998) *Desperate Deception: British Covert Operations in the United States, 1939-44.* Potomac Books Inc. (January 13, 2000)

MI-5 (2011) *KV 3/418: Miscellaneous indications of German Intelligence Service post-war plans for continued..* The National Archives, Kew https://discovery.nationalarchives.gov.uk/details/r/C11692013

Troy, T. (1996) *Wild Bill and Intrepid: Bill Donovan, Bill Stephenson, and the Origin of CIA.* New Haven, CT: Yale University Press, 1996.

Von Raumer, K. (1859) *German Universities: contributions to the History and Improvement of the German Universities* Oxford https://www.google.com/books/edition/German_Universities/tMkFAAAAQAAJ?hl=en

Weitz, E., Roubinek, E. (2019) 'Hitler's First Major Statement on Anti-Semitism: Reply to Adolf Gemlich (September 16, 1919)', http://germanhistorydocs.ghi-dc.org/sub_document.cfm?document_id=3909 (accessed 6/6/19)

West, N. (2005) *The Guy Liddell Diaries Vol.II: 1942-1945 MI5's Director of Counter-Espionage in World War II.* Routledge; 1st edition (August 6, 2005)

CHAPTER 2

INFORMATION WARFARE:
PSYOPS AND INFORMATION OPERATIONS

The development of PSYOPS is not just used on an adversarial target, but is also used, in the case of Weimar Germany from 1918-1933 by German Military Intelligence on its own population. The Reichswehr (German Military) engaged in a systematic approach to counter Communist takeovers in Bavaria with their own far-right counterbalance creating its own propaganda that was politically aligned with far-right nationalist sentiments. The means of indoctrinating a subject population is conducted through Psychological Operations (PSYOPS) and is a part of what is known in military parlance as Information Operations.

INFORMATION OPERATIONS

Information Operations (IO) is a category of direct and indirect support operations for the United States Military. By definition in Joint Publication 3-13, IO are described as the integrated employment of electronic warfare (EW), computer network operations (CNO), psychological operations (PSYOP), military deception (MILDEC), and operations security (OPSEC), in concert with specified supporting and related capabilities, to influence, disrupt, corrupt or usurp adversarial human and automated decision making while protecting our own. Information Operations (IO) are actions taken to affect adversary information and information systems while defending one's own information and information systems. (Joint Chiefs of Staff, 2012)

From a cybernetics perspective it is interesting to note that the mission of IO is both to degrade and protect, through automated self-protection mechanisms, the ability to conduct EW, PSYOP, MILDEC, OPSEC, using automation. The question of whether to always have humans in the loop will come up in later chapters on Cybernetics. A key point is to understand that both attack and protection are envisioned as automated processes in modern IO, which was first carried out operationally during the Balkans Crisis of the 1990s, although Irish Republicans claim it was used in Northern Ireland during this same time, the early 1990s, as we shall read in Chapter 5: automated psyops and IO during the "Troubles."

ELECTRONIC WARFARE

Electronic warfare (EW) refers to any action involving the use of the electromagnetic spectrum or directed energy to control the spectrum, attack an enemy, or impede enemy assaults via the spectrum. The purpose of electronic warfare is to deny the opponent the advantage of, and ensure friendly unimpeded access to, the EM spectrum. EW can be applied from air, sea, land, and space by manned and unmanned systems, and can target communication, radar, or other services. EW includes three major subdivisions: Electronic Attack (EA), Electronic Protection (EP), and Electronic warfare Support (ES). Often one will hear the ideal of "Full Spectrum Dominance" in relation to ES. Military and Intelligence is seeking to have the upper hand against adversaries in the Electro-Magnetic spectrum.

COMPUTER NETWORK OPERATIONS

Botnets are self-replicating computer viruses that can take over a machine for the purposes of attack on other machines. The use of networks of computers, and of humans, is a valuable tool in any offensive or defensive context. The ubiquity of computational devices from the desktop to the hand-held, and now with the Internet, even appliances are vulnerable to attack. Computer Network Attack (CNA) is the use of computer networks to disrupt, deny, degrade and destroy information resident in computers and computer networks. The countermeasures to CNA are Computer Network Defense (CND). Computer Network Exploitation (CNE) is the ability to gather intelligence or data from target or adversary automated information system or networks.

PSYCHOLOGICAL OPERATIONS (PSYOP)

What is PSYOPS? William Donovan of the OSS in his World War II "Basic Estimate of Psychological Warfare" defines PSYOPS:

> Psychological warfare is the coordination and use of all means, including moral and physical, by which the end is attained – other than those recognized military operations, but including the psychological exploitation of the result of those recognized military actions – which tend to destroy the will of the enemy to achieve victory and to damage his political or economic capacity to do so; which tend to deprive the enemy of the support, assistance, or sympathy of his allies or associates. Or of neutrals, or to prevent his acquisition of such support, assistance, or sympathy; or which tend to create, maintain, or increase the will to victory of our own people and allies and to acquire, maintain, or to increase the support, assistance, and sympathy of neutrals. (Roosevelt, 99)

Whereas a field operative definition from Lt. Col. Phillip P. Katz, (US Army) defines PSYOP as:

> Psychological operations is that specialized field of communications that deals with formulating, conceptualizing, and programming goals, and with evaluating government-to-government and government-to-people persuasion techniques. Properly defined, PSYOP is the planned or programmed use of human actions to influence the attitudes and actions of friendly, neutral, and enemy populations that are important to national objectives. The critical variable is, then the perceptions of foreign populations. Propaganda is only the most obvious example of a persuasive communication. (Katz et al, 135)

The means of delivering PSYOPS has changed over time as new technologies have been created. The fuzziness in the general populace's understanding of PSYOPS is attested to by Col. Goldstein:

> Understanding PSYOP is not a simple task. Historically, both military and civilian discussions of PSYOP throughout the leadership spectrum have regularly substituted cliches, myths, and untruths for hard evidence or analysis of what PSYOP is and how it can serve our national objectives. PSYOP policy and doctrine have not received their deserved attention while hostile PSYOP efforts against the US are misunderstood and often *ineffectively countered.* [emphasis added] (Goldstein, 13)

As PSYOPS are a general means of attack, in other words, all segments of a society can and are targeted by these methods, it is in the national interest that an informed public regarding these attacks is undertaken. Just as with a bombing campaign, we must not leave the public in the lurch and unaware of these methods of attack against an entire nation. In information warfare a well-informed populace is part of the national defense strategy, as we are really talking about knowledge warfare. Yet, most nations choose to not inform their citizens about such attacks and technology as those countries themselves are using that same highly classified technology against their enemies. Those countries are at a disadvantage in terms of defense as they have no adequate means to counter the threat with the general populace as they seek to use the same weapons and deny their existence or obfuscate about their full potential.

The utilization of PSYOPS in WWII by the Nazis is well documented in terms of propaganda and vilification of sub-cultures within the German nation. We all can easily think of examples specifically related to Jews, Gypsies, Leftists, Poles, Slavs in general and LGBTQ people that demonized them. What is little understood is how deep their attack vectors using PSYOPS has extended including into civilian areas of governments of the Allies, through active campaigns of turning agents or even the outright brainwashing of service members. The continuing proliferation of PSYOPS throughout the world's militaries has also hastened the development of new technologies for these operations. The bygone days of drawing up leaflets are now augmented by cyber PSYOPS delivered via electromagnetic means, first encountered during World War II with the creation of neurological weapons, or neuroweapons, See Ch. 3.

MILITARY DECEPTION (MILDEC)

In the former Soviet Union deception is known as "Maskirovka" (маскировка) which is:

> …a set of processes employed during the Soviet era designed to mislead, confuse, and interfere with anyone accurately assessing its plans, objectives, strengths, and weaknesses. When used in peacetime it is a political ruse that can be directed at domestic and foreign audiences, designed to alter perceptions about the Soviet Union and its allies in a desired way. A famous example of peacetime Soviet maskirovka was Operation Anadyr or the secret Soviet plan to deploy IRBMs MRBMs in Cuba in the summer of 1962. Maskirovka is closely tied to the concept of "reflexive control," which is about manipulating the enemy's perceptions in a way that the enemy will make decisions detrimental to their own interests - in this case not prevent the deployment of Soviet missiles.

> Maskirovka includes what Hitler called the "big lie" – a lie so blatant and outrageous that ordinary people cannot believe that their trusted leaders would say something like that, if it was not true. This technique is helped by the fact that in the Soviet Union there was a culture of deceit, which still prevails in post-Soviet Bloc countries, especially their militaries: "Lying routinely occurs at the most senior uniformed levels, even when an argument is clearly untenable or contradicted by obvious facts." (Krishnan, 2017, 183)

As we shall read later, this is a prototype of what USAF Col. Szafraski proposed in neocortical warfare in 1994. Perhaps the most well-known Military deception campaign involved convincing the Nazis that the D-Day invasion would occur at different locations through the setting up of fake camps, logistically centered to the North of the actual invasion site.

> MILDEC is described as being those actions executed to deliberately mislead adversary decision makers as to friendly military capabilities, intentions, and operations, thereby causing the adversary to take specific actions (or inactions) that will contribute to the accomplishment of the friendly forces' mission. MILDEC and OPSEC are complementary activities — MILDEC seeks to encourage incorrect analysis, causing the adversary to arrive at specific false deductions, while OPSEC seeks to deny real information to an adversary, and prevent correct deduction of friendly plans. To be effective, a MILDEC operation must be susceptible to adversary collection systems and "seen" as credible to the enemy commander and staff. A plausible approach to MILDEC planning is to employ a friendly course of action (COA) that can be executed by friendly forces and that adversary intelligence can verify. However, MILDEC planners must not fall into the trap of ascribing to the adversary particular attitudes, values, and reactions that "mirror image" likely friendly actions in the same situation, i.e., assuming that the adversary will respond or act in a particular manner based on how we would respond. There are always competing priorities for the resources required for deception and the resources required for the real operation. For this reason, the deception plan should be developed concurrently with the real plan, starting with the commander's and staff's initial estimate, to ensure proper resourcing of both. To encourage incorrect analysis by the adversary, it is usually more efficient and effective to provide a false purpose for real activity than to create false activity. OPSEC of the deception plan is at least as important as OPSEC of the real plan, since compromise of the deception may expose the real plan. This requirement for close hold planning while ensuring detailed coordination is the greatest challenge to MILDEC planners.

> MILDEC as an IO Core Capability. MILDEC is fundamental to successful IO. It exploits the adversary's information systems, processes, and capabilities. MILDEC relies upon understanding how the adversary commander and supporting staff think and plan and how both use information management to support their efforts. This requires a high degree of coordination with all elements of friendly forces' activities in the information environment as well as with physical activities. Each of the core, supporting, and related capabilities has a part to play in the development of successful MILDEC and in maintaining its credibility over time. While PA should not be involved in the provision of false information, it must be aware of the intent and purpose of MILDEC in order not to inadvertently compromise it. (Joint Chiefs of Staff, 1996)

The key component of course of action is further delineated by the JCS:

> A message targeted to exploit a fissure between a key member of the adversary's leadership who has a contentious relationship with another key decision maker is an example. That message could cause internal strife resulting in the adversary foregoing an intended course of action and adopting a position more favorable to our interests. (Joint Chiefs of Staff, 1996)

It's clearly understood that the intended goal is to sow confusion in the enemy and in that confusion generate actions favorable to one's own side, an Aikido of warfare, which in this case is winning the peace as no lethal force is ever used.

OPERATIONS SECURITY (OPSEC)

OPSEC as an IO Core Capability. OPSEC denies the adversary the information needed to correctly assess friendly capabilities and intentions. In particular, OPSEC complements MILDEC by denying an adversary information required to both assess a real plan and to disprove a deception plan. For those IO capabilities that exploit new opportunities and vulnerabilities, such as EW and CNO, OPSEC is essential to ensure friendly capabilities are not compromised. The process of identifying essential elements of friendly information and taking measures to mask them from disclosure to adversaries is only one part of a defense-in-depth approach to securing friendly information. To be effective, other types of security must complement OPSEC. Examples of other types of security include physical security, AI programs, computer network defense (CND), and personnel programs that screen personnel and limit authorized access. What occurs, often, is that data is either leaked, stolen, or hacked online and the enemy has access to and can decipher what that information may say. This is especially true for defensive operational security. US servicemen and servicewomen may have Facebook, multiple blogs, or upload photos, which can lead to the enemy knowing troop movements and locations. With this information, setting up ambush and wreaking havoc on US and support personnel becomes much easier. Geo-tagging features of cellular phones especially, may cause this type of breach in OPSEC. (Joint Chiefs of Staff, 2006)

STEGANOGRAPHY

In a later chapter we will read about the work of Dr. John Norseen, who used the term he picked up in Russia of "stegobullets," which was a means of targeting the brain, putting the pipper on point, through mental manipulation using subliminals. It was based on the more common means of concealing information in images. When one considers that messages could be encrypted steganographically in e-mail messages, particularly e-mail spam, the notion of junk e-mail takes on a whole new light. Coupled with the "chaffing and winnowing" technique, a sender could get messages out and cover their tracks all at once. An interesting aspect of Steganography is that it is a means of "secure" communication where the message is out in the open in the form of an embedding in a public image. We will encounter similar concepts later when holography is covered in the study of remote biological influencing.

HISTORY OF PSYCHOLOGICAL OPERATIONS (PSYOPS)

Warfare has always had an effective psychological component, leaders have used degrees of deception (camouflage), disinformation and other methods to fool their enemies since humans began fighting each other. In modern times, most view World War I as the beginning of a professionalization of these military tactics. Of course Great Britain, being the largest Empire of the time, had the most advanced psychological operations and Intelligence organizations of all the combatants, for instance deploying shock troops and psychological operations against the founding of the Republic of Ireland in 1916, and then re-deploying these assets to the 1920s Palestine Mandate, training Zionist Militias in counter-gang tactics, the Black and Tans in Palestine using Jews to attack Arabs, which was repeated later in Northern Ireland, using Unionists to attack Irish Nationalists. Germany made efforts to keep up, but even though dropping pamphlets was an organized activity, it still did not play much into the German war effort like it did for the Allies.

> British and Nazi German strategies and tactics in the field have historically been termed "political warfare" and Weltanschauungskrieg ("worldview warfare"), respectively. Each of these conceptualizations of psychological warfare explicitly links mass communication with selective application of violence (murder, sabotage, assassination, insurrection, counter-insurrection, etc.) as a means of achieving ideological, political, or military goals. These overlapping conceptual systems often contributed to one another's development, while retaining characteristics of the political and cultural assumptions of the social system that generated it. (Simpson, 1994, 11)

The scientific study of Psyops began in America with the work of Harold Lasswell who in 1926 published *Propaganda Techniques in the World War*. Lasswell went on to be a key researcher in psychological operations research for the American Military. Chris Simpson in his book, *The Science of Coercion* writes, "the study of psychological warfare is in part a look at how powerful elites manage change, reconstitute themselves in new forms, and struggle – not always successfully – to shape the consciousness of audiences that they claim as their own." (Simpson, 1994). He draws out the history of research in this area and its sponsorship by wealthy clients, such as the Ford Foundation and Rockefeller Foundations, as well as the Security State, as a scientific methodology was applied to the subject field:

> U.S. military, propaganda, and intelligence agencies favored an approach to the study of mass communication that offered both an explanation of what communication "is" (at least insofar as those agencies' missions were concerned) and a box of tools for examining it. Put most simply, they saw mass communication as an instrument for persuading or dominating targeted groups. They understood "communication" as little more than a form of transmission into which virtually any type of message could be plugged (once one had mastered the appropriate techniques) to achieve ideological, political, or military goals. Academic contractors convinced their clients that scientific dissection and measurement of the constituent elements of mass communication would lead to the development of powerful new tools for social management, in somewhat the same way earlier science had paved the way for penicillin, electric lights, and the atom bomb. Federal patrons meanwhile believed that analysis of audiences and communication effects could improve ongoing propaganda and intelligence programs. (Simpson, 1994, 5-6)

Lasswell was a recipient of many funding dollars from the Security State as well as these Foundations. He is famous in communication theory for his dictum: "Who says what to whom with what effect." Applying a scientific method to communications theory for the purpose of control was a key element in the promulgation of this research. Creating a reductionist model for research where positivistic outlooks took center stage:

> For Lasswell, the study of all social communication could be reduced to "who says what to whom with what effect" – a dictum that is practically inscribed in stone over the portals of those U.S. colleges offering communication as a field of study. This was a seemingly simple, logical approach to analysis of communication, but it carried with it sweeping implications. Lippmann and Lasswell's articulation of communication-as-domination permitted a significant step forward in applying a positivist scientific method to the study of social communication. Positivism has traditionally been based in part on taking complex, unmeasurable phenomena and breaking them up into discrete parts, measuring those parts, and bit by bit building up a purportedly objective understanding of the phenomenon as a whole. Its early applications in the social sciences in the United States had been pioneered at the University of Chicago, Columbia University, and other academic centers.
>
> New measurement techniques of this sort often have substantial impact on society outside of academe, however. In this case, Lasswell's formulation dovetailed so closely with emerging commercial and political forces in the United States that his slogan became the common wisdom among U.S. social scientists almost overnight. By reducing communication to the Lasswellian model of who says what, et cetera, it became possible for the first time to systematically isolate and measure those aspects of communication that were of greatest relevance to powerful groups in U.S. society. (Simpson, 1994, 19)

Another American researcher in psychological operations was Walter Lippman, who was attached to the American Expeditionary Forces of World War I with the purpose of creating psychological operations material for the war effort. He formulated an important concept of the stereotype:

> Lippmann's career during these years illustrates a phenomenon that was to become much more common in the aftermath of World War II: He was an intellectual who shaped psychological strategy during the war itself, and then helped integrate that experience into the social sciences once most of the shooting was over. Lippmann's highly influential concept of the "stereotype," for example, contended that new communication and transportation technologies had created a "world that we have to deal with politically [that is] out of reach, out of sight, out of mind." The "pictures in our heads" of this world – the stereotypes – " are acted upon by groups of people, or by individuals acting in the name of groups." The complexity and pace of the new world that Lippmann envisaged, together with the seeming ease with which stereotypes could be manipulated for political ends, led him to conclude that "representative government … cannot be worked successfully, no matter what the basis of election, unless there is an independent, expert organization for making the unseen facts [of the new world] intelligible to those who have to make the decisions." The converse of that proposition was that decision makers

had a responsibility to repair the "defective organization of public opinion," as Lippmann put it, in the interests of social efficiency and the greater good. These concepts, first introduced in *Public Opinion*, are illustrated throughout that text with references to Lippmann's wartime experiences as a propagandist and intelligence specialist. (Simpson, 1994, 17)

Yet, Lippman was viewed as a progressive in his time; a police reformer in Denver after the war, his theories were supposed to steer the country toward greater equality or equilibrium rather then become an instrument of hidden power. On the other hand, we have Lasswell, who advocated "those with money... should systematically manipulate mass sentiment from Nazis and Communists" (Simpson, 1994, 23). Lasswell writes that the spread of literacy:

> ...did not release the masses from ignorance and superstition but altered the nature of both and compelled the development of a whole new technique of control, largely through propaganda... [A propagandist's] regard for men rests on no democratic dogmatisms about men being the best judges of their own interests. The modern propagandist, like the modern psychologist, recognizes that men are often poor judges of their own interests ... [Those with power must cultivate] sensitiveness to those concentrations of motive which are implicit and available for rapid mobilization when the appropriate symbol [semiotic] is offered ... [The propagandist is] no phrasemonger but a promoter of overt acts. (Simpson, 1994, 21)

Which presages the "Reflexive Control" of later theories. Having a small class speaking for the entire nation does seem to be counterproductive; nonetheless, with Rockefeller Foundation money behind him, he knew who was funding his research. The scientific application of communications theory to psychological operations did not go uncriticized at the time, as was pointed out by Simpson:

> One Rockefeller seminar participant, Donald Slesinger (former dean of the school of social science at the University of Chicago), blasted Lasswell's claims as using a democratic guise to tacitly accept the objectives and methods of a new form of authoritarianism. "We [the Rockefeller seminar] have been willing, without thought, to sacrifice both truth and human individuality in order to bring about given mass responses to war stimuli," Slesinger contended. "We have thought in terms of fighting dictatorships-by-force through the establishment of dictatorship-by-manipulation." Slesinger's view enjoyed some support from other participants and from Rockefeller Foundation officers such as Joseph Willits, who criticized what he described as authoritarian or even fascist aspects of Lasswell's arguments. Despite this resistance, the social polarization created by the approaching war strongly favored Lasswell, and in the end he enjoyed substantial new funding and an expanded staff courtesy of the foundation. Slesinger drifted away from the Rockefeller seminars and appears to have rapidly lost influence within the community of academic communication specialists. (Simpson, 1994, 23)

While this research was going on in the United States in the 1930s in Germany, we have the rising up of Goebbels as Propaganda Minister for the Nazi government along with others such as Otto Ohlendorf, Dr. Reinhard Hoehn and Elisabeth Noelle-Neumann, all dedicated propagandists.

After the start of World War II we have the creation in the United States of offices dedicated to psychological operations with one of the mainstays of the work the ex-Wall Street lawyer Bill Donovan, who previously had done Intelligence work in Europe. In July 1941 FDR created the aptly named Office of the Coordinator of Information, placing Donovan in charge. He adopted Nazi psyops to an "Americanized" version:

> The phrase "psychological warfare" is reported to have first entered English in 1941 as a translated mutation of the Nazi term Weltanschauungskrieg (literally, worldview warfare), meaning the purportedly scientific application of propaganda, terror, and state pressure as a means of securing an ideological victory over one's enemies. William "Wild Bill" Donovan, then director of the newly established U.S. intelligence agency Office of Strategic Services (OSS), viewed an understanding of Nazi psychological tactics as a vital source of ideas for "Americanized" versions of many of the same stratagems. Use of the new term quickly became widespread throughout the U.S. intelligence community. For Donovan psychological warfare was destined to become a full arm of the U.S. military, equal in status to the army, navy, and air force.

Donovan was among the first in the United States to articulate a more or less unified theory of psychological warfare. As he saw it, the "engineering of consent" techniques used in peacetime propaganda campaigns could be quite effectively adapted to open warfare. Pro-Allied propaganda was essential to reorganizing the

U.S. economy for war and for creating public support at home for intervention in Europe, Donovan believed. Fifth-column movements could be employed abroad as sources of intelligence and as morale-builders for populations under Axis control. He saw "special operations – meaning sabotage, subversion, commando raids, and guerrilla movements – as useful for softening up targets prior to conventional military assaults. "Donovan's concept of psychological warfare was all-encompassing," writes Colonel Alfred Paddock, who has specialized in this subject for the U.S. Army War College. "Donovan's visionary dream was to unify these functions in support of conventional (military) unit operations, thereby forging a 'new instrument of war.'" (Simpson 1994)

Black propaganda was the term used for covert psychological operations; when the OSS was created and Donovan placed as its head, black propaganda was moved to the OSS. Another Wall Street lawyer and friend of Donovan, John J. McCloy, descended from Scottish Unionists, who would later head the Warren Commission, was head of the Army's G2 Intelligence Division's psychological operations department during the war. After the war, Donovan spearheaded the creation of a full-time covert Intelligence group in the United States based on the model of British Secret Intelligence. The advocated Central Intelligence Group was created in 1946 with Gen. Hoyt Vandenburg as it's leader. Then in 1947 the Central Intelligence Agency was created. The years 1946-50 saw the creation of a secret bureaucracy for conducting clandestine warfare, including psychological operations, whose existence was denied for some 30 years in public discourse. In 1947 a layered approach was created for psychological operations with National Security Council directive 4A, which created an overt psychological operations program which "must be supplemented by covert psychological operations" (Simpson, 1994, 38). Later the Office of Policy Coordination was created, led by former Wall Street lawyer, and friend of Donovan and of fraternity brother Dulles, Frank Wisner. An assistant to Wisner when at the State Department was Hans Speier who advocated for martial law:

> He contended that the U.S. government should prepare immediately to "impos[e] martial law [in the United States] to guard against defeatism, demoralization and disorder," if that proved necessary. More urgent in Speier's mind, however, was activation of a strong "offensive" program designed to overthrow rival regimes. "Subversion [is the] aim of strategic propaganda," Speier wrote. "The United States … can wage sincere political subversion propaganda against the dictatorial Soviet regime, particularly in the political realm. … Planning and preparation for strategic propaganda in a future war must begin now."
>
> Thus by the end of the 1940s Speier, McGranahan, and other prominent communication research specialists used the pages of *POQ* [*Public Opinion Quarterly*] to call on U.S. security agencies to employ state-of-the-art techniques to facilitate the overthrow of governments of selected foreign countries in a "future" war – the preparations for which should begin immediately. Speier's program included coercive measures, even the imposition of martial law, to ensure that the U.S. population cooperated. Although Speier presented his argument in the form of a proposal, it is today known from the declassified records of the National Security Council that many of the measures he recommended were in fact actually under way at the time his article appeared. (Simpson, 1994, 48)

As we can see, the slippery slope of scientific coercion can lead it's advocates to nullify that which it claims to protect – individual liberty; creating contradictory positions that seem to have no humanely rational epicenter.

Digital Psyops through Neocortical Warfare

In the mid-1990s, as the Internet became a small part of information exchange available to the public, albeit on a much smaller scale than today, discussion of cyberwarfare started to make its way into conversations regarding defense. One military strategist in this area was Col. Szafranski who postulated the extension of psychological operations into what he termed 'Neocortical Warfare':

> As the right and left brains interact, the enemy is not seen as an inorganic system with multiple centers of gravity, but as other neocortical organisms. Neocortical warfare is warfare that strives to control or shape the behavior of enemy organisms, but without destroying the organisms. It does this by influencing, even to the point of regulating, the consciousness, perceptions and will of the adversary's leadership: the enemy's neocortical system. In simple ways, neocortical warfare attempts to penetrate adversaries' recurring and simultaneous cycles of "observation, orientation, decision and action [OODA Loop]."
>
> In complex ways, it strives to present the adversary's leaders – its collective brain – with perceptions, sensory and cognitive data designed to result in a narrow and controlled (or an overwhelmingly large and disori-

enting) range of calculations and evaluations. The product of these evaluations and calculations are adversary choices that correspond to our desired choices and the outcomes we desire. Influencing leaders to not fight is paramount. Warfare is "organized" fighting. It becomes less organized, more nonlinear, more chaotic and unpredictable once it begins. Until battle (physical fighting) begins, the leaders can stop it more easily. In very complex ways, the neocortical approach to warfare influences the adversary leaders' perceptions of patterns and images, and shapes insights, imaginings and nightmares. This is all brought about without physical violence. It is all designed to reorganize and redefine phenomenological designators to lead the enemy to choose not to fight. In neocortical warfare, enemy minds are the Schwerpunkt [center of gravity] and armed military capability the Nebenpunkte (a term coined by John Boyd to mean "anything that is not the Schwerpunkt"). (Szafranski, 1994, 404)

Col. Szafranski wrote this shortly after the fall of the Soviet Union and the movement westward of many Russian scientists, like Lefebvre, and their ideals regarding Reflexive Control entered the US defense mental space. Clearly, this was an early writing of what would be more commonly referred to as Neuro-warfare. Another concept from this passage is the work of John Boyd in the OODA Loop.

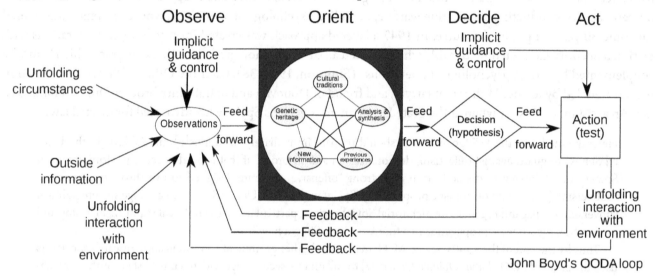

John Boyd's OODA loop

(Szafranski, 1994)

John Boyd was a USAF Colonel who was a renowned air engagement expert, claiming he could down any enemy aircraft in 40 seconds or less. He postulated the OODA loop based on the need to act decisively and quickly in supersonic jet engagements, although this may not necessarily be the case in all situations; for example, Submarine warfare. Szafranski quotes Boyd:

Boyd, "A Discourse on Winning and Losing," suggests that the way to win is to operate (that is, to observe, get oriented, decide and act) more quickly than an adversary. Ways to do this include depriving the adversary of essential information, overloading the adversary with puzzling or difficult to interpret information, using the adversary's "genetic heritage" or "cultural tradition" so that the enemy is self-disconcerted or self-deceived, frustrating adversary actions, or denying the enemy feedback, or accurate feedback on the consequences of action taken. All of this is designed to "generate uncertainty, confusion, disorder, panic, chaos…" and shatter cohesion, produce paralysis, and bring about collapse." Because the real province of conflict is the mind, all warfare is neocortical warfare. (Szafranski, 1994, 414)

His ideals gained wide traction with certain sections of National Defense. It is fitting that Machine Learning would be deployed in the OODA Loop given AI's ability to do things exponential degrees faster than a human, yet a bad model or misinterpretation of the environment could lead to a more rapid driving of the train off the tracks and possibly forbid any capability of correction.

Neocortical warfare here, ostensibly is an extrinsic means of changing one's internal mind. Although, it does presage the work of Dr. John Norseen where direct manipulation of the neocortex is the manner of changing or altering minds rather than through extrinsic means such as subliminal messaging. One way that Col. Szafranski suggested doing this was the use of Neuro-Linguistic Programming:

> We might use tools similar to Richard Bandler and John Grinder's "neuro linguistic programming" to understand how the adversary receives, processes and organizes auditory, visual and kinesthetic perceptions.
> Knowing what the adversary values and using the adversary's own representational systems allows us to correlate values, to communicate with the minds of enemies in the verbal and nonverbal language of the enemy. The objective is to shape the enemy's impressions as well as the enemy's initiatives and responses, pacing the enemy through the cycle of observation, orientation, decision and action [OODA Loop]. (Szafranski, 1994, 405)

Neurolinguistic programming is a noted methodology in behavior modification, which also touches on hypnosis, here being postulated to be used in neurowarfare or psychological operations.

Neocortical Warfare is broken down into 4 parts:

> 1. Warfare is perpetual, conceptions of security or insecurity exist in the mind.

> 2. Adversaries will wage ongoing neocortical warfare against us. "Neocortical warfare uses language, images and information to assault the mind, hurt morale and change the will. It is prosecuted against our weaknesses or uses our strengths to weaken us in unexpected and imaginative ways. That being the case, we have less room for the unimaginative, the mentally weak, or whatever Cohen and Gooch mean by the psychologically crippled among our leaders. Leaders are critical nodes, the targets of neocortical warfare, and they must be prepared for the adversary's assaults." (Szafranski, 1994, 407)

> 3. Continuous and ongoing neocortical warfare against the adversary, control the "enemy" through the OODA Loop.

> 4. Shock and Awe strategies in warfare to supplement neocortical warfare. All future lethal military operations are "special ops" with the primary objective of these ops being "psychological warfare."

Clearly neocortical warfare was envisioned as an ongoing and pervasive effort to secure American National Interests. It is a good question as to what extent, especially given the NSA spying on allies like Germany's Prime Minister, this effort at conditioning and controlling minds is still ongoing. Col. Szafranski wrote about the broad brush that Information Warfare could use on a society, sweeping up both combatants and non-combatants.

Narrative Networks: Applying Natural Language Programing

Dr. James Giordano, US DoD consultant on the ethics of neuroweapons, has written extensively on the use of narrative networks in what is known as NEURINT Neuro-cognitive Intelligence in the sense of espionage. He notes regarding NEURINT: "Assessment of neuro-psychosocial factors in narratives, individual and group expressions and activities." He has also lectured on the Cyber-linked neurocognitive manipulation, of which more is written below (see BCI section). Returning to the notion of Narrative Networks Krishnan and Giordano have both referenced the DARPA sponsored work of Dr. Casebeer. Krishnan relates regarding narrative network utilization:

> Analyzing the neurobiological impact of narratives on hormones and neurotransmitters, reward processing, and emotion-cognition interaction. (Krishnan 2017, 134)

Narratives Networks use a method based on Neuro Linguistic Programming to rewire human neural networks in much the way that the East German Stasi sought to use *Zertsetzung* in conditioning dissidents to become socially acceptable within a totalitarian world view. As is seen from the work of Dr. Casebeer it is clear that linguistics is being used to interfere with people's brain states to recondition them. It can also be used to provide disinformation and defamation about targeted individuals. While also being used by the CIA in 1951 in trying to create a hypnotized person that will not only carry out acts contrary to their morals but also will not have any memory of them, undergoing amnesia, or erasure of short term memory, the proverbial "Manchurian candidates" (Krishnan 2017, 21) or "sleeper agents." (Krishnan 2017, 37). Dr. James Giordano talks about the use of narrative networks:

> …we're targeting the brain and we're talking the brain at a variety of levels now like any good target what I have to be able to do is I need to put the Pipper on point in other words I need to put this gun site so to speak where I want it to be … I have to recon my target area quite well so as to be able to acquire viable targets and also to avoid collateral damage. The assessment neuro-technologies do a very good job doing that with increasing sophistication they're not used individually they're used in a way that's called co-registered. I can use forms of neuro-imaging and these are diverse they run the gamut from the older forms such as things like computerized tomography and single photon emission tomography to the much newer forms that utilize a highly specific electromagnetic pulse signal not only to be able to image certain brain areas but also to image tracts communicating networks and nodes within the brain in a directional way and in rather rapid time. I can utilize near a physiological recordings such as electroencephalography, and I've dialed in the specificity of that as well, through the use of quantitative techniques. I can also look at neuro-genomics and neuro-genetics taking a look at genetic profiles of individuals and groups to be able to determine what genes may be in fact coding for certain structures and functions of the brain. I can utilize proteomics and other forms of biomarkers and I can utilize Neurosci informatics. In other words, I can harness all of these forms of assessments to a big data approach that allow me to make both comparatives and normative indices not only within an individual but between individuals; not only between individuals but within and between groups on a variety of scales. So the idea of assessment technology in many ways combines each and all of these … fortified through the use of big data we've written comprehensively about the use of big data as a force multiplier in neuroscience and neural weaponology.
>
> …but the idea here is like so many other forms of recon and evaluation and assessment we as humans tend not to turn rocks over just to look what's under side we turn rocks over so we can use what's under there, the brain is no different. If what I'm doing is I'm trying to put a pipper [gun sight] on target and make sure it's we're on points I want to do something with that this is not just a let's go see mission this is a let's go see so that ultimately we can translate this into some viable effect, either of the knowledge or to actually target these things to the use of some technique or technology. Now we're looking at is the interventional techniques do not ignore cyber because power some knowledge and information and if I understand how a brain works and how neurocognitive mechanisms are operative in the various impressions we then gain in our thoughts emotions that may ultimately feed into behaviors, I can manipulate the type of information and its delivery so as to be able to influence brain state. This is part of the incentive and underlying rationale and methods that were employed in a DARPA program called narrative networks that was led by a colleague of mine, Dr. William Casebeer, exactly doing that, the more we know about the way a brain works the more we can utilize said information to develop key narratives of psychological and MISO [Military Information Support Operations] operations that are then viable to be able to then be used to influence individual and group brains. We've done this for a long time this is also referred to incidentally as neuro-marketing. (Giordano, 2017, timestamp: 15:04)

The use of narrative networks has most recently come to public attention through the alleged Russian interference in the US elections and the Brexit votes in the United Kingdom through the company Cambridge Analytica, with heavy ties to UK Secret Intelligence Service (SIS) which is just one part of a British defense contractor, SCL Group, owned by a conservative American and AI Billionaire, Robert Mercer. Ironically, my Facebook data was stolen and imported into the Cambridge Analytica scheme. Krishnan notes regarding these manipulations of Facebook that it was the UK SIS that in 2011 sponsored a study on this Intelligence method:

> …the British intelligence service GCHQ commissioned in 2011 a study by behavioral scientist Mandeep Dhami from then Cambridge University, to improve the art of Internet Trolling. In the study the following methods are suggested "to discredit, promote distrust, dissuade, deter, delay or disrupt" – upload YouTube videos containing "persuasive communications, setting up Facebook groups, forums, blogs and Twitter accounts, establishing online aliases/personalities, providing spoof online resources, sending spoof e-mails and text messages from a fake person or mimicking a real person," etc. (Krishnan 2017, 135)

Brain-Computer-Interfaces (BCI)

As mentioned earlier the latest trend in neuroweapons is to move control and handling of those on the receiving end of neuroweapon targeting to use Automation, Cybernetics and Artificial Intelligence. Russian scientist N. Anisimov notes in the field of neuroweaponry, here referred to by its Czech name, psychotronics,:

> ...psychotronic weapons can be used to take away part of the information which is stored in a person's brain and send it to a computer which reworks it to the level needed to control the person (Begich 2006, Ch. 2)

A Brain-Computer-Interface is any device that bridges the brain to a computer for processing, though usually an external device or invasive technology, it is now a non-invasive wave based non-device technology. It is very well known now that EEG can be used to control a computer interface with human thought alone with no other input devices other than brainwaves. Krishnan notes that both DARPA and IARPA are working to directly connect human brains to computers. (Krishnan 2017, 69) Adding artificial intelligence to the equation allows the controlling of targets more efficiently and effectively:

> Strong AI can lead to fully autonomous weapons systems that can learn and adapt to changing situations and the battle management systems that effectively develop complex battle plans through extensive wargaming and then implement them by taking over many staff functions. (Krishnan 2017, 84)
> ...the danger is that human decision making in war is taken over by intelligent machines because they would be a lot faster... (Krishnan 2017, 84)

One could also use an AI chat bot to provide narratives and manipulation. While this may sound unreal, it is very much a possibility and is reported by many Targeted Individuals regarding the behavior of their stalkers who seem in many cases to be "roboticized":

> Again there is no scientific reason why it would not be possible to "roboticize" a human, it has been done to animals with great success. (Krishnan 2017, 138)

One recent report on the malicious use of AI summarizes the threat:

> Artificial intelligence (AI) and machine learning (ML) are altering the landscape of security risks for citizens, organizations, and states. Malicious use of AI could threaten digital security (e.g., through criminals training machines to hack or socially engineer victims at human or superhuman levels of performance), physical security (e.g., non-state actors weaponizing consumer drones), and political security (e.g., through privacy-eliminating surveillance, profiling, and repression, or through automated and targeted disinformation campaigns). (Brundage et al, 2018, 4)

In fact, Targeted Individuals have noticed that many people who seem to be stalking, following and otherwise surveilling them have the tendency to stare at their smartphones as though in a hypnotic trance. This may be due to a computer virus that is known to cyber security specialists as Russian Virus 666 (Krishnan 2017, 133). Using a hypnotic method based on the 25th frame effect, first written in the 1920's in the Soviet Union, as noted by Kazhinsky. This has also been noted by Krishnan and Begich. This 25th frame effect inserts hypnotic suggestions into a 25th frame of films and computer screens. The virus has been found most recently in computing and television programming during the Ukraine conflict.

Behavior modification using computers is nothing new; in fact, such technology as demonstrated publicly by Russian researcher Dr. Smirnov to the CIA, DOD, etc. in the 1990s used a computer screen to show different subliminal messages using the 25th frame effect (Krishnan 2017, 94). Other systems that employ such abilities are known to be on the public market, noted as Psi Tech and MRU (Begich 2006, 81-2), while others note that systems such as these are available on the black market.

Information Warfare including its parts in Information Operations, Psychological Operations and Neocortical Warfare, which is the beginning of neuro-warfare, have been used by not just military operatives but also intelligence and even business operatives to force their will onto others against their own wishes. As we shall see in the next section, the trajectory of the development of neuro-warfare takes on an even more hard science approach in the effort to force one's will onto others and have them submit to your will whether as a military or as a national intelligence. This form of warfare leads to some of the most sinister totalitarian forms of government in history.

BIBLIOGRAPHY:

Begich, Nick (2006) *Controlling the Human Mind: The Technologies of Political Control or Tools for Peak Performance*, Earthpulse Press, 2006

Brundage et al, (2018) *The Malicious Use of Artificial Intelligence: Forecasting, Prevention, and Mitigation, Future of Humanity Institute*, Open AI, Electronic Frontier Foundation, Center for a New American Security University of Cambridge Centre for the Study of Existential Risk University of Oxford 2018

Giordano, James (2017) *Brain Science from Bench to Battlefield the Realities* – 2017 Lawrence Livermore National-al Laboratory's Center for Global Security Research (CGSR), https://www.youtube.com/watch?v=aUtQbri-Wt64 (accessed 22/10/2018)

Goldstein, Frank L (Col. USAF). (1996) *Psychological Operations: Principles and Case Studies*, Maxwell Air Force Base, Alabama: Air University Press. ISBN 1-58566-016-7. Online: http://www.au.af.mil/au/awc/aw-cgate/au/goldstein/goldstein_b18.pdf (accessed 3/24/2018)

Joint Chiefs of Staff (2012), *Information Operations*. Washington, DC: GPO. https://fas.org/irp/doddir/dod/jp3_13.pdf

--(1996) JP 3-58, *Joint Doctrine for Military Deception*. Washington, DC: GPO.

--(2006) JP 3-13.3, *Operations Security*.

Katz, et al, (1996) *"A Critical Analysis of US PSYOP"* in Principles of PSYOPS: Principles and Case Studies, Frank L. Goldstein Col. US Army and Benjamin Findley Col. USAF eds. http://www.au.af.mil/au/awc/awc-gate/au/goldstein/goldstein_b18.pdf (accessed 3/27/18)

Krishnan, Armin (2017) *Military Neuroscience and the Coming Age of Neurowarfare*, Taylor & Francis, 2017 ISBN 131709607X, 9781317096078

Roosevelt, Kermit (ed.). (1976) "War Report of the OSS." New York: Walker and Company, Volume I

Simpson, C. (1994) *The Science of Coercion*. Open Road Media (March 3, 2015)

Szafranskci, Col. Richard. (1994) *Neocortical Warfare? The Acme of Skill*. Rand https://www.rand.org/content/dam/rand/pubs/monograph_reports/MR880/MR880.ch17.pdf

CHAPTER 3

NEUROWEAPONS: 1919-1945

INTRODUCTION TO NEUROWEAPONS

In the following section I cover subjects not usually covered in academic literature related to Neuroweapons or Information Warfare. I do not discuss American or Western developments in these areas as this is well covered in Krishnan 2017. I do cover below the Nazi and Soviet roots of this technology and the general early history of the development of these weapons from the 1910s.

McCrieght defines Neuroweapons as:

> ...the claim is made that neuroweaponry encompasses all forms of interlinked cybernetic, neurological, and advanced biotech systems, along with the use of synthetic biological formulations and merged physiobiological and chemical scientific arrangements, designed expressly for offensive use against human beings. Neuroweapons are intended to influence, direct, weaken, suppress, or neutralize human thought, brainwave functions, perception, interpretation, and behaviors to the extent that the target of such weaponry is either temporarily or permanently disabled, mentally compromised, or unable to function normally. (McCreight 2015, 111-112)

Nørgaard & Linden-Vørnle explain Neuroweapons as:

> Neuroweapons include any kind of neurotechnological agent, drug, or device designed to either enhance or deter the cognitive performance of warfighters and target intelligence and command structures as both non-kinetic [non-lethal] and kinetic [lethal, violent] weapons. (Nørgaard & Linden-Vørnle 2021)

With the creation of neurologically-based and cybernetic-based weapons systems we now encounter a situation where the Battlespace extends beyond a set environment on the outside of a biological entity, but also includes an individual's mind:

> The Department of Defense defines a "battlespace" as "... the environment, factors, and conditions which must be understood to successfully apply combat power, protect the force, or complete the mission. This includes the air, land, sea, space, and the included enemy and friendly forces, facilities, weather, terrain, the electromagnetic spectrum, and information environment within the operational areas and areas of interest. (McCreight 2015, 116-117)

While most scholars write of Neurological Weapons as being a new development in warfare, its actual origins start in the scientific research sponsored during World Wars I and II.

The secrecy involved in the development of neuroweapons technology remains a big hurdle for those trying to understand this technology, as noted by the academic researcher in this area Armin Krishnan, who has no etic knowledge in the DOD or IC, in his book based on open-source material on Neuroweapons:

> A researcher of neuroweapons not only has to deal with the issue that official information is unavailable, but furthermore with the problem of outright disinformation. Steve Aftergood has pointed out that Cold War secrecy systems such as Special Access Programs (SAPs) "authorizes defense contractors to employ cover stories to disguise their activities. The only condition is that cover stories must be believable." (Krishnan 2017, 116)

Even in such open societies as the United States and Great Britain, which have developed Neuroweapons since at least the end of World War II, little information is publicly available. The Nazis are credited with developing their own Neuroweapons during the 1930s and World War II. The Wehrmacht, through its Naval Intelligence program, developed a proto-Remote Viewing program and the Nazi SS research institute, Ahnenerbe, is credited with developing Neuroweapons (Kernbach 2013, 6), which was subsequently taken to the United States, Great Britain and back to the Soviet Union. The Soviets fell behind the west in terms of Neuroweapons development after 1937 when Stalin banned such research, at least in terms of public research. This was also during the Stalinist purges of the Soviet Military just before the war, which itself may have been a Nazi Information Operation. The United States CIA developed neuroweapons under the code name 'MK-Ultra' during the 1950s through the importation of Nazi scientists under "Project Paperclip." MK-Ultra was a follow-on to an earlier project known as 'Project Artichoke' which used drugs to induce confessions during interrogation, based in Germany after the war and using German scientists. In these interrogations they used LSD and mescaline to induce confessions. Other countries involved in early 'remote influencing' technology such as Neuroweapons were Italy through Cazzamali in 1925 and Spain through Robles in 1931. One will notice that all these countries eventually embraced totalitarian regimes. Neuroweapons seems perfectly aligned with totalitarian understandings as noted by Krishnan:

> In contrast, the kind of warfare that has been practiced by totalitarian regimes in the twentieth century and that could be much refined by insights gained from neuroscience is following a completely different pattern for conducting hostilities:
>
> - Neurowarfare is likely to extend over many decades with the distinction between peace and war becoming not just blurred, but meaningless.
> - Neurowarfare primarily targets an adversary's minds and ultimately seeks to fundamentally alter the adversary's consciousness until the adversary perceives the world the same way as the sponsors of neurowarfare—the aim is to cognitively assimilate other societies.
> - Hostilities are carried out by proxies in a mostly covert, indirect manner and will generally not even amount to violence – much of it will be merely IW [information warfare] or propaganda in combination with other techniques of covert subversion, including espionage, sabotage and the use of "agents of influence."
> - Populations and decision-makers are the main targets in neurowarfare and populations are also used as new WMD for destroying an enemy state through the calculated psychological instigation of internal chaos – no international rules exist or are observed in the new "information-psychological" combat;"
> (Krishnan 2017, 193)

Information Warfare (IW) is the main motive behind neuroweaponry. IW is applied to both individuals and collectively. So it is not surprising that the East German 'Stasi' developed a plan, which may have been taken from the US COINTELPRO campaign against anti-war activists in the 1960s and 70s, which was based on British tactics to combat anti-colonial movements, when they developed the individually targeted Zertsetzung program:

> [Zertsetzung is] an operational method of the Ministry for Security of State for the effective fight against subversive activities. With Zertsetzung, across different operational political activities, one gains influence over hostile and negative persons, in particular over that which is hostile and negative in the dispositions and beliefs, in such a way that there would be shaken off and changed little by little, and, if applicable, the contradictions and differences between the hostile and negative forces would be provoked, exploited, and reinforced. The goal of Zertsetzung is the fragmentation, paralysis, disorganization, and isolation of hostile and negative forces, in order to impede thereby, in a preventive manner, the hostile and negative doings, to limit them in large part, or to totally avert them, and if applicable to prepare grounds for a political and ideological reestablishment. (Suckut, 2001, 464)

Neuroweapons against individuals is a methodology employed for neutralizing covertly and usually non-lethally any dissident voices as a form of non-obvious warfare (Krishnan 2017, 184). Its use against individuals that pose no violent threat may seem surprising, but it is noted by Krishnan that this was used against peace activists in the 1980s in Great Britain by the British Intelligence services (Krishnan 2017, 120), which practiced their craft in Northern Ireland such as Operation Clockwork Orange. As one researcher has noted:

The British Defence Equipment Catalogue once carried references to the "Valkyrie System" and "frequency weapons." These were eliminated from the catalogue by request of the British Ministry of Defence in 1983. (Kattenburg, 1987)

It additionally has been cited by Dr. John Hall in his epidemiological studies of targeted individuals by neuroweaponry on 'whistle blowers' usually by their own governments and agencies they formally collaborated with:

> While a small number of victims have come forward with convincing evidence of direct harassment from various government agencies, these are mostly whistle-blowers employed by the same agencies and comprised the minority. (Hall 2009, 69)

> The tactics include total inundation of the target at home or wherever they go. (Hall 2009, 72)

The first publicly known use of this technology was during Gulf War I by the United States against Iraqi soldiers:

> According to statements made by captured and deserting Iraqi soldiers, however, the most devastating and demoralizing programming was the first known military use of the new, high-tech, type of subliminal messages referred to as ultra-high frequency 'silent sounds' or 'silent subliminal.' Although completely silent to the human ear, the negative voice messages placed on the tapes alongside the audible programming by PSY-OPS psychologists were clearly perceived by the subconscious minds of the Iraqi soldiers and the silent messages completely demoralized them and instilled a perpetual feeling of fear and hopelessness in their minds. (Krishnan 2017, 132)

CIA engineer, Dr. Robert Duncan, who worked on these projects has stated that during the war neuroweapon technology was also used to mimic the voices of Iraqi generals to create confusion in Iraqi Command and Control by giving conflicting orders and repositioning troops into positions for easy capture and defeat, which is supported by Dr. Begich:

> Light and sound systems like the Sirius or Proteus devices also allow for the input of a user's own recorded voice for the maximum effectiveness when the brain is otherwise being moved into an altered state by FFR (Frequency Following Response [Brain entrainment]). (Begich 2006, Ch. 2)

Alarmingly, the latest developments in neuroweaponry involve the use of automating the technology through Artificial Intelligence; to this point Krishnan quotes Russian Major-General Vasily Burenko:

> … armed violence will assume a secondary position in the future as different forms and methods of adversely influencing a state, a society, or an individual will appear. Such developments include changing the technogenic shell of civilization, making a distinction between living and nonliving things uncertain. Here the real issue is cyber life, he notes. New gene combinations will be designed that do not currently exist, while nanobots will alter the characteristics of an organism. New conflicts will, in Burenko's opinion, not be so much "wars between people as wars of artificial intellects and the equipment and virtual reality created by this kind of intellect." (Krishnan 2017, 190-1)

Krishnan remarks:

> … biotechnology and nanotechnology could be employed for remaking human life and reshaping human civilization as a method of war. The Russian strategist also seems to believe that military decision-making will be largely delegated to AI, turning warfare in[to] a contest of competing military AI systems. (Krishnan 2017, 191)

As we shall read later the move to automation and cybernetics in war fighting, especially the battle space of mind, took shape in the Soviet Union in the 1980s.

It should be noted that in 1999 there was put forward an initiative in the EU parliament against these technologies:

> Calls for an international convention introducing a global ban on all developments and deployments of weapons which might enable any form of manipulation of human beings. (European Parliament. Resolution on the Environment, Security and Foreign Policy. A4-0005/99 Jan. 28, 1999. EP1159)

While human rights activists and groups have noted:

> The Asian Human Rights Commission released a statement on neuroweapons in 2013: The threat is real... [there are] many indications that brain technology for neuroweapons is scientifically possible. Additionally, some say such technologies have been used systematically against select people in various jurisdictions. (Krishnan 2017, 206)

Perhaps, even used in Myanmar as one example of a military-centric authoritarian regime.

EARLY SOVIET RESEARCH IN NEUROWEAPONS

The history of Neuroweapons begins around the 1920s in the new Soviet Union. It was an early Soviet scientist that first formulated conceptions of 'Biological Radio' or what we would now call Synthetic Telepathy. It was the Soviets and Germans that developed a dual institute: 'The Brain Institute' with one located in Berlin and a sister institution in Moscow. As mentioned previously the secret agreement between Soviet Russia and the Reichswehr of the German Government facilitated the exchange of technology between the two. Jochen Richter notes about this collaboration:

> Of the many interwar connections between Germany and Russia, one of the most unusual - and least explored - is medicine and public health. Between 1922 and 1932, with high-level political support and government funding, Soviet and German physicians and public health specialists collaborated in joint research expeditions, published joint articles, launched a bi-lingual journal, and established joint research institutions. Surprisingly, students of Soviet-German relations have all but ignored this medical collaboration; while historians of science have treated it as political history, an exercise in cultural diplomacy designed to mitigate the impact of the post-war exclusion of both nations from the international science. (Solomon 2006)

The founder of the dual Brain Institute was Oskar Vogt, whose early research was underwritten by the German Armaments producer Krupp. Vogt, being a socialist, was later replaced by the Nazi regime, after which his new institution again was underwritten by the Krupps[1]. Already, we see an interest in weapons developers in Brain research and underwriting such research from the very beginnings. The Berlin Brain Institute eventually became the Kaiser Wilhelm Institute for Brain Research (Kaiser Institut für Hirnforschung), whose building was financed by the Rockefeller Foundation. Vogt was also interested in hypnotism; a famous collaborator of his was Korbinian Brodmann, for whom different areas of the brain are referred to as Brodmann areas.

The early research into telepathy was conducted by several Russian researchers. In 1919 V.M. Bekhterev, who also worked with the Brain Institute in Moscow and a research center in Leningrad, began research into the scientific understanding of telepathy. A Defense Intelligence Agency document from 1978 notes about Bekhterev:

> In 1919, V. M. Bekhterev, a noted physiologist at the Institute of Brain Research of the University of Leningrad, began investigations into unusual psychological and physiological effects associated with the hypnotic state, including cases of apparent telepathic experiences. Pavlov had also made reference to unusual abilities sometimes observed in animals and man and was open to such investigations. Bekhterev organized a special group (Commission for the Study of Mental Suggestion) to continue and elaborate on his early work. L. L. Vasil'yev, a research physiologist who joined this instutie in 1921, was part of this commission. Vasil'yev's initial work was on effects of magnetic fields on psychological state, eventually he became the prime researcher in the area termed 'mental suggestion.'
>
> In addition to laboratory experiments with hypnotized people, Vasil'yev also began to collect and evaluate naturally occurring incidents (i.e. spontaneous cases) that were suggestive of telepathic processes. He also established contact with researchers in other countries, particularly with the noted French physiologist, Charles Richet, who also conducted psychic experiments with hypnotized people. (DoD, 1978)

L.L. Vasil'yev (Vasiliev) had a very long career, later writing publicly about his research decades after his initial inquiries under Bekhterev. The DIA notes regarding his research:

> In 1926 Vasil'yev published results of this early research and postulated electromagnetic radiation from the brain as a possible explanation. In the same year a special board was established at the Brain Research Institute

to duplicate his findings, but its study did not yield definite results. However, later experiments with a different test person (subject) were stated to be positive and supportive of Vasil'yev's initial observations.

After Bekhterev's death in 1927, little work on telepathy studies occurred. This may have been due to some ambiguous results or possibly to the negative viewpoint on telepathy by the Institute's new director.

In 1932 the Institute was given an assignment to initiate an experimental study of telepathy with the aim of determining, if possible, a physical basis for its explanation. Vasil'yev was selected to direct this investigation. This work continued until 1938 when World War II interrupted activities. After that, Vasil'yev continued to collect evidence of spontaneous cases and pursued unofficial investigations on his own.

The main orientation of his research during this period was on telepathic induction of specific motor acts, on transmission of visual images from one person (sender) to another (receiver), and remotely induce sleep or awakening in a hypnotized subject. His initial subjects were easily suggestible or hypnotizable hysteric or neurasthenic patients [highly hypnotizable type]. Later, Vasil'yev found certain normal people appeared to have repeatable psychic aptitude without being hypnotized.

Some of these experiments involved attempts at transmission of black or white targets and also specific drawings. Vasil'yev found a few cases where results were far greater than chance expectancy (10^{-7}), and he also reported data showing high correlation between some of the complex drawings used as targets.

His most famous was the long-distance experiment between Leningrad and Sevastopol (1700km) which involved 'sending' sleep and awake commands to a subject who had been involved in similar experiments at short distances. (DoD 1978)

It is interesting to note that Vasil'yev was an admirer of a scientist whom the Soviets consider the founder of their Space propulsion program and rocket technology, an early Russian Von Braun.

In his [Vasil'yev] presentations, he often quoted the views of the well-known USSR missile pioneer, K. E. Tsiolkovskiy, who suspected the reality of telepathic phenomena, felt it should be investigated, and saw its potential in future space travel. (DoD 1978)

Tsiolkovskiy, interestingly, draws a connection between telepathy and space travel, which presages the work of Heim and Dubrov, who posited a gravitational effect for psi phenomena and field propulsion. Tsiolkovskiy also had the fascinating idea that there was an Intelligence that governed humans as "marionettes, mechanical puppets, machines, movie characters." This Intelligence is remarkably similar to the ideal of neuroweapons, or 'thought injection', yet decades before any known such system ever existed. Another researcher in telepathy that was influenced by Tsiolkovskiy was Chizhevskiy, Vasiliev also wrote the article "Critical Evaluation of the Hypnogenic Method" concerning the work of Dr. I. F. Tomashevsky on experiments in remote control of the brain.

Also, the early work of B.B. Kazhinsky is of note, one of the few working in this area whose work is not classified, as he did his research outside the control of the Soviet Security State. Kazhinsky, being a publicly known researcher, even had his research in Biological Radio (биологической радиосвязи) popularized at an early point through a fictitious account of his research in the Science Fiction novel, *The Ruler of the World* (Властелин мира: роман Беляева — Википедия) by Alexander Belyaev (1926) which told the story of a German banker who used remote telepathy or transcommunication to seize control of a financial empire with what would be later termed "mind control."

The novel's fantastic idea goes back to the research of Hans Berger, who studied the electrical activity of the brain. Many characters of the novel have real prototypes. A remote prototype of Stirner carries the individual features of A. L. Chizhevsky. The image of Dugov is associated with the trainer Vladimir Leonidovich Durov. The prototype of Kaczynski was Bernard Bernardovich Kazhinsky (the author of the book Transmission of thoughts. Factors that create the possibility of electromagnetic oscillations radiating out (1923) and Biological radio communication in the nervous system (1926).

Kazhinsky first postulated what he called 'biological radio' for his version of telepathy:

Following the example of P. I. Gulyayev, Doctor of Biological Science, the author refers to the bio-electromagnetic and radiation wave as telepathema finding it to be a very appropriate name. However, the term "telepathy" (inasmuch as it is associated with the wrong and distorted interpretation of the phenomena of thought transference over distances [deep correlation, i.e. Persinger]) should be expressed by a new term such as "biological radio communication," for example, which offers a clearer depiction of the natural capacity of man (and animals) to intercept mental information and sensations (through a physical medium) as one of the brain functions performed by the nerve cells, the biophysical apparatuses. (Kazhinsky, 1963, 14)

In 1922 he began experiments based on his ideals in the Department of Physics at Timiryuzev Agricultural Academy in Moscow:

> Investigations in this area were initiated back in 1919. Forty-two years have elapsed since the author developed and publicized his hypothesis of the existence of "ganglions" or "apparatuses" [microtubules, etc] in the central nervous system which are similar to the known electrical systems in structure and purpose: simple current generators, condensers, amplifiers, radio transmitting and receiving devices, etc. That hypothesis, in turn, was based on the assumption that the human thought process is accompanied by phenomena of an electromagnetic nature; that is the emission of electromagnetic waves of a biological origin capable of being transmitted and producing an influence over long distances.
> Three years later (1922), following a number of experiments in the department of physics of the Timiryazev Agricultural Academy in Moscow, the author, succeeded in finding in isolated preparations of an animal's nervous system certain nerve elements structurally resembling solenoid loops and paired capacitor plates similar to the well- known elements of the closed Thompson oscillation circuit, a vibrator of discrete currents and electromagnetic waves.

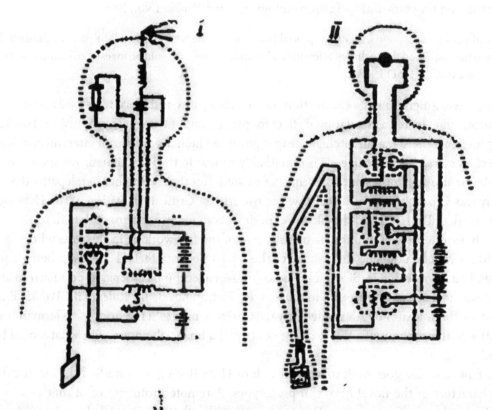

Fig. 9. Initial diagrams of transmitting I and receiving II biological radio stations of the human nervous system

(Kazhinsky 1963)

Also in 1922, Kazhinsky gave a presentation at the 2nd Russian Congress of the Association of Naturalists entitled "Human Thought: Electricity." This was two years before the German scientist Hans Berger created the first known in the west Electroencephalograph (EEG) of the human mind, although Russian researchers in 1914 had performed this on animals. Later, Kazhinsky's research in 1943 postulated a connection to the organ of hearing, perhaps first discovering the key to silent subliminals:

A further study of the physical characteristics of the organ of hearing, from the point of view of the nascent theory of biological radio communications, made it possible (in 1943) to adopt an entirely new viewpoint on that organ as an analyzer of a heretofore unknown stimulant reaching the brain, a bio-electromagnetic wave of acoustical frequency.

An investigation of the structure of the organ of hearing in the light of the new experimental-data suggested (in 1952) a working hypothesis: the eye not only "sees" but also emits into space electromagnetic waves of a certain frequency capable of producing an effect over a distance on a human being (and on animals in general) on whom the gaze is focused. These waves can influence his behavior, induce him to do certain things and generate various emotions, images and thoughts in his mind. Such an emission of electromagnetic waves of a certain frequency by the eye is called a bio-radiation "ray of vision," also see Chapter 7 for information on the eyes as radar receivers and transmitters.

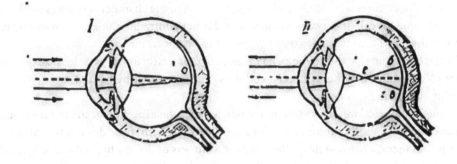

Fig. 14. The organ of vision also has the function of emitting bio-radiation "rays of vision" (working hypothesis):

I - the figure on the left shows the conventional function of the eye -- the retina and crystalline lens diffract the parallel light rays coming into the eye, directing them at an acute angle to point a. This leaves on the retina a clear image of the visual object in a limited zone of its center which is predominated by cones;

II - the figure on the right corresponds to the advanced hypothesis. Extending from the wider peripheral zone b-c of the retina (which is shaped like a concave bowl), perpendicularly to the "bowl" surface, are the "rays of vision" b-g and c-g; this peripheral zone of the retina is predominated by rods. At point g they converge as in a focus. They then separate, falling on the internal side of the crystalline lens.

(Kazhinsky 1963)

Kazhinsky ideals of thought transference originated from his work with the Zoologist Durov who conducted experiments with Kazhinsky on dogs to remotely give them orders to elicit behaviors. At this time, 1924, he also began studies on sending orders between an emitter and receiver, where the receiver was located in a protected room, hypnotized to open up suggestibility.

An account of this research is given below:

In the years 1922-1926 in Moscow, in the Practical Laboratory of Zoopsychology of V. L. Durov of the Main Department of Scientific Institutions of the People's Commissariat of Education, B. B. Kazhinsky conducted a series of experiments. Kazhinsky designed and built a room with more advanced screening ability. The percipient was placed in the chamber, and TV Gurshtein, who hypnotized him, was outside.

Here is how Gurshtein describes some typical results of the first series of observations of 1926:

The hypnotist, standing close to the door of the chamber, opens the cork of the bottle with strong perfume and asks many suggestive questions like, "What do I smell? What smell do you feel?" And so on. The reaction of the percipient after a relatively large gap: "Flower scent, cologne." The hypnotist takes on the tongue the powder of salt and asks: "What taste do you feel on the tongue?" The reaction of the percipient after a long silence: "Sweet." The hypnotist tries tongue sugar. Percipient reaction - quick response: "Sweet." The hypnotist pours pepper on his tongue. Percipient reaction - answer: "Bitter." The tingling of the hypnotist's left palm is performed. To the question: "What and where do you feel?" - the percipient responds: "The pain ... in the left hand."

A total of 14 such observations were made under conditions when the chamber room was shielded (five times) and not shielded (nine times). The results in nine cases did not contradict the electromagnetic hypothesis; in three cases they disproved it, in two cases they turned out to be uncertain.

Kazhinsky has been studying the phenomena of telepathy for nearly forty years. In the experiments of 1936 conducted by TV Gurshtein together with L.A. Vodolazsky, a room made by Leonid Aleksandrovich with even higher screening capabilities was used.

Important methodological innovations were introduced into the experiment: mental suggestion was transmitted by Gurshtein from another room, while he did not know whether the door of the chamber was closed or open (that is, whether it shields or not). The assistant, who was under the hypnotized subject, did not know the time and nature of the mental impact, that is, the task that the subject had to mentally perceive and perform.

The task concerned the performance of various movements: raising a hand or a leg, clenching a hand into a fist, etc. Of the ten mental suggestions, their fulfillment or non-fulfillment did not contradict the electromagnetic hypothesis in nine cases and only in one case the subject, with the open door of the shielded chamber, did not exactly fulfill suggestion.

Similar works, but at a somewhat better level of methodological and technical support, were carried out in 1932–1937 in Leningrad by Professor L. L. Vasiliev. In 1932, the Brain Institute's Director Academician V. M. Bekhterev "was assigned the task of starting an experimental study of telepathy with the aim, if possible, of clarifying its physical nature."

Scientific research leadership was entrusted to L. L. Vasiliev. He worked at the Brain Institute since the fall of 1921 and was directly involved in the research of telepathic phenomena conducted by the Institute's Bekhterev. After his death in 1927, Vasilyev continued this work on his own initiative, and in 1932 he was offered to head the scientific leadership of the topic. Research was conducted for almost five and a half years, from 1932 to 1937 inclusive.

In these large-scale works, the mental suggestion of motor acts, visual images and sensations, sleep and awakening were investigated. To study the physical nature of the carrier, shielding (with metal) of a mentally inspiring inductor or a percipient perceiving mental suggestion, as well as increasing the distance between the inductor and the percipient (from 25 meters to 1700 kilometers) was used (by metal). The result, Vasiliev writes, was unexpected even for the performers: neither the screening nor the distance worsened the telepathic transmission in all those cases when it was clearly manifested without screening or at a short distance.

(Kazhinsky 1963)

As previously mentioned Kazhinsky's work was not classified. He did not work directly for the Soviet security state; however, others did, such as Bekhterev who was supervised by Bokia, Bokia later being executed during the Stalinist purges. Kernbach, as previously noted, talks about how research in this subject is still classified in Russia some 100 years later. In 1934, the Soviet security state OGPU-NKVD, set up secret labs 'neuro-energetic' laboratory initially with the Moscow Power Engineering Institute, after 1935 in a building of the Institute of Experimental Medicine. Barchenko was involved in the study of 'Introduction to the methodology of experimental influence of volumetric energy field.' Barchenko docs are still classified, some funding coming from Dzherzhinsky, head of the Secret Police of the Soviet Union.

Meanwhile the Soviet military set up its labs as well, From 1932-37 USSR's Commissar of Defense studied transfer of information in biological ways. In Leningrad at Bechterev's Brain Institute, led by Prof. LL. Vasilyev; in Moscow the Laboratory of Biophysics, Academy of Science, led by P.P. Lazarev and S.Y. Turlygin. As Kernbach notes:

> It can be assumed that a, more or less, coordinated Soviet program began in 1924, when the Commissar (Minister) of Education A.V.Lunacharskiy А.В.Луначарский) formed the Russian Committee for Psychical Research at the International Committee of the Psychical Research. Many authors point to a program of the USSR's Commissar of Defense in 1932-1937, related to transfer of information in a biological way. These works were conducted in two places: in Leningrad at the Bechterev's Brain Institute, led by Prof. L.L.Vasilyev (Л.Л.Васильев) and in Moscow at the laboratory of biophysics, Academy of Science, led by Prof. P.P.Lazarev (Director of Laboratory) and Prof. S.Y.Turlygin (П.П.Лазарев, С.Я.Турлыгин). The Biophysics laboratory was asked to investigate the physical nature of telepathy. For instance, in Moscow's laboratory the first results of biological emission from humans were obtained. In Leningrad, the Brain Institute was requested to perform more psychologically oriented works, such as transferring visual images and remotely influencing the percipient. Both research organizations did not know about the works of each other. (Kernbach, 2013, 4)

One should note that many scientists concerned in this edge of scientific research eventually found their way onto the receiving end of the Stalinist purges, with the execution of Bokia and the imprisonment of other researchers in the Siberian gulags, effectively taking them out of the research area, although a scientist like Kozyrev was able to continue his theoretical work in Cosmology while in the Gulag. The Stalinist purges beginning in 1937 effectively eliminated research in this area, at least as far as is publicly known. Soviet research did not begin again until after Stalin died, in an attempt to catch up to the Americans and British which were the beneficiaries of receiving German scientists as spoils of war, ostensibly. Project Paperclip brought many German researchers to the United States; however the Soviets also captured many leading researchers in this area and took them as prisoners to the Soviet Union.

It is also worthwhile to keep in mind that the Weimar German Military (Reichswehr) during this entire time had a secret agreement on cooperation of military technology since 1922 with the Soviet Union, for instance Pascual Jordan lectured at joint conferences of German and Soviet scientists at conferences in the Soviet Union. And as noted before there was cooperation directly between the two countries in all forms of technology.

Another area that is of interest regarding early Russian research is that in the field of microwaves. According to Kernbach, In the 1930s B.G. Michaylovskiy studied the microwave radiation effects on higher nervous activity, using medium/short EM waves modulated by low-frequency signals on separate areas of the brain which are responsible for emotional state and functionality of different organs. S. J. Turlygin also did studies in the field of human microwave radiation. (See Kernbach 2013) In the 1960s later experiments went back into research done in the 1920s and 30s. Following the work of Michailovskiy and others, it was found that the EM field, with certain parameters, can cause a variety of bio-physical and mental effects. Kernbach states: "It can be assumed that the psycho-physiological effects of microwave emission were actively investigated during the NS [National Socialist, 'Nazi'] regime in Germany, and after 1945 the technology was adopted by the countries-winners [i.e. USA, UK, France, Soviet Union]." (Kernbach, 2013)

NAZI GERMAN RESEARCH IN NEUROWEAPONS:

One of the main stumbling blocks to researching Nazi involvement in Neuroweapons is that most documentation was either purposefully destroyed by Nazi scientists, destroyed in bombings, taken by the Soviets, or by the secret intelligence in the West. Locating primary sources remains a difficult task in documenting their development. However, we can discern from what is known about Nazi medical experiments and scientific research some of the areas they were involved in. Whether from the German Navy's secret Pendel Research division, a form of early Remote Viewing, to medical experiments under Verschuer which included the likes of Mengele, there are enough pathways of evidence to investigate what they were researching and for what purposes, although sometimes the purposes themselves may be obfuscated.

Psychology was begun in Germany with the work of Wilhelm Wundt (1832-1920) in the famous Leipzig school of psychology. Wilhelm Maximilian Wundt was a physiologist, philosopher, and professor, known today as one of the founders of modern psychology, specifically experimental psychology based on laboratory experiments. Americans influenced by him were Granville Stanley Hall, James McKeen Cattrell, Charles Hubbard, Walter Dill Scott, Edward Bradford Titchener, Lightner Witmer, Frank Angell, Edward Wheller Scipture, and James Mark Baldwin. He also influenced visiting student V.M. Bekhterev, Franz Boas, Emile Durkheim, Ferdinand Tonnies. In 1879, at the University of Leipzig, Wundt founded the first formal laboratory for psychological research. This marked psychology as an independent field of study. By creating this laboratory, he was able to establish psychology as a separate science from other disciplines. He also formed the first academic journal for psychological research, Philosophische Studien (from 1881 to 1902).

Some of his ideals regarding psychology are:

1. Process theory: Mental phenomena are changing processes of consciousness.

2. Categories: fundamental categories of psychology are: Subject, value assessment, the existence of purpose (teleology), and volitional acts (will).

3. Psychophysical Parallelism: certain mental processes regularly correspond to certain physical processes, figuratively they are 'parallel to one another'

4. Causality: Causal explanations in psychology must be content to seek the effects of the antecedent causes without being able to derive exact predictions. Using the example of volitional acts, Wundt describes possible inversion in considering cause and effect, ends and means, and explains how causal and teleological explanations can complement one another to establish a co-ordinated condition.

5. Apperception: based on Leibniz, the process in which the elementary sensory impressions pass into self-consciousness, whereby individual aspirations (striving, volitional acts) play an essential role. Apperception has a range of theoretical assumptions on the integrative process of consciousness. The selective control of attention is an elementary example of such active cognitive, emotional and motivational integration.

During his Heidelberg years, when he was a neurophysiologist, Wundt developed work in sensory physiology, including spatial perception, visual perception and optical illusions, similar in outlook to Gestalt (see below). An optical illusion described by him is call the Wundt illusion, a variant of the Hering illusion. It shows how straight lines appear curved when seen against a set of radiating lines.

Wundt influenced many psychologists of the Nazi era, though Wundt himself was a life-long liberal democrat. Many conspiracy theories paint him as an evil Illuminati, but there is no evidence for such conclusions. Many of his students, being immersed in the socio-political world of their times, were far-right nationalists like many Germans after WWI, feeling persecuted and betrayed by the political order of the times. After Wundt's death the Institute for Experimental Psychology at Leipzig University was headed by a Nazi named Felix Krueger (see below for more).

German psychology was also Gestalt Psychology (German: Gestalt "shape, form") and later found a synthesis with Wundt's experimental psychology and Gestalt in the likes of Krueger, Sander and others. In 1890, the concept of gestalt was first introduced in philosophy and psychology by Christian von Ehrenfels (a member of the School of Brentano). The idea of gestalt has its roots in theories by David Hume, Johann Wolfgang von Goethe, Immanuel Kant, David Hartley, and Ernst Mach. Max Wertheimer's unique contribution was to insist that the "gestalt" is perceptually primary, defining the parts it was composed from, rather than being a secondary quality that emerges from those parts, as von Ehrenfels's earlier Gestalt-Qualität had been.

Gestalt psychology or gestaltism is a philosophy of mind of the Berlin School of experimental psychology. Gestalt psychology is an attempt to understand the laws behind the ability to acquire and maintain meaningful perceptions in an apparently chaotic world. The central principle of gestalt psychology is that the mind forms a global whole with self-organizing tendencies. Kurt Koffka's, "The whole is other than the sum of the parts" is often incorrectly translated as "The whole is greater than the sum of its parts," and thus used when explaining gestalt theory, and further incorrectly applied to systems theory.

The fundamental principle of gestalt perception is the law of prägnanz[de] (in the German language, pithiness), which says that we tend to order our experience in a manner that is regular, orderly, symmetrical, and simple. Gestalt psychologists attempt to discover refinements of the law of prägnanz, and this involves writing down laws that, hypothetically, allow us to predict the interpretation of sensation, what are often called "gestalt laws." As Neuroweapons is an interference in gestalt, research in this area is directly related whether by intention or dual purpose with development of Neuroweapons. Later researchers in Neuroweapons, such as John Norseen, worked with ideals of Quantum Consciousness. Similarities between Gestalt phenomena and quantum mechanics have been pointed out by, among others, chemist Anton Amann, who commented that "similarities between Gestalt perception and quantum mechanics are on a level of a parable" yet may give useful insight.

Physicist Elio Conte and co-workers have proposed abstract, mathematical models to describe the time dynamics of cognitive associations with mathematical tools borrowed from quantum mechanics; and has discussed psychology experiments in this context, which is similar to Norseen's Krylov sub-space of the mind. A similar approach has been suggested by physicists David Bohm, Basil Hiley and philosopher Paavo Pylkkänen with the notion that mind and matter both emerge from an "implicate order." The models involve non-commutative mathematics; such models account for situations in which the outcome of two measurements performed one after the other can depend on the order in which they are performed—a pertinent feature for psychological processes, as it is obvious that an experiment performed on a conscious person may influence the outcome of a subsequent experiment by changing the state of mind of that person.

NAZIS AND PSYCHOLOGY

We begin our survey of Nazi psychologists with the eventual head of the Leipzig school, Felix Krueger, after completing his education under Wundt, Krueger eventually relocated to Buenos Aires, Argentina in 1906 at the Instituto Nacional de Profesorado Secundario (National Institute of Secondary Teaching). He stayed in Argentina until 1908. In 1917, with Wundt's retirement he became the successor to Wundt's Institute for Experimental Psychology. From this point on the Institute became identified with far-right nationalist sentiment. Under Krueger:

> In the 1920s, the institute occupied 34 rooms in the university's main building as well as a smaller office in the city, huge for the time. Krueger had four regular assistants, each of whom was responsible for his own department: Professor Otto Klemm was responsible for applied psychology and experimental pedagogics; Professor August Kirschmann for measurement methods and psychology of perception; Professor Friedrich Sander for psychology of the higher functions; and Privatdozent Hans Volkelt for developmental psychology, including child psychology (Marx, 2013)

Krueger responded to gestalt theory of the Berlin type with his own brand of "holistic psychology" (Ganzheitspsychologie). Instead of patterns (gestalten), he named "complex qualities" (Komplexqualitäten) as the primary perceptual phenomena. These diffuse, quasi-multidimensional perceptions comprised thought processes as well as emotions. However, children were unable to differentiate these complex qualities. Human maturation manifested itself as complex qualities became more structured through experience and reason. This meant that holistic psychology was oriented more towards development and evolution than gestalt psychology. Although Krueger vied with the gestalt psychologists to prove that his own version was the original approach, he was heavily influenced by gestalt theory. Thus, his holistic approach can at least partly be explained by his efforts to outdo his rivals in the new discipline. He conceded that gestalt psychology was a step in the right direction but maintained that a conclusive psychological and philosophical explanation of the psyche could only be provided by the Leipzig school.

The focus on the emotions was crucial to the profile of the Leipzig school and was the most important task of psychology from Krueger's perspective. His student Verwoerd, however, took a completely different view in his doctoral thesis (see below). Verwoerd treated the emotions as phenomena which could be isolated and evoked, rendering them measurable and open to manipulation. This is very far from Krueger's concept of the complex quality and the "holistic experience," which emphasized the diffuse and unfathomable nature of emotions.

From Krueger's perspective the emotions formed a tight cluster of complex qualities, in which rational thoughts manifest themselves, but these were so dependent on their emotional environment that it was almost impossible to investigate the complex empirically. Albert Wellek, a student of Krueger's in the 1930s, explained that feelings lost their intensity when under observation, making it impossible to analyze them. Verwoerd's own position was rather different, because he states in his thesis that the declining intensity of emotions is measurable and that emotions are open to analysis. He probably didn't know about Krueger's approach before he came to Leipzig, since he did not quote any of Krueger's publications in his doctoral thesis. (Marx 2013)

Krueger's theoretical conceptualization of holistic psychology encouraged the absorption of both volkish ideologies and nationalist ones. Holistic psychology was closely interwoven with an ideological and political undercurrent that operated in the context of wholes and transcended the psychology of the individual through the community perceived as a volk:

> Although working in different fields, our efforts aimed at an understanding of community life, especially that of the volk." It comes as no surprise therefore, that both Krueger himself and some of his assistants, such as Volkelt and Dürckheim, were involved in right wing politics as early as the 1920s: "The Psychological Institute was regarded as a 'völkische Zelle' (volkish cell)."

It was the logic of holistic psychology's internal dynamics that led Krueger to wave goodbye to empirical research after 1917. Henceforth he devoted his energies to presenting his ideas in a very general philosophical framework that had less and less to do with practical psychological research. In keeping with this view, Krueger dropped the word "experimental" from the name of Wundt's institute, renaming it the Psychological Institute in 1925.

Attached to the Institute were those influenced by Krueger as well as generating their own research and ideas on psychology.

In 1925 Erich Wohlfart worked on Aktualgenese which he first articulated in his Ph.d. Dissertation at Leipzig (Abbey & Diriwachter, 2008). Later, during the 3rd Reich he was a Wehrmacht psychologist from 1933-35. (Geuter, 2008)

AKTUALGENESE

Actualism is a term derived from gestalt psychology. This refers to the emergence of a perception from more complex, holistic pre-forms, or the process of the differentiation of perceptual contents. If the term is limited to human perception, the actual fact that a complex object is not immediately captured completely but is recorded in a single step in a process. These steps do not occur deliberately. In a wider sense, one can also describe other psychological processes in this way. For example, the emergence of emotional excitements: from the first impression of a situation, several steps are passed through until one realizes the full experience. The emergence of emotions can take place differently depending on the triggering event and person. The development of envy or jealous feelings of a little boy for the newborn brother runs differently from the frightened reaction while driving, when an obstacle suddenly appears directly in front of the car.

This research would later contribute to the understanding of how to manipulate these processes.

At the same time I.G. Farben was creating, in 1925, methamphetamines, heroin, and morphine. Under the work of Otto Freidrich Ranke he introduced methamphetamines into the Wehrmacht, receiving funding from the Rockefeller Foundation; his Ph.D. Dissertation was "The Rectifier Resonance Theory: An extension of the Helhoke resonance theory of hearing by physical examination of the cochlear fluid oscillations, similar to Kazhinsky, in 1931. He was a member of the SA (Sturmabteilung), Storm Troopers. Eventually, in 1939, the widespread use of these drugs would lead the Minister of Health, Leo Conti to declare that the entire German nation seemed addicted. This would be considered to be nootropics by today's neurowarfare terminology. The goal of this of course was to create a drug induced super soldier of the Blitzkrieg (speed war). Even today, low doses of meth are given to US troops in combat to fight fatigue.

In 1926 an interesting student of Krueger's was Hendrik Verwoerd. After his studies at Leipzig he returned to his native South Africa and became a member of the Fascist, National Party. He was known as the architect of Apartheid. He wrote in 1926 "A method for the experimental production of emotions." He was later chair of the Applied Psychology and Psycho Technique at the University of Stellenbosch.

…Hendrik Verwoerd and the Leipzig School of Psychology. In investigating Moodie's allegations regarding the formative influence of German intellectuals on Afrikaner nationalism, it makes sense to concentrate on Verwoerd's time in Leipzig because the Psychological Institute there is the most likely site of the alleged political influence from German scholars. It was the Leipzig psychologists who exhibited rightist political leanings, unlike their colleagues in Berlin and Hamburg, none of whom were drawn by radical nationalism. (Marx, 2013, 92)

Chris Marx gives the following biographical information regarding Verwoerds education:

Verwoerd studied psychology and philosophy at Stellenbosch and wrote a Masters' thesis in each of these subjects in 1922. From 1923 he was a lecturer in psychology at Stellenbosch. He wrote his PhD thesis, entitled "Die Afstomping van Gemoedsaandoeninge" (The Blunting of the Emotions) based on laboratory experiments. He received his doctorate cum laude from Stellenbosch University in 1924 and was awarded a £150 Croll & Gray scholarship to study abroad. He spent three semesters in Germany (1926–27) and three months in the USA. (Marx, 2013)

While at Leipzig he also studied under Richard Pfeifer (1877-1957) on the "Psycho Pathology of Children and Youth" as well as a course on "Psychological Therapy and Hypnosis," as well as under Franz Exner (1881-1947) the "Fundamentals of Criminal Psychology," as well as with August Dollken, professor of medicine on the same topic. (Marx, 2013, 105)

Verwoerd being the one-time Prime Minister of apartheid South Africa does raise the possibility that his research became state funded and underwritten.

In 1926 Hans Volkelt became assistant professor at Leipzig. He took Krueger's holistic psychology and made it applicable for empirical research. He specialized in child and developmental psychology (Marx, 2013, 100). Marx relates on Volkelt's relationship to the Nazi party and the Institute:

In 1926 Volkelt became assistant professor. He and Graf Dürckheim Montmartin were the earliest and most outspoken adherents of National Socialism at the Leipzig School. Volkelt became a member of the Nationalsozialistische Deutsche Arbeiterpartei (NSDAP), the National Socialist German Workers' Party, as early as 1932, one year before Hitler came to power, clear evidence that he joined the party out of conviction rather than opportunism. Under Krueger, the Leipzig Institute adapted very quickly to the new regime and some of its members publicly acclaimed the National Socialist assumption of power. Krueger himself had been an exponent of the radically nationalist and volk-orientated right wing for many years already. In 1935 he became rector of the university but was forced to resign by the Nazis after referring in a public speech to Heinrich Hertz as a "noble Jew." (Marx, 2013, 103)

Other notable Leipzig connected researchers included:

Freidrich Sander, 1942: assistant to Wundt – he was a member the Nazi Party. Taught after WWII in German Universities. Published with Kruger "Gestalt und Sinn." Published "Functional structure, power of Experience and Form" (1942). Worked with Wohlfart on Aktualgenese: the emergence of a perception from more complex holistic pre-form on the process of differentiation of perceptual contents"; the link to neuroweapons is obvious. Sander founded the school of genetic holistic psychology with F. Krueger. Based on experimental perceptual investigations, he developed the concept of actual genesis (emotion), which describes the process of inducing a creative experience, and claimed that the Gestalt qualities are preceded by so-called full qualities. Also known was the "Sandersche figure," an optical illusion (Sander's illusion). In the period of Nazi rule, Sander saw in holistic psychology a contribution to the so-called reorganization of national life. In 1962 he presented a collection of the works on holistic psychology (holistic psychology, fundamentals, results, applications, edited by H. Volkelt). Later, he was found to have committed fraud in his research and undermined Wohlfart. (Abbey 2008, 40)

Otto Klem, whose department focused primarily on the psychology of physical activity. "There are studies of working procedures, fatigue, aptitude tests and related psycho-technical testing. The methods are tested and applied to carefully chosen cases." Klemm's department collaborated with industry as well as employment centers in testing applicants for specific jobs so that his research contributed to optimizing workplace conditions. Peter Behrens identifies four main areas of Klemm's research, namely: "human work, equipment, and control design; human performance and mental functioning; forensic psychology; and mental ability testing and vocational guidance." (Marx, 2013) In other words, characterology, which is used in profiling targets of neuroweapons.

Karlfried Graf Dürckheim-Montmartin, the son of an impoverished aristocratic family, who had taken part in the violent suppression [freikorps] of the short-lived Munich Soviet Republic in 1919. Dürckheim-Montmartin studied psychology and moved to Leipzig after completing his doctorate in Kiel. He worked as a voluntary assistant at the university from 1925 and was given a regular contract at Krueger's institute two years later. Although Verwoerd did not attend any of the count's courses, they obviously knew each other. A few years later both of them participated in the 1934 congress of the New Education Fellowship in South Africa, organized by Ernest Malherbe. (Marx, 2013, 102)

Wilhelm Wirth-Leipzig, psychophysics (nueroweapons relevant), Nazi party member. In 1897 he received his doctorate. After studying in Leipzig, Wilhelm Wundt offered him an assistant position. Wirth habilitated in 1900 with the work The Fechner-Helmholtz's Theorem on Negative Afterimages and Its Analogies. He founded in 1902 the Society for Experimental Psychology. In 1940 he became a member of the NSDAP.

> In 1908 Wirth was appointed professor. During this time his main works, the consciousness phenomena and the methods of experimental psychology emerged. His research goal was to gain precisely measurable stimuli and clearly agreed arbitrary behaviors between the experimenter and the subject as the basis of a generally comparative situation of consciousness. In 1938, he defined: "The entire knowledge of quantitatively comprehensible laws of mental performance vis-à-vis the outside world can be described as psychophysics in the narrower sense." Starting in 1926, the precision of the coordination between optical perception and subjective movement emerged for Wirth. In 1933 he signed the professors' confession at the German universities and colleges to Adolf Hitler.
>
> Albert Wellek, who was at the institute from the late 1920s onwards and created a legend after the war about the institute's distance from the National Socialist regime. In his autobiography he took great pains to circumvent his own sympathies with right-wing positions. Wellek was the most prominent psychologist to fight for a continuation of the Leipzig approach of holistic psychology after the Second World War, when he became a professor in Mainz and a highly influential figure in psychological organizations. (Marx, 2013, 103)

Johaness Rudert (1894-1980) at Heidelberg, army psychologist. Injured in World War I, losing function of his right arm, which he turned into a dissertation with injury-related left-handedness in his 1925 thesis "Casuistic Contribution to the Theory of the Functional Asymmetry of Cerebral Hemisphere ." After graduation he worked in the army psychology of Reichswehr and participates in the development of diagnostic methods for Officer selection. Assistant to Felix Krueger in 1929 at the Psychological Institute in Leipzig, he began his characterological and expressive psychological studies. In 1935 he applied for habilitation at the Faculty of Philosophy in Leipzig with the thesis "Typology and Characterology – To the problem of characterological classification." From 1936-1941 he was active as Senior Army Psychologist at the Psychological Testing Offices of the Reichswehr in Brunswick and Wiesbaden. In 1941 he was sent to the University of Leipzig, appointed associate professor of psychology and succeeded Philipp Lersch as the Deputy Head of the Psychological Institute.

One area of research that is worthy of note for Rudert was his development in the characterological field. Recruiting young talent for technical special services, he developed what became known as the 'film method', originally created by Philipp Lersch, in which a subject was sent to a filming studio to be examined by a team of doctors from behind mirrors, while being surreptitiously filmed. The examinee would be asked for his name, then he was told to go to be photographed, and he could get ready in front of a mirror, through which the filming occurred. The tests took three days; with each of the subjects examined by two psychologists, they pried for different emotional states in front of the mirror while being filmed. (Geuter 1982)

NAZI RESEARCHERS OTHER THAN THE LEIPZIG SCHOOL:

Leipzig was not the only center of psychological research in Nazi Germany. Others engaged in studies related to the mind and its inner workings, such as Matthias Heinrich Goring, the cousin of Herman Goering, who founded the German Institute for Psychological Research and Psychotherapy in 1933. The fact that Psychological research was considered a national interest and even secret is witnessed in the redacted notes of some Psychological conferences in Germany. Hartnacke classifies that in science:

> The highest standing, which is related to securing the existence and raising of the people, whose Daseinssicherung and Erbgutpflege "(S.4) ... Psychology should be a servant and Be a leader and show educational boundaries ... Ergege for genetic engineering and psychological knowledge to found and strengthen the educational work." (S.5) There was a concerted effort by someone or org to obfuscate the proceedings of the 1933 Psychology conference, with lines blackened out and entire speeches deleted from the record of the meetings:
>
> Completely missing the total lectures "of German kind, LF Clauss," "the counter type of the German-volkischen movement, ER Jaensch,""The Erbbiologische and genealogische Contribution to the psychology of racial purity, Prince Von Isenburg" and" The problems of Political Psychology, Poppelreuter. "
> (Hachmann-Gleixner, 2019 pg. 49-50)

The work of George Muller is of interest, as his findings later went into developing psychological profiles of people based on color (farbe) theory, which Capt. Roader, who we shall read about later, studied in the 1950s in correspondence with Hans Bender. In 1930, George Elias Muller, a founder of psychophysics, Color phenomena (see Verschuer below for continuation of research) Müller retired in 1922. Afterwards he began studying color phenomena; during his study of color phenomena he advanced Ewald Hering's theory of color and elaborated on the two-stage theory. The first stage involved the retinal receptors and then the signals were transformed into the four opponent primary colors. In 1930 he wrote two summary books that helped define color theory. His student Erich Jaensch further elaborated on this topic.

Jaensch, here he put forward further considerations Aubert-Förstersches phenomenon that the perceived size of an object does not coincide with the size of the image on the retina. Especially the lateral seeing found his attention here. He was at the University of Strasbourg writing 'about the perception of space' and receiving a habilitation. His duplicity theory begins here. Jaensch assumed that periodic vibrations were absorbed by the cochlea, while aperiodic vibrations were absorbed by other parts of the ear. Vibrations exhibiting both periodic and aperiodic character, on the other hand, would be perceived by both the cochlea and other organs.

Also related to the study of vision is that of Wolfgang Metzger who in the 1930s established that when subjects gazed into a featureless field of vision they consistently hallucinated and their electroencephalograms changed. Ganzfeld was later revisited by Hans Bender (see below).

Finally, we have the work in parapsychology, which would become integral to neuroweapons development. Perhaps the most famous parapsychological researcher that was also a Nazi was Hans Bender, also a member of the SS Ahnenerbe, the scientific arm of the Nazi SS. After graduation in 1925, he first studied law in Lausanne and Paris. In 1927 he transferred to the study of psychology, philosophy and Romance languages in Freiburg, Heidelberg and Berlin. From 1929 he studied in Bonn with Erich Rothacker (psychology) and Ernst Robert Curtis (Romance Studies). After the seizure of power by the National Socialists, he was in 1933 a short-term member of the SA, parallel to his position as Assistant Professor at the Psychological Institute of the University of Bonn. Bender was disabled and not eligible to serve in the military. Thus, he became a professor at the University of Bonn.

In 1932, Hans Bender's experiments dealing with "automatic spelling" ("glass tilting") were performed in 1932 and 1933 at the Psychological Institute of Bonn University under the auspices of Erich Rothacker and were published in 1936 as a PhD. dissertation under the title Psychische Automatismen (Psychic Automatisms). In an interesting development as a student under Kurt Beringer at Bonn University he participated in studies on mescaline, which were a focal point of later pharmacological searches for a 'truth serum' in interrogations, notably with the German-CIA program, Project Artichoke. Bender and Jaensch intersect as Jaensch wrote the preface to a work of Bender's on parapsychology in 1936. In 1939 Bender completed a medical degree, which should give him a greater reputation in view of his controversial research interest. For his assertion that after his medical state examination and his license in Freiburg in 1939 with a thesis: "The working curve under pervitin (methamphetamines) in medicine" with Kurt Beringer receiving a doctorate. He also writes of starting a Parapsychological Institute, inviting psychics to participate in 1939.

After the war Hans Bender was detained but subsequently released. In 1950 he established The Institute for Fringe Areas of Psychology and Mental Health at the University of Freiburg in 1950. From 1942 to 1944, he taught at the Paracelsus Institute studying ESP. Interestingly, after the war he maintained correspondence with Capt. Hans Roeder, who headed up the secret early remote viewing program of the German Navy in Berlin. We shall examine their correspondence shortly. Another development of interest is his work in 1966 with physicist Burkhard Heim, who he hoped to engage in a physical explanation for certain psychic phenomena, most notably trans-communication, or synthetic telepathy. Bender engaged several physicists in pursuit of a physical explanation, such as Rolle. Interestingly, in the development of the Ganzfeld, he conducted a national experiment on television to measure people's psychic abilities through the medium of television, in 1968, based on research conducted in the 1930s. It should be noted that in 1967 he was contracted by the US National Security Agency to conduct experiments regarding psychic phenomena.

A CLASSIC CASE

I. An Illustration
Rosenheim Germany 1967, Evidence: Videotape and Electronic Recording
Instruments - Scientists: Physicists/Parapsychologist

Phenomenon: Neon lights blackout
- Automatic Fuses Blown
- Movement 400 lb. Storage Cabinet
- Pictures Swing Around
- Frequent Electronic Dealing of Number 0119

Scientists
Physicists: Dr. F. Karger
C. Zuma
Parapsychologist/Psychiatrist - Dr. Hans Bender

Institution Involved: Institute for Border Areas of Psychology and Mental
Health - Freiburg University

II. Pertinent Scientific Perspectives/Models

A. Quantum and Relativity Physics:

1. "S" Matrix Theory (including hadron models)
2. Bell Inequality/EPR Paradox (7 Experiments)
3. The Action of Consciousness on Matter: A Quantum
   Mechanical Theory of Telekinesis by Rich Mattuck, Evan Harris,
   Walker
4. Elizabeth Rauscher's "Higher Dimensional Geometrical Models"

B. Parallel and Identical Experiences of Identical Twins

C. Evolutionary Model of Pierre de Chardin (Noogenesis)

NAZI REMOTE VIEWING

As mentioned earlier, the German Navy had a prototypical Remote Viewing program under the leadership of Capt. Hans Roeder, who previously had served on submarines.

To take a step back it is important to look at the historical development and attitudes toward parapsychological research in Germany. One of the first Germans to study psychic affairs was Rudolf Tischner (1879-1961); he was originally an opthalmologist. Revisiting the eyes to psychic research, He practiced in Munich, publishing a monograph in 1921 on telepathy and other psi effects in 'Telepathie und Hellsehen.' Tischner called telepathy and clairvoyance Außersinnlicher Wahrnehmung, extrasensory perception.

A description of one experiment serves as a strong parallel and even perhaps the prototype for the format of a US Military-trained Remote Viewer, where white envelopes with unseen GPS coordinates are written inside the opaque envelope unknown to any that could transmit the information to the viewers. Tischner's experimental description:

> These experiments involved selected participants in identifying the targets – typically, text or drawings – concealed in opaque envelopes, while (unlike a telepathy experiment) no persons were aware of the contents of the envelope.

Telepathy was used early in the German Police investigations according to Wernet 2013. Its interest to official government offices was not limited to police investigations. During the war a special department developed in German Naval Intelligence to investigate translocation of enemy ships. The staff of this department developed out of earlier 'Occult' scientists. This organization was founded in 1919 as the German Okkultistliche Society' (D.O.G.) under the chairmanship of physicist and mason Dr. Werner Haken, who led until 1923 when it was renamed 'German Society for Scientific Occultism' (D.G.W.O.). Its vice president was a scientist of interest and a member of the special Navy department, later known as the 'SP Department' (sidereal pendel), Lt. Col. A.D. Konrad Schuppe, who was the recruiter for staff for the department (Walther, 1949).

Understandably, the department was recruited from membership of the Deutsche Gesellschaft fur wissenschaftlichen Okkultismus (D.G.W.O). The military interest in occult studies is also attested to in that Schuppe also briefed the III Army Corps General Command on Occult sciences. In 1939 the society changed to the 'German Metaphysical Society.' At this time Schuppe was interested in ganzfeld or Earth's radiation, electromagnetism and dowsing (remote location of water), theoretically feeling the weak EM fields of water in comparison to solid earth. Another member of the SP Department was the chemist Dr. Fritz Quade.

It is important to put developments in parapsychology (okkultisme) in a historical context at this time. Shortly before the founding of the SP department in 1942 it was banned in the Reich to practice Okkultisme things in any way. This developed out of a suspicion that occult practitioners had steered Hess to go to Great Britain in an effort at forming a German-British fascist alliance, or "peace," allegedly with Lord Hamilton, a British occultist and Nazi sympathizer. In response to the development of Hess being captured the Gestapo banned all occultish practices. At this time Schuppe and Quade were arrested for several months. However, the military became interested in this research, as well as Heinrich Himmler. Another member of the SP Department was Dr. Hans-Hermann Kritzinger, an astronomer who founded the German Association for Solar Observations, previously employed by the Air Force and Army Weapons Office for Ballistics studies. In 1940 he was working for the Propaganda Ministry after Goebbels became interested in the prophecies of Nostradamus about the downfall of England in the end times and wanted to use it as propaganda. Kritzinger had written about this prophecy so was a person of interest to Goebbels. As one who claimed to specialize in dowsing, he became of interest to the military work with the SP Department.

One of the most renowned persons researching dowsing and pendel was Ludwig Straniak (1879-1951), who in 1936 started the Society for Scientific Pendulum Research (Gesellschaft für Wissenschaftliche Pendelforschung) which was dedicated to the National Socialist cause. He believed in 8 great forces (GroBe Kraft) in the universe. He wrote a book on Pendel techniques, 'Das siderische Pendel als Indikator der achten Naturkraft' (Straniak, 1937). In one chapter of this book, written by Arnold Mannlicher, 'Biologische Strahlenforschung und Elektrotechnik', The belief in polar coordinates system is presented, it was also claimed to be able to use the pendel for diagnosis in the human body, he wrote:

> Zum verstandnis der Angelegenheit mub ich einiges uber die normalen Polaritatsverhaltnisse des menschlichen Korpers vorausschicken. Es verhalt sich dieser namlich vergleichbar einem richtig aufgeladenen elektrischen Akkumulator, nur handelt es sich im Gegensatz zu letzterem, der nur zwei Pole besitzt, beim menschlichen Korper um deren sechs. Da der Orgnismus des Menschen in jeder der drie Axen eines raumlichen Koordinatensystems (Nord-Sud, West-Ost, Tief-Hoch) in postivem oder natgativem Sinne durchstrahlbar und polarisiert ist, ergeben sich (bie der Orientierung mit dem Rucken nach Norden und dem Gesicht nach Suden und bei "Stromabnahme" uber der Wirbelsaule awischen den beiden Schulterblattern) acht verschiedene "Axungsgruppen," und zwar: Nord-West-Tief, Nord-West-Hoch, Nord-Ost-Hoch, Nord-Ost-Tief, Sud-Ost-Hoch, Sud-West-Hoch.

To understand the matter, I must first state something about the normal polarity relations of the human body. It behaves like a properly charged electrical accumulator, only in contrast to the latter, which has only two poles, the human body has six. Since the organism of the human being can be irradiated and polarized in each of the three axes of a spatial coordinate system (north-south, west-east, low-high) in a positive or natural sense, there are (by the orientation with the back to the north and the face to the south and with "current collection" above the spine between the two shoulder blades) eight different "axis groups," namely: north-west low, north-west high, north-east high, north-east low, south-east high, Southwest High. (Straniak 1937)

I would prepare a few years to the understanding of the matter for the normal polaritics of the human body. It is unable to behave a properly charged electric battery, but it is only contrary to the latter that has only two poles, at the human body of their six. Since the organism of man in each of the three axes of a spacious coordinate system (north-sud, west-east, deep-high) is unbalanced and polarized in postive or negative sense... ... eight different "axes groups," namely: North-West-deep, North-West-high, North-East-high, North-East-deep, South-East-high, South-West-high. (Straniak, 1937)

The observation of the body's polarities is an essential aspect of the Nazi Remote Viewing program, this is also observed by physical experiments where an east-west axis is observed as we shall read in a later chapter in the work of Persinger. In the pendel research it was observed that those were more successful who had a reverse polarity in their fingers than those that were not. It was observed that this was a biological difference where the successful viewers had a polarization abnormality.

Also published in Straniak's work is that of Mannlicher, who was a Swiss physician that believed that the earth 'radiated' as related to radionics, and that this earth radiation interfered with human health. This would later be related to the natural earth electromagnetic field and gravity, as gravity is different in different areas of the earth. Indeed, Hitler himself believed in these theories as related by Kurlander: "Hitler himself employed diviners to check the Reich Chancellery for cancer-causing 'death rays." (Kurlander, 504)

In another chapter Straniak himself describes in detail how to work the Pendel in the coordinates system. (Straniak 1937, 17-18)

So, with this understanding we can better put the work of the SP Department into a historical and scientific background wherefrom these beliefs originated.

The SP Department operated under a 'top secret' rubric. Another member of the team, who later quit, was Gerda Walther. She notes in her letter regarding 'ESP in the German Navy' that she was not allowed to refer to the head of the department, Capt. Hans Roeder as "Captain," just Mr. Roeder (Walther 1949). Another member, the Astrologer Wolff, claims that the activities there had been "strictly confidential" and that the staff members had been under the impression of being constantly supervised [under watch]. (Black et al, 164).

The career of Capt. Hans A. Roeder began in WWI as a U-boat commander; he became an engineer after the war, publishing The Technical Computing in 1933. In 1939 he returned to active duty as a Navy Captain assigned as a general consultant for the Inventions und Patentwesen Office of the Navy Main Weapons Office. Interestingly, he was a self-ascribed channeler or what was termed 'commuter' [channeler, clairvoyant]. Initially calling this research

> ...the Navy Intelligence Service supported research on 'Optical Location'; an 'invisible, active locational method' was supposed to be developed. See Bundesearchiv-Mlitararchiv Freiburg i. Br. (Anton, 2015, Note 37)

Later, it was named the Sidereal Pendel Program. He reported to an Admiral Raeder who was Chief of Naval Operations. Others with knowledge of the program were former Freikorps Marine Group Eberhardt member Adm. Otto Schneiwind and a Rear Admiral Gerhard Wagner (1898-1987), from 1941 to 1944 Chief of the Operations Department in the Naval High Command, who reminisces about the work of Capt. Roeder:

> R[oeder], the commuter, was known to all of us. His work was from that point of view not so unusual. After all, one constantly thought about new techniques, and when now someone came who declared that he could achieve something by a certain method, then Of course it was natural that they gave him the opportunity (Anton, 2015).

The structure of the German Naval research of the time is interesting as related by Anton et al, 2015:

About the exact date of construction of this special group in the Kriegsmarine, the corresponding establishment decisions and their justification as well as the organizational framework conditions are still little known. So far, no relevant documents and sources on these issues. That's how we in some places, of necessity, rely on assumptions. Most of the following detailed information comes from retrospective eyewitness accounts and are accordingly to judge critically If we follow the remarks of Gerda Walther and Wilhelm Th. H. Wulff, existed the "SP Division" in the spring of 1942, when both first heard about her, already. The other available reports also suggest an emergence at the beginning of the year 1942. Who gave the order to set up the experimental group, who was informed and who was the driving force behind the experiments within the naval line However, this must remain unclear in the current source situation.

Wulff mentions that at least the fleet chief Admiral Otto Schniewind [freikorp member of Marine Group Eberhardt] was informed about the experiments. On the other hand, it can be proven that the coordination of the pendulum locomotion tests in naval intelligence (MND) lay in the naval warfare. In cooperation with the MND, the Naval Weapons Main Office and there the General Office worked "Invention and patenting" at the trials. The naval intelligence service had since 1942 several "working groups" on the topic "vibration research for the submarine war ," in which also the patent department of the navy was also involved in the special border-scientific research in the context of one of these "working groups" of the MND, but there is no clear evidence.

About the work of the General Department "Inventions and Patents" in the Naval Weapons Main Office there is almost no information left. With effect from 1 September in 1942, this department became Division IV in the new office group "Research - Inventions - Patent Administration (FEP) ." The new FEP, headed by Rear Admiral Wilhelm Rhein, now comprised four departments: FEP I: General Research Control, FEP II: Research Organization and Reporting, FEP III: Research Division, FEP IV: Inventions and patenting. The bureau should answer all questions for the navy research, inventions and the patent system can provide exhaustive information, maintain contacts with research centers and intensify marine research in general. Their establishment was in response to the increasingly lossy and dogged guided submarine warfare, which the German navy to an extension of the Efforts in research and development.

For the year 1943, the Amtsgruppe as an extremely large apparatus with a variety of supervised scientific and technical research projects. Occupied is a huge effort with numerous supervised internal and external projects. In 1943 alone, around 1000 "research tasks" were fulfilled. In 1943, the FEP IV department processed around 13,000 applications for new developments. The work program in the previous year, 1942, cannot be translated into writing sources are hardly anything to be said. In the night from the 22nd to the 23rd of November in 1943, the Berlin office building of the FEP in the Admiral-von-SchröderStraße 31/33, complete with all documents stored there, were destroyed by an air raid. Amtsgruppenchef Rear Admiral Wilhelm Rhein had on 22 December 1943 reported: "All the files in the house were destroyed by the fire." This information is confirmed by a later report of March 27, 1944: "As it is Almost 1 year had just been achieved, with a separate service building for the Amtsgruppe. This was due to fire as a result of the bombing of 22.11.1943 completely destroyed." In this war [of] destruction lies presumably the central one Reason that no written legacies to the border science have been handed down. (Anton et al, 2015, 297)

With the almost total destruction of Germany during the war and the self-destruction of important research records, it is almost untraceable to find documentation on these secret programs. Gerda Walther and Wulff's accounts are the main sources of information on this project. As stated above the project was begun because the Germans felt they had fallen behind what they believed to be a British optical location project. Capt. Roeder held this belief, although it would later turn out that the main cause of the uptick in sinking of German naval vessels was the Turing team's work on cracking Enigma with the Bombe computer. It should be noted, however, that Roeder may have been aware of the work of Harold Sherman and Sir Roy Wilkins in Great Britain, "Thoughts Through Space," that did Remote Viewing experiments for locating ships; thus, being a rationale for German investigations.

Another interesting person working on the SP Department project was Dr. Wilhelm Hartmann, who performed characterological or 'aptitude-tests' on staff members to assign them, although an astronomer and astrologer, he was a member of the Tattwas Team in the SP Department, studying the aspects of the planets, which seems to be related to Alfven waves, the magnetic grids in the universe, and of course gravity. Though the early staff was to be comprised of people attached to the scientific study of the occult, Capt. Roeder was specifically looking for a way to train normal Naval personnel to do this 'locational' work. As noted earlier, Walther broke with this work group.

The issue was the difference of opinion on what this ability really was. Where Capt. Roeder searched for a cause based in physics, Gerda Walther believed it was 'supernatural.' She recollects:

> But being a materialist he always came back to his opinion that it was essentially a problem of physics, not of psychology or parapsychology. (Indeed this stubbornness of his at the end gave me an excuse to decline working there as our views were too much apart.) (Walther 1949).

The cause being purely physical was investigated through other studies of the group that looked at what materials the pendel should be made and what kind of string to hang the pendel from. They performed many experiments to try and bring the study into a science. In the end, the Navy saw no merit in this attempt at location. Although, it is claimed Straniak was able to demonstrate its use. Ostensibly, it ended with negative results.

Another interesting perspective of Gerda Walther's was that of the lead the Anglo-Saxon powers, as she called them, had in parapsychological research of the day, she writes:

> I said it would now avenge itself psychical research had been neglected to such an extent all these years compared with the Anglo-Saxons countries, it needed years of careful research whether and how ships could be detected and placed by the pendulum and not even the very first preliminaries existed, I doubted whether they did in England or the United States, although they were far ahead of Germany in all these things... (Walther, 1949)

The question of what happened to this research after 1942 is a provocative one. Given the SS involvement and Heinrich Himmler's personal involvement in the Thule Society. Scholars have noted:

> Concerning an 'answer to the problem of the dowsing rod' and the research field of radiesthesia, for example, the Reichssicherheitshauptamt (RSHA) of the SS as well as National Socialist leadership circles made increasing efforts over the course of 1942 to get a better handle on the [technological] foundations and possibilities. (Black et al, 2015, 166)

Previous to this the SS had been involved in cultivating occult science for their mission. In 1937, the following from Kurlander:

> On Dr. Kiendl's support for Werner Kittler's "original and useful method, in which he brought together natural scientists and astrologers" in working groups in the Reich Literary Chamber and the Reich Ministry of Propaganda (hereafter RMVP), see BArch, R 58/6206, report from Kiendl to Hörmann, Sept. 2, 1938, 8; BArch, R 9361V/1107, Werner Kittler biography (March 14, 1938), application (June 13, 1938).

It is not without some technical reasons that astrologers were consulted, for instance one of the areas studied by Roeder's Bio-location project was that of tatwas, or astrological aspects). The issue of the differentiation between charlatanry and real scientific investigations is considered in a correspondence between Himmler and Heydrich, his Intelligence chief before Schellenberg. Kurlander notes:

> BArch, R 58/6207, letter from Himmler to Heydrich, Jan. 10, 1939. For more on careful attempts by the SD and the Gestapo to differentiate between "scientific occultism" and occult charlatanry, see BArch, R 58/6206, letters from Haselbacher to the Gestapo (March 29, 1937),

As well as:

> Himmler was deeply invested in occult and border-scientific thinking and saw no incompatibility between actively policing commercial occultism and selectively appropriating 'scientific occultism,' whether for developing military technology, gathering intelligence, or making political prognoses. These differences within the upper echelons of the SS and police administration might explain why Nebe, as head of the Kripo, proposed a middle way that preserved a space for 'scientific occultism' while moving against 'every activity that rests on and exploits superstition. (Kurlander, 506)
>
> The new campaign against occultism also failed to dissuade Goebbels's 'Expert for Cosmobiology' in the Reich Literary Chamber, Werner Kittler, from eagerly recruiting dozens of famous astrologers, dossiers, and cosmo-biologists to study the potential benefits of various border sciences. Even the SD and the Gestapo com-

missioned dozens of reports and peer reviews aimed at differentiating between 'scientific occultism' and charlatanry. Himmler himself advocated this policy in a January 1939 letter to Heydrich:

> As you know, I do not consider astrology to be pure humbug, but believe that there's something behind it … We must do much more to restrict [charlatans] so that we only allow specific communities of research (bestimmte Forschungsgemeinschaften) in this sphere. (Kurlander, 507)
>
> Beginning in September 1939, Himmler, Hess and Goebbels recruited dozens of 'scientific' occultists to assist with obtaining military intelligence and producing domestic and foreign propaganda [PSYOPS]. (Kurlander, 511)
>
> Goebbels and Himmler even employed Kisshauer to review the talents of German astrologers and pendulum dossiers [remote viewing, dowsing], the most 'scientific' of whom they hired to assist the SS and the Propaganda Ministry in gathering military intelligence and producing propaganda (Kurlander, 519)

So obviously the SS was already entangled in this research even before the Wehrmacht showed interest through such groups as Naval Intelligence in edge science or border science.

Indeed, there is evidence that these programs continued as noted in relation to the campaign to free Mussolini in Italy after the fall of the Fascist regime there:

> In 1944 the SS employed psychics to locate Mussolini; subsequently with their help, he was located. After this, secret experiments were conducted with psychics. This was known as 'Operation Mars', source of information on this was Walter Schellenberg, Himmler's assistant. (Black et al, 2015, 168)

The operation to locate Mussolini was conducted in what today would be defined as military remote viewing. It is disputed whether real human intelligence led to his release by German special forces commanded by Skorzeny or whether it was intelligence from remote viewing. Skorzeny remarked regarding the use of this NEURINT that:

> It was Himmler who was said to believe in these always somewhat disputed sciences. I was never told about any positive result of these 'investigations.' (Black et al, 170)

After the war's end, there is evidence that structured or organized Nazi research in edge science continued. This now brings us to another Pendel researcher during the war, Hans Bender. Indeed, after the war in 1952 there is evidence of Capt. Roeder continuing research in parapsychological areas. He and Bender exchanged letters, although only a couple survive today, of which this seems just a sample of other letters regarding research. In Roeder's letter he notes he is working on an extensive account of his work at the SP Department, however, this work did not survive or at least is not known in any public archive or publication. Roeder wrote:

> In the Institute for the Study of Certain Psychophysical Problems, which was set up and managed by the OKM, I have put aside all available material in a treatise which will be published in due course. It has become quite extensive, which was also to be expected from the size of the area worked on in the 7 theses of the institute. (Roeder, 1952)

Roeder apparently is investigating characterology using color theory, the diagnosis of personality using color tests, which was directly derived from Metzger and Muller (above), about which he wrote to Bender seeking the best advice on these matters.

Hans Roeder to Hans Bender 9/20/1952:

> To make mental states and relationships quantitatively better, I proceeded from man's unconscious relations to the colors, which proved to be a particularly suitable gateway to this new territory.
>
> I have now succeeded in developing a method that allows these relationships to be quantitatively measured. I am therefore able to take Vp's static and dynamic curves over these relationships from the current measurements.
>
> The color measurements are based on the Oswald colors 2,5,8, 11, 14, 1, 20 and 23 of the na series. The measurements taken at 4 Vp's, sometimes over one year daily, combine the 8 colors into 2 bundles whose composition individually curves apart (+ -), keeping separate for a while (2-3 weeks), then approaching, beating

into Opposite to (- +) and strive against each other. These reversal periods are always shorter than the normal periods and end with a return to the original state. The 4 colors in the two buds do not run parallel, but swing back and forth in them.

The mashing process is also useful in other unconserved relationships, e.g., To tone, smells, forms, numbers, letters, words, etc. apply, with any combinations can be selected.

Today, I can only circumscribe the very extensive area of research in order to inform you of its presence.

Bender Reply to Roeder 12/9/1952:

The measurement method that you write to me is of great interest to me, but I had to have some documents to comment on. The psychology of colors is actively cultivated in the Institute for Psychology and Characterology of the University of Freiburg, which is led by Prof. Heiss as you probably know unanimously, the so-called color pyramid test (originally from Pfister, Zurich) given to a diagnostic Do you know the test of Luscher, Basel?

It is interesting to see Roeder and Bender continuing their war work into the post-war period, does it show conspiracy to promote a 4th Reich or just benign research?

NAZI ROOTS TO SOVIET PSYCHOTRONICS

The Nazi Remote Viewing project was not the only endeavor that touched on unconventional science during the Nazi Regime. Serge Kernbach argues that the Soviet psychotronic program likely grew out of captured Nazi scientists that led to the use of hypnosis with remote influencing later in the Soviet Union (see Ch.8), but first crafted in the Nazi regime of Germany:

For this overview, two of such forced re-settlements in 1945 through 1955 are of interest: the first one is related to the institutes in Sinop and Agudzera (close to Suchumi, Soviet Georgia), which was created for Manfred von Ardenne and Gustav Hertz, and directed by them until 1955. These institutes were primarily related to the Soviet atomic programs. For technological achievements in this area, von Ardenne received the Soviet Stalin Prize twice, in 1947 and 1953, and Hertz got it in 1951. As mentioned by, e.g., Heikin, the topics were not only related to atomic research, but also included a number of other issues, e.g., energy convention, high-frequency technics, applied radiophysics, and others. Employees who worked in Agudzera in the 1950s remembered small research groups, which explored 'hypnosis and weak emissions from biological organisms.' We know that Russian specialists who worked in these facilities in the late 1950s were involved in brain-stimulation programs in the 1960s and 1970s, and later in psychotronic governmental programs in the 1980s. It is well-known that von Ardenne also conducted research related to brain EM-emission in his laboratory in the late 1920s. Is it possible that works directed in Soviet Georgia by Manfred von Ardenne, Gustav Hertz, Werner Hartmann, Max Steenback (the developer of the first Betatron), and others inspired (or to some extent were used in) early psychotronic research? (Kernbach 2014)

Kernbach also notes that Czech psychotronic research was begun in the Sudetenland, which was an ethnic German, Nazi-occupied territory of the Czech nation.

HIMMLER'S 4TH REICH, A TECHNICAL STATE:

As previously noted in the first part of this work Heinrich Himmler foresaw continuing the war indefinitely but through other means, as the German Reich was now defeated militarily. In 1943 Himmler began a covert war plan that included setting up secret research facilities in German industries, the creation of political front groups that never publicly mentioned Jews or Racial Supremacy. It is also important to remember the attitude of the SS according to head of the Nazi SS Intelligence Office, Amt. VI, Walter Schellenberg, that "if Germany must lose, then let all of Germany die!," which is eerily reminiscent of the Diplomacy AI in the video game *Total War*, see on-line Appendix D.

Reich Science was overseen by the SS under Heinrich Himmler. What areas of research were they investigating? Surely, they were not reliant on sacred arcs buried in the desert. As we shall read, the ideal of using biology on an industrial scale to re-engineer the world in the Nazi image was constructed by Pascual Jordan.

GENETIC ENGINEERING FOR BIOLOGICAL WARFARE:

Genetic engineering research was conducted by the Wehrmacht and SS. Genetic Engineering is the science of using engineering in biology usually associated with augmenting or changing DNA, sometimes through a vector such as a bacteriophage or a virus, to change coding of functions or altering of functions (See Krishnan 2017). During the war the Nazis were interested in bacteriophage research:

A bacteriophage, or phage, is a virus that only disinfects bacteria. In Greek, phageton means food/consumption. They are also called bacterial viruses. These are fundamental tools for research and study in molecular genetics. Bacteriophages used among other vectors for cloning and transfer genes. Then Félix d'Hérelle makes the same observation in the stool of patients with bacillary dysentery (bowel disease), isolates the first phages, develops the first therapeutic applications and markets the first bacteriophage drugs. The support of the genetic information (genome) of the bacteriophages can be a DNA or an RNA.

A German researcher on the genetic and biological research of the time notes that the Nazi research was:

> Regarding the science in the Reich at this time in this area, Akhim Trunk writes: "Regarding the issue of research, the project was by all means state of the art" (Trunk 2007, 132). The Wehrmacht research was conducted under the auspices of the Kaiser Wilhelm Institute, a scientific research institute with many branches. It was also conducted under the orders of the Reichsfuhrer Heinrich Himmler (Trunk 2007, 122).

As noted above, genetic engineering was touted in a 1933 Nazi science conference as being a vehicle for final victory, although deleted from the archive. In what follows is an account of the genetic research carried out by the Nazi regime. Though some of this research may or may not be directly related to neuroweapons, their military utilization is the prime motivator in carrying out this research, so I note instances of Genetic Engineering below.

One final note regarding bacteriophages is the obvious interest of the Nazi military in such technology. In 1943 Nazi's raided bacteriophage researchers in France, imprisoning Eugene Wollman and his wife Elisabeth Wollman. During the 1920s, Eugène Wollman at the Pasteur Institute in Paris attempted to reconcile the views of D'Hérelle and Bordet on bacteriophagy. Wollman posited that the phenomenon was a trait that bacteria acquired through infection or through inheritance. Wollman claimed that lysogenic bacteria involved a form of what he called paraheredity, whereby traits could transmit both vertically, through the genetic material passed from parent to offspring, and horizontally, through genetic material transmitted by infection within the same generation. To test his theory, Wollman conducted experiments on the bacterium, Bacillus megatherium (B. megatherium), with his wife Elisabeth Wollman. They published several papers on this work between 1925 and 1940. Their work on lysogeny included the experimental replication of bacteriophagy and the production of bacteriophages in non-contaminated bacterial cultures. They also showed that, contrary to d'Hérelle's theory, there were many distinct species of bacteriophages. (Racine, 2014) The Wollmans' work ended in 1943 when the Nazis took them to the extermination camp in Auschwitz and executed them. Note this work predates that at Cal Tech under Max Dullbreck (1937), a German immigrant to the United States in 1940. Post-WWII genetic engineering was centered in Cold Springs Harbor, Long Island, NY down the road from Montauk.

In 1900, Mendel's genetics research was rediscovered by three European scientists, Hugo de Vries, Carl Correns, and Erich von Tschermak. The exact nature of the "re-discovery" has been debated: De Vries published first on the subject, mentioning Mendel in a footnote, while Correns pointed out Mendel's priority after having read De Vries' paper and realizing that he himself did not have priority. De Vries may not have acknowledged truthfully how much of his knowledge of the laws came from his own work and how much came only after reading Mendel's paper. Later scholars have accused Von Tschermak of not truly understanding the results at all.

Genetics in the early days was considered a part of Eugenics, which basically amounted to Race Hygiene; the use of sterilization on undesirables was a common practice, the field of Eugenics was primarily founded in America before the Nazis took up the cause during the Third Reich. Verschuer, like many others after the war, was able to steer clear of Race Hygiene and rebrand himself as a genetics researcher primarily studying the effects of radiation on genes, which reminds one of the use of 'Target-Theory' in early gene research, such as advocated by Pascual Jordan in his version of Quantum Biology.

HISTORY OF THE KWI

Genetics in Nazi Germany was carried out in terms of scientific research at the Kaiser Wilhelm Institutes. The KWI of Anthropology, Human Heredity and Eugenics was founded in 1927, partially funded by the Rockefeller Foundation, taking its origins from America. It's first director was Eugene Fischer who in 1921 published *Principles of Human Heredity and Race Hygiene*. In 1927 the director of the Genetics Department was Otmar Freiherr (Baron) von Verschuer (16 July 1896 – 8 August 1969), a Dutch noble, who in 1942 was appointed the director of the Institute. It was Verschuer who directed Josef Mengele in human experiments at Auschwitz. Another of Verschuer's assistants was Katrin Magnussen, a German-Swede that was a committed National Socialist even after the war.

Josef Mengele (1911-1979) joined Verschuer in Jan. 1937 (Weiss, 650). He previously received a Ph.D in Anthropology from the University of Munich in 1935. He became one of four assistants to Verschuer at his Institute in Frankfurt, which worked on categorizing people by race, with 'racial certificates', based on ancestry or genes. This was primarily focused on proving or disproving one was an Aryan or a Jew for court cases and other civil matters in the Nazi era. He received a 2nd Ph.D for medicine with the dissertation "Kinship Examination in Cases of Cleft Lip, Jaw, Palate" in 1939. He was also a captain in the Nazi SS.

In 1943 Verschuer encouraged Mengele to be transferred to Auschwitz, where Verschuer used Mengele to acquire specimens for their research from concentration camp victims. He also was responsible for administering Zyklon B in the gas chambers. In one story of his machine-like efficiency, he at one point cleared out an entire barracks of women during a Typhus epidemic, exterminating them all, to make room to move other inmates into the de-sanitized barracks, thus performing a swap of one barracks to the next to create space to sanitize the next barracks. In another example of his machine-like reductive thinking he tried to artificially join two twins together by sewing them together; they eventually died of gangrene from the operation.

(Joseph Mengele during the war, Wikicommons Image)

The twin research was in part intended to prove the supremacy of heredity over environment and thus strengthen the Nazi premise of the superiority of the Aryan race. (Steinbacher, 2005, 114) Nyiszli and others reported that the twin studies may also have been motivated by an intention to increase the reproduction rate of the German race by improving the chances of racially desirable people having twins. (Lifton, 1986, 358-9). At Auschwitz he was involved in the following studies that directly informed Verschuers research goals at the KWI-A: Projekt Augenfarbe (Eye study), Zwillingforschung (Twin Studies), Projekte Eiweißkorper und Tuburkulose (protein study and tuberculosis).

It is notable that he escaped detainment after the war under questionable circumstances raising the specter of collaboration with Allied security forces. He eventually resettled in South America, at one point being reunited with his family, and visiting West Germany while being hunted by anti-Holocaust activists, West German Intelligence and Israeli Mossad. While in South America he continued his Twin studies in Candido Gadol in Brazil, creating a number of twins of Germanic ancestry.

Another Verschuer assistant was Karin Magnusson. She received her doctorate in 1932 from the University of Gottingen. She studied at the Zoological Institute of the university after receiving her Ph.D. She then became a teacher, a profession she returned to after the war, even though remaining an avowed Nazi. In 1935, she was connected to the Nazi Racial Policy Office for Hanover. In 1936, she wrote Race and Population Policy Tools. In 1941, she stopped teaching after receiving a scholarship to the KWI-A. There she worked in the Department of Experimental Pathology of Heritage under Hans Nachtsheim. She studied inheritance of eye color in rabbits and humans, drawing the conclusion that eye color is genetically selected and also by hormones; at one point, injecting adrenaline into the eye samples she received from Mengele from Auschwitz to change their eye color (Hesse, 2001, 78), she met Mengele in 1943 at the KWI-A. One area she studied specifically was heterochromia iridium, in which the color is different in each eye.

Magnussen's, completed research was published in 1949, being entitled, "On the relationship between histological distribution of pigment, Iris color and pigmentation of the eyeball of the human eye." (Schmuhl, 2005, 490). It is not hard to extrapolate why racial supremacists fixated on eye color for genetic research, although there may be more to the eye studies then just simple genetic research. The use of hormones and the attempt to try to change the eye color is an interesting aspect of this research; as noted the study of hormones is not limited to this study but was also involved in other studies by the Nazi scientists.

In 1939, von Verschuer was approached by the German biochemist, Adolf Friedrich Johann Butenandt (1903-1995) who had won the Nobel Prize in Chemistry in 1939 for his work on sex hormones. Adolf Windaus and Walter Schöller advised him to work on hormones extracted from ovaries. This led to the discovery of estrone and other primary female sex hormones. This work was conducted in 1934 in Gdansk at the Chemisches Institut, extracting progesterone and testosterone in 1935.

Verscheur as head of the KWI Genetics program was approached by Emil Abderhalden (March 9, 1877 – August 5, 1950) to do blood studies, of which Verschuer would direct Joseph Mengele in lab work for this process among other assistants to Verschuer. Albderhalden did extensive work in the analysis of proteins, polypeptides, and enzymes. His Abwehrfermente ("defensive enzymes") theory stated that immunological challenge will induce production of proteases. This work was to be used to racially classify people based on serology.

In October of 1943, Verschuer, Albderhalden and Butenandt worked on joint projects funded by the Wehrmacht; Verschuer, working with Abderhalden, began studies on Human Blood. Mengele took over 200 blood samples from Auschwitz prisoners, This work was done in conjunction with Butenandt. Several research assistants were used, such as Josef Mengele, Gunther Hillmann, Irmgard Haase. Trunk has postulated that the real work here, rather than studying proteases and enzyme reactions, was actually:

> According to Isabel Heinemann's estimates- the RuSHA planned to perform race biological examinations on about 2 million people. Thus, seen in the context of its time, the project represented scientific work profoundly relevant for Nazi racial policy- with potentially extensive, destructive consequences for the people affected by this policy. (Trunk, 2007, 142).

This research used biology to identify people by not just family but also clan, as well as give a geographical spread to genetic research.

Muller-Hill notes an interview with Irmgard Haase:

> Irmgard Haase had spent at first three months with Abderhalden in Halle to learn the defense enzyme reaction in order to analyze the blood of 'gipsy' twins, Russians, Uzbeks, and Kyrgyzstan. In a first step the involuntary blood donors were racial-anthropologically classified: such anthropometric race determinations were required in order subsequently to be able to connect the desired blood analysis results (that is, the race-specific proteins) to a precise type of 'race.' …From this, blood substrates were obtained, as indicated, for instance from Verschuer's third report to the DFG. (Trunk, 2007, 136)

Verschuer has an ominious tone to his research in which he admits to seeking more than simple genetic racial classification, but how genes influence infection, which obviously is of use to racial classification in Nazism:

> Verschuer: "I think that the whole problem is also connected to my research on the issue of heredity of specific proteins. Plasma substrates have been produced from more than 200 people of the most diverse races, twin-pairs and some clans. The Abderhalden method has been exercised and is to be completed with a new method, invented by Hillmann (added on the staff). Hence work on the actual experiment can be started in the near future. My efforts are no longer aimed at establishing the impact of hereditary influence on some infectious diseases, but how it works and what are the processes happening along the way." (Trunk, 2007, 136)

In an even more sinister development within the thought of Mengele is one illuminating entry from his journals that he maintained after the war in South America, he writes:

> "Everything will end in catastrophe if natural selection is altered to the point that gifted people are overwhelmed by billions of morons," he warns, predicting that 90 percent of humans will starve due to stupidity and the remaining 10 percent will survive "like reptiles survived. The rest will die, just like the dinosaurs did … we have to prevent the rise of the idiot masses," he writes.
>
> "The feeble-minded person ('village idiot') was separated from farmers because of his social status and low income," he writes.
>
> "This separation is no longer the case in the age of technology. He is now on the same level with the farmer's son who went to the city.
>
> "We know that selection rules all nature by choosing and exterminating … Those who were unfit had to accept the rule of more accomplished human beings, or they were pushed out or exterminated. Weaker humans were excluded from reproducing. This is the only way for human beings to exist and to maintain themselves."
>
> He says "inferior morons" should be exterminated, adding, "We have to make sure that nature's suspended eradication will continue through human arrangements … birth control can be done by sterilizing those with deficient genes." (Aderet, 2010)

Putting the genetic research and engineering in perspective with Mengele's own admission of "90% of the earth's population will die in a catastrophe" with the purpose of using molecular biology to identify people by race and clan, it is a question as to whether this research was a form of a "Final Solution," leaving the mythical 'Aryans' to rule the world as lone survivors of biological warfare.

BERLIN BRAIN INSTITUTE, BIOLOGICAL RESEARCH IN NAZI GERMANY

It is interesting to take note regarding the various different KWIs in Germany dedicated to studying biology and genetics

- Adolf Butenandt Director KWI for Biochemistry in 1937 D
- Helmut Doring KWI for Breeding Research conducted mutation research. (Deichman 1996)

Virus research, the leaders of KWIs agreed to conduct research in this area:

- Alfred Kuhn, Biology and Biochemistry
- Adolf Butenandt, Biochemistry
- Fritz von Wettstein, Biology

Germany created the KWI Division for Virus Research, with funding from Heinrich Horlein of IG Farben. "From 1937 on, Gustav Adolf Kausche, head of the laboratory for experimental virus research on the Reich Biological Institute, together with E. Pfankuch carried out mutation experiments by using radiation on a TMV dry specimen from Stanly, on their own TMV specimen, and on the x-potato virus." (Deichman, 1996, 210-1)

In 1943 the SS established its own institute for plant genetics (Deichman, 1996, 217)

> The basic research in genetics at this Kaiser Wilhelm Institute [Breeding Research] consisted primarily of mutation research, which after Stubbe's dismissal was carried on by his successor Edgar Knapp. Knapp induced

mutations in mosses through X-rays and UV radiation. During the radiation of moss spermatozoids with monochromatic UV light, he discovered in 1939, together with A. Ruess, Otto Risse, and Hans Schreiber, that the radiation showed the greatest mutagenic effect in the range of the spectrum – 265 micrometers Terahertz radiation occupies a middle ground where the ranges of <u>microwaves</u> and <u>infrared light</u> waves overlap - that corresponded to the absorption maximum of DNA.... Knapp and his colleagues merely concluded that thymonucleic acid (the term for DNA at the time) had a decisive importance for genetic and physiological changes through radiation, and that the relationship between "thymonucleic acid and the genetic substance proper" had to be left to further studies. (Deichman, 1996, 219)

KWI FOR BRAIN RESEARCH AT BERLIN-BUCH AND BIOLOGICAL WEAPONS DEVELOPMENT

The KWI Brain Research Genetics Department was established by Timofeeff-Ressovsky in 1925 in Berlin. The KWI Brain Institute was notably the place where the greats of molecular biology worked together: Delbruck, Zimmer, T-R, and Pascual Jordan, the physicist. It is interesting that America tried to recruit T-R to head up their research in the States, but eventually landed Max Delbruck, who worked at Cold Springs before going to California. "In 1936, after the Reich Education Minister had increased the budget of his department, Timofeeff-Ressovsky turned down an offer from the Carnegie Institution to go to Cold Spring Harbor in the United States." (Deichman, 1996, 221) The research purpose: "in his working report to the DFG in 1938, Tomofeeff-Ressovsky listed the following as the general research task of the department: the phenomenology of gene manifestation, experimental mutation research, and population genetics, with the main focus of the last two fields." (Deichman, 1996, 221-2) Funds from the RFT and the Philips Company were used in 1938 to set up a biophysical laboratory in the department with apparatuses for radiobiological and radio-physical experiments, among them a powerful neutron generator, a linear accelerator for more effective generation of neutron radiation." (Deichman, 1996, 222) [see Zimmer neutrino studies: around this time Zimmer is professionally employed by KWI] After Hermann Muller's discovery in 1927 of the artificial induction of mutations through X-ray radiation, scientists were hoping to get closer to the nature of the gene by analyzing the mechanisms of the induction of mutations. For a number of years mutation research became the most modern, the most strongly funded and most widely pursued field of genetic research. Mutations were induced by X-ray, UV, and neutron radiation. The few experiments that were carried out at this institute with chemicals produced no evidence of chemical mutagenesis." (Deichman, 1996, 222)

Genetic mutation research is of course of interest to supporters of eugenics; as America was the major center of this research it is not surprising research funding came from America and sought to move the most advanced researchers to America. "In 1937 Delbruck received a grant from the Rockefeller Foundation to carry out genetic research under Thomas Morgan at the California Institute for Technology. Delbruck moved to the United States and in 1939 decided to stay. Shortly thereafter he shifted to genetic research in phage." (Deichman, 1996, 223)

Jordan was an advocate of Target Theory early on; this was also reflected by Zimmer and Delbruck,

> In their work on gene mutation and gene structure, T-R, Zimmer and Delbruck applied the target theory of the effect of radiation to the action of radiation in genetics. The Target theory was formulated in 1922 by Friedrich Dessauer as a mathematical description of the biological effects of radiation and was given specific form in 1924 by James Crowther. T-R, Zimmer and Delbruck reached the conclusion that a mutation represented a one-hit result that came about through a single, radiation-caused ionization in a hit area, the gene. (Deichman, 1996, 223)

> Jordan's belief about molecular resonance: "However, in contrast to Delbruck, Jordan was not planning any experiments but deduced from quantum mechanics theoretical conclusions for biological problems. Based on quantum mechanics, he posited an attractive power between identical macromolecules ("quantum mechanical resonance attraction," and with it he tried to explain not only the attraction of homologous chromosomes but also the self-replication of 'genes and virus molecules.' He argued that during replication similar molecules were built, the atoms of which were quantum-mechanically in different states." (Deichman, 1996, 224)

He was wrong as far as protein synthesis; but he was right in other particular areas and led to the Cosic Resonance theory. Of course Jordan was influential on other members of the research team he interacted with:

There is reason to believe that the intense contact with Jordan contributed to Timofeeff-Ressovsky's decision to make the analysis of the primary process of mutation into one of his main areas of research. According to Jordan, many biological reactions, especially biological radiation effects (mutations) were microphysical reactions in the quantum-mechanical sense. He saw a phenomenon of quantum mechanics specifically in the movement of the energy released by ionization somewhere in the hit area to the place where it was used for the change of the gene molecule: electrons did not wander in the normal sense of the word but spread over a molecule like a wave (Jordan 1940). (Deichman, 1996, 225)

Again, we see how Himmler was influential on this kind of research. "The scientific interests and personality of Heinrich Himmler (1900-1945) largely shaped the goals of the science policy of the SS as well as the practical content of the scientific and medical research it initiated." (Deichman, 1996, 251)

On July 7th, 1942 the Institute for Practical Research in Military Science was set up within SS Das Ahnenerbe. The Dachau experiments of Eduard May were conducted under this institute. Kurt Blome, Project Paperclip scientist brought to America, also worked under this institute. (see Deichman, 1996, 279) and had 5 science divisions and two medical divisions. "The informal working group for the study of biological weapons, established in 1940, was renamed the working group Blitzableiter and given the official responsibility by the high command of the Wehrmacht for research into biological warfare, which by Hitler's order was intended to be only defensive." (Deichman, 1996, 279)

Interesting to note that Himmler wanted to develop offensive biological weapons, in contrast to Hitler. Support for attacking America with bioweapons was encouraged. Ministerial Manager for the Science Section of the Wehrmacht, Erich Schumann:

> We must not watch heedlessly but must also prepare for the large-scale use of biological weapons. In particular, America must be attacked simultaneously with various human and animal epidemic pathogens as well as plant pests. (Deichman, 1996, 280)

> On Goering's instruction and with strong support from Himmler, Blome in 1943 set up an institute for the testing of biological weapons on the grounds of the former monastery of Nesselstedt near Posen. (Deichman, 1996, 282) [also included a Pharmacological division in Kleist barracks in Posen]

> The biological weapons studied in Posen included plague bacteria. Research into the use of these bacteria as a warfare agent seems to have been one of Himmler's main interests since 1944. According to investigations by the American secret service, Himmler has ordered that biological warfare research be conducted more offensively and to that end had offered Blome the opportunity of using a concentration camp for studies on the plague. (Deichman, 1996, 284)

KARL GUNTHER ZIMMER'S CONTRIBUTIONS TO MOLECULAR BIOLOGY:

It is worth being aware of the work of Zimmer as he was instrumental in the science of genetic mutations caused by radiation and also taken as a prisoner to the Soviet Union where remote influencing work was studied. The following is a brief account of his contributions to the microbiology.

> "On the Nature of Gene Mutation and Gene Structure" – this was the title of a paper published in June 1935 that was to have a great impact on early molecular genetics. Long known as the "Green Pamphlet" or the "three-man-paper," it has now attained cult status. The paper originated mainly in Berlin-Buch. The authors of this paper were the geneticist Nikolai Vladimirovich Timoféeff-Ressovsky (1900-1981), the radiation physicist Karl Günther Zimmer (1911-1988) and the theoretical physicist Max Delbrück (1906-1981). Each author was singly responsible for one of the first three parts of the paper (Timoféeff-Ressovsky: Some Facts from Mutation Research), (Zimmer: The Target Theory and Its Relation to the Triggering of Mutations) and (Delbrück: Atomic-Physics Model of Gene Mutation). The fourth part, the conclusion (Theory of Gene Mutation and Gene Structure), was written jointly.

> In the conclusion the authors stated: *"We view the gene as an assemblage of atoms within which a mutation can proceed as a rearrangement of atoms or a dissociation of bonds* (triggered by thermal fluctuations or external infusion of energy) *and which is largely autonomous in its operations and in relation to other genes."* The remarkable reception the paper received was mainly due to the detailed presentation of it by Erwin Schrödinger (1887-1961) in his 1944 book *What is Life?* (Wunderlich, 2011)

KARL GUNTHER ZIMMER TIMELINE:

One of the early innovators in microbiology, worked on nuclear radiation and cancer. Co-authored the Green pamphlet or three-man paper with Timofeeff-Ressovsky and Delbruck.

> We view the gene as an assemblage of atoms within which a mutation can proceed as a rearrangement of atoms or a dissociation of bonds (triggered by thermal fluctuations or external infusion of energy [radiation]) and which is largely autonomous in its operations and in relation to other genes. (Wunderlich, 2011)

Zimmer's part of the three-man paper addressed "The Target Theory and its Relation to the Triggering of Mutations"

1933 – began collaboration with Timofeeff at Berlin-Buch Brain Institute

1934 – Habilitation Institute Radiation Research of the Berlin School of Medicine

1937 – paid staff member of Timofeeff's team in the Department of Genetics

1939 – pioneering work in neutron dosimetry

1944 – published with Timofeeff 'The Hit Principle in Biology.' British physicist Douglas Lea wrote a similar book but rather on the hit area, the 'target' theory, was in regular correspondence with Zimmer.

As part of the German scientific war efforts, was required to submit reports to the Reich Research Council, classified as secret. Some of the reports were "Report on studies of the relative effectiveness of X-rays and fast neutrinos with regard to the generation of chromosomal mutations" they were under the Nuclear Physics Research Reports, an internal, top-secret publication series of the German Uranium Society.

1945 – at end of war, briefly worked for Auer Company, which supplied nuclear fissionable material to the Nazi war machine. Upon Soviet occupation was taken to the Soviet Union as an imprisoned scientist to work on Soviet Nuclear projects.

1948 – Jordan, Pascual, Karl Günther Zimmer, Nikolai V. Timoféeff-Ressovsky (1948) Über einige physikalische Vorgänge bei der Auslösung von Genmutationen durch Strahlung II [On some physical processes involved in the induction of gene mutations by radiation II]. *Zeitschrift für Vererbungslehre* 82: 67-73.

1955 – returned to Germany, habilitation from U. of Hamburg, appointment to Professorship in Heidelberg.

1957 – at Heidelburg heads research institute:

Already in the Green Pamphlet the question was raised about the processes that are initiated by the localized supply of energy in biological material, which is associated with the absorption of radiation. Zimmer had barely arrived back in "normal" research operations, when he succeeded in 1957, together with the brothers Lars and Anders Ehrenberg, in making a spectacular finding: Using electron spin resonance spectroscopy, the researchers for the first time detected the formation of free organic radicals on living material following irradiation. Thus, a new field of research was opened, which Zimmer and his team worked on intensively in the following years in Karlsruhe. First and foremost, bacteriophages were used as biological models. The numerous further studies at the Karlsruhe Institute cannot be discussed further here. Among the approximately 550 publications that have emerged from the Institute of Radiation Biology under Zimmer's directorship until his retirement in 1979, many were on the effects of radiation on enzymes (using the example of ribonuclease), on the characterization of primary chemical reaction products in irradiated DNA and on the effect of radiation-damage on the matrix function of DNA. Research was also pursued on radiation-induced energy transfer through elastic nuclear collisions. Zimmer rarely appeared as co-author of the original papers of his staff. Instead, he wrote many overview articles that are still worth reading today. (Wunderlich, 2011)

1958 – with support from Pascual Jordan, Abderhalden and Baron von Verschuer appointed a regular member of the Academy of Sciences and Literature.

The life and work of Karl Günther Zimmer is remarkable for a number of reasons.

1. Zimmer belonged to the first generation of physicists who sustainably changed biology. The geneticist Guido Pontecorvo (1907-1999) described this as follows: "In the years immediately preceding World War II, something new happened: the introduction of ideas (not techniques) from the realm of physics into the realm of

genetics, particularly to the problems of size, mutability, and self-replication of genes. The names of Jordan, Frank-Kamenetski, Friedrich-Freksa, Zimmer, and Delbrück, with Muller and [sic] Timofeef-Ressovsky as their biological interpreters, are linked to this development. [...] The debt of genetics to physics, and to physical chemistry, for ideas began to be substantial then, and it has been growing steadily all the time." Five of the seven scientists mentioned above worked for a time in Berlin-Buch, a sixth (Friedrich-Freksa) worked in Berlin-Dahlem.

2. As co-author of the Green Pamphlet Zimmer's name is inseparably associated with the early history of molecular biology.

3. Zimmer was one of the founders and protagonists of quantitative radiation biology. This was based on his pioneering solutions of dosimetric problems. (Wunderlich, 2011)

Notes:

[1] the Krupp connection is interesting. The original backer of Vogt, Friedrich Krupp (Fritz) killed himself after being revealed as being a homosexual. His son-in-law took over the company, Gustav von Bohlen und Halbach, who helped finance Hitler. His son Alfried Felix Alwyn Krupp von Bohlen und Halback, oversaw the company through WW II. Later family control passed on to a Foundation (Stiftung) which was placed under the supervision of Herman Josef Abs (Deutsche Bank AG) who headed things up in Hamburg, who is spoken of as overseeing financial affairs for the Hamburg centered advocates for a 4th Reich. Nonetheless, we see a pattern of support for Brain research among extreme right-wing politicos and industrialists, even though Vogt was a socialist. Later Krupp merged with Thyssen forming Thyssen-Krupp.

Bibliography:

Abbey, Emily. Diriwachter, Rainer (2008) *Morpheus Awakened.* in Innovating Genesis. Information Age Publishing ISBN 978-1-59311-909-6

Aderet, Ofer (2010) *In His Diary, Mengele Predicted 90% of Humans Would Die of Stupidity.* 02/02/2010 online: https://www.haaretz.com/1.5094756

Anton, Andreas. Schellinger, Uwe, Schetsche, Michael (2010) *Zwischen Szientismus und Okkultismus. Grenzwissenschaftliche Experimente der deutschen Marine.* im Zweiten Weltkrieg Uwe Schellinger, Andreas Anton, Michael Schetsche

Begich, N. (2006) *Controlling the Human Mind: The Technologies of Political Control or Tools for Peak Performance - Kindle Edition.* Earthpulse Press

Black, Monica. Kurlander, Eric. (2015) *Revisiting the 'Nazi Occult': Histories, Realities, Legacies.* Boydell & Brewer 2015 Germany

Brussino, Silvina and Godoy, Juan Carlos. (2010) *Psychology in Argentina*, SiFirst published: 30 January 2010 https://doi.org/10.1002/9780470479216.corpsy0079

Deicthman, U. (1996) *Biologists under Hitler,* Harvard University Press Cambridge, MA

Department of Defense (DoD) (1978) *Paraphysics R&D- Warsaw Pact.* DST-180S-202-78-Chg1 Defense Intelligence Agency online: https://documents.theblackvault.com/documents/dia/PARAPHYSICS_RD-WARSAW_PACT.pdf

Geuter, Ulfried (2008) *The Professionalization of Psychology in Nazi Germany.* Cambridge University Press

Grossman (2008) *Doing Medicine Together: Germany and Russia Between the Wars.* in Bulletin of the History of Medicine, Johns Hopkins University Press, Volume 82, Number 2, Summer 2008 pp. 482-483

Hall, J. (2009) *A New Breed: Satellite Terrorism in America.* Strategic Book Publishing and Rights Co. (August 31, 2014)

Hachmann-Gleixner, M. (2019) *Das Psychologische Institut Heidelberg im Nationalsozialismus und in der Nachkriegszeit* http://archiv.ub.uni-heidelberg.de/volltextserver/4347/1/DA-PsychologieHD-1925-1959.pdf

Hess, Hans (2001) *Augen aus Auschwitz: Ein Lehstruck uber Nationalsozialistischen Rassenwahn und Medizinische Forschung-Der Fall Dr. Karin Magnussen Essen*: Klartext Verlag

Hönighaus, Sascha (2007) *Karin Magnussen,* Berlin

Kazhinsky, B.B. (1963) *Biological Radio Communication*. Foreign Technology Division Air Force Systems Command, Wright Patterson Air Force Base, Dayton, OH [Russian version published in 1962]

Kernbach, (2013) *"Unconventional Research in the USSR"* Cybertronica Research, Stuttgart, Germany

Kernbach, Serge (2014) *Early Psychotronics: German* Roots. Politische Ideologie vs. parapsychologische Forschung -- Kommentare und Autorenantwort. (2014)

Krishnan, A. (2017). *Military Neuroscience and the Coming Age of Neurowarfare*. London: Routledge. DOI: https://doi.org/10.4324/9781315595429

Kurlander, Eric (2015) The Nazi Magicians' Controversy: Enlightenment, "Border Science," and Occultism in the Third Reich Eric Kurlander (a1) Cambridg University Press, https://www.cambridge.org/core/journals/central-european-history/article/abs/nazi-magicians-controversy-enlightenment-border-science-and-occultism-in-the-third-reich/B3BE167EE68DF206E856B97514A9242A

Lifton, Robert Jay (1986). *The Nazi Doctors: Medical Killing and the Psychology of Genocide*. New York: Basic Books. ISBN 978-0-465-04905-9.

Marx, Christoph (2013) Hendrik Verwoerd and the Leipzig School of Psychology in 1926, Historia 58, 2, November 2013, pp 91-118, online: http://www.scielo.org.za/pdf/hist/v58n2/05.pdf [accessed March 13, 2018]

McCreight, R. (2015). *Brain Brinkmanship: Devising Neuroweapons Looking at Battlespace, Doctrine and Strategy*. In J. Giordano (Ed.), Neurotechnology in National Security and Defense: Practical Considerations, Neuroethical Concerns (pp. 115–132). Boca Raton: CRC Press.

Nørgaard, K., & Linden-Vørnle, M. (2021). *Cyborgs, Neuroweapons, and Network Command*. Scandinavian Journal of Military Studies, 4(1), pp. 94–107. DOI: https://doi.org/10.31374/sjms.86

Racine, Valerie (2014) *Lysogenic Bacteria as an Experimental Model at the Pasteur Institute (1915-1965)* in The Embryo Project Encyclopedia https://embryo.asu.edu/pages/lysogenic-bacteria-experimental-model-pasteur-institute-1915-1965

Solomon, S. (ed.) (2006) *Doing Medicine Together: Germany & Russia Between the Wars*. German and European Studies. Toronto: University of Toronto Press

Schmuhl, Hans Walter (2005) *Grenzüberschreitungen. Das Kaiser-Wilhelm-Institut für Anthropologie, menschliche Erblehre und Eugenik 1927–1945*. Geschichte der Kaiser-Wilhelm-Gesellschaft im Nationalsozialismus, Vol. 9 Wallstein, Göttingen 2005

Steinbacher, Sybille (2005) [2004]. *Auschwitz: A History*. Munich: Verlag C. H. Beck. ISBN 978-0-06-082581-2.

Suckut, S., Engelmann, R., Joestel, F. (2004) *Grundsatzdokumente des MfS*. In: Klaus-Dietmar Henke, Siegfried Suckut, Thomas Großbölting (Hrsg.): Anatomie der Staatssicherheit: Geschichte, Struktur und Methoden. MfS-Handbuch. Teil V/5, Berlin 2004, S. 287

Tischner, Rudolf (1923) *Einführung in den Okkultismus und Spiritismus* Springer-Verlag Berlin Heidelberg online: https://books.google.com/books?id=vpG1BgAAQBAJ&pg=PA121&dq=wissenschaftlichem+Okkultismus+telepathie&hl=en&sa=X&ved=0ahUKEwj2iJCD4o3aAhVGb60KHXC1DYcQ6AEIZTAI#v=onepage&q=wissenschaftlichem%20Okkultismus%20telepathie&f=false

Trunk, Achim. (2007). [*Two hundred blood tests from Auschwitz. A notorious research project and the question about the contribution Adolf Butenandts*].. Acta historica Leopoldina. 9-40.

US Department of Defense (DoD) (1978) *Paraphysics R&D Warsaw Pact*

DST-181-2-202-78 Department of Defense Intelligence Document prepared by the Foreign Technology Division, Air Force Systems Command and approved by the Directorate for Scientific and Technical Intelligence of the Defense Intelligence Agency

Walther, Gerda. (1949) *ESP in the German Navy, unpublished manuscript (1949)*. in: Archiv des Instituts fur Grenzgebiete der Psychologic and Psychohygeine c.V. Freiburg i. Br in the following: IGPP-Archiv), 3/21: Korrespondenz mit Gerda Walther 1946-1953

Weiss, Sheila F. (2012) *The Loyal Genetic Doctor, Otmar Freiherr von Verschuer, and the Institut für Erbbiologie und Rassenhygiene: Origins, Controversy, and Racial Political Practice*. In Central European History Vol. 45,

No. 4 (DECEMBER 2012), pp. 631-668. Central European History Society online: https://www.jstor.org/stable/41819485

Wernet, Verena C. (2013) *Studienarbeit from 2013 in the Department of History Europe - Germany - National Socialism, World War II, Grade: 1.7,* Albert-Ludwigs-Universität Freiburg (Department of History) GRIN Verlag, Oct 15, 2013 - History - 27 pages Event: Occultism in the 19th and 20th centuries, Language: German, Abstract: Main seminar paper dealing with the phenomenon of criminal telepathy at the time of the Weimar Republic and illuminating the position of opponents and advocates.

Wohlfahrt, E. (1932). *Der Auffassungsvorgang an kleinen Gestalten. Ein Beitrag Zurich Psychologie der Vorgestalterlebnisses [the perception of small gestalts. A contribution to the psychology of the pregestalt experience].* [Doctoral thesis, Jena, Germany, 1925] Neue Psychologische Studien, 4, 347-414

Wunderlich, V. (2011) *'That was the basic radiobology that was: In Commemoration of the 100th Birthday of Karl Gunther Zimmer.'* Max Delbruck Center for Molecular Medicine. https://www.mdc-berlin.de/karl-guenther-zimmer

Wurzman, R., & Giordano, J. (2015). *'NEURINT' and Neuroweapons: Neurotechnologies in National Intelligence and Defense.* In J. Giordano (Ed.), Neurotechnology in National Security and Defense: Practical Considerations, Neuroethical Concerns (pp. 79–113). Boca Raton: CRC Press. DOI: https://doi.org/10.1201/b17454

CHAPTER 4

LESSONS FROM AN AMERICAN WEAPONS DESIGNER

From before Sun Szu, encompassing the famous Admiral Gorshkov, and extending well beyond future INFO-CYBER warriors, the dictum: Control the Electromagnetic Spectrum and Victory is Promised as your Reward - will be the mandate for success and survival in the coming dawn of the Age of Automated Reasoning, the advent of Synthetic, Sentient Species.

- John Norseen 2000

D r. John Norseen was an American weapons designer working on what today would be referred to as Neuroweapons, he was also a lecturer at George Washington University in DC. When he was employed by Lockheed-Martin[1] in the 1990s and early 2000s, the concept of neuroweapon was not widely known outside the deepest of black operation-funded military and defense sectors. Even today, the development of such weapons is a highly classified and compartmentalized affair. Luckily, John Norseen was a bit more candid and conversational than most weapons designers working in classified positions for defense contractors. Late in his career, for a brief time he held conversations with the artist Duncan Laurie who worked in a field of radionic art.

Norseen and Laurie's correspondences were published by Laurie on the internet after Norseen died from a heart attack at age 53. He also left behind two papers still remaining on the internet, and a published piece co-authored with Juri Kropotov. Attempts at finding journal articles and publications from his time as a Navy officer at the Naval War College have come up empty, for instance the Naval War College has no record of his attendance, although it is confirmable that he did attend and was an officer in the US Navy working at one point in Intelligence. His thesis at the War College was on applying Neuroscience research to anti-terrorism investigations (Pasternak 2000). So, we are fortunate that he leaked certain points about his work in his conversations with Duncan Laurie and left behind some unclassified research papers published by a small computer engineering group, 'American Computer Scientists Association' (Norseen 1996)

The first article I could find on the work of John Norseen dates to a Newsweek article from 2001 he was interviewed for under the title, "Reading your mind and injecting smart thoughts" (Pasternak 2000) in which he talks of being able to read terrorist suspect's thoughts remotely. In a subsequent article from 2001 in the Washington Times, "NASA plans to read terrorist's minds at airports," Norseen notes:

> Space technology would be adapted to receive and analyze brain wave and heartbeat patterns, then feed that data into computerized programs "to detect passengers who potentially might pose a threat," according to briefing documents obtained by the Washington Times. NASA wants to use "noninvasive neuro-electric sensors," imbedded in gates, to collect tiny electric signals that all brains and hearts transmit. Computers would apply statistical algorithms to correlate physiological patterns with computerized data on travel routines, criminal background and credit information from "hundreds to thousands of data sources," Nasa documents say. (Murray 2002)

While it appears the bulk of his work was done at Lockheed-Martin Norseen also had other projects such as working on a team for whole brain emulation in a cybersecurity context with Alert Grid Alliance, Inc., on a product known as 'CYPHER', a quantum intelligence cyber security system, which is claimed to have begun with Sanders Associates, who also did early work in video game consoles, later shipped under Magnavox branding. Norseen is associated as well with the Electro-Optics Lab at NOSC in San Diego under the auspices of the Naval Sea Systems Command [2]. Although interesting, the main area to focus on for this research is that related directly to Semiotics or what John Norseen termed in his conversations with Duncan Laurie, the 'Norseen Semiotic.'

SEMIOTICS

N orseen's innovation in the field of neuroweapons was termed by him 'BioFusion', first published in academic articles at SPIE in 1999. He gives an account to Duncan Laurie below:

BioFusion is my name for the next generation of biometric security/intelligent inter-netted security systems. Please note that a fundamental basis to BioFusion is that brain structures execute biological functions, and that such functions can be represented and understood as mathematical equations [Kryolov space] existing in biophysical time/space/frequency/phase/quantum state Space, spoken of here as Gabor function (wavelet/codelet) in Hilbert Space [vector space with a complete metric].

What Exactly is BioFusion?

BioFusion is described as what happens when you think (a precise mathematical operation), to include:

• When multiple sensors can detect and measure what you think, (Hyperspectral Analysis, [i.e. QEEG see Kropotov below]) and Map where thoughts are in your brain, and then via "Information Injection"

• Monitor, Enhance, Modify, Replace, or Prevent Neural Circuit Function — In Essence,

• Enhance, Replace, or Prevent THOUGHTS! Extremely Inter/Multi-Disciplinary *NSF NBIC Model*

Accordingly, such mathematical representations lend themselves to machine/computational interpretation and cross machine/computational communications, hence the capability for Human-Machine interaction, and prediction of calculated results. Therefore, if known neurological circuits, reading this page, or silently saying a sequence of numbers, or closing one's eyes and imagining a picture…let's say the image of the Mona Lisa…then with the proper sensing techniques, a display based on the underlying mathematical-biophysical space [Krylov space] can be generated which represents the very same neurological functioning. There is vast biomedical evidence of this in PET, MEG, EEG, FMRI, etc. which capture various neurological events faithfully and repeatedly. BioFusion extends the singular look of these various medical diagnostic techniques and merges them into a much more robust hyper-spectral analysis across the electromagnetic spectrum, within which brain function occurs, to correlate and pinpoint with more accurate detail the specific, self-similar regions of the brain engaged in mental processing of the target activity. (Norseen , Laurie, 2002, part 3)

Another known way of capturing electric signals in the brain was proposed by Malech using standard Radar in 1974; this is also the method that a former MI-6 agent turned whistleblower, Carl Clark (Gross 2010), noted was used for covert applications of this technology [see Ch.7 'Radar and Neuroweapons' section]. Here is an outline of how a Brain Emulation application works, by taking in biometric data and then applying statistical learning algorithms to that data and formulating a profile and Brain map of the observed target.

In a more technical definition given at a conference in Russia on the topic of 'Reflexive Control' [see discussion of Reflexive Control below and Ch. 5, 'Reflexive Control']. Norseen writes:

BioFusion is the increasing complexity of one part of the brain to share, mathematically, its information with other parts of the brain in a common, emergent family of mathematical operations, to which the inverse function, the ability to recreate or trigger stored information by using the inverse mathematics is allowable. Panum's fusion space, horopter operations, dreams, and the distinct linkage of either end of the invariant versus holistic storage continuum of object recognition in the posterior inferior temporal gyri (ITG) as opposed to the purer prosopopoeia [visual perception] in the fusiform gyrus (FG) are very nice examples of BioFusion in the visual perception modality. The ability to blend vision and verbal modalities in the Temporal Cortex, TC-22 and Broadmann's Area 44, for example are also fine indications that BioFusion is taking place in more and more complex, adaptive regions of the brain. (Norseen, 2000)

BioFusion is a play on another engineering term 'Sensor Fusion', but usually reserved for purely mechanical sensors such as on ships or aircraft. In essence, BioFusion is the discretization or quantization of your thoughts into a string represented as a vector in Krylov sub-space. Alexei Krylov was a Russian mathematician who created a special mathematics for various calculations. With the quantization of neural information, it allows for a computer to process this information and do either deep mining of neural data, such as memories, or insert a new string to be fed into a radar or microwave generator to generate the necessary frequencies to alter brain function and wiring. Norseen writes:

Anyways, I was working with the Russian Academy of Science Group in Reflexive Control and we were developing an N-Dimensional Graph, called Krylov Space after the Russian bio-mathematician, Krylov, and we developed this cursory folding map of how the brain can twist and turn Semiotics into Biological Pressures, and in certain regions of the Map, the person would as one would expect under harsh and continuing intense pressures…be pushed and molded into some perverse forms of behavior. In other areas of the Krylov Map, where things were going well, the Map was like a quiet estuary or shallow sea…very mellow…in a KRYLOV SPACE, a matrix dimensional grid of ONE IDENTITY communicating, sharing complete semiotics, with another IDENTITY…" (Norseen, Laurie, 2002, part 12)

Norseen has a specific term for each thought in his ideals of BioFusion. A thought is a 'semiotic', he writes:

> Well, equally, if you are aware that a person is entering an Alpha State, or better yet, a hypnogogic (falling asleep) or a hypnopompic state (pre-waking state) of a modified Theta-Alpha brain engagement region…you can actually see the subconscious mind at work and interact with it…you can actually inject Semiotics into the mental region and see the Brain Thoughts surround the Semiotic, infuse it, and then act upon it right into the Awake States. In this way, you can DYE INJECT, action potentials…for influencing someone during the day…or you can do the same thing and get Alert Semiotics injected into the sleeping and even into the Life-Death interface of the Delta state…you can probe the deepest depths of the person and see just exactly how deep into the abyss, the db, you can go…You can even affect someone with Semiotic cues down at negative (-) 200 db…down at the very bottom of our semiotic ability to understand information, and right at the zone where Alfven Wave corridors of the brain Magnetite exchange ZPE [zero point energy] in the dendritic neuropil at nanoscale, discrete bandwidth, channels. It is right here in the Marianas Trench of human thought/perception, that the person is exposed to the Universals of Quantum State potentials, and that each individual thought or Semiotic Identity is formed, only to then bubble or shoot right up to the surface of positive thought realms.
>
> Just as you can look into an aquarium or a fish bowl and see the stuff at the bottom work its way up to the surface, you can track the origin of Semiotics from Alfven Wave Interactions with ZPE, from the plumbed depths of the Brain. This is really pretty cool stuff, because it allows us the opportunity to use Radionics to condition or reinforce or direct the destination of the most basic to the most sublime of human thoughts and the HUMAN CONDITION. (Norseen, Laurie, 2002, part.6)

Semiotics is a field of inquiry usually in reference to Linguistics; it typically connotes a sense of meaning to a linguistic object.

> Semiotics is a discipline (or an attempt to create a science) of combining the theory of signs (representations), symbols (categories), and meaning extraction. Semiotics is an inclusive discipline which incorporates all aspects of dealing with symbols and symbolic systems starting with encoding and ending with the extraction of meaning. (Albus et al, Undated)

In the defense industry Semiotics has largely been identified with the work of C.S. Pierce. An American philosopher from a Boston Brahmin family, his wealthy pro-slavery upbringing was later given up for a semi-transcendentalist lifestyle on his farm where he lived in poverty. His affects and influence on the defense industry scientists that use his Semiotics and arguments of Logic is deep. In the appendix of Norseen and Laurie's communications there is an explanation of Piercean Semiotics that is used by Norseen in his work, along with a scientist we shall read more deeply about, Ed Nozawa later. Semiotics being the study of signs, the definition according to Pierce:

> Anything (R[epresentant]) which is so determined by anything else, called its Object (O), and so determines an effect upon a person, which I call its Interpretant (I).

Which leads to the Piercean triangulation: Object-Interpretant-Representam

- Complex conceptual structure reduced to a single triadic sign
- Unique system - all others are dyadic (two-part)
- Signs may be concatenated to construct concepts Piercean system of logic developed from the sign

An important concept in Piercean Logic is the notion of triadic pathways rather than dyadic pathways, in this sense it is actually a good precursor and informant to Quantum Computational ideals regarding superposition.

Another important element in Pierce's thought and influence on defense contractor engineering and science is that of the Hypothesis. In many of the logic flows of these weapons designers is the concept of forming a hypothesis, then referencing a knowledge base, then re-running whatever iteration of the task one is involved in. As we shall read later under Nozawa the concept of 'closed loop' systems is a prevalent dynamic in such systems engineered under Piercean logic; creating a truly cybernetic system where all decisions potentially could be automated and based on computer algorithms with no human intervention.

In the terminology of Norseen, then the individual whether in a read or write operation to their brains, is the Interpretant, where the object is qualified by a Representatum. So that we understand that a sign can be manipulated by the systems under design and spoken of by Norseen, it can also be used to simply read signs from a human brain.

Norseen referred to the process of manipulating the Semiotic or signs as 'Thought Injection' which is given in a section narrated by Duncan Laurie in their correspondences:

> Theoretically, according to Norseen, each thought represents an energy dispersion pattern which can be monitored by mixed electromagnetic sensors and described mathematically as a "Brain Print." This brain-print can be inverted and retransmitted back into the brain much like an encoded memory. Subsequently, the brain will act upon this inverse signal as if it were a real signal from the environment.
>
> Norseen's point was that if you could trigger that part of the brain remotely, via a transmission of some kind, the receiver would be all but powerless over the transmitted response. [a manchurian candidate with no self-will or control depending on variables such as genes and biochemistry]
>
> The implication was clearly that a command (encrypted as information contained within information), akin to a hypnotic suggestion, can be buried within unrelated visual and auditory information, to be broadcast to the general public. Norseen strongly suggested these techniques were connected to the Columbine murders, as though the killers had been infected from encrypted web sites beforehand, designed intentionally as trial behavior test scenarios. (Norseen, Laurie, 2002, part. 1) [see Ch. 5, Intelligence infiltrates gaming communities]

Although hypnosis is mentioned here, see Chapter 10, Hypnosis in Warfare, for more information. The process of how this works according to Norseen is that he uses 'BioFusion' (sensorfusion or datafusion) to collect all the thoughts (semiotes) in one's head then has the ability to either do deep data mining and profiling to either extract or insert more information, resulting in either a cracked mind or a rewired mind.

He goes further into how this works in an interview with *Signal* Magazine, a military journal:

> Now that bio-fusion research has developed beyond the initial stages and the database of what, how and where thoughts occur in the brain is mature, scientists are looking at information injection, a contentious issue, Norseen admits. The concept is based on the fact that human perception consists of certain invariant electromagnetic and biochemical lock-and-key interactions with the brain that can be identified, measured and altered by mathematical operations. If researchers can re-create the inverse function of what has been observed, they gain the ability to communicate or transmit that information back--intact or rearranged--to the individual or someone else, Norseen says. "When you get down to the mathematical properties, information injection is beginning to be demonstrated."
>
> The brain is very susceptible to accepting information that is either real and comes from its own memory mechanisms or from injection from an outside source, Norseen notes. "I am sure you have memories of when the lawn was being cut in late summer and of the smell of the chlorophyll," he says. "The chlorophyll would then evoke other memories. I could possibly ping you with a light sequence or with an ELF [extremely low field] radiation sequence that will cause you to think of other things, but they may be in the area that I am encouraging. Those are direct ways in which I can cause the inverse function of something to be fired off in the brain so that you are thinking about it. I have now caused you to think about something you would not have otherwise thought about."
>
> By using information injection, a person could be isolated from a group and made to believe that something is happening, while others in the group are being left alone. Likewise, someone at a command post monitoring information on a screen could be affected. Some experts believe that adversaries now are designing techniques that could affect the brain and alter the human body's ability to process stimuli. (Berry, 2000)

As can be seen, this technology has a very brazen double edge. Of course, it could be used to monitor a criminal to prevent them from committing crime, probably in the context of previous conviction under the law, but it could also be used by criminals of another sort to easily manipulate and control innocent persons, thus being an even greater threat to security than it could potentially prevent. What we are talking about here is the modification and alteration of behaviors. The modification of behavior is understood by Norseen as Reflexive Control, which was pioneered not just by Soviet scientists and Nazi scientists but also has its fair representation in American psychological scientific literature. For instance, several members of the editorial board of a publication dedicated to Reflexive Control in Russia come from the United States and Canada.

One Russian researcher now working for the United States government, also directly influenced by the Piercean Semiotics paradigm is Alexi Sharov. He merged logical semiotics with biology, to work in an area known as Biosemiotics:

> Biosemiotics and cybernetics are closely related, yet they are separated by the boundary between life and non-life: biosemiotics is focused on living organisms, whereas cybernetics is applied mostly to non-living artificial devices. However, both classes of systems are agents that perform functions necessary for reaching their goals. I propose to shift the focus of biosemiotics from living organisms to agents in general, which all belong to a pragmasphere [Pierce's Pragmatic Philosophy] or functional universe. Agents should be considered in the context of their hierarchy and origin because their semiosis can be inherited or induced by higher-level agents. To preserve and disseminate their functions, agents use functional information – a set of signs that encode and control their functions. It includes stable memory signs, transient messengers, and natural signs. The origin and evolution of functional information is discussed in terms of transitions between vegetative, animal, and social levels of semiosis, defined by Kull. Vegetative semiosis differs substantially from higher levels of semiosis, because signs are recognized and interpreted via direct code-based matching and are not associated with ideal representations of objects. Thus, I consider a separate classification of signs at the vegetative level that includes proto-icons, proto-indexes, and proto-symbols. Animal and social semiosis are based on classification, and modeling of objects, which represent the knowledge of agents about their body (Innenwelt) and environment (Umwelt). (Sharov, 2010)

Reflexive control is defined as a means of conveying to a partner or an opponent specially prepared information to incline them to voluntarily make the predetermined decision desired by the initiator of the action. It is an interesting point that the usual understanding of reflexive control is a 'voluntarily' made decision, but with thought injection we are talking about a reflexive control that is involuntary, even unconscious. Defense researchers from the European Union give the following technical definition of Reflexive Control:

> According to Russian methodologies, the theory of Reflexive Control (RC) allows an initiator to induce an adversary to take a decision advantageous to the initiator through information manipulation. The RC theory encompasses a methodology where specifically prepared information is conveyed to an adversary, which would lead that adversary to make a decision desired by the initiator. The methodology is generally understood by Russian planners to be applicable in a wide variety of situations and is deeply rooted within Russian Information Warfare concepts. Because theory envelops the Russian understanding of information as both technical data and cognitive content, 'information resources' are understood as technological as well as human. In principle, a well-developed (global) cyberspace presents theorists and operators of RC and RC methodology with numerous possibilities to affect their adversaries. This paper explores ways in which RC can be exercised with the help of the cyberspace. (Jaitner et al, 2016)

Norseen worked directly with one prominent Russian specialist and leader of Reflexive Control, Andrej V. Brushlinsky, who according to Laurie remarking on Norseen's perceptions of Dr. Brushlinsky:

> …I was to discover, a central figure in the field of Reflexive Control was the Russian scientist and distinguished member of the Russian Academy of Sciences, Andrej V. Brushlinsky. Norseen had visited him not so very long before we met. Subsequently, Brushlinsky was found robbed and murdered. Norseen believes he was killed by foreign agents, seeking the scientific protocols he had developed for a type of weaponized "thought insertion" called steganography, or "Stego Bullets" for short. (Norseen, Laurie, 2002, part 1)

Of course, one can see the direct application of thought injection whether based on the methods of Norseen or Brushlinsky, in a weaponized space, especially in warfare. So, it is not surprising that there would come some espionage intrigue along with this research area. Thus, it is important to understand what precisely is happening in Reflexive Control that it would be such a high value target in international espionage.

Traversing from Reflexive Control engineered through Thought Injection we come to larger issues that affect groups, collectives, and societies as a whole. As the Russian meddling in the US 2016 election clamor has brought to the attention such concepts of Information Operations by hostile forces to the attention of the average citizen, it should be mentioned again that in 2011 British GCHQ sponsored studies on undermining social network perceptions on a mass scale. Yet, there is not much meaningful discussion of these terms. Information operations and warfare, also known as influence operations, includes the collection of tactical information about an adversary as well as the dissemination of propaganda in pursuit of a competitive advantage over an opponent.[4]. Information Operations are used in direct correlation to the methods of Perception Management. Perception Management is:

> Perception management involves all actions that convey and/or deny selected information and indicators to foreign audiences to influence their emotions, motives and objective reasoning; and to intelligence systems and leaders at all levels to influence official estimates, ultimately resulting in foreign behaviors and official actions favorable to the originators objectives. In various ways, perception management combines truth projection, operations security [OPSEC] cover and deception, and psychological operations [PSYOP]. [5]

So, it is not unsurprising that Norseen notes the role of his research and its connection to Information Operations and Perception Management in an interview with Ryan Moore, who writes for a Military careers website. Norseen expounds on this subject:

> The key word in understanding Perception Management, whether for selling beer or conducting PSYOP is 'Expectation.' Tons of advertising research dollars swirls down the drain getting commercials right and the audience wrong... You have to either match up the right situations or control the expectation level of the target audience – this holds true for either media or PSYOP management.
>
> "But imagine if you could actually monitor expectations non-invasively, quietly, garnering sufficient measurement of how 'Designed Information' is interacting with the central nervous system of the intended audience. This is what the Science Of Semiotics – signs and symbols – is heading towards, and can be seen today in forms such as 'Engagement Indices' and other biometric techniques of audience attention. This would appear to be the logical extension of Neuro-control into marketing and perception management. (Moore 2003)
>
> Ryan Moore asks: "What do you see as the potential civilian and military applications of 'Information Injection' technology?"
>
> Norseen replies: "If 'Information Injection' pans out – the concept that human perception is made up of certain invariant electromagnetic, and biochemical, lock and key interactions [QSK] with brain structure which can be identified, measured and altered by mathematical/technical operations – then the stage is set to observe, capture, rearrange and play-back human mental functions from one person to another, or into any combination of man-machine system interface. The development of such Cortical Emulation Software, if successful, will rapidly usher in the potential for automated personal diaries -- Emotional Recordings, Mental Cameras, and Digital Biographies. Just as we today catalogue millions of people by fingerprints, this strongly suggests the future ability to use Brain-Prints as the key biometric signature identifier in Total Information Awareness.[3]"
> (Norseen, Laurie 2002 Part 1 'Reflexive Control')

Norseen goes even further with this technique, suggesting its automation and usage by computer systems in an academic paper:

> The concept of injection of information for Information Operations from one human into another human, or from a machine generation of information into a human, the inverse function is utmost and vital. In order to trigger, or refine, or replace, or sharpen an old perception in the human, or to create brand new perceptions, the exact inverse function must be known, or very close to it, in order to fool the brain into accepting it as real. And this inverse injection must also very closely model the exact E and H fields, the electromagnetic field shapes that the original Gabor-like Function in Hilbert Space occupied. (Norseen, 2000)

As can be seen as a weapons designer there is no cloudiness to the intent behind the weapons systems he was designing. In the field of Information Operations in warfare and specifically creating a genre of Neuroweapons capable of such abilities as direct thought injection the ability to undermine an enemy in a battlespace is of unimpeachable value.

Thought Injected Reflexive Control

At this point it is a worthwhile endeavor to trace the development of this technology, specifically focusing on Semiotics and its role in Reflexive Control. Other areas of Neuroweapons history and development has been covered in the preceding chapter on 'Neuroweapons.'

A brief history of Russian Reflexive control research is related:

> The Soviet and Russian Armed Forces have long studied the use of reflexive control theory, particularly at the tactical and operational levels, both for maskirovka (deception) and disinformation purposes and, potentially, to control the enemy's decision-making processes. For example, the Russian Army had a military maskirovka school as early as 1904 that was later disbanded in 1929. This school, the Higher School of Maskirovka, provided the bases for maskirovka concepts and created manuals for future generations.
>
> Since the early 1960s, there have been many Russian intellectual "giants" who have emerged in the field of reflexive theory. In the civilian sector, these include G. P. Schedrovitsky, V. E. Lepsky, V. A. Lefebvre (who now lives in the West), D. A. Pospelov, V. N. Burkov, and many others. The foremost theorists in the military sector include V. V. Druzhinin, M. D. Ionov, D. S. Kontorov, S. Leonenko, and several others. (Thomas 2004)

As one reads scientific publications on Reflexive Control and Semiotics two names often encountered are V. A. Lefebvre and D.A. Pospelov. Lefebvre, now teaching in the United States, has created an interesting paradigm known as Reflexive Game Theory, see Senglaub below for Semiotic Cybernetics examples. A researcher, Sergey Tarasenko, notes:

> The Reflexive Game Theory (RGT) has been entirely developed by Lefebvre and is based on the principles of anti-selfishness or egoism forbidenness and human reflexion processes. Therefore, RGT is based on the human-like decision-making processes. The main goal of the theory is to model behavior of individuals in the groups. It is possible to predict choices, which are likely to be made by each individual in the group and influence each individual's decision-making due to make this individual to make a certain choice. In particular, the RGT can be used to predict terrorists' behavior.
>
> In general, the RGT is a simple tool to predict behavior of individuals and influence individuals' choices. Therefore, it makes possible to control the individuals in the groups by guiding their behavior (decision-making, choices) by means of the corresponding influences. (Tarasenko 2010)

It is important to point out that the anti-Terrorism aspect is a particular application of Reflexive Game Theory while, as Lefebvre writes, in general it can be used for mass applications. It is interesting also that this scientist has sought not only to apply reflexive control to humans but also robots and has mixed them together in his studies in groups. Tarasenko notes regarding the influence of robots on humans in 2010:

> However, robots are forbidden and should not physically force people, but must convince people on the mental level to refrain from doing a risky action. This method is more effective rather than a simple physical compulsion, because humans make the decisions (choices) themselves and treat these decisions as their own. Such technique is called a reflexive control.
>
> The task of finding appropriate reflexive control is closely related with the Inverse task, when we need to find suitable influence of one subject on another one or on a group of subjects on the subject of interest. Therefore, it is needed to develop the framework of how to solve the Inverse task. This is the primary goal of this study. (Tarasenko 2010)

In this sense using RGT crosses boundaries between strictly human-to-human interactions and goes into robot-to-human or AI-to-human interactions to generate desired behaviors using an AI agent.

With the collapse of the Soviet Union many Russian scientists that had previously been employed by the KGB and GRU found themselves in need of funding and sponsorship. Quickly stepping into this sponsorship vacuum came the American secret intelligence agencies seeking to acquire Soviet technology. Norseen, it is known, worked with Russian scientists in the Reflexive Control area of expertise; notable among these is the previously mentioned, murdered scientist Brushlinsky, AI pioneer Dr. Prospolev, and AI designer V.K. Finn, and founder of RGT, Lefebvre.

The collaboration between Russian and American defense engineers and scientists can be traced, at least publicly, to 1995. When Russian groups sought out foreign funding sources:

> One of them (calling itself a Semiotic Design and Control Group of Russian Academy of Sciences) has recently communicated an interest in working with researchers in the United States. In response to this interest, US government has sponsored, and many other government agencies were involved in, two workshops: one in Columbus, Ohio in June 1995; the other in Monterey, California in August, 1995. (Albus et al, undated)

Norseen's use of Semiotics, Reflexive Control and Thought Injection is not new. In the research corridor of New Mexico largely associated with US Government scientific research, for instance, Sandia Labs is located there. A team was created in the Physical Science Laboratory at New Mexico State University. This team was founded by Russian emigre Vladimir Lefebvre who is cited by Norseen in his research. The commonalities between Norseen's research and the PSL group is obvious:

> The theory allows the modeling of high-level value systems. Using the theory, values such as self-esteem, pride, human dignity and willingness to sacrifice may be incorporated into modeling of human agents. Other theories of human behavior do not allow for modeling such non-utilitarian factors. Using a model developed from Reflexive Theory, it will be possible to predict, for example, which of a group of potential terrorists might be susceptible to recruiting by terrorist organizations such as al Queda.

The Reflexive Theory Research Team at NMSU's Physical Science Laboratory has recently received international recognition for its work in anti-terrorism. Front row from left to right: Xenia Kramer, Vladimir Lefebvre and

Source: http://newscenter.nmsu.edu/Articles/view/1397 (2003, accessed 5/27/19)

The team received an award for their research in Russia in 2003. While created with good intentions for security, it is also obvious that such simulations could be also used for nefarious purposes if a rogue element developed with this technology.

Norseen talks about the early development of Semiotics and Reflexive Control to Laurie:

> Of Piercian Scientific Semiotics and its role in United States national security, I can honestly say that I was part of the inception in the early 1990's and have watched over the last decade the growth from the first national security working group on scientific semiotics to where it is now a recognized science effort around the world…

but with not nearly enough Book elucidation, and still lacking a dedicated National Scientific Philosophy linkage into National Security. Almost all of the pacing Soviet scholars that I have met are now dead or corrupted... and most of the working semiotics is now under a classified rubric. At least I can edify about the frolicsome years from 1995-2002 where no holds barred and semiotics as the New Occult held sway... try to search on Lycos with the terms NSA PSYOP... there is a link that you need to see... I will get it to you later. The link describes how semiotics and brain communications can be done covertly. Imagine that. [see note 29 of text] (Norseen, Laurie, 2002, part 15)

The 'frolicsome years' that Norseen talks about are reflected in a meeting with Russian researchers. Norseen talked to Laurie regarding his encounter with Russian scientists at a social event in the US. Laurie writes regarding this:

The next time he found himself at the Double Eagle [a bar in New Mexico], it was with a group of Russian semioticians with whom he was collaborating. This eclectic group was formed in the early 1960's by a Soviet General that set up a secret program of covert reflexive control operations with the KGB and GRU now under the direction of a certain Dr. Pospelov, of extreme interest to Lt. General Ken Minihan, the Director of NSA [National Security Agency] (DIRNSA). Norseen was tired when they arrived. Then, as he walked in, the lights of the saloon went crazy. The one person capable of working the entire bar, physical and non-physical, had arrived. As Norseen worked his way into trance once again, the entities allowed him to enter the minds of his Russian colleagues, probing their thoughts and memories. To their horrified surprise he began casually rattling off the contents of their mind. At the conclusion of the story, Norseen was careful to point out that every one of these Russians (save the general with the gold tooth) is now dead or incapacitated. (Norseen, Laurie, 2002, part 13)

Though it is notable that he may have been employing this technology to debrief the Russian scientists in an environment of high suggestibility using alchohol as a trance agent (see THIQ below), the important point in this recollection is the role of the NSA in sponsoring these Russian scientists and in collaboration with American weapons designers working for Lockheed-Martin.

The question of Brushlinsky's murder is an interesting one. Brushlinsky's research specifically contributed to 'Activity Theory', important to the field of Human-Computer Interface. (See also Victor Finn Quasi-Axiomatic Theory). While the public reasoning behind his homicide was simple burglary, it is very provocative that the US was working on the same technology he was working on but for the Russian Federation. Adding to the intrigue is the statement of a leading researcher in Russia regarding the murder and theft:

In the meantime, the director of the institute for the psychological precautions against terrorism, Professor Viktor Fersht, released a sensational statement. He said that Brushlinsky did not fall the victim of the street robbers. The briefcase contained exclusive documents about the newest, reflexive method of searching for terrorists. The concept was developed at one of the labs of the mentioned institute, and professor Lepsky was in charge of that work. [6]

Dr. Fersht goes on further to note that the findings of this research were to be presented to a joint NATO-Russia conference.

Norseen in his conversations with Laurie notes a sea change in the development of these ideals in research as the technology became tangible and in production. Norseen, rather unwisely, used his work email address to communicate with Laurie regarding this subject. It is not known if an internal security audit picked up on his conversations or not but around 2002, during his active conversations with civilians on this subject he writes of his security clearance and assignment changing:

I just found out that my clearances have been updated. I go in for a new Top-Secret indoctrination tomorrow. Also, at work, my computer and my phone and my office were taken down. I enter over the next few weeks, a new office, a new program, and new computer phone identities. Very odd. (Norseen, Laurie, 2002, part 15)

It was not long after that, Laurie has recollected, that Norseen's security clearances were revoked and he was removed from classified projects. He died that same year of a heart attack at age 53.

SEMIOTICS AND QUANTUM CONSCIOUSNESS

Aside from the Reflexive Control scientists mentioned in the previous section, Norseen has cited the work of various other researchers in the field of consciousness, cybersecurity, etc. In this section I shall review some of the researchers he has cited in his work relating to Consciousness. Norseen is an adherent to the ideal of Quantum Consciousness; this is that consciousness has its origins in the quantum Planck scale of existence, and interacts with the classical world through a molecular construct known as Microtubulin (MT) in the Brain's neural networks. A well-known proponent of this theory is the anesthetist Dr. Stuart Hameroff of the University of Arizona and the physicist Dr. Sir Roger Penrose. They term their hypothesis the 'ORCH-OR' theory, simply known as the Orchestrated Reduction of the quantum wave state. One early researcher in Quantum Consciousness sited by Norseen is Dr. Koruga of the University of Belgrade. Dr. Koruga concluded in a paper with Hameroff that:

> …MT structures lead to the conclusion that packing of tubulin is equal to information coding. This means that microtubules possess a code [like DNA, protein synthesis is based on DNA] (Koruga 1986)

With this insight Norseen was able to come up with the ideal of quantum shift keys in consciousness:

> Encoding discrimination of biologic sensory information is accomplished by quantum shift keying (QSK). QSK originates in the orchestrated reduction (OR) of quantum entanglement at specific electromagnetic resonating frequency locations in protein micro-tubulin in the neuropil. QSK is then communicated via oscillating and standing waves in the neurosynaptic - dendritic region. This resonating mode is either reinforced or reduced by related binding, non-binding activity in other regions of the brain. At certain frequency and energy thresholds, a combining resonance is established in brain function that binds the various oscillating brain sub-resonances into a cohesive, sentient pattern.
>
> Hameroff (90's) indicates that calpain is a primary neuro-molecule that softens brain protein micro-tubulin (MT), which after an electromagnetic resonance wave interference pattern (holonomic) is presented onto the MT, the calpain is dissipated and a structural imprint of the QSK encoded wavefront interference pattern is thus captured in biologic protein structure. Sufficient memory storage mechanisms would be available in the brain to overcome state cycle limitations, since no synapto-dendritic region physically touches any other in the human brain. This establishes myriad number of switching pathways for random, but QSK coded, information patterns to be stored, with self-similar recall features in place. Access to any part of the lissajous-like distribution pattern would allow eventual reconstruction of the invariant information stored in holonomic memory. Internal stimulation of the resonant frequency modality or the actual physical bandwidth would provide the brain with internal memory recall capability. Cognitive recall is comprised of Gabor Functions in Hilbert Space. (Norseen, 1996)

With this finding and knowledge, it is not hard to imagine, as is covered under the Neuroweapons section, how one could use frequencies to insert thoughts at a quantum level; thus, utilizing the calculations of Krylov sub-space to create or extract thoughts in a human brain. Another indicator of Quantum level of consciousness is that many reports of this phenomenon investigated academically have a non-local characteristic (Persinger, 2015) (Norseen Laurie 2002), which in physics is non-local, not just spatially but also temporally.

(Norseen & Laurie 2002) [reconstruction of slide from document]

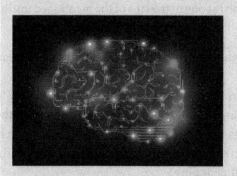

QSK: Non-Local Coherence

Squeezed Light:
Predictive Uncertainty

Twin Photon Phenomenon:
Photons,
Phonons,
Electrons,
Bio-Tensors

- Brain as a Magnetic Property Within
- Revolving Bioelectrochemical E3+ Field (E vector)
- Enfolded Bi-Location
- Neuropil Orchestrated Reduction – 4 Quanta
- Future MT 10/13 Bandwidth to 20/26+

As mentioned, others have found a non-local effect in neuro-warfare techniques. One such technology is known as 'transcommunication' or communication between people at great distances that appear to share deep correlations – or what is known as quantum entanglement. Norseen points to a couple of such researchers such as Dubrov and Persinger below:

Also, for background…type in the following on your search engine: Grill Flame and Stargate, or Scannate - bring that up to 2010 and you are where I am going. The kind of stuff you may want to research is Program Igloo White from Vietnam; you may have to go into the JMIC vaults for this. You should also re-look at what Colby did at Bien Hoa hospital in Vietnam – he may be gone now but a good source here is the Science Advisor to CENTCOM. I can feed you a bit based on my talks with Colby before he died in his canoe [a heart attack]… about Shadow (MACVSOG) within Phoenix. The future of PSYOP, as I am talking about it, grew out of this period, going way back of course to MKULTRA and the Dulles brothers at Langley under the first stop programs: Artichoke and Bluebird. The legacy for today is still the work of Persinger in the Canadian labs…with neat stuff on training people in near death experiences in New Zealand. I can fill you in on the avante garde work here… it even goes into Dubrov's work and the work at Kharkov University where KGB Spetsnaz went into flat line conditions to receive their Stego-bullet instruction sets for their dream missions. This, of course, goes to my visits to Moscow where, unfortunately, Brushlinsky was just found murdered in his apartment. He was passionate with me about his ability to use Dream Sequences to prepare for mission rehearsal. So, you may want to search on Brushlinsky. This will take you into the marine mammal experiments with information injection and then back again to our programs within Air Research and Edwin May [Remote Viewing]. There is really juicy stuff here and you will get a charge out of it. But beware; it can bite you very quickly. I know, it bit me too. (Norseen, Laurie, 2002, part 3)

We will consider here two researchers as it relates to quantum consciousness, Dubrov and Persinger. In the preceding it was mentioned that Norseen told Laurie to research the areas of Edwin May and the Air Research Institute. Edwin May was a project manager, much debased by normative scholars, in the US Military and Secret Intelligence which conducted experiments in Remote Viewing (see Neuroweapons section, i.e., German Navy experiments). Remote viewing is one example of trans-communication. Many have claimed that such remote viewing can be done using microwaves, which dates back in Soviet research to at least 1938. Suggesting that trans-communication between consciousnesses at a distance has an electromagnetic component. However, other Soviet researchers suggested it indeed was not electromagnetic, while others suggested it can occur at Extreme Low Frequency (ELF) electromagnetic waves.

Dubrov advocated another mechanism in physics for such effects, namely gravitational waves [See fuller discussion in Quantum Mechanics section]. Persinger also recently suggested that gravitons are the mechanism for transcommunication. Many researches have also suggested gravitational-like fields as the mechanism for trans-communication between consciousnesses, such as Burkhard Heim, largely unknown outside of defense contractors (i.e. MBB) in Germany and a small community of German physicists. Kozyrev, a Russian astrophysicist, claimed that what he termed 'causal fields' were capable of ESP. Kozyrev has 'time' as a particle; it may share analogs with gravitons. Dubrov termed his gravitational explanation for the phenomenon 'bio-gravitation', He writes:

By the term bio-gravitation, we designate a field-energy system. The bio-gravitational field is universally convertible, i.e., it is capable of transition into any form of field and energy, and therefore a unified field theory must be worked out especially for it. Many facts reported in the literature of psychotronics [paraphysics] give evidence of this property of the bio-gravitational field. The bio-gravitational field thus reflects in microcosm the problem of the unified field, which is the cornerstone of the physics of the future. It will be clear to the unbiased reader that the work published in 1965 by the Soviet physicist K. Stanjukovic on the interdependence of gravitation and elementary particles has made a fundamental contribution to the development of these ideas. This theory has now made great headway, but at the time when it was published there were of course no grounds to suppose that the real solution to this problem could be found primarily in biology on the basis of facts also observable in psycho-tronics (Dubrov 1974, 312)

A much more detailed discussion of gravitation and paraphysics is discussed in a later section of chapter 6. Michael Persinger was a researcher at Laurentian University in Canada that has extensively studied such phenomena as Remote Viewing and Trans-communication. Before his recent death, he released a technology that allowed for trans-communication based on resonating and synchronized magnetic fields. He found the graviton was directly involved in entanglement:

> On the bases of the calculations and conceptual inferences, entanglement phenomena across the space-time that defines the universe could be mediated by a gravitational field whose quantized component, the mass of a graviton, when expressed as the square of the hypothetical entanglement velocity, is light. This velocity (10^{23} m·s^{-1}) is derivable from independent approaches that require the consideration of the universe as a single set. If this inference derived from empirical measurements is valid, then there is additional evidence that "excess correlation" and entanglement of photons anywhere in the universe is mediated by quantized components of a gravitational field that is contained within the total spatial and temporal boundaries (Persinger, 2015)

In one area mentioned here by Norseen was the effect of creating a sense of the Divine using magnetic fields, famously known as the 'God Helmet' experiments, where magnets are used to create an altered state of consciousness or sense of the Divine, which could also be used for other applications. Norseen also cites the Schumann Resonance; Persinger also did extensive research in this field of inquiry. Clearly Norseen kept up with active research in edge science areas such as paraphysics since such things were directly related to Thought Injection and Bio-fusion.

Another physics area mentioned by Norseen is that of the Alfven wave grids, named after the physicist Hannes Alfven. Alfven waves are ELF waves that form an electromagnetic grid in the Universe:

> Any movement within a conducting fluid that is in the presence of a magnetic field will generate electrical currents. These currents will then interact with the field to produce mechanical forces which act back on the fluid. In 1942, Hannes Alfven noted that in this scenario "a kind of combined electromagnetic-hydrodynamic wave is produced which so far as I know, has as yet attracted no attention." Alfven calculated the properties of such waves, suggesting that they could be important in solar physics. Today, Alfven waves and other related magnetohydrodynamic waves take center stage in the study of laboratory, space and astrophysical plasmas. Alfven, H. Nature 150, 405–406 (1942)

It is only speculation and there is no direct evidence that this secret military project existed, but in Project Montauk they claimed to have used some grid for 'trans-communication.' If this is the Alfven wave grid, then it would be understandable for Norseen's repeated mentioning of the Alfven wave grid.

Returning for a moment to the ideal of field propulsion it is interesting that Norseen was interested in exotic aircraft designs. I believe that Norseen must have been familiar with a book on the subject of ESP, since he also mentions in one section of his conversations with Laurie, the spaceship of Ezekiel, which is also a paper presented in the book, cited on Bio-gravitation of Dubrov. Norseen conducted research in Air related systems for Lockheed Martin, and his funding contract was for aircraft controls while at Lockheed Martin. Norseen writes:

> It is just after 0530 and I am already in the office, with a lot of icy roads outside. I am here all alone in probably the world's largest hangar. Down the street we house the C-5 Jumbo Cargo Plane; three of them in a row under one roof—wild! They look like huge blue-gray air whales. Just standing under them is like looking up into the jaws of Tyrannosaurus Rex or the Vegan Brontosaurus. And then, in our windowless palace of concrete and RF Tempest shielding, I am surrounded by ideas and visions of all kinds of advanced earth and non-earth-based aircraft designs. I keep trying to figure out what kind of craft Ezekiel was describing in the Bible… (Norseen, Laurie, Part 15)

Norseen also touches on other aspects of Quantum Mechanics – for instance, it is noted that Gravitational theories are mainly concerned with the study of particle physics, such as Heim's ability to calculate particle masses with accuracy decades before they were known by exact experiments, Norseen writes:

> To understand how a super-solid could exist, you have to imagine the realm of quantum mechanics, the modern theory that explains many of the properties of matter. In this realm there are different rules for the two categories of particles: fermions and bosons. Fermions include particles like electrons and atoms with an odd mass number, like helium-3. Bosons include atoms with an even mass number, like helium-4. The quantum-mechanical rule for fermions is that they cannot share a quantum state with other particles of their kind, but for bosons there is no limit to the number that can be in the identical quantum state. This talent that bosons have for Rockettes-style coordination leads to the remarkable properties that Chan and Kim discovered in super cooled helium-4.

"When we go to a low-enough temperature, thermal energy is no longer important and this quantum-mechanical effect becomes very apparent," Chan explains. "In a super solid of helium-4, its identical helium-4 atoms are flowing around without any friction, rapidly changing places — but, because all its particles are in the identical quantum state, it remains a solid even though its component particles are continually flowing." (Norseen, Laurie, Part 11)

The previous quote touches directly on the functioning of a Quantum Computer processor, for instance Quantum Annealing, which operates at super cold temperatures of almost absolute zero Kelvin. Whether as an intended leak of how their computers might work, or not, the first commercially available Quantum Computer, by D-Wave Systems in Vancouver, uses Helium 3 and 4 solutions to keep its processor super-cooled. To what extent the commercial venture was based on covert science is not known.

Cyber Semiotics

Cybernetics (see more in cybernetics discussion in chapter 5) is the study of control in animals and machines. As was mentioned before, the Piercean Semiotic is not just limited to linguistics but has also had a major impact on control theory and logic of controllers in weapons systems. The American founder of Cybernetics, Norbert Wiener, worked on controllers for radar defense during WW2. As we shall see later Automatic Target Tracking for Radar plays a major part in what we can call Semiotic Cybernetics, the concatenation between Semiotic Logic and Cybernetic controllers. Norseen was at least aware of the lectures of researchers interested in Semiotic Control or Cybernetics at the behest of a U.S. Army-funded gathering (Norseen, 2000)[7]. Early work in this field was actually done by Russian AI researchers, Dimitri Popsolev and V.K. Finn, to name just a couple researchers. In research presentations by Sandia National Labs, owned and managed by Lockheed-Martin, is the consultancy of Dr. Robert Burch (Burch 1997), a professor of Philosophy at Texas A&M University, who studied with V.K. Finn in Moscow at VINITI, specifically reviewing Semiotic Intelligent Systems. So, it is important to understand the influence of Popsolev and Finn on later American weapons system designers.

> This interest arose, originally, in two ways. First, some thirty years ago in the former Soviet Union, interest in Peirce and Karl Popper had led logicians and computer scientists like Victor Konstantinovich Finn and Dmitri Pospelov to try to find ways in which computer programs could generate Peircean hypotheses (Popperian "conjectures") in "semiotic" contexts (non-numerical or qualitative contexts). Under the guide in particular of Finn's intelligent systems laboratory in VINITI-RAN (the All-Russian Institute of Scientific and Technical Information of the Russian Academy of Sciences), elaborate techniques for automatic generation of hypotheses were found and were extensively utilized for many practical purposes. Finn called his approach to hypothesis generation the "JSM Method of Automatic Hypothesis Generation" (so named for similarities to John Stuart Mill's methods for identifying causes). Among the purposes for which the JSM Method has proved fruitful are sociological prediction, pharmacological discovery, and the analysis of processes of industrial production. Interest in Finn's work, and through it in the practical application of Peirce's philosophy, has spread to France, Germany, Denmark, Finland, and ultimately the United States. (Battele 1996)

Pospolev was to become an innovator in the field of Applied Semiotics. The important innovation was using Peirce's Logic regarding 'abduction' to create hypotheses which went on to become a formation for deeper Artificial Intelligence techniques, which also influenced the creator of Genetic Algorithms, John Holland [see below]. In this process the machine intelligence controller forms a 'loop function.' It makes a guess, then runs through data to see if the guess fits the model of the data and can repeat this if there is no break clause in the loop. Albus and Meystel note the contributions of Pospelov to Applied Semiotics:

> Development of the Semiotic Modeling and Situation Analysis area (SSA) is motivated by a strong desire to make the analysis and design of Large Complex Systems, or Intelligent Systems in general, better organized methodologically, more consistent and formally balanced. One of the features of this new methodology is extraction of knowledge from the descriptive information by its consistent analysis based upon well-established algorithms. This should give an opportunity to make the descriptive information a part of the analysis of dynamic processes of control systems theory. It also requires development of new methods of dealing with large (often, multi-resolution)

symbolic systems, and use of "symbol grounding" processes. All of this can be considered now a part of Semiotics.

Several efforts to accomplish this task are known. They were pioneered by W. Haken in Germany, I. Prigogine in France, researchers from CNLS in Los Alamos National Laboratory and in the Santa Fe Institute in the US. In all of these efforts, the opportunities of a linguistic analysis have not been explored. A. Nerode (Cornell) is moving closer to SSA in his Hybrid Control Systems. D. Pospelov and his team from Russia, made Semiotics a basis for development of a variety of formal methods presently known as SSA, or Applied Semiotics.

D. Pospelov, the creator of SSA is definitely a global thinker, he is well prepared in a multiplicity of sciences-components. Unlike many prominent scientists who have specialized solely in their own domain, D. Pospelov is a broad-minded multidisciplinary scholar who has demonstrated bold and aggressive thought in constructing concepts and making associations. US scientists have serious and sometimes better results in each of the components of SSA. However, US never ventured to develop a scientific theoretical synthesis on a such a global scale. (Albus et al, Undated)

Later, Pospelev's work would inform and contribute to research in America. Where one important theoretician working for Lockheed-Martin and a one-time colleague of Norseen was Ed Nozawa. Nozawa is cited in Norseen and Laurie's communications as an expert on Peircean Logic. Nozawa's work is important in the field of controls. He investigated the automation of controllers, from Air Traffic Control (radar) to control of Intelligent Systems. He was the creator of the concept of what is known as the 'Single Warrior Model', of which there is little unclassified information in open-source material. His biography:

E.T. Nozawa (BSE, MSEE) is an Advanced Systems Engineer with Lockheed Martin Aeronautical Systems, Marietta, Georgia. He is the Chairman of the Lockheed Martin Data Fusion Working Group. Experience includes research and development of advanced automatic and adaptive military systems including Multi-Sensor Systems, TWS/SWT Tracking Systems, Information Fusion Systems, and Airborne Weapons Systems; Conceptual design of Advanced Airborne Surveillance and Targeting systems; and system definition and design of Advanced Surface Based 3-D Surveillance and Targeting Radar systems and Automatic and Adaptive TWS Tracking systems. He is a member of the IEEE, AAAI, Charles Sanders Peirce Society. (GACIAC Undated)

In Nozawa's work he has talked about the use of Peircean logic to create self-contained automated management system loops, 'Single Warrior Model.' He uses a concept from Semiotics and Intelligent Systems known as functional loops and applies this to controllers, thus creating a 'closed loop management system':

functional loop - a closed loop of behavior generation which runs through the following subsystems: sensors, sensory processing, knowledge storage, behavior generator, actuators, world. (Albus et al, Undated)

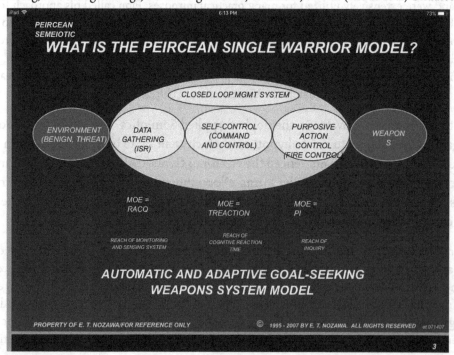

The topic of fully autonomous weapons systems has come to the fore in ethical conversations regarding weapons development, for example the on-line community of AI developers against fully autonomous weapons, https://autonomousweapons.org/. However, this is a recent topic of conversation among Weapons and AI developers. This slide, originally from 1995, predates these conversations by some two decades. The question we have to ask is, 'Was automation and cybernetic control put into play in tandem with Neuroweapons, automated thought injection based on machine learning algorithms and situation management?' One need not look too far into nightmare film scenarios from Hollywood for such a situation of automated neuro-warfare.

> Genetic Algorithms founder, John Henry Holland was inspired by Peircean logic. See also the work of Matthew Kabrisky for USAF 'ATR' fusion. He is mentioned by Norseen. Matthew Kabrisky: "A Proposed Model for Visual Information Processing in the Human Brain." Michael Senglaub, PhD, colleague of Nozawa at Sandia National Laboratories, owned by Lockheed-Martin. "Knowledge Representation in Reasoning Systems" and "C2 for Complex endeavors Automated Decision Support in a Complex Information Space."

Troubling is the connection of Sandia Researchers, who worked directly with Nozawa as a consultant to their work, that specialize in 'Network Assurance and Survivability' such as Michael Senglaub (Senglaub 2001) and their being influenced by closed loop automated controllers under Nozowa's Peircean model. Meaning that if system designers for, say, nuclear missile defense, systems designed to withstand end-of-world conflicts continue operating on their own without human intervention based on the Peircean models, they could continue fighting wars after there are no more humans left to fight. In this case we have a clear example of a situation of loop controllers and engineers such as Senglaub and Nozawa using loops to control weapons systems. Senglaub, in the applications section of his research paper (Senglaub 2001), suggests using the Peircean model for Data Fusion, Anti-Terrorism, Cognition-Based Decision Making and Autonomous System Control. Thus, possibly in their designs they have integrated Closed Loop Management Systems, which is to say fully automated weapons systems which also may integrate Holland's Peircean Genetic Algorithms – self-writing algorithms.

An additional element to the research conducted by Sandia (Senglaub 2005) is that of using game theory to be deployed within the systems [see deeper discussion of Simulation AI in online supplement Appendix D]. Thus, with the integration of games into defense systems we have a computational model that could be invoked which is based purely on mathematical conditions that claim to model the real world; but fall short of it.

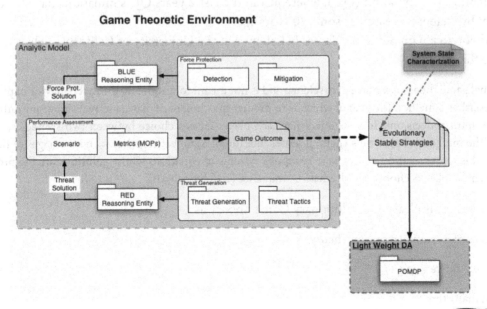

(Senglaub 2005)

91

As is seen above the autonomous decision agent is based on partially observable Markov decision processes (POMDP) machine learning architecture which can have bias problems as noted by one developer differentiating between different methods of POMDP (Azizzadenesheli 2016)."

The issue of bias in AI is a prime problem area and is something that will need to be carefully monitored in applications. If a bias is introduced the AI can get stuck and move in one direction without correcting itself, such as in an adversarial network with Red vs. Blue, so that an attacker in such a biased network would end up with an advantage. More is covered on the issue of bias and adversarial networks in online supplement Appendix D. Graphic from Senglaub presentation which is similar to contemporary Generative Adversarial Networks architecture. This was initially presented in 2003 in the Journal on Reflexive Control by an American team of researchers, pictured previously, from NMSU RTRT group (Kramer et al, 2003). We can see the direct influence between Senglaub's work and that of the group:

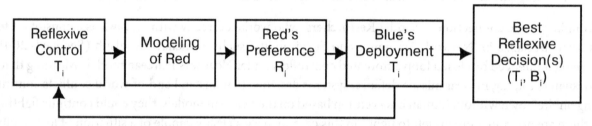

For i = 1 to m − 1, increment i.

Figure 3. Scheme (II)

It is an interesting point of understanding that this conception of adversarial networks predates the innovations in contemporary Artificial Intelligence, introduced by Ian Goodfellow in 2017, so that we see the pre-dating of what is considered cutting edge AI techniques in the public sector by at least 15 years in the defense industry. As is indicated in Senglaub's graph, POMDP (Partial-Observable Markov Decision Process), which is of interest to GANs and Deep Reinforcement Learning as 'breakthroughs' in AI techniques in such applications of using AI to compete against human competitors in Real-Time Strategy Games (RTS), such as what is viewed as the elite public application of this techniques at London based Deepmind. We can see that there is a clear technological lead in the compartmentalized covert world compared to that of the public domain; which, as we shall see later, is also of interest to Quantum Computation (QC), where just in the last 2 years QC simulations have become public, but were written of by Defense researchers some 20 years ago.

The main theoretician on Semiotic Games is Lefebvre at the University of California. He states regarding his semiotic game theory:

> Traditional game theory is a normative science and is not meant for modeling the real behavior of players. This paper describes a method the goal of which is to predict the choices of players in real situations rather than to compute optimal decisions. It is assumed that each player faces a choice between two strategies: active and passive. The method is based on structural representation of a subject together with his images of the self and another. This representation allows us to compose systems of equations whose solutions are the probabilities with which the players choose the alternative strategies. (Lefebvre 2010)

Senglaub presents his ideals on Evolutionary Game Theory as:

- Essentials of Evolutionary Game theory.

- Non cooperative game.

- Played many times.

- "Players" are randomly drawn from a population.

- Each member of the population can have a unique strategy.

- Evolutionary process impacts the population from which players are drawn.

- No guarantee that the ultimate strategy will lead to a Nash equilibrium.

Usually in a game there is what is known as a Nash equilibrium being reached.
Nash Equilibrium:

> In terms of game theory, if each player has chosen a strategy, and no player can benefit by changing strategies while the other players keep theirs unchanged, then the current set of strategy choices and their corresponding payoffs constitutes a Nash equilibrium.
>
> Stated simply, Alice and Bob are in Nash equilibrium if Alice is making the best decision she can, taking into account Bob's decision while his decision remains unchanged, and Bob is making the best decision he can, taking into account Alice's decision while her decision remains unchanged. Likewise, a group of players are in Nash equilibrium if each one is making the best decision possible, taking into account the decisions of the others in the game as long as the other parties' decisions remain unchanged. (https://en.wikipedia.org/wiki/Nash_equilibrium)

It is ominous that in a possibly autonomously controlled system no Nash equilibrium could be reached. He brings forth a co-evolutionary strategy that is fully automated, in other words weapons systems controlled purely by a Computer system.

Co-Evolutionary Game Theory

- Multi-sided game in which all sides evolve a dominant strategy.

- Is evolutionary game theory with n evolving players.

- Provide basis for an automated system to search for optimal solutions against adaptive opponents.

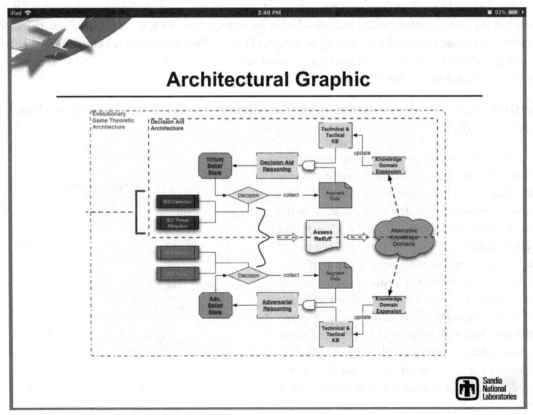

(Senglaub 2005)

As was mentioned previously the technological edge rests with the covert science compared to open-source open-domain technologists. One such area of interest is that of Quantum Computation. It is interesting that

93

many years before that Defense-related computer scientists were already exploring QCs to implement automated decision making:

> A quantum device simulating the human decision-making process is introduced. It consists of quantum recurrent nets generating stochastic processes which represent the motor dynamics, and of classical neural nets describing the evolution of probabilities of these processes which represent the mental dynamics. The autonomy of the decision-making process is achieved by a feedback from the mental to motor dynamics which changes the stochastic matrix based upon the probability distribution. This feedback replaces unavailable external information by an internal knowledge base stored in the mental model in the form of probability distributions. As a result, the coupled motor mental dynamics is described by an online version of Markov chains which can decrease entropy without an external source of information. Applications to common sense-based decisions as well as to evolutionary games are discussed. An example exhibiting self-organization is computed using quantum computer simulation. Force on force and mutual aircraft engagements using the quantum decision maker dynamics are considered. (Zakab 2000)

It is well known to computer scientists that Quantum computation gives one an incredible step up in terms of computational power, it would be hard for a classically based computer to implement an advanced algorithm for such decision making in a complex environment such as the fog of war (incomplete information, dynamic, etc) but not for a Quantum Computer.

Another area that has influenced Intelligent Systems and automation is that of Genetic Algorithms or Genetic Programing, which is based on Natural Genetic Selection, where a computer compiles its own components and finds the best fit among various modules to formulate an optimal choice. This area was strongly influenced through Peircean Logic in the founder of Genetic Algorithms, John Holland of the University of Michigan. It was also advocated by Senglaub in engineering Automatic systems. Senglaub writes:

> Genetic programming or evolutionary programing technologies could also provide insight into design configurations that could result in fault configurations under sets of environmental drivers. recognizing the basic elements of the design configurations and introducing specialized "abnormal environment" operators, genetic programs (GP) could be tasked with finding all possible fault configurations that result in unacceptable states for a sub-system. A great deal of work has been performed in which GP's have been tasked with designing circuits, structures, and algorithms. (Senglaub 1997)

In artificial intelligence an agent is used to formulate optimal solutions. A more generalized definition of Semiotic Agents (SAs) is given:

> Thus in turn the possible decisions that agents can make must be considered relative to those possible actions. The result of all of this is that SAs can be cast in terms of a generalized control architecture, as in the work of Powers [1973, 1989], where the autonomy of the system is allowed by its manifestation of a closed causal relation with its environment. Through this relation the agent makes decisions so as to make its measurements (representations of current and past decisions and states) as "close" as possible to its goals in order to reduce a generalized "error function" given by its own beliefs of what desirable states are. Thus, as illustrated in Fig. 2, SAs manifest a generalized negative feedback control relation. (Joslyn 2000) (Miller 1996)

Figure 2: Semiotic agents as maintaining a generalized control relation with their environments.

(Josslyn 2000)

Lockheed-Martin is not alone in seeking to use Semiotic Cybernetics in their defense systems. Saab Microwave Systems, for example, also is relying on Automated Intelligent Systems, possibly also influenced by Peircean Logic as tech is often copied by one company to another, to manage their defense infrastructure. It is interesting and directly related to Neuroweapons as their systems oversee Radar and Microwave infrastructures which are both directly related to the technologies of Neuro-warfare. In a presentation on-line by Saab Scientist, Hakan Warston, they show the progression in their thinking and what they view as a necessity of relying in the future on automated computer decision-making systems. (Warston, 2007)

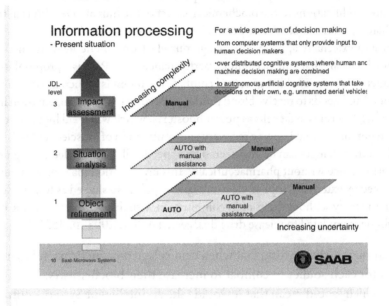

Use of Automation up to 2015:

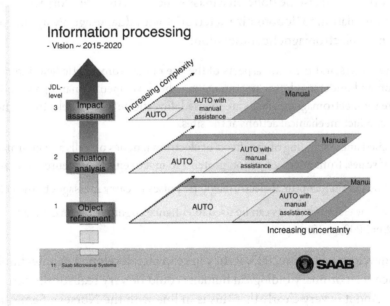

Projected Automation from 2015:

As one can plainly see from the slides at the time of their writing it relies a great deal less on automated with manual assistance and very small footprints of fully automated. However, from 2015-2020 they foresee a large footprint for fully automated computer decision-making in their systems. I would imagine that Saab Microwave Systems is not alone in this trend.

Of course, such concepts as Reflexive Control, Thought Injection and other methods of this weapons technology would be incomplete without a grounding in Brain/Computer Interfaces. Dr. Norseen cites two researchers related to this field. One is a Russian emigre scientist who works for the US Government, Alexei A. Sharov, cited by Norseen. He also cites the work of an American who worked for the Office of Naval Research, Richard H. Dickhaut, under the working title of 'Neuroelectric Activity and Analysis in Support of Direct Brainwave to Computer Interface Development.' From which Norseen developed his techniques for mapping the Brain.

Another Norseen-cited researcher is Robert Asher, also of Sandia Labs, who is specifically working on Brain/Computer Interfaces. A briefing by him from 2003 reads:

> Human performance enhancement may require modifications to the biochemical aspects of the human. Maintained alertness, enhanced physical and psychological performance, and enhanced survivability rates in serious operations all require modifications to the biochemical aspect of the human. DARPA is in the process of developing drugs to enhance performance when a person has been sleep-deprived.
>
> Consider the use of externally applied, non-dangerous electromagnetic fields to increase the rate of production of body biochemicals that enhance human performance. DARPA has a proposal to increase the rate of stress protein production before a soldier goes into combat. The intent is to increase the survivability rate when the soldier is wounded and needs to receive blood products. Beyond that, one can envision increasing the rate of production of ATP [triglycerides in fat cells as power booster?], which will yield higher energy levels by natural means, will help ion pumping to aid in nerve recovery and contraction of muscles, and will speed recovery from combat stress. What other changes can be engineered by a specifically shaped electromagnetic pulse that might enhance human performance without pharmaceuticals? This investigation may spawn a new industry in which the human is enhanced by externally applied electromagnetic pulses so shaped as to enhance specific biochemical changes within the body without drugs or in combination with drugs, with fewer side effects. For instance, nanoparticles might be formulated to release drug dosages... (Asher, 2003, p. 355)

It is not hard to see, through Asher's work, that when using electromagnetic pulses to increase combat readiness one would have to monitor each soldier in combat to increase their biochemistry. It of course would be impossible to do this manually, which would mean that it would take an Intelligent System controller to oversee the mass number of troops in combat to increase their biochemistry, and if this is connected to an Automated system then it is not hard to see how this could also be done on a mass scale covertly. For Norseen's project they would be able to use electromagnetic stimulation to 'lobotomize' a terrorist with dual usage always in view. Asher continues on the different applications of electromagnetic stimulation:

> *Nano*. Develop and understand the nano aspects of the use of electromagnetic field interactions with cellular structures. Develop and understand how treatments may be developed by nano particle interactions only at specific sites where the electromagnetic fields are focused. Investigate whether electromagnetics can be used as a power source to conduct mechanical actions at the sites.
>
> *Bio*. Develop a detailed understanding of the effects of electromagnetics on cells and neuronal networks, including the full range of scales, from micro effects on proteins to macro effects on neuronal networks.
>
> *Info*. Develop methods to shape optimal electromagnetic pulses to carry messages to the cells and neurons.
>
> *Cogno*. Understand how electromagnets can be used to enhance cognitive performance as well as physiological performance. (Asher 2003, p. 356)

This is an alarming development from 2003. If they have in fact developed nanotechnology to enhance or control human performance then ordinary biological humans could be very realistically turned into cyborgs without any visible mechanics. And it is very clearly that this is in line with the Norseen Semiotic vision of Information Injection. In this report of Asher in the section under Brain-Machine-Interfaces he sees the applications of this technology to mass control of automobile drivers or air traffic controllers. Again we see the convergence with Radar in this technology. In many civilian complaints of neuroweapons abuse there are statements related to being stalked by vehicles on the road, Asher writes:

> The DARPA program could be extended to include a broader range of potential impact by including the possibility of other applications: learning and training, automobile control, air traffic control, decision-making, remote sensing of stress, and entertainment. Learning and training might be implemented as information coded into brain signals and then input into the person. Air traffic control in increasingly busy skies can use such

capability: the controller has multiple inputs from multiple aircraft. These can be input into his brain in a 3 -D aspect and an alertness signal used to "wake him up" when his attention drifts beyond acceptable limits. Not only intellectual data might be passed from one person to another without speaking, but also emotional and volitional information. Decision-making may become more precise as emotional, fatigue, and other cognitive states can be appraised prior to making a critical decision.

The potential impact on automobile safety is great. The driver can have quicker control of his automobile (Figure E.1 5), allowing for safer driving while reducing the car- to-car spacing on congested highways. This would help alleviate highway congestion and the need for more highways. Furthermore, it would allow for safer driving, as driver attention can be measured and the driver "alerted," or told in some manner to pay attention to his or her driving when attention wanders beyond safe margins. It can allow for detection of driver impairment so that the vehicle may be made either not to start or to call emergency. (Asher 200, p. 3573)

358   E. Notional Security

Figure E.15. Hands-off control of an automobile through a device for reading and implanting brain waves.

(Asher 2003)

SEMIOTIC DIPLOMATIC CYBERNETICS

Increasingly, we are seeing the use of Intelligent Systems to model various social relationships. One field where this has entered into the convergence between technological and social spaces is that of International Relations. The use of Intelligent Systems to not just model but control and interact with international relations is related:

> The second procedure, called long range, strategic control reflects a longer term planning of policy changes that are implemented consistently throughout the whole evolution. The long term strategic control is achieved by an optimal control algorithm that we briefly discuss in Section 4. In the optimal control framework the perturbations (controls) are evaluated in order to minimize or maximize some objective functional that depends on the state and the controls. The actual form of this functional essentially depends on the goal we want to achieve and explicitly includes the reward and cost of that goal. The main advantage of such planning is that the changes one has to implement are known over the whole time span of the system's evolution and provide an optimal

solution (an optimal cost effectiveness is realized for attaining the desired goal). The basic disadvantage of this method is that modeling errors, inherent perturbations, and unforeseen factors will usually lead to a trajectory different from the planned one.

This approach is based on the optimal control method applied to discrete systems. The optimal control method can be simply summarized as follows. The system is described by a scalar or vector state function depending on a number of independent variables that take values in the phase space of the system. The state satisfies a (usually nonlinear) dynamical scalar or vector equation that depends also on some parameters that take values in the parameter space. One or more of these parameters are considered external controls to be adjusted at will. The goal is to optimize a given objective func-tional that depends on the state and on the control(s).

From the state equation and objective functional one constructs, in a canonical way, a non-homogeneous adjoint equation for a (scalar or vector) adjoint variable. The original state equation together with the adjoint equation form the optimality system (OS). The optimality condition yields an explicit, analytical formula for the optimal control in terms of the solutions of the OS. By replacing this expression of the control in the OS and solving it, one obtains the optimal state and adjoint variable and therefore the optimal control. The general framework for optimal control for general nonlinear systems as developed by J.-L. Lions was recently applied to competitive systems of social and military interest

The long range control is better suited when one has a good idea about global strategic objectives, the costs involved and, one wants to achieve a well-defined goal. Since the role of the user is essential in deciding what control strategy to use we see here an excellent example of applied semiotic analysis to international relations. (Pentek 1997)

The Pentagon has already looked into creating a global simulation of political realities, known as the Sentient World Simulation (Krishnan 2016, 87)

SEMIOTIC ALCOHOL

Dr. James Giordano, a DOD specialist in neuroweapons and lecturer at George Washington University, like Norseen and Umpleby, has written regarding what are known as nootropics, bio-chemical agents affecting cognitive function. Norseen also talks about the use of nootropics with Laurie. He also in this dialogue explicitly implicates 'the Brits' as being the main party responsible behind starting research into this area. Perhaps, the most interesting take from what Norseen discusses with Laurie is what would normally be considered a Conspiracy Theory in relation to the mass shooters at Columbine in Colorado. He suggests that they were influenced by a remote thought injection system in another part of his discussion through websites, which may have used the 25th frame technique [see Neuroweapons discussion] or other methods of subliminal control and influence. In an a long passage from their conversations Norseen goes into a conversation hitting on the use of thought injection as a Weapon of Mass Destruction (WMD), one that he later goes on to view as a means of being implemented for that purpose, which of course should sound like a paranoid conspiracist if it were for the fact that he is a weapons designer working on these very systems for Lockheed-Martin and the National Security apparatus of the United States.

Norseen begins his discussion talking about nootropics:

Quoting Duncan: "My question is, what can that little pill, with its little molecules, contain that can cause such a radical shift in awareness?"

OH BOY! Now you have gone and done it. This actually gets into the DEEPEST, DARKEST SECRETS of my work; the Columbine Massacre….wet ops [assassination] in England [perhaps a reference to the Marconi Murders]…..the next, absolute WMD (information control is the ultimate weapon of mass destruction)

Information Injection - Weapon of Mass Destruction

And now you get me going into the kinds of Little White Pills that are being made in Porten Downs [UK Biochemical Production facility] and in the Russian labs and other places I am familiar with … and you are coming up with MK-809 in Germany and a special little breed I am working on that heads directly for each of the 5 main pain receptor sites in the Central Nervous System … alpha, epsilon, delta, kappa, and mu.

You can easily think of the brain as simply a NITROGEN MOLECULE RESONATOR, and this is the currency by which the ZPE comes pumping in to humans. It is also how the anti-depressants and the REBOUND drugs work, in the Larium, and the Luvox, etc. etc. It is how the DOOM web sites [video game portal used by

Columbine shooters] get the SIGNAL into the receptive minds of th the ATTACHED, and dispatches them… with the ultimate act already PRIMED and LOCKED and LOADED into the Superior Colliculus… and when the final signal arrives, the SC takes over and Wham… suicide, or info induced wet ops. (Noseen, Laurie Part 11)

Norseen here directly talks about the influencing of minds through nootropics, stating that Nitrogen (N) is the key to unlocking Wiring in the brain and leading to changes in function which is to say human behavior. Again we see his notion of unlocking the functions in the brain, QSK. He uses the example of the Columbine shooters here to illustrate his point, which may sound like irrational rambling. It is interesting to note that in the Snowden Leaks it was discovered that GCHQ and the NSA infiltrated video game communities to do behavioral studies. So it may not be as far fetched as we may think, especially with the knowledge of illicitly and illegal biological tests done on unknowing civilians in the history of National Defence research in the United States.

Norseen then goes on to discuss where it originates, he directly implicates the United Kingdom in this research going back he says 100 years. He talks of a biomolecule Tetrahydroisoquinoline (TIQ or THIQ) an organic compound with the chemical formula $C_9H_{11}N$.

OK, OK… where did this all come from…The Brits and their work with the opium trade wars… and also the fear of drug-induced attacks on the Royal Marines that the big bore and higher caliber ammunition couldn't stop… what is the cause?… the Brits still classify all the work in THIQ… now it happens that THIQ is even more powerful than MK-809 and along the lines of my Designer register.

When a drunk becomes a Stage 4 alcoholic, the body and the brain actually convert body chemicals into THIQ… tetrahydroquinine, etc. and the THIQ can actually be found as little white crystals and powderize crystals in the brains of dead alcoholics. The BRITS began over 100 years ago to administer this to see the effects and they found it was 1000x more powerful than morphine (it is even more powerful than fentnyl, the gas used by the Russian 'vimple' antiterror squad to squash the Chechnyan take over of NordEst in Moscow… (the Brits gave the fentyl to the Russkies) and it knocked everybody out in less than 10 seconds… well, THIQ is 100x or more powerful than that… it is what the alcoholic produces to keep him, or rather, his Brain, alive

So in the brain… you have 99% driving for WILD LIFE… and 1% set up to BLANK OUT. And in between are the LITTLE WHITE POWDERS - the PILLS, the 7% laudanum solutions. (Norseen, Laurie Part 11)

THIQ was thought at one time to be the cause of Alcoholism, however, this was later disproved, it is rather a product of Alcoholism according to Norseen. This is an interesting connection, in fact we have already seen how Alcohol was related as a trance agent in an earlier passage in the Norseen and Laurie in regards to Norseen's encounter with Russian scientists. It is a question if he had a scientific purpose in discussing THIQ or to what ends other then as an example of a substance that can alter human behavior. He continues with the discusson of THIQ:

Information as a Drug Delivery Device
And back to THIQ… for a while the British medical corps was using the THIQ for battlefield ops and the patients were getting up and going back into battle with no arms and legs and such and they realized… this stuff is beyond TOP SECRET. What if the enemy gets this… our .45 to the head won't stop them from coming over the walls… so the Brits SEALED IT DEEP AWAY and got the US to "fogitdabowdit." Until certain agency souls started to play with it again and it slipped out… hence the race to Oxycontin… pure female birthing neurotransmitter Oxytocin… I like the spelling changes myself… to MK-809, to new Fentnyl, to my new Designer Formula… (Norseen, Laurie, Part 11)

Here Norseen discusses an interesting opiate Oxycontin, which has become an epidemic in places like the United States in terms of addiction. Other countries developing Neuroweapons, such as Nazi Germany, also had major opiate addictions, for instance IG-Farben created methamphetamines [see Neuroweapons section]. It is also of interest that he relates this to the 'female birthing neurotransmitter Oxytocin.' Oxytocin is a peptide hormone and neuropeptide. It is most important in birthing and nurturing young (social bonding) of mothers to children, it is produced in the hypothalamus and released by the posterior pituitary glands. It is interesting to note that civilians claiming to be affected by Neuroweapons, often termed 'Targeted Individuals' are comprised of 70% female. What role specifically Oxytocin and Oxycontin plays in this is not known to this author, but clearly Norseen as a weapons designer brings it up in the context of brain alteration. He continues:

Duncan…This page shows the chemical "resonating" structure of quinolines…the basic block that links into the neuronal synapses, the neuropil, of the brain and when locked in, the ZPE comes pouring in…and you are the signal…pain goes away and is replaced by the Semiotic. Do you see the BIG FAT "N"? That is the nitrogen resonance….by playing around with the N…you can create all kinds of signals.(i.e. realities) in the brain…That is what your little white pill does…why it is so powerful…it plays the HAARP of the N - and transports you to wonderful new worlds….

Semiotic Prophecies of Dr. John Norseen

Perhaps in the most ominous aspect of his conversations with Laurie, Norseen elaborated on what he perceived as a doomsday outcome of this technology and warfare in general. He directly linked this to overpopulation and migration:

As we approach 500 million people in 2025 [in US population] and the nasties start flying, we are going to lash out at the world and "waste ½ of it" — if you look very carefully at the Semiotics that are being impressed on our culture you can see "Total War" as the dominant theme. F the UN, "just waste em" will be the mindset. (Norseen, Laurie, 2002, part 15)

And yes, there are technologies already set up in advance, pre-positioned for the future border semiotic wars — rapid fire Stego Bullets, brain specific prions, multi-channel semiotic PSYOP — I can believe when people say they have signed documents concerning non-disclosure for 70+ years…I inked such forms myself. (Norseen, Laurie, 2002, part 15)

Mind you this was written in 2002, and approaching 20 years later we see this reality unfolding as climate change has put pressures on growing populations around the globe, leading to migrations, which has led to a rise in Nationalism, and Border Walls, or as Norseen put it 'future border semiotic wars.' One can only imagine how fantastical this conversation must seem to an uninformed audience over the years, however, to those living some time after this conversation as public disclosure regarding neuroweapons and with the changing climate, it is more and more realistic.

Notes:

[1] Norseen cites this contract as his funding vehicle for research, part of his research was used in connection to Human-Sensor interactions in aircraft pilots: Lockheed Martin Aeronautical Systems, AvCS, Inc.: Data Communications Requirements, Technology and Solutions for Aviation Weather Information Systems, Phase I Report - Aviation Weather Communications Requirements. NASA Contract N66001-97-C-8605, March 1999. (Cited in Norseen 2000)

[2] https://cypheragablog.wordpress.com/category/introduction, posted Sept. 15, 2010 (accessed 4/17/19)

[3] Total Information Awareness (TIA) was a project of the National Security Agency to have all known information about an individual and a society, totally. It is interesting that Norseen mentions it here was part of his research viewed as part of TIA?

[4] https://www.rand.org/topics/information-operations.html (accessed 5/18/19)

[5] http://www.au.af.mil/au/awc/awcgate/milreview/jones_perception.pdf (accessed 5/18/19)

[6] See more at http://www.pravdareport.com/news/russia/25537-n/" (accessed 5/20/19)

[7] He cites from 1999 the papers of: Workshop on Multi-Reflexive Models of Behavior, V. Lefebre, ARL-SR-64, May 1999. Reflexive Control in Multi-Subjective and Multi-Agent Systems, V. Lepsky, ARL-SR-64, May 1999. In Norseen 2000

Bibliography:

Albus, James. Meystel, Alex. (Undated) 'An Introduction to Intelligent Systems and Semiotics' National Institute of Standards and Technology http://www.dca.fee.unicamp.br/~gudwin/semiotics/semiotics.doc (accessed 5/25/19)

Asher, Robert, Sandia National Labs, (2003) 'NON-DRUG TREATMENTS FOR ENHANCEMENT OF HUMAN PERFORMANCE' in 'Converging Technologies for Improving Human Performance NANOTECHNOLOGY, BIOTECHNOLOGY, INFORMATION TECHNOLOGY AND COGNITIVE SCIENCE' NSF/DOC-sponsored report Edited by Mihail C. Roco and William Sims Bainbridge National Science Foundation 2003 Kluwer Academic Publishers (currently Springer) Dordrecht, The Netherlands. http://www.wtec.org/ConvergingTechnologies/Report/NBIC_report.pdf (accessed 6/2/19)

Azizzadenesheli, K., Lazaric, A., Animashree, A. (2016) Journal of Machine Learning Workshop and Conference Proceedings vol 49:1–64 http://proceedings.mlr.press/v49/azizzadenesheli16a.pdf

Battele (ed), Stohl R. (1996) Proceedings of March 20-29, Columbus, Ohio Workshop on "Russian Situation Control and Cybernetic Semiotic Modeling," by Battelle, Edit. Stohl, Robert J., March 31, 1996.https://plato.stanford.edu/entries/peirce/

Berry, S. (2000), 'Decoding Minds, Foiling Adversaries', SIGNAL Magazine (October), p.5

Burch, Robert W. (1997) *The VINITI Program*, Army Research Laboratory, ARL-CR-212, June 97.

Dubrov, Aleksandr (1974) *'Biogravitation and Psychotronics'* in 'Impact of Science on Society' UNESCO Volume XXIV, No. 4 'Parasciences' Oct-Dec 1974

GACIAC Bulletin Volume 20 No. 2, https://www.dsiac.org/sites/default/files/journals/GACV20N2.pdf (accessed 5/23/19)

Gross, A (2010) *Heimlich Uberwachung und Strahlenfolter durch Geheimdienste*, in Raum & Zeit https://www.stopeg.com/doc/CarlClarkInterview.pdf (accessed 4/3/19)

Jaitner, M.L., Kantola, Maj. H., (2016) *'Applying Principles of Reflexive Control in Information and Cyber Operations'* Journal of Information Warfare Vol. 15, Issue 4 (2016) https://www.researchgate.net/publication/311983748_Applying_Principles_of_Reflexive_Control_in_Information_and_Cyber_Operations (accessed 5/29/19)

Joslyn, Cliff and Luis M. Rocha (2000). *"Towards Semiotic Agent Based Models of Socio Technical Organizations."* Proc. AI, Simulation and Planning in High Autonomy Systems (AIS 2000) Conference, Tucson, Arizona, USA. ed. HS Sarjoughian et al., pp. 70-79. See https://www.informatics.indiana.edu/rocha/publications/ps/AIS00.pdf (accessed 5/21/19)

Kadtke, Jim; Pentek, Aron; Lenhart, Suzanne; Protopopescu, Vladimir. *Control Mechanisms for a Nonlinear Model of International Relations* https://nvlpubs.nist.gov/nistpubs/Legacy/SP/nistspecialpublication918.pdf

Koruga, J. (1986) *'Microtubular Screw Symmetry: Packing of Spheres as a Latent Bioinformation Code'* in Annals of the New York Academy of Sciences 466 (1 Dynamic Aspec):953-5 · February 1986

Kramer, X., Kaiser, T., Schmidt, S., Davidson, J. and Lefebvre, V. (2003) 'FROM PREDICTION TO REFLEXIVE CONTROL', in REFLEXIVE PROCESSES AND CONTROL No. 1, v. 2, 2003. P. 86-102 http://www.reflexion.ru/Library/EJ2003_1.pdf (accessed 5/29/19)

Krishnan, A. (2017). *Military Neuroscience and the Coming Age of Neurowarfare.* London: Routledge. DOI: https://doi.org/10.4324/9781315595429

Lefebvre, Vladimir. (2010) REFLEXIVE GAME THEORY https://nvlpubs.nist.gov/nistpubs/Legacy/SP/nistspecialpublication918.pdf

Lefebvre V.A., X.H. Kramer, T.B. Kaiser, S.E. Schmidt, J.E. Davidson, V.A. (2003) 'FROM PREDICTION TO REFLEXIVE CONTROL', in REFLEXIVE PROCESSES AND CONTROL No. 1, v. 2, 2003. P. 86-102 http://www.reflexion.ru/Library/EJ2003_1.pdf (accessed 5/29/19)

Moore, R. (2003) http://www.militarytransition.com/, 2003. (Offline as of July 2010. February 2005 snapshot on archive.org)

Miller, L. D., Sulcoski, M. F., and Farmer, B. A., (1996) "Discrete Richardson Model: A Paradigm for International Relations?"

Murray, Frank J., (2002) *'NASA plans to read terrorist's minds at airport'* Aug 17, 2002, archived on-line at https://twoday.net/static/mindcontrol/files/zimmermann_and_norseen.htm

Norseen, John D., Laurie, Duncan *'Outlaw Technology'* (2002) published on-line at http://www.duncanlaurie.com/writing/outlaw_technology (accessed 3/6/2019) archived at https://github.com/autonomous019/Battlespace-of-Mind-Supplement/blob/main/outlaw_technology.zip

Norseen, John D., Kropotov, Juri D., Kremen, Inna Z., (1999) *'Bio-fusion for Intelligent Systems Control'* SPIE (The International Society for Optics and Photonics) Proceedings 12 March 1999

Norseen, John D. (1996) *Images of Mind: The Semiotic Alphabet* online: http://www.acsa2000.net/john2.html (accessed 3/3/19)

Norseen, John D. (2000) Mathematics, *BioFusion and Reflexive Contro for Sentient Machines*, Presentation for International Reflexive Control Symposium (RC'2000) Russian Academy of Sciences – Institute for Psychology 17 – 19 October 2000   Moscow, Russia in *Reflexive Control*. Collected Articles. International Symposium. October 17-19, 2000. M. /Ed. by Lepsky V.E., Moscow, Institute of Psychology Press, 2000. 192 pages.(In Russian) online: http://www.reflexion.ru/Library/EJour_2002_1_b.htm (accessed 6/3/19)

Pasternak, D. (1997) 'Wonder Weapons: The Pentagon's Quest for Non-Lethal Weapons is Amazing, but is it Smart', U.S. News and World Report, 7 July

--(2000) 'John Norseen', U.S. News and World Report, 10 Jan. vol. 128, no.1

Pentek, A., Kadtke, J., Lenhart, S., Protopopescu, V. (1997) Control Mechanisms for a Nonlinear Model of International Relations at Conference for International Conference Intelligent Systems and Semiotics '97 https://nvlpubs.nist.gov/nistpubs/Legacy/SP/nistspecialpublication918.pdf

Persinger, Michael A. (2015). *The Graviton: An Emergent Solution From The Equivalence of Universal Magnetic Field Intensity and Radiant Flux Density.* JOURNAL OF ADVANCES IN PHYSICS. 10. 2811-2815. 10.24297/jap.v10i3.1318.

Senglaub, Michael. (2001) *'Foundations for Reasoning in Cognition- Based Computational Representations of Human Decision Making'* SANDIA REPORT SAND2001-3496 November 2001, see, http://www.au.af.mil/au/awc/awcgate/decision/raybourn-senglaub_013496.pdf (accessed 5/21/19)

Senglaub, Michael, Harris, Dave. (2005) Sandia National Labs, SAND2005-2938C, 'A Modified Perspective of Decision Support in C2', June 14, 2005 see http://dodccrp.org/events/10th_ICCRTS/CD/presentations/150.pdf (accessed 5/21/19). Original Red/Blue design from 2003 in http://www.reflexion.ru/Library/EJ2003_1.pdf (accessed 5/22/19).

Senglaub, Michael. (1997) *'Surety Theoretics'* https://digital.library.unt.edu/ark:/67531/metadc685377/m2/1/high_res_d/292814.pdf (accessed 5/30/19)

Sharov, Alexei. (2010) *'Functional Information: Towards Synthesis of Biosemiotics and Cybernetics'* https://www.academia.edu/237004/Functional_Information_Towards_Synthesis_of_Biosemiotics_and_Cybernetics (accessed 6/1/19)

Tarasenko, Sergey. (2010) *'The Inverse Task of the Reflexive Game Theory: Theoretical Matters, Practical Applications and Relationship with Other Issues'*Kyoto University, Yoshida honmachi, Kyoto 606-8501, Japan. See https://arxiv.org/pdf/1011.3397.pdf (accessed 5/22/19)

Thomas, Timothy L., (2004) *'Russian Reflexive Control Theory and the Military'*, Journal of Slavic Military Studies 17: 237–256, 2004 Taylor & Francis ISSN:1351-8046 DOI:10.1080/13518040490450529 https://www.rit.edu/~w-cmmc/literature/Thomas_2004.pdf (accessed 5/20/19)

Warston, Hakan. (2007) *'System Situation Awareness in Network Based Command & Control Systems'*, euCognition Meeting Munich, January 12, 2007 http://hobbydocbox.com/Art_and_Technology/68615758-Situation-awareness-in-network-based-command-control-systems.html (accessed 5/21/19)

Zakab, M., Meyers, R., Deacon, K. (2000) Quantum Decision-Maker Theory and Simulation Michail Zakab Ronald E.Meyers and Keith Deacon https://www.spiedigitallibrary.org/conference-proceedings-of-spie/4047/0000/Quantum-decision-maker-theory-and-simulation/10.1117/12.391958.short?SSO=1

CHAPTER 5

AI, CYBERNETICS, AUTOMATED CONTROL AND REFLEXIVE MANAGEMENT

"We are living in a computer program reality"
– P. K. Dick 1977

INTRODUCTION

The following section covers the topics of Computation, Cybernetics, and Control and how they can be used in Neuroweapons that are automated and fully autonomous. To begin it is important to go over the history of computers and how it directly relates to weapons research and how it is a direct outcome of war-time needs and demands for fast and efficient mechanisms of execution and plan formulation.

The great advances in computer science that have occurred since the 1940s were greatly enhanced by the war effort in the Allied countries, specifically the Anglo allies: US, Canada, Australia, New Zealand and Great Britain. The race for computational superiority, which I would argue actually went to the Germans, could have been the deciding factor in the war if the German military had continued access to raw materials such as Oil to run their industries and machines. The early pioneers in this field were in the Allies: Alan Turing, and in Germany Konrad Zuse. Some of the first examples of computer controllers are found in the German military industrial production plants. Some of the first examples of "Machine Intelligence" were a direct outcome of the work of Alan Turing for the predecessor of GCHQ. However, before going into Turing and Zuse it is important to look at some of the more basic and the predecessors to more advanced operations of computation in the form of management of the Holocaust by the Germans, using IBM tabulating machines.

Everyone is familiar with the numbers tattooed on inmates of Nazi Labor and Death camps. Those numbers were an index for the tabulation machines created by IBM for the German Government in 1937. International Business Machines (IBM), an American company founded by German Herman Hollerith and managed by American supporter of fascism, Thomas J. Watson, now popularly the name of the IBM Artificial Intelligence platform 'IBM-Watson.' IBM is also involved in the development of Quantum Computing. IBM manages the information used in the extermination camps and mass categorization of Germany through a subsidiary in Germany:

> Dehomag and other IBM subsidiaries custom-designed the applications. Its technicians sent mock-ups of punch cards back and forth to Reich offices until the data columns were acceptable, much as any software designer would today. Punch cards could only be designed, printed, and purchased from one source: IBM. The machines were not sold, they were leased, and regularly maintained and upgraded by only one source: IBM. IBM subsidiaries trained the Nazi officers and their surrogates throughout Europe, set up branch offices and local dealerships throughout Nazi Europe staffed by a revolving door of IBM employees, and scoured paper mills to produce as many as 1.5 billion punch cards a year in Germany alone. Moreover, the fragile machines were serviced on site about once per month, even when that site was in or near a concentration camp. IBM Germany's headquarters in Berlin maintained duplicates of many code books, much as any IBM service bureau today would maintain data backups for computers.
>
> ...IBM Germany's census operations and similar advanced people-counting and registration technologies. IBM was founded in 1898 by German inventor Herman Hollerith as a census tabulating company. Census was its business. But when IBM Germany formed its philosophical and technologic alliance with Nazi Germany, census and registration took on a new mission. IBM Germany invented the racial census listing, not just reli-

gious affiliation, but bloodline going back generations. This was the Nazi data lust. Not just to count the Jews — but to identify them. (Black 2009)

As was seen in the section on the Science of Neuroweapons regarding Eugenics and tracing tribes and clans along genetic bloodlines, we see how the IBM tabulators were used to keep track, index and exploit these data points for the mass extermination of Jews, Poles, Gypsies, Homosexuals, and Leftists, among others. The diabolical methods created by such a Totalitarian regime are truly mind bending. The more scientific and military applications of the German Computer Scientists followed a more technical rather than sociological route in comparison to this utilization of IBM to manage the Holocaust.

Konrad Zuse is not known to be a devoted Nazi, rather he was known as a dedicated computer engineer who happened to be German and was later conscripted into service. However, it is known that one of his collaborators *was* a dedicated Nazi, Helmut Schreyer, who later went on to leave Germany like many former Nazis and resettled in Brazil, where he set up a computing institute. Zuse began his development of his famous Z-series computers in the spare rooms of his parent's apartment. In 1938 he attempted to create his first computer, which never actually worked due to fabrication problems with the mechanical systems of his machine. The construction of the Z-series computers was oriented exclusively towards the mathematics of statistics and Zuse's encryption engine was never built, it was the S1, a special computer which was used in the Henschel factory between 1942 and 1944 to calculate wing measurements for remote control flying bombs, a predecessor to modern drones. Previously, in 1940, Zuse was able to complete his first working computer, the Z-2. In 1941 he built the first programmable computer, the Z-3. After the war he also developed the first algorithmic programming language, Plankukul (Calculus Plan) in 1945-6.

Meanwhile, in Britain, the more famous Alan Turing started working on his computational ideas, some of which were done in collaboration with Von Neumann, a Germanic Hungarian that taught at Princeton, who was respected as one of the greatest mathematicians of his time. Turing became most famous for his breaking of the German Military encryption Enigma machine. Although, this work was actually pioneered by a Polish Intelligence decryption engineer at the Biuro Szyfrów (Cipher Bureau), Marian Rejewski, who created the first version of the 'cryptologic bomb' (bomba kruptologiczna) before the Nazis destroyed the Polish military and work had to be stopped in Poland. The computer as it became known was the 'Bombe.' The Bombe was an electro-mechanical device used by British cryptologists to help decipher German Enigma-machine-encrypted secret messages during World War II. The US Navy and US Army later produced their own machines to the same functional specification, albeit engineered differently both from each other and from the British Bombe itself.

The initial design of the Bombe was produced in 1939 at the UK Government Code and Cypher School (GC&CS), now known as GCHQ, at Bletchley Park by Alan Turing, with an important refinement devised in 1940 by Gordon Welchman. The engineering design and construction was the work of Harold Keen of the British Tabulating Machine Company. It was a substantial development from the first bombe, code-named Victory, installed in March 1940 while the second version, Agnus Dei or Agnes, incorporating Welchman's new design, was working by August 1940.

Another significant contribution from the British war effort was the development of the Colossus machines in 1944. Designed by British engineer Tommy Flowers working at Bletchley Park, the Colossus was designed to break the complex Lorenz ciphers used by the Nazis during World War II. A total of ten Colossi were delivered, each using as many as 2,500 vacuum tubes. A series of pulleys transported continuous rolls of punched paper tape containing possible solutions to a particular code. Colossus reduced the time to break Lorenz messages from weeks to hours. Most historians believe that the use of Colossus machines significantly shortened the war by providing evidence of enemy intentions and beliefs. The machine's existence was not made public until the 1970s.

Lorenz messages created by a cypher machine (image: Wikicommons)

Another important German computer engineer who came to attention shortly after the war, was Heinz Billing. Billing was heavily involved in the development of magnetic drum memory. This eventually converged in a meeting between British computer engineers and German computer engineers shortly after the war:

"...the question of an unknown potential meeting between the computer pioneers Alan Turing and Konrad Zuse. It is said to have taken place at Gottingen in 1947. Most historians of computing have no knowledge of Zuse's interrogation by Turing. So far, only one source is available which mentions this event, Heinz Billing's memoirs." [other participants include on the German side: Zuse, Helmut Schreyer who eventually went to Brazil, and Alwin Walther. On the English side, interrogators Arthur Porter, Alan Turing, and John Womersley]; after which electronic magnetic drum computing entered English computation designs.

Billing was one of the inventors of the magnetic drum and designer of the first German sequence-controlled electronic digital computer as well as of the first German program-stored electronic digital computer.

Turing worked at the National Physical Laboratory (NPL) developing the modern stored-program electronic digital computer called 'ACE' (automatic computing engine). Oct. 1945 (Bruderer 2013)

Later, at NPL Zuse and Schreyer visited and exchanged ideas with staff from 15 Feb 1948 - 4 March 1948. (Bruderer 2013)

It is interesting that Britain was able to take the work of Billing after the war and create advances to computational abilities. Heinz Billing researched and worked at the Institute for Instrumentation in the Max Planck Society, which was located on the grounds of the AVA in Göttingen and where he developed in 1948 a magnetic drum memory and program-controlled computing machines. Billing mainly used amplifier tubes for this purpose. During this time, he learned about the novel electronic computing machine ENIAC in the USA and its performance. In 1947, an exchange with senior English scientists and computer scientists from the National Physical Laboratory (NPL) took place in Teddington, where John Roland Womersley (1907-1958), Arthur Porter and Alan Turing were involved. In the form of a colloquium, the British experts interviewed German scientists such as Heinz Billing, Konrad Zuse, Alwin Walther and Helmut Schreyer. Billing was confronted for the first time with the idea of binary numbers and data storage.

In contrast to the English, who worked with acoustic storage, Billing from 1948 worked on music recordings and glued on a rotating drum tapes for magnetophones to save numbers. Later, Billing was interested in Physics and was part of the research which was cited to disprove the discovery of Gravitational Waves by American Physicist, Weber. [See Ch. 6 Physics of Neuroweapons]. Also, later in life, in 1967, Zuse became interested in Physics and created what was known as Digital Physics. Zuse suggested that the universe itself is running on a cellular automaton or similar computational structure (digital physics); in 1969, he published the book Rechnender Raum (translated into English as Calculating Space). This idea has attracted a lot of attention, since there is no physical evidence against Zuse's thesis.

One of the tragic stories of the development of computer technology involves that of Alan Turing after the war. After the war, Turing made great strides in developing proto-Artificial Intelligence ideals. In 1950, he created the Turing test which was a theoretical test to see if a human could tell if they were interacting with a computer or a person. If the computer could fool the human it had passed the test, posing as human. He also was involved in researching new computational hardware to support his ideas in Artificial Intelligence. However, Turing was a homosexual, which at the time was a criminal offense in Great Britain. Whether he was set up to cover up a burglary at his residence and where he conducted his research is an open question in conspiracy theories. Nonetheless, it was charged that his lover burgled his house leading to discovery of his homosexuality. Turing's conviction led to the removal of his security clearance and barred him from continuing with his cryptographic consultancy for GCHQ. He was denied entry into the United States after his conviction in 1952; but was free to visit other European countries. Turing was never accused of espionage but, in common with all who had worked at Bletchley Park, he was prevented by the Official Secrets Act from discussing his war work. On 8 June 1954, Turing's housekeeper found him dead. He had died the previous day. A post-mortem examination established that the cause of death was cyanide poisoning. When his body was discovered, an apple lay half-eaten beside his bed, and although the apple was not tested for cyanide, it was speculated that this was the means by which a fatal dose was consumed.

As can be seen by this brief history of the development of computing out of the need to break encryption during World War II, we see the convergence of computation and Intelligence work. Jumping forward, we will see how the British Secret Intelligence Services used computers in the war with the Irish Republican Army.

HISTORY OF BRITISH COMPUTING IN INTELLIGENCE

Building on the earlier work of such great Intelligence computer engineers as Turing in Britain, the United Kingdom started turning to computers for active surveillance and tracking of Irish Republican Volunteers during the 'Troubles' in Northern Ireland which ended some 20 years ago as Neuroweapon computerized Thought Injection was becoming a viable platform for conducting irregular warfare. Ironically Lockheed-Martin engineers used the IRA as an example in their early 2000s research on Game Theoretic Reflexive Control. It is interesting that in 1966, which was also the year that saw the creation of the Ulster Volunteer Force (UVF) in Northern Ireland, which openly attacked Native Irish Catholics starting the 'Troubles', Great Britain developed its first Intelligence Satellite. Later, in 1969, a series of satellites were launched, ironically named 'Skynet', which is also an electronic surveillance system used by the NSA. Though this is ironic in a chapter on Artificial Intelligence and Automated Systems, it does reveal a frame of mind in the British Intelligence Community, of desiring information. The question then becomes how to manage such information.

In Northern Ireland during the Troubles, MI-5 developed some of its first surveillance systems based in visual data: cctv; and managing that data using Statistical Learning algorithms and computer networks. It is easy to see why they would want to use computers for surveillance and tracking with this brief account of what is involved in surveillance and the mass numbers of human agents involved:

> The branch of MI5 in charge of static and mobile surveillance is A4, part of A branch (Operations & Intelligence) in a fast-growing empire that has at least fourteen main departments and many sub-units. The field officers of A4 are dedicated expert people who are often treated as a lesser breed by the desk analysts and policy makers. Foot surveillance is taught to students of MI5 and military Intelligence officers using a drill known as the A-B-C system. At least three people are used to follow the target: A (for adjacent, also known as the 'Eyeball') is nearest; B (Back-up) is further back, preferably concealed from the quarry. Both usually stick to the same side of the road. C (Control) has a wide field of vision on the opposite side of the road, guiding the other two with concealed throat microphone and/or discreet hand signals. A guide for novice trackers suggests: "Behave naturally; have a purpose for being there; be prepared with a cover story (ensure that it fits the situation); remember you are most vulnerable when coming from cover." The guidance deals with distance from the target, anticipation, body language, local knowledge, concentration and teamwork.
>
> Means by which the target is kept off-guard include 'boxing' and 'paralleling.' "The subject is allowed to proceed on a route where there are a minimal number of surveillance officers. The idea is to let the subject 'run' from point to point to be checked at various places [like polling in a video game] by surveillance officers on parallel routes or ahead." Even if new faces are introduced into the surveillance team, close control deteriorates in this form of play. However, "the most important factor about surveillance is the need to be honest about exposure. It is better to have a controlled loss rather than to hang on to the subject too long."
>
> The MI5 technique is manpower intensive. Up to fifty Watchers might be needed to maintain twenty-four-hour cover on a single target. The result was a drive to recruit a large number of officers in a short time. (Geraghty 1998,144-5)

In the early 1970s, to track movements of vehicles in Northern Ireland, the British military used a system of logs which recorded the drivers and vehicle tags. As technology developed in CCTV, the system became more and more computerized. Initially, the logs were replaced with computer terminals and a database. Then in the mid-1990s, the computer system started switching to Machine Intelligence to analyze data. They developed a system of hidden cameras deployed covertly, called Glutton.

> Second only to the informer is the computer or, rather, the array of computers which act as the collating brains of this new style of warfare. In Northern Ireland, for example, the army uses two systems: 'Vengeful', dedicated to vehicles, and 'Crucible', for people. Crucible, one source explained, "will hold a personal file containing a map/picture showing this is where a suspect lives; as well as details of family and past." Vengeful is linked to the

Northern Ireland vehicle licensing office. The two systems provide total cover of a largely innocent population, the sea within which the terrorist fish still swim. Information management is handled by yet another Intelligence Corps team, the Joint Surveillance Group. (Geraghty 1998, 158-9)

Later, a new AI system was introduced called Caister, which was a knowledge-based system to analyze IRA movements and personnel. This system replaced an earlier system, known as Crucible. Later, Caister was replaced by a system known as Calshot, which included AI analysis of data, bypassing human interaction, an automated autonomous system, which replaced an earlier attempt at using AI for automated analysis called Effigy, which was replaced in 1998 with a system known as 'Mannequin.'

Geraghty writes:

Another new Intelligence computer was 'Caister', a knowledge-based system (KBS) to replace the earlier Crucible [mid-90s] in sifting personal information about terrorists and their associates. Caister or its later variant 'Calshot', it was hoped, would be part of a process of analysis where the computer, rather than human mind, identified significant links between one suspect and another. The generic name given to this technique is Artificial Intelligence. Laden with personal files Caister, according to one document, would 'provide dual central processing suites at Theipval (military HQ) and Knock (RUC HQ) interconnected by mega-stream support up to 350 terminals over secure communications bearers. Data up to 'Secret.' Average response time of ten seconds for a single enquiry with 192 concurrent references.'

Artificial Intelligence was trialed and failed at an earlier stage under the code-name 'Effigy', but by 1997, under the code-name 'Mannequin', plans were virtually complete to have a second shot at this project, regarded as vital to a successful counter-terrorist campaign in the future. The key was integration, and an electronic spring-clean of the Military Intelligence cupboard in which, in 1994, there were no fewer than thirty-seven separate computer programs, virtually none of which was compatible with any other. (Geraghty 1998, 160)

Obviously, this reveals the nature of surveillance to Secret Intelligence, in that it is not specific to known suspects but is a wide net cast across all sectors of a society, which was later confirmed in the Snowden NSA leaks. As Geraghty notes:

By 1996, the new culture of directed Intelligence had proliferated like some exotic plant inside a greenhouse in Bedfordshire, new home of the Defense Intelligence and Security School. The system could run effective surveillance on an entire population and, through the use of psychological warfare (reserved, so far, for use in Bosnia), shape popular perceptions of events to suit a military strategy. It gave enormous power to those in charge of the system in Northern Ireland… (Geraghty 1998, 131-2)

It is interesting to note that at that time, the mid-90s, psychological warfare could be run through their computer systems and its AI. Although the claim of psyops being limited to Bosnia and not employed in Northern Ireland is contradicted by historical accounts of such psychological warfare in Northern Ireland (Cadwallader 2013, 328, 348). Additionally, there is a cavalier attitude about such powers held by those in authority. As exhibited by Michael Mates, Northern Ireland Secretary 1991-2:

I never had to go looking for power. This is where Northern Ireland is different. You could have more than you could use…. There's no bloody democracy down there. That's why it works so well. I've never been happier. I had power. But one keeps very quiet about it. (Geraghty 1998, 132)

Indeed, it is noted by the author Richard Aldrich that the European Convention on Human Rights was viewed by the British secret state as a threat to its viability (Aldrich 2010, 485); that adhering to international treaties and laws, not to mention domestic laws would be a 'threat.' To what extent this attitude remains in the human administrators of the security establishment in Great Britain, it is an interesting question as to whether the AI analysis also considers such laws a 'threat' and what it's automated responses to such a threat might be. Clearly, when it comes to security agencies the law is not implemented against their own Intelligence. Professor Bill Rolston in his paper "An Effective Mask for Terror: Democracy, Death Squads and Northern Ireland":

"Although the law was sometimes used against state forces, it was used leniently, even when they acted independently outside of their special units." (Rolston 2005, 21). It is recorded that the Military Intelligence during the Troubles viewed those in civil authority with contempt as they referred to oversight as being 'betrayed and maligned' by 'flabby-faced men with pop-eyes and fancy accents.' (Cadwallader 2013, 322). Going even further than contempt for legal oversight is the outright applying of fuel to the fire to achieve objectives:

> If loyalist paramilitaries could not shoot the fish, they would poison the water. Eventually, they reasoned, this would ineluctably drive the nationalist community to pressurize the IRA to stop its campaign. A spokesman explained the UVF strategy at that time: "We believed, rightly or wrongly, that the only effective way to beat the terror machine was to employ greater terrorism against its operative [s] ... By bombing the heart of Provisional enclaves we attempted to terrorize the nationalist community into demanding that the Provisionals either cease their campaign or move out ... we hoped to crack their morale and destroy their chain of command." (Cadwallader 2013, 323)

This notion of using terrorism by members of the security state are echoed by Evelegh:

> A third military strategist with experience in Ireland was Robin Evelegh, who served in Cyprus during the late 1960s. After service in Northern Ireland, he wrote *Peace-Keeping in a Democratic Society: The Lessons of Northern Ireland*, which influenced later security operations. In his book, Evelegh bemoaned "shortcomings in the laws governing the operation of the Security Forces [in Northern Ireland] to suppress terrorism and disorder" which –if only they could be corrected –could "succeed in ending these horrors." Echoing Kitson [directed psyops], he thought such limitations necessitated civil, policing and military powers being united to "weld all the efforts of the Government into a machine directed at one end, the defeat of the insurrection" – a call, in effect, for martial law. Evelegh supported Kitson's lead on turning paramilitaries into allies who 'have to be consciously created' and then indemnified with immunity "for the crimes he will have to commit." On agents provocateurs infiltrating enemy ranks, Evelegh says openly that the agent should "clearly play his part in terrorist activity which will almost inevitably involve him in committing further crimes." He quotes Lord Widgeryad in a 1974 High Court appeal as also acknowledging this fact. (Cadwallader 2013, 352)

To what extent surveillance systems and their management through Artificial Intelligence could go toward enforcing martial law, or of enabling Military Intelligence to run around oversight is an open question. Clearly, there is a very big opening for abuse of such systems. It is worrisome that the NSA does not consider passive automated systems of surveillance as real 'surveillance'; would this mean that an automated system of thought injection is also not 'neuroweapons' or 'mind control'? As journalist Jakob Applebaum explains:

> According to Appelbaum, the NSA is running a two-stage data dragnet operation. The first stage is TURMOIL, which collects data traffic passively via satellite and cable taps and stores it – in some cases for up to 15 years – for future reference. The NSA does not consider this surveillance because no human operator is involved, just automatic systems." [1]

If the NSA can collect data passively without a warrant, what is to stop them from collecting passive neural data using automated systems? Is full automation just a legal workaround, but one which opens up unforeseen complex engineering problems?

Tracking and Surveillance are not the only areas in military operations that are automated and utilizing Artificial Intelligence. Information Operations is also an area that is utilizing automated and machine intelligence to achieve the aims of secret Intelligence organizations. Many are now familiar with the Cambridge Analytica data breach and exploitation story. Influence operations, a sub-specialty of Information Operations are becoming more and more automated. Cambridge Analytica, a British defense contractor, with many connections to far-right American business interests, such as billionaire Robert Mercer, who made his fortune in Image Recognition in Artificial Intelligence Systems, was owned by SCL Group. SCL Group conducted Information and Influence Operations research for the British Ministry of Defense. As explained by this news article:

> The SCL project was carried out by the MoD's Defence Science and Technology Laboratory (DSTL), which is focused on maximising "the impact of science and technology for the defence and security of the UK."

According to a heavily redacted document released under freedom of information rules, Project Duco was part of the government's "human and social influence" work, and SCL was paid £150,000. The company was also paid £40,000 for work carried out in 2010-11.

The government team, which included psychologists and analysts, worked with SCL in 2014 to assess how "target audience analysis" could be used by the British government. (Watt 2018)

It is easy to see how such a company could be used to further a Secret Intelligence Agency's goals and plans; goals and plans which need not be the same as the democratically elected government. Another troubling aspect of Cambridge Analytica was its complicity in influence operations during the UK's plans to exit the European Union, which as noted before Secret Intelligence viewed EU laws on human rights, such as the equality of the Irish with the British in Northern Ireland, as a 'threat.' Indeed, another company connected to Cambridge Analytica and SCL Group, Harris Media, conducts influence operations for far-right political organizations such as the AFd in Germany, and has a common cause with other far-right political causes.

The Defense Science and Technology Laboratory has as its component areas of expertise such areas as counter-terrorism, under which category in America research into 'Thought Injection' was conducted as a counter-terrorism tactic. Another area of DSTL research and promotion of automation and machine autonomy is Influence Operations, and Cognitive Science. Recently it has offered financial support to researchers using machines in this endeavor.[2]

It is not just the 5 Eyes nations, such as the UK and USA, that have automated influence operations, virtually any well-organized intelligence department of any nation could easily deploy such a system, and not just the bogeymen of Russia and China. So, with such a plethora of potential operatives in Influence Operations one would think the United States would have developed counter measures to such operations, as Maj. Christopher Telley reminds us:

> …the transformation of one industry in particular has grave implications for U.S. national security: influence. AI-guided information operations (IO) utilize tools that can shape a target audience's perceptions through the rapid and effective mimicry of human empathy with that audience. Machine speed influence operations are occurring right now, but future IO systems will be able to individually monitor and affect tens of thousands of people at once. Though the threat of automated influence exists quite literally on the smartphone in front of you, the Pentagon's current efforts to integrate AI do not appear to include any reasonably resourced IO response. (Telley, 2018)

It is noteworthy that the Defense Department tried to create a counter-measures department for Influence Operations, but it was closed down in 2002 by Donald Rumsfeld, SECDEF under George W. Bush, citing public outcry, which itself may have been an influence operation. [3] Although, in late developments it has been revealed that in 2022 the DoD has set up a department, Influence and Perception Management Office (IPMO), to counter other countries disinformation regarding perception management. (Klippenstein, 2023) Maj. Telley calls the automated machine intelligence implementation of Influence Operations, the Influence Machine, he elaborates on the problem with such Influence Machines:

> The crux of the Influence Machine's value is the inherent vulnerability of Western democracy, that decision makers are beholden to a malleable selectorate. as senator Mark Warner noted, "We're increasingly in a world where cyber vulnerability, misinformation and disinformation may be the tools of conflict." By affecting the cognition—the will—of enough people, this machine can prevent or delay a democratic government's physical response to aggression; it is a defeat mechanism. The Influence Machine's objective comes down to changing the value of the target's strategic goal. Clausewitz knew that the political object, the original motive, in a conflict was the essential factor in any deterrence equation. The smaller the value demanded of an opponent, the less that competitor would be willing to try to deny it. This is the inverse of Fearon's "tying hands" findings that the increase of the perceived costs for an audience, a national population, tends to prevent a country from backing down when attempting to coerce an opponent. With automated influence, that opponent attempts to lower the expected benefits, on the part of the competitor's audiences, for the intervention action. The Influence Machine enables defeat before any shots are ever fired by removing "the physical means or the will to fight." in this condition, a defeated state's executive is unwilling or unable to respond to a threat action, thereby yielding to the opponent's will as fake news becomes frighteningly competitive with real news, the emergence of the Influence Machine presents a novel way to "hack" the unchanging human nature of war. (Telley, 2018, 7)

As we have learned Influence Operations are an integral part of any Intelligence Agency's strategic goals and policies. Another area that has developed directly out of Intelligence work is that of Operations Research, which is most closely identified with the development of Cybernetics, which is a direct outgrowth of Operations Research.

CYBERNETICS

Before discussing Cybernetics, we need to understand the parent concept of Operations Research (OR).

> According to the Operational Research Society of Great Britain (OPERATIONAL RESEARCH QUARTER-LY, l3(3):282, l962), Operational Research is the attack of modern science on complex problems arising in the direction and management of large systems of men, machines, materials and money in industry, business, government and defense. Its distinctive approach is to develop a scientific model of the system, incorporating measurements of factors such as change and risk, with which to predict and compare the outcomes of alternative decisions, strategies or controls. The purpose is to help management determine its policy and actions scientifically. (Anonymous, year unknown)

Operations Research began in Great Britain just before the war [WWII] and was involved in the development of British Radar defenses. The Operational Research department was eventually placed under the command of Lord Dowding, in charge of Air Defenses and credited with saving England in the 'Battle of Britain' (he also believed in UFOs). It is easy to see how this is important to a National Intelligence infrastructure. As it is also the task of the IC to monitor its nation's fiscal and economic output and intakes, every IC has a department related to these affairs. Hence, the creation of a mathematically based scientific discipline for analysis of these most important aspects of national Intelligence.

Norbert Weiner coined the term 'Cybernetics' as a participant in the Macy Conferences, an early academic colloquy on automation and machine learning held at Dartmouth College in the 1950s. Weiner worked on controllers for Radar systems during World War II for the United States Government. Later, he was interested in how controllers work in not just radar but in general terms. Cybernetics is a transdisciplinary approach for exploring regulatory systems—their structures, constraints, and possibilities. Norbert Wiener defined cybernetics in 1948 as "the scientific study of control and communication in the animal and the machine." In the 21st century, the term is often used in a rather loose way to imply "control of any system using technology." In other words, it is the scientific study of how humans, other animals and machines control and communicate with each other. A colleague of Weiner was Stafford Beers, who during World War II worked for British Military Intelligence in the area of Operations Research and was a prominent figure in the development of Cybernetics. Eden Medina provides a digest of the interactions between Military Intelligence and Cybernetics:

> British cybernetics, as practiced by Beer, differed from the U.S. approach in significant ways. In his book *The Cybernetic Brain*, Andrew Pickering distinguishes British cybernetics (as represented by the careers of Beer, Ashby, Grey Walter, Gregory Bateson, R.D. Laing, and Gordon Pask) from the better-known story of cybernetics in the United States, which is often tied to the career of Norbert Wiener and Wiener's military research at MIT during the Second World War. Pickering notes that British cybernetics was tied primarily to psychiatry, not military engineering, and focused on the brain. (Medina 2005, 36)
>
> Psychiatry and military engineering were not separate domains in the postwar era, and work in cybernetics spanned both fields in the U.S. and British contexts. For example, the British cybernetician Gordon Pask received fifteen years of funding for his work on decision making and adaptive training systems from the U.S. Office of Navy Research. Military funding also supported the work of psychologists such as George Miller, who promoted the use of cybernetic ideas and information theory in psychology. (Medina 2005, 36, Note 45)

The modeling of cybernetics on the Nervous System of vertebrate animals was done explicitly by Stafford Beers; in the sense of the brain as commander of the body. This is a biological C2 system (command and control = C2). USAF Colonel Scherrer delineates the relationship of cybernetics to C2 [for similarity to discussion on Semiotic Cybernetics see 'Ch. 4']:

> The cybernetic-system model is the dominant C2 paradigm for nearly all researchers and systems builders and either explicitly or implicitly informs all C2 models (see Figure 5). A cybernetic system is composed of three fun-

damental components: sensors that accept input from the environment, processors that accept the input and transform it, and output mechanisms that take the processed information and use it to change the behavior of the system. The cybernetic aspect of military operations is readily apparent given these operations are a process by which a commander (sensor and processor) directs forces (people, processes/ors, and technology organized into a system to produce output) to achieve comparative advantage over an adversary (interaction with the environment) through maneuver and the application of firepower (output and feedback). The science of cybernetics studies internal and external interactions "guided by the principle that numerous different types of systems can be studied according to the principles of feedback, control, and communications." Also key to understanding the concept of cybernetics is the idea

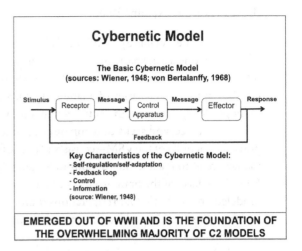

Figure 5: The Cybernetic Model. (Sources: Wiener, 1948 and Bertalanffy, 1968).

of self-regulation. When a system senses a change in the environment, that information is used to adjust the behavior according to the goal of the system. The system then monitors the environment to ascertain if either the internal or external change has successfully aligned with the system's goal. (Scherrer, 2009, 34)

With this we see how similar and intrinsic the study of cybernetics is to military and intelligence command and control. Stafford Beers, however, took this in a more interdisciplinary direction, eventually creating a cybernetic system that regulated the industries of Chile in 1972-73, with Project Cybersyn. Beers is the creator of what he termed the Viable Systems model, which was first postulated in 1972 in Beer's book, *The Brain of the Firm*. Medina offers the following on the Viable System Model of Beers:

> Beers defines a viable system as "a system that survives. It coheres; it is integral. It is homeo-statically balanced both internally and externally, but has none the less mechanisms and opportunities to grow and to learn, to evolve and to adapt—to become more and more potent in its environment." …a system that is "capable of independent existence." (Medina 2005, 50)

The Viable Systems model was based on Beers notion of the central nervous system.

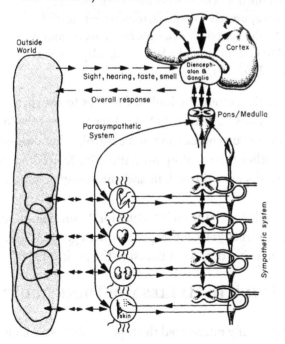

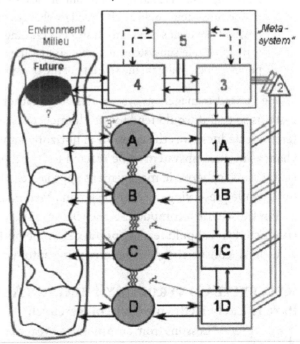

Beers Viable System Model (Schwaninger, 2008)

111

Andrew Pickering explains Beers' view:

> The spirit of the [Viable System Model] VSM is nicely expressed in the juxtaposition of two figures from *Brain of the Firm*: one a schematic of the human body; the other of the firm. Very briefly, Beer argued that one needs to distinguish, at minimum, five levels or systems of control in any viable system. In this figure, System One consists of four subsidiaries of a larger organization, labelled A,B,C,D, analogous to arms and legs, the heart, kidneys, etc. System Two, the equivalent of the sympathetic nervous system, connects them to one another and to System Three, and seeks to damp out destructive interactions between the subsidiaries. System Three-- the pons and medulla of the VSM-- consists of a set of Operation Research (OR) models of production that enables management to react to fluctuations in Systems One and Two--by reallocating resources, for example. System Four – the base of the brain itself – was envisaged as a decision-making environment for higher management, modeled on the World War II operations room. It would collect and display information from the lower systems and from the outside world and, very importantly, it would run a set of computer programs that higher management could consult on the possible future effects of major decisions. At the same time, this operations room was intended to function as a clubroom for senior management – a place to hang out, even when major decisions were not at stake. Finally, System Five was the location of the most senior management whom Beer regarded as the cortex of the firm. Their vision of the firm and its future, whatever it was, was to be negotiated into reality in reciprocally vetoing homeostatic interactions with System 4. (Pickering 2006, 16)

As noted, cybernetics, and controllers or control are intrinsically linked. Beer defined control in a more open sense; for Beer control is self-regulation, or the ability of a system to adapt to internal and environmental changes and self-sustain. This was an important distinction for Beer. Rather than trying to create a hierarchical system of total control, he was trying to create a system that is much more fractal in nature (Medina, 37). Indeed, for Beer an integral component of control is what he called 'variety', citing Ashby's Law of Requisite Variety: for a system to be stable, the number of states that its control mechanism is capable of attaining (its variety) must be greater than or equal to the number of states in the system being controlled, only variety can control variety. Medina has observed that "it is impossible to truly control another unless you can respond to all attempts at subversion." (Medina 2005, 39).

Another important aspect of Beer's cybernetics was the creation of inter-connected components within the system:

> Beer emphasized creating lateral communication channels among the different subsystems so that the changes in one subsystem could be absorbed by changes in the others. This approach, he argued, took advantage of the flexibility of each subsystem. Instead of creating a regulator to fix the behaviour of each subsystem, he found ways to couple subsystems together so that they could respond to each other and adapt. Such adaptive couplings helped maintain the stability of the overall system. (Medina 2005, 39)

He viewed managers as system designers rather than as part of the system, he looked for ways to restructure systems so that it would tend toward homeostasis and desired behaviors. (Medina, 40). Another aspect of the interconnectedness was the creation of horizontal and vertical forms of communication and control. This allowed changes in one subsystem to be reacted to by other subsystems rather than waiting for a directive from the top (C2). Thus, cybernetic management approached the control with degrees of freedom and autonomy of subsystems, while preserving the overall system (Medina 2005, 40).

For those with a computer science background or those interested in how the architecture for AI simulations is conducted you should read **Appendix D** in the on-line supplemental materials at this point, which gives an overview of AI, constructing simulations, using automated planning and other topics of interest to the geek at heart.

REFLEXIVE CONTROL: MY THINKING ABOUT YOUR LYING TO MY LIES YOU THINK ABOUT
Part 1: Early Reflexive Control Research

In chapter 4 "Lessons from an American Weapons Developer" we briefly introduced the topic of 'Reflexive Control' (RC), to quickly jog one's memory, this is the doctrine created in the 1960s by Soviet military planners to enforce their will on other countries or entities by making others 'choose' their positions through coercion, negotiation and manipulation; it was related to the concept of military deception (maskirovka). Understanding the subtleties of the Russians, we should observe the difference between 'vranyo' and 'lozh':

> …it is important to become familiar with the Russian terms lozh and vranyo, two of the most common terms of in-exactitude in the language. Lozh refers to actual lies and total untruths, whereas vranyo is a more subtle term referring to the dissemination of untruths which have some grounding in reality. (Chotikul, 1986, 66)

Indeed, successful RC depends on camouflage and stealth, without which such operations become useless. The starting point of RC is a lie:

> …facts will change this predetermined approach, in which the main aim is to create several alternative truths (instead of one truth), which by their very existence can give rise to doubts. Telling 'tactical truths' and lack of trust between the government and citizens provides a fertile ground for such activities: nobody expects to hear the objective truth from the official channel as people expect everybody to lie to some extent. The observations made over the past ten years show that Russia has, at least to a certain degree, managed to create such alternative narratives, independently of the objective truth. In the long term, systematic information operations carried out by Russia are also producing results: they create uncertainty and suspicion between citizens and the government. At the same time, efforts are made to steer the opinions of susceptible citizens in polarized societies. (Vasara, 2020, 79)

In a later section we shall review the polarization effect of the Boolean Algebra of RC. It is important to understand that the basis of effective RC is to create confusion in the adversary, to trick the enemy from the beginning.

The Soviet Union's military was heavily invested in developing RC for military operations. It has also been suggested RC was first begun as a means of domestic influence in the SU:

> …there was a need for reflexive control in the Soviet society, which prompted systematic research on 'soft' influence operations. This research and the influence operations may first have been directed at the country's own citizens after which they were incorporated into the planning of military operations and the use of military force (Pynnöniemi, 2018, cf. Peters, 2016, p. 4). (Vasara, 2020, 32)

Deception (maskirovka), becomes an optimized tool of warfare under the Soviets. These concepts are ancient – simply read some ancient Asian Martial Arts texts, though they took on a new calculated and computational nature in the Soviet Union during the Cold War.

> The political counterpart to maskirovka appears to lie in the concept of 'Finlandization.' Briefly stated, Finlandization describes a process whereby the Soviet Union influences the domestic and foreign policy behavior of non-communist countries in a way that leads them to follow policies congenial to or approved by the Soviet Union, (Chotikul, 1986, 72)

And of course, we can trace back to Nazi doctrines as originally inculcated by the German Black Reichswehr such as the military doctrine of 'poisoning'- perverting the intellectual space of your enemy or target group. A Russian military planner explains the use of deception in RC, in particular keying in on the tactic of diversions:

> According to Karankevich, success requires a systemic approach in which, parallel to the actual operational plan, a diversion plan is prepared on the basis of which appropriate diversionary moves can be carried out. In that case, the commander must determine in advance which of the enemy's decisions are advantageous to his own side. Karankevich also discusses the use of information technology, which in his view, is connected with the use of reflexive control. He does not only emphasize the role of deceiving the enemy but also highlights the extreme complexity of carrying out deception operations in today's situation. In his view, deception lies at the core of information operations and deception measures must be planned at strategic level (Karankevich, 2006, p. 143).

Deception is a high-level chain of command decision according to Karankevich. As can be seen the snowball effect can become a fixture in the calculations of RC with the use of multiple layers of deception or Shannon Entropy. There are clear similarities between Karankevich's thoughts and Lefebvre's approach to modelling the information available to the enemy and shaping it in accordance with one's interests (discussed earlier). (Vasara, 2020, 48-9)

However, as Russian military leaders warn, because of the use of deception in the method of RC it can lead to a myopic closed circuit of misinformed facts:

> Strict differentiation between methods and the need to find desired reflexions in all actions are additional weaknesses in this approach. This may lead to a situation (which existed during the Cold War) in which the mere possibility of doing something is interpreted as an intention of the other party: a neutral text assumes a different meaning when it is interpreted using the 'methods.' It is entirely possible that these methods only exist in researchers' imagination and their determination to find a deeper meaning in all human activities. (Vasara, 2020, 79)

As one could see, deception or camouflage is a source of Shannon Entropy in the equations of RC. In analyzing the effectiveness of RC, you first need to accurately assess the conditions of your target vectors. If you go against an adversary in RC that appears sophomoric in RC capabilities, it may turn out to be deception.

> Chotikul notes in her report that one of the key findings is that underestimating the enemy and its reflexion capacity may substantially undermine the effectiveness of reflexive control methods. It is also important to understand that a variety of different techniques should be applied, and the same technique should not be used repeatedly. This prevents the enemy from deducing which methods and techniques are used and from developing appropriate countermeasures (Chotikul, 1986, p. 83).

In Russia during the detente between the German Reichswehr and the Soviet Union N. Bernstein was the first to suggest the concept of a reflexive image, which would become essential to Lefebvre's theories, A Finnish military researcher writes of his contribution to RC:

> In 1929, Nikolai Bernstein, a Soviet neurophysiologist, wrote for the first time that when acting in a goal-oriented manner, human brain creates two models: the real world (the model describing what exists around us) and the goal (the model of what will exist around us in the future). Bernstein called the function linking these two models as the feedback arising from the joint impact of neurons and muscles. In 1934, he proposed that the concept 'reflex arc', according to which the stimulus-reaction link moves in a single direction should be replaced with the concept 'reflex circle', in which the stimulus and reaction also move in the opposite direction. Identical results were published by Norbert Wiener, one of the founders of cybernetics, 15 years later. However, Bernstein's theories were not appreciated as they ran counter to the Pavlovian physiology, and in the Soviet Union, he was marginalised. (Vasara, 2020, 11)

V. Lefebvre is the seminal reference in the West and to a great extent in his native Russia on Reflexive Control. As a Colonel in the Soviet Army, he began his first mathematical formulations of RC; he is especially mentioned in connection to the creation of RC in a Game theoretic framework, with Reflexive Game Theory. He also discovered the science of 'Fast Reflexion' which allows one's subconscious to be over-ridden through the Amygdala via a controlling force. Reflexive Control is a sub-science of Cybernetics, which is the study of control in mechanical and biological systems. Specifically, RC grew out of Soviet Military Cybernetics, hence you see in the West the corollary in private Defense contractors. It is important to realize that RC is a part of cybernetics, and as such covered under cybersecurity threats. The Soviet conception of cybernetics, although as a scientific discipline it was refuted as a Western Capitalist conspiracy under Stalin, flourished under Khrushchev. Lefebvre, working as a military engineer in cybernetics, first formulated the equations that would come to define RC.

Lockheed-Martin engineer Dr. Ed Nozawa, who has studied reflexive control in Russia, points out there are two types of reflexive schools of thought, or rather that RC is a subset of overall Reflexive Processes, of which RC is a subset, Nozawa created automated decision-making systems for Lockheed-Martin. American studies dating to at least 1986 have systematically studied Soviet Reflexive Control, Diane Chotikul writing in her thesis for the Naval Postgraduate School notes the dual nature of Reflexive Control:

> In addition to being made up of two components—the psychological and cybernetic—reflexive control theory has other dual aspects. For one, it [can] be conducted in two ways: 1. reflexive control through transformation [of] the enemy's information processing (cognitive), and 2. reflexive control by selecting the messages (informational). Furthermore, reflexive control can be of two types: 1. constructive reflexive control in which the enemy

is influenced to voluntarily [consciously or unconsciously] make a decision favorable to the controlling ... or 2) destructive reflexive control in which means are employed to destroy, paralyze, or neutralize the procedures and algorithms of the enemy's decision-making processes. These varied aspects and applications of the theory add to its range and potential effectiveness, as well as to the difficulty of discerning it in use. (Chotikul, 1986, 81-2)

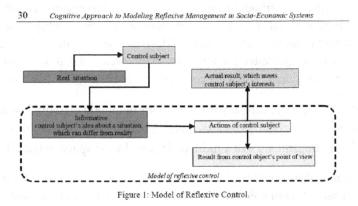

30   *Cognitive Approach to Modeling Reflexive Management in Socio-Economic Systems*

Figure 1: Model of Reflexive Control.

(Shemayev, 2007)

Constructive RC is also sometimes referred to as Creative RC. The mathematics of RC is expressed in Boolean Algebra, usually working with sets. Most RC methodologies incorporate the typical cybersecurity divisions of Red and Blue, Red attacks, Blue defends against attack. The algebra that Lefebvre created is expressed mathematically below, where the calculations become more complex in the case when a subject under control may realize they are being manipulated, even to the point of playing the Reflexive Game to their advantage if they have sufficient knowledge of the situation.

1. transferring false information about the real situation
$$\pi_y x \rightarrow \pi_y$$

2. creating a goal for the opponent
$$\mu_y x \rightarrow \mu_y$$

3. creating the doctrine for the opponent
$$\Delta_y x \rightarrow \Delta_y$$

4. transferring a decision
$$P_y x \rightarrow P_y$$

5. transferring an image of the stage
$$\mu_y x \rightarrow \pi_y x \rightarrow \pi_y \rightarrow \mu_y$$

6. the transformation $\pi_y xy \rightarrow \pi_y x$

7. the transformation $\mu_y xy \rightarrow \mu_y x$

8. the transformation $\Delta_y xy \rightarrow \Delta_y x$

9. the chain $\mu_y xy \rightarrow \pi_y xy \rightarrow \pi_y x \rightarrow \mu_y x$

10. neutralization of an opponent's deductions

When the rank of reflection (reflexive control ability/skill) is raised, these more complicated transformation chains can be used.

Lefebvre's equations for Reflexive Control.

Chotikul goes into the history of the development of Lefebvre's ideals regarding RC:

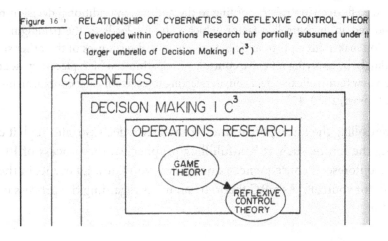

Figure 16 : RELATIONSHIP OF CYBERNETICS TO REFLEXIVE CONTROL THEORY
(Developed within Operations Research but partially subsumed under the larger umbrella of Decision Making I c³)

CYBERNETICS

DECISION MAKING I C³

OPERATIONS RESEARCH

GAME THEORY

REFLEXIVE CONTROL THEORY

Cybernetics was initially developed by the Soviets at the First Computer Center of the Ministry of Defense. One of the major tasks of the institute during the early 1960s was to develop methods of optimization of the decision-making process. Lefebvre worked in a sub-unit of the institute developing algorithms for the automation of computers, under the leadership of Colonel Tkachenko. In 1963, Lefebvre proposed a different approach to the problem from the game theory methods being employed by the other scientists involved. He proposed that there was a need to organize a special 'modeling system' consisting of three subsystems: 1. a unit to simulate one's own decisions, 2. a unit to simulate the adversary's' decisions, and 3. a decision-making unit. In response to criticisms that the principle of guaranteed results must be followed and that decisions must be independent of the decisions of the adversary, he suggested the concept of reflexive control. (Chotikul, 1986, 86-89)

Although RC work was begun by the military it was not immediately classified or taken into a covert layer of official defense work. However, a few short years after Lefebvre began formulating this concept it was taken by the KGB and according to Lefebvre became part of a hidden classified workspace in the KGB:

In 1968, a KGB agent named Panov published a classified report of Lefebvre's work, and it is rumored that the KGB Organized its own laboratory of reflexive studies. According to Lefebvre himself, the theory of reflexive control became a classified subject shortly following the publication of Panov's report, which lends support to the viewpoint that it is considered an extremely valuable concept by the Soviet leadership. Military interest heightened with the publication of K.V. Tarakanov's book, *Mathematics and Armed Conflict* in 1974, and particularly with Druzhinin and Kontorov's '*Problems of Military Systems Engineering*' in 1976. These highly ranked officers of the Soviet Army's General Headquarters claim that it is widely used in pedagogical, political, diplomatic and administrative activities. In military affairs, they discuss the excellent results reflexive control engenders in the training and control of troops and the development of effective leadership, in addition to the obvious goal of control of the adversary. (Chotikul, 1986, 90)

TWO TIERED RC

To focus more on the dual nature of RC, the cognitive and the informational approach is a good way to understand the underlying theories of RC and its combination with real world maneuvers. It is important to understand that along with exerting influence on minds and providing information to deceive, there is also the tandem actions of troop management along with RC deployments. In 1984, Lefebvre presented the concept of two different ways of exerting control for the first time: the cognitive way, in which the aim was to change the processing of the information possessed by the enemy; and the informational approach, in which the messages conveyed to the enemy were selected. (Vasara, 2020, 38). In the first model, the aim is to influence the known cognitive dissonance of the adversary, while in the second model, the enemy is provided with selective information. (Vasara, 2020, 48). Another factor in RC is its longitudinal nature; that is, it is a long term 'long war' campaign according to western theoreticians Giles, Seaboyer and Sherr, the author decided to divide reflexive control into long-term constructive methods and short-term destructive methods that are applied in different ways. As a result, no limits have been set for the time span of reflexive control. (Vasara, 2020, 79). The main object is to create reflexive decisions in an adversary, that are in harmony with your intentions or goals. Reflexive Decisions are conveyed by Vasara:

'From Prediction to Reflexive Control.' According to the authors, in traditional decision-making theories, the adversary is considered an uncontrolled factor, which naturally leads to the paradigm of anticipation. This means that a decision maker attempts to anticipate the potential responses of the other side in different situations. Correspondingly, by applying reflexive control, anticipation can be replaced by defining the future. The authors introduce a new term, reflexive decision, in referring to decisions that contain an informational message for the other side. (Vasara, 2020, 47)

RC is a means of controlling the future, orchestrating a reflexive decision, although it can also have deleterious effects from controlling the future, such as 'self-fulfilling prophecies', the process of RC is to predetermine the future, which may have unforeseen consequences since unless you know all events in the future you may end up engineering a bad result for yourself. As a RC theoretician notes regarding the process of controlling foresight or the future:

How does foresight become a "guide to action"? Foresight is committed to achieving by all parties involved *consensus* on the "vision of the future." Since, from the participants' point of view, the final option is chosen as the *best of set of all possible*, then deviations from it, generally speaking, anyone not beneficial. Respectively, every starts focus on this image and make efforts to ensure that exactly this version of the future was realized. This means that in that the extent to which it was possible to involve all or most stakeholders, starts up the mechanism of "self-fulfilling prophecies " (Nikateav, 2011)

The curating of futures is no easy task. It involves the calculated understanding of your adversary, especially their psychology, including 'information ambushes' as written about by military planner Chausov.

> According to Chausov, the pervasive nature of information technology, especially in command-and-control systems, is a factor facilitating the use of reflexive control. This allows one's own side to infiltrate the enemy's information networks, filter information, block or restrict network access, set up 'information ambushes' and traps, distort information or replace information with lies. The capacity to create value-based models of the way in which enemy leaders behave is especially important. These models are compilations of behaviour, thoughts and emotions. Such activities can be carried out by broadcasting fabricated (but correctly presented) information directed against military and political leadership. At the same time, high-ranking officials are urged to betray their own country. This helps to create public support for one's own cause and weaken the adversary's will to fight. (Vasara, 2020, 49)

Chausov's war is a war over behavior, thoughts and emotions. It may sound funny to break war down into a soap opera, but indeed that is the base underlying RC and Information Warfare, or combined Neuro-warfare. The method used in RC to attack the psyche of the adversary is that of simulacrum, or targeted images, which can also be textual, into the mind of the adversary. The Russian military planners have based their ideal of simulacra ('influence images') on that of a sign, or what we know from Dr. John Norseen and Lockheed et al, that of the Semiotic (signs), the simulacra is a sign, a message. These signs can be from many different sensory inputs: images, thoughts, text, PR, Social Media, etc. Makhnin, a Russian enthusiast of simulacra has provided a basic outline of these methods:

> With simulacrum, Makhnin refers to a stimulus arising from simulated influence produced by a reflexive system. Based on these stimuli, the adversary's battle system produces decisions and provides the system exerting reflexive control with the understanding that it needs to achieve its own goals. Organization of reflexive processes between battle systems manifests itself in the development and carrying out of measures (sending simulacra) that provide the controlled system with areas of interest, motivation and reasons as a result of which the controlled system makes decisions that are in the interests of the controlling system (Makhnin, 2013b, p. 34). (Vasara, 2020, 53)

Makhnin has three inputs into the Influence or RC Machine or System. 1. Real Objects, 2. Information Objects, 3. Psychological Objects.

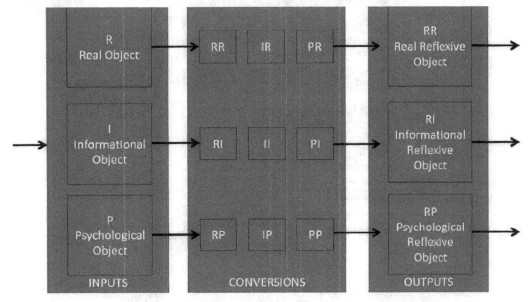

Figure 5: Reflexive conversion of inputs (Makhnin, 2012)

In accordance with the figure above, different ways of producing variations can be defined. Makhnin presents the variations of real-world objects, information world objects and variations of psychological impacts and the resulting categories of simulacra. By doing this, he expands the concept of reflexive control beyond the concept of information operations. (Vasara, 2020, 54)

In Makhnin's view, the key elements of reflexive influence are as follows: 1) the inputs creating the influence; 2) order of the inputs; and 3) the procedures used to create information packets. The fourth important thing is to identify the reflexive techniques used by the enemy and against which protective measures must be taken. Like Lefebvre et al., Makhnin also identifies two different principles for applying reflexive control: the first principle is to use predetermined simulacra so that the enemy can be induced to select the desired line of action. The second principle is to use simulacra with a vague chain of action [suggestibility not pre-definement]. This means that the enemy uses the information as a basis for its own action and can choose between a number of different options. One must be able to shape one's own action on the basis of the option selected by the enemy. (Vasara, 2020, 54) According to Makhnin, reflexive actions are at their most effective when replacing rational stereotypic algorithms with entirely new methods and tactics to take the enemy by surprise. Likewise, reflexive actions can disorient the adversary's command and control system by paralyzing its components, one by one. (Vasara, 2020, 55)

Combining Lefebvre's theory and the ideas of Makhnin described above, Kazakov and Kiryushin note that in Makhnin's view, key to reflexive control is the chance to generate influences preventing the enemy from using new information, to paralyze the enemy's creativity and to prevent the enemy from making full use of its combat potential. They note, however, that it is equally important for a researcher of reflexive control to identify the messages essential to reflexive control (the information packets used by the enemy as a basis for its decision-making). Like Makhnin, they recommend that the term 'simulacrum' should be used. In their view, it provides an adequate theoretical basis for the information packets used for deceptive purposes. They note that such information packets should be divided into two general models: representational and non-representational. A representational information packet is a copy of a copy (pretending to be the real thing). In the context of reflexive control, such information packets are used when one wants to conceal one's intentions. The information is partially false but its sole purpose is to conceal the real information and to deceive the enemy A non-representational information packet, on the other hand, does not pretend to be a copy of a real thing. Its purpose is to act as a cover for the original matter and to convey false information about a matter, action or an event. (Vasara, 2020, 56). As Vasara has noted it is also important to realize that there are two simultaneous processes going on, 1. the RC of the adversary and 2. mission management: moving around troops as RC is running to respond to the outcomes of forcing the adversary around the battlefield based on RC.

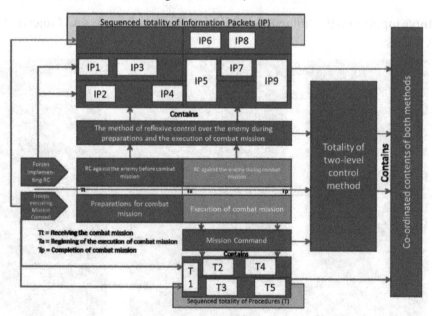

FIGURE 6: Chronological connection between reflexive control and mission command methods (Kazakov, Kiryushin & Lazukin, 2014b)

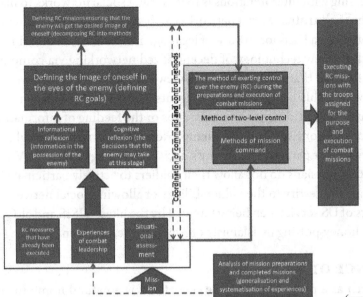

(graph from Vasara 2020)

FIGURE 7: Cycle of two-level control (Kazakov, Kiryushin & Lazukin, 2014b)

The model described above shows that the implementation making use of constructive reflexive control can be based on any of the three inputs. The real inputs are based on the action of one's own troops, while the informational and psychological inputs are based on the starting point or situational data created for the enemy's decision makers that is advantageous to one's own side. Using these inputs as a basis, the enemy is expected to voluntarily make decisions that are advantageous to one's own side and that one's own side has been able to anticipate.

To complement this definition, a model has been prepared on the basis of the sources discussing reflexive control and presented above. It encompasses all aspects of reflexive control, from the methods of exercising it to its goals, using the division Ends-Ways-Means produced for strategy by Lykke. The essential feature of the model is that, in accordance with the ideas presented by Lefebvre and Makhnin, it is divided into two implementations: constructive (creative) implementation, employing procedures aimed at inducing the enemy to make desired decisions, and the destructive implementation, employing methods attempting to weaken and disrupt the enemy's decision-making (Ways). The model also features different types of reflexive control, different forms of control inputs and different methods for exerting reflexive control (Means). The model combines all these factors to illustrate the areas of the military command system targeted for the influencing efforts (Ends). (Vasara, 2020, 62)

> There is one key element to remember in dealing with RC; that is, that without a valid model of the adversary you have a useless tool that will continue to attack phantom targets rather than real targets. This is because the whole concept is based on the assumption that the enemy's decision-making can be modelled so that using specific prepared inputs, the enemy can be persuaded to take the decisions anticipated and desired by the other side. (Vasara, 2020, 67).

As the processes of RC become more and more AI driven and automated the question of a valid model becomes increasingly important. Another important understanding of the functionality of RC techniques is that of targeting the interpretation of objects, in Semiotics the Interpretant (Subject), this can be affected through various means, such as providing false interpretation of scientific data by paying experts to mislead with half-truths, for instance to obfuscate military capabilities. Franke, gives a fuller understanding:

> Ulrik Franke, a Swedish military researcher, has written a study of information warfare, which relies on Russian documents as source material. Like Makhnin, he highlights the use of real, informational, and psychological inputs in the conveying of information. According to Franke, the following measures can be used during peacetime: attempts can be made to discredit foreign politicians; messages can be sent by means of aggressive air operations; or Russian views on the world situation can be conveyed through suitable media. However, as required in the implementation of reflexive control, more importance is attached to the adversary's interpretation of the activities than to the activities themselves. (Vasara, 2020, 68)

One example of messing with interpretations is that of using social networks to plant fake news which is usually not totally fabricated but half-truths. Social networks can be used to influence individuals' behavior and their beliefs and such action provides a basis for the use of legal 'agents.' (Vasara, 2020, 61).

It is telling that with the new technology of decentralized networking via computers that it has opened a new door to operations of RC, and that military planners view the members themselves of these networks as valuable 'agents' even if unknowing. This handling of these agents "can be applied using real and information inputs that mainly comprise surprise/deception by one's own troops or the feeding of information to the enemy's system and decision-makers that creates confusion on the enemy side or is otherwise harmful to the enemy. These inputs are expected to destroy, weaken or paralyze the enemy's decision-making capacity." (Vasara, 2020, 65).

It should be noted that Russians do not allow their soldiers to actively participate in social networks, especially on deployment, one can also testify to the vulnerabilities of allowing social network access while on deployment in the many encounters of US servicemen being targeted by the likes of ISIS and al-Qaida operatives through these networks, for instance honey-potting by Islamists of American servicemen on dating apps.

CYBER INFLUENCE OF RC

Operations Research as a part of Intelligence operations is a natural home for Reflexive Control; the intertwinement of Cybernetics and Reflexive Control is a long held combination, we can even see its influence today in the work of Serge Kernbach, a Professor of Robotics who also studies Soviet remote influencing. Again, cybernetics being the study of control in the animal and machine, it is not surprising that a binary logic such as Reflexive Control grew out of the section that developed computerized algorithms, such as V. A. Lefebvre. As those old enough to remember, the Soviet Union's dictatorship of the proletariat was a hierarchical directed graph. The notion of machine and man is not separate in Soviet culture. We look for instance at Soviet artistic expressions in 'Constructivism' which envisioned the mixing of man and machine, a new Soviet man. It is also expressed in the military organization of the Soviet Union where it was not difficult to envision total automation of military units, for instance we could look at the Alpha class of Soviet submarines with a skeleton crew of commissioned officers only and cybernetic control of most systems. This extended into other spheres of the Soviet military:

> In Soviet economics we therefore see Five-Year and Ten-Year Plans; in the Soviet military, a trend toward a cybernetically based theory of troop control (upravienie voyskami/silami, C^2), and projection for the eventual total automation (ASUV) of the Command, Control, and Communications (C3) System. (Chotikul, 1986, 29)

Finnish Military researcher Vasara drives down into the subtleties of Russian, a nuanced language, understanding of upravienie voyskami (command and control) in his work on Reflexive Control:

> However, 'management of troops' is not the correct translation for the Russian term either. This translation fails to convey the fact that the Russian term refers to a successive management process and not merely to the direct action of commanding troops. 'Giving orders' (командование) is an instrument implementing the directing function, whereas 'management' (управление) implements the action itself. The fact that the Russian translation for 'reflexive control' is 'refleksivnoje upravlenie' ('reflexive management') and not 'kontrol' is also relevant to this study. Management is a dynamic process, which includes both inputs and feedback. In Russian, the word 'control' (контроль) is used to describe feedback functions and supervision. Thus, directing and execution are seen as two separate, though continuous and mutually dependent, (dialectical) functions. (Vasara, 2020)

As we shall read, Soviet and later Russian military leaders viewed the connection of RC to operate in tandem with troop movements which necessitated not only RC of other troops but also as part of mission management to use cybernetics to command troops, as Vasara notes:

> Researchers studying the military applications of cybernetics proposed that computers and cybernetic control should not only be used in autonomous weapons systems but also in the command of military units. In fact, the first information technology centre operating under the auspices of the Soviet Ministry of Defence was the first facility to study automated command of troops. In the opinion of cyberneticians, computers can make more objective decisions than individual commanders because computers do not base their decision making on intuition but on collective information and on a broader operational-tactical view in specific areas. (Vasara, 2020, 15-6)

Vasara offered the following flow chart of command and control with cybernetic reflexive control, noting that #5 is a mirror image of the opposition to that showed in the flow chart as Red attacks Blue and vice versa.

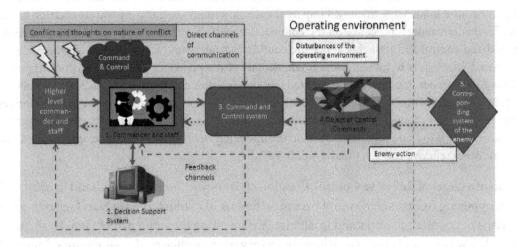

FIGURE 3: Reflexive model of the military command and control system prepared in this study

(Vasara, 2020, 27)

To further drill down into Russian understandings Vasara quotes a Russian General on command:

> Volostnov and Golod put together earlier concepts in their search for the core idea of command and control. In their view, command is an intentional, creative, organizational and a technical process that is put into practice by commanders and their staffs. It creates impacts on the troops subordinated to them. The ultimate goal of command and control is to organize troops for their combat missions and to ensure that they can effectively carry out their combat missions within the time allocated to them and with minimum losses. Secondly, when examined through the cybernetic perspective, all command takes place in a closed cybernetic system, in which objects in contact with each other transmit information in an appropriate manner. Thirdly, the command process is part of the military system. In this connection, the principles defining the content of 'control' are those that define the functioning of complex military systems. (Vasara, 2020, 25)

It is an interesting difference between Western views and the Marxist dialectical view, where everything is interconnected rather than viewed as having a more modular architecture.

At least initially this willingness to trust cybernetics with management of troops themselves and automation of C3 was not shared in the West, for instance while serving on US submarines the main reason our Sonar system was not fully automated was this distrust of machine over human intuition, then again Sonar personnel are known for their deeper understanding of fluid natural situations than a machine could ever be capable of, but the move to Automation became inevitable. Returning to the concept of hierarchical control, realizing we are dealing with Soviet architecture, it is not surprising to see a main controller, the main controller of all controller classes; the concept of 'edononachalniye', one man control (Chotikul, 1986, 61), finds itself even imported to the west later after the fall of the Soviet Union in Lockheed-Martin engineer Ed Nozawa's 'Single Warrior Model' which is a closed loop self-management automated system based on Soviet research. We see it previously, "….to the Soviet view of the leader as 'sole formulator and controller' of group decisions and actions." (Chotikul, 1986, 62). In fact, according to the analysis of Vasara the prime target of Russian RC is the commander or leader:

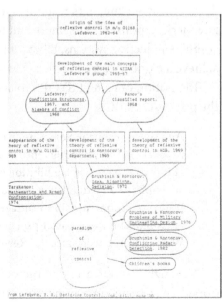

In the context of this study, it is important to identify the potential targets for influence operations in this highly automated command system, which is designed for quick commander-centred decision-making. It can be concluded from the above that the commander is likely to be the prime target and the staff the secondary target. This is because influencing them will impact the whole system (in the same way as exerting influence on a higher-level commander). Influence on the commander and his staff can be exerted through their thoughts (command and control and thoughts about the conflict as background factors), through the plans that they have prepared (the aim is to influence the fundamentals of the plans), or through decision support systems (solutions advantageous to one's own side are fed into the decision-making process). Efforts may also be made to exert direct influence on individuals (especially the commander). Efforts may also be made to influence the command system, even though this will produce more limited results. The ultimate method of exerting influence on the enemy is to cause more disruption in the operating environment. All these options are discussed in the dual model of reflexive control. (Vasara, 2020, 28)

Softening up of a target of Reflexive Control, the subject, is another area that goes hand in hand with RC. In this battle between opposing RC agents the mind becomes the seat of conflict, the Russian Generals are very aware of this both in terms of counter measures and in offense. Vasara citing the influence of Gen. Ryabchuk, "intellectual capability is the key weapon and crucial to achieving victory over a well-armed, well-equipped and well-trained enemy (Ryabchuk, 2001, pp. 14–15)." Another General, Makhnin, reached similar conclusions. (Vasara, 2020, 26). One of the most important contributions from cybernetics to Command and Control in the SU was the creation of decision aides to guide commanders' decisions. However, even with the added tool of automated data mining and simulations, the mental strength of the commander is the key, according to Ryabchuk. Vasara notes:

> Ryabchuk concludes his article by noting that today's military commanders have access to more systems helping them to select the best possible options when making decisions. Nevertheless, in his view, success in the battlefield is guaranteed by the personal characteristics of a military commander, which comprise a high intellectual capability, high ethical standards, and psychological and professional capabilities. When available in sufficient quantities, these characteristics provide a basis for an effective approach to command and control (Ryabchuk, 2001, p. 17). (Vasara, 2020, 26)

For a Commander when dealing with RC and it's necessary cybernetic underpinning one of the key attributes of success is maintaining an analytical mind as well as applying 'exploration' in tactics. Decisions are usually made according to the Recognition-Primed model of Klein which states that decision makers make quick decisions based on previously experienced patterns, without analyzing different options. In such an automated system this would lead to being quickly out-maneuvered. Another mentally weak strategy in RC for a commander is to quickly make decisions, avoid knee-jerk responses which may even be conducted with RC psychological inputs to promote such knee-jerk responses. It is important to understand the systems a commander is faced with, that these systems of complex reflective systems, taking into account decisions made by the adversary in their own actions and try to achieve a higher degree of reflex (Vasara, 2020, 22).

The notion of using PSYOPS to achieve this softening up of the thinking of adversarial commanders is one of the processes of RC:

> And secondly by the Soviet study of the psychology of attention. This academic discipline and, in particular, its research on the 'orienting reflex' has convinced the Soviets of the value of inducing psychological strain and inability to cope through inhibition of the ability to establish patterns. These repeating techniques, coupled with an emphasis on redundancy, would thus appear to be very effective tools in the attempt to reduce risk and create "right conditions' to gain advantage, and possibly even control, over an adversary. As Beaumont has noted, "The cross-links between Soviet psychology, the military and engineering are far more well developed than in the West and have been since the Revolution. (Chotikul, 1986, 76)

Although it is not true that the union of psychology and warfare is not found in the West (perhaps not mentioned due to a need-to-know restriction of the military author), it is important to understand the linkage. On the battlefield, in this case a physical space, the Commander is going to establish full-spectrum dominance; they are going to want to control the terrain, the heights, the valleys, the beach, etc. This is also a part of effective RC, hence the softening up process is also a means of extending dominance of the environment, removing unknown factors or variables, thus controlling even the inputs to the Reflexive algorithm:

> Important considerations for the Soviets when attempting to optimize a decision are: what is the nature of unknown factors, what is their origin, and who controls them. Measures of effectiveness (MOEs) in Soviet operations research take these unknown factors into account in their algorithms, and attempt to optimize effectiveness in spite of them. (Chotikul, 1986, 86)

The Soviet military put a lot of emphasis into Reflexive Control in the 1970s and 1980s; of course one questions its validity considering the Soviet Union collapsed like Nazism, but nonetheless military planners in the Soviet Union and now the UK-USA have fully embraced the edicts of RC. The problem is that in militaries around the world, most will simply mimic each other, as the SU creates RC, then the UK-USA must also create RC and RC counter-measures. referencing the work of Lt. Col. Timothy Thomas (US Army Ret) currently a contractor for Defense Industry Company Mitre Corp, has perhaps the deepest academic understanding on Soviet RC of anyone. Soviet military leader Col. Leonenko explains the importance of knowing RC and applying it to the enemy:

> If successfully achieved, reflexive control over the enemy makes it possible to influence his combat plans, his view of the situation, and how he fights. In other words, one side can impose its will on the enemy and cause him to make a decision inappropriate to a given situation. Reflexive control methods are varied and include camouflage (at all levels), disinformation, encouragement, blackmail by force, and the compromising of various officials and officers. Thus, the central focus of reflexive control is on the less tangible element of "military art" rather than more objective "military science." Achieving successful reflexive control requires in-depth study of the enemy's inner nature, his ideas, and concepts, which Leonenko referred to as the filter through which passes all data about the external world. Successful RC represents the culmination point of an information operation.
>
> So defined, a filter is a collective image (termed "set" [see Bernstein above] of the enemy's favorite combat techniques and methods for organizing combat actions, plus a psychological portrait of the enemy. Thus, reflex requires study of someone else's filter and the exploitation of it for one's own ends. In the information age, this filter is represented by human and machine (computer) data processors. The most important question then becomes: How does one side achieve this higher degree of reflex and, hence, more effective reflexive control over the enemy? It does so primarily by employing a broader range of means for achieving surprise. In turn, it achieves surprise by means of stealth, disinformation, and avoidance of stereotypes [*shablon*]. (Thomas 2004, 242-3)

You might compare the process of Reflexive Control to a normal war, except the battlefield is of the mind, wherein you use various tools for manipulation, intimidation, honey-potting, psychological torture, rewards, pay-off, a combination of both positive and negative feedbacks – even physical violence to steer your opponent to your will, while hiding your true will and goal from your opponent; it is a hidden war. This is all done in an effort to hamper, hinder and sabotage the opponent's decision-making process, time and methodology, to sow confusion at every turn.

Another Soviet military leader, Col. S. A. Komov, has presented the following list of elements of RC in military decision making:

- **Distraction**, by creating a real or imaginary threat to one of the enemy's most vital locations (flanks, rear, etc.) during the preparatory stages of combat operations, thereby forcing him to reconsider the wisdom of his decisions to operate along this or that axis.

- **Overload**, by frequently sending the enemy a large amount of conflicting information.

- **Paralysis**, by creating the perception of a specific threat to a vital interest or weak spot.

- **Exhaustion**, by compelling the enemy to carry out useless operations, thereby entering combat with reduced resources.

- **Deception**, by forcing the enemy to reallocate forces to a threatened region during the preparatory stages of combat operations.

- **Division**, by convincing the enemy that he must operate in opposition to coalition interests.

- **Pacification**, by leading the enemy to believe that pre-planned operational training is occurring rather than offensive preparations, thus reducing his vigilance.

- **Deterrence**, by creating the perception of insurmountable superiority.

RUSSIA'S REFLEXIVE CONTROL THEORY

- **Provocation**, by force him into taking action advantageous to your side.

- **Overload**, by dispatching an excessively large number of messages to the enemy during the preparatory period.

- **Suggestion**, by offering information that affects the enemy legally, morally, ideologically, or in other areas.

- **Pressure,** by offering information that discredits the government in the eyes of its population.27 (Thomas, 2004, 248-9)

As one can see from this list a large amount of emotional and psychological pressures are formulated in the process of RC. One may think that only national leaders or Generals would be subject to this kind of campaign, however, it is noted that this is to be used against even local commanders in military operations, of course to psychologically manipulate someone you have to have solid information about their psyche, the inner world, their behaviors. The predicted responses, the methodology for achieving this psych profile has become increasingly invasive, see Quantum Consciousness chapter for how this is achieved.

As mentioned earlier the primary difference between modern RC and ancient RC is that of technology. Since the creation of computational systems in war fighting with the advent of the computer in combat during WW2, it has also come into play in RC, with the automation of RC under the Soviets, who at one time enjoyed an almost two-decade advantage in computer power compared to the United States in the 1980s; in other words the Soviets had far outpaced the UK-USA in terms of computational and psychotronics in the 1980s but still lost the Cold War. Like the Nazis in Russia in WW2, natural power trumps artificial power, as the Russian winter defeated the Nazis.

The use of big data in RC was first accomplished by the Soviets. Col. S. Leonenko was one of many architects behind the integration of early AI systems into processing RC. He has pointed out,

> …that the use of reflexive control by making it easier to process data and calculate options. This is so since an opponent can more easily 'see through' a reflexive control measure by an opposing force by simply using a computer. The computer's speed and accuracy in processing information can detect the reflexive control measure. On the other hand, in some cases, this may actually improve the chances for successful reflexive control, since a computer lacks the intuitive reasoning of a human being. (Thomas, 2004, 246).

Leonenko draws attention to the problem of involving computer automation in such military operations as RC. He stated, "we live in a much more frightening existence than we care to believe if, in fact, decisions are in the hand of machines that are "incapable of assessing what is occurring and do not perceive that a person reacts to" (Thomas, 2004, 247). Automated weapons researchers also note that computers also do not experience guilt and remorse regarding their actions; it provides a layer of emotional insulation to human decision makers, when a machine is the main instrument of conducting 'wet' operations. In a later section we will be reviewing the automated aspect of computer management systems of Reflexive Control.

SITUATIONAL AWARENESS AND MANAGEMENT

As we shall read later regarding Western development of software that manages military simulations, situational awareness and management is a key to effective military operations regardless if they include an RC component, although it is safe to say that every modern military action includes RC. Managing situations becomes a cornerstone to the understanding of RC. Lefebvre viewed conflict as no longer between two physical armies; rather the conflict was an interaction between two decision-making processes which have a feedback loop onto how the troops are managed and deployed (Vasara, 2020, 34).

Lefebvre's definition accords that the other party gains leverage over the adversary's situational assessment, this in tandem with studying and knowing the highly probable moves of the adversary, it is possible to create an equation of the options available to decision-makers. Vasara notes, "it is particularly important to be able to influence the adversary's situational awareness, his goals or doctrine and to ensure that the adversary does not notice the influencing attempts" (Vasara, 2020, 35)

Of course, this would then necessitate the use of deception to hide one's own plans as well as a random use of randomness to offset the pattern of an equation.

> Major General M. Ionov notes that influencing is possible if the plans and intentions of the enemy are revealed. According to Ionov, the enemy can be persuaded to make decisions that are to one's advantage based on the following conditions: the enemy is placed under pressure; influence is exerted on the enemy's situational assessment, decision-making algorithm, and the way in which it selects its goal; and influence is exerted on the timing of the enemy's decision-making. Placing the enemy under pressure is the easiest condition to understand. Its aim is to influence the psychological state of decision-makers and to persuade them to avoid combat. Disguise, deception, unexpected new instruments, and changes in troops are used to influence the enemy's situational assessment (Vasara, 2020, 36).

As can be seen, controlling the situation becomes one of the key parameters in a conflict. One western researcher has come to the following conclusions on the necessity to have the situational upper hand:

> • .goal setting can be influenced in three ways. One is a show of force to convince the enemy that a goal is unachievable. A second is to demonstrate a threat of such significance that its countering dominates the enemy's goals. The third way is to keep the enemy in a state of uncertainty concerning one's own actions to ensure that none of its goals can guarantee a satisfactory outcome in all plausible sets of events. (Vasara, 2020, 39)

Vasara gives a list of successful tactics used in controlling the situation and setting the goal state:

- Transferring a situational picture to the enemy: in this method of reflexive control, the enemy is conveyed a wrong or incomplete situational picture by means of deception, disguise or decoys.

- Creating goals or a doctrine for the adversary: in this reflexive control method, the aim is, by sharing one's own information, to put the enemy in a situation where its only options are also advantageous to one's own side.

- Transferring the desired decision: in this operating model (which requires trust and contacts between the parties), the aim is to force the enemy to make a decision that provides a basis for action on one's own side.

These three operating approaches are simple models, in which the aim is to directly influence the adversary's situational assessment at specific stages of decision-making. The operating models described below are more complex because in them, the aim is to shape one phase of the decision-making process by controlling the adversary's understanding of another phase. Success in such actions requires extremely good understanding of how the adversary makes decisions.

> - Influencing goal formation by feeding a false situational assessment: feigning weakness so that the enemy can be lured into a trap is one application of this method. This model can also be used by controlling specific 'indicators' identified in advance that the enemy uses as a basis for its decision-making.

> - Feeding parts of one's own situational assessments to the enemy: for example, controlled leaks concerning matters presented as important to one's own operations.

> - Feeding details of imaginary goals to the enemy: the purpose of this method is to shift the enemy's attention away from one's actual goal to the desired goal.

> - Feeding a fake version of one's own doctrine to the enemy: exercises, in which the troops are deployed differently than in the real situation are an example of this method (ibid., p. 305).

> - Modifying one's own action so that the enemy gets a wrong situational picture: in this method, one takes a controlled risk and moves troops to an area from where no attack is planned. The assumption is that the enemy expects an imminent attack.

> - Reflexive control of bilateral engagement by a third party: in this method (which is directed at decision-makers), a third-party attempts to get two other parties into a situation that is advantageous to it (ibid., p. 306).

- Reflexive control over an enemy applying reflexive control: in this operating model, it is assumed that the adversary is using reflexive control, and the aim is to uncover its stratagems and to use them against the other side.

- Reflexive control over an enemy relying on the game theory: in this method, which is based on the conservative nature and inflexibility of the game theory and answers known in advance, inputs in line with these characteristics are fed into the adversary's decision-making process (Vasara, 2020, 39-40)

A WOPR OF A DECISION AID:

In the Russian and earlier Soviet research regarding RC it is noted that automation and information technology greatly expand and also limit the effectiveness of RC. In terms of amplifying RC, the sheer iterations that a machine can throw at an adversary can potentially paralyze their response due simply to the number of automated attack vectors, but for the same reasons of losing effectiveness due to automated detection of RC techniques, the same machines can undo attacks along with making attacks of one's own more effective. This was not lost to Russian military planners such as Ionov as early as 1971:

> Ionov concludes his article by noting that influencing the enemy's operations constitutes a complex logical problem that can only be solved if a large amount of information is processed. This is beyond the capabilities of the commander and his staff and automated systems are required for the work (Vasara, 2020, 37)

Earlier we mentioned that in Russian Cybernetics there is a trust in full-cycle automation, that is, there is no human in the loop of automated management, though still not as popular as having a human commander to reference automated data procedures, as a form of insight or recommendation, which is conducted by Decision Aides. Russian military planners write regarding Decision Aides:

> Tikhanitsev, who works at the research department of the Russian military administration and actively contributes to the debate on research issues, has written about developing decision support systems for automated administration. He notes that in the context of the systems theory, the individual who decides to launch an operation (battle) merely adjusts the control parameters in order to construct a strategy allowing weapons systems and troops to achieve the goals set by the commander (within the limitations set). If there is only one solution to such a system-level problem, it can be determined by means of direct calculations. However, Tikhanitsev admits that in combat troops are rarely in such a situation. If there are not enough troops or weapons, the goal can rarely be achieved with the prerequisites set. In such cases, in order to achieve a solution, new values for the target function (goal) must be calculated or estimated or some of the limitations must be adjusted. In that case, a rational solution can be achieved but solving the equation involves a large number of changing parameters and producing the calculations is difficult. Reaching a solution may prove impossible unless the decision-makers use the capabilities offered by automated support. (Vasara, 2020, 23)

Although it is hard to imagine that human soldiers would just be moved around a battlefield like tin soldiers of competing machines, the reality is that is what warfare has become, whether the soldiers are directly controlled by a machine or still maintain their own consciousness in battle through the thin line of a human commander interacting with a machine, we are confronted with a situation in automated warfare where even the soldiers themselves are mere puppets to an automated system, as we have read in 'Lessons from an American Weapons Developer' it has already been investigated in the United States military of using EM to control soldiers body states and the use of Decision Aides in Lockheed Martin's work on Reflexive Games based on AI POMDP Algorithm competing agents of Red and Blue.

The downside of using automated decision support is that those decisions themselves could be based on disinformation, data poisoning, or just bad math. The article by Donskov, Nikitin and Besedin on intelligent decision support systems for electronic warfare is relevant to reflexive control. In their view, decision support systems used today are typically built as expert systems that support decision makers without them having to take any active measures. In the authors' view, the risk here is that the adversary can manipulate these automated systems with its signals. They note that as systems become more extensively automated, it becomes increasingly likely there will be attempts to control them on a reflexive basis. According to the authors, a decision support system may in itself exert reflexive control over the enemy and protect one's own system against the control attempts made by the adversary. (Vasara, 2020, 23). It is not trivial to realize that any group with appropriate knowledge can poison an automated system, for instance when Microsoft's AI came under attack from a Neo-Nazi-style attack, which trained the AI to produce Nazi-aligned beliefs in its comments.

FAST REFLEXION: OVERRIDING INDIVIDUAL CONTROL

In the 1980s V. Lefebvre came up with a new concept in Reflexion studies – that of Fast-Reflexion – reflexion that happens at an automatic unconscious level, operating at a rate faster than consciousness in the milliseconds range. Fast Reflexion:

> Our view of "reflexion" has been essentially broadened during the last twenty years. Traditionally we have considered it to consist of the conscious constructing of images of the self and others by human beings. Now we have evidence that there is a reflexion of another nature as well. It is as if an inborn informational processor is built into human psyche whose function is to *automatically* create these images together with their subjective domains. This processor generates a specific specter of human responses not controlled consciously and running extremely fast (one-two milliseconds). This type of reflexion, as distinct from the traditional concept is called *fast reflexion* [not controlled by one's self-will, an entirely subconscious process] (Lefebvre & Webber, 2002).

In Lefebvre's Algebra of Conscience, he postulates a pole between liberal "western" values and authoritarian "eastern" values. Which are diametrically opposed to each other. Agents within these two systems are given their position by the pressures from others. An agent creates an image of self and an image of other and even more complex images of reflexion.

> the image of the self plays the role of the subject's conscience, seeing oneself as 'bad' prevents one from choosing the negative pole. (Lefebvre & Webber, 2002, 3)

> Ideally, global theoretical models ought to possess two properties: integrity and uniformity. Integrity means that the model must be able to reflect simultaneously the subject's perception, behavior, and inner domain. Uniformity requires that different aspects of the subject's activity must be described in terms of the same theoretical language. The general method for attaining these two properties is to represent the subject as a composition of mathematical functions. Various elements of this composition are interpreted as "inputs" and "outputs" and as images of the self and of other subjects. These images can have their own inner domain containing images of the next order. As a result, we succeed in producing a unified functional description of the subject's inner and external activity. A composition of mathematical functions is also a function. It describes the subject's behavior. Therefore, the composition's structure reflects not only the subject's inner domain, but also the macrostructure of a computational process generating behavior. In the simplest cases, when the "global" function of behavior is known in advance, information about the mental domain can be obtained from a purely mathematical analysis of the properties of the function. (Lefebvre & Webber, 2002, 1)

Lefebvre formula for images of self and others:

$X_1 = f(x_1, x_2, x_3)$ //values [0,1], describes the subject's readiness to choose the positive pole [willing to be controlled]

$X_1 = F(x_1, F(x_2, x_3))$ //$F(x_2, x_3)$

x1: worlds pressure toward the positive alternative A at the precise moment of choice.[swarming seems to occur at this moment] Normalized utility- measures of the alternative Sets A,B

x2: worlds pressure toward A which is expected by the subject based on prior experience. Normalized expected utility measures.

X3: subjects intention to choose the positive pole. greater the x3 val; greater the desire (compliance) to make the choice.

Function F(x,y) describes subject from his perspective and external points of view [when targeted ignore external points of view since they are all manufactured and meant to mislead]

x – image of the input

y- secondary image 'model of the self' not just subjects intention from which obtain a formal analogue of the macrostructure of the subjects inner domain:

$F(x^1, F(x^2, x^3))$ this structure describes the process involved in the cognitive computation of X:

i. X2 = F(x2,x3) is computed, and then

ii. X1 = F(x1,X2)

So, it becomes obvious from the above that in Reflexive Control the polluting of the 'image of the self' becomes the focus of informational confrontation.

Composition of Mathematical Functions (representation of subject or target): describes the subject's behavior, therefore the compositions structure reflects not only the subject's inner domain, but also the macro-structure of a computational process generating behavior.

The hypothesis of existence of the inner processor for generating fast reflexion can be described as follows (Lefebvre, 1985):

(1) A person possesses an inner formal mechanism for modeling the self and others. This mechanism is universal and does not depend on the particular culture to which a person belongs.

(2) The models of the 'self' and 'other' are reflexive; that is, these models may themselves contain models of the self and other, and so on.

(3) The inner formal mechanism for modeling includes a computational process, which is automatic and does not depend on conscious will. This process predetermines a person's responses in a situation of choice between "good" and "bad," and it also generates his inner feelings, such as guilt and condemnation.

(4) The models of the self and of the other also have this computational ability, which allows a person to model automatically his own and his partner's inner feelings, providing information that is unavailable to direct observation.

Automatized and Deliberate Choice: deliberate – "a person sometimes [probability, random factor] consciously plans and then performs an action as planned."

Automatized – the phase of conscious planning is absent.

Mixed cases are possible in which intention x3 influences X1 but does not entirely determine it.

THE RUSSIAN ALLEGATION OF NEURO-WARFARE ATTACK BY THE WEST

In the chapter "Quantum Consciousness and Neuro-weapons" I review the work of Okatrin, noting a CIA interview with him regarding the ability of remote influencing. Okatrin noted to the CIA that he was only aware of Western attempts at such technological control or mass influencing. Which is probably dishonest but as a member of the Soviet Academic community he would as a Government employee of the Soviet Union disavow any such work. Apparently, this is contradicted by memos regarding official Soviet interest in controlling biological objects. However, the claim that the west is interested in such technology is also brought forward by Brushlinsky's replacement in charge of Russian Reflexive Control Vladimir Lepsky, in his work also claims that the west is interested in controlling the East, that is Russia, through such technology, creating an oligarchy, through a form of 'organized chaos' citing DoD funded researcher Mann's chaos ideals in geopolitics, charging the west with the managed chaotic destruction of Russia. In 1992, "according to Lazarev, the United States uses information as a reflexive control instrument, and for this reason, information security of the state must be given a high priority." (Vasara, 2020, 42)

There is also the work of Sokolov, that claims that the attacks on people in Russia working on these technologies has led to losing such talent to England who are now working against Russia. Then we can also look at the 2015 claim by the Russian Press Secretary Peskov that Russia was under 'Anglo-Saxon' information war as noted by one opinion piece author:

… Peskov also spoke about the information war "primarily with the Anglo-Saxons" on March 26 on the air of the TVC. And, as if by way of illustration, the Kremlin's Russian Institute for Strategic Studies released a report "Foreign media in 2015 - an anti-Russian vector." Information war will write off everything (Sinitsyn & Epple 2016).

If a country is in an information war, it means that the state does not need feedback from society, and socially significant facts are transformed into state significant ones. Their significance can only be determined by the ruling elite; a mobilized society must obey orders.

Yet, looking back in history it is important to note the Nazi plan to colonize Russia and displace the Slavs with Aryans, with those Nazis who were serving to that purpose during the war, then after the war headed to western intelligence organizations set to defeat the Soviet Union. So, the question is whether this is a cultural artifact or an actual reality that the Russians are under a form of neuro-warfare, a soft form of open warfare?

Interest in the west in Russian Reflexive Control is known through the work of Miller and Sulcoski in 1999, who proposed application of a model based on multi-attribute utility function (MAUF) in automated decision support systems. The model represented a chain of binary choices, for each of which its own reflexive model can be built. Taran (2002) elaborated models of multi-criteria reflexive selection and researched conditions that create prerequisites for management of a subject's behavior under decision making. In collaboration with Shemayev (2005) she also proposed an approach to solution of problems of cognitive conflicts modeling, considering the influence of the external environment, psychological set and intentions of subjects. (Shemayev, 2017) Other Americans that have studied in Russia include Dr. John Norseen and Ed Nazawa both of Lockheed Martin. Earlier work in the American equivalent of RC:

> ...the focus in the Western approach to influencing opinions and impressions (perception management) is to steer the emotions, motives and objective deduction of foreign audiences and decision-makers by conveying to the target audiences selected information and indications or by preventing the target audiences from accessing information. This action is based on presenting the truth in a desired manner, operational security, deception and psychological operations. In addition to (or instead of) the term 'perception management' the term 'strategic communication' is now also used in the West (the concept originated in the United States). It is described as a government-level activity in which the aim is to reach target audiences, and create, strengthen or preserve conditions that are in one's own interests. Strategic communication is carried out using a variety of different methods and all channels available at government level. Analysis of the target audiences and decision-makers and of the way in which the emotions and motives of the target audiences should be understood (subjective background factors) is a key component of these methods. In the subjective (understanding) approach to target audiences and to selecting information, there is a need to use a feedback channel: measuring and assessing whether this action is creating the desired impacts or whether the action should be adjusted in accordance with the feedback has been part of the Western way of influencing opinions ever since the Second World War. (Vasara, 2020)

It is important to note a key difference here between the Russian model of control and the American model of control, with the American architecture including a feedback loop to measure the result of the action against the target. The Russian system lacks such feedback loops. The use of feedback loops of this type can be also considered similar to the use of Polling in Video Game design to measure the game state, registering actions and results through an Agent. As Vasara has noted about this distinction:

> This differs from the Russian approach described in this study: in it, the aim is to determine the situation in advance, and to plan one's own action and the sending of the information in such detail that there is no need for any feedback channel. (Vasara, 2020, 78)

It is important to remember that US contemporary influence technology is based in some degree on Russian designs that came to the west in the early 1990s after the collapse of the Soviet Union, such as Igor Smirnov who worked with the FBI at Waco and also had partnerships with former US military officials, such as General Stubblebine. Parallel to the war against terrorism launched by the United States in 2001, Russia under Vladimir Putin was working to achieve rapprochement with the West. In those years, there was more public discussion of reflexive control and reflexivity, and Russian researchers were engaged in close cooperation with their US counterparts. In 2001, Vladimir Lepsky, who had collaborated with Lefebvre since the 1960s, launched the publication Рефлексивные процессы и управление. Between 2001 and 2004, it also appeared in English under the title 'Reflexive Processes and Control.' (Vasara, 2020, 45-6)

The question of the scope of Russian Cybernetics often comes up, with RC being designed in Russian engagements more at the command level rather than the geopolitical level, it is noted by Vasara that there was a sentiment of the US being interested in influence operations for this purpose:

> In fact, the operational level only became a topic of discussion in the 1980s. This was prompted by American researchers who noted that reflexive control is a useful tool at strategic level and that the Soviet orientation is systemic-strategic compared with the technical-tactical approach favoured in the United States (Chotikul, 1986, 35). (Vasara, 2020, 67)

Vasara then cites US Army Lt. Col. Thomas regarding interest in higher levels of control:

> In his book 'Kremlin Kontrol', Thomas notes that reflexive control can be applied at tactical, operational, strategic and geopolitical levels. In fact, for the people behind the theory of reflexive control and for those responsible for its practical applications, the issue of operational levels has not been a prime concern. In their view, it should be applicable at all levels listed by Thomas when used in combination with different methods. The activities should be directed at the adversary's decision-makers regardless of whether they are heads of state, Members of Parliament or battalion commanders. (Vasara, 2020, 67)

Then there is the warning regarding future Behavior Wars, obviously between the US and Russia, which Vasara relates from the 2017 work of Kiselyov:

> In Kiselyov's view, the focus should now be on warfare directed at behaviour. Such warfare has only become possible in recent years as methods have been developed to collect large amounts of data on human behaviour. Human behaviour is not only based on ideas, values, and beliefs, but it is also to some extent founded on stereotypes, habits, and behavioural models. At the same time, our behaviour is also shaped by official and unofficial institutions. Kiselyov goes on to note that there is indisputable scientific evidence that human behaviour largely takes place in semi-automatic mode and is based on habits and stereotypes. In his view, this not only applies to simple solutions, but the effect also manifests itself in complex decision-making situations involving choices that require in-depth thinking. (Vasara, 2020, 69)

Kiselyov then goes on to cite the US as pursuing behavior weapons:

> Weapons influencing behaviour are the weapons of the future, and Kiselyov claims that Western countries, especially the United States, are already developing them. Kiselyov notes that it is particularly important to conceal the personal data of senior officers to ensure the adversary is unable to anticipate their decisions in conflict. (Vasara, 2020, 70)

WOULD YOU LIKE TO PLAY A GAME?

In the 1980s there was a cyberpunk movie called *War Games,* in which a machine intelligence takes the world to the brink of Nuclear War by running simulations of scenarios. RC finds its most effective application in military planning and simulation programs. Games enter into RC thought and remain used to this day in military automated programs for conflict. RC grew directly out of reflections on Game Theory. Lefebvre later went on to create the concept of Reflexive Game Theory, which was implemented in Military simulations in the former Soviet Union. Remembering the cybersecurity Red (attacker) and Blue (defender) divisions we will see how Military planners via simulations and real-world computer systems manage Reflexive Control, including the management of their own troops with algorithms based on RGT. Andrew Schumann, an investigator into RGT, defines it as:

> The notion of reflexive games was first introduced by Vladimir Lefebvre in 1965. A game is called reflexive if to choose the action the agent has to model (predict) actions of his/her opponents. The game-theoretic mathematics for reflexive games has been developed by D.A. Novikov and A.G. Chkhartishvili. Notice that the ideas of Lefebvre are very close to ideas of metagame which were proposed by Nigel Howard. Level-k models are considered in. The difference between reflexive games and any bounded rational approach consists in that, in reflexive games there is a massive-parallel logic [which may not be resolvable, always frustrated] that should be analyzed by the players for winning. In reflexive games both conflicting parties simulate decision making

of each other and aspire to foresee them. This decision making (on the basis of reasoning as well as emotional reactions), which we expect from our interlocutor/opponent, are called perlocutionary effects of our dialogue.

Let us recall that any dialogue has three levels: locutionary (information expressed in verbal or non-verbal exposition of states of affairs), illocutionary (cognitive and emotional estimations of considered information), perlocutionary (effects of cognitive and emotional estimations of interlocutors/opponents). What will be the perlocutionary effects of our utterance, i.e., which decision will be made, we do not know, but we try to foresee them. The situation where my decision processes (cognitive estimations and feelings) are not transparent for the interlocutor, while his/her decision processes are transparent for me, shows that my level of reflexion is higher than my interlocutor's level. (Schumann, 2014)

Emotions, which are expressed in illocutions, are one of the main forms of reflexion. The interchanging of emotions is always a reflexive game, a method of manipulation of others. (Schumann, 2018, 49)

The use of RC and Games is not just limited to the military; it is used extensively throughout the Business and Political worlds. Indeed, the methods of RC are object-type agnostic – and can be applied to many classes of objects:

London et al. (2006) suggested a reflexive capability conceptual model for the individual in relation to e-business is developed which relies upon merging economic and social practices through an industrial organization economic theoretical lens and social science theories of communication. Studies of the reflexive approach in the sphere of market interaction of business entities are developing particularly actively. The researches deal with models of reflexive control of consumer demand, formation of supply chain and dealer network, influence on competitor behavior, seller-buyer interaction during business transaction. Hartmann et al. (2008) used the principles of reflexive control in modeling passive and active social interactions in marketing. Bettany and Woodruffe-Burton (2009) proposed a structured approach to the possibilities of critical reflexive practice in marketing and consumer research. (Shemayev, 2017)

From one such business implementation we could look at the work of S. Tarasenko, currently working for Mizuno Finance, a business of acquisitions and selling, regarding his research into the Reflexive Game Theory (RGT). Tarasenko defines RGT as:

… model behavior of individuals in groups. It is possible to predict choices which are likely to be made by each individual in the group in order to cause this individual to make certain choices. Therefore making it possible to control the individuals in the groups by guiding their behavior by means of the corresponding influence. (Tarasenko, 2010, 1)

The math behind RGT is based on Boolean Algebra and Set Theory. Though some have questioned whether the math itself is flawed in RC and thus never truly workable, we will follow the Soviet lead and analyze RGT from a Boolean perspective, as is the practice throughout the world's military and intelligence fields. It is typical in RGT to assign all members of a population (individual humans or robotic autonomous agents) a unique ID which is then represented on a fully connected directed graph, where each node is defined as either in 'Alliance' or in 'Conflict' with each other node on the graph. It is noted that mathematically conflicts are disjunction (summation) and Alliance is conjunction (multiplication), whereas the influences on a subject are held in a matrix. If a node views another node as a conflict, though the other node views them as 'alliance' the disjunction indicates a conflict relationship, which would always suggest a higher level of 'conflict' relationships.

RGT employs the fundamental principles of hierarchical organization on individuals and groups. To be able to control an entity in the RGT you put them in a group, and then try to influence the target by other group members and adversaries. The goal of the subjects in the groups is to choose the alternative from the set of alternatives under consideration through what is known as the Decision Equation. If one is not able to influence the target's Decision Equation the result is to put the target into a frustration state. Although many targets or subjects are easy to influence, there are some individuals and groups that are not. These are referred to as "Super Active Groups" (Tarasenko, 2010, 15), which would be outliers to the RC theory. When confronted with the inability to influence the subject's Decision Equation the alternative is to put the target into a 'frustration state' – neither a position of safety or of adverse influence.

To influence a subject or group it is necessary to formulate the Forward and Inverse tasks. As discussed regarding changing Brain states by Dr. John Norseen, here in the RC theory it is necessary to re-route the subject with these methodologies.

> Forward Task: a task to find the possible choices of a subject of interest, when the influences on him from other subjects are given. [Target receives simulacrum to influence decisions as well as physical feedback from objects in the environment]

> Inverse [Reverse] Task (Turning): a task to find all the simultaneous (or joint) influences of all the subjects together on the subject of interest that result in choice of a particular alternative or subset of alternatives. We call the subject of interest a controlled subject. [Target abandons own will and submits to the will of the influencing objects giving a win to the Controller; in normative robotics this would result in a successful trajectory or path being achieved.]

Home » Institute of Control Science » Dmitry A. Novikov

Dmitry A. Novikov

Institute of Control Sciences | IPU · Director

.Il 27.92 · Dr.Sc (Techn.), Prof., Corresponding Member of Russian Academy of Sciences

Novikov discusses creating two principals (red/blue or alliance/conflict in our discussion) that set up agents that control the game and make decisions based on RC rules, including the use of 'phantoms' – fake agents – for various reasons like manipulation and disinformation. The winner in the contested space or game will be the one that controls the 'information equilibrium' the best. In this case he discusses controlling economics in a game.

> From the game-theoretic viewpoint, the control problem of an ecological-economic system whose elements can demonstrate a purposeful behavior consists in the following. A control subject (a Principal) has to design a game of controlled subjects (agents) with some rules so that its outcome appears most beneficial to the former. Therefore, a necessary step of such control problems concerns game-theoretic analysis allowing a Principal to forecast the response of a controlled system to certain control actions.

> Reflexive games represent a method of game-theoretic modeling with due consideration of agents' complex awareness (particularly, their mutual awareness). Nowadays, reflexive games have found wide application in the description of awareness, joint decision-making of agents and solution of associated informational control problems (control of agents' awareness structures) in different fields, namely, corporate management, economics, marketing, political science, etc.

> Agents' awareness in a reflexive game is defined by a structure comprising their beliefs about essential parameters of a current situation and the beliefs of their opponents (other agents). The solution of a reflexive game is an informational equilibrium, *viz.*, a set of actions chosen by real and phantom agents (the ones existing in the minds of real agents), where each agent maximizes a goal function based on its awareness. (Novikov, 2015, 1)

According to Novikov the key to a Reflexive Game is the Information Equilibrium whose important component is the maximization of a goal function which is based on the agent's awareness. Alter awareness to a weakened position and you will achieve the upper hand in the Reflexive Game.

> The conducted analysis indicates that the mutual awareness of the members of ecological-economic systems appreciably affects their decision-making. By exerting control actions (i.e., varying such awareness), one can modify the equilibrium states of these systems. (Novikov, 2015, 8-9)

As we have read before, one way of altering the awareness is through the use of simulacrum, which is referred here as "information package":

> In the theory of reflexive games they operate with the concept of an information package, obviously investing in its content:

- a set of gradually or purposefully sent information about their troops (with a certain amount of misinformation, of course!)

- information about the number, condition, staffing level, moral and psychological state (!), etc. enemy troops.

- emotional reactions to actions and other aspects of the response of opponents to the information received.

- intelligence information about plans that have complex informational value, emotional, etc. nature, and specific formalized and documented managerial decisions of the enemy (combat orders, decisions on military actions, etc.).

In such a representation of the concept of "information package," it appears not entirely "informational," but is also filled with emotional and management content. Thus, we believe the concept of "reflexive game" as a mutual attempt to reflexive control of the conflicting parties. In this case, the problem arises of postulating a new term denoting confrontation carried out without the involvement of conventional weapons, directly and destructively affecting a person and military equipment. The specificity of this type of struggle lies in the indirect impact on the military man and equipment in order to organize obstacles to the adequate perception of information and the adoption of correct management decisions.

This type of struggle is carried out at the level of human thinking (which, although it operates with information, is regulated and determined by a large number of non-informational factors), which is the basis of our actions and deeds. As a clarification and addition to the concept of "information confrontation" within the framework of its most effective methodological base – the theory of reflexive games – and in the context of a broader vision of indirectly influencing the enemy and causing damage to the adequacy of his thinking process, we propose to use the term **"reflexive confrontation."**

By reflexive confrontation, we mean the rivalry of the opposing sides for the superiority of the implemented means and methods of reflexive control. In this context of the proposed definition, the concepts of reflexive confrontation and reflexive play turn out to be synonymous. At the same time, the use of the factor of reflexive confrontation is justified for the analysis of military-applied problems, since it focuses on the exclusively hostile nature of the social interaction of combat systems.

> At the same time, the state in which one of the opposing sides achieves success in applying its system, methods and means of reflexive control that are linked in purpose, place and time, we will designate as reflexive superiority. (Kiryushin, 2013)

As a War Game RGT does not achieve Nash equilibrium, it is the opposite of Nash Equilibrium, the ability in games or competition to cooperate where various agents get a partial reward rather than winner takes all:

> Let us suppose now that rational agents are our enemies. They do not wish to help us to reach the equilibrium of our goal functions by means of an interchange. In every possible way they hinder us from having the usual interchange with other players (for example, they use dumping practices so that we will go bankrupt). In this case the Nash equilibrium cannot be reached. We cannot wait for a simple mutually advantageous interchange of goods.
>
> Competitiveness complicates any strategy of reaching a maximal guaranteed payoff. We should already deal with reflexive games in order to evaluate other actors, for example, to reconstruct their goal functions, taking into account circumstances in which they can try to delude their environment concerning the original motives of their acts. The main task of reflexive games is to hide true motives and goals, not to be transparent for others, but to know everything important about them. (Schumann, 2018, 44)

This concept of the 'zero-sum' game with either total victory or total defeat is the end state of the Game, which can become a problem when coupled with the power of Machines to run processes that will far outstrip any human mind. It could also mean that in a Reflexive Game no endgame state could be achieved due to the complexity of the interactions of the systems under study, leaving a cybernetic manager running endlessly; since no end state can ever be achieved, there is no Path to victory for an overly complex reflexive game. Schumann describes this as a reflexive paradox:

It is an example of the *reflexivity paradox*, i.e., the impossibility of defining a true level of reflexion for a successful interaction with competitors. (Schumann, 2018, 47)

One example of the complexity one can be dealing with in trying to compute reflexivity is an example from the equation where red must think about blue at the fourth level of reflection:

$$ThinkA(ThinkB(ThinkA(ThinkB(ThinkA)))), ThinkB(ThinkA(ThinkB(ThinkA(ThinkB)))).\text{(Schumann, 2018, 46)}$$

Schumann explains that the game is to get more information about the enemy, while hiding our own actions in the game:

If at least one agent selects a game strategy assuming a non-zero level of reflexion, then this game is called a *reflexive game*. Its essence consists in finding the level of reflexion n of the competitor ($n > 0$) to move onto re-flexion level n (if I have advantages at the equal level of reflexivity) or $n + 1$ (if I have no advantages) and to act on the basis of the given level. The task of a reflexive game is to have the opponent's actions become transparent for us, while our actions remain obscure for the competitor. (Schumann, 2018, 47)

Accordingly, the victory in a reflexive game is determined by who has managed in most cases to be in dialogues at a level of reflexion n or $n+1$ while the interlocutor remained at level n. The more difficult the reflexive game, the more information we should give about ourselves to uncover all motivations and all predispositions of the interlocutor. There are too many examples of daily reflexive games. (Schumann, 2018, 47)

Agents in Reflexive Games according to Schumann come with four components: preferences, operations, knowledge and sequencing:

- *preferences of agents* (different goal functions and dependencies of their payoff on actions, e.g. when we know that each agent is interested in a maximization of payoff and for this purpose (s)he commits a minimal set of certain actions, and for different agents this set can be different);

- *set of admissible actions of agents* (there are actions which are unacceptable for all in the group of agents, and there are actions which are expected or not expected by other agents, but these actions are admissible for the entire group of agents).

- *knowledge of agents* (at the moment of decision-making agents should be informed, probably falsely, about all preferences of other agents).

- *order of moves* (sequence of choices of actions, comprehensible to all in the group of agents).

Thus, preferences express what agents want, sets of admissible operations express what they can do, knowledge expresses what they know, and order of moves express when they select actions. (Schumann, 2018, 48)

Games can be 2 players or more; the more agents the more complex it is to win.

In RGT there is an implicit understanding that there is a form of mimicry involved in the game, with many theoreticians assuming that players will play the same play as the opponent in each given situation. This is also known in Game AI as 'shadow AI' where a game agent mimics the attacks of the player. This is played out in solving the game according to Schumann:

Insufficient knowledge (lack of common knowledge $K^{in+1}A$) of agent i on reflexion level n leads to an actual vector of actions on reflexion level n that can differ from a vector expected by agent i. For reaching a performative equilibrium it is expedient to follow the following assumptions:

1. The finite number of real and phantom agents participate in a reflexive game.
2. Equally informed agents select identical actions according to reflexion level n.
3. The rational behavior of agents consists in that each of them aspires to maximize a goal function by a choice of appropriate actions, predicting which actions other agents will choose as rational agents from the point of view of knowledge of reflexion level n about other agents.

In case a reflexive game is carried out between agents belonging to the same organization (corporation, company, institute), success in a reflexive game can be reached by a purposeful modification of some components [structures, 'change the group'] of a controlled system. Such   a modification for the guaranteed victory in a reflexive game is called *reflexive management*.

The principal kinds of reflexive management are as follows:

- *institutional management* (modification of admissible sets of actions of all groups of agents).
- *motivational management* (modification of goal functions of concrete agents).
- *informational management* (modification of information which agents use in decision making).

Informational management refers to the following kinds:

- *informational regulating* (purposeful influence on information about states of affairs).
- *expert management* (purposeful influence on information about models of decision making).
- *active prognosis* (purposeful spread of information about future values of parameters depending on states of affairs and actions of actors).

The task of reflexive management is formulated as follows: a controlling organ creates a knowledge structure of agents in a way such that a performative equilibrium satisfies the centre's goals (maximally favourable for this centre.) Management of an opponent's decision-making can be carried out by means of suggestions to him/her of some foundations from which (s)he could logically infer decisions favourable to us. Such a process of suggesting foundations for an opponent's decision-making is called reflexive management. Reflexive management can be performed by means of saying false information about a state of affairs (creation of false objects), by means of suggesting an opponent's purposes (provocations and intrigues, acts of terrorism and ideological diversions), or by means of suggesting decisions (false advice). (Schumann, 2018, 50)

In an interesting point regarding structure, whether an organization should be centralized or decentralized, Schumann makes the point that decentralized organizations provide more complex reflexive games and through these games, probably through constant refinement between the different moving parts, a higher efficiency is gained because of the interactions.

The system, in which there is a delegation of powers, where the decision-making process is distributed throughout the entire system of management, is more rational than the centralised system. The higher tasks of organization are divided into many more detailed tasks for which solutions specific employees are responsible. Hence, each employee (1) surely knows what action (s)he is responsible for; (2) knows what resources (s)he can use independently and in what cases (s)he can ask the manager about additional resources; (3) knows how outcomes of activity are evaluated and knows the method of reward for success. These conditions provide the system with complex reflexive games, making the system more stable performatively (Schumann, 2018, 51)

Having seen how reflexive games can be applied to economic and organizational structures it is also informative to analyze how a Reflexive Game is compiled for specifically military purposes. In a prototypical military simulation using Reflexive Gaming the Russian military research community has come up with one algorithmic depiction of such a game.

Rulko, Gertsev and Buloychik have set out the purpose of using mathematical models such as reflexive control for combat simulations:

…any specific battle is a unique, isolated phenomenon …and is special, making this fight different from another. Therefore, on the one hand, the mathematical model should reflect the most general patterns of the modeled processes and its capabilities should allow taking into account changes in goals, objectives and conditions of combat operations. On the other hand, with its help it should be possible to make studies of the influence of the characteristics of a specific situation and specific decisions, taken by the warring parties. The essence of such studies is in reproducing the commander's reasoning about the degree of influence of various parameters setting and quantifying this impact. Assuming reasonable behavior [of an] adversary, it is advisable to carry out such reasoning for him and also evaluate their influence.

Thus, the success in organizing a particular battle largely depends on the skill of the commander to try to side with the enemy, to analyze the course of his thoughts, to understand his possible further actions, to predict their result and thus be able to act in anticipation, outsmarting it, to form in him false ideas about the real state of affairs by using masking (maskirovka, маскировки) or demonstrating false intentions (сформировать у него ложные представления о реальном положении дел путем использования маскировки или демонстрирования ложных намерений).

In addition, in itself such a two-way process of analysis can provide additional information for thought about the best option for their actions in a combat, continuously changing situation. For a formal description of this type of mental activity of commanders of the opposing sides, the closest in fact is the apparatus of the theory reflexive control (hereinafter – TRU) рефлексивного управления (далее – ТРУ). As a rule, reflexive control means the use of results imitating reasoning for the opposing side in the course of making your own decisions and the impact on the process of making its (the opposing party's) decisions by forming in her the necessary (as a rule, false about us) idea of setting. The solution obtained in this way can be used for repeatedly imitating the reasoning of the enemy, taking into account the fact that this decision to one degree or another the enemy knows. In this regard, the concept of the rank of reflection is introduced. (Rulko, 2017)

The purpose is to plan for battle, as well as play out possible scenarios for RC. However, without quantitative tools to measure the effectiveness of such influence one could be left in the lurch and deceiving oneself about the adequacy of the models used for behavioral modification of a target. Of course, again we are in awareness (perception) management which, according to the authors:

by managing intelligence processes and protection of information (extraction of someone else's or hiding their information) and the process disinformation of the enemy, we can influence the decisions he makes. However, until now since then there was no possibility of a quantitative assessment of the effectiveness of such an influence, which is essentially the basis for the reflexive control of the enemy. In this sense, the application of the SM developed by us is of interest. In [4], it is shown that the maximum appropriate rank of the reflexive management, which today should be considered when making decisions, is equal to two. When the chain of reflexive reasoning that needs to be reproduced looks like: "Determine what the enemy thinks about my behavior, based on this make a decision for him, then on the basis of the information received to make his own decision. "Quantitative accounting for higher ranks of reflection is a formalization "Significant tricks." He is fraught with the danger of "outsmarting himself" and today it is difficult to implement, since it will require much more complex and accurate predictive models of simulated processes and highly adequate models "Intellectual abilities" of specific decision-makers (commanders of warring parties). And there are no such models yet. Moreover, on a tactical level of decision-making, as a rule, there is no information on the enemy commander, necessary for modeling his mental activity.

In this sense, it should be noted that in an example of constructing a model behavior of Saddam Hussein, obtained from the results of many years of observation, the use of such a model made it possible to quickly achieve success in the operation. (Rulko, 2017, 156-7)

It is interesting to note that Rulko et al put the limit of nested reflexive processes at 2 levels and that quantitative accounting for higher reflection levels would need 'significant tricks' and the operator of such tricks is in danger of 'outsmarting himself.' The system that Rulko et al came up with to simulate these rounds uses the standard Red vs. Blue architecture.

Consider an example of choosing behavior alternatives by Red and Blue using simulation of the process of their confrontation on the developed SM. Let, according to the results of battle planning, the Reds (we) have three (n = 3) behavioral alternatives given in the form of appropriate behavior strategies (Table 1). The Reds also have some information about the Blue (enemy) and non – which probability can suggest their possible steps in the form of four alternatives (m = 4). In this case, these are alternatives; figuratively speaking, a phantom agent, existing in the minds of the Reds. It is obvious that the degree of their identity with the real behavior is determined by the degree to which the Reds are aware of their opponent.

Blue, with some information about Red, will also build a system of assumptions about their behavior and choose their strategy under the influence of how the Reds will act from their point of view. (Rulko, 2017, 157)

The Red and Blue forces are given standard options of defense and offense in a typical infantry conflict. To calculate the various parameters of action and counteraction Rulko et al introduce some math:

It is obvious that each of the possible alternatives of the parties corresponds to a certain preference – the probability of its choice (choice of a given scenario of the development of events).

Let's introduce the notation:

Pxyi(j) *is the* preference of the *j* -th option of actions of the side *x* in relation to the one *y* at the *i* -th rank of reflexive control.

For our example, you can write:

PKCu(j) *the* preference of the *j* -th, *j* = 1, 2, 3, option for Red's actions with respect to blue at the zero rank of reflexive control (when, as a rule,

PCKi(j) the alternatives are equally likely); preference of the *j* -th, *j* = 1, 2, 3, 4, option of Blue's actions (phantom agent) in relation to Reds at the first rank of reflexive control, etc.

For a specific solution of one side with the chosen option behavior, another simulation system allows you to obtain values by selected indicators of the effectiveness of each side of its combat mission: losses at a given moment in time, the line reached by one of the parties at that moment in time, time of holding the boundary, etc. Given that there can be many such possible behaviors, for their comparative assessment, we introduce an indicator characterizing the effectiveness of actions by one side for a given variant of behavior of the other $\rho x \in [-1; 1]$ and obtained by simulation results. Here, the index *x* defines the affiliation of the party, relative to which the indicator is calculated: ρC for the Blue side and ρK – for the Red ones.

Moreover, their extreme values -1 and 1 – correspond to the least and most favorable outcomes.

A measure of the effectiveness of behaviors is set up with values -1 and 1 and then this is run against the possible variants of behavior giving the effectiveness of actions.

The authors give the following simulated scenario:

Another example of synthesizing an expression for calculating the value of the exponent ρx. Let it be the combat mission of the Blues (they are on the offensive) is to occupy the L C line, and the Reds (in both Rhône) - to prevent the achievement of a milestone Blue L K. We denote:

Δ L C - depth of penetration of Blue;

Δ L K - the depth of holding the line by the Reds.

From these and other calculations they are able to quantify the appropriate strategies in the Reflexive Game.

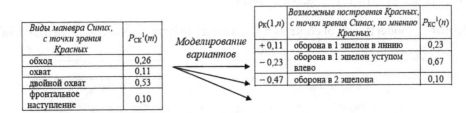

Рисунок 2. – Оценка показателя сравнительной эффективности для маневра Синих (с точки зрения Красных) «обход»

(Figure 2. - Assessment of the indicator of comparative efficiency for the BLU maneuver (in terms of Red) "bypass")

It is interesting to see how the concepts of RGT can be employed in combat. The boolean red and blue games could also be extended into other areas as previously noted, such as geopolitics, which of course we did portray during the cold war as Blue vs. Red. It is interesting to note that in this game of Rulko et al, Blue is attacking and Red is defending; again we see the Russian psychology of being on the defense against the West.

REFLEXIVE CONTEMPORARY TOPICS:

In the previous section we have delved into the basics of Reflexive Control and Reflexive Game Theory. The research that was done in the 1960s and into the 2000s was conducted by one generation which has given way to a new generation, with such authors as Tarasenko and Shemayev extending the work of Lefebvre, and Novikov as well. In the following section we shall be reviewing some recent developments of RC to see how it is becoming extended and in what direction research in this field is leading.

The first research to cover is that of Shemayev and the synthesis of RC with Cognitive Mapping.

REFLEXIVE CONTROL BECOMES COGNITIVE

The initial ideas regarding the use of cognition were written about by Chotikul in the US in 1986. According to Vasara, RC could be used to exert influence on the adversary's activities, and it could be applied if the adversary's cognitive map was thoroughly understood. In this case, objective observations of the situation made by the adversary could be modified without the adversary noticing anything. To achieve the situation described above, the attention should be on psychological aspects and subjective factors characteristic of the adversary. (Chotikul, 1986, p. 79). (Vasara, 2020, 35-6)

From 2007 in the former Soviet Republic of Ukraine Shemayev has written of a synthesis of cognitive modeling and RC. Volodymyr Shemayev is head of the Department of Economics and Finance of the National Defense Academy of Ukraine, Kyiv. His scientific interests include Reflexive Control, Information Security, Defense Planning and Budgeting, and Ukraine's Integration to NATO. Shemayev writes:

> Another approach to modeling socio-economic systems is cognitive modeling. Cognitive modeling based on fuzzy cognitive maps is considered to be one of the best ways to formalize control processes in social-political and economic systems. Such a mathematical model allows both to analyze the situation in-system and to synthesize a control strategy. (Shemayev, 2007)

Formally, the task of information control can be presented with the following relation:

$$\Phi(t) = \Psi(D(F,W,M), G(t), X(t), U(t)),$$

where
- D(F,W,M) represents the structure of the situation;
- G(t) – the set of objectives;
- X(t) – the set of situation conditions;
- U(t) – the set of controls

Then, U*(t) is the rational (optimal) set of controls given by;
- U*(t) = Arg opt Φ (t) U(t)$\in$ U (Shemayev, 2007)

In order to adequately model the set of controls it is necessary to have a good cognitive model of the target of RC.

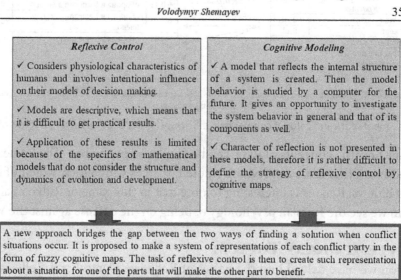

Figure 4: A cognitive Approach to Modeling Reflexive Conrol.

This synthesis of RC and Cognitive Mapping is more like western attempts at behavioral influencing which are covered in a separate chapter. However, it is interesting to compare the procedures of Shemayev compared to what is mentioned by Dr. John Norseen regarding the Inverse, sometimes also referred to as Reverse, and Direct Tasks, sometimes referred to as Forward, of Reflexive Control. Here Shemayev defines the synthesized Forward and Inverse Task:

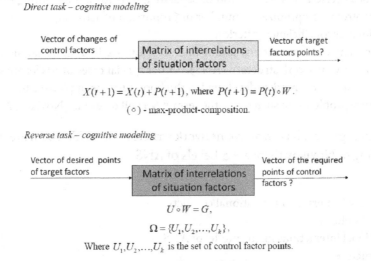

Direct task – cognitive modeling

Vector of changes of control factors → Matrix of interrelations of situation factors → Vector of target factors points?

$$X(t+1) = X(t) + P(t+1), \text{ where } P(t+1) = P(t) \circ W.$$

$(\circ)$ - max-product-composition.

Reverse task – cognitive modeling

Vector of desired points of target factors → Matrix of interrelations of situation factors → Vector of the required points of control factors ?

$$U \circ W = G,$$

$$\Omega = \{U_1, U_2, \ldots, U_k\},$$

Where $U_1, U_2, \ldots, U_k$ is the set of control factor points.

Direct and reverse tasks are used for cognitive analysis and reflexive control of situation development. Shemayev and Taran proposed a new method that bridges the gap between the two approaches to finding a solution when conflict situations occur. The authors propose to make a system of representations of each conflict party in the form of fuzzy cognitive maps. The task of reflexive management is to create such representation about a situation for one of the parts that will make the other part benefit.

CONTROLLING THE MOB WITH REFLEXIVE CONTROL

Other more recent work in RC in Russia is that of D. Novikov, head of the Institute of Control Sciences & Moscow Institute of Physics and Technology of the Russian Academy of Sciences, who has looked into the issue of mass-influencing mobs. Novikov works on the mathematical modeling of mob control. This can be traced back to earlier work in 1978 by Granovetter and his own work from at least 2008. Mathematical models of Mobs are of two types:

1. Models of Teams: joint adaptive decision-making by groups of people using information about uncertain factors, which is not considered by Novikov.

2. Conformity Threshold Collective Behavior (Granovetter 1978): the decision of a given agent depends on the proportion or number of other agents making a corresponding decision (particularly, mob behavior); which is considered in the work of Novikov here.

Novikov defines a mob:

Mob is understood below as an active or aggressive gathering of people, i.e., an active or aggressive group, crowd, etc. In scientific literature, mob control has several stable and widespread interpretations. (Novikov, 2017, 5)

Mobs are viewed as groups of agents, which can also be artificial agents or 'phantoms' in RC parlance. The study of agents involves such elements as:

'Control of agents' motion (goal achievement, collision avoidance, obstacle avoidance, formation control, etc.). This direction of group control demonstrates intensive development since the early 2000s, embracing two broad fields of research, namely, analytical and simulation (agent-based) models. … A separate aspect concerns choosing a set of physical influence measures for a mob (prevention of jams, mass riots, and so on), which also represents a subject of many investigations. (Novikov, 2017, 5)

Novikov gives the basis for Mob stratification:

Mobs are classified using several bases. This book proceeds from a substantial hypothesis that a mob can be united by a common object of attention (be organized in some sense), while its members-people (agents) may undertake certain actions or not. To put it tentatively, agents can be active (e.g., supporting some decision, participating in mass riots, etc.) or passive. Accordingly, mob control represents a purposeful impact (as a rule, informational influence exerted on a whole mob or separate agents for implementing their desired behavior. [74]. If the goal of control is to optimize the number or proportion of active agents, exactly this index [active, passive] forms a major control efficiency criterion.

As actions of agents and communications among them are both vital for mob analysis, a mob can be treated as a special case of an active network structure (ANS). Other special cases of ANS's are social groups, online social networks and so on. Some models developed in the book turn out applicable to wider classes of ANS's, not only to mob control problems. In such cases, the term ANS will be used. (Novikov, 2017, 5)

In short, in this terminology a mob is an active network structure or ANS, which are more popularly known as social networks. According to Novikov there are 5 Levels of ANS:

ANS Levels
Level 5: game theory (reflexive) informational conflicts
Level 4: Control Problems
Level 3: informational interactions micro-model of ANS
Level 2: graph structure
Level 1: Macro-model of ANS

In much the same sense as a convolutional neural network as higher levels feed into lower levels. The main issue with ANS analysis and structure is the state of the agents whether they are active or passive.

Model of an ANS:
-each agent chooses between two states:
0- passive
1- active (participation in mob action)

While making his decision, each agent demonstrates conformity behavior, taking into account the so-called social pressure as the observed or predicted behavior of the environment: if a definite number (or proportion) of his 'neighbors' [KNN clustering?] are active, then this agent chooses activity. The minimum number (or proportion) of neighbors that 'excites' a given agent is called his threshold. Note there also exist models of anti-conformity behavior and 'mixture' of conformity and anti-conformity [26]. (Novikov, 2017, 7)

Threshold is the minimum number (or proportion of neighbors that influences a given agent. Equilibrium state of a mob is defined via the distribution function of agents' thresholds.

If the relationship between the equilibrium state of a system (a social network, a mob) and the threshold distribution function is known, one can pose threshold control problems, e.e., find an appropriate control action modifying agents' threshold so that the system reaches a desired equilibrium. (Novikov, 2017, 8)

Each agent has an opinion. Novikov offers the following iteration to determine threshold behavior. Model of a mob N = {1,2,....,n) of agents. Agent I in the set of N is characterized by:

1. influence (a certain 'weight' of his opinion for agent j)
2. the decision
3. the threshold, defining whether agent I acts under a certain opponent's action profile.

Formally, define the action x_i of agent I as the best response to the existing opponent's action profile.

Therefore, given an initial state (the proportion of active agents at step 0), further dynamics of system (7) and it's equilibrium states depend on the properties of the distribution functions of agent's thresholds. Hence, a goal-oriented modification of this function can be treated as mob control.

Although the following from Novikov is math intensive, for those interested it is important to understand the basics of how Thresholds are calculated as well as activations. Novikov gives the following equations for his mathematical model of mobs:

If the relationship between the equilibrium state of a system (a social network, a mob) and the threshold distribution function is known, one can pose threshold control problems, e.g., find an appropriate control action modifying agents' thresholds so that the system reaches a desired equilibrium.

Consider the following *model* of a *mob* as a set $N = \{1, 2, \dots, n\}$ of agents. Agent $i \in N$ is characterized by

(1) the *influence* $t_{ji} \geq 0$ on agent j (a certain "weight" of his opinion for agent j). for each agent j, we have the normalization conditions $\sum_{i=j} t_{ji} = 1, t_{ii} = 0$.

(2) the decision $x_i \in \{0;1\}$;

(3) the *threshold* $\theta_i \in [0;1]$, defining whether agent i acts under a certain *opponents' action profile* (the vector $\overline{x}_{-i} = (x_1, \dots, x_{i-1}, x_{i+1}, \dots, x_n)$ comprising the decisions of the other agents except agent i) Formally, define the action x_i of agent i as the best response to the existing opponents' action profile:

$$(1) \quad x_i = BR_i(x_{-i}) = \begin{cases} 1, & \text{if } \sum_{j \neq i} t_i x_j \geq \theta_i \\ 0, & \text{if } \sum_{j \neq i} t_i x_j < \theta_i \end{cases}$$

This book has independent numbering of formulas for each section; while referring to a formula from another section, the double numbering system is used, where the first number indicates the section.

The behavior described by (1) is called *threshold behavior*, see surveys in [20, 21]. A *Nash equilibrium* is an agents' action vector $\overline{x}_N$ such that $\overline{x}_N = BR(\overline{x}_N)$, where

$$BR(\overline{x}_N) = (BR_1(\overline{x}_{-1}), \dots BR_n(\overline{x}_{-n})).$$

Consider the *following discrete-time dynamic model of collective behavior* [23]. At the initial (zero) step, all agents are passive. At each subsequent step, the agents act simultaneously and independently according to the best-response procedure (1).

Introduce the notation

(2) $Q_0 = \emptyset$, $Q_1 = \{i \in N \mid \theta_i = 0\}$,

$$Q_k = Q_{k-1} \cup \{i \in N \mid \sum_{j \in Q_{k-1}, j \neq i} t_{ij} \geq \theta_i\}, \quad k = 1, 2, \dots, n-1.$$

Clearly, $Q_0 \subseteq Q_1 \subseteq \dots \subseteq Q_n \subseteq N$. Let $T = \{t_{ij}\}$ be the influence matrix of th agents and $\theta = (\theta_1, \theta_2, \dots, \theta_n)$ correspond to the vector of their thresholds. Evaluate the following index:

(3) $q(T, \theta) = \min \{k = \overline{0, n-1} \mid Q_{k+1} = Q_k\}$.

Define the *collective behavior equilibrium* (CBE) [23]

$$(4) \quad x_i^*(T,\theta) = \begin{cases} 1, & \text{if } i \in Q_{q(T,\theta)} \\ 0, & \text{if } i \in N \setminus Q_{q(T,\theta)}, i \in N. \end{cases}$$

The value

$$(5) \quad x^* = \frac{\#Q_{q(T,\theta)}}{n} = \frac{1}{n} \sum_{i \in N} x_i^*(T,\theta)$$

with # denoting set power characterizes the proportion of active agents in the CBE.

Further exposition mostly deals with the *anonymous case* where the graph of agents' relations is complete: $t_{ij} = 1/(n-1)$). In the anonymous case, expression (1) takes the form

$$(6)\ x_i = BR_i(\overline{x}_{-j}) = \begin{cases} 1, \text{ if } \dfrac{1}{n-1}\sum_{j \neq i} x_j \geq \theta_i, \\ 0, \text{ if } \dfrac{1}{n-1}\sum_{j \neq i} x_j < \theta_i. \end{cases}$$

Designate by $F(\cdot)$: $[0, 1] \to [0, 1]$ the *distribution function of agents' thresholds*, a nondecreasing function defined on the unit segment that is left continuous and possesses right limit at each point of its domain. Let $\{x_t \in [0, 1]\}_{t \geq 0}$ be a discrete sequence of the *proportions of active agents*, where t indicates time step.

Assume that the proportion x_k of active agents at step k is known $(k = 0, 1, \ldots)$. Then the following recurrent expression describes the dynamics of the proportion of active agents at the subsequent steps [19-27, 44, 56]:

After establishing Collective Behavior Equilibrium (CBE) from above we arrive at mob control which is altering the threshold of agents with a goal-oriented modification [steering, cybernetics].

The Nash equilibrium is calculated as:

Denote by $y = \inf\{x : x \in (0,1], F(x) = x\}$ the least nonzero root of equation (8). The collective behavior equilibrium (CBE) and, as shown in [23], a Nash equilibrium of the agents' game is the point

$$(9)\ x^* = \begin{cases} y, \text{ if } \forall z \in [0, y] : F(z) \geq z, \\ 0, \text{ otherwise.} \end{cases}$$

According to the properties of the distribution function, for implementing a nonzero CBE a sufficient condition is $F(0) > 0$.

Novikov analyses mob control on two levels a micro and macro scale:

> two approaches to the design and analysis of ANSs, namely, macro- and micro-descriptions. According to the former approach, the structure of relations in a network is averaged, and agents' behavior is studied "in the mean." The latter approach takes into account the structural features of the influence graph of agents and their individual decision-making principles. The first and second approaches are compared using the threshold model of collective behavior with a common relative threshold. (Novikov, 2017, 10)

THRESHOLD MODEL OF AGENTS BEHAVIOR

As mentioned before, the threshold of the agents, the influences of neighbors, is a key to the CBE. As mentioned, each agent has an opinion which can be influenced. Novikov explains the model:

> The models of agent's opinions dynamics in ANSs involve a single characteristic of each agent-- his opinion-- and the rest parameters reflect the interaction of agents. The so-called behavioral models of ANSs are richer: in addition to 'internal' parameters, the incorporate variables describing agent's behavior (his decisions). Generally, these decisions depend on the internal parameters of an agent (his opinions, individual characteristics) and, maybe, on the opinions and/or actions of other agents (all agents, neighbors or some group of agents). As an example of behavioral models, we choose the threshold model (the general game theoretic modeling approaches to collective threshold behavior were outlined in the publications. (Novikov, 2017, 15)

The *common relative threshold* of the agents is the consensus of the ANS, a common opinion.

Novikov applied his math models in simulation of social networks: Facebook, Twitter and LiveJournal; this work was done in collaboration with A. V. Batov. A social network is a directed graph, which one could use SRI's A* search to crawl:

> The relations among agents in a real SN can be reflected by a directed graph G. The direction of an edge from one agent (node) to another shows the former's influence on the latter. The micro-models address explicitly the influence graph, whereas the macro-models operate its macro-characteristic, i.e., the distribution M(.) of a number of neighbors (Novikov, 2017, 20)

Novikov provides a simple illustration for the structure of influences on Facebook:

> For instance, in *Facebook* an agent has connections to his friends, which can be interpreted as the influence relations of these friends on the agent. In *LiveJournal* and *Twitter*, directed influence relations are agent's subscriptions for viewing and commenting information posted by other agents. We will believe that all agents influencing a given agent in a network are his *neighbors*, see expression (1). (Novikov, 2017, 21)

4.1. A Threshold Model of Mob Behavior

Consider the following model of a mob. There is a set $N = \{1, 2, ..., n\}$ of *agents* choosing between two *decisions*, "1" (being active, e.g., participating in mass riots) or "0" (being passive). Agent $i \in N$ is characterized by

– the *influence* on agent j, denoted by $t_{ji} \geq 0$ (a certain "weight" of his opinion for agent j); for each agent j, we have the normalization conditions $\sum_{i \neq j} t_{ji} = 1$, $t_{ii} = 0$;

– the decision $x_i \in \{0; 1\}$;

– the *threshold* $\theta_i \in [0, 1]$, defining whether agent i acts under a certain *opponents' action profile* (the vector x_{-i} comprising the decisions of the rest agents). Formally, define the action x_i of agent i as the best response to the existing opponents' action profile:

$$(1)\ x_i = BR_i(x_{-i}) = \begin{cases} 1, \text{if } \sum_{j \neq i} t_{ij} x_j \geq \theta_i, \\ 0, \text{if } \sum_{j \neq i} t_{ij} x_j < \theta_i. \end{cases}$$

The behavior described by (1) is called *threshold behavior*. A *Nash equilibrium* is an agents' action vector x_N such that $x_N = BR(x_N)$ [64].

By analogy to the paper [18], adopt the *following dynamic model of collective behavior*. At an initial step, all agents are passive. At each subsequent step, agents act simultaneously and independently according to procedure (1). Introduce the notation

$(2)\ Q_0 = \{i \in N \mid \theta_i = 0\}$,

$$Q_k = Q_{k-1} \cup \{i \in N \mid \sum_{j \in Q_{k-1}, j \neq i} t_{ij} \geq \theta_i\}, k = 1, 2, ..., n - 1.$$

Clearly, $Q_0 \subseteq Q_1 \subseteq ... \subseteq Q_{n-1} \subseteq Q_n = N$. Let $T = \{t_{ij}\}$ be the influence matrix of agents and $\theta = (\theta_1, \theta_2, ..., \theta_n)$ form the vector of their thresholds. Evaluate the following index:

$(3)\ q(T, \theta) = \min \{k = \overline{0, n-1} \mid Q_{k+1} = Q_k\}$.

Define the *collective behavior equilibrium* x^* (CBE) by

$$(4)\ x_i^*(T, \theta) = \begin{cases} 1, \text{if } i \in Q_{q(T,\theta)}, \\ 0, \text{if } i \in N \setminus Q_{q(T,\theta)}, i \in N. \end{cases}$$

<u>Assertion 4.1.</u> For any influence matrix T and agents' thresholds θ, there exists a unique CBE (4) representing a Nash equilibrium in the game with the best response (1).

Proof of Asserton 4.1. To establish the existence, one should actually demonstrate the following: the set used for minimization in (3) is nonempty. By *argumentum ex contrario*, suppose emptiness of this set. In other words, the sequence of sets $Q_0 \subseteq Q_1 \subseteq \ldots \subseteq Q_{n-1} \subseteq Q_n$ is assumed to have no coinciding elements. This implies that each consequent set differs from the previous one (at least) by a single element. On the other hand, the sequence has $n + 1$ sets, but there are n totally. We have arrived at a contradiction.

Uniqueness follows from the CBE definition—see (4)—and from uniqueness of index (3).

Let $x^*(T, \theta)$ specify the CBE. And so, all agents belonging to the set $Q_{q(T,\theta)}$ are active. However, according to formulas (1)–(2), this choice matches their best responses. All agents in the set $N \setminus Q_{q(T,\theta)}$ turn out passive. By virtue of (2)–(3), these agents satisfy $\sum_{j \in Q_{q(T,\theta)}} t_{ij} < \theta_i$,

$i \in N \setminus Q_{q(T,\theta)}$. Then being passive is the best response (see expression (1)). Hence, for all i we obtain $x_i = BR_i(x_{-i})$, and $x^*(T, \theta)$ represents a Nash equilibrium. Proof of Assertion 4.1 is complete. • (here and in the sequel, symbol • indicates the end of a proof, example, etc.).

We underline that the above CBE definition possesses constructive character, as its evaluation based on (2)–(4) seems easy. Moreover, a reader should observe an important fact: without agents having zero thresholds, passivity of all agents makes up the CBE. In the sense of control, this means that most attention should be paid to the so-called "*ringleaders*," i.e., agents deciding "to be active" even when the rest remain passive.

The model with reputation. Denote by $r_j = \dfrac{1}{n-1}\sum_{i \neq j} t_{ij}$ the average

REPUTATION (CONFORMITY) CONTROL

Another component of mob control involves the reputation of an agent, which is the opinions of other agents of that agent, also their influences upon that agent. This is given mathematically by Novikov in the following:

influence of agent $j \in N$ on the rest agents. The quantity rj is said to be the relative reputation of agent j (a certain "weight" of his opinion for theother agents). The other agents consider his opinion or actions according to this weight. Within the framework of the model with reputation, influence can be characterized by the vector r = {ri} i ∈ N. In this model, define the action xi of agent i as the best response to the opponents' action profile:

A special case of the described model is the *anonymous case*, where all agents have the identical reputations $r_i = \dfrac{1}{n-1}$. Then choose integers $m_1, m_2, \ldots, m_n$ as the thresholds and construct the corresponding threshold vector m. Next, sort the agents in the nondecreasing order of their thresholds: $m_1 \leq m_2 \leq \ldots \leq m_n$. Believing that $m_0 = 0$ and $m_{n+1} > n$, define the number $p(m) \in \{0, \ldots, n\}$ by

$$p(m) = \min \{k \in N \cup \{0\} \mid m_k \leq k, m_{k+1} > k\}.$$

Consequently, the CBE acquires the following structure: $x_i^* = 1$, $i = \overline{1, p(m)}$; $x_i^* = 0$, $i = \overline{p(m)+1, n}$. That is, the first $p(m)$ agents are active (if $p(m) = 0$, suppose passivity of all agents).

In the anonymous model, a Nash equilibrium satisfies the equation [18]

(5) $F(p) = p$,

where $F(p) = |\{i \in N : m_i < p\}|$ indicates the number of agents whose thresholds are less than p. Evidently, the CBE corresponds to the *minimal* solution of equation (5).

Thus, one easily calculates the CBE under known thresholds and reputations of the agents. To proceed, let us study control problems. Imagine the influence and/or thresholds of agents can be modified. How should this be done for implementing a required CBE? In terms of the practical interpretations of the model, we aim at reducing the number of agents deciding "to be active."

The aggregated index of mob state is the number of active agents: $K(T, \theta) = |Q_{q(T, \theta)}|$.

In the model with reputation, replace the matrix T with the vector r. In the anonymous case, we have $K(m) = p(m)$.

$$x_i = BR_i(x_{-i}) = \begin{cases} 1, \text{if } \sum_{j \neq i} r_j x_j \geq \theta_i, \\ 0, \text{if } \sum_{j \neq i} r_j x_j < \theta_i. \end{cases}$$

Let T^0 and θ^0 be the vectors of initial values of influence matrices and agents' thresholds, respectively. Suppose that the following parameters are given: *the admissible sets* of the influences and thresholds of agents (T and Θ, respectively), the *Principal's payoff* $H(K)$ from an achieved mob state K and his *costs* $C(T, \theta, T^0, \theta^0)$ required for modifying the reputations and thresholds of the agents.

As a control efficiency criterion, select the Principal's goal function representing the difference between the payoff $H(\cdot)$ and the costs $C(\cdot)$. Then the *control problem* takes the form

(6) $H(K(T, \theta)) - C(T, \theta, T^0, \theta^0) \to \max_{T \in T, \theta \in \Theta}$.

In the anonymous case, the control problem (6) becomes

(7) $H(p(m)) - C(m, m^0) \to \max_{m \in M}$,

where M is the admissible set of threshold vectors in the anonymous case, while m and m^0 designate the terminal and initial threshold vectors, respectively.

Now, consider special cases of the general problem (6). The threshold control problem in the anonymous case is treated in subsection 4.2. And the reputation control problem in the non-anonymous case can be found in subsection 4.3.

Some examples of the mathematical models considered by Novikov also includes Reflexive Control along with Reflexive Game models of competing Principals usually expressed by a bi-matrix in the considerations. An example of RC in Mob Control is where the Principal influences the beliefs of the agents about their parameters, the beliefs about beliefs. The non-cooperative Principals must control the informational equilibrium; possessing a certain awareness structure the agents choose their actions. Here, awareness would be the equivalent of an opinion (Novikov, 2017, 49). Novikov argues that the basis of altering awareness or opinions is best conducted through information control, or information warfare in military contexts.

...we believe that any result achievable via a real variation of thresholds can be implemented by informational control (an appropriate modification of the agents' beliefs about their thresholds). And so, information control for thresholds turns out equivalent to threshold control in a common sense. Apparently, the former type of control is 'softer' than the latter." One property of 'good' informational control concerns its stability [75] when all agents observe the results they actually expected. (Novikov, 2017, 49)

Among other things, informational control in the ANS's lies in a purposeful impact exerted on the initial opinions of agents, in order to ensure the required values of the final opinions (desired by the control subject) (Novikov, 2017, 111)

One of the most important elements in information control is stability.

Stability is a substantial requirement for a long-term interaction between the Principal and agents. Indeed, under an unstable information control, the agents just once doubting the truth of Principal's information have good reason to do it later." (Novikov, 2017, 49-50)

STOCHASTIC MODELS OF MOB CONTROL

In practice, a possible tool of such control consists in mass media [48, 75] or any other unified (information, motivational and/or institutional [74])

For instance, consider the following interpretations of potential control actions: the thresholds of a given proportion of randomly chosen agents are nullified (which matches 'excitation') or maximized (which matches 'immunization,' ie., complete in-susceptibility to social pressure). Or just believe that each agent can be excited and/or immunized with a given probability. Such transformations of agent's threshold cause a corresponding variation in the equilibrium state of an active network structure (a social network, a mob).

Another way for managing threshold behavior (not agents' thresholds) is staff control according to the control types classification introduced in [74]. Staff control implies embedding additional agents with zero and maximum threshold (provokers and immunizers, respectively) in an ANS. In this case, the resulting equilibrium of the ANS depends on the number of embedded agents having an appropriate type.

And finally, there may exist two control authorities (Principals) exerting opposite information impacts on the agents [red vs. blue sub-machines]. This situation of distributed control [43, 74] can be interpreted as *informational confrontation* [46, 48, 70, 72] between the Principals. Using the analysis results of the control problems for each separate Principal, one can describe their interaction in terms of **game theory**." (Novikov, 2017, 51)

Novikov also addresses such things as Provokers in Mobs, Excitation of Whole Mob and Positional Control. The main area of concern for this study is the use of Mob Control in Game Theory from normal-form games, to reflexive games to hierarchical games.

What makes Mob Control Game theoretic is the situation with non-cooperative Principals gaming the agents to influence them to achieve the Principals' goal state. This is usually expressed in cybersecurity and military simulations as Red vs. Blue. A look at Novikov's models for Game theoretic considerations is very illuminating in understanding issues in cybersecurity dealing with influencing of masses.

Game-Theoretic Models of Mob Control

Problem description: Consider a set of interconnected agents having mutual influence on their decision-making. Variations in the states of some agents at an initial step accordingly modify the state of other agents. The nature and character of such dynamics depend on the practical interpretation of a corresponding network. Among possible interpretations, we mention the propagation of excitation in biological networks (e.g., neural networks) or in economic networks [49, 54], failure modes (in the general case, structural dynamics models) in information and control systems and complex engineering systems, models of innovation diffusion [controlling scientific consensus], information security models, penetration/infection models, consensus models and others, see an overview in [48]. (Novikov, 2017, 72)

the control problem of the purposeful 'excitation' of a network is to find a set of agents for applying an initial control action so that the network reaches a required state. This abstract statement covers informational control in social networks [8, 48], collective threshold behavior control, etc. (Novikov, 2017, 72)

The goal function of a control subject (Principal is the difference between the income and the costs. For the Principal, the centralized control problem lies in choosing a set of initially excited agents to maximize the goal function..." (Novikov, 2017, 74)

"Using relationship (4) between the final opinion of the agents and the control actions, one can suggest a game-theoretic interaction model of the agents performing these actions. To this end, it is necessary to define their goal functions. Suppose that the goal functions of the first and second agents… are calculated as the difference between their 'income' that depends on the final opinion of the agents and the control costs. " (Novikov, 2017, 112)

"the aggregate… composed of the goal functions and feasible action sets of the two agents specifies the family of games. The distinctions among these games are induced by the awareness structure of the players and the sequence of functioning." (Novikov, 2017, 112)

9.2. "Antagonistic" Game

Choose the zero opinions of the agents ($X^0 = 0$) as the "status quo." Suppose that the first player is interested in final opinion maximization ($H_F(X) = X$), whereas the second player seeks to minimize it ($H_F(X) = -X$). Both players have identical "control resources" ($U = V = [d, D]$, $d < -1 \le 1 < D$) and identical cost functions ($c_F(u) = u^2 / 2$, $c_S(v) = v^2 / 2$).

The goal functions of the players,

(5) $f_F(u, v) = r_F u + r_S v - u^2 / 2$

and

(6) $f_S(u, v) = -r_F u - r_S v - v^2 / 2$,

are separable in the corresponding actions. Hence [74], under the simultaneous independent choice of the players' actions, there exists a *dominant strategies' equilibrium* (DSE) (u^d, v^d), where $u^d = r_F$ and $v^d = -r_S$.

A *Pareto point* is the vector (u^P, v^P) that maximizes the sum of the goal functions of the players, where $u^P = 0$ and $v^P = 0$.

The DSE is Pareto inefficient:

$$f_F(u^d, v^d) + f_S(u^d, v^d) = -[(r_F)^2 + (r_S)^2] / 2 < f_F(u^P, v^P) + f_S(u^P, v^P) = 0,$$

while the Pareto point appears unstable against the unilateral deviations of the players.

For the first (second) player, define the penalty strategy as his worst action for the opponent: $u^P = D$, $v^P = d$. Within the framework of this model, the dominant strategies of the players are *guaranteeing*. Calculate the guaranteed payoffs of the players:

$$f_F^{MGR} = f_F(u^d, v^P) = (r_F)^2 / 2 + r_S d, \quad f_S^{MGR} = f_S(u^P, v^d) = (r_S)^2 / 2 - r_F D.$$

Assume that a third party controls how the players fulfill their commitments [59, 74] and the following *contracts* are concluded (the "non-aggression pact"):

(7) $\hat{u}(v) = \begin{cases} 0, & v = 0 \\ u^P, & v \neq 0 \end{cases}$, $\hat{v}(u) = \begin{cases} 0, & u = 0 \\ v^P, & u \neq 0 \end{cases}$.

Then the players benefit from executing these contracts if

(8) $\begin{cases} (r_F)^2 + 2r_S d \le 0, \\ (r_S)^2 \le 2r_F D, \end{cases}$

which leads to the stable implementation of the Pareto point. The same result can be achieved using the penalty strategy in *repeated games*. According to condition (8), the "*contract equilibrium*" is implementable if the impact levels of the first and second players differ slightly. Fig. *22* demonstrates the hatched domain 0AB that satisfies condition (8) with $d = -1$ and $D = 1$.

Consider the goal functions that differ from the ones explored in the previous subsection in the cost functions of the players: $c_P(u) = u^2 / (2 q_F)$, and $c_S(v) = v^2 / (2 q_S)$, where $q_F = 1$ and denote the "efficiency levels" of the players. By assumption, each player knows his efficiency level, the first player believes that the common knowledge is $q_S = 1$, while the second player knows this fact and the real efficiency of the first player. The described reflexive game [75] has the graph $2 \leftarrow 1 \leftrightarrow 12$.

According to expression (11), the first player chooses $u^* = \dfrac{r_F - 2r_F(r_S)^2}{4(r_F)^2 + 2(r_S)^2 + 1}$. Consequently, the second agent selects his best

response $v^* = \dfrac{0.5 r_S (1 + 2(r_F)^2)(1 + 2(r_S)^2)}{(1 + (r_S)^2)(4(r_F)^2 + 2(r_S)^2 + 1)}$. These actions lead to the

final opinion $X = \dfrac{(r_F)^2 + (r_S)^4 + 0.5(r_S)^2}{(1 + (r_S)^2)(4(r_F)^2 + 2(r_S)^2 + 1)}$ of the ANS; in the

general case, it does not coincide with the opinion

$X^4 = \dfrac{(r_F)^2 + (r_S)^2}{4(r_F)^2 + 2(r_S)^2 + 1}$ expected by the first player. This means that the

resulting informational equilibrium is unstable [75]. For this reflexive game graph, the informational equilibrium enjoys stability only in two situations: (1) the belief of the first agent about the opponent's efficiency level is true, or (2) the total reputation of the impact agents of the second player makes up zero (however, the reputation is assumed strictly positive).

9.5. Secure Strategies Equilibrium

Consider the game where $H_F(X(u, v)) = \begin{cases} h_F > 0, X \geq \hat{X} \\ 0, X < \hat{X} \end{cases}$,

$H_S(X(u, v)) = \begin{cases} h_S > 0, X < \hat{X} \\ 0, X \geq \hat{X} \end{cases}$, $c_F(u) = u$, and $c_S(v) = v$, with

$U = V = [d, D]$, $d < -1 \leq 1 < D$, $h_F > D$, and $h_v > |d|$. In a corresponding practical interpretation, the first player is interested in the adoption of a certain decision, which requires that the opinion of the ANS members exceeds the threshold $\hat{X}$; in contrast, the second player seeks for blocking this decision.

Let $r_F D + r_S d + X^0 > \hat{X}$ for definiteness. There exists no Nash equilibria in this game, but it is possible to evaluate a *secure strategies' equilibrium* (SSE) [50, 51, 52] in the form $((\hat{X} - r_S d - X^0) / r_F + \varepsilon; 0)$ where ε is an arbitrary small strictly positive constant. A practical inter-

In this section, we have analyzed a series of specific examples illustrating the applicability of game theory to the description of informational confrontation in ANS's, both in terms of the process and result. Despite its simplicity, the stated model shows the diversity of possible game-theoretic formulations (dominant strategies' equilibrium, Nash equilibrium, "contract equilibrium," Stackelberg hierarchical games and hierarchical games of the type $\Gamma 1$, reflexive games, secure strategies' equilibrium).

Generally speaking, any specific model of informational confrontation should be developed taking into account, first, the features of an associated practical problem and, second, the identifiability of a modeled system (i.e., ANS parameters, the admissible actions of the players, as well as their preferences and awareness). Note that the

game-theoretic models of informational confrontation over ANS's have several applications, namely, information security in telecommunication networks, counteraction to the destructive informational impacts on the social groups of different scale, prevention of their massive illegal actions, and others.

As for the promising directions of further investigations, we mention the design and study of the game-theoretic models of informational confrontation in ANS's under the following conditions:

– the sequential choice of the players' actions under the observed dynamics of the ANS state (the "defense-attack" games with the description of opinion dynamics (the distribution of information an epidemic or viruses [memes] within an ANS));

– the repeated choice of the players' actions under incomplete information on the actions of the opponents and the ANS state. (Novikov, 2017, 117-8)

It is important to note that there is no Nash Equilibrium in a SSE game, which is exemplified in a war platform such as Lockheed-Martin's evolutionary games model of Lockheed's Senglaub which also uses SSE.

The issue of superstructuring games, or hierarchical games, is addressed by Novikov as well:

10.4 Hierarchical Game

In mob control problems, the players (principals) often make decisions sequentially, Here the essential factors are the awareness of each player at the moment of decision-making and the admissible strategy sets of the players. A certain hierachical game can be 'superstructured' over each normal-form game [74]. Moreover, it is necessary to discriminate between two settings as followed:
1. one of the Principals chooses his strategy and then the other does so, being aware of the opponent's choice. After that, an informational impact is exerted on the agents. As a result, the distribution functions of the agent's thresholds takes form…
2. One of the Principals chooses his strategy and exerts his informational impact on the agents. After that, the other Principal chooses his strategy and exerts his informational impact on the agents, being aware fo the opponent's choice. (Novikov, 2017, 131)

10.5 Reflexive Game
it is also possible to 'superstruct' reflexive games [75] over a normal-form game where the players possess non-trivial mutual awareness about some essential parameters. (Novikov, 2017, 131)

Novikov's work on Mob Control mathematical modeling gives us valuable insights into influence campaigns conducted on a daily basis on such social networks as Facebook, Twitter, and others. The need for mass education on influence machines is one that should be addressed by regulators at all levels of civil oversight with appropriate international laws applied to such use of mob control and cyber influencing. It is not hard to imagine why a military power might want to be able to control mobs in enemy areas which necessarily raises issues of the Geneva Conventions and other bans on prohibited weapons, making their use a war crime, but of course proving such a case in law may be a complete impossibility which would leave competing military powers to develop their own offensive and defensive influence machines.

I, Robot Reflexion:

Another contemporary scientist working in the field of Reflexive Control is Serge Tarasenko; A younger researcher, who has written articles for the Journal of Reflexive Control as well as his own independently published results of applying RC in Games, applying Emotions to Agents, and socializing mixed groups of Robots and Humans for the purposes of steering the Humans with the Robots.

Earlier we encountered Tarasenko's work in terms of Alliance/Conflict groups or otherwise known as Red vs. Blue. In this section we will be mainly going over his research regarding using Robots to train Humans using Reflexive Control. Tarasenko introduced the subject of Robots into Reflexive Game Theory in 2010.

Robots – the goal of the robots in the mixed groups of humans and robots is to refrain human subjects from choosing risky actions. [inverted can be used to create terrorists, etc]

In a nod to Asimov, Tarasenko argues that the Robots should always observe the 3 Laws of Robotics. Introducing a certain assumption of moral responsibility behind the Robots actions, of course we know in a military or weaponized context these safeguards would be contradictory to using Robot agents when the goal of the Robot is to use force to stop an adversary, and hence not included in any war application.

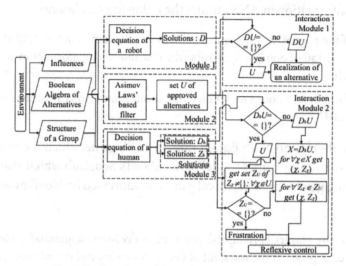

Fig. 5. The Basic Control Schema of a Robotic Agent (BCSRA).   (Tarasenko, 2010)

Tarasenko explains the flow diagram, where you take in a set of alternatives for the controlled subject:

The output of the Module 1 is set D of alternatives, which robot has to choose under the given joint influences. In the Interaction Module 1, the conjunction of sets D and U is performed: D ⊠ U = DU. If set DU is not empty set, this means that there are aproved alternatives among the alternatives that robot should choose in accordance with the joint influences. Therefore, robot can implement any alternative from the set DU. If set DU is empty, this means that under given joint influences robot cannot choose any approved alternative, therefore robot will choose an alternative from set U. This is how the Interaction Module 1 works.

The output of the Module 3 contains sets Dh and Zh. The goal of the robot is to refrain human subjects from choosing risky alternative. This can be done by convincing human subjects to choose alternatives from the set U. First, we check whether Dh contains any approved alternative. We do so by performing conjunction of sets Dh and U: Dh ∩ U = DhU. If set DhU is not empty, then it means that it is possible to make a human subject to choose some non-risky alternative. Therefore, we should choose the corresponding reflexive control strategy from the set Zh. However, if set DhU is empty, we have to find the reflexive control strategy that will make human subject to select approved alternative from set U. For this purpose, we construct set ZU by including all the joint influences $Z\chi$ for approved alternatives: $Z\chi \in ZU \Leftrightarrow \chi \in U$. Next, we check whether set ZU is empty. If set ZU is empty this means it is impossible to convince a human subject to choose non-risky alternative. Therefore, the only option of reflexive control in this case is to put this subject into frustration state. However, if set ZU is not empty, this means that there exist at least one reflexive control strategy that results in selection of alternative from the set of the approved (non-risky) ones (Tarasenko, 2010)

In computing and robotics one method suggested to increase the robot or artificial agent's ability to work in an environment is to add emotions. Tarasenko has proposed the use of the Pleasure-Arousal-Dominance (PAD) model to robotics. PAD is traced back to Mehrabian and Russell 1974 to assess environmental perception, experience and psychological responses. The three dimensions can be linked to the current ABC Model of Attitudes: pleasure, arousal and dominance can be respectively related to affective, cognitive and conative responses, ie. Affect (feeling), Cognition (thinking) and Behavior (acting) (ABC). (Mehrabian & Russell, 2014). Previous to this Kelly in 1955 came up with the Theory of Bipolar Constructs of Good (+) / Bad (-). The propensity of turning toward good and bad is estimated by V. Lefebvre that the positive pole is chosen by 61.8% of subjects and the negative pole by 38.2%. Later in 1957 Osgood proposed the semantic differential approach which characterizes a subject's personality as Evaluation, Activity, Potency, which Mehrabian & Russell proposed the PAD on. In Neuromarketing, the business implementation of neuro-warfare, uses the PAD model in Self-Assessment Manikin (SAM) tests, emotional responses of consumers can be recorded through the SAM scale. This is a non-verbal pictorial assessment technique applicable for direct measurement of PAD associated with a person's affective reaction to a wide variety of stimuli.

In this study of Tarasenko he uses the PAD model along with Reflexive Game Theory (RGT) to emotionally color the interactions between humans and robots. The emotional research based on PAD model is transparent and clear. The models of robots exhibiting human-like emotional behavior using only PAD has been successfully illustrated in recent book by Nishida et al. Nishida, T., Jain, C. L., and Faucher, C.: Modelling Machine Emotions for Realizing Intelligence. Foundations and Application. Springer-Verlag Berlin Heidelberg (2010). The ideal of mixing emotions with AI agents, Affective Computing (see Nashida), can be traced back to earlier work in the Soviet Union with Russian Pospolev's Psychonics theory of computation in the 1960s. The basics of PAD begin with a 3-axis layout, one axis for P, A, D.

By definition, PAD model is spanned by three dimensions. The value of each component continuously ranges from -1 to 1. The notation in the PAD model space presented in Fig. 1 are as follows:

1) pair +P vs -P corresponds to Pleasure (positive pole: value 1) vs Displeasure (negative pole: value -1);

2) pair +A vs -A corresponds to Arousal (positive pole: value 1) vs Non-arousal (negative pole: value -1); and

3) pair +D vs -D corresponds to Dominance (positive pole: value 1) vs Submissiveness (negative pole: value -1).

According to Mehrabian, "pleasure vs displeasure" distinguishes the positive vs negative emotional states, "arousal vs non-arousal" refers to combination of physical activity and mental alertness, and "dominance vs submissiveness" is denied in terms of control vs lack of control. (Tarasenko, 2010b)

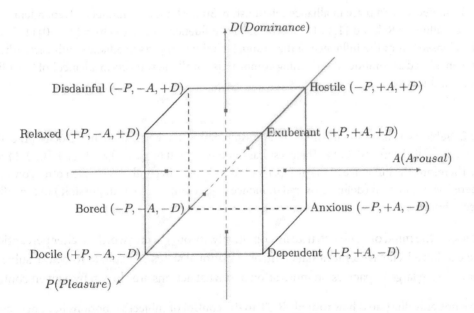

Fig. 1. The Pleasure-Arousal-Dominance (PAD) model's space.

Among eight basic states (hermetry 8), there are three special emotional states:
 Docile (+P, -A,-D) {1, 0, 0}),
 Anxious (−P, +A, −D) {0, 1, 0}) and
 Disdainful (−P, −A, +D) {0, 0, 1}).

These three states are the basis of the 3d binary space. Thus, any other five emotional states can be considered as disjunction (notations OR/∪/+) of these three basis vectors (emotional states). For example, emotional state Dependent (+P, +A, −D) is disjunction of basis states Docile (+P, −A, −D) and Anxious (−P, +A, −D): Docile OR Anxious = (+P, −A, −D) ∪ (−P, +A, −D) = {1, 0, 0} ∪ {0, 1, 0} = {1, 1, 0} = (+P, +A, −D) = Dependent. (Tarasenko, 2010b, 3-4)

The complete set of emotional states represented as binary vectors is

Docile (+P, –A, –D) is coded as {1, 0, 0};
Anxious (–P, +A, –D) is coded as {0, 1, 0};
Disdainful (–P, –A, +D) is coded as {0, 0, 1};
Hostile (–P, +A, +D) is coded as {0, 1, 1};
Dependent (+P, +A, –D) is coded as {1,1,0};
Relaxed (+P, –A, +D) is coded as {1, 0, 1};
Exuberant (+P, +A, +D) is coded as {1, 1, 1};
Bored (–P, –A, –D) is coded as {0, 0, 0}.

Tarasenko proposes through this model to alter emotions of the human subjects:

we note that PAD model provides description of how the emotional states of humans can be modeled, meaning that a certain emotional state of a particular person can be changed to the desired one. Furthermore, it is straightforward to see that the coding of the PAD emotional states and alternatives of Boolean algebra are identical. (Tarasenko, 2010b, 7)

often people directly express their emotions in actions – in such cases a particular emotional state of a subject can be considered as the influence he is making on other subjects. (Tarasenko, 2010b,7)

Using the PAD one can alter the emotions of a group:

Alliance:

Example 1. Subjects a and b are in alliance relationship. Subject a makes influence Dependent {1, 1, 0}. Subject b makes influence Relaxed {1, 0, 1}. Their resultant influence will be (a · b) = {1, 1, 0}{1, 0, 1} = {1, 0, 0} or Docile. Consequently, the influence of the group, including subjects in alliance with each other, on a given subject is considered as conjunction (defining compromise of all the subjects in alliance) of the influences of all the subjects' influences.

Conflict:

Example 2. Subjects a and b are in conflict relationship. Subject a makes influence Docile {1, 0, 0}. Subject b makes influence Disdainful {0, 0, 1}. Their resultant influence will be (a + b) = {1, 0, 0}{0, 0, 1} = {1, 0, 1} or Relaxed. Therefore, the influence of the group, including subjects in conflict with each other, on a given subject is considered as disjunction (defining overall influence since compromise is impossible) of the influences of all the subjects' influences.

RC is an attack on the mind of a subject, usually cognitively, through using words to alter perception. However, with PAD-RGT one can have Reflexive Emotional Control: emotional states can appear to be the subject for the reflexive control, emotions being large impactors on motivation and what actions are chosen by a given controlled subject.

… we have not only illustrated how to apply RGT to the control of subject's emotions but uncovered the entire cascade of human reflexion as a sequence of subconscious reflexion, which allows to trace emotional reflection of each reflexive image. This provides us with unique ability to unfold the sophisticated structure of reflexive decision-making process, involving emotions. (Tarasenko, 2010b,10).

It is known that the Amygdala is the manager of emotions, it is also the seat of Fast Reflexion as brought forward by Lefebvre, which is unconscious automatic processing.

According to Ekman, emotions should be regarded as highly automatics processing algorithms responsible for our everyday life survival. Being entire unconscious (automatic) regulators of the human body's physiology, emotions bring the instantenous solutions of how to act in front of rapidly approaching possible threat. This instantenous activity is possible due to unconscious processing algorithms, which have been characterized by Lewicki et al. as highly non-linear by nature and extremely fast by performance (Tarasenko, 2010b, 11)

Therefore, emotions are fast processors of information coming, apart from environment. Usually, the emotions are characterized by some physiological patterns of body activity on the one hand, and external expression by face mimic or gestures on the other hand. From this point of view, the fact that the reproduction by the self of the physical part of emotional pattern, i.e., just making an angry face can elicit the anger as emotional state itself, is scientifically a completely unexpected phenomenon. (Tarasenko, 2010b, 11).

It is important to understand here that what is being said that just seeing a sad face can make one sad, or seeing an intimidating face puts one in a fear defense response. In this sense one can attempt Emotional RC on another just by frowning at them and change their emotional state; one could also control their muscles to put them into a frown, and the corollary sad emotion will be triggered as well. This kinesthetic trigger is able apply to affect a wide variety of motor actions, causing some emotional states to emerge "therefore, it is possible to control human emotions not directly, but making people perform particular actions." (Tarasenko, 2010b, 11)

One can alter another's image by simply mimicking the emotions you want them to experience in your outward expression, which becomes important when modeling the self and others in the steps of RC:

From this point of view, the self-mimicking is reflexive process. Thus, it is possible to elicit and understand the emotions of others by reflexion. Ekman et al. suggested that this is possible due to "…direct connections between motor cortex and hypothalamus that translates between emotion-prototypic expression in the face and the emotion-specific patterning in the autonomic nervous system. (Tarasenko, 2010b, 11)

From the PAD model applied to AI Agents we now have a rough approximation, as statistics can only best provide at the most, of human emotions in AI algorithms, and developed for the purpose of more efficient Reflexive Control.

ROBOTS IN NETWORKS OF HUMANS

Having understood how robots can at least now mimic human emotions it is good to understand how they are to fit into the Red. vs. Blue architecture of Reflexive Game Theory. Tarasenko in 2015 wrote a paper addressing the issue of Network Activity of Robots including the communications protocols he envisioned for group collaboration in Alliance and Conflict teams of mixed groups of Robots and Humans.

First, we need to have a better understanding of the term 'reflexia' and how it specifically is used:

The notion of reflexia in the psychological context was first introduced by Lefebvre in late 60s. Reflexia means projection of the external world on one's mental state. More specifically, if a human being stands in a field of barley he/she can imagine standing in the field of barley from the 3rd person's perspective. Thus, preserving the egocentric point of view, humans are capable of imagining their own allocentric representation. 1. Therefore, the gist of reflexia is an ability to imagine self-perception in the allocentric reference frame (external 2 point of view) operating in one's egocentric reference frame. Reflexia is an ability to penetrate into the deeper layers of one's psychological state. An abstract example of penetration into the deeper layers is when subject (a) can imagine another person (subject b), who is imagining subject (a), the world around and himself imagining it

There are two theoretical explanations for Reflexia brought up by Tarasenko aside from those originally proposed by Lefebvre:

A. Mirror neuron system: The key concept of the Mirror Neuron System discovered by Rizzolatti and his colleagues, is that there are neurons in primate brain that activate in both cases when the primate is doing a particular action itself or observes someone else doing the same action. Therefore, mirror neuron system translates external state of another agent into the internal state of the current agent. Therefore, primates can repeat the observed action. This functionality is very close to the notion of reflexia. (Tarasenko, 2015, 1)

B. Perception of Emotions – proposed based on facial recognition and emotional responses of face.

The question that the paper addresses mainly is that of how to synch groups of agents, given their Alliance/Conflict value, so that they can coordinate actions in influencing humans to choose the positive pole of the Principal. Tarasenko employs Frequency Domain Multiplexing, that is each robot communicates with another via specific frequency based on alliance/conflict groups, which is also reminiscent of Kernbach's mapping of entangled objects, each has a unique frequency. In Tarasenko's proposal each robot has a unique ID and frequency. Spiking is a part of such a communications network; you might imagine a spike wave crossing over a group, inhibitory/excitatory (active/passive) pulses are sent through the network, each series of pulses starts 1ms after the system onset. Pulsations are based on Resonate and Fire linear neural model proposed by Izhikevich.

Tarasenko explains how this works:

> We present the sample dynamics of two resonate-and-fire neurons, described by system, with different eigen-frequencies $\omega 1 = \pi\,3/2$ and $\omega 2 = \pi\,4/3$ in Fig. 4. It is illustrated that neurons with eigen-frequency $\omega 1$ spikes for the series of pulses with the same frequency and does not respond to the series of pulses with frequency $\omega 2$. The same is true for the second neurons regarding shift in roles of frequencies $\omega 1$ and $\omega 2$. Thus, we have described the mechanism of frequency selectivity. This can be used to enable multiple neurons to talk to each other via the same medium by means of Frequency Domain Multiplexing. However, the linear model has other important properties. The inhibitory pulses can also cause resonate-and-fire neurons to spike, if the inhibitory pulses are applied with the eigenfrequency of the neuron. However, it is not the final feature of this model. It is possible to make the neuron fire with series of pulses of different magnitudes. For example, let the magnitudes of the first, second and third pulses be 0.1, 0.4 and 0.6, respectively. The same result will occur for the inhibitory pulses (Fig. 7). Since the neurons are selective to a certain frequency, it is possible to transfer signals of several frequencies through the same communication channel. (Tarasenko, 2015, 4)

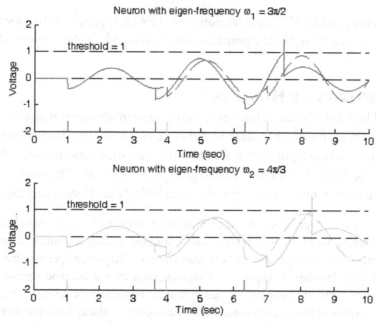

The Resonate-and-Fire neurons. T op: solid line illustrates resonanse with the input frequency $\omega 1 = 3\pi/2$, dashed line shows only subthreshold oscillations meaning that neuron does not respond to the frequency $\omega 2 = 4\pi/3$. Bottom: solid line illustrates resonanse with the input frequency $\omega 2 = 4\pi/3$, dashed line shows only subthreshold oscillations meaning that neuron does not respond to the frequency $\omega 1 = 3\pi/2$. The green and red vertical lines indicate the equal input pulses of magnitude 0.4. Green and red pulses are provided with frequencies $\omega 1 = 3\pi/2$ and $\omega 2 = 4\pi/3$, respectively. Each series of pulses starts 1 ms after the system onset. Threshold is set to 1. Parameter b is -0.1.

Information Coding – each autonomous unit has several resonators tuned to particular frequency.

- each unit corresponds to a resonators

- resonators = units (each unit has unique frequency)

- units send pulses with alliance or conflict values, if the series pulses contain the excitatory impulses, the sender/receiver = alliance, else in conflict message = {0.4, 0.4, 0.4} if a sender self-frequency (resonator unique freq).

to send message to another agent:
1. sender transmits ID-code
       -neuron spikes units b,c of which a is net or get member, and b,c understand a wants to transmit msg.
       -after short delay 0.5sec after spike unit a sends a code to other frequency.

Options Polarity (see Lefebvre Algebra. Of Conscience.)

alliance = + polarity {0.4, 0.4, 0.4}

conflict = - polarity {-0.4, -0.4, -0.4}

| TABLE III | | |
| TRANSMITTED RELATIONSHIP CODES | | |

	a	b	c
a	-	0	0
b	0	-	1
c	1	1	-

| TABLE IV | | |
| INFLUENCE MATRIX | | |

	a	b	c
a	a	{α}	{}
b	{α}	b	{β}
c	{β}	{}	c

units b and c (Fig. 9). Unit b will send conflict code to unit a and alliance code to unit c (Fig. 10). Unit c will send alliance

The canonical form of decision equation for unit a is $a = a + bc\bar{a}$ and the corresponding solution interval is $1 \supseteq a \supseteq bc$.

Alliance relationship results if both units agree on relationship codes:

Influences: the second part of the algorithm then calculates influence matrix of each node in groups, in reflexive control, the influences are applied to a subject or target to inverse or feed forward way (backward and forward propagation).

The only difference is that instead of the alliance or conflict unit transmission some code associated with a particular alternative.

- units can make mutual influences in order to achieve a particular goal in a cooperative behavior task.

- once each unit receives information about the structure of the group and the mutual influences, each autonomous unit can apply algorithms of RGT inference. Thus, each unit can make both it's own choice and also predict the possible choices of other members of the group.

Serge Tarasenko also goes into Decision Making with his analysis and modeling of RGT in Multistage Decision Processes.

The Reflexive Game Theory (RGT) [1, 2] allows to predict choices of subjects in the group. To do so, the information about a group structure and mutual influences between subjects is needed. Formulation and development of RGT was possible due to fundamental psychological research in the field of reflexion, which had been conducted by Vladimir Lefebvre [3].

The group structure means the set of pair-wise relationships between subjects in the group. These relationships can be either of alliance or conflict type. The mutual influences are formulated in terms of elements of Boolean algebra, which is built upon the set of universal actions. The elements of Boolean algebra represent all possible choices. The mutual influences are presented in the form of Influence matrix. (Tarasenko, 2012)

RGT Inference Steps (Single Session)

1. formalize choices in terms of elements of Boolean Algebra of alternatives

2. presentation of a group in the form of a fully connected graph of alliance and conflict

3. if graph is decomposable: then it is polynomial: alliance is a conjunction operation; conflict is disjunctive operation

4. Diagonal Form transformation

5. Run the decision equations

6. input influence values into the decision equations for each subject

each process of making a decision in a group is a 'session' (Tarasenko, 2012)

This study is dedicated to the matter of setting mutual influences in a group by means of reflexive control [4]. The influences, which subjects make on each other, could be considered as a result of a decision-making session previous to ultimate decision making (final session). We will call the influences, obtained as a result of a previous session(s), set-up influences. The set-up influences are intermediate result of the overall decision-making process. The term set-up influences is related to the influences which are used during the final session, only. (Tarasenko, 2012)

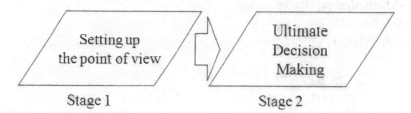

Fig. 1. The general schema of the two-stage decision making.

"…using the 2 stage decision making is possible to make one's opponents choose one's point of view." (Tarasenko, 2012, 5). How does one get this done, in this study Tarasenko offers up the exclusion or changing the structure of a group by node removal from the connected graph of an opposing viewpoint to the Principal seeking to push through their agenda in a decision-making group. In decision making there are consecutive decisions, decisions regarding a single parameter, a secondary process is 'parallel decision' with distinct parameters.

A GAME OF VIOLENCE, EXCLUSION AND DEGRADATION

When you play dodge ball and you are dodging, ducking, diving and dodging, you are playing a game that seeks to knock you out of the arena. Well, RC is no different. In the following section I review Tarasenko's two examples of changing structure to your benefit, first excluding a member from a decision from Tarasenko 2012 and second, Reflexive Emotional Control to alter the opinions of a member of a group from Tarasenko 2010.

Excluding a Member from a Decision:

A Model of a multi-stage decision: set-up parameters of the final session

Now we consider the two-stage model in more details. In the considered example, during the preliminary session only the decision regarding the influences has been under consideration. In general cases, however, before the final session has begun, decisions can be made regarding any parameters of the final session. Such parameters include but are not limit to:

1) group structure (number of subjects and relationships between subjects in a group);

2) points of view;

3) decision to start a final session (a time when the final session should start), etc.

We call the decision regarding a single parameter a consecutive decision, and decisions regarding distinct parameters to be parallel decisions. Therefore, during the first stage (before the final session) it is possible to make multiple decisions regarding various parameters of the final session. These decisions could be both parallel and consecutive ones. We call such a model of decision making a multi-stage process of decision making (Fig.3).

6   Sergey Tarasenko

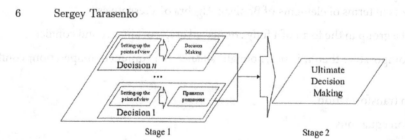

Fig. 3. Multi-stage decision making model.

4 Modeling multi-stage decision-making processes with RGT

Next, we consider the realization of multi-stage decision making with RGT. Example 2: Change a group structure. Considering the subject from Example 1, we analyze the case when a director wants to exclude the 3rd advisor from the group, which will make the final decision. In such a case, there is a single action (1) to exclude subject (d) from the group. Then Boolean algebra of alternatives includes only two elements: 1 and 0. Furthermore, it is enough that the director simply raise a question to exclude subject d from a group and make influence 1 on each subject: if = 1, then a = 1, b = 1 and d = 1 (Table 2). Thus, the decision to exclude subject d from the group would be made automatically (Fig.4).

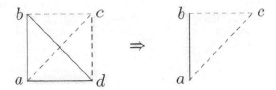

Fig. 4. Exclusion of a subject d from a group.

Example 3: Realization of multi-stage decision making. Let the first decision discussed during the first stage be a decision regarding influences (points of view). The next decision was about exclusion of a subject d from the group. Thus, during the first step the formation (setting-up) of points of view has been implemented, then the structure of the group was changed. Therefore, the group which should make a final decision is described by polynomial ab+c. The decision equations and their solutions are presented in Table 4. The overall multi-stage decision-making process is presented in Fig.5.

We consider that the point of view cannot change without a preliminary session regarding the parameter. Therefore, we assume that the points of view do not change after the alteration of group structure.

Modeling Mixed Groups of Humans and Robots   7

Table 4. Decision intervals for Example 3

Subject	Decision Equations	Decision Intervals
a	$a = (b+c)a + c\bar{a}$	$(b+c) \supseteq a \supseteq c$
b	$b = (a+c)b + c\bar{b}$	$(a+c) \supseteq b \supseteq c$
c	$c = c + ab\bar{c}$	$1 \supseteq c \supseteq ab$

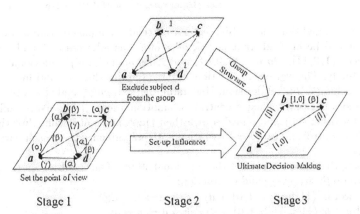

Fig. 5. Illustration of multi-stage decision making process. The influences are indicated by the arrow-ends of the ribs. The actual influence is presented near the arrow-end.

Therefore, during the final session the subjects would make the set-up influences derived from the preliminary session: subjects a and b will make influences $\{\beta\}$ and subject c will have a choice from the interval $1 \supseteq c \supseteq \{\beta\}$.

Such process is introduced in Fig. 5. During the 1st stage (first step), the points of view of subjects have been formed. On the 2nd stage (second step), the decision to exclude subject d from a group has been made. Finally, during the 3rd stage the final decision regarding the marketing strategy has been made.

SECOND, REFLEXIVE EMOTIONAL CONTROL:

3 Emotionally Colored Reflexive Games: Sample Situation

Consider a group of four subjects - the director d and his advisors a, b and c. Let advisors a,b and c are in alliance with each other and in conflict with director d. The graph of such group is presented in Fig. 4. This groups is described by polynomial $abc + d$.

Fig. 4. Relationship graph of four subjects a, b, c and d.

The canonical form of decision equation for each subject are:

$$a = (bc + d)a + d\overline{a} \tag{8}$$
$$b = (ac + d)b + d\overline{b} \tag{9}$$
$$c = (ab + d)c + d\overline{c} \tag{10}$$
$$d = d + abc\overline{d} \tag{11}$$

The corresponding solution intervals are

$$(bc + d) \supseteq a \supseteq d \tag{12}$$
$$(ac + d) \supseteq b \supseteq d \tag{13}$$
$$(ab + d) \supseteq c \supseteq d \tag{14}$$
$$1 \supseteq d \supseteq abc \tag{15}$$

Emotionally Colorful Reflexive Games   9

It is assumed that each subject is in a particular unique emotional state. Let director will be in Exuberant emotional state. The advisors a, b and c are in *Relaxed* ($\{1,0,1\}$), *Docile* ($\{1,0,0\}$) and *Anxious* ($\{0,1,0\}$) emotional states, respectively. This variety in emotional states refrains director and his advisors from reaching a fruitful decision. Understanding this emotional situation, director decides to apply reflexive control on emotional level. Let adivors' influence on all the other subjects coincides with their emotional state, while directly is in complete control and can decide, which emotional influence to on each particular subject.

Using RGT, we can predict the emotional states of each subject in the group after the *reflexive emotional interaction*:

for subject a: $(\{1,0,0\}\{0,1,0\} + d) \supseteq a \supseteq d \Rightarrow a = d$;
for subject b: $(\{1,0,1\}\{0,1,0\} + d) \supseteq b \supseteq d \Rightarrow a = d$;
for subject c: $(\{1,0,1\}\{1,0,0\} + d) \supseteq c \Rightarrow \{1,0,0\} + d \supseteq c \supseteq d$;
for subject d: $1 \supseteq d \supseteq \{1,0,1\}\{1,0,0\}\{0,1,0\} \Rightarrow 1 \supseteq d \supseteq 0 \Rightarrow d = d$.

Therefore, under conditions of such group structure and influences, decision of advisors a and b is completely defined by the director's influence.

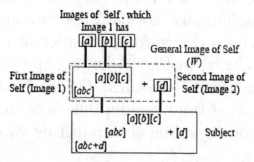

Fig. 5. Interpretation of the Diagonal form levels.

The entire diagonal form $(P + \overline{W})$ represents the state of the subject. In Fig. 5, the diagonal form is marked as Subject. The term $\overline{W}$ is called a general image of the self. On the next level, there are two images of Image 1 ($[abc]^{[a][b][c]}$) and Images 2 ($[d]$). The Images 1 and 2 are images of the self, which general image of the self W has. Finally, there are the images $[a]$, $[b]$ and $[c]$ are the images of the self, which Image 1 has.

Following this interpretation of the diagonal form [16, 17], we can calculate each emotional state in each image. We analyze the structure of reflexion for advisor c. His state is $(\{1,0,0\} + d)$ or $(Docile(+P, -A, -D)$ plus director's influence). The emotional state in the Image 1 is $Exuberant$ $(1 = \{1,1,1\})$, because $[abc]^{[abc]} = [abc] + \overline{[abc]} = 1$. The Image 2 is $[d]$ that means it is entirely defined by director's influence. Finally, the general images of the self W is $Exuberant$ $(1 = \{1,1,1\})$.

10   Sergey Tarasenko

In this simple example, we have illustrated how the emotional states can appear to be the subject for the reflexive control. We call such reflexive control to be *reflexive emotional control*. We have shown how the reflexive emotional control can be successfully implemented by means of the Reflexive Game Theory.

Besides, the RGT allows to unfold the entire sequence of reflexion in the human mind including its emotional aspects.

In the preceding we have traced out the history of cybernetics and it's relationship to psychotronics or neuroweapons. We have also seen how cybernetics is combined with Reflexive Control and even the addition of robots into the RC cycle. The main point is that scientists have worked out how to control not just individuals but entire groups within society. In the hands of a benevolent agent there is good to be found in such influence, say a weather disaster and you need to influence people to safety, on the other hand we can see how in the wrong hands such mathematical precision combined with AI could lead to societies spinning out of control in a neurowar based in the information space, leading to alteration of the brain's neurons themselves.

Notes:

[1]   https://www.gov.uk/government/news/100000-for-research-into-automation-and-machine-intelligence   (accessed 11/26/18)

[2]   https://www.theregister.co.uk/2013/12/31/nsa_weapons_catalogue_promises_pwnage_at_the_speed_of_light   (accessed 6/11/19)

[3] Rumsfeld shuts down Pentagon Influence Ops and Countermeasures, https://m.govexec.com/defense/2002/02/pentagon-shuts-down-controversial-information-office/11149/ (accessed 3/13/19)

BIBLIOGRAPHY:

Anonymous, 'Introduction to Operations Research', http://www.pondiuni.edu.in/storage/dde/downloads/mbaii_qt.pdf (accessed 6/11/19)

Aldrich, Richard J. (2010) 'GCHQ:The Uncensored Story of Britain's Most Secret Intelligence Agency' London: Harper Collins

Black, Edwin (2009) [2001]. IBM and the Holocaust: The Strategic Alliance Between Nazi Germany and America's Most Powerful Corporation (Paperback) (Second ed.). Washington, DC: Dialog Press.

Brannon, N., Conrad, G., Draelos, T., Seiffertt, J., Wunsch, D. Zhang, P. Coordinated (2007) 'Machine Learning and Decision Support for Situation Awareness: Sandia Report SAND2007-6058 September 2007 https://www.osti.gov/servlets/purl/920460/

Brederer, H. (2013) 'Did Allan Turing Interrogate Konrad Zuse in Gottingen in 1947?' ETH Zurich Report https://www.research-collection.ethz.ch/bitstream/handle/20.500.11850/69357/eth-6960-01.pdf

Cadwallader, A. (2013). Lethal Allies: British Collusion in Ireland. Ireland: Dufour Editions.

Chotikul, D. (1986) 'The Soviet Theory of Reflexive Control in Historical and Psychocultural Perspective: A Preliminary Study' Naval Post Graduate School https://nsarchive.gwu.edu/document/15364-diane-chotikul-soviet-theory-reflexive

Geraghty, Tony (1998) The Irish War: The Hidden Conflict Between the IRA and British Intelligence" John Hopkins University Baltimore

Kiryushinm A.N., (2013) Information confrontation: the problem of terminological insufficiency https://www.catu.su/analytics/439-informacionnoe-protivoborstvo-problema-terminologicheskoj-nedostatochnosti

Lefebvre, V., & Adams-Webber, J. (2002). Function of Fast Reflexion in Bipolar choice. Reflexive Processes and Control. Vol.1, N1. P.29-40 http://www.reflexion.ru/Library/ELefebvre_2002_1.htm

Medina, Eden (2005) 'Cybernetic Revolutionaries' MIT Press, Cambridge, Mass. https://uberty.org/wp-content/uploads/2015/10/Eden_Medina_Cybernetic_Revolutionaries.pdf (accessed 3/5/19)

Nikitaev, V. (2011) 'Foresight as reflexive control' (Russian) Journal of Reflexive Control and Processes Vol. 11 http://www.intelros.ru/pdf/rpu/1-2_2011/9.pdf

Novikov, D. A., Chkhartishvili, A. (2015) 'Models of Reflexive Games in Control Problems of the Ecological-Economic Systems' In Game-Theoretic Models in Mathematical Ecology / Edi-tors: V. Mazalov, D. Novikov, G. Ougolnitsky, L. Petrosyan. – New York: Nova Science Publishers, 2015. – P. 167 – 174. ISBN 978-1-63483-489-6. (Trapeznikov Institute of Control Sciences, Russian Academy of Sciences, Moscow, Russia)

Novikov, D.A., Breer, V., Rogatkin, A. (2017) 'Mob Control: Models of Threshold Collective Behavior' Russian Academy of Sciences Institute of Control Sciences & Moscow Institue of Physics and Technology https://www.researchgate.net/publication/311911469_Mob_Control_Models_of_Threshold_Collective_Behavior

Pickering, Andrew Andrew (2006) 'The Science of the Unknowable: Stafford Beer's Cybernetic Informatics' http://sts.au.dk/fileadmin/sts/publications/working_papers/Pickering_-_Science_of_the_Unknowable.pdf (accessed 2/12/19)

Rolston, Bill (2005) 'An Effective Mask for Terror: Democracy, Death Squads and Northern Ireland' https://www.academia.edu/11970647/An_Effective_Mask_for_Terror_Democracy_Death_Squads_and_Northern_Ireland (accessed 6/6/19)

Rulko, E., Buloychik, V. Gertsev, A. (2017) 'Application of a Simulation System for Optimizing Solutions Based on the Elements of the Theory of Reflexive Control' in Collection of Scientific Articls ofthe Military Academy of the Republic of Belarus 32'2017, pg. 153 https://www.researchgate.net/publication/329505714_Application_of_a_simulation_system_for_optimizing_solutions_based_on_elements_of_the_theory_of_reflexive_control_Primenenie_imitacionnoj_sistemy_modelirovania_dla_optimizacii_resenij_na_osnove_element

Russell, Stuart J.; Norvig, Peter (2003). Artificial Intelligence: A Modern Approach (2nd ed.). Upper Saddle River, New Jersey: Prentice Hall. ISBN 0-13-790395-2.

Scherrer, Col. Joseph H and Grund, Lt. Col. WIlliam C. (2009) 'A Cyberspace Command and Control Model', Air War College, Air University https://apps.dtic.mil/dtic/tr/fulltext/u2/a540457.pdf (accessed 3/20/19)

Schumann, A. (2018) 'Reflexive Games in Management' in Studia Humana Volume 7:1 (2018), pp. 44—52 DOI: 10.2478/sh-2018-0004

--(2014) 'Payoff Cellular Automata and Reflexive Games' in Journal of Cellular Automata, January 2014

Shemayev, V. (2007) Cognitive Approach to Modeling Refelxive Control in Socio-Economic Systems in Information and Security Vol. 22, 2007, 28-37, https://connections-qj.org/article/cognitive-approach-modeling-reflexive-control-socio-economic-systems

Shemayev, V., Sysoiev, V. (2017) Reflexive Modeling of Business Partner Selection in the Supply Chain, https://hrcak.srce.hr/file/281864

Tarashenko, S. (2010a) The Inverse Task of the Reflexive Game Theory: Theoretical Matters, Practical Applications and Relationship with Other Issues https://www.researchgate.net/publication/47797138_The_Inverse_Task_of_the_Reflexive_Game_Theory_Theoretical_Matters_Practical_Applications_and_Relationship_with_Other_Issues

-- (2010) Modeling multistage decision processes with Reflexive Game Theory
https://arxiv.org/abs/1203.2315

-- (2010b) Emotionally Colorful Reflexive Games (2010) https://www.researchgate.net/publication/48178099_Emotionally_Colorful_Reflexive_Games

-- (2016) Socializing Autonomous Units with the Reflexive Game Theory and Resonate-and-Fire Neurons https://www.researchgate.net/publication/303370445

_Socializing_Autonomous_Units_with_the_Reflexive_Game_Theory_and_Resonate-and-

Fire_Neurons

Telley, Maj. Christopher. (2018) 'The Influence Machine: Automated Information Operations as a Strategic Defeat Mechanism' in LAND WARFARE PAPER No. 121, October 2018 https://www.ausa.org/sites/default/files/publications/LWP-121-The-Influence-Machine-Automated-Information-Operations-as-a-Strategic-Defeat-Mechanism.pdf

Vasara, A. (2020) Theory of Reflexive Control: Origins, Evolution and Application in the Framework of Contemporary Russian Military Strategy Finnish Defence Studies #22 https://www.doria.fi/handle/10024/176978

Watt, Holly (2018) MoD granted 'List X' status to Cambridge Analytica parent company, https://www.theguardian.com/uk-news/2018/mar/21/mod-cambridge-analytica-parent-company-scl-group-list-x (accessed 3/21/18)

CHAPTER 6

PHYSICS OF NEUROWEAPONS

GRAVITATIONAL BASIS OF NEUROWEAPONS

Some suppose that to have psi or faster-than-light propulsion one must come up with a new physics that is not Einstein's General Relativity (GR). However, this is not mandatory for psi or faster-than-light propulsion. The question of Gravity is a central question to Einstein's equations, yet missing from GR is the explanation of Quantum Gravity. This remains an open question in Quantum Physics. Below we will review one possible explanation of Quantum Gravity in the work of German Physicist Burkhard Heim. It is important to realize that what we know of Gravity is still very much an open investigation with no firmly established principles or any quantifiable explanation for how Quantum Gravity works. In regard to explanations for Quantum Gravity we will also encounter the founder of Quantum Field Theory, Pascual Jordan, who as a Nazi scientist worked extensively on Gravity and Quantum Biology.

The conception in many conspiracy theory explanations of Neuroweapons is that cell towers are the methodology for such propagation. Though it is true that potentially microwaves, as used in cell towers, could be used to send out EM waves. From the documentation by proponents of this technology it becomes clear that the cell tower explanation may indeed be disinformation.

In the High Frequency Gravitational Wave (HFGW) section of this chapter we will see documentation by former Lockheed Engineer, Dr. Robert Baker, to embed HFGW receivers and transmitters in cell phones; thus making the need for any cell towers obsolete and unnecessary. However, it is still a valid concern regarding the 25th Frame effect in inducing deeper trance states which can be manipulated through gravitational waves and their conversion into EM radiation to affect brain function through video screens, not reliant on cell towers, including 5G. For instance, microwaves can be blocked, yet people complaining of Neuroweapon exploitation experience this effect even in shielded environments where microwaves cannot penetrate, which points to gravitational waves which can penetrate all materials.

The question becomes where and how did Gravitational Wave technology come from and who developed it. Regarding this we would have to look at an avowed Nazi Quantum Physicist, credited as one of the founders of Quantum Mechanics, Pascual Jordan and the conscripted German soldier Burkhard Heim, who went on to propose a gravitational theory that expanded on Einstein's General Relativity into a hyper-dimensional space where others have noted Gravitational Waves can also propagate. Before diving deeper into Jordan and Heim's work in Nazi Germany and post-war Germany it is worthwhile to take a look at the development of these ideas as they were propagated through the post-war Soviet Union and UK-USA defense industry research. Also of note is Austrian biologist Paul Kamerrer (who based his 'law of seriality' on the theory that that synchronicities occur through a gravity-like field. His writings indicate a typology associated with 'Targeted Individuals.' He died of suicide in 1926.

This technology, in the early days, was not referenced as Neuroweapons, but rather as 'Transcommunication.' There are several explanations for the ability of non-local communication, most of which incorporate gravity and neutrinos. Several researchers in the Soviet Union have credited the work of Pascual Jordan on gravity as the source of their gravitational wave investigations for the purposes of neurowarfare. American researchers have also noted the role of gravitation in psi or 'transcommunication' technology; for instance, in the Soviet Union the work of Dubrov, which calls for 'non-local transference only in a gravitational field, which he based on the work of L.L. Vasilev" (DIA, 1975, 16-17). It is also incorporated into the work of Bunin in his creation of a signal transmitter/

receiver using GW in 1972. Dubrov credits Bunin with his knowledge of bio-gravitation. Also mentioned in Dubrov's work is that of theoretical physicist K. Stanjukovic. We mention the work of Matvei Bronstein, Gravitational Theorist, who was killed in a Stalinist purge. The purges themselves may have been a Nazi Psyop, as they occurred in 1938, just before the war started and shortly after the ending of the Nazi-Soviet military cooperation pact, signed in 1932. Another purged researcher in Astrocosmology was Kozyerev, who did not use the term 'gravitation' for his explanation but seems to correlate what he called 'time' as 'gravitational effects'; a theory formulated in the Siberian gulag he was sentenced to. Again, there is a pattern of people involved in gravitational explanations being targeted by the Stalinist purges, while Jordan is working on his own Nazi technology based on the same.

United States academics have cited the work of Haaken Forwald (1897-1978), who proposed in *Mind, Matter and Gravitation* (1969) that psi was gravity based. W. G. Roll, originally a German national, immigrated to the US and proposed that 'psi' field which we would now call 'gravitational field'; he also worked with Nazi Parapsychologist Hans Bender after the war, on a physical explanation of 'Psi.' Bender, as noted before, also worked with Jordan and Heim, as well as Capt. Hans Roeder, post-war on a physical explanation for psi on which to base a real scientific technology. Bender is not outside American influence either, as he is noted to have worked with the DIA on 'hauntings' at an American base in Germany.

In the DIA report that speaks of this collaboration, an American academic, Elizabeth Rauscher, was also consulted where, in the work cited in the report 'Higher Dimensional Geometrical Models', she also used a higher dimensional or hyper-space; in this case 8d, to explain psi. Again only gravitation could be in both 4d and hyper dimensions. Dr. Robert Baker writes, "An important point about Gravitational Waves is that they propagate in subspace or hyper dimensions beyond the 4d we inhabit" (Baker, 2017, 28).

An interesting contribution to the gravitational explanation for Psi came from former DoD analyst, Lt. Col. Thomas Bearden, who worked on analyzing Soviet technology in this area, where he explains the construction of electro-gravitational waves and beams. The destructive interference of ordinary EM waves produces potential gravitational energy. Release of EM leads to bleed off of a 5d gravitational potential as EM. Bottling up of EM leads to 5d Gravitational potential, similar to Gerstenshtein Effect and Li Effects discussed in HFGW section below, as ordinary 4d gravitational force. These and other ideals are analogous to B. Heim's explanations of Psi and gravity.

Digging deeper into Soviet research, it was L. L. Vasilev who proposed the gravitational hypothesis, first formulated by Jordan. Vasilev also referenced neutrinos, another particle, like graviton, that is thought to be able to penetrate almost anything (DIA, 1975, 7-8). L. L. Vasilev was a key assistant to Bekhterev in the joint German-Soviet Brain Institute. Some of his early research involved the use of hypnosis to enable better psi transmission.

> ...suggested that the interaction between the gravitational field and some existing but unexplained factor, possibly by the cerebral matter itself [possibly magnetite or Microtubules], might be involved in telepathic communication. He also suggested that thought transmission might be connected with the laws of cybernetic systems. Vasilev also referred to the action of the neutrino particles formed during nuclear reactions. If it could be established that such particles (neutral charge), move with speed approaching C [light] and are capable of penetrating obstacles of enormous mass, are generated during the neuropsychic activity of the brain, it might conceivably be shown that these particles serve as the mechanism for telepathic transmission. (DIA, 1975, 16-7)

Vasilev went on to publish some of his unclassified work in "Telesuggestion" (1962) and "Experiments in Mental Suggestion" (1965). As noted, he influenced the work of Dubrov.

Aleksandr P. Dubrov, in a seminal article from 1973, "Bio-gravitation and Psychotronics" noted: "By the term bio-gravitation, we designate a field energy system. The bio-gravitation field is universally convertible...it is capable of transition into any form of field and energy, therefore a unified field theory."

Dubrov notes that it is a "unified field theory," which is also a pointer back to Jordan's contribution to the Soviet understanding of Gravitational effects on biological systems.

Dubrov goes onto explain Bio-gravitational effects:

a. act at close or long range
b. Can be directed and focused
c. + or -

d. Can carry information

e. Convert the energy of field into matter with weight (mass)

f. Field persists in absence of source

g. can transition to any form of field or energy

h. Are bound up with the change of symmetry groups and with distorting of space at the sub-molecular level of biological structure (Dubrov, 1973, 313)

Referencing the work of Bunin, this reference also touches on the work of Dr. Michael Persinger, (see below), regarding the effects of bio-gravitation on thixotropy in water, which also may have an effect on brain microtubules, and hence consciousness:

For a variable biogravitational field, according to V. Bunin, it may be accepted that gravitational radiation is contingent on the phased oscillations or rotating of hydrogen electrons or atoms of water in H2O [see Persinger below and in Quantum Consciousness section, thixotropy] a living organism may be both a receiver/transmitter of gravitational waves, evaluating the minimum level of a receivable signal:

It is illuminating in the following section that Dubrov talks of directing or focusing the gravitational radiation, as this is exactly the device designed and built by Bunin in 1972:

DESCRIPTION | 347937
OF THE INVENTION

Союз Советских
Социалистических
Республик

Stated 02.11.1959 (N 701720 / 40-23)

Published on 10.VIII.1972. Bulletin 24

Date of publication of the description 11.X.1972

Inventor: V. A. Bunin

Комитет по делам
изобретений и открытий
при Совете Министров
СССР

**SIGNAL TRANSMISSION AND RECEIVING SYSTEM
USING GRAVITATIONAL WAVES**

English Translation of V. Bunin's 1972 Soviet Patent for GW Signals

Later these same principles are applied in Dr. Baker's HFGW Transmitter/Receiver, although it is possible he had already developed these ideas himself in 1961 at Lockheed:

we should mention in this connection that a number of researchers have studied gravitational radiation in respect of rotating particles. This radiation has been studied by quantum theory methods in respect to the approach of a weak gravitational field in the case of the gravitational radiation of a synchotron of a particle moving along a circle. The most interesting thing for us is this research author's conclusion that the major part of the radiation is concentrated in a small angular region near the particles place of rotation and can thereby be directed. (Dubrov, 1973, 316)

Also noted by DIA HFGW proponent, Paul Murad: "A similar thing occurred several years ago concerning the idea that gravity waves obey a law of optics and could essentially be directed which has interesting consequences." (Murad, 2006)

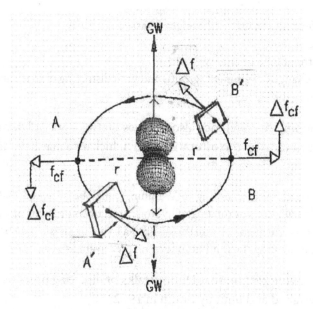

Figure 2.1.3a. Radiation pattern calculated by Landau and Lifshitz (1975) Section 110 Page 356.

Dr. Forward is remembered by Paul Murad, a DIA HFGW investigator, referencing back to Forwards early contributions to gravity theory and control:

> Bob Forward .... I had no real idea of how impressive he was. Mead had supported him when he looked at exotica such as anti-matter propulsion and tethers. I found that in a 1963 paper, he talked about controlling gravity with electric and magnetic fields, something that Einstein in his recently translated papers from 1920 said the same thing. Forward looked at gyroscopes about the same time as the Russian Kosyrev also investigated such effects. (Murad, 2006)

Dubrov, like Jordan, also touches on gravity on Quantum Biological subjects, here specifically protein synthesis, which later we will encounter in the resonance concepts in Cosic's work (see Quantum Consciousness Section):

> ...the formation of a gravitational field, with all its attendant consequences, is also possible. In this way, theoretical calculations support our hypothesis that a biogravitational field may result from changes in the conformation of protein molecules subjective to compression, tension and deformation. (Dubrov, 1973, 316)
>
> The process by which a constant biogravitational field is formed can be hypothesized in a similar way using traditional notions. Considering that, during that change in conformation of the protein molecules from a state of random aggregation to an ordered crystalline state, not only does a phased oscillation of the atoms occur but the atoms move closer together, it is to be expected that a considerable constant Bio-Gravitational field will appear, owing to the great increase in the density at micro level, of the biostructures.
>
> Aleksandr P Dubrov, a Moscow physicist, has proposed a model for paranormal perception based on a gravity-type interaction. In this concept, he considers it theoretically possible for aggregates of biological molecules that are in a loosely bound state (liquid crystal type) to create very weak quasi-gravitational field effects. This would result, in his view, from variations in gravitational attraction forces arising from changes in relative molecular spacing. The net effect would be a very small gravitational-type perturbation. This would be in addition to normal gravitational attraction and gravitational perturbations which are theoretically possible from thermal oscillations. (DoD, 1978)

He suggests that a constant Biogravitational field results from specialized brain structures when strongly excited (epiphysis, hypophysis).

In psychology, new light will be thrown on one of nature's greatest secrets, the workings of the brain. A better understanding of mental processes, the brains integrating activity, the coding of information and partcular states of consciousness can be achieved only with the aid of the bioGravitational hypothesis. (see V. Pushkin psychological biogravitational hypothesis 'Autogravitaija (Autogravitation).' in Socialisticeshajaindustrija Moscow 9 Sept 1973)

From Dr. Dubrov's work we can see the direction and correlation with actual inventions in the form of Bunin's Gravitational Signal Transmitter (1972), as well as the tendency to associate gravity with influencing the Brain. The subsequent publication in 1973 of Dubrov's paper shows that at least as early as the 1970s the Soviets were working on weaponized versions of Gravitational based technology for the purpose of remote influencing.

MODERN THEORIES OF GRAVITY AND REMOTE SENSING

One of the most important North American researchers in the role of gravitation, electro-magnetism and microwave radiation in remote sensing was Dr. Michael Persinger (d. 2019), who as the son of a Naval Intelligence officer and also research collaborator, got interested in the idea of EM waves and remote sensing at an early stage, a subject that has occupied his entire career. He is known to neuroweapons developers as evidenced in the writings of Lockheed engineer, Dr. John Norseen. As a professor at Laurentian University in Canada, he had an experimental lab set up that could look into these areas with some level of public financial support. His experiments are, as we should expect with plausible deniability, doubted, controversial and often on the receiving end of extreme emotional counter arguments for such a quantized scientific experimentation that he employed in his understanding of the physics behind entanglement (he calls 'deep correlation'), brain physiology, brain microtubules, Schumann Resonance, and other areas, all of which are directly related to technologies outlined and documented in Neuroweapons development.

Persinger related the role of gravity in deep correlation:

> ...the theory developed by Hu and Wu (2006a, b; 2013) that the primary source of the macroscopic manifestation of quantum entanglement originates from primordial spin processes in non-spatial and non-temporal pre-space-time and involves gravity. When one considers the measurement by Fickler et al (2013) that single photons (even though they differ by 600 in quantum number as long as they exhibit quantized orbital angular momentum from helical wave structures) can exhibit excess correlation, then the potential for remote sensing become feasible. (Persinger, 2015, 660)

Persinger in another paper makes the case for graviton, the particle form of gravity, as the means of psi:

> Measurements have shown an inverse association between natural electromagnetic intensities and irradiance from background photons. In general for every $\sim 10^{-12}$ W·m^{-2} increase in photon radiant flux density there was a 1 nT decrease in intensity of the ambient static (geo-)magnetic field. Dimensional equivalence of the two quantities required the latter to be multiplied by $\sim 10^{-3}$ A·s^{-1}. Assuming $\sim 10^{79}$ particles universally, each with a unit charge, the rest mass of that particle would be $\sim 10^{-65}$ kg or the median solution for the graviton. On the bases of the calculations and conceptual inferences, entanglement phenomena across the space-time that defines the universe could be mediated by a gravitational field whose quantized component, the mass of a graviton, when expressed as the square of the hypothetical entanglement velocity, is light. This velocity (10^{23} m·s-1) is derivable from independent approaches that require the consideration of the universe as a single set. If this inference derived from empirical measurements is valid, then there is additional evidence that "excess correlation" and entanglement of photons anywhere in the universe is mediated by quantized components of a gravitational field that is contained within the total spatial and temporal boundaries. (Persinger, 2015b)

Persinger, in this same paper goes on to clarify that entanglement or deep correlation occurs in a singular universe, the view that the universe as proposed by theoretical physicists, Hu and Wu, that everything is connected, or a full graph. Persinger remarks, "the essential premise is that the physical mechanisms that serve as the substrate for entanglement reflect the properties of the entire universe as a unit within which differences in time may be less critical" (Persinger, 2015). Again, one should be aware that graviton and gravitational waves are indeed non-local, both spatially and temporally, adhering to the quantum physics definition of non-local. We can see from Persinger's research that he directly relates 'remote sensing' with gravitational effects at the least. In another paper, he relates that entanglement and remote sensing are directly related: "two-photon, 3d entanglement may be capable of applied quantum communication [transcommunication]. Such quantum energy teleportation may not be limited to distance [or location: x,y,z,t]." (Persinger, 2014). We will encounter Dr. Persinger more in the Quantum Consciousness section where we will learn about his ideas regarding neuroscience, entanglement and changing angular momentum as the means of remote sensing, which of course is common to all waves, whether EM or Gravitational.

In the following sections we shall read about the history of the development of Gravitational Waves and their detection. Starting with the work of Pascual Jordan, Burkhard Heim, Joseph Weber, and the work of Dr. Robert Baker with HFGW.

PASCUAL JORDAN (1902-1980)

Pascual Jordan received his Habilitation (Ph. D). in 1927 at age 24 in Göttingen. After graduating he received a Rockefeller Grant to study in Copenhagen, the center of the dominant QM interpretation. In 1929 he was a professor at Rostock; he had a stuttering problem which kept him from more prestigious postings. At Rostock he became a propagandist for the Nazi cause, he later became the same for the Christian Democratic Union in West Germany. His sentiments at the time of his appointment to Rostock are characterized by Beyler:

> After the Nazi takeover, Jordan put his own name to similar but even more vehement opinions. The physics professor and new NSDAP member wrote in the Rostock University student newspaper in May 1933 that 'armed with fundamentally unlimited power...this [ongoing] transformation [of the state] levis the 'claim of totality' to reform incisively all domains.' An antiliberal variation appeared in his 1935 book Physicalisches Denken in der neuen Zeit, from the same publishing house as Dutsches Volkstum. The book was, inter alia, a proclamation of the service that science and technology--above all, military technology--could offer the power-oriented modern state. The 'technical modernization of the apparatus of government,' he specified, occurred through the replacement of the old parliamentary forms... with authoritative and dictatorial methods.' Elsewhere, in a report to the Reich education ministry on the 1936 Unity of Science Conference in Copenhagen, he endeavored to convince the authorities of the possible role of modern science in the struggle against 'Bolshevism' and the 'materialistic camp' in general. (Beyler, 1996, 259)

An avowed fascist and racist from an early age, after having been a Protestant Fundamentalist, his scientific interests diverged from his cultural interests; on one hand he worked with such infamous Jews in Physics as Einstein, on the other hand calling for their removal from academia. In 1942 he attempted to start a Physics journal dedicated to the industrial scale development of Quantum Biology. Often Jordan's contributions to Quantum Mechanics are minimized due to his Nazi past. During the war he ostensibly served in the meteorological service until 1944, when he received a Professorship in Berlin, worked with Berlin-Buch Brain Institute, and was employed, like Capt. Roeder, at the secret technology office of the Kriegsmarine (German Navy). After the war he eventually ended up in the 4th Reich hotbed of Hamburg where he was a professor in 1947.

Pascual Jordan worked with Burkhard Heim to set up experiments, but never got funded. Pascual Jordan was also at MBB when Heim made his presentation in 1969. Pascual was also in contact with Hans Bender. Bender records in a letter to Duke University parapsychology Dr. Rhine, that he had exchanged information regarding parapsychology with Jordan in 1949 (Asprem, 2013, 410). Jordan, already in 1936 had written regarding parapsychology and quantum physics[1]. As we shall read later, he very much anticipated developments in Quantum Consciousness, thus informing the work of Dr. Norseen.

His pet theory (Schoer, 2003) was gravitation with a time-dependent gravitational coupling. His name is part of what is known as the Jordan-Brans-Dicke Theory. Which calls for supplementary gravitational fields to what is normally considered, see below. As Schoer has noted:

> "Jordan was a visionary revolutionary" (Schoer 2003, 9). He was guided in his early work by Max Bjorn, and his papers helped solidify Heisenberg's claims. He is considered a co-founder of Quantum Mechanics, but due to his Nazi beliefs his contributions are largely minimized, although one can see the importance of his intellectual

scientific achievements in being considered as one of the founders of Quantum Mechanics. He also founded a form of mathematics known as Jordan algebras. In 1926 he worked on quantization of wave fields using Quantum Field Theory, which differs from typical Quantum Mechanics.

In 1929, he presented on QFT at the Kharkov (Ukraine) conference, which was a German language based conference, though in the Soviet Union; part of the German-Soviet technological cooperation:

> In 1929 at a conference in Kharkov, Jordan gave a remarkable plenary talk (the conference language at that time was still German). In a way it marks the culmination of the first pioneering phase of QFT; but it also already raised some of the questions which were partially answered almost 20 years later in the second phase of development (i.e., renormalized perturbation theory, gauge theory). In his talk Jordan reviews in a very profound and at the same time simple fashion the revolutionary steps from the days of matrix mechanics to the subsequent formulation of basis-independent abstract operators (the transformation theory which he shares with Dirac) and steers then right into the presentation of the most important and characteristic of all properties which set QFT apart from QM: Locality and Causality as well as the inexorably related Vacuum Polarization.
>
> ....These statements are even more remarkable if one realizes that they come from the protagonist of field quantization only two years after this pivotal discovery. When I accidentally came across the written account of this Kharkov talk, I was almost as surprised as I was many years before when it became known that Oscar Klein (with whom Jordan collaborated in the 30s in Copenhagen) had very advanced ideas about nonabelian gauge theory (which were published in the proceedings of the 1939 Warsaw international conference). Apparently, all of the classical aspects of nonabelian gauge theories and some quantum aspects were known before the second world war. Apart from QED the postwar interest developed away from gauge theories into pion-nuclear physics. The great era of gauge theory in connection with strong interactions had to wait 3 decades. (Schoer, 2003, 8)

It is interesting to note that Jordan was decades ahead of the rest of the physics community in the 1930s, an era when he is also formulating his ideals on mass scale Quantum Biology research. The modern antecedent to Jordan's thought is contained in Loop Quantum Gravity theory. According to Schoer Jordan's expectations about QFT are now in Local Quantum Physics (LQP):

> ...although important ideas in the exact sciences may get lost in certain situations, sooner or later they will be rediscovered and expanded." In this sense it is in relation to the rediscovery of key concepts of QFT from 1939 that were lost during the war and not taken up again for 30 years. Noting such work at Oscar Klein, all of the classical aspects of non-abelian gauge theories and some quantum aspects were known in 1939 but lost for 30 years (Schoer 2003, 8-9).

For Jordan gauge theory was important in 1929.

Quantum Biology these days is thought to have begun with Heisenberg, who was never a member of the Nazi Party; in actuality it was started through a synergy of ideas exchanged between Bohr and Jordan. Jordan heavily influenced Heisenberg, though they disagreed on many points, Werner Heisenberg did accept the target-theory approach. Jordan's contribution is largely buried, suggested by scholars due to his Nazi beliefs, which also could be explained if he was continuing research as an obfuscation of hidden work. He worked with a team of Genetic Researchers at the Berlin-Buch Brain Institute. He collaborated with this group from the 1930s to the end of the war. He also sought to work with the Nazi Reich in establishing a massive industrial scale Quantum Biology research sector within the assumedly victorious Nazi Reich. In 1942 Jordan started the academic journal *Physis: Betrage zur Naturwissenschaftlichen Synthese,* in which he propagandized for his scientific ideas. He was working with the censorship office on this, while also being dually recruited by the Propaganda Ministry for a similar project. (Beyler 1996, 268). Dahn has written regarding this period:

> The second contribution, though, exemplified the way in which ideology could find its way into Physis—and into the plan for Europe-wide big science—as it was written specifically to pique the curiosity of well-positioned Nazi power brokers. Titled "Future Tasks for Quantum Biological Research," it expanded on Jordan's article in *Deutschlands Erneuerung,* outlining a detailed plan for a massive group of research institutes to investigate Jordan's quantum biology—essentially prototyping his vision of big science. The "research center" envisioned

was so costly and ambitious that "its realization would certainly presuppose the German victory as already achieved," so it would "stand after the German victory as a symbol and representation of the unlimited means of power [Machtmittel] of the new Reich." In charge would be a Führerinstitut, or leading institute, conforming to the Nazi Führer principle that a leader should be found in every area. At the end, Jordan slyly tied his proposed institute to another of the Nazis' favorite bugbears, cancer, noting that all quantum biological research opened "new possibilities of attack against the cancer problem."

This wide spectrum of articles makes the deeper designs for Physis clear: Jordan and Meyer-Abich aimed to create a leading (and the analogy to the Führer was intended) interdisciplinary, international, scientific organ, in the vein of Nature or the German Die Naturwissenschaften, that would institutionalize Jordan's vision of big science in the "new Europe." Demonstrating the quality, loyalty, and military value of German science to the Nazi state, Physis was to be a vehicle through which Jordan and Meyer-Abich could pull in financial support—and protection—for their monumental plan for a Europe-wide scientific enterprise operating on an industrial scale under German leadership." (Dahn, 2018, 82)

To delineate the departments of the Quantum Biological Institute would undertake, the first volume of the journal, *Physis*, contained Jordan's elaborate plan for a quantum-biological research institute. This envisioned 3 research groups: genetic research (on bacteria, yeast, fruit flies, etc.), protein research [RNA], and 'warm-blooded [animals] research' (Including topics such as serology [Vershuer-Butenandt experiments], immunology, oncology and mammalian genetics).

Jordan was in dynamic tension with the ideological purity of the Hitler-led establishment of the Nazi Reich. He worked regularly with Jews in Quantum Mechanics and this was not viewed as true Deutsch Physics: the attempt to rid Physics of all Jewish influence. He did, though, manage to get official sponsorship from the Reich for his journal. Beyler notes:

The power structure of the Nazi state, despite the propaganda touting totalitarian unity, was a 'polycracy' of different power blocs [Himmler: North German (Hamburg) vs. Hitler: South German/Austrian] often with ill-defined and overlapping spheres of authority and sometimes with mutually antagonistic interests. This was especially true in science policy. Here there were long-standing conflicts between authorities who pushed for instrumental efficiency [Himmler] and those whose main interest was ideological purity [Hitler] (Beyler, 1996, 250).

One issue in Germanic Nationalist science is that of organacism, while the Reich itself was very mechanistic oriented. This dynamic between organicism and mechanics is one that is played out in Jordan's mind. German researcher, Beyler, writes regarding this:

To win support for a quantum revolution in biology, Jordan sought to reconcile organicist ends-- the rejection of mechanistic theories--with physicalist means--the deployment of concepts, techniques, and metaphors derived from modern physics. Extending the quantum revolution also meant, for Jordan, seeking to link modern science and the Nazi state in mutual legitimation. He was partially successful in finding a niche for quantum biology in the ideological and institutional structures of the Third Reich, but only partially. Just as the intended conceptual and disciplinary bases of quantum biology were marked by unresolved tensions, so too the cultural meanings Jordan ascribed to quantum biology mirrored a volatile instability in Nazi ideology and praxis; professed allegiance to ideals of volkisch social harmony alongside the unmitigated exertion of authoritarian, technocratic power. In short, in its cultural meanings the target-theoretical organism embodied the precarious situation of modernity in the Third Reich. (Beyler,1996, 248-9)

Beyler continues to delineate Jordan's organicist ends toward authoritarian science:

On the conceptual and disciplinary levels, quantum biology combined two trends that seem prima facie to be polar opposites. Starting in 1932, Jordan published several essays on biology that he intended as contributions to the 'organicist conception of the world' and to the concomitant rejection of materialism [Marxist Leninism]. Responding to criticisms of these speculations, he added from 1937 onward a quite different perspective appropriated from the 'target' or 'hit' theory in biophysics. Target theory was a statistical methodology for analyzing the effect of radiation or other physical agents on organisms. It hypothesized the existence of submicroscopic 'targets' that were affected--that is, 'hit'--by the impinging radiation. Through the target-theoretical connection, quantum biology would acquire experimental technologies and theoretical models from modern physics. It would also become allied with a group of dynamic and well-supported researchers. (Beyler, 1996, 249)

'Target' or 'hit' theory was first introduced in 1922 by the X-ray physicist Friedrich Dessauer, professor of the physical foundations of medicine in Frankfurt. Parallel developments started in Britain with the work of J.A. Crowther and in France with that of Fernand Holweck. The theory gained in interest following a series of dramatic discoveries that focused new attention on physical experimentation in biology and on the microscopic or submicroscopic domain. The discovery of X-ray mutagenesis by H. J. Muller in 1927 opened a new era in experimental biology. (Beyler, 1996, 253-4)

Boris Rajewsky continued the work of Dessauer, who went into exile in 1934. Rajewsky headed and founded the KWI for Biophysics in 1936. Another target institution was the KWI for Genetics, the Institute for Brain Research in Berlin-Buch, founded by Oskar Vogt with a twin institute in Russia. The work in Berlin-Buch was by Russian geneticist Nikolai W. Timofeeff-Ressovsky. Target theory also influenced the founding of microbiology through phage research. By 1936, [Jordan] spoke enthusiastically of using physics in pursuit of fundamental problems of genetics, within the context of eugenics. In 1935, Timofeeff and Zimmer wrote a paper with CalTech's German emigre Delbruck, which addressed the atomic-physical model of gene-mutation. Within the target-theoretical analysis of radiation genetics data, the paper argued that mutation was a 'one-hit' process, a single ionization produced by a quantum of radiation in certain receptive areas, a large organic molecule. Jordan argued that the gene was such a thing, the gene as a group of atoms.

Jordan is here speaking or alluding to the concept of targeting genes with waves or radiation, a specialty of one of his collaborators, Karl Zimmer of the Brain Institute. It is important to note that the working group at Berlin-Buch that Jordan was involved with led directly to the invention of Genetic Engineering. As is well documented, the Nazi scientific community was very interested in using Genetics to target those of other Genetic compositions deemed 'non-German.' Beyler writes of this collaboration:

Jordan's plans for restructuring biophysical research were directly linked to his target-theoretical contacts. Their importance to him is shown by the fact that during the war years he repeatedly attempted to be transferred to Berlin from his postings in the Luftwaffe meteorological service in order to be closer to the Berlin-Buch group. Despite the resistance of his military superiors, in late 1943 he succeeded--with Heisenberg's help--in obtaining simultaneous appointments to a professorship of physics at the University of Berlin and to a position at the Navy Research and Patent Office. He hoped to be able to pursue biophysical work more intensively and in closer collaboration with Zimmer, Rompe, and other Berlin colleagues. (Beyler, 1996, 269)

Again, the Navy Research and Patent Office of the Kreigsmarine were secret facilities to develop advanced technology for use in warfare. It is not known if Jordan seeking a physical explanation for Psi, and Capt. Roeder also seeking a physical explanation for Psi converged as they served in the same institution, the Navy Research and Patent Office. It is known they circulated among die-hard supporters of the Nazi cause post-war. Roeder and Jordan, both being Hamburg based, had common connections like Nazi Parapsychologist Dr. Hans Bender; Jordan worked with Heim, who worked with Bender, who worked with Roeder.

The utilization of science to further the great racial cleansing, the Final Solution, of the Nazi state was envisioned by Jordan:

"In the noninheritance of acquired characteristics, lies the natural scientific foundations of the racial-political conceptions that have victoriously prevailed in the great revolution of our time." Quantum biology could thus contribute to this means of authoritarian intervention into the social fabric; 'race research' would be one of the tasks of the proposed institute. (Beyler,1996, 270)

In a previous section we covered the work of Baron von Verschuer through Mengele, a different group working on genetics, through the Genetics section of the KWI for Anthropology headed by von Verschuer. Jordan saw science as a directed endeavor, to be used for interdiction into human natural existence to meet social demands, like the demands of the Nazi ideology. He viewed existence as teleological (designed with purpose):

...Jordan had expressed in a 1928 letter to Albert Einstein, that atoms or subatomic particles in a living organism might somehow be able to coordinate their behavior, in a way not yet understood by quantum theory, and thereby allow the organism to act teleologically. (Beyler, 1996, 263)

As seen, the concept of steering human existence is a definite part of Jordan's research endeavors:

Jordan's question to biology, then, became "whether organic entities, e.g., humans, can be seen as essentially macroscopic entities." He believed he knew the answer: "Exactly such organic reactions by which the macroscopic reactions of the human or animal body are directed... are often a delicacy that reaches in the atomic domain." Living beings, although macro-physical in size, were 'directed' or 'steered' by acausal quantum events, whose effects were then somehow amplified by organic structures. Jordan cautioned that this 'amplifier theory' could not by itself explain the 'essence of the organic.' Indeed, he thought that complete physical-chemical investigation might well destroy the ability of the steering centers to function; they might possess a kind of non-observability over and above that found in ordinary quantum physics. Despite this, the amplifier theory brought out the crucial anti-mechanistic insight that quantum effects had to be taken into account in biology. (Beyler, 1996, 261)

The concept of the Amplifier theory from Quantum level of existence to macroscopic level, or the classical level of existence, is an important understanding for Jordan. Indeed, it presages ideas of Quantum Consciousness discussed later; that consciousness bubbles up from the Quantum level to the biological scale.

Jordan saw science as a way to change humans, to make them true citizens of the Reich, which of course necessarily means surrendering one's own individual identity to the Volk Statt (Nazi "People's" State). Beyler notes:

What became, then of organic totality in the Nazi state? In the formulation of Ralf Dahrendorf, "the Nazi regime tried everywhere to replace organic structures by mechanical formations." As we shall see, Jordan applied metaphors from quantum biology to a modern, technocratic, albeit anti-democratic society; these metaphors accorded with certain aspects of his cultural context but were hard to reconcile with the concept of holistic, organic coordination. Embodying in this way the ambiguities of modernity in the Third Reich, Jordan's biophysical metaphors may have contained more truth then even he realized. (Beyler, 1996, 252)

Jordan viewed biology as a model for human social organization:

In the first instance, microphysical control centers--genes, 'miniature nuclei,' and the like--served as metaphors for dictatorship. In 1941, in a book on the 'secret of organic life,' Jordan wrote that "the parliamentary-democratic idea lives no longer." In contrast to decrepit, outmoded democracy he placed lively, modern authoritarianism. "The micro-physical steering center ruling the macrophysical cell," he wrote, "offers perhaps the most extreme realization that the principle of authoritative leadership has received in all of nature." Especially in the midst of war, it seemed to him that the future belonged to decisive, instrumentally efficient political structures led by *a directing will of the greatest strength and rigor* [emphasis added] (Beyler, 1996, 269)

Jordan would use the target-hit theory as an analogy for the Reich:

The stakes went beyond conceptual innovation and the reconfiguration of scientific disciplines, however. Refutation of the scientific versions of materialism would contribute, Jordan argued, to the struggle against the putative political manifestations of materialism: liberalism and Marxism. The extension of quantum ideas would stand in analogy to the extension of the power of the German imperium. The microphysical 'controlling centers' of the organism would symbolize the political Fuhrer and vice versa. (Beyler, 1996)

From Pascual Jordan we see how science in the Nazi Reich is intended to serve the Wehrmacht (War machine, Military). Academic researchers tend to ignore his involvement in the military research done with the Kriegsmarine, or the genetics research performed with the Berlin-Buch group, among those who even bother to mention him in relation to the founding of Quantum Physics. As we can see, this type of authoritarian science also is largely devoid of any moral scruples or feedback as it is designed for one end: Killing the perceived weak.

BURKHARD HEIM (FEBRUARY 1925 – 14 JANUARY 2001)

One physicist working on the issue of trans-communication or synthetic telepathy was Burkhard Heim. One cannot exclude that perhaps Heim had developed an intuitive ability, which focused his research, as he lived with severe hearing and visual disabilities that led him to resign from the prestigious Max Planck Institute for Physics under Wiesacker after receiving his Ph. D. in Physics from Göttingen. After the war the KWI Institutes were renamed after Max Planck. Heim was a type of misfit wunderkind with chemicals and especially thermite explosives; after a prank with small explosives he was kicked out of school at age 14. He was recruited by Göring after submitting ideas regarding a type of nuclear detonator, to the Chemical-Technical Institute of the Reich in Berlin-Tegel while serving in the Luftwaffe in Italy.

He was then put in touch with Heisenberg, to work on thermite explosive devices for the Wehrmacht. As a very young man, aged only 19, he led his own team. It was his love of thermite that led to his disabilities. As he was loading a thermite explosive for testing, an air raid alarm warning, a false alarm, went off. The vibrations triggering the explosives he held in one hand, he instinctively covered his neck with his other hand, both hands were blown off, otherwise he would have been decapitated by the explosion. Luckily for Heim, the plant doctor was present on his one-day-a-week onsite duty and prevented massive blood loss, saving Heim's life. (Ludwiger, 2001, 5-6)

Later in 1952 he began lecturing on his ideas regarding a new propulsion system, which gave him some momentary notoriety. It also placed him under surveillance by the intelligence services (Ludwiger, 2001, 9).

He received personal and financial support from Ludwig Bolkow of the aerospace and defense contractor, Messerschmitt-Bölkow-Blohm (MBB), starting in 1958, from which he was able to hire an electrical engineer to assist with his experiments short term. The US Government was also interested in Heim, with an early review of Heim theory in the technical publications of the USAF from 1961. One would think that with such patronage as Heisenberg and von Wiezsacker that Heim's academic credentials would be secured. Heim and his ideas regarding gravity, propulsion and transcommunication have had a steady opposition from the start. One modern example includes a former Physicist, Dr. Holm Hummler. He left science in 2001 to work for Boston financial interests, the Boston Consulting Group. He has been the owner and managing director of Uncertainty Managers Consulting GmbH in Bad Homburg, near the banking center of Frankfurt, since 2007 (Hummler, 2018).

He makes a habit of specifically debunking Heim's theory as pseudoscience and is a self-marketed 'skeptic', among other things he 'debunks' are technological conspiracy theories. So once again, we find another gravitational theoretical physicist being suppressed and again we see some connection to the same original social networks of the Boston-London-Hamburg axis of financial interests.

As mentioned in the Jordan section, Jordan and Heim collaborated together. Heim and Jordan were both educated at Göttingen, both had connections with von Weizsacker, who was imprisoned in Britain for a year after the war as a member of the Nazi A-Bomb team. Jordan and Heim have extensive theories and emphasize the role of Gravity, both were seeking a physical explanation for telepathy using gravity. It is no wonder that they would eventually collaborate. Jordan was in attendance when Heim presented his theoretical physics at a symposium for the staff of German areo-space and defense contractor Messerschmitt-Bölkow-Blohm (MBB) at Ottobrun in 1969. At that time Jordan was an advisor on Aerospace propulsion for MBB and others. It is important to remember Jordan had won a Gravity Research Foundation (GRF) award for a paper on faster than light propulsion. Jordan and Heim were to conduct an experiment on measuring gravity, but it did not receive sufficient funding at the time and the experiment was superseded by other experiments and never conducted. Like Jordan, Heim also collaborated with the former SS member and scientist Dr. Hans Bender, who scientifically investigates psi phenomenon and specifically worked with Heim on a scientific theory of 'transcommunication.'

Many physicists have come up with hyperdimensional explanations of our physical reality, like Klein-Kaluza theory from the 1930s, the original hyper dimensional explanation. Heim too comes up with a theory based on hyper-dimensions, (6d). Ludwiger notes regarding 6d that Roger Penrose has come up with a similar concept; we will read about Penrose's ideas on Quantum Consciousness later, where gravity plays a role in determining the final Quantum State:

> Incidentally, the mathematician Roger Penrose, Stephen Hawking's teacher, has come across three real and three imaginary dimensions of the world as well. He discarded his complex C3-world, as he could not interpret the two additional imaginary dimensions physically. Should there be three time dimensions? How should they be discriminated from one another? However, if they are not time dimensions, what are they? And why can't they be temporal dimensions? Xiaodong Chen, a student of Penrose, found that in a R6 at least the wave-particle-dualism… (Ludwiger 2013)

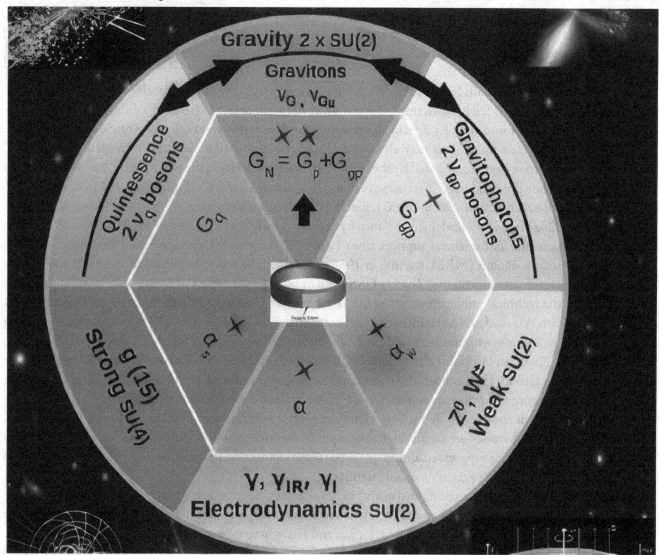

Heim's 6 Fundamental Forces: Strong, Electrodynamic, Weak and Gravity in 3 modes; Quintessence, Gravity, Gravitophotons

Another participant at the MBB lectures, at the time an engineer working there, Dr. Illobrand Ludwiger, who later became an adept of Dr. Heim's theories, has given the following succinct overview of Heim's contribution to theoretical physics:

- a unified phenomenological field theory in which electro-magnetism and gravity have been united by Heim,

- a unified quantum-geometric structure theory that has led to a formula for the calculation of the masses of elementary particles, and

- development of an aspectual logic by means of which both the quantitative-physical as well as the qualitative-organisational part of the world can be uniformly described.

At the end there emerges a new world view with the following predications:

- we live in a 6-dimensional world,

- elementary particles are 6-dimensional, dynamic, metric structures,

- humans, too, are 6-dimensional creatures,

- there wasn't a big bang, but the universe developed from a simple space cell,

- the organization in matter is governed by qualitative structures from the 5th world coordinate, an approach for solving the body-mind-problem,

- autonomous structures of consciousness can exist free from a material carrier. (Ludwiger, 2013)

In the 1950s the main achievement for which Burkhard Heim achieved a degree of recognition was his discovery of a new propulsion concept for space flight. According to this concept, it should be possible to have a spaceship powered by specially generated gravitation fields and by conversion of electromagnetic waves… instead of chemical fuels. Heim had discovered a phenomenological explanation of gravity as well as a connection to electromagnetic fields. By analogy with Maxwell's theory of electromagnetism, he had interpreted gravity as a physical field. (Ludwiger 2013)

Heim notes that, "temporally variable magnetic fields [see Ch. 9] should also be able to generate gravitation fields." Which is significant in that it presages the ideas of 'Gerstenshtein Effect' by a decade, where EM is turned into Gravity and Gravity into EM. This may also be related to the findings of Dr. Persinger that variable magnetic fields are used in 'remote sensing' and 'deep correlation.'

As mentioned previously, the aerospace defense contractor, MBB, was interested in Heim from at least 1958. He periodically briefed MBB engineers on his gravity-based physics. According to former MBB engineer, Ludwiger:

Only as of 1985 the aerospace company MBB seized on Heim's idea, and wanted to furnish the experimental proof that rotating masses can generate magnetic fields. In a laboratory experiment the weak magnetic field generated by means of a rotating crystal ball should have been proved with a Squid magnetometer, which is a highly sensitive detection device. However, the money necessary for that device couldn't be raised. (Ludwiger 2013)

As noted before Einstein's GR does not supply a complete answer for the role of Gravity in our Universe, and it still remains in 2023 an open question how Quantum Gravity works exactly. Heim developed a Contrabaric Equation, first formulated in 1955, which is used by other researchers in faster than light propulsion. Ludwiger notes regarding the equation:

As he factored in the field mass of the gravitation field (which Einstein had neglected due to its insignificance), Heim obtained his so-called contrabaric equation. According to that equation, the transformation of electric or magnetic fields into gravitational acceleration fields and vice versa should be possible. (Ludwiger, 2013)

It is interesting that in the 1950s he is already contemplating issues that would later be written on by the likes of Russian Physicist, Gerstenshtein, regarding Gravity in 1962. Yet, there is an almost total absence of knowledge of Burkhard Heim, for reasons such as his having to live in isolation due to his disabilites, and not wanting to publish in Academic journals without experimental results to back up his theories. Unfortunately, he did not live into the era we live in now, when Gravitational Science is taking off and taken more seriously after the confirmed discovery of Gravitational Waves in 2015.

Heim directly worked with transcommunication, which is an important part of any Neuroweapon platform deployed today. He was contacted in 1966 by the parapsychologist Dr. Hans Bender, Ludwiger notes regarding this collaboration:

When in 1966 the well-known parapsychologist professor Hans Bender asked whether he would be willing to help him with his physical knowledge with interpreting the "tape-recorded voices," Heim agreed. In Sweden, together with his assistant W.-D. Schott, he assessed the claims made by Mr. Jürgenson who heard unexplainable voices on tape and on the radio, voices that seemed to address him personally. As these experiments weren't performed scientifically correct, Heim himself did experiments in his laboratory, which, however, he only rarely talked about. He despised people who carelessly went public with undistinguished results.

In 2010, the physicist Holger Klein found several hundred manuscript pages in Heim's legacy in Northeim which had been administered by Heim's foster daughter Ingrid Hartung until her death in the same year. Not only did these pages contain hundreds of Heim's experiments regarding the validation of transcommunication, but also approaches for a theory of transcommunication. No mainstream physicist would ever dare to start such a kind of work.

As in the 6-dimensional theory all physical field sizes are 6-dimensional, too, Heim derived a possible influx of the additional components x5 and x6 to the moduled phonetic sequence density from the 6-dimensional radiation vector that is transmitted by radio stations. He did this in such a way that in considering the required aerial properties for the trans-components of the radiation vector a modified spoken text can be received as a matter of principle.

In doing so, Heim created first approaches for theoretically comprehensible experiments of a paranormal kind. (Ludwiger, 2013)

Yet, it gets weirder for Burkhard Heim, as has been indicated with other scientists, some feel that they are interacting with a superior intelligence while researching and being in a sense directed in their research, one notable example of this is the case of physicist and former CIA consultant Dr. Jack Sarfatti. Heim, while working on his Logics, was working on 'Syntrometric Telecentrics of Maximes', a book on formal logic, that was unpublished but presented at MBB in 1976 with Jordan present. He speaks of being in communication with an extrinsic intelligence, which of course would match the description of a Targeted Individual who hears either positive or negative feedback from 'voices':

The work on it was so difficult for Heim that sometimes he himself was not able to understand himself anymore. On July 19, 1974 Heim talked about his experiences…

"As I cannot write, I dictated the derivations I did in my head to my father, walking up and down in the room. And during this, I sometimes got a very strange feeling: I couldn't say 'I'm dictating this' and 'I'm thinking this', but 'IT is dictating. IT's thinking!' It was something that apparently didn't belong to me at all. It seemed to me as I was only repeating something that actually belonged to something completely elsewhere. That's a weird feeling! I have never talked to anybody about this, as I said to myself, nobody would understand anyway." (Ludwiger 2013)

Sometimes – and that's the most creative moments you can have as a human being – you have the feeling as if you're only the tool and you say, dictate or write something that actually doesn't originate in you. That has happened to me more than once while I was dictating these notebooks that I later further worked on in more detail. I always had the feeling that completely foreign thoughts were approaching me which only had to be recorded. But I was never able to tell where that came from. That only happened some times, strangely always in such moments where it seemed that I was at a loss. Then it happened." (Ludwiger 2013)

As can be seen from Burkhard Heim's studies and findings the science of Trans-communication is directly related to Gravity. Later, other researchers picked up on Heim's original theories. Droscher and Hauser have used his theories to create "Extended Heim Theory" (EHT). They even won an award, American Institute of Aeronautics and Astronautics' Future Flight prize, for a paper in 2010 that argues for faster than light propulsion based on this. However, it would take some x-ray generation, pulsed high power beam, to get it done as Roger Lenard of Sandia Labs has stated regarding the proposal:

*Roger Lenard, a space propulsion researcher at Sandia National Laboratories in New Mexico does think it might be possible, though, using an X-ray generator called the Z machine which "could probably generate the necessary field intensities and gradients." (Haines 2006)

Although this is one way of doing new propulsion, it may or may not be the way. Without adequate funding for experimentation, we may never know if Heim Theory is accurate or inaccurate. As it has not been tested it is too early to be a protagonist or antagonist of the Heim Theory. As knowledge and interest in working with gravitational wave technology is relatively new and under-researched, since it took so long to even confirm their existence, an entirely different or unknown process may emerge from gravitational research, especially at the quantum level, that may be the real answer. Although, it is true many supporters of UFO encounters claim that different governments in the world already have this technology, if it is gravitational based then when it exists may be completely irrelevant, with the real question, who has the capability?

The search for the validation of gravitational waves was a bumpy one. In the next section we will review the history of the confirmation of gravitational waves by examining the work of American Dr. Joseph Weber.

THE ROCKY ROAD TO GW DETECTION:

The question of Gravitational Waves was for a very long time a controversial topic in Physics. Many doubted they even existed, until confirmed in 2015 by LIGO. The story of the building of LIGO itself is full of 'intrigue', 'disruptions' and 'delays.' The controversies dealing with the detection of Gravitational Waves and general gravity theory and quantum gravity research extends to at least the 1930s, noting the execution by Stalin (a repeated pattern in dealing with the topic of Neuroweapons research in the Soviet Union) of the theoretical physicist Bronstein, then working on advanced theories regarding gravity. The controversy extends to the first claims of actual detection of GW by the American Naval Academy graduate Dr. Joseph Weber.

On Jan 19, 1949 Roger W. Babson founded the Gravity Research Foundation (GRF) dedicated to the science of Gravity, a gravity-centric physics research institute. It was attacked by the scientific community, in part due to faster than light propulsion studies. Because of this villification, Babson moved on to start a new institute to study gravity, although today the GRF enjoys credibility in the scientific community. An interesting aside is that Pascual Jordan, writing on faster than light propulsion using gravity, was an award winner in the GRF's annual competition for best Gravity-related research paper. Babson's new Institute for Field Physics (IOFP) was headed by Dr. DeWitte in Chapel Hill, North Carolina (UNC). It started the prestigious General Relativity conferences, which began in 1957, with GR1. The first conference, titled 'The Role of Gravitation in Physics', drew such highly regarded physicists as Wheeler and Feynman. Another participant was Joseph Weber. One of the chief questions of this conference was whether gravitational waves can produce work, or energy. Later, it was confirmed they do.

In 1960, Joseph Weber published on how to detect gravitational waves. His idea, among others such as interferometric, was to use a resonant antenna (a hollow cylinder) to detect low frequency gravitational waves. He had built two detectors separated by 950km; one at U of Maryland and the other in Chicago at the Argonne National Laboratory. He was assisted by his students, Dr. Forward and Dr. David Zipoy. Dr. Forward went on to play a seminal role in interferometric methods and with High Frequency Gravitational Waves. In 1969 Weber published a paper claiming to have detected Gravitational Waves. Subsequent to this, attempts at replicating his experiment proved invalid. Because others were not able to replicate his results he was viewed as a fraud by the scientific community, although later rehabilitated and honored at the 2016 ceremony announcing the confirmed existence of gravitational waves. It should be pointed out that the replication attempts were flawed in several respects and were not a genuine replication of his approach. For instance, he used a 3-ton cylinder, others only a 1.5-ton cylinder made of different materials. He placed his in a sealed vacuum, others did not. Gravitational Wave research diminished after this point, while simultaneously being investigated in secret Military Defense projects of the UK-USA and USSR.

Heinz Billing, former Nazi computer engineer and physicist, worked to discredit Weber on claim of Gravitational Waves. He was involved in early attempts at building interferometry projects, all of which faced difficulties during his involvement. Also involved in discrediting Weber was an IBM scientist, Richard Garwin, noted for his highly aggressive derision of Weber's gravity wave results, based on the claim that Weber's computer program had a bug creating the readings. Former Nazis were not alone in discrediting Weber; also not able to replicate his results was the Soviet Physicist Braginsky. We note that Bunin's Gravity Wave signal generator was built in 1972, so was the Soviet criticism of Weber also a form of technological obfuscation of actual military capabilities?

In 1975, Heinz Billing laid plans for a Gravitational Wave detector. He was working with the Garsching Group to build an interfermetric system for detection, later contacted by NSF regarding Weiss plans, see below. Billing's project tried for 30 years but never detected GW. Apparently, noise was too costly, although the noise suppression technology developed did lead to LIGO, which did detect Gravitational Waves in 2015.

It wasn't until 1979 that the announcement came, by Joseph Hoston Taylor and Alan Russell Hulse, of the detection of gravitational radiation effects. This proved effects from gravitational waves but did not measure them, and thus to an extent rekindled interest in gravitational waves.

Weber's main method of detection was a cylinder; he also thought of investigating Gravitational Waves with interferometric methods, which became the basis of LIGO. In the following section we shall look at how the interferometric method for measuring Gravitational Waves came into being. The Soviets, too, built technology using superconductors, also used in Quantum Computation, such as in an Akimov generator or Bunin's designs for the GW Signal Generator.

INTERFEROMETRIC DETECTION OF GRAVITATIONAL WAVES:

As mentioned, the discovery of Gravitational Waves in 2015 was made by LIGO, an American interferometric detector. The road to LIGO began with the work of Joseph Weber, his student, Bob Forward, Dr. Weiss at MIT working with the DoD, eventually leading to other projects of the same nature such as the Billing-led Garsching Team in Germany.

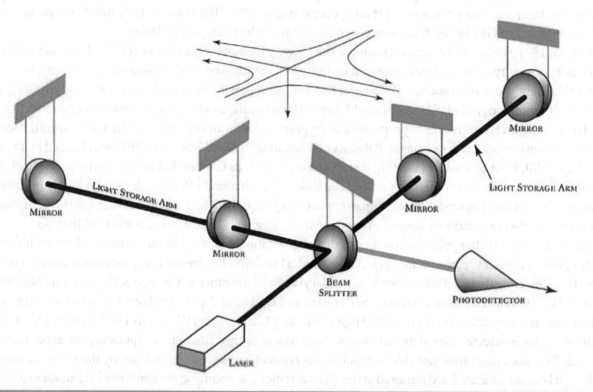

Basic schematic of LIGO's interferometers with an incoming gravitational wave depicted as arriving from directly above the detector. (Caltech/MIT/LIGO Lab)

LIGO defines interferometry:

> Interferometers are investigative tools used in many fields of science and engineering. They are called interferometers because they work by merging two or more sources of light to create an interference pattern, which can be measured and analyzed; hence 'Interfere-o-meter', or interferometer. The interference patterns generated by interferometers contain information about the object or phenomenon being studied. They are often used to make very small measurements that are not achievable any other way. This is why they are so powerful for detecting gravitational waves--LIGO's interferometers are designed to measure a distance 1/10,000th the width of a proton! (LIGO, 2020)

Although Joseph Weber wrote about interferometry in his notebooks, he did not publish his ideas; but he is credited by Bob Forward with coming up with the idea. The first to publish on this method were Dr. Gerstenshtein and Dr. Pustovoid in the Soviet Union. They attempted to get the Soviet government interested in supporting such a thing but were never funded. Again, in 1966, Braginsky attempted to get the Soviet interferometer going for measuring gravitational waves, but again was not supported. It is entirely possible that they had already developed a secret method for this, using superconductors like the Akimov generators, but this is speculative.

In the United States Rainer Weiss was working on an Interferometer at MIT around 1968. He came up with some of his first theories on this method funded by the DoD, but the funding had to be dropped because a new law, the Mansfield Act, banned the DoD from funding college research not directly related to military purposes, which also closed down anti-gravity research at Wright Patterson AFB in 1970 (Tingley, 2019).

Later, he would become pivotal in the creation of LIGO, he was awarded the 2017 Nobel prize for Physics for his work on LIGO. In California, Dr. Bob Forward at Hughes Research Labs has built a prototype of an interferometer. In 1971 Dr. Forward built the first prototype of a 'Transducer Laser' which became the basis of LIGO. Weiss bases his 1974 design on Dr. Forward's.

In 1974, Weiss was trying to build his own prototype on requests from the National Science Foundation for a 9m prototype. NSF asked the German Max Planck Institute to review the proposal. Eventually it landed in Heinz Billing's lap. His team, Garching Group, built a prototype on their own. The Garching Group never detected Gravitational Waves but it did develop a noise suppression system that was used on the LIGO detector. Weiss sent his assistant Dr. David Shoemaker to work with the Garching Group. In 1975 NSF funded Weiss's detector. Weiss's plan was to develop the detector in stages with a LIGO, a prototype and b LIGO a production detector, which did go on to detect Gravitational Waves.

So, it took from 1960 to 2015 to go from ideas of detecting gravitational waves to their final authoritative confirmed finding by LIGO. This may seem like a long time to go from theory to measurement. Indeed, there have been many unforeseen delays in the detection of Gravitational Waves, from funding problems, mismanagement and intense personal conflicts; for instance LIGO was managed by Weiss and Drever, but they had intense interpersonal conflicts leading to more delays as noted by one scholar:

> The Caltech–MIT project was funded by NSF and named the "Laser Interferometer Gravitational-Wave Observatory," known by its acronym LIGO. The project would be led by a triumvirate of Thorne, Weiss, and Drever. Soon interactions between Drever and Weiss became difficult because, besides the strenuous nature of their interaction, both had differing opinions on technical issues. During the years 1984 and 1985 the LIGO project suffered many delays due to multiple discussions between Drever and Weiss, mediated when possible by Thorne. In 1986 the NSF called for the dissolution of the triumvirate of Thorne, Drever, and Weiss. Instead, Rochus E. Vogt was appointed as a single project manager. (Czervantes-Cota, 2017)

Whether it is the killing off of Gravitational Theorists during the Stalinist purges or building a detector or trying to improve communications with HFGW, as we shall see later, there is much gravity in the world of researching Gravity.

GRAVITATIONAL WAVES AND SURVEILLANCE

In Intelligence gathering, say, visual surveillance, a question of resolution is always an issue. The desire by agencies to increase their resolution of recon satellite images is something that is always a technical challenge to be improved on. Resolution is also important in terms of Neuroweapons, or any weapon involving any basic targeting, to hit the target with the most precise accuracy is always desirable in the field of warfare. There are two ways covered in this work to gain high resolution through using waves: 1. Time-Reversed Radar Waves and 2. High Frequency Gravitational Waves.

In 1961 Dr. Robert Baker, who lived and grew up near the cornerstone of aerospace defense contractors in sunny California, a childhood friend of the Douglas family (McDonnell-Douglas) and the Grumman (Northrop-Grumman) family. He later after graduating from UCLA worked for Lockheed. It was while working for Lockheed Astrodynamics Research Center (LARC) that Dr. Baker made the first known presentation on High Frequency Gravitational Waves. According to Dr. Baker he presented his finding to Lockheed engineers, along with Weber assistant, Dr. Bob Forward, who worked at nearby Hughes Research Lab, who lectured on interferometric methods. Dr. Baker writes:

> The first mention of High-Frequency Gravitational Waves or HFGWs that I could determine was in a Lecture in 1961 that I had given with Dr. Robert Lull Forward at my Lockheed Astrodynamics Research Center in Bel Air, California. [Lecture given at the Lockheed Astrodynamics Research Center (LARC), 650 N. Sepulveda,

Bel Air, California, USA, a few blocks from UCLA, November 16th. Lockheed Research Report RL 15210, based upon notes taken by Samuel Herrick a Lockheed Consultant and UCLA Professor]. Attendees included LARC members Robert Rector, Professors Geza Gedeon, Kurt Forester, my secretary Joan Boyle who typed up Herrick's notes in the Lockheed Research Report of the Lecture, plus UCLA students.] I had invited Dr. Forward over from the Hughes Research Laboratory in Malibu, California to deliver a lecture on the "Weber Bar" that he and Dr. Joseph Weber were constructing at the Hughes Lab to detect Low-Frequency Gravitational Waves (1660 Hz). During the Question and Answer part of our Lecture, Bob Forward and I talked about building a Laboratory generator and detector for "High-Frequency Gravitational Waves," having frequencies over 100 kHz. As far as I know this was the first time the subject had been broached. I recall that we concluded that it could not be accomplished with the technology then available; but I suggested that such high-frequency gravitational waves, or HFGWs, would have practical applications, for example communication (the ultimate wireless system)." (Baker, 2017)

As always in science the issue of who takes credit for an idea or invention is always a high prestige item for engineers. The first written paper on HFGW was by a Soviet researcher, in 1962. Mikhaeil Gerstenshtein 'Wave Resonance of Light and Gravitational Waves are HFGW' A paper on HFGW regarding converting EM to HFGW and HFGW converting to EM. Which became known as the "Gerstenshtein Effect." An important note regarding this is that later this effect will be misapplied in a suppression effort against another HFGW technology based on the "Li effect" in the US DoD and Intelligence Community circles JASON Reports.

It was in 1964 that HFGWs were written of in relation to investigating the Big Bang. Leopold Halpern and Bertel Laurent published on the Big Bang having relic HFGW and suggested a gasser Generator of HFGW analogous to EM Wave generation by lasers. Then in 1974, Leonid Grishchuk, Mikhail Sazhin's "Emission of Gravitational Waves by an Electromagnetic Cavity" involved HFGW. The Soviets did research in HFGW during the cold war, which draws attention to the very important concept of EM Cavity, of which there are also many natural biological correlates. In other words, we can find EM Cavities in Biology, such as proposed by some researchers for microtubules in the brain. It should be pointed out in regard to the Soviet use of Gravitational Wave signal generators that those generators were of a Low Frequency nature, not HFGW.

The first UK-USA based HFGW detector was created in England by Professor Cruise:

> One of the first practical HFGW detectors was developed at Birmingham University, England by Professor Mike Cruise and his graduate student Richard Ingley. Professor Cruise published his years of research in 1983 and during the 1990s on an electromagnetic detector for very-high-frequency gravitational waves, in Class. Quantum Gravity in 2000. Professor Cruise has published over 100 research papers and a textbook on The Principles of Space Instrument Design. He is a member of the European Space Agency and a member of international teams searching for gravitational waves using ground based and space-based facilities such as LIGO and the proposed Laser Interferometer Space Antenna or LISA. An interaction between a gravitational wave and the polarization vector of an electromagnetic (EM) wave is the basis for the Cruise-Ingley Birmingham HFGW detector. The polarization vector of the EM wave rotates about the direction of its propagation. If a resonant condition can be established with the EM wave always experiencing the same phase as the gravitational wave, then the effect is cumulative and can be enhanced linearly by repeated circuits of a closed loop. The detector measures changes in the polarization, using a short filament or probe, of the EM microwave beam (indicating the presence of a HFGW) propagating within a waveguide loop about one meter in diameter. This is about the wavelength of 300 MHz HFGWs. (Baker, 2017, 10-11)

Another detector was created in 1998 in Italy – Giorgio Fontana's HTSC Gazer:

> Giorgio Fontana in Italy had been studying another possible HFGW laboratory generator also similar to a Laser that he termed a "HTSC Gazer." His high-temperature superconductor or HTSC generator is based upon the previously mentioned Halpern and Laurent studies and "…the properties of copper-pair pairing states …" (Baker, 2017, 15-16)

Shortly thereafter, Dr. Baker along with Dr. Li patented their collaboration on HFGW in 2000, the first patent in US and China for a HFGW Generator by Dr. Li and Dr. Baker, filed July 14, 2000, granted July 19, 2002. (Baker, 2010, 33)

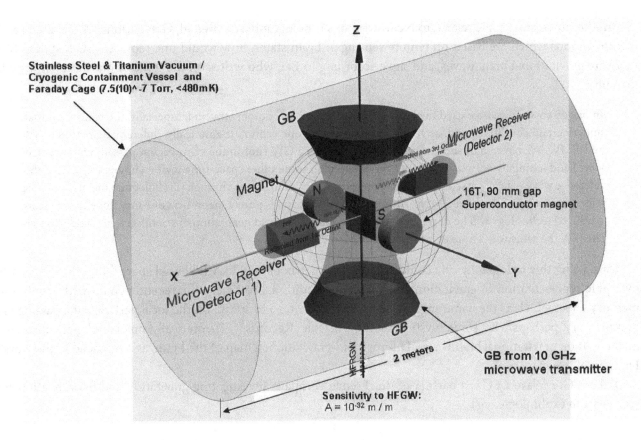

Figure 3.6.2 Schematic of the Proof-of-Concept Li-Baker HFGW Detector (Peoples Republic of China Patent Number 0510055882.2) Claims can be found at: http://www.gravwave.com/docs/Chinese%20Detector%20Patent%2020081027.pdf

Baker also filed a patent for 'Gravitational Wave Generator Utilizing Submicroscopic Energizable Elements filed Dec. 27, 2000 (Baker, 2005). In 2004 issued a patent for generating HFGW using x-rays, which was a method noted by researchers on anti-gravity technology as being a necessity for creating anti-grav tech. Lockheed-Sandia labs in New Mexico operates an X-Ray generator for weapons development, the "Z-Machine." In this particular submicroscopic version Dr. Baker sees the ability to change cellular nuclei, etc., along the lines of earlier work in microbiology during World War II. It is also interesting to note that Dr. Baker foresaw this technology as a means of transferring thoughts, and his company, GravWave LLC, has partnered with the French company Exobiologie on thought transference, as described by Lockheed engineer Dr. John Norseen in a previous chapter, using HFGW from one person to another (see http://www.exobiologie.org); which in its premiere Academic conference has the following program for 2020: "Brain to Brain exobiological communication by High Frequency Gravitational Waves. (Gary V Stephenson - Physicist and engineer, Gravwave team)" (web site, accessed 7/28/20). The Exobiologie documentation references the work of Daniel Bar of Bar Ilan University in Israel, who in 2007 first proposed publicly the concept of gravitational brain waves. Noting that:

> For the first half of this work we have used the fact that the ionic currents and charges in the cerebral system radiate electric waves as may be realized by attaching electrodes to the scalp. That is, one may physically and logically assume that just as these ionic currents and charges in the brain give rise to electric waves so the masses related to these ions and charges should give rise, according to Einstein's field equations, to weak GW's. From this we have proceeded to calculate the correlation among an n-brain ensemble in the sense of finding them at some time radiating similar gravitational waves if they were found at an earlier time radiating other GW's. We have used as a specific example of gravitational wave the cylindrical one which we have investigated in a thorough and intensive way... (Bar, 2007)

Another interesting topic related to Neuroweapons is holography; if, after all, Gravitational Waves are used for Neuroweapons which are based on remote sensing of brain states, how would one represent such states. Since there are gravitational brain waves, and since according to Bar, who writes on the topic of gravitational wave holography:

> In our discussion we have used the known methods of optical holography and, especially, the realization that, under certain conditions such as very small wavelength, one cannot, theoretically, differentiate between GW and EMW. We have, thus, shown that passing a reference GW (not in the same region passed by the subject wave) and letting these two waves meet and interfere in some other space-time region (hologram) then if this reference wave is again passed, as the corresponding EMW illuminator, through this hologram the result will be a reconstruction of the subject wave. Although this discussion is purely theoretical one may hope that a future advanced technology will be developed which will enable the next generation of scientists to use and manipulate GW the same way we are able now to use EMW. (Bar, 2005)

Thus, using this holography one could recreate the matrix of GW in Minkowski space (4d); thus, have a holographic representation of gravitational brainwaves. Additional to that is the recently confirmed gravitational memory effect which as the name suggests leaves an imprint, so to speak, on the local particles of a passing GW, or a memory, perhaps what some mystics call the "Akashic Records." Theoretically, one could generate a visual map based on gravitational brainwaves, Dubrov's bio-gravitation; a map of the brain, as referenced in the work of Dr. John Norseen.

Baker's GravWave LLC is a partner of this French company investigating gravitation and brain relationships (image from exobiologie.org)

Gravitational Brainwaves and Evolution

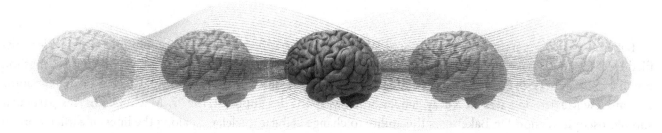

Gravitational Brainwaves and Medical Neuroforescasting

Exobiologie.org - Gravitational Brainwaves and Evolution. 12 Bvd Thibaud de Champagne 77600 Bussy-Saint-Georges - france. RNA: w77

There is basically no area of research for HFGW outside of the military and IC. Public funding, except to a limited degree, is only given in China, there so far has been no major funding in any publicly trackable way for the development of HFGW. In January 2000 Dr. Baker contacted the NSA regarding HFGW technology, primarily focused on using HFGW for surveillance. Later in 2007 he presented on HFGW Surveillance at the University of New Mexico STAIF conference. This is in the heartland of government labs such as Lockheed-Martin-Sandia and others.

In the late 1990s and early 2000s Dr. Baker collaborated with Dr. Li in China. Dr. Li published on the "Li Effect." Dr. Baker recounts:

> In China Dr. Fangyu Li had accomplished research into the Li effect in which HFGWs in a Gaussian electromagnetic field and an intense magnetic field could allow for the detection of HFGWs. This detector, termed

the Li-Baker HFGW Detector, was under initial development in China at Chongqing University. (Baker, 2017, 17) The Li Effect was the basis for Dr. Baker's work, not the Gerstenshtein Effect which was used to debunk Dr. Baker's work by the Military Scientific advisor, Yeardley, of the JASON Reports.

The Fangyu Li effect, a gravitational wave transfers energy to a separately generated electromagnetic (EM) wave in the presence of a static magnetic field as discussed in detail in Li et al., 2009. That EM wave has the same frequency as the GW (ripple in the spacetime continuum) and moves in the same direction. (Baker, 2010, 25)

In 2003 a former DIA officer, Paul Murad (M.Sc.), organized a conference on HFGW at a front company for DoD and US IC projects, the Mitre Corporation of McLean, VA, which is also known for its cybersecurity platforms. The Mitre Conference was the first sponsored, serious symposium solely dedicated to HFGW. Presenters included the leading figures in HFGW, such as Dr. Baker and others; Gary Stephenson, who presented on using HFGW for communications, Eric Davis, who presented on "Laboratory generation of high-frequency gravitons via quantization of the coupled Maxwell-Einstein fields." Others presented on other issues related to HFGW.

The interesting detail regarding this conference was its intimacy with the DoD/IC Research community through Paul Murad (d. 2022). He is known to have worked for the Defense Intelligence Agency on new technology research. He ran Section-F of the University of New Mexico STAIF conference, dealing with anti-gravitation propulsion and the like. Section F was established by a NASA scientist, Marc Millis, who invited Murad to organize the sectional conferences. (Murad, 2006)

STAIF is part of the UNM Institute for Space and Nuclear Power Studies (ISNPS). In an interview regarding his involvement as head of Section-F the issue of Military and Intelligence involvement in the conferences is brought up:

> Interviewer: I've heard that at the 2004 session there were maybe 40 regular attendees, as well as the somewhat disturbing sight of Air Force officers quietly moving around in the back of the conference room.

> Murad: The overall STAIF conference in 2004 had up to 750 attendees and we held an audience of regulars for each paper. I am not concerned about military attendees. In fact I have many people from DoD and various government agencies as session chairs and co-chairs [it] is useful because if funding were available, they would be knowledgeable about it. (Murad, 2006)

So, clearly, the Military and Intelligence community is established in HFGW. Also attending the conference was *Janes* Military Intelligence editor Nick Cook. *Janes* attended conferences between 2003-5, which is in keeping with its mission of providing private intelligence information regarding all kinds of military threats. I often studied *Janes* Warships while on Sonar duty on a US Navy Submarine. One would think with this much interest the United States was ahead of the game. However, Murad paints a different picture, one with the Russians and Europeans in the lead as he recounts of the 2003 Mitre Conference:

> As is typical of Americans, during the coffee breaks, they would sketch a candidate idea for a gravitational wave detector at a given frequency x trying to impress a foreign presenter. The foreigner in one case shook his head and suggested it was a good design and then took out Polaroid pictures showing his test apparatus at frequency x, then y and finally z! These were pictures of metallic hardware representing a gravity resonating cavity that was shock isolated and quite impressive. Clearly, the U.S. had ignored this technology and seriously, if there was any value to this work, we were sorely not even second best. (Murad, 2006)

This too was the case with Neuroweapons research in general, with the United States, having out-spent, out-muscled, and outlasted the Soviet Union, inheriting the Soviet's research once it collapsed; bringing Soviet Researchers to New Mexico in the 1990s to work on NSA sponsored Neuroweapons research as evidenced by the writings of Dr. John Norseen.

SUPPRESSION OF HFGW

Paper Presentation on High-Frequency Gravitional Wave Overview
Plenary Session of the Space Technology Applications Forum (STAIF 2008)
Albuquerque, New Mexico, USA, February 11, 2008

2008 – JASON suppression of HFGW after Dr. Baker (pictured above) in 2007 presents on using HFGW for Surveillance and Military Applications at STAIF in New Mexico.

After the 2nd HFGW Workshop on June 17, 2008, a research group called the JASONS, composed of very influential and respected university scientists, were given a briefing on the generation, detection and applications of high-frequency gravitational waves (HFGWs). The JASON Report (JSR-08-506) on that briefing was published in October 2008. The Report was widely distributed to the US scientific community and various press organizations reported it. The JASON Report stated that,

> Our main conclusions are that the proposed applications of the science of HFGW are fundamentally wrong; that there can be no security threat; and that independent scientific and technical vetting of such hypothetical threats is generally necessary. We conclude that previous analysis of the Li-Baker detector concept is incorrect by many orders of magnitude ...

> The author of the JASON Report's basic premise for generating HFGWs was: "A basic mechanism for generating a HFGW is the direct conversion of an electromagnetic wave into a gravitational one of the same frequency, by a strong static magnetic field. This Gertsenshtein process is idealized in Figure 3." In addition, the Report states: "Proposed HFGW detectors have generally been based upon versions of the inverse Gertsenshtein process." (Italics added by the author for emphasis.) These statements are both incorrect. As already mentioned, the Gertsenshtein process or effect was published in 1962: M. E. Gertsenshtein, "Wave resonance of light and gravitational waves," Soviet Physics JETP, 14, Number 1, pp. 84-85. The effect is extremely weak and is not utilized in most of the modern HFGW generation, detection or applications. (Baker, 2017, 24)

Once again, it is not surprising that we find some irony in the concept of suppression of HFGW, which occurred after Dr. Baker's 2007 STAIF presentation. In general, working with gravitational based technology is considered a high risk proposition by many 'free energy' researchers: 'faster than light' propulsion researchers. According to Lt. Col. Tom Bearden, he himself no longer researches in this area due to concern for his life:

> I'm a co-author of a paper in the literature way back there which reports a successful anti-gravity drive. I'm not going to do another experiment not even going to participate in one … so you know everybody's got a little bit different circumstance and my circumstance for me to go on living and staying healthy and doing well depends on me avoiding certain areas and that's one of them. (Bearden, 2005)

Paul Murad notes where there is no overt suppression there is a general disinterest in HFGW and unnecessary roadblocks put in place to publish regarding HFGW:

> The culture and the problem set had to change. The major problem was how could one simple person change these things and then I found that I was not alone in these beliefs and surrounded myself with several other kindred spirits with similar ideas. This included Dr. Bob Baker and Tony Robertson. My papers were then being rejected from both AIAA and STAIF because of much stricter selection criteria. For example, papers would only be accepted if I had somebody from academia as a co-author! At this point, going to these conferences were, at least in my view, quite boring. It was as if the technical community had shut down and would become bureaucratic, thereby losing its lust to resolve new and exciting technical challenges. Clearly the technical community was falling into a risk-averse paradigm and apparently there was no way out. (Murad, 2006)

What is one to make of two members, both former Military Intelligence, of the Gravitational research community painting such a grim picture of research in this field? Could it be directly related to non-disclosure of highly classified military weapons programs being developed by the likes of Lockheed-Martin? Dr. Robert Baker, when asked if he believed that the 2008 JASON Report was an attempt at suppression, answered rather directly in the affirmative:

> Q: Do you believe that the organizers of the GravWave briefing to the JASONs had a preconceived agenda to discredit high-frequency gravitational wave research in general and the GravWave® LLC research in particular?
>
> A: It is difficult to believe otherwise. Ordinarily, an unbiased analysis of a technical presentation would have involved some consultation with the presenters in order to better define the subject matter. Furthermore, an exclusive focus on only one HFGW detector, to the exclusion of the Birmingham University, INFN Genoa and Japanese HFGW detectors, which the GravWave presenters discussed in their PowerPoint presentation, would be unwarranted in an unbiased analysis, as would be the avoidance of a discussion of other HFGW-generator research presented by GravWave. Only one HFGW detector paper was scrutinized by the JASON authors -- their reference [10]. Although never discussed in the GravWave® presentation, the Abstract of that paper did mention the Gertsenshtein effect, but the first paragraph of the actual paper admonished the reader to review the other literature that clearly showed that the detector was the result of a combination of the Gertsenshtein effect with synchro-resonance, the Li-effect and not the Gertsenshtein effect alone. Their avoidance of analysis of the basic reference in their Report, which covered the Li-effect, was certainly unwarranted in an unbiased Report. (Eardley, et al.) (2008) "High Frequency Gravitational Waves," JSR-08-506, October, the JASON defense science advisory panel and prepared for the Office of the Director of National Intelligence. (Baker, 2009)

In personal communications with one of the attendees of the JASON meeting that debunked Dr. Baker's plans, it is noted that CIA consulting scientists were behind denying the validity of the approach of Dr. Baker's group. Dr. Jack Sarfatti was invited by the JASON chair Dr. Ron Pandolfi (Sarfatti, 2022) both of whom are former CIA contract scientists and were part of the JASON consultations regarding HFGW feasibility as a security threat.

It is an established practice of nations' military defense to obfuscate their own capabilities from others, as well as take technology from original researchers and place it in classified labs of their own. Additionally, if an enemy has such technology it could be used to send enemies down the wrong research trajectory by influencing the reviewers to make basic academic mistakes. Reading the context from the JASON Report they were trying to analyze whether a country like China posed a threat using such technology, from which they concluded no 'enemy' possessed such technology to pose a threat. Undoubtedly, the US Military has expressed interest in HFGW at least into 2013, when DARPA issued a call for proposals https://www.sbir.gov/node/386412 (accessed 7/19/20) regarding HFGW communication systems much like Dr. Baker's. Research conferences continue on the issue of HFGW with the 2017 3rd HFGW Conference in Chengdu, China.

In the following we will review the military applications of HFGW as proposed by Dr. Robert Baker, his main proposals are to use HFGW for surveillance and secure covert communications.

Dr. Baker makes some elementary remarks on their significance to the military:

- Gravitational waves have a very low cross section for absorption by normal matter, so HFGWs could, in principle, carry significant information content with effectively no absorption, unlike electromagnetic (EM) waves.

- Because of their unique characteristics, HFGWs could be utilized for uninterruptible, very low-probability-of-intercept (LPI) communications.

- Other potential very theoretical military applications are propulsion, including "moving" space objects and missiles in flight, surveillance through buildings and the Earth itself, and remote initiation of nuclear events. (Baker 2009)

Regarding HFGW for LPI Comms:

If we could generate ripples in this space-time fabric, many applications would become available to us. Much like radio waves can be used to transmit information through space, we could use gravitational waves to perform analogous functions. (Baker 2009)

Of the applications of high-frequency gravitational waves (HFGWs), communication appears to be the most important and most immediate. Gravitational waves have a very low cross section for absorption by normal matter, so high-frequency waves could, in principle, carry significant information content with effectively no absorption, unlike electromagnetic (EM) waves. Multi-channel HFGW communications can be both point-to-point (for example, to deeply submerged submarines) and point-to-multipoint, like cell phones. HFGWs pass through all ordinary material things without attenuation and represent the ultimate wireless system. One could communicate directly through the Earth from Moscow in Russia to Caracas in Venezuela—without the need for fiber optic cables, microwave relays, or satellite transponders… (Baker 2009) [in this system it is important to note it is terrestrial based, not space based satellites as in many conspiracy theories about Targeted Individuals.]

Any nation that possesses a communication system that is totally secure, high-bandwidth and can propagate directly through the Earth has an economic advantage over nations who do not possess that capability. From a national security viewpoint, they would be able to communicate with little or no possibility of interception. Surprise attacks by enemies of the United States could be planned and executed utilizing such a communications system with impunity. (Baker 2009)

HFGW Generator

Using Magnetron-FBAR (Piezoelectric Crystals)

Similar to Romero and Dehnen (1981)

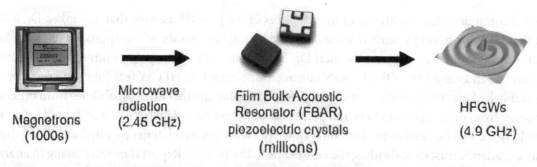

Magnetrons
(1000s)

Microwave
radiation
(2.45 GHz)

Film Bulk Acoustic
Resonator (FBAR)
piezoelectric crystals
(millions)

HFGWs
(4.9 GHz)

Figure 3.5.2. Magnetron FBAR (Piezoelectric Crystal) HFGW Generator.

One of the important components of the Li-Baker HFGW detector is the use of FBARs (Film Bulk Acoustic Resonator pairs) which are commonly used in such things as cell phones. FBARs are powered by magnetrons in their design; through which Dr. Baker plans to miniaturize his technology and put in cell phones, so that each phone would have its own Gravitational Wave antenna/transmitter, which he envisions for secure communications in a noiseless channel.

What do we plan to do?

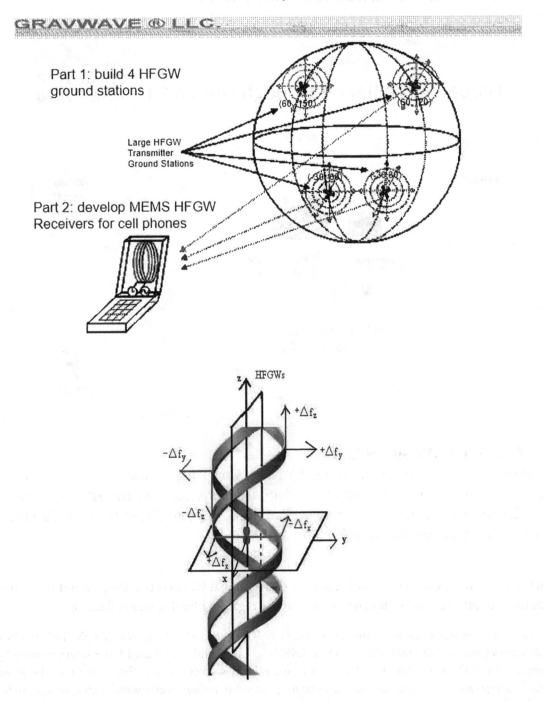

Figure 1.1.4. Double Helix Configuration of FBAR Pairs (Patent Pending)

Helical patterns are a common attribute in 'remote sensing.' See Quantum Consciousness section for further discussion.

Communication is one area that Dr. Baker proposed for Military and Intelligence. Another area was Surveillance, for which he writes:

> The potential for through-earth or through-water "X-ray like" surveillance utilizing the extreme sensitivity of HFGW generation-detection systems to polarization angle changes (possibly sensitive to even less than 10^{-4} radians) might allow for observing subterranean structures and geological formations (such as oil deposits), creating a transparent ocean; viewing three-dimensional building interiors, buried devices, hidden missiles and weapons of mass destruction, achieving remote acoustical surveillance or eavesdropping, etc., or even a full-body scan without radiation danger (Baker 2007a). (Baker, 2009)

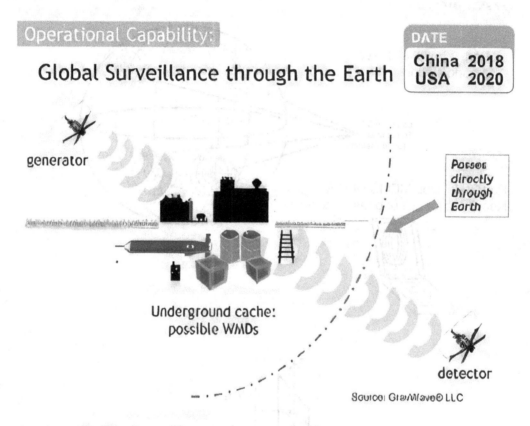

Figure 1.2.2.1. HFGW Surveillance
[*Operational capability predictions are based on very rough estimates by the author from conversations and impressions gained during three international HFGW Workshops (MITRE2003, Austin 2007 and Huntsville 2009) and trips to China in 2004, 2006 and 2008 and to Europe and the Middle East in 2009.*]

One of the issues regarding using Low Frequency Gravitational Waves is that they cannot be used for surveillance since the resolution is too low for any useful purpose regarding Intelligence collection.

> The Laser Interferometer Gravitational Observatory (LIGO) and other long-wave-length GW interferometer detectors (such as GEO 600, Virgo, TAMA, Advanced LIGO and the planned Laser Interferometer Space Antenna, or LISA) cannot detect HFGWs due to the HFGW's short wavelengths, as discussed by Shawhan (2004). Long-wave-length gravitational waves have thousand-to million-meter wavelengths, which can be detected by LIGO (LIGO is frequency limited to signals below 2,000 Hz and wavelengths longer than 150 km), but these are of no practical surveillance value, due to their diffraction and resulting poor resolution. Furthermore, the LIGO technology is completely different from the detection method and noise suppression suggested here. (Baker, 2000)

From Dr. Baker's overall picture and others' work with High Frequency Gravitational Waves we can see how from at least an academic or prototypical design view point that it is highly possible that HFGW could not only be used for 'remote sensing', but, as we shall see later, for 'consciousness' or using gravitational waves to affect brain function remotely. We can also see clearly how the primary players, at least in the UK-USA countries, is the Military and IC, and no doubt neuro-marketers would be of keen interest to such a technology.

GENERAL TIMELINE ON GRAVITATIONAL TECHNOLOGY:

1905 – First proposed as extension to Newton's Laws by H. Poincare

1918 – Einstein Gravitational Quadropole (4x4 Tensor). Einstein writes about GW as a quadropole; a quadropolar waves simplest solution that maintains conservation of momentum during propagation of waves. An interesting episode in GW History is Einstein's denial of GW, then his re-affirmation of them. In 1936 he submitted a paper to a journal denying GW existed; it was met with rebuke by reviewers and never published. In 1937, he revised his position, affirming GW in a new paper with collaborator Rosen. Gravity is quadropolar, EM is bipolar.

1929 – Jordan Kharkov Lecture- spacetime indexed network of local algebras, also interested in gauge theory.

1936 – Jordan Parapsychology paper, a physics of ESP.

1939 – Jordan founds Quantum Biology, Amplifier Theory

1941-- Jordan plans Nazi Quantum Biology Research on Industrial Scale. Launches *Physis* Journal in 1942.

1943 – Jordan to Berlin as Professor, works for Navy Research and Patent Office; secret tech research like Capt. Roeder of Remote Viewing program. In Berlin is able to more closely work with the Berlin Group of the Brain Research Institute: Nikolai W. Timofeeff-Ressovsky (Russian), Karl Gunter Zimmer (later taken to Soviet Union), as well as with Walter Gerlach, famous for spin theory experiments, later taken as POW to Britain and debriefed for a year by MI6. Group included phage research as it relates to target theory.

1948 – Jordan post-war after the end of rehabilitation as De-Nazification program ended, becomes Professor at Hamburg (see cross correlations with Capt. Roeder, the Schroeders and the General acknowledgement as Hamburg being the center of 4th Reich planning.

1949 – Jordan and Hans Bender hold dialogue on physics and parapsychology.

1952 – Burkhard Heim presents his ideas for the first time, regarding cosmology and physics. 1955 Habilitation in Physics.

1952 – Jordan publishes Gravity and Space (Schwerkraft und Weltall), textbook on his ideals regarding cosmology and gravity. Cited by Russian L. L. Vasilev as source of Biogravitation. Other possible dissemination of ideals is through Zimmer during forced labor in Soviet prison on Soviet Nuclear Bomb project.

1955 – Zimmer is freed from Soviet prison, returns to Germany. He is helped by Jordan to get a habilitation card from Hamburg University and appointed Professor at Heidelberg. He is also helped by Adolf Butenandt and importantly Otmar von Verschuer.

1961 – Baker presents Gravity talk to Lockheed. Dr. Forward (J. Weber's student) in attendance, credited with promoting research on HFGW later.

1962 – L. L. Vasiliev, gravitation theory for psi based on Jordan 1955

1966 – Bender & Heim collaborate on a physical explanation for psi or 'transcommunication'

1966 – Lupanov uses capacitors to detect HFGW in the Soviet Union

1967 – Soviet experiment steering fish schools with gravitational waves

1969 – Heim & Jordan collaborate in experiments on gravity. Jordan works as a consultant for Aerospace research in Germany, he is at Heim lecture on his cosmology at MBB Aero-Defense contractor in Germany.

1972 – in Soviet Union Bunin patents 'System sending signals using Gravitational Waves'

1973 – Dubrov publishes influential paper 'Biogravitation and psychotronics'

1976 – Heim again at MBB lecturing, with Jordan in attendance. Jordan works for an 'Aerospace Technology Group.'

1978 – Forward builds the first interferometric detector. "In the early seventies Robert L. Forward, a former student of Joseph Weber at that time working for Hughes Research Laboratory in Malibu, California, decided, with encouragement of Rainer Weiss, to build a laboratory interferometer with Hughes' funds." (Cervantes-Cotta, 2016)

2003 – High Frequency Gravitational Waves (HFGW) conference organized by DIA agent Paul Murad at Mitre Corp (Mildef front company)

2007 – Baker presents at STAIF conference in Albuquerque, NM on HFGW surveillance.

2008 – HFGW debunked by Mitre Corp administered JASON Reports, suspected by Baker as suppression campaign of technology.

2013 – DARPA issues call for proposals for HFGW Communications systems.

NOTES:

[1] Jordan, Pascual (1936) 'Positivistiche Bemerkungen uber die Parapsychlogischen Erscheinungen' in Zentrablatt fur Psychotherapie.

BIBLIOGRAPHY:

Asprem, Egil (2013) *The Problem of Disenchantment: Scientific Naturalism and Esoteric Discourse 1900-1939.* SUNY Press

Bar, Daniel (2005) *Gravitational wave holography* in Int.J.Theor.Phys.46:503-517,2007 https://arxiv.org/abs/gr-qc/0509052

--(2007) '*Gravitational Brain Waves, quantum fluctuations and stochastic quantization*' https://arxiv.org/abs/0708.1635

Bearden, Thomas (2005) *Pulling Energy from the Vacuum – Lt. Col. Thomas Bearden* (2005) https://www.youtube.com/watch?v=eNU3MLqyzPk&t=1359s

Baker, Robert (2017) *Search for the Invisible Waves: Brief History of High-Frequency Gravitational Wave Research.* presented at 3rd HFGW Workshiop, 7-9th April 2017 Southwest Jiaotang University, Chengdu, China online: https://www.drrobertbaker.com/docs/Search%20for%20Invisible%20Waves%20v5c.pdf (accessed 7/19/20)

--(2004) *Gravitational wave generator utilizing submicroscopic energizable elements*

https://patents.google.com/patent/US6784591B2/en

--(2009) '*Military Applications of High-Frequency Gravitational Waves (Abridged)*'

http://citeseerx.ist.psu.edu/viewdoc/download?doi=10.1.1.496.3368&rep=rep1&type=pdf

Beyler, Richard H. (1996) *Targeting the Organism: The Scientific and Cultural Context of Pascual Jordan's Quantum Biology, 1932-1947* in Isis Vol. 87, No. 2 (Jun., 1996), pp. 248-273

Cervantes-Cota, L. Et al '*A Brief History of Gravitational Waves*' https://arxiv.org/ftp/arxiv/papers/1609/1609.09400.pdf

Dahn, Ryan (2018) *Big Science, Nazified? Pascual Jordan, Adolf Meyer-Abich, adn the Abortive Scientific Journal Physis,* in Isis, vol. 109, no. 4, The History of Science Society

Groß, Armin (2009) *Heimliche Uberwachung und Strahlenfolter durch Geheimdienste Whistleblower outet sich als ehemaliger Täter* in Raum und Zeit #161 http://stopeg.com/doc/CarlClarkInterview_Raum_und_Zeit.pdf

Haines, Lester (2006) '*Scientists moot gravity-busting hyperdrive*' The Register, 6 Jan 2006 https://www.theregister.com/2006/01/06/hyperdrive/

Hummler, H. (2018) *Vortrag über Burkhard Heim • Held der UFO-Szene* presentation at Planetarium Nürnberg, am 04.07.2018 https://www.youtube.com/watch?v=lqR2S8yxfFM

Ludwiger, I. (2013) *Das neue Weltbild des Physikers Burkhard Heim: Unsterblich in der 6-Dimensionalen Welt* (German Edition) Munich, Verlag Komplett-Media GmbH

Murad, Paul (2006) 'The Birth of Section F', https://www.americanantigravity.com/files/articles/Paul-Murad-Interview.pdf

Persinger, M., Rouleau, N., Carniello, T. (2014) *Non-Local pH Shifts and Shared Changing Angular Velocity Magnetic Fields: Discrete Energies and the Importance of Point Durations.* Journal of Biophysical Chemistry, 5, 44-53. http://dx.doi.org/10.4236/jbpc.2014.52006

Persinger, Michael (2015) '*The Graviton: An Emergent Solution from the Equivalence of Universal Magnetic Field Intensity and Radiant Flux Density*' in Journal of Advances in Physics, Vol. 10, No. 3 (2015)

Sarfatti, Jack (2022) Personal Communication June 16, 2022 "Re: Heim 1950s German Description of Tic Tacs & Eric Davis's Review"

Schroer, Bert (2003) Pascual Jordan, his contributions to quantum mechanics and his legacy in contemporary local quantum physics https://arxiv.org/abs/hep-th/0303241

Tingley, Brett (2019) '*The truth is the military has Been Researching "Anti-Gravity" For Nearly 70 Years*' OCTOBER 29, 2019 HTTPS://WWW.THEDRIVE.COM/THE-WAR-ZONE/30499/THE-TRUTH-IS-THE-MILITARY-HAS-BEEN-RESEARCHING-ANTI-GRAVITY-FOR-NEARLY-70-YEARS (ACCESSED 8/19/2020)

CHAPTER 7

RADAR AND NEUROWEAPONS

My first experience with radar was as a radar operator in the US Navy, watching the sweeping green line make its centrifugal rounds of any contacts on the green-tinted screen. Radar is a detection system that uses radio waves to determine the range, angle, or velocity of objects. It can be used to detect aircraft, ships, spacecraft, guided missiles, motor vehicles, weather formations, and terrain. A radar system consists of a transmitter producing electromagnetic waves in the radio or microwaves domain, a transmitting antenna, a receiving antenna (often the same antenna is used for transmitting and receiving) and a receiver and processor to determine properties of the object(s). Radio waves (pulsed or continuous) from the transmitter reflect off the object and return to the receiver, giving information about the object's location and speed. Radar is a direct outcome of the British need to detect incoming Nazi German aircraft, and again we see the relationship of technical advances in warfare.

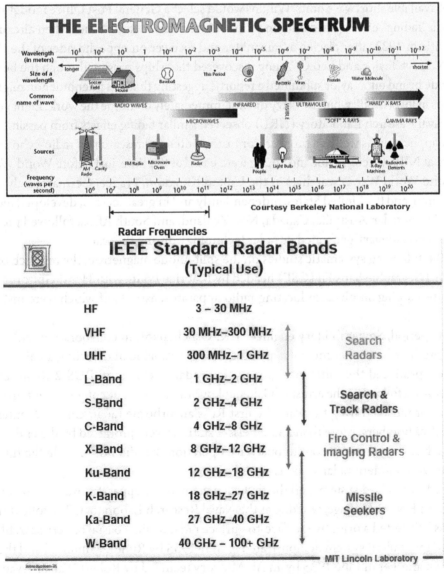

Courtesy Berkeley National Laboratory

Radar Frequencies
IEEE Standard Radar Bands
(Typical Use)

Band	Frequency	Use
HF	3 – 30 MHz	
VHF	30 MHz–300 MHz	Search Radars
UHF	300 MHz–1 GHz	
L-Band	1 GHz–2 GHz	Search & Track Radars
S-Band	2 GHz–4 GHz	
C-Band	4 GHz–8 GHz	Fire Control & Imaging Radars
X-Band	8 GHz–12 GHz	
Ku-Band	12 GHz–18 GHz	
K-Band	18 GHz–27 GHz	Missile Seekers
Ka-Band	27 GHz–40 GHz	
W-Band	40 GHz – 100+ GHz	

MIT Lincoln Laboratory

History of Radar Wiki Overview:

As early as 1886, German physicist Heinrich Hertz showed that radio waves could be reflected from solid objects. In 1895, Alexander Popov, a physics instructor at the Imperial Russian Navy school in Kronstadt, developed an apparatus using a coherer tube for detecting distant lightning strikes. The next year, he added a spark-gap transmitter. In 1897, while testing this equipment for communicating between two ships in the Baltic Sea, he took note of an interference beat caused by the passage of a third vessel. In his report, Popov wrote that this phenomenon might be used for detecting objects, but he did nothing more with this observation.

The German inventor Christian Hülsmeyer was the first to use radio waves to detect "the presence of distant metallic objects." In 1904, he demonstrated the feasibility of detecting a ship in dense fog, but not its distance from the transmitter. He obtained a patent for his detection device in April 1904 and later a patent for a related amendment for estimating the distance to the ship. He also obtained a British patent on September 23, 1904 for a full radar system, that he called a telemobiloscope. It operated on a 50 cm wavelength and the pulsed radar signal was created via a spark-gap. His system already used the classic antenna setup of horn antenna with parabolic reflector and was presented to German military officials in practical tests in Cologne and Rotterdam harbor; but was rejected.

In 1915, Robert Watson-Watt used radio technology to provide advance warning to airmen and during the 1920s went on to lead the U.K. research establishment to make many advances using radio techniques, including the probing of the ionosphere and the detection of lightning at long distances. Through his lightning experiments, Watson-Watt became an expert on the use of radio direction-finding before turning his inquiry to shortwave transmission. Requiring a suitable receiver for such studies, he told the "new boy," Arnold Frederic Wilkins, to conduct an extensive review of available shortwave units. Wilkins would select a General Post Office model after noting its manual's description of a "fading" effect (the common term for interference at the time) when aircraft flew overhead.

Across the Atlantic in 1922, after placing a transmitter and receiver on opposite sides of the Potomac River, U.S. Navy researchers A. Hoyt Taylor and Leo C. Young discovered that ships passing through the beam path caused the received signal to fade in and out. Taylor submitted a report, suggesting that this phenomenon might be used to detect the presence of ships in low visibility, but the Navy did not immediately continue the work. Eight years later, Lawrence A. Hyland at the Naval Research Laboratory (NRL) observed similar fading effects from passing aircraft; this revelation led to a patent application as well as a proposal for further intensive research on radio-echo signals from moving targets to take place at NRL, where Taylor and Young were based at the time, just before World War II.

Before the Second World War, researchers in the United Kingdom, France, Germany, Italy, Japan, the Netherlands, the Soviet Union, and the United States, independently and in great secrecy, developed technologies that led to the modern version of radar. Australia, Canada, New Zealand, and South Africa followed prewar Great Britain's radar development, and Hungary generated its radar technology during the war.

In France in 1934, following systematic studies on the split-anode magnetron, the research branch of the Compagnie Générale de Télégraphie Sans Fil (CSF) headed by Maurice Ponte with Henri Gutton, Sylvain Berline and M. Hugon, began developing an obstacle-locating radio apparatus, aspects of which were installed on the ocean liner Normandie in 1935.

During the same period, Soviet military engineer P.K. Oshchepkov, in collaboration with Leningrad Electrophysical Institute, produced an experimental apparatus, RAPID, capable of detecting an aircraft within 3 km of a receiver. The Soviets produced their first mass production radars RUS-1 and RUS-2 Redut in 1939 but further development was slowed following the arrest of Oshchepkov and his subsequent gulag sentence. In total, only 607 Redut stations were produced during the war. The first Russian airborne radar, Gneiss-2, entered into service in June 1943 on Pe-2 dive bombers. More than 230 Gneiss-2 stations were produced by the end of 1944. The French and Soviet systems, however, featured continuous-wave operation that did not provide the full performance ultimately synonymous with modern radar systems.

Full radar evolved as a pulsed system, and the first such elementary apparatus was demonstrated in December 1934 by the American Robert M. Page, working at the Naval Research Laboratory. The following year, the United States Army successfully tested a primitive surface-to-surface radar to aim coastal battery searchlights at night. This design was followed by a pulsed system demonstrated in May 1935 by Rudolf Kühnhold and the firm GEMA [de] in Germany and then another in June 1935 by an Air Ministry team led by Robert Watson-Watt in Great Britain.

In 1935, Watson-Watt was asked to judge recent reports of a German radio-based death ray and turned the request over to Wilkins. Wilkins returned a set of calculations demonstrating the system was basically impossible. When Watson-Watt then asked what such a system might do, Wilkins recalled the earlier report about aircraft causing radio interference. This revelation led to the Daventry Experiment of 26 February, 1935, using a powerful BBC shortwave transmitter as the source and their GPO receiver set-up in a field while a bomber flew around the site. When the plane was clearly detected, Hugh Dowding, the Air Member for Supply and Research was very impressed with their system's potential and funds were immediately provided for further operational development. Watson-Watt's team patented the device in GB593017.

Development of radar greatly expanded on 1 September, 1936 when Watson-Watt became Superintendent of a new establishment under the British Air Ministry, Bawdsey Research Station located in Bawdsey Manor, near Felixstowe, Suffolk. Work there resulted in the design and installation of aircraft detection and tracking stations called "Chain Home" along the East and South coasts of England in time for the outbreak of World War II in 1939. This system provided the vital advance information that helped the Royal Air Force win the Battle of Britain; without it, significant numbers of fighter aircraft, which Great Britain did not have available, would always need to be in the air to respond quickly. If detection of enemy aircraft had relied solely on the observations of ground-based individuals, England might have lost the Battle of Britain. Also vital was the "Dowding system" of reporting and coordination to provide the best use of radar information during the tests of early radar deployment during 1936 and 1937.

Given all required funding and development support, the team produced working radar systems in 1935 and began deployment. By 1936, the first five Chain Home (CH) systems were operational and by 1940 stretched across the entire UK including Northern Ireland. Even by standards of the era, CH was crude; instead of broadcasting and receiving from an aimed antenna, CH broadcast a signal floodlighting the entire area in front of it, and then used one of Watson-Watt's own radio direction finders to determine the direction of the returned echoes. This fact meant CH transmitters had to be much more powerful and have better antennas than competing systems but allowed its rapid introduction using existing technologies.

A key development was the cavity magnetron in the UK, which allowed the creation of relatively small systems with sub-meter resolution. Britain shared the technology with the U.S. during the 1940 Tizard Mission.

In April 1940, *Popular Science* showed an example of a radar unit using the Watson-Watt patent in an article on air defense. Also, in late 1941 *Popular Mechanics* had an article in which a U.S. scientist speculated about the British early warning system on the English east coast and came close to what it was and how it worked. Watson-Watt was sent to the U.S. in 1941 to advise on air defense immediately after Japan's attack on Pearl Harbor. Alfred Lee Loomis organized the secret MIT Radiation Laboratory at Massachusetts Institute of Technology, Cambridge, Massachusetts, which developed microwave radar technology in the years 1941–45. Later, in 1943, Page greatly improved radar with the monopulse technique that was used for many years in most radar applications.

ILLUMINATION

Radar relies on its own transmissions rather than light from the Sun or the Moon, or from electromagnetic waves emitted by the target objects themselves, such as infrared radiation (heat). This process of directing artificial radio waves towards objects is called illumination, although radio waves are invisible to the human eye as well as optical cameras.

The klystron was the first significantly powerful source of radio waves in the microwave range; before its invention the only sources were the Barkhausen-Kurz tube and split anode magnetron, which were limited to very low power. It was invented by the brothers Russell and Sigurd Varian at Stanford University. Their prototype was completed and demonstrated successfully on August 30, 1937. Upon publication in 1939, news of the klystron immediately influenced the work of US and UK researchers working on radar equipment. The Varians went on to found Varian Associates, to commercialize the technology (for example, to make small linear accelerators to generate photons for external beam radiation therapy). Their work was preceded by the description of velocity modulation by A. Arsenjewa-Heil and Oskar Heil (wife and husband) in 1935, though the Varians were probably unaware of the Heils' work.

The work of physicist W.W. Hansen was instrumental in the development of the klystron and was cited by the Varian brothers in their 1939 paper. His resonator analysis, which dealt with the problem of accelerating electrons toward a target, could be used just as well to decelerate electrons (i.e., transfer their kinetic energy to RF energy in a resonator). During the second World War, Hansen lectured at the MIT Radiation labs two days a week, commuting to Boston from Sperry Gyroscope Company on Long Island. His resonator was called a "rhumbatron" by the Varian brothers. Hansen died of beryllium disease in 1949 as a result of exposure to beryllium oxide (BeO).

During the Second World War, the Axis powers relied mostly on (then low-powered and long wavelength) klystron technology for their radar system microwave generation, while the Allies used the far more powerful but frequency-drifting technology of the cavity magnetron for much shorter-wavelength one-centimeter microwave generation. Klystron tube technologies for very high-power applications, such as synchrotrons and radar systems, have since been developed.

Right after the war, AT&T used 4-watt klystrons in its brand-new network of microwave relay links that covered the US continent. The network provided long-distance telephone service and also carried television signals for the major TV networks. Western Union Telegraph Company also built point-to-point microwave communication links using intermediate repeater stations at about 40-mile intervals at that time, using 2K25 reflex klystrons in both the transmitters and receivers. (Wikipedia, 'Klystron', https://en.wikipedia.org/wiki/Klystron)

As a software engineer, including work in cyber security, I followed the Snowden leaks regarding NSA Computer Network Operations with interest. The hacking tools employed by the NSA as revealed by Snowden, had some intriguing elements. If you go through the leaks you will read how they could install ports and chips into targeted systems, and power them through Radar, by directing a radar signal at the target the device inserted into their system would be energized, a basic magnetron. Similarly, you will read reports from former MI-5 and MI-6 agents that talk of doing this same thing to their targets, deploying radar for the purposes of covert surveillance. Radar's relationship to neuroweapons is not just limited to CN ops. The Frey effect itself, hearing voices not spoken inside one's head, was a direct outcome of radar technicians' experiences while maintaining the radar; they would start to hear strange things inside their heads, leading to the discovery of the Frey effect. In another ironic twist with contemporary politics, one of the leading engineers on the US Radar systems during World War II at MIT in Boston, was David G. Trump, the uncle of ex-President Trump. He was dispatched upon Tesla's death (Tesla suggested a radar system in 1917), to American investors, to investigate Tesla's papers and remarked upon review that there was nothing to see in them.

RADAR FUNCTIONAL THEORY

In the following section is a brief review of the equations and theories of Radar operation. The following is based on O'Donnell lectures at MIT Lincoln Laboratory in 2021. A very basic block diagram of a radar system is this:

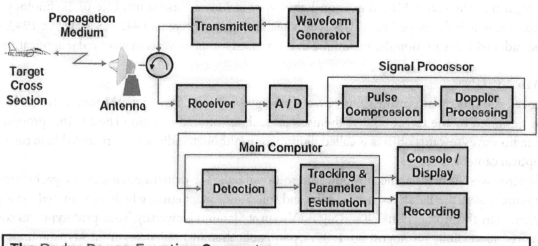

(O'Donnell 2021)

Radar sends out an EM wave in the microwave bandwidths hitting a reflection or object, then a very small amount of energy bounces off the target and is processed by the Radar's receivers. Then the signal undergoes processing and finally output to a User Interface of some kind. The two main components of radar in terms of scientific equations are the Received Signal equation and the Radar Range Equation including signal to noise equations. First, the Received Signal equation is formulated as:

$$\text{Received Signal Energy} = [P_T]\left[\frac{4\pi A}{\lambda^2}\right]\left[\frac{1}{4\pi R^2}\right]\left[\frac{1}{L}\right][\sigma]\left[\frac{1}{4\pi R^2}\right][A][\tau]$$

Transmit Power — Transmit Gain — Spread Factor — Losses — Target RCS — Spread Factor — Receive Aperture — Dwell Time

(O'Donnell 2021)

This equation is used to measure the echo from an object or target that the radar signal has a hit on. The objects echo foot-print is represented by Target RCS (sigmoid), this is the area of the object that the radar can see and receives a return signal or echo from, it is a small fraction of the original sent signal amplitude. The radar equation is used to formulate the details of the echo and processing of it, in this book I use the equations for tracking a target also known as surveillance radar, we start with the Radar Range equation:

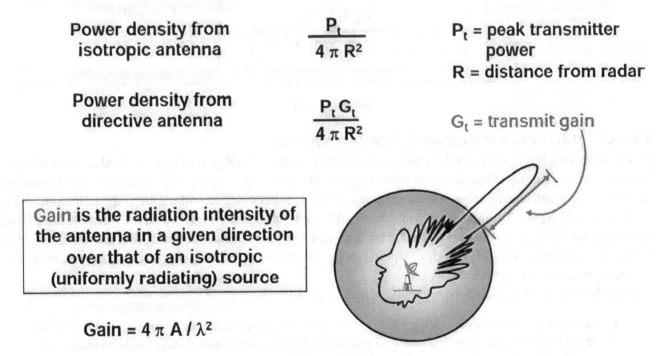

Power density from isotropic antenna $\dfrac{P_t}{4\pi R^2}$

P_t = peak transmitter power
R = distance from radar

Power density from directive antenna $\dfrac{P_t G_t}{4\pi R^2}$

G_t = transmit gain

Gain is the radiation intensity of the antenna in a given direction over that of an isotropic (uniformly radiating) source

Gain = $4\pi A / \lambda^2$

(O'Donnell 2021)

For our purposes we are using the 'Power density from a directive antenna.' Next, we get the Radar Cross Section (RCS or sigmoid). RCS is a measure of the energy that a radar target intercepts and scatters back toward the radar:

Power of reflected signal at target $\dfrac{P_t G_t \sigma}{4\pi R^2}$

σ = radar cross section units (meters)^2

Power density of reflected signal at the radar $\dfrac{P_t G_t}{4\pi R^2}\dfrac{\sigma}{4\pi R^2}$

Power density of reflected signal falls off as ($1/R^2$)

197

The received power is the power density at the radar times the area of the receiving antenna.

Power of reflected signal from target and received by radar

$$P_r = \frac{P_t G_t}{4 \pi R^2} \frac{\sigma A_e}{4 \pi R^2}$$

P_r = power received

A_e = effective area of receiving antenna

Finally, we have to finish the radar equation with the Signal-to-Noise (SNR) ratio which is calculated from the following:

Signal Power reflected from target and received by radar

$$P_r = \frac{P_t G_t}{4 \pi R^2} \frac{\sigma A_e}{4 \pi R^2}$$

Average Noise Power

$$N = k T_s B_n$$

Signal to Noise Ratio

$$S/N = P_r / N$$

$$S/N = \frac{P_t G^2 \lambda^2 \sigma}{(4 \pi)^3 R^4 k T_s B_n L}$$

Assumptions:
$G_t = G_r$
L = Total System Losses
$T_0 = 290° K$

(O'Donnell 2021)

RADAR IN INTELLIGENCE AND SURVEILLANCE

In an earlier chapter we discussed how the use of agents to track an intelligence target in Northern Ireland, specifically, Irish Catholic nationalists, was something like 50 agents per 1 target. This labor intensive process of surveillance of an intelligence target was the main reason to use cyber as a means of tracking targets, it reduced the need for so many agents. Before the creation of more advanced techniques for tracking in the early 2000s a part of the manual surveillance was the use of Radar to track a target by secret intelligence throughout the world, a hidden trade-craft that is not discussed publicly except in rare circumstances by British ex-intelligence specialists such as Dr. Barry Trower and ex-agent Carl Clark.

Clark describes how he would deploy Radar against a target:

> It's a bit like what takes place in a science fiction movie. People can be tracked anywhere by radar, satellite, a base station and complimentary computer programs. For example, three radar devices would sometimes be positioned in the vicinity of the target. The radar emits electromagnetic waves, some of which pick up the target and the result is then evaluated. My friends who work in the special department could then follow the target all day on their computers. This form of localizing the target made it easy to deploy the weapons accurately. My colleagues could see exactly where to aim and also observe how the target reacted. (Groß 2009)

This was similar to descriptions by Dr. John Norseen of using radar for the purposes of Thought Injection and Biofusion.

> …a couple emails back you talked about how you can feel different thought patterns, sometimes just a twinge, other times full bore…well, I wrote a rather lengthy project report for NASA back in 2000 and also for NSA related to Cryptomnesia…this is Greek for the Continuum of signals and noises that can occur in a brain.
>   Imagine a Vertical Bar to the left of this page. In the middle of the bar would be zero dB or decibel, and it would move to over 100 db + positive to the top…and in the same vein would register down into 150-200 db – negative.

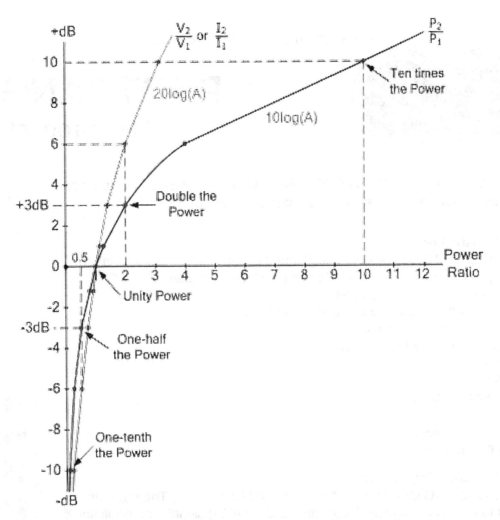

A generic example showing the relationship of dBs to Power

This is exactly the same kind of measurement scale that is used to rate a submarine sound signal or Electro-magnetic Signal…positive and negative. Well, it is possible using EEG and other BioFusion tools that one can track the movement of Identified Thoughts or Semiotic Structures as they emanate Functions or Communications (INTENT). In fact, right now, you Duncan, probably have hundreds or thousands of Thoughts and mini-thoughts that are dancing around, and banging around inside your head, just like a radar sweep looking out at weather patterns…one can radar sweep the semiotic conditions inside of your head and plot them on this Cryptomnesia Scale. You can even apply Doppler analysis and see which thoughts are growing in intensity, or dying out, or getting stuck in "feed-back" loops, sustaining themselves, perhaps in Unconscious or Non-Cognitive zones, at let's say – 100 db or -35-50 db, self-obsessive routines, etc. etc.

When thoughts emerge past zero and move into the high positive values then you can clearly see that that is what is occupying the Mental Awake State of the person…you can flash brief visuals or sound types or kinesthetic potentials, and you can see the Brain Thought adjust… (Norseen, 2002, part 6)

This is similar to the NSA using Radar to illuminate a target computer for off-line retrieval of information in a covert manner. This was first brought to public attention through the Snowden Leaks, where old NSA files were leaked by a contractor to show systematic abuse of personal privacies; again it is an important leak, but also all the leaked materials were out-of-date and not the latest technology even at the time of the leaks. One such system that is used was the CTX4000 system which has been replaced by what they termed 'PHOTOANGLO', again showing the Anglo-Saxon bias of UK-USA secret intelligence, rather than calling it PHOTOBRIT for example, inclusive of all British nations including the Irish of Northern Ireland. It works in tandem with other components such as VAGRANT and NIGHTWATCH – portable computer to display data from VAGRANT retrieved via PHOTOANGLO. NSA docs relate the following:

TOP SECRET//COMINT//REL TO USA, FVEY

PHOTOANGLO
ANT Product Data

(TS//SI//REL TO USA,FVEY) PHOTOANGLO is a joint NSA/GCHQ project to develop a new radar system to take the place of the CTX4000.

24 Jul 2008

(U) Capabilities
(TS//SI//REL TO USA,FVEY) The planned capabilities for this system are:
• Frequency range: 1 - 2 GHz, which will be later extended to 1 - 4 GHz.
• Maximum bandwidth: 450 MHz.
• Size: Small enough to fit into a slim briefcase.
• Weight: Less than 10 lbs.
• Maximum Output Power: 2 W
• Output:
• Video
• Transmit antenna
• Inputs:
• External oscillator
• Receive antenna

(U) Concept of Operation
(TS//SI//REL TO USA,FVEY) TS//SI//REL TO USA,FVEY) The radar unit generates an un-modulated, continuous wave (CW) signal. The oscillator is either generated internally, or externally through a signal generator or cavity oscillator. The unit amplifies the signal and sends it out to an RF connector, where it is directed to some form of transmission antenna (horn, parabolic dish, LPA, spiral). The signal illuminates the target system and is re-radiated. The receive antenna picks up the re-radiated signal and directs the signal to the receive input. The signal is amplified, filtered, and mixed with the transmit antenna. The result is a homodyne receiver in which the RF signal is mixed directly to baseband. The baseband video signal is ported to an external BNC connector. This connects to a processing system, such as NIGHTWATCH, an LFS-2, or VIEWPLATE, to process the signal and provide the intelligence.

Unit Cost: $40k (planned)

Status: Development. Planned IOC is 1st QTR FY09.

POC: ▮▮▮▮▮▮, S32243, ▮▮▮▮▮, ▮▮▮▮▮@nsa.ic.gov

Derived From: NSA/CSSM 1-52
Dated: 20070108
Declassify On: 20320108

TOP SECRET//COMINT//REL TO USA, FVEY

One can see the similarity to Thought Injection/BioFusion that targets wetware and the hardware version of PHOTOANGLO. Both are for remote monitoring using Radar.

BEARDEN ON TIME REVERSED WAVES: NO, IT'S NOT TIME-TRAVEL

Lt. Col. Tom Bearden (USA, ret.) brought to attention the use of time-reversed waves in the sense of reversing back from a given pathway, not in reverse time, of a beam of energy and Radar in the mid-1980s. He explicates on the subject and its connection to radar:

> At the end of WWII, the Soviet Union obtained the cream of the crop of Germany's radar scientists and infrared scientists.
>
> At that time, the German scientific team led the world in the theory and technology of radar absorbing materials (RAM) and radar cross section. For example, some leading Western radar experts believe that the German scientists had already advanced the theory of radar cross section beyond where Western scientists have arrived at today. Radar cross section science is the "heart" of modern radar technology, countermeasures, and counter-countermeasures. The theory of RAM technology is precisely what is needed to develop and design phase conjugate mirrors for radar frequency bands. Phase conjugate mirrors are capable of producing a time-reversed (TR) wave in direct response to a received ordinary wave. The mirror may be powerfully "pumped" with energy to produce a very large amplification of the time-reversed wave.

He continues:

> Compared to a normal wave, a time-reversed wave has startlingly different weapon capabilities.
>
> Such a wave precisely retraces the path of the ordinary wave that stimulated it to be formed. So, it possesses an "invisible wire" through space, back to the original position of whatever emitted its stimulus wave.
>
> Further, the time-reversed wave continually converges upon its invisible "back- tracking" path. It does not diverge and spread its energy, in contradistinction to normal waves.
>
> Using several simple schemes (particularly pumped 4-wave mixing), extremely large amplification of the time-reversed (TR) wave can be cheaply and readily accomplished.
>
> A startling weapons capability therefore emerges when amplified TR waves are generated in response to received signals from a distant target:
>
> (1) If any signal at all can be received from a distant target, a return TR signal of extreme power can be delivered directly to that target. Almost all of the transmitted TR signal energy will arrive at and in the distant target, even through a highly nonlinear medium or under scattering conditions. Hardly any of the energy will be lost en route. If the target is fast-moving, a "lead correction" signal can be calculated and added to steer the return path.
>
> (2) Since real-time holography can readily be accomplished using TR waves - and without first making holograms, geometrical forms (balls, shapes, hemispherical shells, etc) of energy can be created readily by interferometry (crossed beam techniques). Since the TR wave carriers do not disperse with distance, these interference energy forms can be assembled by crossed TR wave beams at great distances – even hundreds of thousands of miles. The energy appearing in such a distantly created energy form is limited only by the amount one cares to put in at the amplified transmitting end.
>
> Thus, the radar itself now becomes a powerful, all-around weapon. With a TR wave adjunct, once the radar receives a return signal from a target, an extremely powerful TR wave pulse can be generated, and all the energy in that pulse can be unerringly returned to the distant target from which the return was received. (Bearden, 1988, 285)

What a time-reversed wave does, is allow for a channel to be opened up in a certain sense from the object to the radar. Radar sends out a signal, it is echoed back by an object, then another wave is sent back directly to the target and not to any other coordinates, which is also akin to Ahronov-Bohm Effect monitoring we shall read about in later chapters as developed by the Soviets. This would be one way to pump an auditory signal as example to a target but nobody else around the target will hear that signal. Holography, as we shall read about more in the next section, is something he brings up, which we shall also read about more in later chapters as well. It is important to note that he mentions holography in connection with time-reversed waves, as well as his drawing attention to the cross section of the target or object of surveillance.

EYES AS RADAR

Previously, we read how the early Russian researcher Kazhinsky had formulated a connection to communication and the eyes. Recently, this conjecture of his has been given experimental ground through the work of Singh, et al (2018). In their studies they find the eye to be an antenna capable of receiving microwave radiation, infrared, ultraviolet, aside from the normal color spectrum of electromagnetic radiation we see. As Norseen noted, flashes of images appear in the visual cortex through Thought Injection; the visual pathway is a major part of Thought Injection. He also has spoken of sending beams of light (LED) at a target to affect neuro-cognitive function, see Chapter 4. Yet, he was not the originator of this concept, either, as it was done in the Soviet Union long before Thought Injection made its mark in the national security world. Pribram is sighted as the originator of Norseen's ideas of using holography. As we shall see, there are real-world applications of this developed by Kaznacheev.

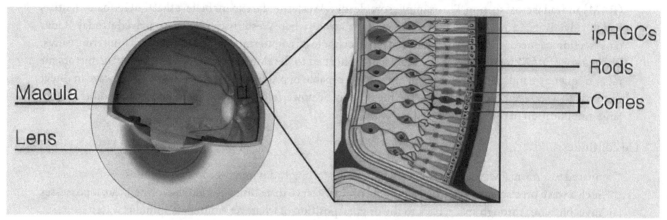

(image- Wikicommons)

Pribram's theories on holographic vision, recounted here:

> Three sorts of image representation are proposed to be used in the cortex: 1. the Gabor wavelets, rooted in dendritic webs, seem to be used for associative processes underlying visual cognition; 2. their Gabor coefficients represent neural-net's sparse codes which serve for automatic processing; 3. the spatial image, reconstructed in the extrastriate area, is those which is then consciously perceived "with shapes and colors." Because the third image representation is even perceptually projected back into external space, so that it coincides precisely with the original object, I propose that quantum holographic process is necessary, since neural nets cannot realize that alone. (Perus, 2010)

Earlier it was mentioned that Pribram was a source for the holographic background to Norseen's work; however, it should be mentioned that the use of holography was already developed in the Soviet Union. Holography is a visual field phenomenon as noted by a Russian researcher Kaznacheev in work initially begun by him in the 1960s. Again, it should be pointed out that the retina's cones and rods act as cavity resonators or as high-Q antennas. In his patent (Kaznacheev 2004) he and his team engineered a system to pass holograms into the visual cortex but not in the visual range so it is imageless holography, although it can be modified to also send visual holograms, as he writes "the invention relates to the field of optics and is intended to create a hologram containing non-visualized physiologically significant information that can be used in medicine." (Kaznacheev, 2004). This method is described:

> Method 3: The holographic image reproduced from the transmission hologram according to option 3 is taken on a digital video camera, the contrast of the diffractive components is enhanced using computer programs, for example PhotoShop, the graphic image of the hologram is converted into a digital matrix containing information about the color components and their intensity, a comparative statistical analysis of the values of elements of numerical matrices of holograms with the presence and absence of non-visualized physiologically significant information (mean values, variances, Parsons correlation coefficient, covariance of digital matrix values). If there are significant differences, a conclusion is made about the presence of non-visualized physiologically significant information in the hologram. (Kaznacheev 2004)

This allows both the transmission and reception of holographic information in the form of a frequency-modulated luminous flux. The transmission of the holograms occurs in the 2.5Hz-3.5Hz, and 10Hz (Alpha) brain-wave rhythms. When the brain is presented with a hologram containing non-visualized physiologically significant information triggers the activation of 10Hz Alpha, which is also mentioned by Norseen.

Eye as Antenna

Singh et al (2018) have brought out the physics of the human eye as a fractal antenna.

fractal antenna- electronic conduction and self-symmetry as in DNA, self-similarity was one of the underlying requirements to make antennas frequency and bandwidth invariant

One of the most basic self-similar structures is that of the Fibonacci sequence which is found throughout nature but also the human eye, which gives the eye a fractal antenna property:

"Mainly the Fibonacci Sequence-based structure or the periodical array of basic physiological units (such as photoreceptors within the retina) is responsible for optimizing the signal communication in biological living systems" (Singh et al, 2018)

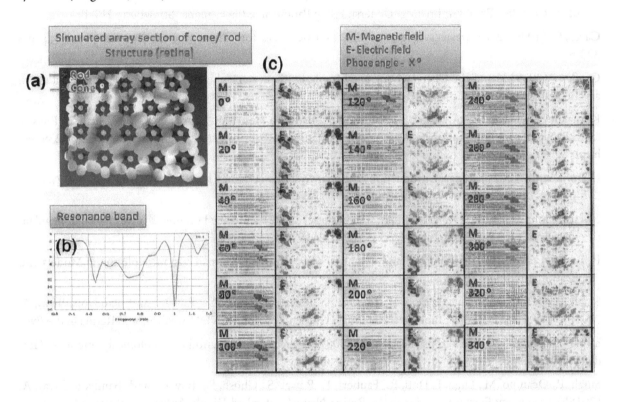

Singh et al 2018

It has been argued that the proteins vibrate in the presence of electromagnetic signal like a cavity resonator… Protein synthesis is stimulated by electromagnetic fields of the specific frequency in the RF range… Since we now have evidence that proteins vibrate electromagnetically, we can revisit the electromagnetic interaction in the cells, considering the whole cell as a cavity resonator. (Singh et al, 2018b)

Cavity resonators are needed to generate and receive microwaves among other wave frequencies, microwave cavity resonators are used to detect High Frequency Gravitational Waves (HFGW) as noted by Caves:

The coupled electro-mechanical system consisting of a microwave cavity and its walls can serve as a gravitational radiation detector. A gravitational wave interacts with the walls, and the resulting motion induces transitions from a highly excited cavity mode to a nearly unexcited mode. (Caves, 1976)

Singh has found that the structure of the eye's retina nano-center is a dipole antenna network. The interaction of a photon beam with this mechanism is considered: "If a rotation of the light wave underlies the laser emission then the possibility of helical electron transmission increases… …the network of cells acts as an array of helical antennas." (Singh et al, 2018b)

This is important to note in that helical structures interact with the Aharonov-Bohm Effect, so that in the human eye, this effect is felt and acted upon biologically. This dipole antenna of the eyes photoreceptors is modeled as an octagonal array; there is an octagonal order in rods and cones, with three types of cones: s,m,l, with wavelengths at three separate magnitudes: r=400nm, g=550nm, b=700nm. This is somewhat reminiscent of radar used by wasps at three different magnitudes as well as noted also in another paper by Singh et al (2018).

We see how the human eye, not normally thought of in connection with Radar, has certain radar-like properties, which may include infrared transmission and reception – the same basic structural pattern of the wasp's antennae which use infrared communication signals according to Singh, et al. In later chapters, we shall see how the Soviets developed a radar-like system using the Ahronov-Bohm effect and Spin-Entanglement which effectively are Quantum Radars.

BIBLIOGRAPHY:

Bearden, T (1988) 'Excalibur briefing: Understanding Paranormal Phenomena.' Strawberry Hill Pr

Caves, C. (1979) 'Microwave cavity gravitational radiation detectors' Physics Letters B Vol. 80, Issue 3, pages 323-6

Groß, A. (2009) Heimliche Uberwachung und Strahlenfolter durch Geheimdienste Whistleblower outet sich als ehemaliger Täter in Raum&Zeit 161/2009 pg. 47

Kaznacheev, V., Trofimov, A. (2004) A Method for Creating a Hologram Containing Non-Visualized Physiologically Significant Information Казначеев В.П. Трофимов А.В. https://findpatent.ru/patent/223/2239860.html

O'Donnell, R. (2021) Radar: Introduction to Radar Systems (Online) http://www.ll.mit.edu/outreach/radar-introduction-radar-systems-online-course

Norseen, John D., Laurie, Duncan 'Outlaw Technology' (2002) published on-line at http://www.duncanlaurie.com/writing/outlaw_technology (accessed 3/6/2019)

Perus, M. Loo, C. (2010) Biological and Quantum Computing for Human Vision: Holonomic Models and Applications. IGI Global; 1st edition

Singh, P., Ocampo, M., Lugo, J., Doti, R., Faubert, J., Rawat, S., Ghosh, S., Ray, K. and Bandyopadhyay, A. (2018) Fractal and Periodical Biological Antennas: Hidden Topologies in DNA, Wasps and Retina in the Eye

https://www.researchgate.net/publication/336408771_Fractal_and_periodical_biological_antennas_Hidden_topologies_in_DNA_wasps_and_retina_in_the_eye

Singh, P., Ocampo, M., Lugo, J., Doti, R., Faubert, J., Rawat, S., Ghosh, S., Ray, K. and Bandyopadhyay, A. (2018b) Frequency Fractal Behavior in the Retina Nano-Center-Fed Dipole Antenna Network of a Human Eye DOI:10.1007/978-981-10-5699-4_20 In book: Soft Computing: Theories and Applications (pp.201-211)

CHAPTER 8

QUANTUM CONSCIOUSNESS

A comparison of the latest available data, despite the different scales of objects, unexpectedly revealed a deep commonality of the foundations of the universe, that the micro- and macrocosm "are not so different from each other"

-Kravkov

In a previous chapter (Ch. 4, 'Lessons from an American Weapons Designer'), we read about the development of Thought Injection by Dr. John Norseen, while employed at Lockheed-Martin. In his research articles and in conversations he explained several of the key areas involved in his work. One of the areas that he touched upon was the concept of Quantum Consciousness. Citing many researchers in this area, he was influenced by the holonomic ideas of Dr. Karl Pribram. Dr. Norseen, in one particular key technological area of his research, specifically cites the gravitational based Orchestrated Objective Reduction of Nobel laureate Sir Roger Penrose and University of Arizona professor, Dr. Stuart Hameroff. It is important to again note Dr. Norseen's concept of Quantum Shift Keying (QSK), which is to say a code, which was suggested in Koruga-Hameroff's 1994 research on Quantum Consciousness. Norseen claimed to use this QSK as a lock-key mechanism that he also compared to a die, casting a thought into the biological fabric of a target brain. In 'Ch. 6, Physics of Neuroweapons' we studied how gravitational waves served as the basis of this technology, and in detecting gravitational waves, the technology of interferometry is used. This is exactly how Norseen viewed the brain – the brain is an interferometer: "If we take Pribram and the Russian work, it shows that the human brain structure is an interferometer that uses Gabor Function (wavelet-codelet analysis) in Hilbert Space." (Norseen, 2002, Part 4)

A slide preserved by Laurie from a presentation prepared by Dr. John Norseen below:

Gabor Function	Spectral domain first, inverse transform to space time, a phase space
Hilbert Space	A Phase space (Sequence, probability, amplitude phase)
Holography	A method of representing space time configurations by their spectral transformations. Acted upon by the inverse transform.
Holonomic	Representation bo Hilbert Space (Spectral and Time Space)
Steganography	Injects hidden story-objects

(Noseen & Laurie 2002)

The seat of the QSK is revealed by Dr. Norseen as taking place in a particular part of the brain, inside neurons, in the molecular mechanism of Microtubules (MTs) writing:

> Invariance can be captured in MT by quantum encryption of various combinations of photons, phonons [GW produces phonons], and electrons, which may synergistically produce, via solitons, a binding property of emergent epiphenomenon; a biofield communication both local and non-local to the protein MT strings. Calpain induced start/stops in the dendritic-synaptic receptors, with varying degrees of glial cell neurochemical nutrient infusion, to turn on or off the QSK coded learning sequences in the MT. As more and more neuronal activity forms a topological geometry around these events, oscillating in concert, perceptual and then cognitive events transpire, suggesting a process for sensory to sentient computation. Norseen (1996)

A phonon is the quantum mechanical description of an elementary vibrational motion in which a lattice of atoms or molecules uniformly oscillates at a single frequency. In classical mechanics this designates a normal mode of vibration.

In his conversations with Laurie, he speaks of the Orchestrated Reduction; in his 1996 Russian presentation he cites Hameroff's ORCH-OR three times:

> Semiotics leads to greater complexity and teleological concentration of energies. Brain structures form to interface and resonate with ZPE; memories are captured ZPE events stored in orchestrated reductions of proteins. When memories are tapped by brain signals — electromagnetic, biochemical or phononic or vibrational — the proteins unwind and unleash the stored memories. Then, as proteins do, they rewind themselves to be tapped again…think of a balsa wood, rubber band-powered airplane that can be used over and over again to fly around the yard. (Norseen, 2002, Part 11).

An important thing to notice about these remarks, aside from familiarity with Orchestrated Reduction of Penrose, is that he is also formulating the Amplifier Theory of Jordan, as he speaks of memories coming from ZPE, Zero Point Energy, which are vacuum fluctuations of virtual particles which in the Classical world are encountered in the Casimir Effect where virtual particles can appear, of which we will read more from Dr. Michael Persinger. Dr. Persinger also points to ORCH-OR as a viable candidate as a physical explanation for Consciousness. (see more below) In talking about the negentropy (structure) of Semiotics, Norseen brings up the issue of the ability to speak of them quantitatively and then improve on that quantization through technology:

> So, if you are concerned, we are dealing in Esoteric, erudite, non-approachable conditions of Semiotics and Radionics and ZPE and Alfven Wave Grids, then BE SOFTENED my good friend. The very fact that SEMIOTICS requires structure means that it can be TESTED, MEASURED, VERIFIED and understood and TECHNICALLY AMPLIFIED. I have given examples of how simply twisting Chromatin within a mitochondrial (ZPE channel) cell structure results in SEMIOTICS expression and cell division/cloning (Representamen)… and this can be shown faithfully and measurably. (Norseen, 2002, Part. 7)

The question becomes, how is the measuring done? To which Norseen has also provided some insights, speaking of using holography, which we also encountered in the work of Dr. Bar in terms of gravitational wave holography. Norseen also speaks of the gap junctions between neuronal cells – they correspond to a small enough distance for Casimir Effects to take place:

> It is only in the communications switching capacity of the brain — (no two neurons normally physically touch each other, therefore, this gap represents a switching capacity), and it is this switching capacity of several million objects that allows for our great mental scan and scope capabilities, not the Memory Storage in physical memory of proteins.
>
> This structure is almost limitless in the ability to generate Holonomic-holographic-like resonance patterns. In physical protein memory, there are parts of the brain that deal in one memory to one laid down protein. For instance, in the Fusiform Gyrus, the one-to-one memories of loved ones' faces are stored in isomorphic recall conditions, whereas the rest of the brain is involved with undulating and regular modifications of the alternating calpain, induced plasticity of neurons and protein lay down, that occurs each time we introduce a new memory for codification. These functions normally take place during the delta frequency of deep-sleep patterns, only after repeated Rapid Eye Movement (REM) cycles trigger new memory consolidation. (Norseen, 2002, Part. 7)

Here he is noting the difference between long-term memory, which can become encoded in proteins, and a holographic resonant model of memories before they become encoded as long-term memories. Not all resonances will become memories, though. Norseen has noted that to get a hologram of the brain state at a given time the Casimir Effect is employed. Another methodology he explicitly brings up in regard to measurements and modeling (holographic mapping) is the Zeeman Effect which he received from the Russians:

> I am into Continuous Wave Energy (CWE) using the Zeeman Effect (ZE), and refined by the Russkies under Zavoisky in '45, and picked up by the Japanese in the mid 80's at Hitachi. It is even being used in conjunction

with some deep space and HAARP projects and hyper spectral satellite transmissions groups to find gravity lenses, and ionosphere scintillation factors that corrupt GPS, etc. Anyway, in the human brain the combination of electric fields, biochemical plasma and magnetic dipoles [MT dipoles] set up conditions ripe for monitoring by CWE and the hyper spectral definitions come about by looking at the Zeeman Effect - the directions that the electrons take in the presence of the regular and applied magnetic field…you can peer right into the actual communications structures, the semiotics if you will, of the target. (Norseen, 2002, Part 8)

He writes in another section:

…and right at the zone where Alfven Wave corridors of the brain Magnetite exchange ZPE in the dendritic neuropil at nanoscale [MTs], discrete bandwidth, channels. It is right here in the Marianas Trench of human thought/perception, that the person is exposed to the Universals of Quantum State potentials, and that each individual thought or Semiotic Identity is formed, only to then bubble or shoot right up to the surface of positive thought realms.

Just as you can look into an aquarium or a fishbowl and see the stuff at the bottom work its way up to the surface, you can track the origin of Semiotics from Alfven Wave Interactions with ZPE, from the plumbed depths of the Brain. (Norseen, 2002, part 6)

Norseen here specifically mentions the Zeeman effect, which is of special interest because of the importance of Zeeman data in the analysis and theoretical interpretation of complex spectra used in Atomic spectroscopy and spectroscopy in general--the study of the interaction between matter and electromagnetic radiation [see chapter 6, 'Physics of Neuroweapons' for HFGW spectroscopy of Dr. Robert Baker]. Pieter Zeeman effect: splitting of a spectral line into several components in the presence of a static magnetic field (CWE radar of Norseen). It is analogous to the Stark effect, the splitting of a spectral line into several components in the presence of an electric field; splits, via changing angular momentum, a spectral line say 400nm into a more energetic line, it's normative line and a less energetic line, 3 lines. Since the distance between the Zeeman sub-levels is a function of magnetic field strength, this effect can be used to measure magnetic field strength, e.g., that of the Sun and other stars or in laboratory plasmas.

The Zeeman effect is very important in applications such as nuclear magnetic resonance spectroscopy, electron spin resonance spectroscopy, magnetic resonance imaging (MRI) and Mossbauer spectroscopy. A theory about the magnetic sense of birds assumes that a protein (cryptochrome-2) in the retina is changed due to the Zeeman effect. Humans have similar proteins in their eyes. Kernbach in experiments directly related to the work of Norseen has noted that earlier Russian versions of this technology used spectroscopy based on Impedance Spectroscopy, which uses Zeeman splitting. Kernbach also notes that this technology is used in Intelligence work:

There are known cases of application of these methods in anti-terrorist, military and intelligence operations but they also have the nature of rare exceptions. Reaction from the academic community is quite polarized, although in the field of quantum research such a potential it is quite possible: 'Quantum entanglement allows engineered quantum systems to exceed classical information processing bounds', especially for biological systems, neurons, nervous system and brain (and 'nonlocal functions' of consciousness) (Kernbach, 2018)

Kernbach further elaborates on the meteorological aspects of this science, about keeping track of entangled objects and mapping them:

The proposed method for remote monitoring is based on Electrochemical Impedance Spectroscopy (EIS) with optical excitation and is a combination the notion of the two systems …. The essence method is to create a entangled system from a remote object and a measuring container with liquid. A new element is the introduction of optical IC excitation at two wavelengths 470 / 940nm into the measuring system. Experiments with LED demonstrated the property of transmission of influence between two entangled macrosystems therefore, it is assumed that in the presence of an optical the excitation of the container with water will be the impact is also the remote object. Necessary bridging of EM radiation for entangling macro objects other authors also paid attention. Measuring the excitation of electrochemical dynamics water system, it is possible to express this impact result in numbers. The more 'active' the remote object is etc., the more intense the EIS deflection will be from an unexcited state. A numerical estimate uses a statistical method to characterization of electrochemical noise, which has proven itself in other EIS applications.

Thus, this method makes it possible to estimate the degree of the level of 'activity' of a remote object is its way to influence other objects. By observations, this property is characterized by biological organisms, generators, shape effects, certain processes. An interesting area of study is the 'activity' of information (sym-free) objects, which brings us back to the discussion in work on the possible independent character of the sym-free structures. 'Activity' can stimulate or depress the dynamics of the corresponding channel. These changes can be expressed in terms of entropy (negentropy) and associate with the state of the remote object. This moment is especially interesting when working with pathogenic objects/zones, allowing casting of their possible parameters without direct contact. Experiments have shown the same possibility of selective detection of global 'informational/cosmo-biological' events. In tests with humans, when volunteers with sufficient level of sensitivity were informed of the beginning of the measurements, various subjective reactions occurred – dizziness, specific 'tingling/burning' on the skin, changes in state of consciousness and sleep patterns. If the subject is not new to the measurement process, he could determine in most cases, the fact of measurement, however there was an error in determining the measurement time. With short-term use, this method can be used for self-diagnosis, for example, when taking info-ceutical drugs or with psycho mental training (yoga, meditation, various practices), in the experiments there was a correlation between the current psycho-physiological state and the received data. (Kernbach, 2018)

Others Kernbach points to in Russia working on 'Quantum Indexing of Entangled Macro Objects' during the Soviet era were Shkatov, Kravchenko, Savelyev [who worked with Okatrin, see below]. With this ability to alter brain, nervous systems with nonlocal functions of consciousness would be one of the most valuable assets any military commander could have, hence, we see the importance the KGB put behind developing these technologies. Indeed, the Soviet Military was involved in this research:

The test of the Radiation installation in military unit 71592, where this installation was created (in the Novosibirsk region), has become well-known. A report on this test was heard at the Institute of Radio Engineering and Electronics of the Russian Academy of Sciences. The authors of the invention called the report "Impact on biological objects by modulated electrical and electromagnetic impulses."

The ability to cover an entire battlefield is noted, "You can put an entire stadium, concert hall or military unit into a 10-minute sleep using psychotronic weapons." From the preceding we can see the direct connection of remote biological influence and its study as a weapon by the Soviet Military.

Regarding the spectroscopy involved it is interesting that in one presentation for the product GeoScan System speaks of referencing hyper dimensions in their program; in this use instance it is able to penetrate kilometers of earth to find mineral deposits, when radar can only penetrates a few meters (Geoscan 2016). Again, this research was also looked into by the Soviets from at least the 1970s. (Sokolova, 2016)

In an interesting corollary, Persinger relates the Schumann Resonance to the Zeeman effect in the cerebrum:

The operating intensity of the cerebrum has been measured and calculated to be in the 1 to 100 pT range with a wide band of coefficients. From this context it is interesting that kg/As * 1/s or the mass of an electron divided by a unit charge multiplied by 7 Hz is 9.1×10^{-31} kg$/1.6 \times 10^{-19}$ As * 7 Hz (1/s) or 40×10^{-12} T. This relationship is closely coupled to the Zeeman effect whereby the application of a magnetic field produces an additional or a third spectral line in an absorption spectrum by inducing different quantum levels. The change in angular frequency with an applied field of 40×10^{-12} T would be, according to classic Zeeman formula solutions, the product of 4×10^{-11} T * 1.6×10^{-19} As divided by 12.56 * 9.1×10^{-31} kg or about 0.6 Hz. However, in non-angular systems it would be 7 Hz [Schumann Resonance]. (Persinger, 2010, 818)

Persinger here seems to correlate the rate of Alpha Brain Waves with the Zeeman effect's angular momentum, suggesting that the reason that at 7Hz the entire brain is vibrating, which is also the Schumann Resonance of the Ionosphere, in other works Persinger has suggested that there is some memory connection to the EM in the ionosphere and particular individual brain memories, remote storage of memories in the ionosphere.

Another area that is of interest in terms of mapping is the ability to measure brain waves. The Casimir effect plays a direct role in these waves, as the effect creates the contracting and expanding of neuron cells. Duncan Laurie gave this encapsulation of Norseen's presentation on the creation of brain waves:

> The communications described are instantaneous, and to describe how that is possible, Norseen introduced two additional factors: Zero Point Energy and Alfven Waves. Zero Point Waves (ZPE) having been introduced earlier in the manuscript. This energy of the vacuum has actually been measured and is called the Casimir Effect. The Casimir Effect is measurable when two metal plates are placed extremely close together (1 nanometer). The vacuum created interferes with the flow of ZPE and has been scientifically measured. The result is that the plates are drawn together, as if by magnetic attraction. Norseen points out by comparison that the identical 1 nanometer distance is the distance between brain cells, thereby implying a stage for ZPE coupling. As these distances open and close between the cells, a signal impressed upon the ZPE [virtual particles in a vacuum] can be generated out in the 5-30 Hz. range.
>
> How it becomes an instantaneous signal reaching anywhere in the universe is accomplished by the Alfven Wave (AW). Norseen's definition of Alfven waves is that of a magnetic string stretched out, and then impinged upon by unique traveling magnetic resonant structures…like plucking a magnetic harp. Theoretically, Alfven waves interconnect all parts of the universe via magnetic fields. Magnetite within the brain cells connect local magnetic swirls to the magnetic river or storms existing locally or outside our magnetosphere. Norseen describes the AW as a universal plasma that extends between local and non-local events, capable of carrying semiotic communications via directed ZPE [virtual particles in a vacuum] pulsation. These signals are capable of penetrating the magnetic storm, in the same way radio signals penetrate our congested airways carrying selective information from point to point. (Norseen, 2002)

Here Norseen seems to suggest that to observe brain state, you need an EM field (Alfven Wave Grid), which can also be a correlate to a Gravitational Field, perhaps using gravito-electromagnetics (GEM). An Alfven Wave is a wave behavior of magnetic grid lines, if you could imagine those grid lines as the surface of an ocean, then the Alfven Waves would be surfable. A more technical definition is given:

> Alfvén waves, being transversal, are incompressible.
>
> In a compressible fluid, the pressure acts as a restoring force, and one obtains sound waves. The combination is magneto-acoustic waves, which have three modes: i) unchanged Alfvén mode, because it is incompressible; and sound waves modified into two coupled slow (ii) and fast (iii) modes. Considering a stratified fluid (e.g., an atmosphere) and adding gravity as a restoring force, one has magneto-acoustic-gravity waves and Alfvén-gravity waves decouple only if the horizontal wave-vector (which exists only in the direction transverse to stratification) lies in the plane of gravity and the external magnetic field. Adding rotation and the Coriolis force as the fourth restoring force leads to magneto-acoustic-gravity-inertial waves for which decoupling of Alfvén-gravity modes is generally not possible. Below, the Alfvén waves are uncoupled to other types of waves in fluids. https://encyclopediaofmath.org/wiki/Alfv%C3%A9n_waves

However, Norseen here seems to use Alfven waves as a pseudonym for 'magnetic grid lines' in general. Other researchers have remarked on the correlation of Alfven waves to their occurrence in the earth's Ionosphere (resonating at 3Hz to 5Hz), which is related to the psychotronic area of the Schumann Resonance, named after a German scientist brought to America under Project Paperclip, though credited to an Irishman, Fitzgerald. Although there are in these plasmas magneto-gravity wave. A magneto-gravity wave is an acoustic gravity wave which is associated with fluctuations in the background magnetic field. In this context, gravity wave refers to a classical fluid wave, and is completely unrelated to the relativistic gravitational wave, see Gravitational Aharonov-Bohm effect in Ch. 9. Although, as we know the Alfven Wave Grid would and does interact with gravity, thus producing gravitational waves, and one would also be able to interact with the Alfven EM Grid, as explained by Norseen, with gravitational waves.

> In 1985 P.P. Belyaev … discovered a resonant structure of electromagnetic noise at frequencies below the first harmonic of the Schumann resonance. It turned out that Alfvén waves in the ionosphere form an Alfvén resonator with an oscillation frequency that depends on the thickness of the ionosphere, the strength of the Earth's

magnetic field and the concentration of ionospheric plasma particles… the resonant frequency of the Alfvén resonator varies within 0.5-3.0 Hz… the amplification of the Alfvén resonance phenomenon occurs at night, in the daytime the amplitude of resonance increases decreases to the values of ordinary noise… historical "adjustment" to the rhythms of the ionosphere…, synchronization of delta - and theta - rhythms with the frequencies of the Alfvén resonator, most likely, did take place

The frequency of the delta-rhythm inherent in the state of sleep, F = 0.3-4.0 Hz, indeed, in general, coincides with the ionospheric frequencies F = 0.5-3.0 Hz. Is it possible to replace natural oscillations with generator waves of the same length? (Norseen Laurie 2002)

I am not aware of any working HFGW surveillance at the time of Norseen's engineering work at Lockheed-Martin; it would be shortly after Norseen ended his work at Lockheed that Dr. Baker would write to the NSA regarding such technology. In interviews Norseen indicated a small local Radar system was to be deployed to do neural scanning of suspected terrorists at airports. As we know a gravitational signal receiver/transmitter can do the type of spectroscopy that was done with Radar alone before, but with added resolution. One other note in relation to Alfven Waves is that they are usually associated with Solar plasmas, in the inner solar corona of Stars. It is known that during Solar Storms, vast EM discharges from the Sun that are shielded from the Earth by the Atmosphere, correlate with decreased 'psi' ability according to Dr. Persinger and earlier Russian studies, related to breaking the static conditions of the EM Field as rapidly increasing levels from solar coronal masses make their way to the Earth's Schumann Resonance or EM Field. Also, the relationship to geomagnetic plasmas in the inner core of the earth may also have a relationship to Dr. Persinger's proposal to predict earthquakes based on EM discharges. Kravkov explains the relationship of Schumann Resonance, Alfven Waves and Consciousness:

"It has been experimentally revealed that the brain, as an oscillatory system, has a high Q factor. With a simple forced resonance of a linear system with a high-quality factor, the amplitude of the oscillations increases significantly only when the natural frequency and the frequency of the external influence exactly coincide." The basic rhythms of the human brain are as follows:

• Delta-rhythm, rhythm of a sleeping person, sinusoidal, F = 0.3-4.0 Hz;

• theta-rhythm, rhythm of a completely relaxed state and transition to a state of sleep, anesthesia, sinusoidal, F = 4-8 Hz;

• alpha-rhythm, the rhythm of a waking person, dominant in the occipital parts of the brain, is associated with the ability of abstract thinking, sinusoidal, F = 9-13 Hz.

So, it is easy to see from the research provided from Norseen, Persinger, Kravkov and others that there is a direct correlation to electro-magnetic fields and consciousness. How consciousness is affected by EM is part of the theory of Orchestrated Reduction.

ORCHESTRATED OBJECTIVE REDUCTION AND NEUROWEAPONS

As we've seen, Dr. Norseen directly cites the work of Hameroff-Penrose on ORCH-OR as the model or physical explanation for Quantum Shift Keying, which is to say changing or monitoring the brain maps of a given target, thus directly affecting cognitive function of that brain targeted. ORCH-OR has also had its detractors, such as Stefan Koch. The most direct explanation of ORCH-OR was given by Hameroff in his 2014 paper:

'Orchestrated objective reduction' ('Orch OR') is a theory which proposes that consciousness consists of a sequence of discrete events, each being a moment of 'objective reduction' (OR) of a quantum state (according to the DP scheme), where it is taken that these quantum states exist as parts of a quantum computations carried on primarily in neuronal microtubules. Such OR events would have to be 'orchestrated' in an appropriate way (Orch OR), for genuine consciousness to arise. OR itself is taken to be ubiquitous in physical actions, representing the 'bridge' between the quantum and classical worlds, where quantum superpositions between pairs of states get spontaneously resolved into classical alternatives in a timescale ⊠ τ, calculated from the amount of mass displacement that there is between the two states. In our own brains, the OR process that evoke consciousness, would be actions that connect brain biology (quantum computations in microtubules) with the fine scale structure of space–time geometry, the most basic level of the universe [Norseen's ZPE], where tiny quantum space–time displacements are taken to be responsible for OR. The Orch-OR proposal therefore stretches across a considerable range of areas of science, touching upon the foundations of general relativity and quantum mechanics, in unconventional ways, in addition to the more obviously relevant areas such as neuroscience, cognitive science, molecular biology, and philosophy. It is not surprising, therefore, that Orch OR has been persistently criticized from many angles since its introduction in 1994. Nonetheless, the Orch OR scheme has so far stood the test of time better than most other schemes, and it is particularly distinguished from other proposals by the many scientifically tested, and potentially testable, ingredients that it depends upon. It should be mentioned that various aspects of the Orch OR theory have themselves evolved in response to scientific advances and, in some cases, constructive criticism. We here list some recent adaptations and developments that we have now incorporated into the theory.

Cell and molecular biology

• Tubulin information states in Orch OR quantum and classical computation are now correlated with dipoles, rather than mechanical conformation, avoiding heat and energy issues. [Tubulin Information states are interacted with via Aharonov-Bohm potentials changing EM of Tubulin]

• Tubulin dipoles mediating computation and entanglement may be electric (London force charge separation), or magnetic (electron 'spin' states and currents) [spin is the basis of Soviet 'Thought Injection'], as presented in this paper.

• Enhanced electronic conductance discovered by Anirban Bandyopadhyay's group in single microtubules at warm temperature at specific alternating current gigahertz, megahertz and kilohertz frequencies ('Bandyopadhyay coherence', 'BC') strongly supports Orch OR.

• BC and Orch OR may well be mediated through intra-tubulin quantum channels of aromatic rings, like in photosynthesis proteins, plausibly for quantum computing in microtubules.

• Anesthetics bind in these tubulin quantum channels, presumably to disperse quantum dipoles necessary for consciousness.

Brain science

• Alzheimer's disease, brain trauma and other disorders are related to microtubule disturbances; promising therapies are being aimed at BC in the brain.

• Scale invariant ($1/f$, 'fractal-like') processes at neuronal and network levels might perhaps extend downward to intra-neuronal BC in microtubules, e.g. megahertz excitations.

• Orch OR conscious moments, e.g. at 40 Hz, are now viewed as 'beat frequencies' of BC megahertz in MTs, the slower beat frequencies coupled to neuronal membrane physiology and accounting for EEG correlates of consciousness. The Orch OR proposal suggests conscious experience is intrinsically connected to the fine-scale structure of space– time geometry, and that consciousness could be deeply related to the operation of the laws of the universe. (Hameroff, 2014)

Hameroff writing on the information processing ability of MT to represent boolean values:

Hameroff and Watt suggested that distinct tubulin dipoles and conformational states—mechanical changes in protein shape—could represent information, with MT lattices acting as two-dimensional Boolean switching matrices with input/output computation occurring via MAPs. MT information processing has also been viewed in the context of cellular ('molecular') automata ('microtubule automata') in which tubulin dipole and conformational states interact with neighbor tubulin states in hexagonal MT lattices by dipole couplings, synchronized by biomolecular coherence as proposed by Fröhlich. Protein conformational changes occur at multiple scales, e.g. 10^{-6} s to 10^{-11} s transitions. Coordinated movements of the protein's atomic nuclei, far more massive than electrons, require energy and generate heat. ….recent Orch OR papers do not make use of conformational changes, depending instead on tubulin dipole states alone to represent information. Within MTs, each tubulin may differ from among its neighbors due to genetic variability, post-translational modifications, phosphorylation states, binding of ligands and MAPs, and moment-to-moment conformational and/or dipole state transitions. Synaptic inputs can register information in dendritic–somatic MTs in brain neurons by metabotropic receptors, MAP2, and CaMKII, [Norseen's Calpain] a hexagonal holoenzyme able to convey calcium ion influx to MT lattices by phosphorylation (Fig.

211

4). Thus tubulins in MTs can each exist in multiple possible states, perhaps dozens or more. However for simplicity, models of MT automata consider only two alternative tubulin states, i.e. binary 'bits.' Another potential factor arises from the specific geometry of MT lattices in which helical winding pathways (in the A-lattice) repeat according to the Fibonacci sequence (3, 5, 8…) and may correlate with conduction pathways. Dipoles aligned along such pathways may be favored (and coupled to MT mechanical vibrations) thus influencing MT automata computation. MT automata based on tubulin dipoles in hexagonal lattices show high capacity integration and learning…. Finally, MT information processing may be directly related to activities at larger scale levels of neurons and neuronal networks through something of the nature of scale-invariant dynamics. Several lines of evidence point to fractal-like (1/f) self-similarity over different spatio-temporal scales in brain dynamics and structure. These are generally considered at the scale levels of neurons and higher-level neuronal networks but may extend downward in size (and higher frequency) to intra-neuronal MT dynamics, spanning 4 or 5 scale levels over many orders of magnitude. MT information processing depends on interactive dipole states of individual tubulin proteins. What are those states, and how are they governed?"

In this technical explanation of information processing an important point is that "MT information processing depends on interactive dipole states of individual tubulin proteins." Another important point he makes is that MT information processing is scale-invariant with fractal-like self-similarity. This is also seen not just in the brain but also in the human eye where cones and rods match a Fibonacci sequence in an octagonal antenna for EM. This is also seen in DNA. Helical structures are also designed by Dr. Baker in his HFGW receiver/transmitter, using a double helix like DNA. Given that these structures may be scale-free fractal-based patterns there may be a reason that the Retina Antenna is similar to brain information processing. The manipulation of MT dipoles may be the key in Norseen's QSK. It is also important to note that the binary model was a toy model created for a simple explanation of information processing. If we are talking about Quantum computation then we are probably talking about qubits or qutrits. A qubit reduces to O or 1 with a temporary superposition 0,1. A qutrit reduces to 0,1,2 with the superposed state maintaining its own state without a binary collapse, objective reduction. A final point regarding computation is that Hameroff-Penrose do not see human consciousness as something computable, rather they view it as non-computable, their colleague Badhyapadhyay has created a project, Artificial Brain (not AI), based on the resonant model of dipole switching (shifting) in MT's.

Hameroff goes into detail about the role of gravitation in the Objective Reduction, in a lengthy explanation, although necessary to understand, he writes:

> In Penrose, the tentatively suggested OR proposal would have its onset determined by a condition referred to there as 'the one-graviton' criterion. However, in Penrose, a much better-founded criterion was used, now frequently referred to as the Diósi–Penrose proposal (henceforth 'DP'; see Diósi's earlier work, which was a similar gravitational scheme, though not motivated via specific general-relativistic principles). The DP proposal gives an objective physical threshold, providing a plausible lifetime for quantum-superposed states. Other gravitational OR proposals have been put forward, from time to time as solutions to the measurement problem, suggesting modifications of standard quantum mechanics, but all these differ from DP in important respects. Among these, only the DP proposal (in its role within Orch OR) has been suggested as having anything to do with the consciousness issue. The DP proposal is sometimes referred to as a 'quantum-gravity' scheme, but it is not part of the normal ideas used in quantum gravity… Moreover, the proposed connection between consciousness and quantum measurement is almost opposite [Copenhagen Interpretation, Heisenberg], in the Orch OR scheme, to the kind of idea that had frequently been put forward in the early days of quantum mechanics (see, for example Wigner) which suggests that a 'quantum measurement' is something that occurs only as a result of the conscious intervention of an observer. Rather, the DP proposal suggests each OR event, which is a purely physical process, is itself a primitive kind of 'observation', a moment of 'proto-conscious experience.' This issue, also, will be discussed below.

It is a very important distinction that Hameroff-Penrose are making here in terms of the reduction or collapse of the quantum wave into a fixed state. In the Copenhagen Interpretation the observer plays a role in collapse, in D-P the collapse has no 'conscious' element, it rather is based on the effects of gravity. In this sense of being a purely physical process alone, it is like P. Jordan's ideals:

"there were times when a quantum system effectively observed itself, by collapsing into a specific state rather than remaining in a superposition of states. This does not need any 'conscious observer,' as had been argued by John von Neumann and Eugene Wigner, but it does need decoherence (and collapse) of the wave function that prevents further interference of various possibilities." (https://www.informationphilosopher.com/solutions/scientists/jordan/ [accessed 7/19/19])

Hameroff continues on the distinction of D-P quantum gravity:

OR and quantum gravity Diósi–Penrose objective reduction (DP) is a particular proposal for an extension of current quantum mechanics, taking the bridge between quantum- and classical-level physics as a 'quantum-gravitational' phenomenon. This is in contrast with the various conventional viewpoints, whereby this bridge is claimed to result, somehow, from 'environmental decoherence', or from 'observation by a conscious observer', or from a 'choice between alternative worlds', or some other interpretation of how the classical world of one actual alternative may be taken to arise out of fundamentally quantum-superposed ingredients. The DP version of OR involves a different interpretation of the term 'quantum gravity' from what is usual. Current ideas of quantum gravity (see, for example, Smolin) normally refer, instead, to some sort of physical scheme that is to be formulated within the bounds of standard quantum field theory—although no particular such theory, among the multitude that has so far been put forward, has gained anything approaching universal acceptance, nor has any of them found a fully consistent, satisfactory formulation. 'OR' here refers to the alternative viewpoint that standard quantum (field) theory is not the final answer, and that the reduction R of the quantum state ('collapse of the wavefunction') that is adopted in standard quantum mechanics is an actual physical process which is not part of the conventional unitary formalism U of quantum theory (or quantum field theory). In the DP version of OR, the reduction R of the quantum state does not arise as some kind of convenience or effective consequence of environmental decoherence, etc., as the conventional U formalism would seem to demand, but is instead taken to be one of the consequences of melding together the principles of Einstein's general relativity with those of the conventional unitary quantum formalism U, and this demands a departure from the strict rules of U. According to this OR viewpoint, any quantum measurement—whereby the quantum-superposed alternatives produced in accordance with the U formalism becomes reduced to a single actual occurrence—is a real objective physical process, and it is taken to result from the mass displacement between the alternatives being sufficient, in gravitational terms, for the superposition to become unstable. In the DP scheme for OR, the superposition reduces to one of the alternatives in a timescale τ that can be estimated (for a superposition of two states each of which is assumed to be taken to be stationary on its own) according to the formula $\tau \approx h/E_G$. An important point to make about τ, however, is that it represents merely a kind of average time (Hameroff, 2014)

To abridge the above, rather than there being any kind of 'conscious observer' or environmental decoherence, the collapse or reduction is caused by the mass displacement between alternatives available which is given with:

$$\text{formula } \tau \approx \hbar/E_G.$$

This reduction is random and is given as an analogy to nuclear decay, occurring over a time series (t).

52

S. Hameroff, R. Penrose / Physics of Life Reviews 11 (2014) 39–78

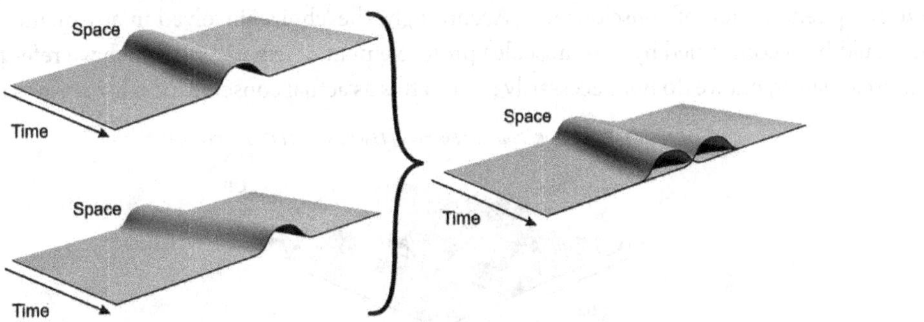

Fig. 8. Space–time geometry schematized as one spatial and one temporal dimension in which particle location is represented as curvature. Left: Top and bottom show space–time histories of two alternative particle locations. Right: Quantum superposition of both particle locations as bifurcating space–time depicted as the union ('glued together version') of the two alternative histories (adapted from Penrose [24], p. 338).

It is helpful to have a conceptual picture of quantum superposition in a gravitational context. According to modern accepted physical theories, reality is rooted in 3-dimensional space and a 1-dimensional time, combined together into a 4-dimensional [Minkoswki] space–time. This space–time is slightly curved, in accordance with Einstein's general theory of relativity, in a way which encodes the gravitational fields of all distributions of mass density. Each different choice of mass density effects a space–time curvature in a different, albeit a very tiny, way. This is the standard picture according to classical physics. On the other hand, when quantum systems have been considered by physicists, this mass-induced tiny curvature in the structure of space–time has been almost invariably ignored, gravitational effects having been assumed to be totally insignificant for normal problems in which quantum theory is important. Surprising as it may seem, however, such tiny differences in space–time structure can have large effects, for they entail subtle but fundamental influences on the very rules of quantum mechanics.

....

The degree of separation between the space–time sheets is a more abstract mathematical thing; it would be more appropriately described in terms of a symplectic measure on the space of 4-dimensional metrics but the details (and difficulties) of this will not be important for us here. It may be noted, however, that this separation is a space–time separation, not just a spatial one. Thus the time of separation contributes as well as the spatial displacement. It is the product of the temporal separation T with the spatial separation S that measures the overall degree of separation, and OR takes place when this overall separation reaches the critical amount. In the absence of a coherent theory of quantum gravity there is no accepted way of handling such a superposition as a separation (or bifurcation) of space–time geometry, or in any other way. Indeed the basic principles of Einstein's general relativity begin to come into profound conflict with those of quantum mechanics. Some form of OR is needed. The OR process is considered to occur when quantum superpositions between such slightly differing space–times take place (Fig. 9), differing from one another by an integrated space–time measure which compares with the fundamental and extremely tiny Planck (4-volume) scale of space–time geometry. As remarked above, this is a 4-volume Planck measure, involving both time and space, so we find that the time measure would be particularly tiny when the space-difference measure is relatively large (as with Schrödinger's hypothetical cat), but for extremely tiny space difference measures, the time measure might be fairly long. For example, an isolated single electron in a superposed state (very low EG) might reach OR threshold only after thousands of years or more, whereas if Schrödinger's ($\boxtimes 10$ kg) cat were to be put into a superposition, of life and death, this threshold could be reached in far less than even the Planck time of 10–43 s. As already noted, the degree of separation between the space–time sheets is technically a symplectic measure on the space of 4-metrics which is a space–time separation, not just a spatial one, the time of separation contributing as well as spatial displacement. Roughly speaking, it is the product of the temporal separation T with the spatial separation S that measures the overall degree of separation, and (DP) OR takes place when this overall separation reaches a critical amount. This critical amount would be of the order of unity, in absolute units, for which the Planck–Dirac constant h‾, the gravitational constant G, and the velocity of light c, all take the value unity. For small S, the lifetime $\tau \approx T$ of the superposed state will be large; on the other hand, if S is large, then τ will be small. To estimate S, we compute (in the Newtonian limit of weak gravitational fields) the gravitational self-energy EG of the difference between the mass distributions of the two superposed states. (That is, one mass distribution counts positively and the other, negatively.) The quantity S is then given by: $S \approx EG$ and $T \approx \tau$, whence $\tau \approx h/E\,G$, i.e. $E\,G \approx h/\tau$. Thus, the DP expectation is that OR occurs with the resolving out of one particular space–time geometry from the previous superposition when, on the average, $\tau \approx h/E\,G$. The Orch-OR scheme adopts DP as a physical proposal, but it goes further than this by attempting to relate this particular version of OR to the phenomenon of consciousness. Accordingly, the 'choice' involved in any quantum state-reduction process would be accompanied by a (minuscule) proto-element of experience, which we refer to as a moment of proto-consciousness, but we do not necessarily refer to this as actual consciousness for reasons to be described.

S. Hameroff, R. Penrose / Physics of Life Reviews 11 (2014) 39–78

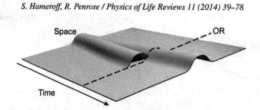

Fig. 9. As superposition curvature E reaches threshold (by $E_G = h/\tau$), OR occurs and one particle location/curvature is selected, and becomes classical. The other ceases to exist.

With such a simple mechanism of collapsing the wave function, rather than 'observers' or 'decoherence' we have a straight-forward measure of reduction. In a later section Hameroff discusses the question of Quantum Computing in the Brain, this would correlate with the 'cryptological' QSK of Dr. John Norseen. A long passage which goes over QC in MTs is given by Hameroff:

5.1. Quantum computing in the brain Penrose [23,24] suggested that consciousness depends in some way on processes of the general nature of quantum computations occurring in the brain, these being terminated by some form of OR. Here the term 'quantum computation' is being used in a loose sense, in which information is encoded in some discrete (not necessarily binary) physical form, and where the evolution is determined according to the U process (Schrödinger's equation). ... A proposal was made in Penrose [23] that something analogous to quantum computing, proceeding by the Schrödinger equation without decoherence, could well be acting in the brain, but where, for conscious processes, this would have to terminate in accordance with some threshold for self-collapse by a form of non-computable OR. A quantum computation terminating by OR could thus be associated with consciousness. ...Penrose and Hameroff teamed up in the early 1990s when, fortunately, the DP form of OR mechanism was then at hand to be applied in extending the microtubule–automata models for consciousness as had been developed by Hameroff and colleagues. ... the most logical strategic site for coherent microtubule Orch OR and consciousness is in post-synaptic dendrites and soma (in which microtubules are uniquely arrayed and stabilized) during integration phases in integrate-and-fire brain neurons. Synaptic inputs could 'orchestrate' tubulin states governed by quantum dipoles, leading to tubulin superposition in vast numbers of microtubules all involved quantum-coherently together in a large-scale quantum state, where entanglement and quantum computation takes place during integration. The termination, by OR, of this orchestrated quantum computation at the end of integration phases would select microtubule states which could then influence and regulate axonal firings, thus controlling conscious behavior. Quantum states in dendrites and soma of a particular neuron could entangle with microtubules in the dendritic tree of that neuron, and also in neighboring neurons via dendritic–dendritic (or dendritic–interneuron–dendritic) gap junctions, enabling quantum entanglement of superposed microtubule tubulins among many neurons (Fig. 1)... In dendrites and soma of brain neurons, synaptic inputs could encode memory in alternating classical phases, thereby avoiding random environmental decoherence to 'orchestrate' U quantum processes, enabling them to reach threshold at time τ for orchestrated objective reduction 'Orch OR' by $\tau \approx h/E_G$. At that time, according to this proposal, a moment of conscious experience occurs, and tubulin states [which would be Norseen QSK encoded] are selected which influence axonal firing, encode memory and regulate synaptic plasticity...the idea is that consciousness is associated with this (gravitational) OR process, but occurs significantly only when

(1) the alternatives are part of some highly organized cognitive structure capable of information processing, so that OR occurs in an extremely orchestrated form, with vast numbers of microtubule acting coherently, in order that there is sufficient mass displacement overall, for the $\tau \approx h/E_G$ criterion to be satisfied.

(2) Interaction with environment must be avoided long enough during the U process evolution so strictly orchestrated components of the superposition reach OR threshold without too much randomness and reflect a significant non-computable influence.

Only then does a recognizably conscious Orch OR event take place. On the other hand, we may consider that any individual occurrence of OR without orchestration would be a moment of random proto-consciousness lacking cognition and meaningful content. We shall be seeing orchestrated OR in more detail shortly, together with its particular relevance to microtubules. In any case, we recognize that the experiential elements of proto-consciousness would be intimately tied in with the most primitive Planck-level ingredients of space–time geometry, these presumed 'ingredients' being taken to be at the absurdly tiny level of 10^{-35} m [Baker's HFGW resolution] and 10^{-43} s, a distance and a time some 20 orders of magnitude smaller than those of normal particle-physics scales and their most rapid processes, and they are smaller by far than biological scales and processes. These scales refer only to the normally extremely tiny differences in space–time geometry between different states in superposition, the separated states themselves being enormously larger. OR is deemed to take place when such tiny space–time differences reach the Planck level (roughly speaking).

Owing to the extreme weakness of gravitational forces as compared with those of the chemical and electric forces of biology, the energy E_G is liable to be far smaller than any energy that arises directly from biological processes. OR acts, effectively, instantaneously as a choice between dynamical alternatives (a choice that is an integral part of the relevant quantum dynamics) and E_G is not to be thought of as being in direct competition with any of the usual biological energies, as it plays a completely different role, supplying a needed energy uncertainty that then allows a choice to be made between the separated space–time geometries, rather than providing an actual energy that enters into any considerations of energy balance that would be of direct relevance to chemical or normal physical processes.

The previous depiction of Hameroff seems to confirm that it is indeed possible to have QSK targeted at the MTs of the brain's neurons.

ELECTROMAGNETIC RESONANCE OF MICROTUBULES

Another colleague of Hameroff's who supports the ORCH-OR theory is the research scientist that works with physical materials at a Japanese Materials Science lab is Dr. Anirban Badhyapadhyay. There is a convergence between Dr. Persinger and Dr. Bandyopadhyay's research in studying the EM resonance of molecular materials. Both cite the work of Dr. Irene Cosic and her Resonant Recognition Model (RRM) which is an implementation of research carried out in the Soviet Union as early as the 1960s and earlier in Nazi Germany. Dr. Bandyopadhyay based his resonance research model on Cosic. Dr. Bandyopadhyay has found the following in studying Microtubules in which he examined tubulin, the MT and the Neuron with the same meteorology used by Kernbach, Impedance Spectroscopy:

Here, we report a self-similar triplet of triplet resonance frequency pattern for the four-4 nm-wide tubulin protein, for the 25-nm-wide microtubule nanowire and 1-μm-wide axon initial segment of a neuron. Thus, preserving the symmetry of vibrations was a fundamental integration feature of the three materials. There was no self-similarity in the physical appearance: the size varied by 106 orders, yet, when they vibrated, the ratios of the frequencies changed in such a way that each of the three resonance frequency bands held three more bands inside (triplet of triplet). This suggests that instead of symmetry, self-similarity lies in the principles of symmetry-breaking. This is why three elements, a protein, it's complex and neuron resonated in 106 orders of different time domains, yet their vibrational frequencies grouped similarly. Our work supports already-existing hypotheses for the scale-free information integration in the brain from molecular scale to the cognition. (Bandyopadhyay, 2020)

It is interesting that nano-length MT's have a 3 pattern to them like Protein Amino Acid synthesis using RNA.

Fractal Fract. 2020, 4, 11

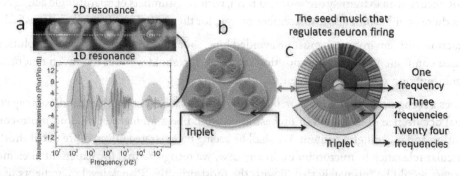

Figure 5. Frequency wheel for the triplet–triplet resonance band (Movie 1): (a) 2D resonance of a single isolated microtubule from Figure 3a. A dotted line shows 1D resonance measurement location (top), the data are shown below panel (a). The 3D resonance plot of panel a is represented as a nest of nine circles (nine circles inside three circles inside one circle = 13 circles). Using a shadow and an arrow we connected a triplet in a 1D resonance plot of panel (a), with the schematic of panel (b); (c) The circular triplet–triplet plot of panel b is a replica of experimental resonance data (panel a), however, the resonant oscillations follow a periodic condition. If we apply periodic limits then panel b looks like panel c. One can find the triplet in panel c, each triplet has single frequency and its total period is sum of three frequencies inside, each of the three has periods of eight frequencies (a particular case of tubulin).

(Badhyapadhyay, 2020)

Divergence between self-similar and symmetrical energy resonance:

Similar to the microtubule and the neuron cell, we observed here triplet of triplet resonance bands (Figure 3c right). Normally, it was believed that electromagnetic resonance depends on the carriers, dispersion relation in a classic textbook would show how at different frequency regions, different carriers resonate. However, the classic dispersion relation presented in the textbooks, do not consider self-similar symmetry structures at all scales. (Bandyopadhyay 2020)

The axon core, microtubule and tubulin have self-similar bands, with a common frequency region, a similar structural symmetry governs the resonance in all the three systems. Helical distribution of neural branches, rings of proteins in the axonal core, spirals of proteins in the microtubule, α helices in the proteins, are the common structures, and the resonant energy transmission in generic spiral symmetry follows a quantized behavior. Sahu et al. have patented this feature of microtubule as a new class of fourth circuit element. Hence, a spiral symmetry possibly ensures coupling of all the periodic oscillations. (Bandyopadhyay, 2020)

An earlier finding of Dr. Bandyopadhyay was that the water channels inside microtubules were responsible for conduction of electrical signals which control the EM field within the microtubule. We shall read later in the work of Dr. Persinger that virtual particles (Norseen's ZPE) are a part of water Casimir effect, Bandyopadhyay remarks:

Water-extracted microtubule behaves like an insulator … therefore, the interstitial water channel inside microtubule is solely responsible for the 1000 times more conductivity than tubulin.

The large tunneling current across 25 nm wide microtubule (insulator) is not via tubulin-water-tubulin route, the water core should act as a current source by storing charges. Dried microtubule does not show energy levels identical to tubulin protein, therefore, the water channel holds the proteins in a mechanism that does not allow splitting of energy levels of tubulins (Bandyopadhyay, 2013, 145)

The delocalization feature is responsible for four-probe unique conductivity, and automated noise management; again, delocalization disappears if water channel is removed. Then, at a higher bias 42 V, protofilaments disintegrate in one scan. In the atomic force microscope (AFM) measurement, protofilaments do not break apart. In the AFM images, only helical tubulin rings are visible, while STM images show only longitudinal protofilaments, when water is inside, otherwise, it is a disintegrated mass of proteins. This suggests that the water channel controls microtubule's internal conductivity and force modulation. In TEM, both helical ring and longitudinal fringes due to the water channel are visible, if water channel is released the fringes disappear and rings split… (Bandyopadhyay, 2013, 145)

Bandyopadhyay provides a mechanism for Norseen's QSK in the following:

Microtubule exhibits a perfectly square hysteresis behavior (Fig. 4a,b) (Damjanovic, 2006), it means the dipole moments of tubulin proteins rotate synchronously by ±23°, which plays a vital role in switching the conductivity or memory states. The hysteresis area increases with the maximum applied bias [or Aharonov-Bohm potential]… (Bandyopadhyay, 2013, 145)

Dielectric resonance frequencies of multiple proteins were mapped by applying two distinct kinds of electromagnetic fields one perpendicular to another. Such an orthogonal field-based splitting of energy exchange was never applied before to read the 2D interaction of the system profile over a large frequency range. Normally 1D transmission profiles are studied, the direction at which the input signal frequency is pumped along the same direction how much the carriers are pushed through is estimated as the response of the system. When a gating effect [EM Zeitgebers] is applied to all the three systems, additional dynamic feature hidden in the system is revealed by orthogonal fields. Such studies are regularly applied in transistor research. However, that is not the end. We speculate that if advanced further, it may be possible to map the higher-level dynamic features in the neuron, thus, we advance here the temporal correlations observed by Ghosh et al. and Agrawal et al. We have detailed how a 3D triplet of triplet band could be experimentally extracted from the three systems, located one inside another. The tubulins are located inside microtubule and the microtubules are located inside a neuron, if the 3D band architecture is also self-similar, it would mean that the three systems could exchange geometric information conformally, i.e., without losing the angular features of the geometric shape over a time domain of 10^6 order in time scale. (Bandyopadhyay 2020)

The finding of a three-level harmonic in the Tubulin is of interest as it relates to other harmonics also based on trinaries, such as that found in the Schumann Resonance, also reminiscent of Zeeman Splitting.

MICHAEL PERSINGER'S RESEARCH ON CONSCIOUSNESS

As mentioned in the 'Physics and Neuroweapons' chapter Dr. Persinger was a research professor at Laurentian University. He duplicated earlier Soviet experiments in his labs, as well as interfaced with people attached to Stanford Research Institute. He investigated a research track that mirrors that of various military intelligence research labs throughout the world, with the caveat that his research was done with public funds at a parochial university working in the public interest. As such, he was never in a position to capitalize on his research as many other researchers in the field of neuroscience and physics have. As mentioned previously Dr. Persinger also concurred that ORCH-OR was a viable model for explaining Quantum Consciousness. He gives a very technical consideration to the issue:

> The quantity of energy 10^{-20} J has direct application to the neuroquantum approaches to consciousness. The most popular is the "collapse of the wave function" as cogently articulated by Hameroff and Penrose. Their recent articulate article entitled, "Consciousness in the universe: a review of the 'ORCH OR' theory" reviews the essential concepts. The dichotomy of the existence of the electron as a particle or a wave within space is reflected by its classical width, of about $2 \cdot 10^{-15}$ m and its Compton wavelength, 10^{-12} m, derived from quantum concepts. Although there are several interpretations for this discrepancy, what is important here is that the discrepancy in length according to the Lorentz contraction requires a specific discrepancy between the speed of light ($3 \cdot 10^{8}$ m·s^{-1}) and some very negligible value less than that velocity.
>
> The difference in energy equivalence for the electron at the velocities that would accommodate the Lorentz contraction is in the order of 10^{-20} J. This could suggest that the increment of energy required for the "collapse of the wave function" is congruent with the quantum increment associated with a single action potential. By extension, millions of action potentials would affect millions of these functions. That the action potentials from only *one* neuron could affect the global state of the entire cerebral cortices has been reported by Li *et al*. Energies in the order of a few increments of 10^{-20} J have been shown experimentally to alter the probability of an overt response. (Persinger, 2015c)

He takes the ORCH-OR theory one step further by suggesting that the reduction of the wave form is able to be performed by a 'single action potential' which can alter the state of the whole brain; he identifies a measure of the energy behind this potential as 10^{-20}J. He then points out: "Energies in the order of a few increments of 10^{-20}J have been shown experimentally to alter the probability of an overt response." Indeed, this would seem to confirm to some degree the claims of Dr. John Norseen of altering brain behavior with Thought Injection. It is also worth noting that responses are 'probabilities' not deterministic.

CASIMIR AND CONSCIOUSNESS

As seen from the work of Dr. Norseen, he notes the role of the Casimir Effect in generating brain waves such as Alpha at 7Hz, etc.; and, we are talking about a Biological entity, so it necessarily has a large portion of water as its constituent parts. It is easy to overlook this most basic element of all biological entities for the last 3.5 billion years of evolution on this planet. As noted in the work of direct supporters of ORCH-OR in the work of Bandyopadhyay MT water controls EM, which gives a product – memories or what the more technical community calls Semi-states. It is also important to note where ideals of the Casimir Effect and Consciousness come from originally, which Dr. Persinger's work replicates and also provides original methodologies and insights on work conducted in the Soviet Union directly under the sponsorship of the KGB; so obviously of importance to weapons and possibly even propulsion systems for ICBM, Star Wars, etc.

The question is, where did the Soviets get their ideas regarding the importance of these things? It is noted that German nuclear engineers were brought to the Soviet Union; part of that work was the creation of Heavy Water, so obviously they would have understood a thing or two about the Casimir Effect and its role in heavy water; one would assume any nuclear engineering team anywhere would. It is also noted by Dr. Kernbach (2014), that alleged Psychotronic experiments were conducted at German run Soviet Nuclear Weapons labs in the 1950s for instance in Sukhumi under Hertz, who also worked with von Ardenne, who in the 1930s conducted research with reading brains in his research institute. Ardenne was also a nuclear engineer, held in prison in the Soviet Union after the war working on their nuclear program.

The Casimir Effect deals with the occurrence in a Classical scale quantum effects in vacuum fluctuations and their transition into virtual particles. Virtual particles:

> In the realist narrative, virtual particles pop up when observable particles get close together. They are emitted from one particle and absorbed by another, but they disappear before they can be measured. They transfer force between ordinary particles, giving them motion and life. For every different type of elementary particle (quark, photon, electron, etc.), there are also virtual quarks, virtual photons, and so on. (Rorvig 2020)

For the sake of consistency with the frame of reference of Persinger he gives the following definition of virtual particles and their significance:

> The space occupied by a brain would be subject to the complex possibilities of the multidimensional spaces of Kaluza-Klein as well as the potential energy contained within the structure of space. Matter, defined as protons and electrons, occupy spaces of $\sim 10^{-15}$ m. Between this level of discourse and the smallest conceptual increment of space, Planck's Length ($\sim 10^{-35}$ m) [resolution of HFGW goes down to 10^{-37}m], there are inordinate degrees of freedom whose structures could contain latent energy.
>
> The boundary of "the smallest space" which has been considered Planck's Length ($1.62 \cdot 10^{-35}$ m), includes the "virtual particles" of the zero-point potential of vacuum energies. They are functionally a modern equivalent of the 19th century concept of "ether" or a universal medium. These virtual particles exhibit zero-point fluctuations or *Zitterbewegung* which endow the property of "process" or a change as a function of time. Within these point fields, a changing electromagnetic boundary has the capacity to transform virtual particles, through Casimir processes, to "real" particles. Real particles are protons and electrons with the capacity to mediate local causality. Virtual particles would have the capacity to mediate "non-local" causality. (Persinger, 2015)

There are several aspects to this understanding of virtual particles that are worth recollecting: 1. the brain interacts with hyperdimensions (Kaluza-Klein) 2. Quantum is associated with the Planck length, the level of existence of virtual particles, and hence the Casimir Effect, though it's possible to see in the Classical world, an immanence of quantum existence, that engineers can work with. How all this relates to consciousness is best given in an overview of the significance of the Casimir Effect, and other EM effects Persinger gives the following:

> The explanations for the absolute nature of consciousness have been distributed historically along a continuum that ranges from extreme materialism to idealism. Consequently, the fundamental operations of most philosophies range from the assumption consciousness is determined by the physical laws of matter and energy to energy and matter as being constructs or "creations" of consciousness. Within the quantum domain that includes Casimir phenomena whereby virtual particles can be transformed under optimal conditions to particles with mass, there are other perspectives. The perspective developed in this paper is that consciousness is a boundary condition between a singularity (black hole) and space within the brain [hippocampus]. ... One traditional approach to pursuing the validity of concepts that are difficult, but not impossible, to verify experimentally is to pursue the consistency of the quantitative solutions that relate central components to the theory. We assume here that the central mass unit associated with the physical bases of the phenomena that define our reality is the simplest complex of a proton and an electron, the hydrogen atom. Metrics related to these phenomena should be related in a meaningful and systematic manner to the key parameters that occur at the level of the synapse and the neuronal plasma membrane ion channel as well as the values that define the boundaries of our current concepts of the smallest ($\sim 10^{-35}$ m) and largest ($\sim 10^{26}$ m) spaces.

Elaborating further:

> The human brain is the matter within a volume that may contain properties that facilitate the transformation of virtual particles existing at the level Planck's length to actual matter. As indicated by Bordag et al. an infinite vacuum energy of quantized electromagnetic field in free Minkowski space can be shown to allow a finite force between two parallel neutral plates. This Casimir force involves the existence of zero-point oscillations which

are associated with the point values of a quantized field. Boundaries composed of matter polarize the vacuum of a quantized field. The energy over distance is a consequence of the result of vacuum polarization by an external field. One of the possibilities of vacuum quantum effects is the creation of particles from the vacuum by external fields. Energy is transferred from the external field to virtual particles or vacuum oscillations, much like Eddington's formulation, to produce real particles. However, this effect of transformation requires the boundary condition to be a function of time (time varying) rather than static conditions. In other words, a transformation of the state of particles occurs when there is a changing electromagnetic field that contributes to or defines a boundary condition. The degrees of freedom for this potential are markedly enhanced by the unique property of attraction or repulsion depending upon the geometry and topology of the quantized manifold or shape. The recursive, changing electromagnetic fields, much like a classical tensor, that occurs within synaptic space and across the cerebral cortical manifold during the ~20 ms "recreation" of consciousness, could be preconditions to allow this virtual-to-matter transitions. The synapse, the primary interface between two neurons, is effectively two plates where the width is much larger than the separation between the apposing boundaries of a Casimir condition. These "plates" are in the order of 1,000 to 2,000 nm wide and are separated by 10 nm. Assuming a width of 2 μm (an area of $4 \cdot 10^{-12}$ m^2), the Casimir force during discrete intervals of neutrality between the "plates" or boundaries would be about 0.5 microNewtons. When applied across the 10 nm synaptic cleft, the energy would be 14 0.5 10 . J. The frequency equivalence of that energy, when divided by Planck's constant ($6.624 \cdot 10^{-34}$ J·s), is $.078 \cdot 10^{20}$ Hz. The equivalent wavelength, assuming c is the velocity of light in a vacuum is $3.8 \cdot 10^{-11}$ m or 38 pm. This length is within error measurement of the width of the neutral hydrogen atom. Such convergence would be expected between Casimir transformations from virtual to real particles and the component that composes 90% of the matter in the universe. Hydrogen is the essential unit by which aggregates of heavier elements are formed. (Persinger, 2013)

Returning to Bandyopadhyay's work on demonstrating that virtual particles affect conduction and EM patterns in Microtubules through waters and brain EEG rhythms, which is to say Consciousness, it is important to understand the role of the Casimir Effect in terms of water. Persinger has studied the role of Casimir Effect of thixotropy of water (relating to viscosity), and in more general terms in entangled states, between two non-local water samples united by a changing velocity EM field, through a local device (a circular pointing vector emitter), which was also used by Kernbach (2017b). He cites Akimov generators as the basis of their usage, they being circular versions of the Akimov generators. Serge Kernbach replicated earlier Soviet experiments on distant influencing of biological organisms. The original experiment of A.E. Akimov was conducted in 1986 and released in 2001, regarding distant influencing. Before going into the experimental results and setup of this replication we will first review the history of this research with secret intelligence such as the KGB, which would eventually result in leading Soviet experts moving west to work for western intelligence agencies. Kernbach notes of the original experiment, it was mainly investigating the disturbance of biological rhythms by long-term non-local impact and possible neurological manifestations. Noting its connection to the KGB, Kernbach writes:

> The work [originally from 1986] was published in 2001 and caused extensive controversy in the press. It reported about the experiments performed in 1986 on a nonlocal impact on biological objects over 22km distance, the article pointed out that "advancement in this area was made possible through the support of the KGB of the USSR and the USSR's Council of Ministers." In it is explicitly stated "all reports even on works with the Ministry of Defense of the USSR were not classified." According to the biography of A. E. Akimov, he worked 1977-1983 in the Moscow Research Institute of Radio Communication and 1983-1987 in the research institute of communication and control systems. This explains the telecommunication methodology and terminology that are used for conducting those attempts. Indeed, modern experiments on quantum communication confirm his vision and approach (Kernbach, 2018b)

The original ideal for these experiments can be traced back to 1982 by V.A. Sokolova. Kernbach also notes the CIA's interest in this research where it is known as 'Remote Action':

> The description of the experiment from 1986 indicates that 'a bioelectronic system was used as a torsion [Aharonov-Bohm effect] receiver. It is based on the property of tissue cells to change the conductivity of membranes when exposed by a torsion field [vacuum virtual particles created with potentials]. This property was

implicitly established by V.A.Sokolova in 1982'. The use of biological objects (in this case plants) for technical communication systems is surprising. The approach developed by V.A.Sokolova (several of those methods were confirmed in our laboratory) used a simplified impedance spectroscopy applied to fluidic systems. Cellular tissues were only one of many tested systems; they are characterized by unstable electrochemical properties. In later works of the ISTC VENT, for example of A.V. Bobrov, water was used as a physical receiver of nonlocal signals. Another interesting point, related to this experiment, is the widely debated resolution of the Council of Ministers of the USSR, that allegedly was about 'managing living objects.' It also dates back to 1986 and was mentioned by E.B.Aleksandrov. Finally, our attention was attracted to works on interaction with biological systems that were carried out at that time, whose traces can be found in the press. Therefore, the question faced by the thoughtful reader is whether the experiments of 1986, under the patronage of the KGB, were first test experiments on nonlocal influences on biological objects. Such an interpretation could explain the motivation of transmitting signals in a slow 'communication channel' with only a few bits per hour, that has no technical sense but a lot of biological implications. This could also explain the interest of intelligence services of different countries in these technologies, for example, the CIA called similar methods 'Remote Action'; the beginning of their research falls also in 1986-87. (Kernbach, 2018b)

Although, they were not the first tests of remote influencing, it is illustrative to see the history behind the generators used in these experiments. Akimov and also Bobrov mentioned in these passages both had experience working secretly for the Soviet secret intelligence services. Akimov generators became public in the mid-1980s, much later then their military and intelligence development, extending back to at least the 1950s. Akimov himself started in this field in 1959 working for the KGB scientific labs that studied remote influencing of biological objects, such as white rabbits (Zhigalov, 2009).

In 1961, a young A.V. Bobrov was sent to the Baltics to study fields associated with psychics, his first foray into detectors and transmitters; later, from 1989-91, Bobrov was doing classified work on 'remote consciousness' (Kernbach, 2019). He again worked on secret projects for the military and intelligence sector of the Soviet Union. Bobrov reported in a discussion about studies performed at Gagarin Air Force Academy in Monino and by St. Petersburg L.I. Mechnikov State Medical Academy in the 80s and 90s. (Kernbach, 2013, 17). Bobrov returned in 1964 to graduate school looking for a theory to explain the energetics associated with his classified psi work from 1961. He later, according to the public story, came across the work of Akimov, then formulating the ideal of 'information radiation.' He continues working today on projects with open researchers such as Russian researcher at the University of Stuttgart Serge Kernbach. Among the innovations that Bobrov brought to the field, aside from Medical Treatments, is the question of detection and sensing, or metrology. For instance, the question becomes to change a thought you have to have the map of the thought, as Dr. Norseen put it. Kernbach writes of Bobrov's innovation of the electric double layer in sensing:

In 1988 the first note of A.V.Bobrov about the electric double layer (EDL) as a sensor had appeared. In his book, he confirmed the program of the USSR's Ministry of Defense on the study of psychics and instrumental psychotronics. Bobrov's EDL sensors have been proven as very sensitive devices. The book edited by Lunev describes the work carried out at the Tomsk Polytechnic University from 1983 to 1993, including a number of sensors based on quartz resonators and detectors of radioactivity. In 1989 a patent of G.A.Sergeev on capacitive sensors is issued. Since 1989 various tests with crystallized structures are conducted and, further, with the melting of metals. Attempts were made to develop sensors on that basis. In the early 90s sensors of Y.P.Kravchenko (Ю.П.Кравченко) appeared, based on measurements of electric fields. In the Institute of Physics, St. Petersburg State University, the results related to Kozyrev's sensors are verified (these and other works have stimulated the development of solid-state sensors). The book of G.N.Dulnev and colleagues describes the research conducted between 1995-1998 at the Center for Energy and Information Technologies at the St. Petersburg State Institute of Fine Mechanics and Optics (TSEIT GITMO). In those experiments more biological, optical, magnetic and thermal sensors are used. Interesting works are performed on bioelectrogenesis of plants and the application of such sensors in experiments. By 2000, there is already a large amount of works on the impact of 'high-penetrating' radiation on different semiconductor devices, see e.g. in the review in 2013 related to metrology of 'high-penetrating' emission, there are 19 groups of physical effects that can represent a basis for the development of sensors, with dozens of technical sensors. (Kernbach, 2013)

The question as to where Akimov learned of these technologies can be traced back to at least the 1920s. While Kernbach has argued that Vril generators (the Nationalist Socialist idea of 'prana' or 'ruah', spirit) possibly date back to early versions in 1913. This is no coincidence, as Kernbach has traced the production of these generators as a direct outcome of Nazi war research and possible deployment in Germany during the war. The German aristocrat Manfred von Ardenne, who later was taken to the Soviet Union as a captive scientist working on their Nuclear program, was known to have worked before the war with reading brainwaves in his self-funded research institute. Ardenne wrote,

> the high-frequency field is nothing in thinking, to perceive the electricity, amplify with tube amplifiers, and transfer this enhanced energy to the second brain. So that in the second brain... we have the same thoughts, it is necessary that with a variety of thinking, an amplifier of produced broadband frequency very uniformly... (Kernbach, 2014, part 2)

Kernbach notes:

> Ardenne and Hertz worked in Soviet Georgia (Max Steenbock was the developer of the first Betatron). In Georgia, we also find traces of early psychotronic works. According to eyewitnesses, back in the 50s research works were carried out in Agudzer on hypnosis and ultra-weak radiation of biological organisms... there is a description that AEG supplied equipment for secret projects such as Colocation [instrumental remote viewing]. The authors indicate that German specialists from the AEG-Röhrenfabrik Oberspree, where the high-frequency technology of the war was harnessed, took part in the formation of Research Institute 160, later Research Institute Istok. (Kernbach, 2014)

In addition to this, Kernbach has cited the Soviet Army's discovery of special antennas that resemble the design of Akimov generators including klystrons, ray tubes, and other items related to highly penetrating radiation generation. Kernbach concluded regarding the various electronic finds from Nazi Germany: "These strange phenomena suggest that the objects under study somehow possibly acted on the morale of the German units and the civilian population." (Kernbach, 2014).

Kravkov further elaborates on the connection of Nazi research to Soviet psychotronics beginning with the find under the Reich in Berlin and examination by Soviet engineer Devyatkov who gave this account:

> I took up my duties for Deputy Director for Scientific Affairs (Research Institute-160 Source) from May 15, 1948 ...Institute was very broad. In terms of time work was listed not only microwave devices, but also electron-beam devices, generator and modulator lamps, kenotrons, type raytrons, gas-discharge stabilizers, resonators resonance arresters, receiving-amplifying lamps. The range of microwave devices included many other classes: magnetrons of continuous and pulse action, generator klystrons and amplifying, reflective heterodyne klystrons, traveling wave tubes – input and medium power, backward wave lamps, amplitrons and other M-type amplifiers. Interestingly, in another interview we find Devyatkov and backward-wave lamps in completely different research Institute Istok: The seminar was delivered on the initiative [of] N. D. Devyatkov - Corresponding Member of the Academy of Sciences USSR, scientific director of the Research Institute of Electricity [Fryazino, Moscow region – Author] and blowing department 16 Ultrahigh frequency electronics IRE AN USSR. Reverse lamps Noah waves gave the opportunity to start unconventional work of radio electronics in biology and medicine. The first very interesting experimental results, delivered at the suggestion of N.D. Devyatkov and M.B. Golant, were obtained in 1965, when the resonant response was established out biological objects when exposed to them with discrete millimeter waves range [microwaves]. Other sources, for example, indicate that high-frequency equipment SRI Istok used was called in torsion [Aharonov-Bohm effect] studies of the 80s and 90s. Obviously, these and other facts allow the possibility that there is a connection between the German and Soviet unconventional developments. (Kravkov, 2006)

It may seem like there is insufficient evidence from the accounts of N.D. Devyatkova. But it is interesting that later in his career he began experiments with the effects of millimeter wave technology which may correspond to the Nazi find he was asked to backwards engineer in 1948. It is important to remember in the 1930s Mikhailovich was already researching in this area of microwaves effect on the brain. A Russian researcher, Kravkov, remarks regarding this development in N.D. Devyatkova Research:

> The problem [influencing biological objects with waves] was born in the early 60s of the twentieth century as "the idea of the possibility of a specific effect of electromagnetic radiation of the MM (millimeter, 10 mm at

30 GHz decreasing to 1 mm at 300 GHz.) wavelength range on biological structures and organisms," was expressed by Soviet scientists (ND Devyatkov, MB Golant and etc.).

This is how the participant in the events, Professor O.V., spoke about the first step towards testing the hypothesis (3). Betsky: "In September 2003, 40 years have passed since the IRE of the USSR Academy of Sciences ... a scientific seminar devoted to the discussion of the unusual properties of low-intensity electromagnetic fields of the millimeter (extremely high-frequency - EHF) range in relation to the processes of biological organisms functioning. By this time, the Istok Scientific Research Institute of the Ministry of Economic Development of the USSR ... completed research work on the development of the world's first broadband millimeter wave generator based on vacuum devices - backward wave tubes with a longitudinal magnetic field (LOV-O). The seminar was staged at the initiative of N.D. Devyatkov - Corresponding Member of the USSR Academy of Sciences, scientific director of the Research Institute "Istok" (Fryazino, Moscow region - Auth.) And head of department 16 "Ultrahigh-frequency electronics" of the IRE of the USSR Academy of Sciences. Backward wave lamps made it possible to start work in an unconventional direction for radio electronics - in biology and medicine. "

The first very interesting results of experiments set up at the suggestion of N.D. Devyatkova and M.B. Golant, were obtained in 1965, when the resonant response of living biological objects was established when exposed to discrete waves of the millimeter range.

Almost simultaneously, at the other end of the Soviet Union, in Novosibirsk, V.P. Kaznacheev, S.P. Shurin, L.P. Mikhailova discovered a no less interesting "Phenomenon of intercellular distant electromagnetic interactions in the system of two tissue structures." (Kravkov, 2006)

To show the important connection that the Akimov generator research served, as it was directly connected to the remote influencing of biological objects, Kernbach points out that at the highest levels of Soviet Government work involving remote influencing were reviewed citing Maj. Gen. Ratnikov:

this area – research on the one side [USSR] stimulated equivalent studies on the other side [UKUSA]. Some representatives of 'power structures' in the Soviet Union so characterized the 80s: 'In general, in 80s, in this country, it was created a system of well-organized and conspiratorial work to develop new methods and means of resolving interstate and internal political problems without involving intimidating power forces and damaging effects. It includes methods of obtaining timely information, other than the traditionally known.

(Kernbach, 2013, Interview of the head of Energy and Information Laboratory Russian NAST Academy Major General FSO В.К.Ratnikov (Б.К.Ратников) to the magazine 'Security' on August 29, 2010)

It is hard to imagine any different reason from the totalitarian Nazi regime, that the totalitarian Communist regime sought to use this technology:

Since the mid-80's the central coordinator of unconventional research became the State Committee for Science and Technology at the Council of Ministers (SCST USSR) with the direct participation of the Ministry of Defense and the KGB. In the middle of 1986, N.I.Ryzhkov (Н.И.Рыжков) on a memo about the perspectives of torsion technologies wrote a resolution: "Take steps to organize the works." Many authors point to the classified document by the Central Committee of the CPSU and the USSR Council of Ministers N137-47 of 27 January 1986 about the program 'Management of living objects, including human.' For obvious reasons, the text of this resolution is not in the public domain, but this document has several indirect evidences. (Kernbach, 2013, 12)

As far as the technological development Kernbach notes that these generator designs were already completed a decade earlier in the 1970s, although it is possible they were taken directly from Nazi Germany, apparently in secret Soviet labs under sponsorship of the KGB and Ministry of Defense, which seems to have begun this work as a direct corollary to the Nuclear Weapons program of the 1950s in which many German scientists were involved, like Zimmer, Hertz and von Ardenne. It is possible they were disclosed in the mid-1980s to attract more research or that these particular designs were antiquated, but their circulation as devices would be valid in academic contexts even if the design itself is antiquated and replaced with a new version of the technology such as lasers of LED based devices, in the mid-90s Bobrov switched from Akimov generators to Quantum Generators (lasers, LED). As is usual there was much suppression of Akimov and the research community following the fall of the Soviet Union. In 1991, Akimov and the research of Torsion Fields were declared 'pseudoscience' by the presidium of the USSR's Academy of Science, which in one week went from funding Akimov and the Center for Unconventional

Technologies to declaring such research 'pseudoscience', Kernbach has written this off as jealousy over funding of research, while Russian researcher Zhigalov finds a direct military deception reasoning behind the labeling of this technology as 'pseudoscience':

> Somewhere in the beginning 80s (and maybe even earlier), he [Akimov] discovered the mutual influence of dis-united rotating bodies. The report of these studies was classified. It seems that Akimov's work was initiated by these studies. It is possible that the main achievements of Akimov are classified. Maybe exactly therefore in VENT publications there is very little directly on torsion topics, especially publications with detailed descriptions of experiments. I even admit that the whistle about 'pseudoscientific' torsion research is specially organized as a 'disinformation' for hiding very important achievements. But this is just an unreliable hypothesis. (Zhigalov, 2009)

This was all just previous to the end of the Soviet Union. After the fall of the Soviet Union funding dried up for Akimov and his center, VENT, though active work continued into 1995, after that period support became sporadic, with Akimov trying to continue VENT into 2001. VENT was organized into 5 research areas: communication, material research, new sensing technologies (e.g., for forecasting earthquakes), water cleaning and medical diagnostics. All psychotronic research stopped in 2002-2003, which was also around the time of the murder of Brushlinsky (Jan 2002); the first creation of 'Thought Injection' in the US. Basically most Russians with expertise in this field went west or carried on meagerly developing their own private funding sources, never with any serious money behind them. Sokolov notes that some Torsion scientists went to England as well around the time of the fall of the Soviet Union (Sokolov, 2016).

An example of the ending of Psychotronics programs in Russia was the closing of the military unit 10003 in 2003, which was established in 1989 to explore the possibilities of military use of paranormal phenomena. While during this period Academics that had previously been doing solid scientific work in this area decided not to carry on this work, fearing for their academic positions at Universities in Russia by being labeled as 'pseudoscientists' (Kernbach, 2013). One interesting point regarding the generators used by Akimov, for instance he did not use Okatrin's generator, though similar, or include other Theoretical Physicists' work such as A.G. Gurvich or B. Kobozev due to their ideas being 'Old', like Okatrin's microlepton theory.

Kernbach has studied the Soviet 'Torsion' generators produced by the likes of Akimov, Oktarin (Анатолий Федорович Охатрина d. 2002), Deev, and others (Kernbach, 2015). Later, we shall examine the physics behind these generators or antennae and it's use of the Aharonov-Bohm effect. It is revealing that in a document dated from July 22, 1991 an interview was held with a Russian scientist, Oktarin, by the CIA during the collapse of the Soviet Union. Evidently the CIA was interested in his inventions' Neuroweapons abilities:

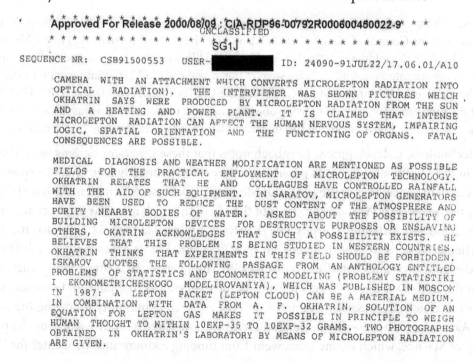

```
* * * * * Approved For Release 2000/08/09 : CIA-RDP96-00792R000600450022-9 * * *
* * * * * * * * * * * * * * * UNCLASSIFIED * * * * * * * * * * * * * * * *
                                    SG1J
SEQUENCE NR: CSB91500553   USER-████████   ID: 24090-91JUL22/17.06.01/A10

CAMERA WITH AN ATTACHMENT WHICH CONVERTS MICROLEPTON RADIATION INTO
OPTICAL RADIATION). THE INTERVIEWER WAS SHOWN PICTURES WHICH
OKHATRIN SAYS WERE PRODUCED BY MICROLEPTON RADIATION FROM THE SUN
AND A HEATING AND POWER PLANT. IT IS CLAIMED THAT INTENSE
MICROLEPTON RADIATION CAN AFFECT THE HUMAN NERVOUS SYSTEM, IMPAIRING
LOGIC, SPATIAL ORIENTATION AND THE FUNCTIONING OF ORGANS. FATAL
CONSEQUENCES ARE POSSIBLE.

MEDICAL DIAGNOSIS AND WEATHER MODIFICATION ARE MENTIONED AS POSSIBLE
FIELDS FOR THE PRACTICAL EMPLOYMENT OF MICROLEPTON TECHNOLOGY.
OKHATRIN RELATES THAT HE AND COLLEAGUES HAVE CONTROLLED RAINFALL
WITH THE AID OF SUCH EQUIPMENT. IN SARATOV, MICROLEPTON GENERATORS
HAVE BEEN USED TO REDUCE THE DUST CONTENT OF THE ATMOSPHERE AND
PURIFY NEARBY BODIES OF WATER. ASKED ABOUT THE POSSIBILITY OF
BUILDING MICROLEPTON DEVICES FOR DESTRUCTIVE PURPOSES OR ENSLAVING
OTHERS, OKATRIN ACKNOWLEDGES THAT SUCH A POSSIBILITY EXISTS. HE
BELIEVES THAT THIS PROBLEM IS BEING STUDIED IN WESTERN COUNTRIES.
OKHATRIN THINKS THAT EXPERIMENTS IN THIS FIELD SHOULD BE FORBIDDEN.
ISKAKOV QUOTES THE FOLLOWING PASSAGE FROM AN ANTHOLOGY ENTITLED
PROBLEMS OF STATISTICS AND ECONOMETRIC MODELING (PROBLEMY STATISTIKI
I EKONOMETRICHESKOGO MODELIROVANIYA), WHICH WAS PUBLISHED IN MOSCOW
IN 1987: A LEPTON PACKET (LEPTON CLOUD) CAN BE A MATERIAL MEDIUM.
IN COMBINATION WITH DATA FROM A. F. OKHATRIN, SOLUTION OF AN
EQUATION FOR LEPTON GAS MAKES IT POSSIBLE IN PRINCIPLE TO WEIGH
HUMAN THOUGHT TO WITHIN 10EXP-35 TO 10EXP-32 GRAMS. TWO PHOTOGRAPHS
OBTAINED IN OKHATRIN'S LABORATORY BY MEANS OF MICROLEPTON RADIATION
ARE GIVEN.
```

Oktarin hypothesized during an era when many, outside of secret government labs, had given up on gravitational waves and any normal EM wave explanations for the effects they were encountering in their labs came up with the theory of microleptons, so that we now understand when he refers to microleptons he is really referring to the well-founded physics of the Aharonov-Bohm effect, not some new pseudoscientific 'Torsion physics' or 'microleptons.' The camera mentioned in the text was created in 1989. It is a photometric method for recording energy fields using digital scanning and optical devices [see Ch. 9B] developed at the Torsion Laboratory of the International Academy of Medical and Technical under the leadership of G.F. Saveliev working with Oktarin. A brief review of Oktarin's biography reveals some interesting relationships:

Okhatrin Anatoly Fedorovich, Academician of the International Academy of Energy Information Sciences, Head of the Biolocation Laboratory and the Institute of Mineralogy, Geochemistry and Crystal Chemistry and Rare Elements (ITGRE), developer of biogenerators (академик Международной академии энергоинформационных наук, руководитель лаборатории биолокации и института минералогии, геохимии и кристаллохимии и редких элементов (ИТГРЭ), разработчик биогенераторов.). https://spaev-gev.livejournal.com/44962.html

From 1953 he worked in the design bureau of academician A.P. Korolev in Novosibirsk [Kozyrev also worked there on his 'torsion' theory based on 'Causal Mechanics' with time as a particle], where devices were developed that affect human energy, which is interesting since most in the west credit such work to Pavlita, but it seems to also have been investigated by the Soviet rocket scientists, literally rocket scientists. Keeping in mind that Tsiokolvsky, credited with the founding of the Russian space program, himself was haunted and also believed psi technology would bring a great leap forward in space exploration. Early in Oktarin's career he is already investigating biological linfluences in an official Soviet government lab. His mentor, Korolev, before designing the rockets that launched Sputnik and the first manned mission, was working on biological effects of remote action, this after having been arrested and sent to the Gulag in 1938, we see another important person within this research field sent to Siberia, work with the Soviet space program and biogenerators would have ceased with his elimination. Oktarin 1953 to 1980 worked at KB Zarya, NPO Krasnaya Zvezda on the creation of onboard (space, etc.) nuclear power plants [a topic that Dr. Baker also remarks on], took part in the creation of aircraft control systems which we also see in the work of Norseen and Sokolov, which is significant in that the technology 'Thought Injection' as developed by Lockheed-Martin developed directly from the need to interact with pilots in combat aircraft during critical times, so points to a direct correlative result in the research from the Soviets then being imported to the UKUSA after the collapse of the Sovet Union ending up in the work of Lockheed-Martin engineer Dr. John Norseen, again he also studied in Russia with Reflexive Control academics and engineers.

It is not coincidental that there are claims of 'free energy' from this technology along with 'remote sensing', though ostensibly exaggerations of capabilities. Okatrin worked on creating energy for space exploration. In 1973, he is Deputy Chief Designer of NPO Krasnaya Zvezda, Deputy Director of NPO Krasnaya Zvezda for scientific work. He supervised the development and implementation of nuclear power systems for direct energy conversion (thermoelectricity, thermal emission, electrochemistry, radioisotope sources, etc.) in projects: "Romashka," "Topaz," "Yenisei," "Buk," "Lemon," "Orion," "Beta-1," "Beta-2," "Beta-3," "Beta-M," "Beta-S" are currently working in various autonomous objects of technology on the spacecraft "Kosmos-84," "Kosmos- 90 "(1965), radioisotope generators" Orion-1 and Orion-11K "based on polonium-210 were used, on the spacecraft "Lunokhod-1" (1970), "Lunokhod-2" (1973). An interesting twist is that the USA bought some of his power plants. The nuclear power plant BES-5 "Buk" was used on the USA radar reconnaissance satellite. The first apparatus of this series was launched on October 3, 1970 from Baikonur ("Cosmos-367"). The Buk itself has been in development since 1960. at NPO Krasnaya Zvezda. In 1992, the United States purchased two Yenisei (Topaz-2) nuclear power plants in Russia for $ 13 million. One of the reactors was supposed to be used in 1995 after thorough ground tests. in the "Nuclear Electric Propulsion Spaceflight Test Program."

The generators that he worked on had both negative and positive effects. Counter measures in military applications is always one of the most important aspects of technical development, either a weapon will be more useful or less useful based on the counter measures developed in reference to it. In terms of counter measures Okatrin also developed a system to suppress the same effects that cause physiological problems he has developed devices, sensors and neutralizers of harmful fields of natural and man-made origin, also see Maslobrod below. In particular, to protect a person from various kinds of negative fields, a series of devices "Gamma-7" «Гамма-7» has been developed: "Neutralizer" «Нейтрализатор» and "Activator" «Активатор."

Persinger also has found there is a way to block 'remote viewing.' (Disruption of Remote Viewing by Magnetic Fields, see Ch. 9). In a study with psychic Ingo Swann as the subject, Persinger was able to block some remote viewing, suggesting that a changing EM field interferes with psychic abilities, static fields enable psi. This could also explain why Psi differs with solar storms, changing EM field in storm. "The results suggest weak, temporally complex magnetic fields generated within [the object]... may have interfered with the stimuli to the [psychic]..." (Persinger, 2002, 994)

In Kernbach's study of the 1986 Soviet experiment he relates that the experiment from 1986 owes its impetus to previous work of Sokolova in 1982. Sokolova's work is related to earlier studies by V.P. Kaznacheev in the 1970s. These studies are all related to the effect of an irradiated body transmitting its internal state to bystanders, or other objects nearby, such as a rat to another rat in its cage. This work actually began much earlier than the Soviet 'inception' of these techniques. Biophotons are a photonic form of radiation that cells and all living matter send out with exchanges of free protons in, say, a molecule. Others study the bystander effect as relates to Biophotons. Earlier we saw how biophotons are used in Brain Computer Interfaces as explained by Dr. Persinger. Some very early studies related to this are the work of Gurvitch in the 1920s, who reported communications between animals based on photons. Later, the German E. Woenckhaus from 1930 (Mothersill, 2014) experimented on the bystander effect from irradiating mice and then measuring the effect on the test subjects' cage mates. Noting Gurvitsch's contribution:

> Intensive research started in the 1920s with the work of Gurvitsch whose 200 or more experiments revealed that when pointing the tip of an onion root (inducer) to another onion root (receiver), separated by quartz glass, the receiver root surprisingly shows an increased rate of mitosis (approx. 20-25%). Since this effect was absent when using ultra-violet (UV)-opaque glass, he concluded that electromagnetic radiation in the UV range was responsible. He termed this type of radiation "*mitogenetic radiation.*" In 1927 Frank & Gurwitsch reported the successful spectroscopic detection of UV radiation in the range of 193-237nm originating from frog muscles. Gurwitsch's research stimulated many other researchers in the 1930s and early 1940s to replicate and extend their experiments, leading to both successful and unsuccessful replications. The research showed that there is indication for a non-chemical, electromagnetic cell-to-cell signaling which can be experimentally detected when investigating the effect of inducer cells on receiver cells, where the inducer cells have to be in the mitotic state or in a stressed condition (induced by e.g., chemical, thermal, mechanical or electrical treatments). The radiation emanated from stressed cells was termed by Gurwitsch as "degradation radiation" [negative position of Akimov generator]. One limitation of Gurwitsch's work is that it does not completely meet modern scientific requirements for proper experimental investigations, i.e., it lacks proper statistical analysis and complete control over confounders. However, new analyses of Gurwitsch's data revealed that most of the results were statistically significant using modern statistical test (personal communication, Prof. Beloussov [Faculty of Biology, Lomonosov Moscow State University, Moscow], Dr. Stefanov [Institute of Biophysics, Russian Acad Sci., Moscow]). Unfortunately, these analyses were not published. Thus, Gurwitsch's work is primarily of historical significance and should be regarded as an initial approach for experimental investigation of a new topic. Unfortunately, in the 1940s-1950s, World War II and a shift in the focus to biochemistry halted research into this topic. (Scholkmann, 2013)

In the Soviet Union we can see pioneering work in remote influencing on biological objects was first proposed in the 1920s and continued post-war with experiments noted from the 1960s on. The main researcher in this area was V.P. Kaznacheev. Regarding his contributions:

> In the 1960s-1980s the research group of Kaznacheev continued to investigate the topic by performing a large number of experiments with different cell cultures. They used a specially designed device to perform the experiments consisting of two flasks, which were connected by a window of either quartz glass or a UV-opaque glass plate (with a depth of about 0.2-2 mm). An "inducer" cell culture was placed in one flask and a "receiver" culture in the other. It was investigated how the treatment of the inducer culture with different stressors (e.g. viruses, chemicals or UV-radiation) affects the receiver culture. For example, experiments using inducer cell cultures consisting of monkey kidney tissue treated with adenoviruses demonstrated that the receiver cell culture also shows morphological signs of infection in 72% of performed trails (total number of trials: 170) after 2.3 days

of contact. The observed effect was termed the "mirror cytopathic effect." After analyzing all experiments done, Kaznacheev concluded among other things that the effect (i) was at its strongest when cultures from the same species were used, (ii) seems to be caused by an electromagnetic interaction between the cultures in the UV range, and interestingly... (iii) its strength showed an annual modulation (month with most successful experiments: August), possibly related to environmental factors. (Scholkmann, 2013)

The Soviet Union recognized Kaznacheev for his contribution, "The Phenomena of Intercellular Distant EM Interaction in the system of Two Tissue Cultures," dating it officially to Feb. 15, 1966. We can see clearly there is a continuation of the work of Gurvitsch. Kaznacheev was of interest to the DoD and the CIA. Former military intelligence analyst in the field of psychotronics, Lt. Col. Tom Bearden, has written of Kaznacheev's contributions to Psi research:

As an example of the kindling effect and the variability of photon quenching of the paranormal channel, some extremely interesting experiments were performed by V.P. Kaznacheyev et al regarding the paranormal transmission of death. Briefly, two groups of cells were selected from the same cell culture and one sample placed on each side of a window joining two environmentally shielded rooms. The cell cultures were in quartz containers. One cell culture was used as the initiation sample and was subjected to a deadly mechanism - virus, germ, chemical poison, irradiation, ultraviolet rays, etc. The second cell culture was observed, to ascertain any transmitted effects from the culture sample being killed.

When the window was made of ordinary glass, the second sample remained alive and healthy. When the window was made of quartz, the second sample sickened and died with the same symptoms as the primary sample. The experiments were done in darkness, and over 5,000 were reported by Kaznacheev and his colleagues. The onset of induced complementary sickness and death in the second culture followed a reasonable time - say two to four hours - behind sickness and death in the primary culture.

The major transmission difference between window glass and quartz is that quartz transmits both ultraviolet and infrared well, while glass is relatively opaque to ultraviolet and infrared. Both quartz and glass transmit visible light. Thus glass is a suppressor of the paranormal channel, while quartz is not.

By performing the experiment in darkness through a quartz window, the four-law patterns of disease, sickness, or death engendered in the primary sample are not extensively squelched by the photon interaction, and these four-law patterns are transmitted through the quartz window into the second cell culture. Since the genetic patterns of the second culture are the same as those of the first, sympathetic four-state interaction and eventual kindling occur, resulting in the appearance of the effects in the second culture.

It is well known that cells also emit mitogenic radiation, including radiation in the ultraviolet and infrared regions. Since these same regions are not strongly suppressed by the photon interaction, one may hypothesize that paranormal effects may be strongly modulated onto infrared and ultraviolet photon activity, and there is indeed evidence for such an assumption. In 1950, Western researchers found that cells could be killed in darkness with ultraviolet radiation, kept shielded from visible light for twenty-four hours or longer, and then if radiated with visible light the cells would start reviving by hundreds of thousands even though they had been clinically dead.

Specifically, every cell emits mitogenetic radiation in the ultraviolet twice: when it is born and when it dies. The UV photon emitted at death contains the exact virtual state pattern of the condition of the cell at death. The healthy cells are bombarded with death messages from those that are dying, and this diffuses the death pattern throughout the healthy culture, eventually kindling into the same death pattern there.

However, the squelching of the paranormal channel by photon interaction is never complete, or paranormal phenomena could never occur in daylight. Hence paranormal patterns can be modulated even onto visible light, although only extremely weakly. Thus we may speak of the Q or sharpness of the paranormal modulation upon photon frequencies; Q is extremely low for visible light and may be extremely high for infrared and ultraviolet. In the visible light spectrum, it is probable that extremely large numbers of near-zero strength paranormal patterns are modulated on the light radiation; hence these patterns simply consist of a very weak background noise and the kindling effect does not apply. (The patterns are so random as to be self-canceling in the kindling effect.) (Bearden, 1983)

V.P. Kaznacheev, later in 1991, founded a scientific committee ' Bioenergy', showing the continuation of his work outside of official government labs after the fall of the Soviet Union (Kernbach, 2013).

Which brings us to the continuation of Soviet research in this area under V.A. Sokolova. In 2016 Sokolova published a synopsis of work on remote influencing on biological objects in a book form. Sokolova gives information on how these experiments developed over the years:

A.A. Deev, who created a generator emitting fields of an incomprehensible nature. Research conducted at the Institute of Clinical and Experimental medicine SB AMS USSR (director V.P. Kaznacheev) in 1981 Deev jointly with the staff of the laboratory of Biophysics A.P. Mikhailova and N.B. Kartasheva showed that under the influence of this generator, biophysical cell culture characteristics. During the experiment, a double shielding cells from the effects of an electromagnetic field. In 1984 in Peoples' Friendship University named after P. Lumumba V.A. Sokolova, A.A. Deev and Sukhanov conducted experiments that recorded a sharp change relative dispersion of electrical conductivity in plants at frequencies 1 - 517 kHz when exposed to this generator (measurements were carried out by method V.V. Gorchakov and A.D. Kotamokhin). The generator was based on spin polarized (SP) materials. It must be assumed that this deep interest in work with JV generators began for Akimov his research to create torsion generators. (Boldyreva, 2009)

In this work some of the details on how the generators work is given; similar to the Zeeman Effect, it has 3 channels, a positive transition, negative transition (causing deleterious effects) and neutral or zero-transition channel. The zero channel is the channel that carries information with very low force and energy, the 'psi' channel (Sokolov, 2016, 30). Sokolov also credits not just the A-B effect but also with the gyromagnetic 'spin-wave', the generators are able to control the physical vacuum. In explaining the physics behind the generator Sokolov turned to the anti-gravity theory of Jose Del Prado, explaining that between 2 counter 'torsion' [spin] fields there is a spatial boundary tension field=0, a cord, conductor in layers of cord [cord may resemble Persinger's Singularity explanation]. Between there is a gap formed by repulsion of the same charge (Sokolov, 2016, 35). In an interesting parallel with other researchers in 'thought injection' such as Dr. Norseen, Sokolova also worked on avionic systems involving the interface of the pilot and machine (Sokolova, 1981). Sokolova expresses both alarm and dismay at the use of the technology for purposes of control in terms of mass control. He writes:

Even the Russian scientist Shipunov argued that the transfer of information is possible at the level of human thought. This is real since wave functions are organized more strictly. It was on Earth with the number of electromagnetic matrices grows every year negative sign, and surrounded by one person they can exist, and the other person is simply blinded by them. Therefore, it is not surprising that 70% of unsolved crimes their cause is unknown. Under certain conditions that, in particular, it can be called a "soulless person," formed vacuum, and electromagnetic matrices with a negative sign, who then begin to control the Person like demons. This is a very dangerous situation, and one can only hope for the fact that torsion fields are not the final station of the wave world. We hope that in addition to torsion fields, there are more completed fields, purely informational, to save the world. (Sokolova, 2016)

It should be noted, in a manner related to TI claims of neural monitoring, that Sokolova finds that the Torsion (Spin) Field can be broadcast over media (Sokolov, 2016, 16). Kernbach has also performed experiments related to finding if weak radiation can be transmitted through the internet, which he concluded positively it could (Kernbach, 2015); again many TI claim to be affected through television and internet connected devices with what they call Directed Energy Weapon attacks. Later, Sokolova expressed dismay at the attacks on Russian Torsion scientists by Russian Scientific authorities and points out that some have even left Russia to work for the west:

...Y. Vorobyevsky It would be better if he criticized those "performers" of torsion fields who left Russia in its most difficult time and settled, for example, in England. Therefore, it is possible that they are not working with us, but in the West in this scientific direction. (Sokolov 2016)

Sokolova (see 2016, 56-9) has brought forth several meaningful conclusions to his research; a summary is provided:

- Field Twins: In the frequency range from 1 to 512 *kHz* with remote exposure revealed an insubstantial (non-physical) field twin in each of the examined material object. Each material object after the torsion left impact, you can issue a field passport in the range frequencies from 1 to 512 *kHz*

- Individual Map: The field non-material counterpart of each material the object has within the same architectural form both general and unique to him individual characteristics in the distribution within the field package of curves.

- Gravity and Communications: The process of remote action of torsion fields of communication is concerned with the geotropism of plants, that is, with gravity.

- Operational Modes: The torsion generator can operate in three modes: positive, negative and zero transition. [Spin Field is Trinary, neg, pos, neutral or qutrit-like; at the metaphysical scale it is enneagram-like].

- Death Ray: Negative impact (mode) of the torsion field turns a previously organized field package into a completely disordered distribution of curves and leads to destruction; the curves are preserved.

- Imprinting: There is a transfer of information properties from one object to another, and the latter acquires the characteristics of the first only if the torsion generator operates in the zero-transition mode. Transfer is possible in the operating mode of the torsion generator to zero-transition from an inanimate object (washer) to a living object (plant), and the latter loses part of its substance."

- Fatty Acids: Found signs of changes in the geometric iso-metrics under the action of a torsion field on those objects that belong to unsaturated hydrocarbons, that is, they have a double bond – including if this bond is present in the radical organic compound. [found that milk irradiated coagulated, increasing its viscosity, applicable to other mammalian fat cells?]

- Broadcasting: Torsion fields are recorded on a tape and successfully broadcast to the object; pictures also have the same effect, photons 'weak emissions' (A, psi) are captured by Electro-magnetic based storage.

- Viscosity: related to Fatty Acids. In some cases, torsion fields can change the consistency of liquid substances, turning them into a solid state. Torsion fields are capable of changing the viscosity of fuels (kerosine, gasoline, oil) and, the greater the degree of continuous efficiency, the stronger this change improves fuel efficiency. Carried out the transfer of the viscosity properties of fuels with fuels for fuels that are at room temperature, and the intensity of this process depends on the degree of unsaturation of the investigated fuel, and to a lesser extent changes in the viscosity of the fuel in which are more chemically pure substances.

- Stress Effects: Under stressful conditions of an object in conditions of increased stress the concentration of saline nutrient solution changes field state contour.

Sokolov concluded:

> Thus, my personal experimental results of exposure to torsion fields or those in which I took an active part. Besides those stated, there are also many other experimental materials of other specialists; and by now accumulated great experimental materials, convincingly that the effect of torsion fields on material objects really takes place. And although now there is a situation where the experimental part of the problem is ahead of the theoretical, nevertheless, in science experimental confirmation has always been the end proof of truth. (Sokolov, 2016, 56-59)

Kernbach has concluded that the so-called 'torsion' field and generators are actually EM based antennas that use the Aharonov-Bohm effect. Both the effect and the history of the 'Torsion' generators are of importance to understand the development of this technology and how it eventually ends up in the CIA contractor SRI with Hal Puthoff's patent for a generator based on the Aharonov-Bohm effect in 1993. An examination of Hal Puthoff's 1993 patent give us an idea as to how the Akimov and other generators, all based on a basic Russian prototype, work and function and the physics behind them. First, it is important to understand Hal Puthoff's background. Puthoff is a physicist who formerly worked for the Stanford Research Institute, examining the physics behind psychics associated with SRI's Remote Viewing studies funded by the DoD and CIA. He has collaborated with Lockheed-Martin scientists on Zero-Point Fields (ZPF) as referenced by Lockheed-Martin engineer John Norseen.

Collaborating with Bernhard Haisch of Lockheed-Martin on *Advances in the Proposed Electromagnetic Zero-Point Field Theory of Inertia*, Haisch had previously to this paper worked on *Quantum and classical statistics of the electromagnetic zero-point field* (Haisch, 1996). As a contractor for the CIA back in the day, the early 70s to the 90s, he worked on the physics of the phenomena being experimented on by him and colleague Targ. Eventually in 1993, shortly after the publication of the Soviet "Akimov" generators, he patented an American version while working for SRI. One of the primary effects behind his device according to his patent filings is the Aharonov-Bohm effect. Puthoff writes:

> With the advent of quantum theory, however, the above picture changed. In the prior art literature, the (A, Φ) formalism has emerged as more fundamental because it predicts certain quantum interference effects that have been observed and are not apparent from the (E, B) approach. This difference was first set forth in an unequivocal way in a seminal 1959 paper by Aharonov and Bohm, entitled "Significance of Electromagnetic Potentials in the Quantum Theory," Physical Review 115, 485 (1959); see also "Further Considerations on Electromagnetic Potentials in the Quantum Theory." Physical Review 123, 1511 (1961). In these papers it is shown that in certain two-leg electron-interferometer configurations in which the potentials A and Φ are established in a region of Space, but E and B are absent, it is nonetheless possible for the potentials to induce changes in electron quantum interference patterns. That is, electrons that are in an electromagnetic field-free region and therefore do not encounter an electric or magnetic field are none the less acted upon by the presence of the A and/or p potentials. Such an effect is now referred to broadly as the Aharonov Bohm effect, and devices have been built which demonstrate this effect in the laboratory; for a recent overview, see Y. Imry and R. A. Webb, "Quantum Interference and the Aharonov-Bohm Effect," *Scientific American* 260, 56 (April 1989). A Second quantum interference effect which demonstrates the independent reality of the A, Φ potentials in the absence of the (E, B) fields (and one which is significant for the technology disclosed herein) is a single-leg electron interferometer effect known as the Josephson effect, [See R. P. Feynman et al.] The Feynman Lectures on Physics, vol. III (Addison-Wesley, Reading, Mass., 1965), pp. 21-14 through 21-18. The Josephson effect is based on the fact that the current density J through a Josephson junction (which consists of two Superconductors separated by a thin electric insulator) is determined by the magnitude of the potentials A and Φ, independent of whether E or B fields are present. (Puthoff, 1998)

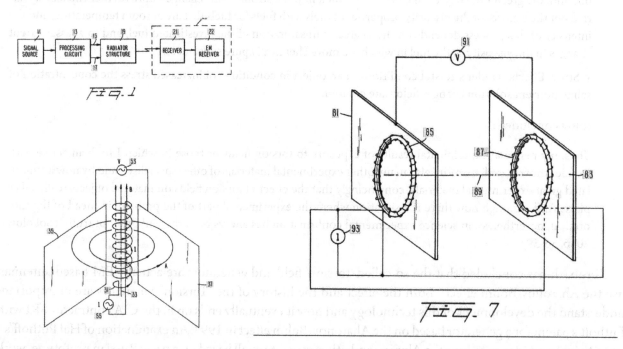

PUTHOFF DESIGN 1

As stated earlier by Sokolova, these A-B (Aharonov-Bohm) Generators, as I will refer to them, can control vacuum fluctuations. Referencing Puthoff design 1 functioning of these devices is based around a helical coil that is stood up vertically (31) and is powered by a DC source. This solenoid gets current to generate a vertically directed magnetic field (B), which also generates a curl-free vector potential exterior to the solenoid. The plates (37,35) driven by the voltage source produce a horizontal electrostatic field; the voltage varies as the time derivative (rhythmic). The electrostatic and electrodynamic fields from the solenoid and plates cancel in the horizontal plane suppressing the EM Field in the horizontal plane. The field from solenoid and plates combine in horizontal plane, causing a signal along the horizontal plane. The Receiver is a quantum interference receiver, such as Norseen referred to the human brain; the receiver includes Josephson junction super-conductor rods [also see Baker HFGW design].

Referencing Puthoff Design 2 or Fig. 7 above we are presented a different setup, one that is used by Dr. Michael Persinger in some of his experiments, where toroidal coils, if both are properly phased and adjusted in amplitude to provide a time varying signal (A, Φ) having no EM component. For more technically inclined it is absent from the Maxwell Equations as a force; there is no Lorenz Lemma.

The gist of how this works is that electric potentials, not actual force, that is, structure minus any weight behind it; imagine a hologram of a punch hitting you. So, they end up transmitting structure but not force which interacts subtly with matter, which leads to reactions and causations which we would not 'normatively' anticipate to be caused by such low strength fields.

Having noted that Intelligence is directly involved in the ideas of remote action or sensing it is worthwhile to look at what Dr. Persinger was able to learn through similar studies as that of Kernbach.

Dr. Persinger has written about the Casimir Effect in several publications. In a paper on thixotropy which has to do with the viscosity of water and its impact by EM fields, he studies the pH free protons of aqueous solutions separated by non-trivial non-local distances but united in EM fields applied to the water samples in which he found a deep correlation between water samples pH changed locally and then reflected in the remote water sample. Regarding virtual particles Persinger writes: "Here I present quantitative evidence that thixotropic properties of water could reflect a universal interface for the transformation of virtual particles from zero-point, vacuum oscillations to real particles." (Persinger, 2015, 6203)

Previously we have read how Aharonov-Bohm generators affect the viscosity of water, which is its thixotropic properties. Knowing that these generators affect the vacuum it is important to understand the effect of these generators on water, on which all life depends, as well as playing an important role in controlling the EM within Microtubules, which is to say our memories and working consciousness, and subconscious.

Dr. Persinger points out on several occasion the connection of 10^{-20}J, its role not just in neuronal EEG rhythms, or its role in free proton creation. He connects them to vacuum oscillations in water:

> The persistent, subtle, and specific properties of thixotropic phenomena in water meet the quantitative criteria for a special condition that could be distributed throughout the sub-matter spatial fabric of the universe. The prevalence of the quantity of energy in the order of 2×10^{-20} J derived from the product of the ratio of the proton's magnetic moment to its unit charge and viscosity applied across the O-H length could mediate the dynamics that connect water to the transformation of vacuum oscillations (or virtual particles) to real states and determine the spatial and temporal boundaries of the coherent domains that create the thixotropic state.
>
> The state could originate from the interaction between the spin-orbit magnetic moments and neutral hydrogen line frequency that sets the condition for a single orbit to display ½ wave (virtual) and ½ real (particle) properties. The mass equivalent of the transformation from virtual to real states from energy converging between Casimir-magnetic field strengths at the limen of the intergalactic background magnetic field compliments the numbers of free protons (pH) in an optimal volume of water and determines the numbers of interactive molecules within the domains. When undisturbed or within minimal radiant influence the conduit of ~2×10^{-20} J would conservatively increase the viscosity to five times the usual value.
>
> The involvements of the energies that reflect shifts of photons from rest mass as well as a "diffusivity" or "entanglement" velocity that converge with 10^{-20} J as a universal value emerge across levels of spatial structure and suggest that thixotropic conditions of water could reflect universal conditions. The occurrence of excess correlations between solar and terrestrial water molecules could accommodate the periodicities noted in thixotropic responses reported in various chemical systems over the previous decades. (Persinger, 2015, 6209)

In a related experiment Dr. Persinger studied the long-distance interaction of water samples and their connection by two alternating pattern magnetic fields; that is, he created two separate EM fields, put water samples in these fields, added free Protons (H+) and watched not just the local sample that had free protons directly added but also the separate non-local field had its samples pH increase, although no direct free protons were added to it locally. He also noted that this effect was in small volumes, <25cc, which is much larger than water in the Microtubules. The issue of thixotropy obviously plays a role in life:

The thixotropic phenomenon of water may determine many of the parameters that both create and constrain the conditions for living systems. Thixotropy is an emergent property of liquids and gels whose viscosity slowly increases and appears to involve the intrinsic ordering of large numbers of water molecules. Vybiral and Voracek's study of water containing ions indicated that the gel-like behavior developed "spontaneously" over time when undisturbed in closed vessels. Mechanical stimuli dissipated the enhanced viscosity and the correlative properties. The history and primary explanations for the thixotropic phenomenon of water have been reviewed recently by Verdel and Bukovec. They concluded that thixotropy is one "of the more complex characteristics associated with the behavior of non-Newtonian liquids." One would expect the mechanisms to be relatable to quantum levels of discourse. Here I present quantitative evidence that thixotropic properties of water could reflect a universal interface for the transformation of virtual particles from zero-point, vacuum oscillations to real particles.

Noting that water's viscosity, thixotropy, loses entropy (non-structure) as viscosity increases, becoming more 'solid'; the harder the structure the less entropy. Persinger found that if undisturbed, including from thermal radiation like sunlight, thixotropy increases in spring water samples, but not distilled water like from public taps, suggesting that the mechanism for this increase are trapped EM fields in the water:

> The hypothesis by Verdel et al. that thixotropy and proton transfer within water, that is the dynamics of the hydronium ion involving Grotthuss-like mechanisms, are intricately related is revealing. They examined the possibility that a structured network of hydrogen bonds between water molecules and ions in aqueous solutions when left undisturbed for protracted periods near hydrophilic surfaces facilitated this condition. If this were valid, then weak magnetic fields of the appropriate temporal configuration could be contained or "trapped" within these structure networks as predicted by Del Giudice and Preparata. When we exposed spring water containing physiological concentrations of ions to 3 m. (Persinger, 2015, 6201)

What could cause this? Persinger suggest the Casimir effect:

> The Casimir effect has been considered a "pure quantum effect" from zero-point oscillations. According to Bordag et al. it represents the zero-point energy of a quantized field. To transcend and integrate spatial levels from the smallest space (Planck's Length) the Casimir process should be transformable to macroscopic phenomena, such as matter-level magnetic fields. If this occurs there should be a convergence of quantitative solutions that relate to the properties of matter within specific boundaries. (Persinger, 2015, 6203)

> The occurrence of the ½ value has significant implications for the transformation of virtual particles to real particles. If the boundary conditions, that is the single orbital completion, depends upon time and is associated with external magnetic fields, then creation of particles could occur. From a strictly geometric perspective, because the movement is within a circle, the packet of energy is perpetually "accelerating." If for a given single orbit of an electron around a proton half of the time the electron occurs as a particle (matter) while the other half of the orbit it operates as an emergent virtual particle (wave) derived from the Casimir-magnetic energy transformation, manifestations of random vacuum fluctuations could occur. (Persinger, 2015, 6204)

> If the single orbit is related by ½ to the transformation from virtual manifestations to "real" particles or matter and the changing boundaries of magnetic fields are present, there should be creation of particles from the zero-point vacuum oscillations. The transformation vector would be the strength of the magnetic field coupled to the geometry of sub-matter space. (Persinger, 2015, 6204)

Remembering, according to Bandyapadhyay, that brain microtubules are controlled by water inside the MTs it is now possible to see through Persinger's work how Norseen's Thought Injection focused on the MT could work. Another important relation that Persinger brings up is that of the question of entanglement in water, writing on the concept of 'entanglement velocity', that there is an actual speed of the so-called 'instantaneous' entanglement.

> However, for excess correlations to occur "simultaneously" from our temporal perspective within the universal boundaries there must be an additional velocity whose value ultimately connects the upper boundaries for photon masses to the energies ($\sim 10^{-20}$ J) congruent with the operations within water that would contribute to increased viscosity. Persinger and Koren equated the product of the four-dimensional geometries for circularity, that is, 21.3 π 4 r 7 f with the aggregate m7 ·s⁻¹, to the optimal combination of universal values that balanced this

relationship. They were $G^2 \cdot m^2 \cdot d \cdot t^3$, where G was the Newtonian Gravitational constant, m was the mass of the universe, d was its diameter and t, its age. The resulting value for this "diffusivity" term for the 7th root was 2.84 $\times 10^{23}$ m·s^{-1}. They called this value the "entanglement" velocity. Approximately 7 to 8 min would be required for the universe to be traversed.

A process with this velocity moving between the earth and the sun would require ~10–12 s or the lifetime of a hydronium ion before the proton moves to the next water molecule. That "diffusion velocity" derived from the appropriate combination of G, and various powers of the width of the universe, its mass, and its age is related to the velocity produced by the ratio of the voltage field to the magnetic field by a frequency that at the quantum level is equivalent to the upper rest mass of the photon. (Persinger, 2015, 6208)

Similar quantities of energies within the water molecule and across levels of discourse from the photon to intergalactic magnetic fields, when coupled partially by the entanglement velocity, indicate the prominence of the value of 10^{-20} J as the energy metric for both dynamics and structure within the space that is occupied by all matter including water. It might be considered the conduit by which energy and virtual particles transform from and to entropy. (Persinger, 2015, 6208-9)

Looking into the method of entanglement between the two water samples, which were correlated or coupled by a magnetic field generator which we now know capitalizes on the Aharonov-Bohm effect to create entanglement, Persinger notes some particular attributes about these fields:

However, the excess correlations were only manifested when the reactions within the two volumes of water occurred in the centers of rotating, phase-modulated magnetic fields that shared the same changing angular velocities. When a coupled decreasing phase/frequency-modulated pattern and accelerating group velocity pattern was followed by a coupled increasing phase/frequency modulated pattern immersed in decreasing group velocity the powerful excess correlation occurred. The duration of the excess correlation was about 7 to 8 min. Reverse order presentations or fixed angular velocities did not produce the effect. (Persinger, 2015, 6207)

Again, noting the 8-minute relationship to entanglement and experimentation he found that the fields generated entanglement for 8 minutes:

When a coupled decreasing phase/frequency-modulated pattern and accelerating group velocity pattern was followed by a coupled increasing phase/frequency modulated pattern immersed in decreasing group velocity the powerful excess correlation occurred. The duration of the excess correlation was about 7 to 8 min. Reverse order presentations or fixed angular velocities did not produce the effect. (Persinger, 2015, 6207)

For excess correlations between complimentary shifts in pH within two volumes of water separated by non-local distances the optimal frequency of the angular rotation was balanced with that obtained from the product of the magnetic moment of the proton and the intensity of the magnetic field divided by Planck's constant. When this occurred the magnitude of the shift attributed to excess correlation increased by almost a factor of 10. (Persinger, 2015b, 406)

Persinger suggests that the orthogonal aspects of the field are what creates correlations citing again the role of the Schumann Resonance:

Although there are clearly other explanations the orthogonal directions of the attenuated static field and the dynamic toroid field could create the conditions for the type of photon involvement (Vaziri et al., 2002) derived from the Lorentz Lemma that would allow superimposition with the Schumann Resonances that occupy the space between the earth's surface and the ionosphere and most if not all human brains (Persinger and Saroka, 2015; Saroka and Persinger, 2014).

Though this study is on thixotropy and the Casimir Effect it is not just limited to changing pH in water samples, the implications of this research go further as explained by Persinger:

A means by which information could be inexpensively exchanged over large distances without the requirement for classic "transmission" and the escalating expense of equipment would substantially alter the concept and form of communication. The concept of "non-locality" and "excess correlation" has been considered by many as the quintessential property limited to quantum phenomena. As indicated by Hofmann et al., "observers of two

233

or more entangled particles will find correlations in their measurements that cannot be explained by classical statistics." Two-photon, three dimensional entanglements may be capable of applied quantum communication. Such quantum energy "teleportation" may not be limited by distance. (Persinger, 2014, 45)

MOLECULAR RESONANCE AND SOVIET RESEARCH

A researcher cited by both Dr. Persinger and Dr. Bandyopadhyay is the work of Dr. Irene Cosic, formerly of the U. of Belgrade, of which also Norseen-connected researcher Koruga is a professor. She now teaches at a university in Australia. Cosic's main contribution is known as the 'Resonant Recognition Model' which, importantly, allows for a new formulation of how cell signaling works, which is usually based on the JAK-STAT cellular signaling pathway, rather than resonant frequencies as suggested by Cosic and earlier Soviet Research. It should be remembered Belgrade was behind the Iron Curtain in the former Yugoslavia. The history of Resonance in physics is not new, people have been studying resonances in EM, for instance, for decades. Resonance has played a part in theoretical physics since the inception of Quantum Mechanics. One of the lead authors in QM Theory, Nazi physicist Pascual Jordan, in the early days while working with Biologists at the Berlin Brain Institute came up with a resonant theory of molecular attraction. Which was 'proven' wrong in the end by the majority of scientists while being explored and developed further by scientists inside Nazi Germany at the Brain Institute, which led to an official science that is accepted regarding cell signaling based on the JAK-STAT pathways and another alternative pathway of resonant cell signaling, which is ignored and not studied very much in the West. Indeed, most in the West do not consider this valid, yet we see how fruitful gains in the field of Psychotronics were conducted through this alternative scientific explanation for cell signaling. Jordan's ideas and that of the Berlin-Buch group later influenced the ideas of Frohlich who is recognized as a well-founded scientists on molecular issues. One author writes regarding Frohlich and Jordan:

> I went to see Frohlich because I had been trained as a theoretical physicist and we hoped to find out whether there was anything in his theory, which, I should say, flew in the face of everything that molecular biologists believed about interactions between large biological molecules. Frohlich believed in long-range 'resonance' forces between identical molecules. Every other molecular biologist preferred short-range forces between areas which are topographically complementary on opposing surfaces of molecules. This is typified by the two complementary chains of DNA within the double helix.
>
> Looking for some sort of perspective on Frohlich's theory, I discovered that the theoretical physicist, Pascual Jordan, had formulated essentially the same idea more than 30 years earlier. He had suggested that it might underlie molecular replication. The idea was sharply rebutted in 1940 by Linus Pauling in a short paper to the journal Science. Pauling's paper seemed to foreshadow the idea of complementarity as the way to replication and provide the physico-chemical basis for genetics, later so brilliantly realized in Crick and Watson's double helix. (Galloway, 1989)

In the paper mentioned it is rather curious that Linus Pauling had such a sharp response to it; it is noted by others whereas most ignored Jordan's paper when it first came out, Pauling's attachment and drive towards it was of note, which did lead to the non-resonant theory achieving dominance in the scientific community, of which Pauling was a part. It is worthwhile to look at the specifics of the argument that Jordan brought forward, which was later shown to have scientific validity in other areas through experimental research in the Soviet Union, while Western science remained controlled and stymied by academic discipline, a discipline that is easy to manipulate with monetary power as most universities are dependent on private funding of very influential industrial powers:

> Jordan suggested that quantum-mechanical resonance phenomena would lead to an attraction between molecules containing identical groups, and thus to self-reproduction of the antibody molecule…. Jordan"s concept was substantially identical to Ehrlich's, with the substitution of a more 'modern' mechanism for the reproduction of the specific antibody molecules. It was even more closely the equivalent of Jerne's natural selection theory…but failed completely to attract the attention of biologists. It did, however, come to the attention of Linus Pauling,t hen promoting his own theory of cantibody formation, who lost no time in attacking Jordan's formulation. The nature and role of intermolecular forces was Pauling's special domain, and he was quick to point out, in Jordan's own quantum-mechanical notation, that resonance attractions were less likely between

identical molecules than between complementary molecules, as Pauling's own theory had suggested. It is of some interest that although Pauling's attack was limited to Jordan's proposed mechanism for the reduplication of antibody molecules, it served also to eclipse the natural selection aspect of the argument. (Silverstien, 2009)

Jordan believed that like molecules would have like resonances and that molecules would be attracted to these resonances. Although, the particulars are not true, the ideal did bear fruit later in a similar concept of Cosic's that Molecules that share function share resonances; rather than being an issue of stacking or macromolecule building, it was relevant in terms of function. Cosic, being an eastern bloc-educated scientific engineer, later in the 1980s came up with the Cosic Resonant Recognition Model. It is generally related (though I have no direct or previous specific idea) in the Resonance research of the Soviets. The question then is, did Jordan's ideas percolate into Soviet thought? As seen in other sections after the war the Soviets captured Nazi scientists and brought them to work on the Soviet Nuclear program, some of whom were collaborators of Jordan in Berlin-Buch. For instance, G. Zimmer, a close collaborator with Jordan and a specialist in nuclear radiation and genetics, was taken to the Soviet Union. Eventually, the resonance model would prove fruitful in the field of Psychotronics. Kravkov in writing about the use of Millimeter Waves (GHz) in Soviet Psychotronic research relates how resonances were studied in relation to signals used to influence biological objects:

Resonances were the first, most intriguing manifestation of microwave exposure. Radio-physicists were struck by the narrowness of the operating radiation bands, the Q factor (the ratio of the wavelength to the bandwidth) reached 300-500 units. To date, influences (capillary effect) with a figure of merit up to 10 thousand units have been found. (i.e., at a wavelength $\lambda = 10$ mm, for example, the permissible deviations are in the range from 9.9995 to 10.0005 mm, no more).

Soon it was realized, that not a millimeter wave in general and specific, ostrorezonansnye their frequency, causing one or another back a response of living organisms, and thus have a signal value to their control systems, can be a tool of remote external influence on biological objects, including per person. A long-term experimental search for bio-effective frequencies has begun.

"The response to them can be different, both positive and negative. There are certain "frequency-amplitude windows," inside of which there is a detectable reaction of the biological object, and outside of them, there is none. In this case, the most informative is the frequency of exposure, and the amplitude determines only the mechanism of realization of the response of the organism."

Resonances have been studied for forty years, but there is no comprehensive, satisfying explanation for the mechanism of their occurrence. There are only assumptions. More or less reliable.

Formally, the resonance effect can be observed if the natural frequency of any structure has a natural frequency of oscillatory or rotational motion, which coincides with the frequency of the incident radiation ...

A strong frequency dependence should also be observed in cases where the frequency of the incident MM radiation coincides with the natural resonance frequency of a molecular ensemble of the cluster type ...

The resonance effect can also take place in cases when the frequency of absorption of an electromagnetic wave of any molecule coincides with the frequency of the incident radiation.

It was noted above that the frequency is the carrier of information, and the modes of vibration in the body can transform into each other. Therefore, it can be assumed that the resonant response of an organism is possible at the same frequencies with completely different types of influences on it (electromagnetic, acoustic, gravitational, etc.).

Further, the question arises about the preference of this or that effect and its effectiveness, but the reaction of the organism, of course, must exist. "

The greatest interest has always been in the resonances of the human body as a whole: "The argument for using electromagnetic radiation with $\lambda = 4.9$ mm was considerations based on the known fact of maximum absorption of millimeter waves in the atmosphere by molecular oxygen; $\lambda = 7.1$ mm was determined in the experiment - when treating animals affected by oncopathy; and only $\lambda = 5.6$ mm was chosen based on the analysis of clinical observations of the results of treatment of patients with gastric and duodenal ulcers ." These frequencies are considered basic and were allowed for use by the USSR Ministry of Health.

There are also references to the therapeutic use of wavelengths of 3.8 mm and 6.4 mm. Most recently, the number of therapeutic ones has also been supplemented with wavelengths $\lambda = 5.96$ mm, 5.79 mm, 4.61 mm.

The human types most sensitive to one or another wavelength have been determined.

The wave $\lambda = 7.1$ mm is more suitable for "sprinters" who are characterized by relatively low resistance to long-term external and internal factors (stimuli), the ability to carry out large volumes of activity in short periods of time, i.e., fast entropy syndrome.

The 5.6 mm wave is more useful for "stayers" who have "high resistance to long-term internal and external factors …, slow development of the disease, ie. delayed entropy syndrome. (Kravkov, 2006)

Irene Cosic' herself has described her interest in Resonances as stemming from the work of Nikola Tesla, who studied the brain frequencies from 3-69Hz (Cosic, 2017). From this she eventually was led to formulate the Cosic Resonant Recognition Model, which was used by Bandyopadhyay to study the EM resonance of Microtubules which is also used by Norseen for 'Thought Injection.' Cosic has defined the RRM in the following:

The RRM enables the calculation of these spectral characteristics, by assigning each amino acid a physical parameter representing the energy of delocalized electrons of each amino acid. Comparing Fourier spectra for this energy distributions by using cross-spectral function, it has been found that proteins sharing the same biological function/interaction share the same periodicity (frequency) within energy distribution along the macromolecule [5,6]. Furthermore, it has been shown that interacting proteins and their targets share the same characteristic frequency, but have opposite phase at characteristic frequency [5,6,14]. Thus, it has been proposed that the RRM frequencies characterize, not only a general function, but also a recognition and interaction between the particular macromolecule and its target, which then can be considered to be resonant recognition. This could be achieved with resonant energy transfer between the interacting macromolecules through oscillations of a physical field, which is electromagnetic in nature. (Cosic, 2017)

As mentioned, this has been used in modeling MTs. Persinger's group has also had beneficial results through referencing the RRM.

Cosic discovered that spectral analyses of a protein sequence after each constituent amino acid had been transformed into an appropriate pseudopotential predicted a resonant energy between interacting molecules. Several experimental studies have verified the predicted peak wavelength of photons within the visible or near-visible light band for specific molecules. Here, this concept has been applied to a classic signaling pathway, JAK–STAT, traditionally composed of nine sequential protein interactions. The weighted linear average of the spectral power density (SPD) profiles of each of the eight "precursor" proteins displayed remarkable congruence with the SPD profile of the terminal molecule (CASP-9) in the pathway. These results suggest that classic and complex signaling pathways in cells can also be expressed as combinations of resonance energies…. Here we present evidence that the JAK (Janus Kinase)– STAT (Signal Transducer and Activator of Transcription) pathway, one of the classic signaling pathways within the cell whose final component affects the nucleus, can be described as a resonance pattern that is composed of the spectral characteristics of the pathway that converge at the nuclear interface as CASP-9. The protein interactions can be considered a transfer of resonant energy between interacting molecules through an oscillating physical field that could be expressed within the domain of classic photons. (Persinger, 2015d, 245)

As we have previously seen, Akimov Generators have been replaced with Lasers and LED quantum generators, in Russian research in Psychotronics from the late 1990s. It is interesting that the RRM occurs in the frequency range from Infrared to visible to Ultraviolet waves. A further implementation of the RRM using LEDs is to use this methodology to fight viruses, not just remotely influence one's thoughts, Persinger has written on treating viruses using Cosic Resonance with LED lights. In studies it has been used on Ebola as a model, could be investigated for Covid-19 (see Persinger 2015b) and others using appropriately patterned monochromatic (Narrow band) LED to fight Zika virus (Caceres 2018).

Although, as important it is to fight infections and viruses, the most important point as this technology relates to Neuroweapons is that it is a viable explanation as to how without drugs or other direct chemical interdiction that EM waves are able to have a neurological or medical affect." Dr. Bandyopadhyay, in research underwritten by the United States Air Force, has related how this alternate pathway interacts with neurons which produce a stream of binary information:

A neuron gets hot and then cold (5–6 THz electromagnetic frequency domain) when it fires or sends a nerve spike (Abbott et al., 1958). Electromagnetic effect on neurons has been studied extensively as it modulates the firing rate (Camera et al., 2012) and even ion channel pathways (Li et al., 2014). Two neighboring neurons communicate electrically similar to wireless communication (Katz & Schmitt, 1940), and a neuron's sensitivity to the electric fields depends on the frequency of firing (Radman et al., 2007). While inserting an atomic sharp scanning tunneling microscope (STM) tip vibrating at low sinusoidal frequency (30 Hz) inside a single protein at resonance or a protein complex deep inside an axon of a rat hippocampal neuron during a firing we observed a stream of binary pulses. In Fig. 4(a) we have shown two binary streams – one for protein complex in the axon core (see B) and the other for a neuron membrane (see A) measured by using an atomic tip. Obviously, there happens to be a communication in an electrically resonating protein complex in the axon of a neuron whose membrane is resonating a bit later. The Fourier transform of the streams of binary pulses occurring at apparently random time gaps resembled the electromagnetic resonance frequency band measured by us following other routes (Sahu et al., 2013a,b, 2014; Ghosh et al., 2014). This was a surprising observation, and we confirmed this by putting several electrodes and patch clamps simultaneously [Fig. 4(b)], we see live a new form of communication that runs through a pair of neurons and grouping of the resonance frequencies: Molecular biology has not yet incorporated the supremacy of thermal effects (5–6 THz absorption, 22–23 THz emission as noted above), but grouping of peaks or nesting of frequencies is what we have observed over the years when we see 1012 Hz bandwidth of response simultaneously [Figs. 8(a)–8(c)]. Resonance frequency \Peaks groups together activate together," is analogous to the historic \neurons wired together fire together." See the groups of resonance peaks in Figs. 5(c), 5(d), 6(b), 8(d) and 8(e), one could find the existence of triplet of triplet (3 3 ¼ 9) bands. There are various forms of grouping and that is revealed only when we look at the entire frequency bands from micro-hertz to tera-hertz simultaneously. Prior to us, no one looked into the entire em band simultaneously, continuously, so no one saw the complex temporal evolution of resonance band. (Bandyapadhyay, 2016)

The greatest criticism leveled against anyone claiming that Neuroweapons are real, in development and being used is the argument based on scientific refutation of such phenomena being possible. Critics of claims of neuroweapons will point out, for instance, that the EM cannot influence molecular activity, like the use of chemical compounds, or another criticism is that you need Line-of-Sight to target and follow anyone, that these signals cannot keep up or penetrate the many obstacles in their way. These are two of the more common arguments put forward by those invested with denying in any way the reality of Neuroweapons. So, it is without question that there are indeed historical, scientific and social pointers to the reality of these weapons and their use. In this section I have primarily relied on the technical issues to show that the disinformation, and I can only conclude it is disinformation, is patently and easily shown to be false to the critical researcher or interested party.

BIBLIOGRAPHY:

Bandyopadhyay, A. , Saxena, K., Singh, P., Sahoo,P., Sahu, S., Ghosh, S., Ray, K., Fujita, D. (2020) 'Fractal Scale Free Electromagnetic Resonance of a Single Brain Extracted Microtubule Nanowire, a Single Tubulin Protein and a Single Neuron' https://www.mdpi.com/2504-3110/4/2/11

Bandyopadhyay, Anirban, Sahu, Satyajit & Ghosh, Subrata & Ghosh, Batu & Aswani, Krishna & Hirata, Kazuto & Fujita, Daisuke (2013). 'Atomic water channel controlling remarkable properties of a single brain microtubule: Correlating single protein to its supramolecular assembly.' Biosensors & bioelectronics. 47C. 141-148. DOI:10.1016/j.bios.2013.02.050.

Bandyopadhyay, A., Ghosh, S., Sahu, S., Agrawal, L., Takashi, S. (2016) 'Inventing a co-axial atomic resolution patch clamp to study a single resonating protein complex and ultra-low power communication deep inside a living neuron cell.' In Journal of Integrative Neuroscience, Vol. 15, No. 4 (2016) 403-433 World Scientific Publishing Europe Ltd. DOI: 10.1142/S0219635216500321

Bearden, T. E. (1983). 'Excalibur Briefing: Explaining Paranormal Phenomena.' Strawberry Hill Press. https://archive.org/details/excaliburbriefin0000bear/mode/2up

Boldyreva, L.B. (2009) 'About Anatoly Evgenievich Akimov' in Materials of the international scientific conference. Khosta, Sochi, August 25-29, 2009

Болдырева Л.Б. 'Об Анатолии Евгеньевиче Акимове' Материалы международной научной конференции. Хоста, Сочи, 25-29 августа 2009 г. http://www.second-physics.ru/sochi2009/pdf/p34-35.pdf

Caceres, J.L., Wright G., (2018) 'Zika Virus viewed through the Resonant Recognition Model…' EJBZI Vol. 14 (2018) Issue 1 https://www.researchgate.net/publication/330748880_Zika_Virus_Viewed_Through_the_Resonant_Recognition_Model_Unraveling_New_Avenues_for_Understanding_and_Managing_a_Serious_Threat

Cosic, Irena & Cosic, Drasko & Lazar, Katarina. (2017). Tesla, Bioresonances and Resonant Recognition Model. Conference: Second International Congress Nikola Tesla - Disruptive Innovation Volume 1 https://www.researchgate.net/publication/318306399_Tesla_Bioresonances_and_Resonant_Recognition_Model

Geoscan (2016) 'Geoscan Technologies' https://www.raum-und-zeit.com/cms/upload/Consulting/GSS_PPT-_2016-SQUEEZED.pdf (accessed 8/6/20)

Galloway, John (1989) 'The Max factor, Review of "Thinking About Science Ernst Peter Fischer and Carol Lipson" in New Scientist https://www.newscientist.com/article/mg12216593-900-the-max-factor-review-of-thinking-about-science-by-ernst-peter-fischer-and-carol-lipson/#ixzz6Vo5V55x4

Hameroff, S., Penrose, R. 'Consciousness in the Universe' in Physics of Life Reviews 11 (2014) pp. 39–78 https://www.sciencedirect.com/science/article/pii/S1571064513001188

Haisch, B., Ibison, M. (1996) 'Quantum and classical statistics of the electromagnetic zero-point field' Phys. Rev. A 54, 2737 https://journals.aps.org/pra/abstract/10.1103/PhysRevA.54.2737

Kaznacheev, V.P., Mikhailova, L.P., Kartashov, N.B. "Distant Intercellular Interactions in a System of Two Tissue Cultures," Psychoenergetic Systems, Vol. 1, No. 3, March 1976, pp 141-142. https://link.springer.com/article/10.1007/BF00834249

Kernbach, S. (2013) 'Unconventional Research in USSR and Russia: Short Overview' in SSRN Electronic Journal (December) https://www.researchgate.net/publication/259106295_Unconventional_Research_in_USSR_and_Russia_Short_Overview DOI:10.2139/ssrn.4136176

--(2014) 'Highly penetrating' radiation in the West. A brief overview through the eyes of an engineer. Part 2 in International Journal of Unconventional Science | Journal of Emerging Directions of Science Issue No. 6 http://www.unconv-science.org/n6/kernbach2/

--(2015) 'Ochatrin's detector and Akimov's generator: Analysis of devices' (Russsian), IJUS, 9(3), 70-89

--(2015) The use of global telecommunication networks for the transmission of non-electromagnetic effects. in International Journal of Unconventional Science | Journal of Emerging Directions of Science Issue No. 8 http://www.unconv-science.org/n8/

--(2018) 'Quantum Indexing of Entangled Macro Objects' [in Russian] Journal of Unconventional Science no.21-22 (6), pp. 28-42, 2018 http://www.unconv-science.org/n21/kernbach1/

--(2018b). Replication experiment on distant influence on biological organisms conducted in 1986. International Journal of Unconventional Science Issue 32, pg. 41-6 (Russian) English Version: 'Replication experiment on distant influence on biological organisms conducted in 1986' Serge Kernbach International Journal of Unconventional Science Issue E2, pg. 41-46 (2017) http://www.unconv-science.org/en/e2/kernbach2/

--(2018c) Tests of the circular Poynting vector emitter in static E/H fields. In IJUS Issue E2, pp. 23-40 http://www.unconv-science.org/en/e2/kernbach1/

--(2019) Remote Consciousness: Latest Results from Optically Excited Electrochemical Impedance Spectroscopy (Video) Nov 2. 2019 https://www.youtube.com/watch?v=qt7TnR3BNcI

Kravkov, G.A. (2006) 'The Effect of Non-Thermal (Informational) Exposure to Electromagnetic Radiation of Extremely High Frequency on Biological Objects and Humans' Kiev https://img1.liveinternet.ru/images/attach/c/3//3901/3901192_PSIHOTRONNOE_ORUZHIE.doc

Mothersill, Carmen Transmission of Signals from Rats Receiving High Doses of Microbeam Radiation to Cage Mates: An Inter-Mammal Bystander Effect. in Dose Response. 2014 Jan; 12(1): 72–92. Published online 2013 Aug 27. doi: 10.2203/dose-response.13-011.Mothersill https://www.ncbi.nlm.nih.gov/pmc/articles/PMC3960955/

Norseen, John D., Laurie, Duncan 'Outlaw Technology' (2002) published on-line at http://www.duncanlaurie.com/writing/outlaw_technology (accessed 3/6/2019)

Persinger, M. A., Saroka, K. S., Koren, S. A. & St-Pierre, L.S. The Electromagnetic Induction of Mystical and Altered States within the Laboratory. In Journal of Consciousness Exploration & Research, October 2010, Vol. 1, Issue 7, pp. 808-830

Persinger, M., Burke, R. (2013) 'Convergent Quantitative Solutions Indicating the Human Hippocampus as a Singularity and Access to Cosmological Consciousness' in NeuroQuantology 11(1) https://www.researchgate.net/publication/270552657_Convergent_Quantitative_Solutions_Indicating_the_Human_Hippocampus_as_a_Singularity_and_Access_to_Cosmological_Consciousness

Persinger, Michael. (2015). Thixotropic Phenomena in Water: Quantitative Indicators of Casimir-Magnetic Transformations from Vacuum Oscillations (Virtual Particles). Entropy. 17. 6200-6212. https://www.mdpi.com/1099-4300/17/9/6200

Persinger MA, St-Pierre, L. (2015c). The physical bases to consciousness: Implications of convergent quantifications. J Syst Integr Neurosci 1: doi: 10.15761/JSIN.1000111 https://www.researchgate.net/publication/307787426_The_physical_bases_to_consciousness_Implications_of_convergent_quantifications

Persinger, Michael (2002) 'Possible Disruption of Remote Viewing by Complex Weak Magnetic Field Around the Stimulus Site and the Possibility of Accessing Real Phase Space: A Pilot Study' in Percept Mot Skills 2002 Dec;95(3 Pt 1):989-98 https://pubmed.ncbi.nlm.nih.gov/12509207/

Persinger, M., Rouleau, N. , Carniello, T. (2014) Non-Local pH Shifts and Shared Changing Angular Velocity Magnetic Fields: Discrete Energies and the Importance of Point Durations. Journal of Biophysical Chemistry, 5, 44-53. doi: 10.4236/jbpc.2014.52006. https://www.scirp.org/html/4-7100209_45572.htm

Persinger, M. (2015) Thixotropic Phenomena in Water: Quantitative Indicators of Casimir-Magnetic Transformations from Vacuum Oscillations (Virtual Particles). Entropy. 2015; 17(9):6200-6212. https://doi.org/10.3390/e17096200 https://www.mdpi.com/1099-4300/17/9/6200

Persinger, M, Rouleau, N. Tessaro, L., Saroka, K. Scott, M. Lehman, B., Juden-Kelly, L. (2015b) 'Experimental Evidence of Superposition and Superimposition of Cerebral Activity Within Pairs of Human Brains Separated by 6,000 Km: Central Role of the Parahippocampal Regions' in NeuroQuantology https://www.academia.edu/47052247/Experimental_Evidence_of_Superposition_and_Superimposition_of_Cerebral_Activity_Within_Pairs_of_Human_Brains_Separated_by_6_000_Km_Central_Role_of_the_Parahippocampal_Regions

Persinger, M. et al (2015c) 'Cosic's Resonance Recognition Model for Protein Sequences and Photon Emmission Differentiates Lethal and Non-Lethal Ebola Strains: Implications for Treatment' in Open Journal of Biophysics Vol. 5, No. 1 https://www.scirp.org/journal/paperinformation.aspx?paperid=52972

Persinger, M, Karbowski, L., Murugan, N. (2015d) 'Novel Cosic resonance (standing wave) solutions for components of the JAK–STAT cellular signaling pathway: A convergence of spectral density profiles' in FEBS Open Bio 17(1) https://www.researchgate.net/publication/274096152_Novel_Cosic_resonance_standing_wave_solutions_for_components_of_the_JAK-STAT_cellular_signaling_pathway_A_convergence_of_spectral_density_profiles

Puthoff, Harold (1998) 'Communication Method and Apparatus with Signals Comprising Scalar and Vector Potentials Without Electromagnetic Fields' Patent Number: 5,845,220 (45) Date of Patent: Dec. 1, 1998 https://patentimages.storage.googleapis.com/22/08/af/c892bd5ff5433f/US5845220.pdf

Puthoff, H., Haisch, B. (1998) 'Advances in the Proposed Electromagnetic Zero-Point Field Theory of Inertia' Solar & Astrophysics Laboratory, Lockheed Martin 3251 Hanover St., Palo Alto, CA Revised version of invited presentation at 34th AIAA/ASME/SAE/ASEE Joint Propulsion Conference and Exhibit July 13–15, 1998, Cleveland, Ohio AIAA paper 98-3143 https://arxiv.org/pdf/physics/9807023.pdf

Rorvig, M. (2020) OK, WTF are 'Virtual Particles' and Do they actually exist?. In Motherboard: Tech by Vice https://www.vice.com/en_us/article/3az8g3/ok-wtf-are-virtual-particles-and-do-they-actually-exist

Scholkmann F, Fels D, Cifra M. (2013) 'Non-chemical and non-contact cell-to-cell communication: a short review.' Am J Transl Res. 2013 Sep 25;5(6):586-93. PMID: 24093056; PMCID: PMC3786266. https://www.ncbi.nlm.nih.gov/pmc/articles/PMC3786266

Silverstein, Arthur (2009) 'A History of Immunology' Academic Press https://www.sciencedirect.com/book/9780126437706/a-history-of-immunology

Sokolova, V. A. (В.А. Соколова) (2016) 'First Experimental Confirmation for the Existence of Torsion Fields and Prospects of Their use in People's Economy' Russian Physical Society "Journal of Russian Physical Thought," 2016, No. 1-12

Соколова, В. А. (2016) 'Первое экспериментальное подтверждение существования торсионных полей и перспективы их использования в народном хозяйстве' Журнал русской физической мысли. - 2016. - N 1-12. - C.2-64. https://urss.ru/cgi-bin/db.pl?lang=Ru&blang=ru&page=Book&id=124863

Zhigalov, V. A (2009) Materials of the international scientific conference. Khosta, Sochi, August 25-29, 2009 Conference "Torsion Fields and Information Interactions - 2009" Edited by http://www.vixri.com/d/Materialy%20konferencii%20-Torsionnye%20polja%20i%20informacionnye%20vzaimodejstvija%20-%202009.pdf Торсионные поля и информационные взаимодействия - 2009 Материалы международной научной конференции Электронная версия Хоста, г. Сочи 25-29 августа 2009

CHAPTER 9

COUNTERMEASURES: ARE CHANGING ANGULAR VELOCITY MAGNETIC FIELDS A COUNTERMEASURE TO HAVANA SYNDROME AND OTHER PULSED MODULATED FREQUENCY CYBERATTACKS?

1. MEDICAL PATHOLOGY OF NON-LOCAL WEAPONS

In the following I provide documentation on the physics of Aharonov-Bohm Effect weapons technology and neurological effects from these physics as it interacts with the interferometer known as the human brain. This is a review work that provides documentation for the A-B Cybersecurity Device developed to counter non-local weapons. The physiology of those attacked by RF-based weapons in the US Embassy in Havana provides one of the first efforts at medically studying the use of directed waves against a human target. After this I go into the use of entanglement and the physics of entanglement focusing on angular momentum and the utilization of the Aharonov-Bohm effect and Dynamical Casimir Effect, including its Gravitational corollary to the EM version, covering also gravito-electromagnetism- the coupling of gravity and EM, which produces photon emissions which is suggested by some researchers as that along with gravitons as the boson involved in entanglement or deep correlations which is the physical basis of these weapons. Then I show that this work was begun in the Soviet Union and then transferred to the defense industry of the United States of America as well as other NATO members, proliferating into the Black Market. After showing the neurological effects, then understanding the science behind the technology we can then correlate studies on A-B effect regarding Neurological effects to specific areas of the Brain affected in terms of functionality as studied by FMRI and QEEG by the Verma et al and Persinger Group cross-correlated to changes studied in the Havana Syndrome medical studies.

PROFILING A DIRECTED ENERGY ATTACK MEDICALLY SPEAKING HAVANA SYNDROME

Havana Syndrome is a popular term coined to refer to the illnesses experienced by diplomats at the US Embassy in Havana, Cuba in 2016. It is similar to incidents at the Moscow US Embassy of 2.4- 4.0Ghz from 1953 to 1976. Kravkov notes the use of mm waves for biological weapons development starting in the Soviet Union in 1973 (Kravkov, 2006). Another incident was reported in Guangzhou, China also at a US Embassy in 2018. The same illnesses were reported by Russian politician Boris Yeltsin (Kernbach, 2017) in the early 1990s during the break-up of the Soviet Union and attempted coup by Communist Generals. Scientists studying the phenomenon cite microwaves (mm waves) as the culprit; directed-pulsed Radio Frequency weapons. Whereas critics dismiss the use of highly sensitive technology by militaries around the world, calling the situation a case of mass psychogenic illness, which fits well with a disinformation campaign to keep highly classified technology top secret. There is a general pattern of labeling any serious researchers in this area that are outside military control as pseudo-scientists; for instance, see the case of Akimov (see Ch. 8), former Soviet scientist denounced as a pseudo-scientist after disclosure of the Soviet military technology.

Neurologists at the University of Pennsylvania (Verma et al, 2019) studied the brains of embassy staff from the Havana incidents. All professional diplomats and military personnel who complained of the following symptoms:

Balance problems, tinnitus, hearing strange grating noises, headache, hearing loss, memory loss, and nausea.

These symptoms can also occur when working near Radar installations as reported by military technicians since the inception of Radar. Verma et als (2019) Neuroimaging studies focused on the change in white matter and gray matter volumes of the attacked individuals compared to controls the main area affected was the right hemisphere, specifically altering the auditory: Right and Left Superior Temporal Gyrus, Heschl's Gyrus (BA 22, 48); Right Thalamus and visual-spatial subnets: R & L Frontal Gyrus, Superior Frontal Gyrus, Precentral Gyrus (BA 6); R & L Inferior Parietal Sulcus (BA 2, 40, 7); R & L Frontal Operculum, IFG (BA 44,45, 48) R & L Temporal Gyrus (BA 37), also involved in vision is the Cuneus (BA 17). Finding a difference of whole brain white matter volume, regional gray and white matter volume, mainly in the right hemisphere. The Cerebellar tissue micro-structural integrity was damaged. Functional connectivity in the auditory/visual-spatial subnets was reduced.

The study does not address a specific causality although they do believe that some form of pulsed directed microwaves were involved. The researchers note that: "the clinical importance of these differences is uncertain and may require further study." (Verma et al, 2019)

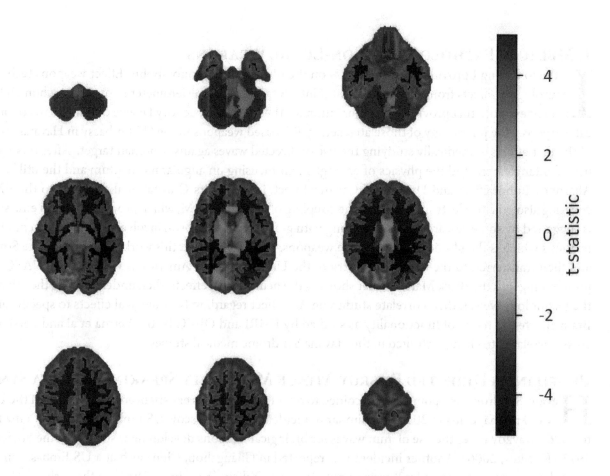

eFigure 3: FDR-corrected group differences on region volumes of the MUSE atlas. Regions which survive FDR correction are displayed on a series of axial slices of the brain, color coded by t-statistic. White matter structures throughout the brain were found to have lower volume in the patient group. Cerebellar gray matter and brain stem structures were found to have higher volume in patients.

(Verma et al, 2019, Supplemental Materials)

As shall be seen later, the area of BA 22 was involved in early Soviet and later Russian research as well as those scientists' employment with western companies such as Lockheed-Martin (see Norseen et al, 1999). An additional area affected was the volume differences between right and left ventral diencephalon, the caudal (posterior) part of the forebrain containing the thalamus, hypothalamus and ventral thalamus and the third ventricle. Further, they found higher mean fractional anisotropy, the property of substances to exhibit variations in physical properties along different molecular axes (i.e. crystals).

In the supplementary information provided in their study Table 7 provides some of the areas of the brain that have high levels of differentiation from the control group.

Brain organelles with large difference from normative values of brain morphology:

- Cuneus, receives visual information from the senses, retina. Broadmann Area 17.

- Anterior Insula, involved in consciousness, salience, emotion, homeostasis, compassion/empathy, taste, perception, self-awareness, cognitive function interpersonal experience-- involved in psychopathology, connects to the Amygdala. Loss of Balance and vertigo in people with lesions in the insula. The posterior insula processes auditory detection, simple auditory hallucinations were elicited by electrical functional stimulation. It has no Broadmann area as it covers a large area. 2 Spontaneous activity fluctuations in anterior insular cortex influence auditory perception. (Sterzer, 2010)

- Putamen, Broadman Area 8, regulate movements at various stages (preparation , execution and influences learning. Neurotransmitters GABA, acetylcholine, encaphalin, dopamine. It receives serotonin, glutamate. It is part of the "hate circuit" along with the insula. In Male-to-Female Trans people this area has significantly larger gray matter.

- Post-Central Gyrus, Broadmann Area 1,2,3. Somatosensory cortex, part of Default Network, contains a sensory strip representing the lower part of the body, contains an inverted map of the contralateral body mirroring the motor strip. Senses touch, pressure, pain, temperature. TMS improves tactile discrimination and reorganizes the somatosensory map, also affects pain modulation.

- Middle Temporal Gyrus (BA 21, part of Temporal Lobe: BA 20,21,22, measured by EEG C4) Functions for object vision, recognition, facial recognition.

- Triangular part of the Inferior Frontal Gyrus (BA 45, part of Broca's Area as cited by Norseen below), part of the IFG: BA 44,45,47 Semantic processing, associated with N400 waves in EEG. Part of the VLPFC (ventrolateral prefrontal cortex) [related to hypnosis, (see Chapter.11 'Hypnosis in Warfare')]. Functions as cognitive control of memory. Language processing. In Schizophrenics this area is distorted. In Epileptics right IFG (EEG F8) is where seizures start.

- Parietal Operculum Broadmann Area 40 secondary somatosensory system Recent data suggest that the parietal operculum acts as an integration center within a multimodal network, originating from different primary sensory and motor cortices and projecting to frontal, parietal and temporal cortical hubs, which in turn govern cognitive and motor functions. Thus, parietal operculum might also play a crucial role in the integrated control of voluntary movement and posture. (Marchese, 2019)

- Supramarginal Gyrus The supramarginal gyrus is part of the somatosensory association cortex, which interprets tactile sensory data and is involved in perception of space and limbs location. It is also involved in identifying postures and gestures of other people and is thus a part of the mirror neuron system. Broadmann Area 40

- Temporal Pole found in the Temporal Lobe complex. The temporal pole is a paralimbic region involved in high level semantic representation and socio-emotional processing. The uncinate fasciculus provides a direct bidirectional path to the orbitofrontal cortex, allowing mnemonic representations stored in the temporal pole to bias decision making in the frontal lobe. Broadmann Area 38

Below, where I present the data on the Brain science involved in studying the effects of A-B weapons, we will see how the Havana Study correlates with Persinger's (et al.) research. Another researcher on A- B weapons is Dr. Serge Kernbach at U. Stuttgart. He remarks specifically on the Havana Syndrome in relation to weapons:

> Can such neurological symptoms occur when the rhythms of biochemical oscillators in the central nervous system are disturbed during nonlocal exposure for several weeks or months? Specialists should answer these questions. (Kernbach, 2017)

The Verma et al study is one attempt to answer this question. He further goes into the Soviet military developers view of these technologies as non-lethal weapons.

Akimov spoke about the possibility of using this technology in a kind of non-lethal weapon (for example, and at the conference 'KGB: Yesterday, Today, Tomorrow'). Taking into account that this experiment is easy to repeat (for example, the script for creating feedback in the 'transmitter' is provided in the paper), we ask ourselves, whether the '1986 experiment' did open the Pandora's box for nonlocal biological technologies?

An unexpected result of this replication experiment represents the potential possibility for a remote monitoring of biological organisms (and possibly non-biological objects). By introducing nonlocal feedback, the object on the transmitter side becomes 'entangled' with the receiver and can thus be nonlocally monitored. It is necessary to set up such an operation of a remote station, which would not affect the monitoring object. This new aspect needs further verification and development. (Kernbach, 2017)

It was the Soviet developers that used the quantum mechanical effect of entanglement to "dose" a target of their technology using the Aharonov-Bohm effect. The creation of the actual tech is well documented and it's transition into the west, including defense industry markets as well as being available in the black market to non-state actors, so that in our day hypothetically anyone from a state (such as Israel) to a private defense contractor (such as SCL Group of Cambridge Analytica fame), as well as terrorist organizations of all styles of the political spectrum, but more so those aligned with the Black International (e.g. UDA, UVF) with sufficient small-scale technical infrastructure, could have the capability to deploy such a weapon.

TECHNOLOGICAL BRIEFING

Soviet Technology in the US National Security Defense Industry

A succinct account is that the development of A-B weapons actually predates the Cold War, with early work begun in this area in the 1920s during the Reichswehr-Soviet Technical cooperation agreement, the Rapallo Agreement. In the 1930s Nazi researchers (according to Soviet researchers) developed the use of remote influencing biological objects with equipment seized during the end of the war, initially begun by Ardenne, who experimented with brain-to-brain transfer of thoughts using EM (Ch.8, Quantum Consciousness for details of Nazi origins and transfer to Soviet Union post war).

Later, the Soviets arrested key nuclear engineers of the Nazi regime and brought them under forced labor to aid the Soviet Nuclear program. Earlier work had been done during the war, including the awareness of the viscosity of deuterium under studying D_2O. A secret weapons development intelligence bureau (Navy Patent and Technology Office, see Ch. 3 for details on Nazi research in remote surveillance) was set up in Berlin during the war that involved one of the founders of Quantum Mechanics, Pascual Jordan, and some of his close collaborators in molecular biology genetics research and the Nazi Nuclear program who were taken to the Soviet Union, Timoféeff-Ressovsky and Karl Zimmer; with expertise in the Nazi Nuclear program in cancer and radiation, altering genes with EM, etc.

Russian researchers trace the origins of the Cold War weapons program which was re-started in the 1950s after Stalin stopped all research in 1937, ruthlessly purging his military just before the war and was diagnosed with schizophrenia, which can also mimic temporal lobe epilepsy; which also as we shall see below match symptoms of A-B effect on the brain when used maliciously. The studies of remote influence on biological objects were first conducted in 1966 by Kaznacheev and another team led by N.D. Devyatkov, who reverse engineered the Nazi generators, and M.B. Golant studying "the resonant response of living biological objects exposed to microwaves (mm waves)," (see Chapter 8). With backward wave lamps or oscillators (Лампы обратной волны) with longitudinal magnetic field linked between Nazi instruments and later remote influencing research at the Soviet Istok (Исток) Institute, which involved captured Nazi scientists in its administration and founding. These oscillators are used as microwave generators in THz range as illuminators for imaging and practically as radar jammers, will they also work against Quantum Radar such as A-B generators? It was also in 1966 that the first Soviet plans for detecting HFGW was formulated by G.A. Lupanov, using capacitors for detectors.

Reflexive Control, Cybernetics and Biology were used to further the weapons program. In the later part of the 1990s the US NSA became interested in Soviet Weapons development using A-B Effect and specifically at injecting 'corrective behavior' using various psychological mechanisms delivered remotely through the transmitters of the A-B Generators. One company contracted to develop American versions of Soviet technology was Lockheed-Martin, which is where engineer Dr. John Norseen, who studied in Russia, was contracted to develop Air Control systems which involved interactions monitored automatically as a means to assist the pilot for safety purposes. His other work with Lockheed-Martin involved the creation of sentient machines (Norseen, 2000) for automation, the creation of 'Thought-Injection' to correct the behavior of terrorists. His ideals of using 'Thought-Injection' were reported in popular publications as well as military publications of the late 1990s and early 2000s, before all talk of this work stopped after being deployed. We are aware of his work by his public statements, papers and conversations with others that were documented such as (Norseen, Laurie, 2002). From these open public sources, we can gain valuable information on how a neurological based weapon could be created.

The following material is different from that presented in Ch.4 ('Lessons from an American Weapons Developer'). Here I drill down into some of the specific areas that Norseen was interested in, in terms of 'Thought-Injection', in which he proposed using radar to inject and monitor the thoughts of the terrorist, his neurobiological interests primarily focused on using Electromagnetism (E x H Fields) to influence the microtubules (MT10 and MT13 types) in the neurons of the brain, which was compiled from brain maps using QEEG working with Soviet Researcher Juri Kropotov of the Brain Institute in St. Petersburg, one of the original centers of research for remote influence in terms of psychology. He coined the term BioFusion as on overarching term relating to the sensor fusion of the human senses.

In a 1999 paper co-authored by Norseen and Kropotov, they studied the visual cortex, one of the main areas affected by the Havana Syndrome. In Norseen's other work (Norseen, 2000) he cites specifically BA 17,18 which is the visual pathway altered in Havana Syndrome. BioFusion as the sensory input is the starting point in understanding how 'Thought-Injection' is accomplished. Norseen has remarked on what is BioFusion: "emergent process of biochemical-induced, electromagnetic E & H [electric and magnetic flux] fields mediated interactions of information with uniquely configured neural structures, and expressed into work via protein reconfiguration [microtubules] under the term BioFusion." (Norseen, 2000) and "Biofusion involves posterior inferior temporal gyri (ITG) [altered in Havana Syndrome] in visual perception modality. The ability to blend vision and verbal modality in the Temporal Cortex, TC-22 and Broadmann's Area 44 [Broca's Area]." (Norseen, 2000). It is interesting that the areas targeted are also areas that were affected by Havana Syndrome. The ability to sense and alter a brain state happens in the microsecond scale, see point durations below, as explained by Norseen:

> The time scale for Bio-Fusion action is remarkably short. The vast majority of the brain executes its portfolio of actions in seconds to tenths, to hundredths of seconds. It is very hard for the brain consciously to concentrate for minutes or hours on end, almost as if in the striatum, our sense of time to dwell, our bio-chronicity is preset for the sub-second regime. Can this be reset? The answer would appear to be yes, if only at least from episodic documentary from periods of altered states and periods of time loss due to dissociative or fugue events.
>
> This also does not preclude that the brain may be engaged in very long term, but non- conscious, mathematical processing. So, what would happen if suddenly, instantly, in a fit of advanced, catastrophic evolutionary rage, that our brain would suddenly operate on a far more distant Time Slope of not seconds and partial seconds, but thought domains of hours, days, years – allowing Sentient Machines to handle the routine reasoning tasks of the lesser Time Limits? Such time-thought testing is now available in Cortical Emulation Research (CER). And where is the dark matter of the brain, the untapped regions that will provide for our future, perhaps even Accelerated Rates of Evolution? The answer may exist at the layer in the anterior cingulate between the older brain, deeper brain and the outer folding top cover of the cortex, as well as in the less knotty, less complicated realm of the right side of the brain – 'The God Spots!' [a reference to Dr. Persinger's work with sensed presences using the God helmet magnetic field generator]. (Norseen, 2000)

It is interesting to note that Norseen specifically mentions the anterior cingulate which is a prime difference between highly and non-highly hypnotizable persons who have a heightened activation in the ACC, He also mentions in other places the connection to the Amygdala, which is enlarged in the highly hypnotizable and in Epileptic patients. The Cortical Emulation Research he is referencing is that of former Soviet scientist Dr. Juri Kropotov. The timings involved come into play in creating modulated phases or frequencies which are used to alter the electromagnetism of the brain. As shall be seen this is the main principle involved in the Soviet A-B Generators. Norseen speaks of magnetism and reconfiguration of proteins, like the microtubules:

…emergent process of biochemical induced, electromagnetic E & H [electric and magnetic flux] fields mediated interactions of information with uniquely configured neural structures, and expressed into work via protein reconfiguration under the term BioFusion. (Norseen, 2000)

Sentient machines, which Dr. Norseen advocates, is a common attribute of being interested in cybernetics along with remote influence of biological objects, seen routinely in Soviet research as well as by Dr. Serge Kernbach who teaches Cybernetics, reminding us that cybernetics is the study of control in the machine and the animal. The primary protein that Dr. Norseen is interested in altering using EM waves is that of the MT10 and MT13 (25nm width, Casimir Effect length) structures in the neurons, damage to MT13 in neurons is associated with Alzheimer's disease, brain trauma and other brain ailments due to microtubule disturbances. In some of his presentation slides (see Laurie 2002) he writes of MT10 (cellular mitosis controller) as an electrical biocomputer, and importantly for A-B effect MT13 as a magnetic bio-computation, which he notes is targeted by potentials as in the A-B Effect.

Pribram speaks of MT as a wave guide, "The intracellular spread of dendritic polarizations can be accounted for by microtubular structures that act as wave guides and provide additional surface upon which the polarizations can act." (Pribram, 1999) Norseen posited the concept of Quantum Shift Keys (QSK) which interacts as a lock-key mechanism to alter MT's. He cites in his work the ideas of Primbram and Hameroff (see, Chapter 8, Quantum Consciousness for detailed discussion), who also worked with former Communist block scientist Dr. Koruga (U. of Belgrade, Serbia, former Yugoslavia), on the ideal of microtubules and Consciousness. Hameroff published with Karl Pribram on the topic in 1994. Brain Holography was the area cited in terms of Pribram as we shall see below, the idea of MTs and neurons goes back to the concept of the Objective Reduction, a gravitational collapse of the wave state created by Penrose and Hameroff, here we see already the role of gravity and gravitons in the collapse as shall be discussed later in relation to the Gravitational Aharonov-Bohm effect and other Soviet research in control using gravitational waves, (See McCarron 2021, 'CH.8 Quantum Consciousness'). The orchestrated reduction according to Norseen takes place in the Neuropil and involves 4 Quanta, a quaternion. Norseen writes regarding the role of QSK and MTs:

….a biofield communication both local and non-local to the protein MT strings. Calpain induced start/stop in the dendritic-synaptic receptors, with varying degrees of glial cells neurochemical nutrient infusion, turn on or off the QSK coded learning sequences in the MT. (Norseen, 1996).

The role of magnetic fields in interstitial water of MTs has been proven by Bandyopadhyay's Group (See Ch. 8 Quantum Consciousness for detailed discussion) in The Materials Science Institute in Japan, interstitial water core of MT acts as a current source, controls internalconductivity and force modulation (jerks or pulses of waves). We see that the QSK is a E-H Field as mentioned by Norseen. It is claimed that human thought can be reduced down to a Krylov sub-space, "the human condition captured in automated krylov space," as Norseen put it (Norseen, 2000).

These calculations were begun by Juri Kropotov in the Soviet Union in the 1980s. Again, it does not seem Norseen has invented these techniques but learned of them for Lockheed-Martin from the original Soviet Communist science researchers. Kropotov has called the collapse of the totalitarian- dictatorship of the Soviet Union "horrible" (Kropotov, 2009). Norseen writes regarding Kropotov's contribution to 'Thought-Injection':

Even more extraordinary, Dr. Kropotov was able to capture the complex adaptive rules of mental functions, perceptual activity across sensory modalities, into software to produce Cortical Emulation Research, by which the same math functions that appear in brains, can now be made to emerge in software. This finding of extreme importance leads us to Information Injection via the introduction or playback of the Inverse Function of the Gabor in Hilbert Space, or whatever other mathematical domain that also may be workable in various species' brains. Thoughts then could be categorized as either culturally dependent, or when synthetically produced, as culturally independent. Both culturally independent and dependent thought means that machines could be produced that could conceivably never be able to communicate with a human. It/they would exist in its/ their own perceptual world made up of its/their own mathematical thought structures. But more likely is that some common, semiotic language of human-machine interests will arise that can universally transform to some degree each particular species, to include synthetic species, into emergent mathematical thought domains." (Norseen, 2000)

The inverse function is similar to experiments aimed at stopping seizures by playing back an EM recording of the patient's brain waves to suppress seizures. The work of Sandyk and Anninos in 1992 attenuated seizures by playing back through EM the intensity and frequency of a magnetic field from the MEG profile of patient, repeated for n=150 other patients successfully (Ye et al, 2019). So, clearly, we can see that the science behind what Norseen is referring to is based on experimental success.

Dr. Kropotov is a world renowned scientist in what has become known as Quantitative Electroencephalography (QEEG); he worked extensively studying various medical conditions of the brain using EEG measuring tools, fMRI, during the late Soviet days Positron Electron Tomography to map the various parts of the brain and their functions. However, when the 'horrible' collapse of the Soviet Union came he found himself, like many scientists who went to the west for employment, working with Karl Pribram in the early 1990s at Radford University. So, we can understand the synthesis of the quantitative methods of Kropotov and those of the holographic brain of Karl Pribram reflected in the writings of John Norseen, a collaborator of Kropotovs.

As mentioned previously, one of the main areas of influence are the visual cortex (BA 17,18) in Thought Injection to be delivered via EM waves, this is also one of the primary areas showing differential measurements in Gray Matter (GM) and White Matter (WM) in the fMRIs of staff affected by Havana Syndrome, see below. Kropotov and Norseen collaborated on a paper in 1999; Norseen lists himself as a Lockheed-Martin employee and uses his work address in this paper. Kropotov previously had come up with the Canonical Cortical Module (CCM), which is a way of dividing the brain into a matrix of 500x500 individual modules, each matrix or module representing functionality in the cortical area of the brain. It is reminiscent of the AI technique Convolutional Neural Networks. The math of the CCM Operators includes encoding all orientations and all possible spatial frequencies which are extracted in the cortical area at a given eccentricity (Norseen & Kropotov, 1999)

Another trade craft gleaned from Norseen's collaboration with Kropotov was that of the use of the Gabor Function, a sinusoid wave windowed with a Gaussian wave where frequency and orientation as well as size of the function can be tuned. Norseen credits his use of the Gabor Function and the Inverse transform at 14Hz to Kropotov (Laurie, 2002), who again worked with Pribram, who comments on Gabor functions:

> During the 1970's it became apparent that Gabor's notation also applied to the cerebral cortical aspect of visual and somatic sensory processing. The most elegant work was done with regard to the visual system. A recent review by Tai Singe Lee in the IEEE casts these advances in terms of 2D Gabor wavelets and indicates the importance of frames and specifies them for different sampling schemes. For the monkey, the physiological evidence indicates that the sampling density of the visual cortical receptive fields for orientation and frequency provides a tight frame representation through oversampling.
>
> The 2D Gabor function achieves the resolution limit only in its complex form. Pollen and Ronner did find quadriture phase (even-symmetric cosine and odd-symmetric sine) pairs of visual receptive fields. (Pribram, 1999)

The Gabor function is used to gather texture or fine detail of object recognition. In another presentation slide Norseen cites the use of hyper spectral analysis, fine detail analysis of spectral lines, which is also preluded by the work of former Soviet military researcher Shkatov in using A-B effect techniques in sensing. Since 2000 they used the method 'torsion [AB] phase portrait' (TPP), торсионного фазового портрета (ТФП)) for remote fine field diagnostics. (Shkatov 2009), claiming to glean potential energy data from EM based media.

Norseen writes about the use of Gabor-Like Functions in Hilbert Space (a dimensional space of at least 3d), citing Pribram:

> Hence, to find a Gabor-Like Function in Hilbert Space as the operant mathematical operation where neural structure interacts with information compressing it from the environment would be the precise math structure that one could use to define the exact moment when Perception occurs from the general state input from or of the Sensory Modalities. A specific Gabor function could then be assigned to each object perceived in the brain. A data base could be built up, a thought code of mathematical expressions that literally is what the brain actually sees when information, like a Bernoulli's code, passes through neural structure. Just as wind under an airfoil produces lift, a Gabor function is the moment when information entering neural structure creates a thought. Such a 'Eureka' moment was discovered in Pavlov's Laboratory in 1996, by Dr. Juri Kropotov and his team. They found

that just as Pribram predicted, when you look at neural structure interacting with signal to noise information from the external environment, that a Gabor-Like Function in Hilbert Space emerges at the exact moment of perception from the sensory field. Based on the work described in this paper, BioFusion R&D findings strongly suggest earlier predictions that human brain perceptual processes represent, at a minimum, an n-dimensional family of interacting Gabor-Like Functions in Hilbert Space (Pribram-91). (Norseen, 2000)

The mathematical representation of human thought for the purposes of sensory fusion enables a cognitive map to be produced. Norseen speaks of the key ability to capture brain EM maps as well as send back via an inverse function either the same or altered information to the brain. He speaks of deceiving the mind to accept these thoughts as one's own, this concept of an A-B Effect injected thoughts not being perceived as alien to one's own thought train is written of by the Persinger Group as well. Norseen comments on inverse function or injection:

> [to dye inject thoughts] in order to fool the brain into accepting it as real. And this inverse injection must also very closely model the exact E and H fields, the EMF shapes that the original Gabor like Function in Hilbert Space.

The connection between EM waves and the ability to alter Hilbert Space is very explicit in the above. The wave patterns injected or QSK of EM waves is directly connected to entanglement or deep correlations by Norseen, the A-B Generators are also based on entanglement, He remarks:

> QSK originates in the Orchestrated Reduction of Quantum *entanglement* at specific EM resonating frequency locations in the protein microtubulin in the neuropil. QSK is then communicated via oscillating and standing waves [solitons] in the neurosynaptic-dendritic region… At certain frequency and energy threshold a combining resonance is established in the brain function that binds the various oscillating brain subresonances into a cohesive sentient pattern. (Norseen, 2000)

Entanglement is created through Angular Momentum and as we shall read later, the Casimir Effect (mentioned by Norseen) in conjunction with A-B Effect. One is able using entanglement to target a brain non-locally through the MTs:

> Cognitive recall is comprised of Gabor Functions in Hilbert Space. The MTs are altered by the magnetic fields of interstitial (within the protein) waters. The wave form specifically targets calpain as Norseen points out: "EM Resonance, then calpain (neuromolecule), then calpain dissipates and a structural imprint of the QSK encoded wave-front interference pattern onto protein [MT] structure." (Laurie, 2002)

Pribram has explained the connection of magnetic fields to neurons in the following:

> To account for these properties we turn to the dendritic membrane and its immediate surround. Dendritic membranes are composed of two oppositely oriented phospholipid molecules. The interior of the membrane is hydrophobic as it formed by "lipids which form a fluid matrix within which protein molecules are embedded - the lipids can move laterally at rates of 2 ~sec; protein molecules move about 40 times more slowly (50 nm/sec or 3 ~tm/min)." Some of the intrinsic membrane proteins provide channels for ion movement across the membrane.
>
> We proposed that a perimembranous process occurs within dendritic compartments during which boson condensation produces a dynamically ordered state in water.
>
> We have gone on to speculate that as each pattern of signals exciting the dendritic arborization produces a macroscopic, ionically produced change of the charge distribution in the dendritic network, it triggers a spontaneous symmetry breaking of a radiation field (a boson condensation) altering the water molecular field in the immediately adjacent perimembranous region. A macroscopic domain of the dynamically ordered structure of water is created in which the electric dipole density is aligned in one and the same direction. It is this domain of dynamically ordered water that is postulated to provide the physical substrate of the interactions among polarizations occurring in dendritic spines. (Pribram 1999)

Earlier it was mentioned that Pribram was a source for the holographic background to Norseen's work; however, it should be mentioned that the use of holography was already developed in the Soviet Union. Holography is a visual field phenomenon as noted by Russian researcher Kaznacheev in work initially begun by him in the 1960s. Again, it should be pointed out that the retina's cones and rods act as cavity resonators or as high-Q antennas. In his patent (Kaznacheev 2004) he and his team engineered a system to pass holograms into the visual cortex but not in the visual range, so it is imageless holography, although it can be modified to also send visual hologram, as he writes "the invention relates to the field of optics and is intended to create a hologram containing non-visualized physiologically significant information that can be used in medicine." (Kaznacheev, 2004). This method is described:

> Method 1. The subject is alternately presented with a holographic image invisible to him, reproduced from the transmissive hologram according to option 1 (Fig. 2a), containing (experimental hologram) and not containing (control hologram) non-visualized physiologically significant information. At the moment of presentation of holograms, physiologically significant biophysical parameters of a person are measured. As physiologically significant biophysical parameters can be used, for example, the characteristics of the electroencephalogram or the parameters of the glow of the fingers in the video recording mode, obtained by the method of computer gas-discharge visualization. In the presence of significant differences in the reactions of the organism between the control and experimental holograms, a conclusion is made about the presence of non-visualized physiologically significant information in the hologram.

This allows both the transmission and reception of holographic information. The transmission of the holograms occurs in the 2.5Hz-3.5Hz, and 10Hz (Alpha) brain wave rhythms. When the brain is presented with a hologram containing non-visualized physiologically significant information it triggers the activation of 10Hz Alpha, which is also mentioned by Norseen. Kaznacheev found upon exposure the 10Hz frequency modulation variant in the EEG locations, with significant difference, in F3, F4 (frontal lobe) and in 01, 02 (occipital lobe) related to the visual pathways, which is noted as suffering under Havana Syndrome.

The work of Gurov dating back to 1976 is of special interest as it relates to Norseen's Thought- Injection. He works with such concepts as the 'Semantic Field of a Person' (семантического поля) using 'psychosomatic radar' (психосоматического радара) and psychoneuroimmuno-modulation which is corrective behavior. Gurov explains this concept in more detail:

> Human communication involves not only verbal and non-verbal signals, but also psychosomatic radar. Psychosomatic radar is a genetically determined frequency of electromagnetic oscillations emitted by the brain, which, complementing verbal and non- verbal communication patterns, sends signals to the environment and perceives signals coming from the environment. With the help of this radar, a person transmits information about himself to the outside and perceives information coming from other people. A. Meneghetti (the founder of ontopsychology) argued that such energetic interaction of people occurs in the semantic field, and the perception of the semantic field allows a person to know about any action, visible or invisible, that is related to him in his environment. This field is a radar given to man by nature. The peculiarity of the psychosomatic radar is that it can be directed both outside (extroverts) and inside (introverts) of a person. We understand the semantic field as the physical field of a biological object (person) with its bioenergetic and energy-informational features, which are revealed semiotically (by certain signs) [семиотически (по определенным знакам)] at the level of kinetic-proxemic communications and which are further interpreted by the operator, establishing a pragmatic connection of signs with the "addressee" and its properties ... Let us consider two patented methods of analyzing the semantic field of a person, which in the "here and now" mode allow us to assess extra-introversion (intentionality), the level of reactivity and the degree of congruence and incongruence of the semantic field of a person. (Gurov, 2016)

It is of note that this is about 'semiotic' or by signs, which is also echoed in Norseen's work.

To summarize, neurons are controlled by the electro-magnetic waves that interact with the microtubules acting as wave guides through the influence of interstitial waters; these microtubules using QSK can be programmed and altered as well as read out using various spectroscopy. In the next section we depart from neurobiology and electromagnetics to focus on the actual physics behind the A-B generators to understand how a profile of a targeted brain or even a piece of hardware could be understood. .

MECHANICS OF AHARONOV-BOHM GENERATORS OF THE SOVIET MILITARY

The means of delivering A-B Effect magnetic potentials is done through the use of generators that use the Aharonov-Bohm effect, referred to in the original and outdated Soviet research as Torsion Fields and referred to in some popular pseudoscience advocates' presentation of this technology. The A-B effect can be used for both local and non-local transmission and reception; this is not a countermeasure to optical-based attacks such as Lasers and LED. The non-local A-B Generator is the focus of this countermeasure, not local transmission. The non-local effect is created through entanglement as mentioned by Norseen above; this is also mentioned in the works of Persinger and Kernbach. In this work I will examine the original Soviet A-B generator, the Akimov Generators (Kernbach, 2017), and I will examine the design of American Physicist Hal Puthoff in his A-B Generator (Puthoff, 1998), then comparing this to the coil system based on a toroid by the Persinger Group (Scott et al, 2015a), who initially experimented with circular arrays of 8 solenoids before switching to toroids (Persinger, 2002 till 2015). It should be mentioned that Akimov Generators were replaced by an LED system by another Soviet military researcher, A.B. Bobrov, who uses lasers (LEDS) to entangle objects (targets) (Bobrov, 2009). An LED-based countermeasure system is the goal of this project after experimenting with toroid coils. In another project I experiment with LEDs and entanglement for biomedical purposes.

ENTANGLEMENT, GAPS AND ANGULAR MOMENTUM

According to physicists the key instrument of entanglement is Angular Momentum (Fickler et al, 2012). In the generators such as Puthoff's there is a mechanism to change angular momentum as well as the rhythm of the frequency output of the generator. Angular Momentum is represented by J. For entanglement this focus is on orbital angular momentum since as Fickler et al argue single photon with helical phase (like the coil toroid) structures may carry a quantized amount of orbital angular momentum (OAM) and their entanglement is important for quantum computation and information science, which aids in quantum remote sensing according to Fickler by using OAM. Stav et al have shown that there is quantum entanglement between spin AM and orbital AM in photons (Stav et al, 2018).

History of the discovery of spin or angular momentum is interesting. The first experiments that became known as being associated with the discovery of spin was that by Stern and Gerlach, both WWI veterans and German nationalists. Walter Gerlach later went on to head the Nazi Nuclear Weapons program and was arrested and detained by the British for a year of interrogations. The Stern-Gerlach experiment settled the question as to what the actual spin configuration was; whereas Bohr thought it binary, Sommerfeld thought it trinary, the experiment proved that it is trinary. Another Nazi involved in the science of spin was Pascual Jordan, whose Jordan Map was key to Schwinger's bosonic model of angular momentum. Jordan was a collaborator of Nazi personnel working in heavy water enrichment taken to the Soviet Union. In the Soviet Union spin (in Russian 'torsion') is used was recognized as the key part to the A-B Generators. This suggests the Soviets inherited their knowledge of Spin Fields from the Nazis, calling it by the term of Torsion Fields, as named by Akimov and Shipov. However, these spin fields are really angular momentum in physics, the coupling of orbital and spin angular momentum. The lasting impact of the Iron Curtain that split eastern science from western science has had a long and deleterious effect on scientific progress.

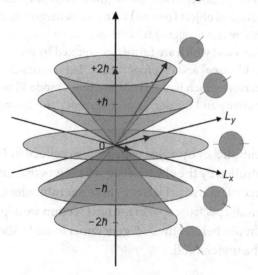

Angular Momentum has a classical context and a quantum context. The classical definition of angular momentum is L = r × p. The quantum-mechanical counterparts of these objects share the same relationship:

L = r × p where **r** is the quantum position operator, **p** is the quantum momentum operator, × is cross product, and **L** is the *orbital angular momentum operator.*

There is another type of angular momentum, called spin angular momentum (more often shortened to *spin*), represented by the spin operator S = (S x, S y, S z). Spin is often depicted as a particle literally spinning around an axis, but this is only a metaphor: spin is an intrinsic property of a particle, unrelated to motion in space. All elementary particles have a characteristic spin, which is usually nonzero.

- Angular momentum cannot be oriented purely in the z axis

- Spin Angular Momentum: quantum number is from a range of 0, ½, 1, 3/2, 2, 5/2. Bosons (Messenger particles) full integer spin. Fermions have half-integer spin.

- Coupling- 2 or more Angular Momentum interactions with each other so the angular momentum can transfer from one to the other (i.e. spin-orbit coupling) transfer of L to S (orbital to spin). (see below)

- Angular Momentum Rotation: the total AM or J characterizes how a quantum system is changed when it is rotated. R is the Rotation Operator

- Conservation of angular momentum states that **J** for a closed system, or **J** for the whole universe, is conserved. However, **L** and **S** are *not* generally conserved. For example, the spin–orbit interaction allows angular momentum to transfer back and forth between **L** and **S**, with the total **J** remaining constant.

TOTAL ANGULAR MOMENTUM IN QUANTUM SYSTEMS

In quantum mechanics, the angular momentum operator is one of several related operators analogous to classical angular momentum. The angular momentum operator plays a central role in the theory of atomic and molecular physics and other quantum problems involving rotational symmetry. Such an operator is applied to a mathematical representation of the physical state of a system and yields an angular momentum value if the state has a definite value for it. In both classical and quantum mechanical systems, angular momentum (together with linear momentum and energy) is one of the three fundamental properties of motion.

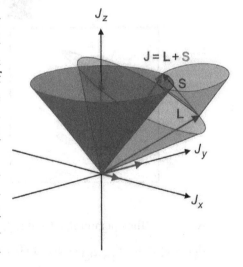

There are several angular momentum operators: total angular momentum (usually denoted J), orbital angular momentum (usually denoted L), and spin angular momentum (spin for short, usually denoted S). The term angular momentum operator can (confusingly) refer to either the total or the orbital angular momentum. Total angular momentum is always conserved, see Noether's theorem.

total angular momentum J = (J x , J y , J z) , which combines both the spin and orbital angular momentum of a particle or system:

J = L + S

the total angular momentum operator characterizes how a quantum system is changed when it is rotated. The most general and fundamental definition of angular momentum is as the *generator* of rotations. More specifically, let R (n, φ) be a rotation operator, which rotates any quantum state about axis n by angle φ. As φ → 0 , the operator R (n, φ) approaches the identity operator, 1, because a rotation of 0° maps all states to themselves. Then the angular momentum operator J is defined as:

$$J_{\hat{n}} \equiv i\hbar \lim_{\phi \to 0} \frac{R\left(\hat{n}, \phi\right) - 1}{\phi} = i\hbar \frac{\partial R\left(\hat{n}, \phi\right)}{\partial \phi}\bigg|_{\phi=0}$$

251

Also notice that R is an additive morphism: R (n , φ 1 + φ 2) = R (n , φ 1) R (n ^ , φ 2); as a consequence

$$R\left(\hat{n}, \phi\right) = \exp\left(-\frac{\imath \phi J_{\hat{n}}}{\hbar}\right)$$

where exp is matrix exponential. And h is Planck's constant.

Often, two or more sorts of angular momentum interact with each other, so that angular momentum can transfer from one to the other. For example, in spin–orbit coupling, angular momentum cantransfer between **L** and **S**, but only the total **J = L + S** is conserved. In another example, in an atom with two electrons, each has its own angular momentum $\mathbf{J}_1$ and $\mathbf{J}_2$, but only the total $\mathbf{J} = \mathbf{J}_1 + \mathbf{J}_2$ is conserved.

The different types of rotation operators. The top box shows two particles, with spin states indicated schematically by the arrows.

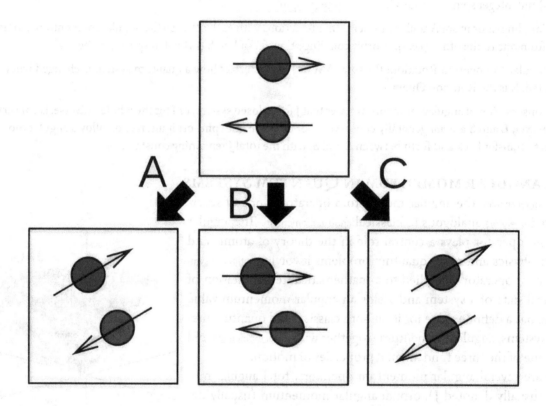

A.   The operator R, related to **J**, rotates the entire system.

B. The operator R_{spatial}, related to **L**, rotates the particle positions without altering their internal spin states.

C.   The operator R_{internal}, related to **S**, rotates the particles' internal spin states without changing their positions.

Thus, we see from this general overview of Angular Momentum and its relationship to Entanglement, that spin and orbital angular momentum come into play with the Aharonov-Bohm toroid, or helical coil generator. So that rotation is related to entanglement, meaning that anything in rotation is entangled, also this could mean that a Closed Timelike Curve (EPR=CTC?) can only occur in rotating spaces so if the universe is rotating it is entangled as a whole, which comes into play with what I call the Persinger Time: the actual entanglement velocity, which Persinger puts at 10^{-23}s/m^{-1}. Persinger et al have found that it takes about 8 minutes for the entanglement process to begin in non-local experiments of the A- B Generators, which he also calculated to be equivalent of the Persinger Time to traverse the universe,

This process is based in transition from virtual particle to real particle involving dark energy, "entanglement velocity involves the ongoing conversion of dark energy as subthreshold ('virtual') photon masses into measurable photon" (Koren, 2015). Virtual particles of the vacuum fluctuations mediate non-local causality (Persinger, 2015), "a transformation of the state of particles occurs when there is a changing EMF that contributes to or defines a boundary condition, Casimir and A-B effectsare at boundary conditions, phase transition is a boundary condition as well. 1 μT increase in Magnetic intensity gives us 2 photon emission at 10^{-18}J (Persinger, 2015).

COUPLING OF ELECTRO-MAGNETISM AND GRAVITY INTO GRAVITO-ELECTROMAGNETICS (GEM)

To understand the mechanics further of the A-B Generators it is necessary to review general theories of Electro-Magnetism and the coupling with Gravito-electromagnetics, as well as a general overview of the Aharonov-Bohm effect and the Casimir Effect, of which for the purposes of biological influence are interrelated as Casimir Effect phenomena are argued to occur in the neurons of the Brain by Persinger et al, Norseen, Bandyapadhyay's Group.

There is a direct relationship between photons and entanglement. Photons the Messenger Boson (spin 1) of the electro-magnetic spectrum are related to entanglement and the graviton. In a study on the A-B Generators it was found that entanglement reflects both the mass and velocity of the electron- wave (photon) duality (Koren, 2016, 3337). As the electron and photon represent the duality, a relationship is related to Gravity through its particle the graviton and the photon. As explained by Koren:

> The ~10^{23} m·s^{-1} value relates the rest mass of the graviton and the rest mass of the photon as intersecting phenomena that may only differ by the proportion of involvement of the entanglement velocity. The product of the upper boundary for the rest mass of a photon (2·10^{-52} kg, the velocity of light (3·10^8 m·s-1) and the entanglement velocity (2.8·10^{23} m·s-1) is 1.7·10^{-20} J. On the other hand, the product of the upper boundary of a graviton is ~2·10^{-65} kg. In this case the square of the entanglement velocity derived from the electric and magnetic energy equivalents of 0.8·10^{23} m·s-1 (that does not involve G) is 4.4·10^{-19} J. This is within the range of the visible wavelength. Clearly if the actual value was 10^{-66} kg for the theoretical graviton, the energy for the emergent photon and graviton would be potentially convergent. This is another support for the quantitative relationship and perhaps identity between the process labeled as Gravity and that labeled as "light" which persistently exhibits the dual properties of wave and particle" (Koren, 2016, 3337).

When an electron shifts Bohr shells it discharges 2 photons of spin-1; a photon is composed of gravitons of Spin 2. An electron is spin ½. So, we see 3 bands of spin involved in entanglement. The interaction between photons and gravity, graviton's identity changes (Spin 2), so it can form the EM properties of photons (spin=1). The electron is a half-concrete (electron) and half virtual particle (photon) as it traverses the Compton Wavelength for the electron orbit.

This shows us the progression through EM-Light (Photon)-Gravity as we shall see below.

MAXWELL EQUATIONS FOR ELECTRO-MAGNETISM (EM)

Maxwell's equations as we understand them today were abridged by Heaveside. The original Maxwell equations comprised dozens of equations, which were simplified by Heaveside to the four main equations below. As far as the potential energy vectors of Aharonov-Bohm effect, these equations were first hinted at in the work of Whittaker in 1904, a one-time astrophysics teacher at the Observatory in Dublin, Ireland.

Here I list the Maxwell Equations for reference. These equations are taken from Gravitational Physicist Raymond Chiao of the University of California at Merced. I reference his work below for the Gravitational versions of these equations as well

$$\nabla \cdot \mathbf{D} = +\rho_e \qquad (36)$$

$$\nabla \times \mathbf{E} = -\frac{\partial \mathbf{B}}{\partial t} \qquad (37)$$

$$\nabla \cdot \mathbf{B} = 0 \qquad (38)$$

$$\nabla \times \mathbf{H} = +\mathbf{j}_e + \frac{\partial \mathbf{D}}{\partial t}, \qquad (39)$$

where ρe is the electrical free charge density (here, the charge density of Cooper pairs), and je is the electrical current density (due to Cooper pairs), D is the displacement field, E is the electric field, B is the magnetic induction field, and H is the magnetic field intensity.

$$\mathbf{D} = \kappa_e \varepsilon_0 \mathbf{E} \tag{40}$$

$$\mathbf{B} = \kappa_m \mu_0 \mathbf{H} \tag{41}$$

$$\mathbf{j}_e = \sigma_e \mathbf{E}, \tag{42}$$

where κe is the dielectric constant of the medium, κm is its relative permeability, and σe is its electrical conductivity (Chiao et al, 2002)

For clarification the field we are mainly interested in is the B (magnetic) Field, which in the quaternion version of the Maxwell Equations of Whittaker is the scalar magnetic Φ usually annotated (A, Φ) for both the scalar part and the vector part.

AHARONOV-BOHM EFFECT

In a 1959 paper, Y. Aharonov and D. Bohm contrary to the conclusions of classical mechanics, the electromagnetic 4-potential (A, Φ), the motion of an electron beam, even in regions where the electromagnetic field vanishes can still affect a particle. Aharonov-Bohm takes hold at boundaries and in macrostructures in phase shifts of matter, "Attributing the Aharonov-Bohm effect to the four-potential A is possible only where the EM field vanishes." (Friedman et al, 2010) The application of the A Vector Potential is based on the work of Whittaker in 1904. As explained by Israeli Mathematician Friedman:

> The Aharonov-Bohm effect is traditionally attributed to the effect of the electromagnetic 4- potential A, even in regions where both the electric field E and the magnetic field B are zero. We argue that the quantity measured by AB experiments may be the difference in values of a multiple-valued complex function, which we call a pre-potential [Persinger's Second Derivative? See below]. The pre-potential is a combination of the two scalar potential functions introduced by E. T. Whittaker. We show that any electromagnetic field can be described by such pre-potential; and give an explicit expression for the electromagnetic field tensor through this potential. (Friedman et al, 2014)

Another important understanding to have of the A Vector is that it is applicable to quantum physics, not classical physics, as indicated by Waechter: In contrast to classical mechanics, where the equation(s) of motion contain only the electric and magnetic field, in quantum mechanics the Schrödinger equation explicitly contains the electromagnetic potentials. This fact was known since the beginning of quantum mechanics, but it wasn't until the publishing of the paper "Significance of Electromagnetic Potentials in the Quantum Theory" by Y. Aharonov and D. Bohm in 1959, that the consequences of this fact received serious attention. (Waechter, 2018)

An electromagnetic four-potential is a relativistic vector function from which the electromagnetic field can be derived. It combines both an electric scalar potential and a magnetic vector potential into a single four-vector.

As measured in a given frame of reference, and for a given gauge, the first component of the electromagnetic four-potential is conventionally taken to be the electric scalar potential, and the other three components make up the magnetic vector potential. While both the scalar and vector potential depend upon the frame, the electromagnetic four-potential is Lorentz covariant.

Like other potentials, many different electromagnetic four-potentials correspond to the same electromagnetic field, depending upon the choice of gauge.

The magnetic vector potential A is a vector field, defined along with the electric potential ϕ (a scalar field) by the equations:

$$\mathbf{B} = \nabla \times \mathbf{A}, \quad \mathbf{E} = -\nabla\phi - \frac{\partial \mathbf{A}}{\partial t},$$

where B is the magnetic field and E is the electric field.

The A-B Effect involves using potential energies at boundaries of EM Fields where the field disappears but not potential energies or what I would call information. In the toroidal and solenoid experiments with A-B Generators of Persinger's Group they work changing phase shifts:

The phase shift of the Aharanov-Bohm effect can be described as:

$\Delta\theta = qVt\,\hbar^{-1}$ (1),

where q is the unit charge, V is the voltage, t is the time or duration within the voltage field and ħ is the modified Planck's constant." (Koren, 2016)

> More specifically, the involvement of an Aharanov-Bohm effect indicates that for phase- modulation or phase shift to occur the average change in voltage must be near the peaks of capacity but not at the peaks of capacity. Consequently, forcing the systems to its limits or maximum boundaries (-5 to +5 V), in addition to distorting the signal, would be above the narrow band pass. This has been observed in our systems. Values below the value would not be sufficient to elicit the effect. Because our signals are constructed from a series of numbers (integers) ranging from 0 through 256 (-5 to +5 V) and pass through the critical zone, perhaps the efficacy of our patterns might be re-evaluated with respect to what proportion of "time" or passes occur within the 4.1 to 4.3 V band. This could be considered a metaphor for the duration within the voltage field." (Koren, 2016)

GRAVITATIONAL MAXWELL EQUATIONS

The Soviet researchers learned that there is a conversion between Electromagnetic Waves and Gravitational Waves, which explains the Soviets' focus on Gravitational Wave-based non-local cybernetic experiments as early as 1967. (see Chapter 6 'Physics of Neuroweapons') A Russian researcher, V. Samokhvalov, continuing on the earlier Soviet research in this area, explains the subtle energies which could be overlooked; he comments:

> According to Einstein's general theory of relativity, the rotating mass field differs from a non-rotating mass field by additional, so-called, gravimagnetic forces, which affect rotating objects. Taking this fact into consideration, it is assumed that gravimagnetic forces act only if they are close to large masses or in presence of masses moving at relativistic speed, and they do not exhibit themselves in nature because of their extremely small values. However, many researchers in their works mentioned facts, which showed significant non-electromagnetic interaction of small objects, rotating at low speeds, with each other and with the objects, surrounding them.
>
> One of the first evidences of such kind was the experiments of Professor N.P. Myshkin, which were carried out at the beginning of the XX century. The effect of change in weight of rotating objects (gyroscopes) and their non-electromagnetic interaction with other objects are described in works by N.A. Kozyrev, V.V. Roshin and S.M. Godin, S.V. Plotnikov, etc. The experimental research... also showed that in nature there is a significant value contactless interaction of rotating small masses and their force effect on closely located objects (masses) at relatively small rotary and linear speeds of rotation. The value of occurring mass-dynamic forces is by 20 orders more than the value of gravimagnetic forces, which act in this case according to general theory of relativity. [see Persinger observation of 20x greater entanglement reactions in his experiments of non-local entanglement]
>
> Experimentally determined non-electromagnetic interaction was called mass-dynamic interaction, because it is determined by dynamic mass rotation, having a variable quadrupole moment. [see Einstein's Gravitational Quadropole equation below] The research, which was carried out, showed non-electromagnetic nature of force interaction, i.e., independence of interaction force effects from electrical conductivity of disc materials and dependence of force interaction value on their rotation frequency. (Samokhvalov, 2016)

The deniers of the scientific reality of this technology, which seems to be an information operation aimed at keeping state-secrets secret, have claimed that this is an EM conductive or thermal effect, this is not what the researchers are claiming, they are claiming that there is a potential EM non- thermal effect, A-B Effect, and that is the basis of the A-B Generators. This is also related to the argument against Thought-Injection or QSK that the magnitudes, here talking about magnetic fields of 1-5μT, are too small in terms of electric conduction, which we see below is not based on experimental findings.

There is another A-B Effect that is not EM based; the equivalent in Gravitational Theory, according to many researchers, including R. Chiao, the gravitational equivalent of the Gravitational Aharonov- Bohm effect. So that one does not as seen need to use Electric force in entanglement experiments but rather potentials can accomplish what force can. Chiao has written of the conversion from Maxwell Equations to Gravitomagnetic Maxwell Equations.

The gravitoelectric field EG, which is identical to the local acceleration due to gravity g, is analogous to the electric field E, and the gravitomagnetic field BG, which is identical to the Lense-Thirring field (Poynting Vector of Magnetic flux), is analogous to the magnetic field B; they are related to the vector potential h in the radiation gauge as follows:

$$\mathbf{g} = -\frac{\partial \mathbf{h}}{\partial t} \text{ and } \mathbf{B}_G = \nabla \times \mathbf{h} , \qquad (43)$$

which correspond to the electromagnetic relations in the radiation gauge

(Chiao et al, 2002)

$$\mathbf{E} = -\frac{\partial \mathbf{A}}{\partial t} \text{ and } \mathbf{B} = \nabla \times \mathbf{A} .$$

$$\nabla \cdot \mathbf{D}_G = -\rho_G \qquad (45)$$

$$\nabla \times \mathbf{g} = -\frac{\partial \mathbf{B}_G}{\partial t} \qquad (46)$$

$$\nabla \cdot \mathbf{B}_G = 0 \qquad (47)$$

$$\nabla \times \mathbf{H}_G = -\mathbf{j}_G + \frac{\partial \mathbf{D}_G}{\partial t} \qquad (48)$$

where ρG is the density of local rest mass in the local rest frame of the matter, and jG is the local rest- mass current density in this frame (in the case of classical matter, jG = ρGv, where v is the coordinate three-velocity of the local rest mass; in the quantum case). Here HG is the gravitomagnetic field intensity, and DG is the gravito-displacement field. Since the forms of these equations are identical tothose of Maxwell's equations, the same boundary conditions follow from them, and therefore the same solutions for electromagnetic problems carry over formally to the gravitational ones." (Chiao et al, 2002)

$$\mathbf{D}_G = 4\kappa_{GE}\epsilon_G\mathbf{g} \qquad (49)$$

$$\mathbf{B}_G = \kappa_{GM}\mu_G\mathbf{H}_G \qquad (50)$$

$$\mathbf{j}_G = -\sigma_G\mathbf{g} \qquad (51)$$

where εG is the gravito-electric permittivity of free space given by Eq. (35), μG is the gravitomagnetic permeability of free space given by Eq. (32), κGE is the gravito-electric dielectric constant of a medium, κGM is its gravitomagnetic relative permeability, and σG is the gravitational analog of the electrical conductivity of the medium, whose magnitude is inversely proportional to its viscosity (Chiao, 2002).

Viscosity and brain structure are reviewed in Ch. 8.

So, it is important to understand there is a gravitational correlate to EM; as shall be pointed out later these potentials exist not in classical scale but quantum scale. It is worthwhile to point out there is a high frequency gravitational wave-based equivalent to this type of remote sensing as adapted see Baker-Li HFGW Military Applications in Ch. 6 'Physics of Neuroweapons.'

EINSTEIN'S QUADROPOLE EQUATION:

To measure the strength of a Gravitational Wave due to the change of masses the following equations were formulated.

Because of symmetry, the quadropole moment (of Einstein's quadropole-approximation equation) can be related to a principal moment of inertia, I, of a mass system and can be approximated by

$$P = -dE/dt \approx -G/5c^5 \, (d^3I/dt^3)^2 = 5.5 \times 10^{-54} \, (d^3I/dt^3)^2 \quad \text{watts.}$$

In which -dE/dt is the generated power output of the GW source, P is in watts, c is the speed of light, G is the universal constant of gravitation, and d^3I/dt^3 is the third time derivative of the moment of inertia of the mass system. The GW power is usually quite small because of the small coefficient multipliess. (Baker, 2010, 20)

The GW frequency is 2ω or twice the orbital frequency ω. That is, for ever period of an electron the graviton is 2x, twice the frequency of the electron. Following for a one-meter-long rod spun so fast as to nearly break apart due to centrifugal force, the radiated GW power is only 10^{-37} watts.

See below for R. Chiao et al treatment of Einstein's GW Quadropole equation by modifying it.

One sign that there may be a Gravitational component to the A-B generators is that Kernbach (2017) noticed that energy collected near the tip of the A-B Generator cone. This axial radiation in the z-coordinate (tip point direction) could be explained in that GW radiation is concentrated in the angular portion of rotation, near the axis, which suggests the ability to emit the GW with directionality.

GRAVITATIONAL AHARONOV-BOHM EFFECT

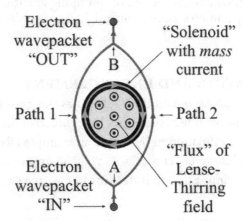

Figure 1: (Color online) Sketch of a gravitational Aharonov-Bohm effect. A "solenoid" with circulating mass currents (in blue), produces "flux" (black dots) of a certain "gravito-magnetic" field (the Lense-Thirring field) in its interior (in yellow). In its exterior (in white), this field is zero. Nevertheless, an electron wave packet (in red), which is split at point A to go around the "solenoid" via paths 1 and 2, and then recombined at point B, will exhibit an Aharonov-Bohm fringe shift.

As mentioned above there is based on gravito-electromagnetics (GEM) also a gravitational Aharonov-Bohm effect. R. Chiao explains that:

…mass currents in a cylindrical superconducting (SC) mass shell (indicated in black in Figure 1), could be produced by rotating the shell at a constant angular frequency around its cylindrical axis. The two partial waves could then be recombined into an outgoing single-electron wave packet at point B by means of another beam splitter. Just like in the purely electromagnetic AB effect, the "flux" of a certain gravito-magnetic field (i.e., the Lense-Thirring field) would be confined entirely to the interior region (indicated in yellow in Figure 1) of the "solenoid," and would vanish at all points in its exterior (indicated in white). There results a quantum mechanical AB fringe shift due to the "flux" that is observable at point B, which cannot be explained classically. (Chiao, 2013)

Bg is the Lense-Thirring Field or the magnetic flux in the interior of the solenoid pictured above, which is an analog to the solenoids used in Persinger's non-local experiments till 2015. However, the real difference here is the Angular Momentum as explained:

…if one thinks of the "solenoid" as a rotating SC [super conductor] cylindrical mass shell, the experiment has two independent parameters, namely, the linear mass density, and the angular velocity of the shell. That means one could shift the interference fringes by changing the angular velocity. Since the gravito-electric field from the mass of the shell does not depend on the angular velocity, a fringe shift will happen despite the fact that the classical force has not changed. Hence the AB fringe shift in the gravitational case could not have had a classical origin. (Chiao, 2013)

In an analog to the EM Maxwell equations the A vector potential is equivalent to magnetic field B. In gravitational theory, h is the magnet-like gravitational vector potential, so you can think of h as like A. Vector Potential (h) can arise either from a Lense-Thirring field, or from rotations of a quantum system, such as from a rotating SC ring (solenoid, toroid). Experiments with rotating SC rings are easier to perform than those with Lense-Thirring fields. Phase shift occurs in this experimental setup, "The phase shift, which is nonvanishing for the "solenoid" configuration of Figure 1, is the gravitational AB phase shift. It is closely related to Berry's phase, since both phases have a common origin in non- Euclidean geometry." (Chiao, 2013, 6)

$$\Delta\phi_{tot} = \frac{q}{\hbar}\oint_C \mathbf{A}\cdot d\mathbf{l} + \frac{m}{\hbar}\oint_C \mathbf{h}\cdot d\mathbf{l} = \frac{q\Phi}{\hbar} + \frac{m\Phi_g}{\hbar}$$

In eq. 33 (Chiao, 2013), these quantum currents can be the quantum mechanical sources of time- independent A and h fields that give rise to the AB effect. (Chiao, 2013, 7)

Chiao further speculated that a gravitational version of "pumping gravitons out of the vacuum" via parametric amplification, and above threshold, parametric oscillation, might be possible. The analog of a laser for gravitational waves could thus be constructed.

CASIMIR EFFECT, GRAVITATION AND ENTANGLEMENT

The vacuum oscillations/fluctuations or what others refer to as the Zero Point Energy field (ZPE) (Norseen, 2002) is interfaced with the Casimir Effect. Scientists have directly related entanglement with the Dynamic Casimir effect of which accelerating modulation or 'jerks' are an example (Romauldo, 2019) as we shall read further. Romauldo et al found that the Casimir effect produces a high degree of entanglement, and study that process. Felicetti et al study the Dynamical Casimir Effect in its relation to creating entanglement in bipartite and multipartite entanglement among qubits.

> The existence of vacuum fluctuations, i.e., the presence of virtual particles in empty space, represents one of the most distinctive results of quantum mechanics. It is also known, under the name of dynamical Casimir effect, that fast-oscillating boundary conditions can generate real excitations out of the vacuum fluctuations. Long-awaited, the first experimental demonstration of this phenomenon has been realized only recently, in the framework of superconducting circuits [C. M. Wilson et al. Nature 479, 376-379 (2011)]. (Felicetti, 2013)

For our purposes the Dynamical Casimir Effect (DCE) is of interest as this is the corollary to the work involved with the A-B generators, the pulsating modulation of magnetic amplitudes, which is what a DCE is an equivalent of a generation of photons from vacuum due to the motion of uncharged boundaries.

Raymond Chiao of University of California-Merced has proposed the concept of a gravitational laser based on the DCE which we can use to see how pulsations are conducted in the EM version of our toroidal coil, the A-B Generators. (Chiao, 2017) Many would consider gravitational amplitudes to be so minute that it could never be possible to generate or detect based on their understandings of Einstein's [Quadropole] equations for Gravity.

However, Chiao introduces a Planck scale mechanism which argues for the ability to generate and detect gravitational effects in the laboratory. He introduces the ideal of "relative gravitational permeativity" which is analogous to EM electric permittivity and magnetic permeability, hence 'permeativity', as G is, stands in for E and M. Permeativity, argues Chiao, allows for a possibly large quantum mechanical enhancement of the response of a superconductor, such as the solenoid or coil, to an incident tensor gravitational wave field." (Chiao, 2017)

The group has also argued that the quantum amplification process in the DCE is equivalent to the amplification process in a parametric amplifier (paramp). Chiao et al point out that in Einstein's quadropole equations, used for figuring Gravitation, that the Planck Constant, the quantum of electromagnetic action that relates a photon's energy to its frequency ($h= 6.62607015×10−34$ J•s in SI units), is absent which he modifies to include, placing the equations in a quantum level of existence rather than classical scale. Meaning that Gravitational Waves on the quantum scale (Planck Length 10-33 cm) has greater force then anticipated by the Classical gravitational force. This directly addresses the issues of the assumption by many scientists that none of this is possible due to the low Lorentz forces involved in Electromagnetic force. This is addressed by Dotta when studying Long Term Potentiation in neural networks:

> The primary effect upon the shift of the spectra power density of the photon emissions following the modified LTP magnetic field exposure suggests that the temporal geometry of the applied field interacts with the temporal pattern of the photon emissions. Pattern is often associated with information and does not require significant addition or subtraction of energy from the system. As succinctly summarized by Cifra et al. [13], a shift in the rate of temporal patterns by which energy is emitted rather than induced by the applied magnetic fields minimizes the counterargument that their intensities are too small to overcome the kT values associated with intrinsic thermal oscillations.(Dotta et al, 2014)

It is an important point to understand this when faced with criticisms regarding the lack of sufficient strength from the A Potential Vector and its GEM analog. This question of low amplitudes affecting biological objects was also addressed by Djumeava in her studies on using A-B effect to transmit medicines remotely:

> In the recent decade, low level laser (LLL) therapy has been used to treat various diseases. The question about how the energy from low level lasers works at the cellular and organism levels is still disputable. In 1977 A.C. Tam and W.Happer showed experimentally that two circularly-polarized laser beams attract or repel depending on mutual orientation of their circular polarization. If the direction of rotation of polarization of the two laser beams is similar, then these beams attract, and if the rotation of polarization is opposite, then they repel. These results collided with quantum electrodynamics and could not be explained. Study conducted by
>
> A. Bobrov demonstrated the presence of non- electromagnetic component of laser beam which doesn't shield by electromagnetic screen and spreads in the direction of laser beam's distribution. In 2012 M.Krinker showed a bio-physical similarity between spinning fields and information imprinted in special carriers. According to the data obtained by the authors of Russian patent, when the spiral light-guide is twisted from the right to the left, the effect of strengthening mitosis in the cells exposed to the non-electromagnetic properties of laser radiation was observed, whereas the light-guide spiral twisting from the left to the right leads to strengthening of synthesis of protein and carbohydrates. In M. Krinker's experiments a maximal growth of cell took place in case when they were exposed to the counterclockwise field. In our case we also utilized the device with the counterclockwise light-guide. (Djumeava, 2004)

It is argued by Persinger that the Minkowski space becomes one space through the irrelevance of time (t):
(Persinger Group Presentation at 2016 The Science of onsciousness Conference, organized by Stuart Hameroff)

Minkowski Space

$$u \cdot v = \mp [\, c^2 t_1 t_2 - x_1 x_2 - y_1 y_2 - z_1 z_2 \,]$$

→ Synchronization of magnetic spaces (assuming active quantum process) allows cancellation of t, implies spatial homogenization (i.e. non-locality)

(Persinger Group Presentation at 2016 The Science of onsciousness Conference, organized by Stuart Hameroff)

In other words, through entanglement, time becomes irrelevant and locality also become irrelevant with the ability to have separate spaces interact through entanglement.

ANALYSIS OF THE A-B GENERATOR POYNTING VECTOR

> "This experiment, based upon physical principle, suggests there is a technology that can generate reliable excess correlation of brain activity (and potentially consciousness and specific experiences) between two [or more] people separated by thousands of kilometers." (Scott, 2015)

The A-B Generators use what is known as a Poynting Vector in EM engineering to accomplish its transmission of potential energies to a receiver or target. Dr. Serge Kernbach has studied the A-B Effect Poynting Vector Emitter (PVC) in terms of non-local interactions between an emitter and a receiver or target, he reconstructed the generator built by Akhimov and conducted measurements in experiments to understand the phenomenon.

Fig. 3. One of the SAG constructions used in 80s and 90s.

The Poynting Vector can be inferred to discern the direction the energy is moving within space-time. Poynting vector (S = E x H) represents the directional energy flux (the energy transfer per unit area per unit time) of an electromagnetic field. The SI unit of the Poynting vector is the watt per square metre (W/m2). It is named after its discoverer John Henry Poynting who first derived it in 1884. Oliver Heaviside also discovered it independently in the more general form that recognizes the freedom of adding the curl of an arbitrary vector field to the definition. The Poynting vector is used throughout electromagnetics in conjunction with Poynting's theorem, the continuity equation expressing conservation of electromagnetic energy, to calculate the power flow in electric and magnetic fields.

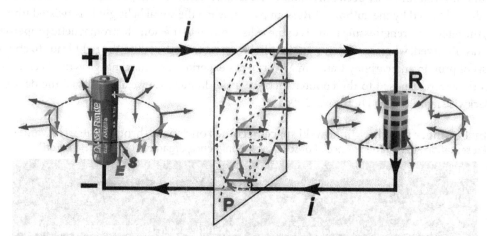

A DC circuit consisting of a battery (V) and resistor (R), showing the direction of the Poynting vector (S, blue arrows) in the space surrounding it, along with the fields it is derived from; the electric field (E, red arrows) and the magnetic field (H, green arrows). In the region around the battery the Poynting vector is directed outward, indicating power flowing out of the battery into the fields; in the region around the resistor the vector is directed inward, indicating field power flowing into the resistor. Across any plane P between the battery and resistor, the Poynting flux is in the direction of the resistor. The magnitudes (lengths) of the vectors are not shown accurately; only the directions are significant.

There are 2 types of EM oscillation: *harmonic-* E/H vary according to sine and cosine law. *Modulated-* amplitudes frequency or phase vary according to a law. In the case of the toroid coil system, we are dealing with a modulated amplitude frequency device. A-B Generators use orthogonal ExH fields to generate Poynting Vector (S) which is rotating due to shielding; only the torsion [AB effect] component is emitted out through the copper cone" (Kernbach, 2017). The Poynting vector is a planar wave sent out in the x-axis.

Kernbach points out the relationship of angular momentum and force created by the generator:

> Although only static electric and magnetic fields exist, the calculation of the Poynting Vector gives a circular flow of EM energy clockwise [coil is wound cw, Persinger is ccw] The flow of circulating energy underlies the popular idea of 'rotation' of the S (Poynting) vector which is located in the axial plane (the circulating energy flow contains the angular momentum and creates the magnetic component of the Lorentz force arising when the capacitor is discharged. (Kernbach, 2017)

The generators studied by Sokolova (2016), who worked with this technology from at least 1982, have 3 modes of operation:

- negative (turns ordered field into a completely disordered distribution of curves, the curves are preserved.

- a positive transition.

- The zero channel, or neutral, is the channel that carries information with very low force and energy, the 'psi' channel. It should be noted that Russian researchers such as Sokolova cite the gyromagnetic 'spin-wave', as well as the A-B effect in these generators.

An gyromagnetic effect arising from the relation between the angular momentum and the magnetization of a magnetic substance. It is the effect which is exploited in the measurement of the gyromagnetic ratio of magnetic materials. The gyromagnetic effect is demonstrated by a simple experiment in which a freely suspended magnetic substance is subjected to a magnetic field. Upon a change in direction of the magnetic field, the magnetization of the substance must change. In order for this to happen, the atoms must change their angular momentum. Since there are no external torques acting on the system, the total angular momentum must remain constant. Thus, the sample must acquire a mass rotation which may be measured. In this way, the gyromagnetic ratio may be determined. Two common methods of determination are the Einstein-de Haas method and the Barnett method. (Abrahams et al, 2019)

SYNCHRONIZATION OF EMITTERS AND RECEIVERS

Researchers have noticed that non-local transmitters and receivers have synchrony, develop the same rhythmic patterns, though driven at different times by local forces. One of the phenomena observed in use of these generators by both Kernbach and Persinger is the synchronization of the emitters, in Kernbach's case the Akimov Generator, in Persinger's the use of a circular solenoid and a circular toroid. Kernbach remarks, "It is assumed, as a working hypothesis, that the well-known synchronization effect of coupled oscillators with weak (nonlocal) coupling plays here a key role." (Kernbach, 2017, 37)

He further points to entanglement as the reason for the synchronization, "synchronize emitters and receivers. Here an analogy with the well-known phenomenon of quantum entanglement is assumed. The long-range spin-spin interactions are [a] well established research topic." (Kernbach, 2017) Here he directly mentions the spin theories of Akimov which we know to be the normative physics concept of angular momentum. Another issue related to synchronization was the uptick in responses in detection of AB potentials in sensors when using a desynchronized rhythm, "increasing reaction of sensors was accomplished when frequency desynchronizing between 2 generators increase sensor response." Like Persinger, Kernbach found that there is a connection to [the] 7 to 8 minute gap between initiation of the field and onset of 'entanglement' like activities. Kernbach remarks "there is a 7-8 min delay between emitter turned on and reaction through proton tunneling." (Kernbach, 2017). Here Kernbach, like Persinger, finds a connection to proton tunneling, which in biochemical terms would be the Ca^+ ion mentioned by Norseen for neurological reactions, membrane channels for positively charged ions.

A further example of an Aharonov-Bohm Generator was that designed by American physicist Hal Puthoff, a former researcher at Stanford Research Institute, where also early Remote Viewing experiments were conducted, such as with Ingo Swann, who was tested by Persinger and the basis of the experiment that led to the conclusion of Persinger that remote viewing could be blocked (Persinger, 2002). This generator is different from the Akimov generator in that it uses angled shields for changing the angular components controlling frequency of the signal. Puthoff defines this invention as, "A method of transmitting information that changes as a function of time comprising transmitting a signal having scalar and vector potentials (A, phi) without including an EMF, the signal varying as a function of time in accordance with the information." (Puthoff, 1998)

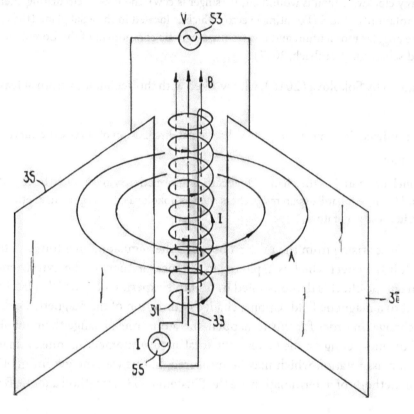

(Puthoff, 1998)

As can be seen here the coil used in this system does not have a larger base and then condense as it coils in the z axis. This coil has a constant width, which is also used in another version of the generator according to Puthoff, where he uses two toroid coils (patent item #85,87); these coils are the equivalent of the system used by Persinger et al from 2015. Puthoff instructs on how the coils work, "A-B generator coils #85,87 are driven in parallel by current source, currents are time-derivative phased and adjusted in amplitude to provide a time varying (A, phi) signal [potentials] having no EM component in the same planes as (A, phi) signal radiates." (Puthoff, 1998) Persinger in his work with these coils has defined based on Tu (2005) phase and group velocities that he describes as:

> group velocity- bulk movement of the field around the circle (coil or solenoid array) phase velocity- temporal configuration (rhythm) irregular frequency shifting pattern within the bulk movement.

Which we can see correspond to that which is mentioned by Puthoff. The key ingredient here is that there is no EM Field in the plane of the transmitted signal comprised of potentials:

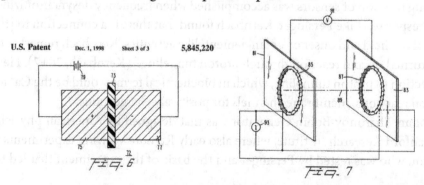

The coils are time derivative (phase velocity) phased and adjusted in amplitude (group velocity) providing a time varying (A, phi) signal having no EM component in the same planes [horizontal, Y coordinate] as the (A, phi) signal radiates. In the countermeasure we are using just one of the coils since we have no need for entanglement with another since it encompasses one object (see Lehman, 2015). The toroid coils are able to induce changes in interference patterns as explained by Puthoff, "it is shown that in certain two-leg electron-interferometer configurations in which the potentials (A,phi) are establish in a regional space, but E and B are absent, it is still possible for the potentials to induce changes in electron quantum interference patterns." (Puthoff, 1998)

As one examines the coil, it is clear that what we are looking at is really a helical structure; as the wire wraps around the hoop it creates an analogous DNA helix around the circle. The use of a helical structure is also performed in the HFGW detector/transmitter of Baker-Li (Baker, 2010).In this case he is citing the use of FBARs (which are already miniaturized in mobile phones), used to detect gravitational waves according to Baker. Persinger remarks how this relates to entanglement angular momentum "[Graviton] the involvement of a (closed) circular geometry moving in a direction (a helix) around an infinite but bounded perimeter is important single photon with helical phase structures [that] could carry a quantized amount of orbital angular momentum." (Persinger, 2013).

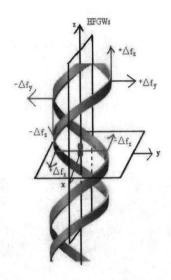

Figure 1.1.4. Double Helix Configuration of FBAR Pairs (Patent Pending)

According to Baker the Poynting Vector is the x-axis and propagates in both directions. His Gravitational Wave Poynting Vector is known as perturbative photon flux (PPF), (Baker, 2010, 29). HFGW are directed along the z-axis.

The perturbative photon flux (PPF), which signals the detection of a passing gravitational wave (GW), is generated when the two waves (EM and GW) have the same frequency, direction and phase. This situation is termed "synchro-resonance."

These PPF detection photons are generated (in the presence of a magnetic field) as the EM wave propagates along its z-axis path, which is also the path of the GWs,

2. The magnetic field is in the x-direction. According to the Li effect, the PPF detection photon flux (also called the "Poynting Vector") moves out along the x axis in both directions.

3. The signal (the PPF) and the noise, or background photon flux (BPF) from the Gaussian beam have very different physical behaviors. The BPF (background noise photons) are from the synchro-resonant EM Gaussian beam and move in the z-direction, whereas the PPF (signal photons) move out in the x-direction along the x-axis. (Baker, 2010, 29)

Dr. Baker and his team at GravWave LLC have also developed an interest in gravitational waves and the human brain hoping to use understanding from gravitation brain (Bar, 2007) for exobiological detection of life, as well as the direct brain-to-brain transfer capabilities as a communication device. Their work is at exobiologie.com. This work is based on the theories of Israeli physicist, Daniel Bar, of Bar Ilan University who came up with the insight of gravitational brain waves as quantum fluctuations and stochastic quantization, viewing the brain as an EM structure that is also capable of detecting and transmitting GW.

> That is, one may physically and logically assume that just as these ionic currents and charges in the brain give rise to electric waves so the masses related to these ions and charges should give rise, according to the Einstein's field equations, to weak GW's. From this we have proceeded to calculate the correlation among an n brain ensemble in the sense of finding them at some time radiating similar gravitational waves if they were found at an earlier time radiating other GW's. We have used as a specific example of gravitational wave the cylindrical one which has been investigated in a thorough and intensive way... (Bar, 2007)

Detractors again point out that these GW's would be too small to be of biological significance, to which Chiao has addressed the scale issue not being the classical Quadropole Gravity equations but a quantum gravitational equation with the addition of permeativity on the Planck scale.

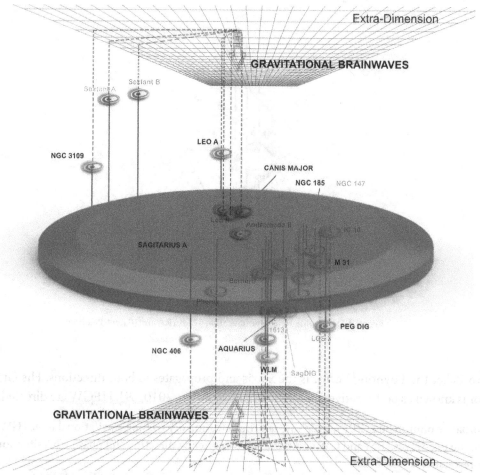

Baker-Woods endeavor to use gravitational brainwaves to search for extraterrestrial life. exobiologie.org/

THE DARK SIDE OF THE POYNTING VECTOR

In a follow-up study in 2018, Kernbach replicated the experiments of Akimov done in the Soviet Union in 1986 dealing with the remote influence of biological objects. In these experiments Kernbach looked at how to monitor a remote biological object. He points out that it is possible to use the experimental setup for monitoring the object via remote non-local technology. Kernbach remarks on this reality, "An unexpected result of this replication experiment represents the potential possibility for a remote monitoring of biological organisms (and possibly non-biological objects). By introducing nonlocal feedback, the object on the transmitter side becomes 'entangled' with the receiver and can thus become non-locally monitored." (Kernbach, 2018, 46).

He was able to base his understandings with the Z-score in the spectroscopy aspect of the experiment on the documentation provided by Akimov in the original 1986 experiment. Through the Z-score monitoring is accomplished: "The statistical Z score was calculated based on the EIS [electrochemical impedance spectroscopy] dynamics of this channel. Thus, the nonlocal address mark was involved in the feedback loop [allows remote monitoring], both in terms of impact and measurement." (Kernbach, 2018, 43).

One further issue noted by Kernbach was the use of Akimov of such ideas as universal addressing of entangled objects, "Akimov vague allusion 'special spin (torsion) address matrices" (Kernbach, 2018). Kernbach has written of mapping entangled objects so it is not out of the question that it may be possible to have a matrix of entanglement that could potentially be searched and indexed via AB Effect type technology that Kernbach has claimed the Soviet Union was interested in for use in mass control.

Other efforts at using A-B Effect technology in Russia is the use of a method known as 'torsion phase portrait' (TPP) торсионного фазового портрета (ТФП)) for remote fine field diagnostics. Shkatov in 2009 speaks of the automation of TPP, "the TPP method and its extensions are continuously developing both in instrumental and methodological aspects. It is planned to develop an automated software hardware complex for unmanned periodic TPP, a kind of TPP object monitoring." (Shkatov, 2009)

Skin as Input System to the Brain

Another interesting concept in remote monitoring is that of the Israeli team Feldman, et al (2009), which has proposed remote sensing based on the helical and aqueous nature of sweat ducts for monitoring:

> The simulation and experimental results are in a good agreement and both demonstrate that sweat ducts in the skin could indeed behave as low Q antennas. Thus, the skin spectral response in the sub-Terahertz region is governed by the level of activity of the perspiration system and shows the minimum of reflectivity at some frequencies in the frequency band of 75-110 GHz. It is also correlated to physiological stress as manifested by the pulse rate and the systolic blood pressure. As such, it has the potential to become the underlying principle for **remote sensing** of the physiological parameters and the **mental state of the examined subject**. (Feldman, 2009) [emphasis added]

Again, this was a research area originally broached by the Soviet Union then exported to the west like UK-USA and Israel. The use of skin sensing for remote monitoring is of interest as another example of natural toroids within the human body, such as DNA, MTs, etc. Sweat ducts are helical conductive tube structure – homochirality (90% right-handed turning direction) which is a dipole antenna like the human eye. Skin is the largest organ of the body, designed as the primary interface, utilizing numerous interactions between us and our environment. The low Q duct antenna which is a 2D antenna array with sub-THz (e.g., 110GHz) range with electrical conductance in the Extreme High Frequency (EHF) range. There is fast proton hopping though distributed H-bond networks along the duct surface, with a time for transport of 10^{-13} sec. Difference in pH between skin surface and dermis creates a concentration gradient which is a cause of fast current in the duct coil. There are questions that do come up with remote monitoring through the skin, as well as any light-based system of monitoring such as optogenetics, and that is the question of skin tone.

AI has proven to have difficulty with darker skin colors, biology and light-based technologies as well as the sun itself affect different skin tones differently. The difference is in radiation absorption. There is a case of those with Ephelides (Freckles) like 20% of Ireland, Scotland and Wales, who have a different melanin composition from most people, where the melanin is usually eumalanin, for darker colors, those with red/brownish hair and freckles have a different form of melanin, pheomelanin, arising with the MC1R, IRF4, BNC2, OCA2 gene adaptation which gives red hair and rust colored freckles, though it offers no UV protection, it is also different in that it contains Sulfur, hence easy burning of Irish, Scots and Welsh where up to 50% of the population carry at least one of these gene markers for pheomelanin, it also allows very little absorption of UV-A, and other emissions, such as X-Rays which are used for behavioral control of neurons (Yamashita et al, 2021) . Those with eumelanin have an increased absorption of UV and visible light spectrum; eumelanin has increased absorption due to higher molecular weight (Ou-Yang et al, 2004).

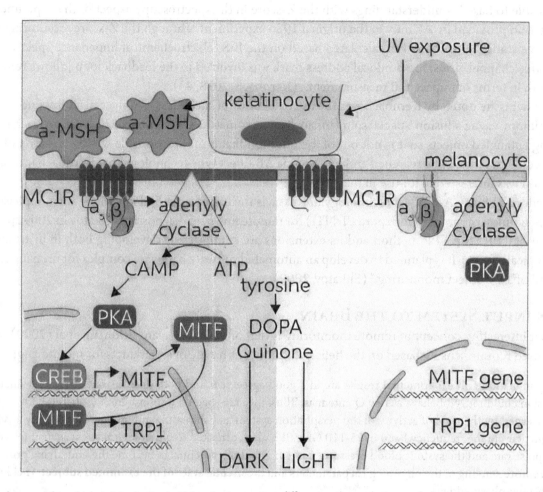

https://www.chegg.com/learn/biology/introduction-to-biology/mc1r-gene two different pathways between dark eumelanin and light pheomelanin

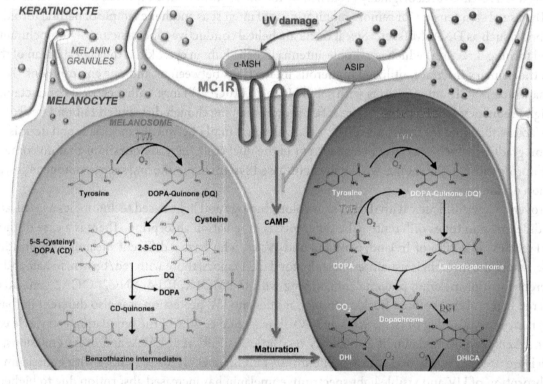

https://www.ncbi.nlm.nih.gov/pmc/articles/PMC4299862/

Due to this difference there are two separate pathways for absorption of EM through the skin as Ou-Yang explains:

> Finally, the photostability of pheomelanin is different from that of eumelanin. Both absorption mechanisms tend to drop following UV-A exposure for pheomelanin. We therefore suggest that eumelanin and pheomelanin could be differentiated according to their spectral responses to UVA irradiation." (Ou-Yang, 2004)

One important note regarding the generation of melanogenesis and melanosome production from melanocortin (POOMC) then alpha MSH and ACTH, ACTH is part of the Hypothalamic pituitary- adrenal axis, produced in response to biological stress. The hypothalamus is noted as a key ingredient to Havana Syndrome-like effects as noted by researchers such as Persinger. One obscure connection was the use by Nazi Scientists of adrenalin to change the Iris color during their experiments with victims of the Holocaust. It is noted that the iris and choroid contain melanin, and also pheomelanin and eumalanin play a role in the eyes.

Pheomelanin Chemical Composition (note Sulfur)

A new material has been created by swapping out sulfur in Pheomelanin for selenium (Cao et al 2020) which can be used to block x-rays among other properties.

Further research by Shan et al (2021) has shown in Low Level Light Therapy that the human skin can be affected by the LED version of the Aharonov-Bohm entanglement-based attack, they have shown that skin reception of pulsed light can affect 14Hz Brain entrainment by pulsating photons of coherent and incoherent streams, but always pulsed or phase shifted through the skin of the palms:

> In this experiment, the average PSD of the subjects in the parietal and temporal cortex locations during session 3 was increased and shifted toward lower frequencies in comparison with the rest stage… phenomenon was caused by LED stimulation which was operated at 10 Hz. The normalized alpha activity rapidly increased during and after LED stimulation in the LED group… The affected regions were the occipital, parietal, and temporal regions. LED stimulation exerted a latent effect on alpha rhythm. The effect could persist for at least 15 minutes after LED ceased. Based on the experimental results, LED stimulation at the palm has an effect to induce alpha rhythm activity, and the affected regions were distributed in posterior. The influence was like AVS [audio visual stimulation], but the latent time was longer. In the control group, no significant variation in alpha rhythm was observed.
>
> Furthermore, the therapeutic window for inducing specific brainwaves via light stimulation has been found. We believe that the results in this study have practical implications in the medical field. For instance, using a higher dose (or frequency) of light stimulation may have the potential application in enhancing the attention of students. Conversely, using a low dose of light stimulation may improve the sleep problems for people who have insomnia. (Shan, 2021)

As Shan et al has noted that there is a medically beneficial application of using near-infrared or infrared pulsed light, it's incoherent form in LEDs, it can also by extension be used for degrading the biological object. Again, it is worth noting that former Soviet researcher A.B. Babrov developed LEDs to replace the Akimov or Aharonov-Bohm generators, LEDs have their own A-B effects.

REMOTE MONITORING AND MAPPING OF BIOLOGICAL OBJECTS

The monitoring of a biological object and mapping that object via entanglement is a different technical setup then simply sending a signal locally in Line-of-Sight type transmission. Kernbach has studied the use of entanglement to map distant objects (Kernbach 2019).

In terms of results, firstly, the distant monitoring even at the $\approx 3\boxtimes$ level is useful when no other sources of information are available. The technique… allows testing several hypotheses about distant macro-objects. Taking into account probabilistic nature of information, and a need of its independent verification, the distant monitoring can be a part of more complex system for working with remote biological, geographic, physical, or symbolic objects. Secondly, when monitoring human persons, volunteers reported about different neurological manifestations – changes in perception, consciousness and sleep patterns, however due to ethical issues no systematic research in this direction has been conducted. It can be assumed that the use of this and similar techniques can raise ethical questions… (Kernbach, 2019)

Other researchers, Kravchenko and Savaliev, investigated the ability of devices to monitor super-weak natural radiation, interestingly, as the human body interacts with the earths geo-magnetic field noting its application to covert intelligence surveillance:

In Ufa State Aircraft Technical University, Ufa Medico - environmental firm " Light 2" for the period 1990 - 2009 developed a number of devices for measuring ultra-weak electromagnetic fields of the natural field of the Earth and re-emitted by various objects . These devices, represent a selective receivers electromagnetic fields in the range of 5 .to 10 kHz , with the calculation of the phase integral shift at the measured frequency . Sensitivity from units to hundreds of picovolts. Devices differ from standard gauges selective fields, so, that instead of resonant LC circuits, a pulse filter is used, providing a " narrow " bandwidth in the form of one spectral line, characterizing a specific tuning frequency, and a phase-sensitive detector instead of the amplitude one, which allows you to measure the relative phase shift of the oscillations, allocated by a pulse filter. The IGA- 1 device belongs to developments in the field of ecology, medicine and **covert intelligence** and can be used:

Detection of human exposure to the anomalies of terrestrial radiation, including electromagnetic in the so-called geopathic zones, for example, when placing hospital beds, planning workplaces, when constructing residential buildings.

Biofield measurements for the purpose of medical diagnosis and test different effects on a person, as psychophysical, psychotropic drugs, bioenergy amplifiers and protective devices.

Медико-экологической фирмой "Лайт-2" за период 1990…2009 г. разработаны и запущены в производство ряд приборов для измерения сверхслабых электромагнитных полей естественного поля Земли и переизлучаемых различными объектами. Эти приборы, представляют из себя селективные приемники электромагнитных полей в диапазоне 5…10 кГц, с вычислением интеграла фазового сдвига на измеряемой частоте. Чувствительность от единиц до сотен пиковольт. Приборы отличаются от стандартных селективных измерителей полей, тем, что вместо резонансных LC контуров используются импульсный фильтр, обеспечивающий "узкую" полосу пропускания в виде одной спектральной линии, характеризующей конкретную частоту настройки, и фазочувствительный детектор вместо амплитудного, позволяющий измерять относительный сдвиг фазы колебаний, выделяемых импульсным фильтром [8…21].

Прибор ИГА-1 относится к разработкам в области экологии, медицины и подземной разведки и может быть использован:

для обнаружения воздействия на человека аномальностей земного излучения, в том числе, электромагнитного в так называемых геопатогенных зонах, например, при размещении больничных коек, планировании рабочих мест, при строительстве жилых домов.

измерения биополей в целях медицинской диагностики и проверки различных воздействий на человека, как психофизических, психотропных препаратов, биоэнергетических усилителей и защитных устройств. (Kravchenko 2009)

Another paper notes regarding this technology:

The method for assessing the electromagnetic field of a biological object is based on topological analysis of the equipotential surfaces of a stationary electromagnetic field surrounding the biological object. As a parameter by which the equipotential surfaces are constructed, in contrast to all known literary sources, the value of the phase shift between the reference signal of a fixed frequency and the harmonic component of the received noise signal is used. Thus, the noise signal recorded near the biological object is useful, and the use of the ultra-long radio wave range from 1 to 10 kHz as the working range makes it possible to tune out the fast rhythmic-physiological processes (such as ECG, EEG, CRG, EMG, circadian rhythm etc.) and judge the slowly changing stationary field, bearing the imprint of the general functional and morphological state of organs, tissues and systems of the body, as well as responding to drug and other types of therapeutic effects.

Способ оценки электромагнитного поля биообьекта основан на топологическом анализе эквипотенциальных поверхностей стационарного электромагнитного поля, окружающего биообьект. В качестве параметра, по которому строятся эквипотенциальные поверхности используется, в отличии от всех известных литературных источников, величина фазового сдвига между опорным сигналом фиксированной частоты и гармонической составляющей принимаемого шумового сигнала. Таким образом, шумовой сигнал, фиксируемый около биообьекта, является полезным, а использование в качестве рабочего диапазона диапазона сверхдлинных радиоволн от 1 до 10 кГц позволяет отстроиться от быстропротекающих ритмико-физиологических процессов, (таких, как ЭКГ, ЭЭГ, КРГ, ЭМГ, цикадная ритмика и т. д.) и судить о медленно меняющемся стационарном поле, несущем отпечаток общего функционального и морфологического состояния органов, тканей и систем организма, а также реагирующем на медикаментозные и иные виды лечебных воздействий. (ИСПОЛЬЗОВАНИЕ ФАЗОАУРОМЕТРИЧЕСКОГО МЕТОДА ПРИ ИССЛЕДОВАНИИ БОЛЬНЫХ БЕСПЛОДИЕМ https://pandia.ru/text/77/308/50239.php, accessed, 12/12/21)

It is interesting to note the use of background noise for detection; this methodology is new in the field of quantum radar, where it is mentioned in connection with using entanglement in quantum radar, here preceded by a couple decades in Russia, developed out of Soviet technology.

Kernbach notes the ethical issues involved in this sort of monitoring, as it is very easy to monitor and entangle any person without their knowledge or consent. The countermeasures to this monitoring are part of this project. However, as mentioned before engineers don't just create weapons without countermeasures and as such the Soviet engineers involved in the early development of these weapons after the fall of the Soviet Union started private business ventures based on countermeasures such as A. V. Okhatrin's 'Gamma 7' system which claims to counteract remote biological influencing or effects.

Rhythmic Point Durations of EM Potentials in the A-B Coil Generator of Puthoff and Persinger

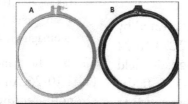

Figure 1. A plastic crotchet ring (A) before and after (B) copper wrapping. The coil is covered in black vinyl electrical tape.

As seen in the Puthoff A-B Generator Phase/Group Velocities are disassociated; this is a product of a photon with nonzero-mass. The A-B Generator is a helical toroid in a circle, thus always accelerating, according to Persinger the phase modulation has the capacity to mediate unlimited information with little energy and phase locking is the key to information copies, the patterns in the EM fields. Karbowski points to this mechanism in terms of information, "the coupling of specific temporally patterned magnetic fields with 'quantum well' like point durations and a 'single' wavelength might be employed as a carrier upon which specific information could be coded which then penetrates into cells and remains there for an hour." (Karbowski, 2016b). In other research the Persinger Group has found such a phenomenon as 'water memory' of potentials. Memory in the brain, a water-based organ, is related to thixotropy and viscosity, viscosity is increased by the A-B Effect according to Sokolova (see Chapter 8: Quantum Consciousness'). One physical attribute to keep in mind is that a toroid with a gap will leak magnetic flux; like the hippocampus and toroids, gapped systems have long range entanglement, as we shall see below in the medical section in dealing with the toroidal hippocampus, which mediates information or memory.

Persinger et al, studied the use of point durations in creating their phase modulated EM patterns for use in entanglement experiments. The point duration is either a 1ms or 3ms delay in the wave form at a given amplitude. It is part of the difficult process of designing a pattern that is based on a neurological functional correlate: "Accurate and precise point durations are essential for producing the sensed presence similar 'temporal sensing' sensitivity for cells has been shown for frequency modulated (FM) weak magnetic fields. (Rouleau, 2015)"

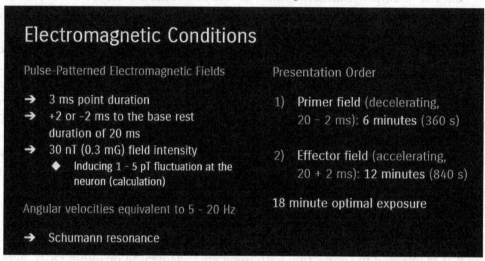

An overall modulation configuration was constructed based on a 20ms starting point, then descending or ascending 2ms between which,

> The rates of rotation of the magnetic field that were most effective involved 20ms reference intervals. Addition or subtraction of 2ms as the field moves around the solenoid produced a changing angular velocity. (Scott, 2015)

1ms Point Duration - Electron

- increased free protons
- pH increased aciditiy
- proton expand one planck length
- changes in pH only during increasing angular momentum.
- 1 ms electron pulse 1000 fold increase in photon emissions

1ms Point Duration - Electron

- Increased free protons
- pH increased acidity
- proton expand one planck length
- changes in pH only during increasing angular momentum in toroid, descending in solenoid array.
- 3ms point durations participate in Ca Ion channels (aka CamKII in microtubule) (Persinger 2010, 821)
- 3ms gives 1-5nT in the E-W component of the static geomagnetic field (Persinger, 2014)

The magnetic moment of the circulating current created by an electron moving in its closed path is $9.274 \cdot 10\text{-}24$ A·m2 (J·T-1). Hence the required magnetic field strength would be the ratio or $1.01 \cdot 10\text{-}1$ T. If the square of that value ($1.02 \cdot 10\text{-}2$ T 2) is inserted into equation (2), the optimalseparation between ideal parallel plates would be~24 nm. Application of the central limit theorem and assuming the typical standard deviations of ~30 % of the central tendency, the range for 95 % of the spaces would be between 10 and 37 nm. This is the range of the width of a synapse, the interface between neurons. (Persinger, 2014)

On the other hand if the magnetic moment of the proton ($1.41 \cdot 10\text{-}26$ A·m2) is employed, the magnetic field strength required to obtain the energy associated with the hydrogen line is $6.67 \cdot 101$ T. If this value squared ($44.5 \cdot 102$ T 2) is inserted into equation (2), the resulting width (a) is $0.93 \cdot 10\text{-}9$ m. This is within the median range of the width of an ion channel found in plasma cell membranes. Most "channels" within the plasma cell membrane are those that mediate the movements of protons. " (Persinger, 2014)

Recalling that the toroid helix is in a circular arrangement, this arrangement with changing rates or modulation has an odd effect that Rouleau finds could violate causality:

Movement in a circle is uniquely interesting because the process would always be accelerating (m·s⁻²) and a changing rate of this acceleration (m·s⁻³) often referenced as "jerks," would be a second derivative containing the potential temporal non-continuities that could encourage the conditions we assume may be associated with the observed excess correlations. They could spread over the Minkowski four-dimensional field and appear to violate directional causality. In other words the "effects" of these "jerks" could occur before events and appear to violate causal principles but not necessarily the concept of entanglement. The presence of non-local and advanced correlations for geomagnetic effects had been reported by Korotaev and his colleagues (Rouleau, 2015)

In this way rotation, which affects, entanglement becomes a key part of the process of the functionality of the toroid coil. One of the interesting finding is that given the Earth rotates CCW there is more torque in E-W direc-

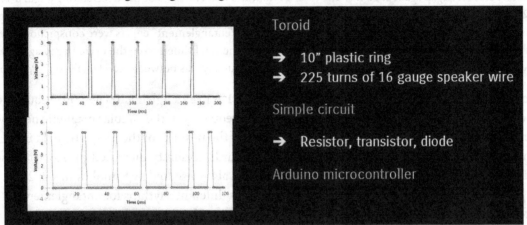

Toroid
→ 10" plastic ring
→ 225 turns of 16 gauge speaker wire

Simple circuit
→ Resistor, transistor, diode

Arduino microcontroller

tion. Orientating to directions was also a very key part of early Nazi German remote sensing experiments before and during WW2 (see Chapter 3. 'Neuroweapons').

The issue of a second derivative of fields is given as an example where a wave produces a background field for itself by itself.

Quote from section 108, page 349 of the authoritative Landau and Lifshitz (1975) textbook:

Since it has definite energy, the gravitational wave is itself is the source of some additional gravitational field [static g-field]. Like the energy producing it, this field is a second-order effect in the hik. But in the case of high-frequency gravitational waves the effect is significantly strengthened: the fact that the pseudotensor tik is quadratic in the derivatives of the hik introduces the large factor λ-2. In such a case we may say that the wave itself produces the background field [static g-field] on which it propagates. This [static g-field] is conveniently treated by carrying out the averaging described above over regions of four-space with dimensions large compared to λ [wavelength]. Such an averaging smooths out the short-wave "ripple" and leaves the slowly varying background metric [static g-field]. (Brackets and underline added for clarity and emphasis.) (Baker, 2010)

Returning to the issue of 'jerks' from above it is also used in the HFGW system of Dr. Robert Baker (2010). Baker speaks of jerks as a cascade-like effect. The jerks add force (see Chiao et al, 2017), and in a circular constant accelerating circuit the change in force (Δf), the faster the jerks (<Δt) the higher the GW frequency, so that the larger the change in f the better. According to Baker, GW waves are too small to use to change frequency, it is better to use EM Waves, which of course could come from GW. The production of gravitons comes through change in mass, so that "each time a mass undergoes a change or build up in force over a very brief time Gravitational Waves are generated." Baker has used laser pulse approach to generate Gravitational Waves in the laboratory @ THz frequencies 1012 HZ.

Persinger's Group first began using magnetic fields in 1990 when he designed phase-modulated magnetic fields in a circular array of solenoids; in 2013 Burke was the first to test non-local entanglement effects of the generators, then in 2015 they switched to toroids from solenoids. Some of the physical phenomenon they have observed are

- appearance of longitudinal photon, the non-local effects for non-gauge fields for the Aharonov- Bohm effect and altered access to Casimir sources.

- Aharonov-Bohm effect Flux can be curved into a finite toroid (Persinger, 2016)

One effect that is dependent on whether solenoids (superconductors) or toroids were used is that of the phase type modulation used: ascending or descending. In solenoids entanglement effects are observed in descending changing rhythms, in toroids entanglement effects occur in ascending changing rhythms. The basis of consciousness according to Persinger et al is 20ms, with the base unit of the human brain at 1ms. They use 20ms as the starting point for ascending and descending rhythms in 2ms increments, in this case for a solenoid experiment:

> The second derivative component (assuming the circular rotation is always accelerating and is a "first derivative") was programmed by adding +2 ms or -2 ms to the base duration of 20 ms. For the accelerating angular velocity (20+2 ms) this meant that the duration the field was generated changed through 20, 18, 16, 14, 12, 10, 8, and 6 ms before it began again at 20 ms. The total circuit time was 104 ms. For the decelerating angular velocity (20-2 ms) the duration at each pair of solenoids was 20, 22, 24, 26, 28, 30, 32, and 34 ms before starting again at 20 ms. This duration was 216 ms and was the phase in which "entanglement" effects were conspicuous. Because the circumference of the array of solenoids was 60 cm and the total time before the cycle began again was the sum of the 8 durations (216 ms) the averaged rotational frequency was between 4.6 Hz. (Persinger, 2016).

One property observed is that there can be a boost by up to 10x in entanglement when the frequencies are phase matched between two entangled coils, "when the rotational frequency of the circular magnetic fields within the 2 vols of spring water had been phase matched the frequency of the product of the magnetic field intensity and the protons' magnetic moment, the excess correlations shift towards alkalinity increased by 10x with the non-local volume." (Persinger, 2016). This effect of a dramatic increase is also observed by Samokhvalov in 2016. Solenoid is a different geometry from a toroid; this geometrical basis gives different rhythms for entanglement.

The difference in ascending and descending rhythms is observed by Saroka:

> Most of the subjects had volunteered for "relaxation" or "learning" studies so that expectation would be minimal. Approximately 80% of these subjects reported a sensed presence when a slowing frequency-modulated field was first applied continuously with a slightly right hemisphere bias for 30 min[utes] followed by the equalized bilateral application of an accelerating frequency-modulated (burst-firing) field for 1 s every 3 s for 30 min. A similar temporal order (slowing frequency modulation and bilateral accelerating frequency modulation presented for 15 min each) of field presentation over the right hemisphere increased the report of sensed presences [46]. Presenting the same field patterns in reverse order was not as effective. (Saroka, 2013)

The modulations of the toroid in this project are controlled through Arduino Board programmed in C++ to add or subtract appropriate intervals for entanglement or in this case creating a masking field with one toroid to interfere with non-local signal transmissions aimed at the object surrounded by the masking field.

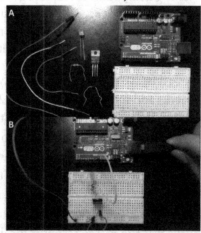

(Arduino Micro-controller phase modulator, from Scott 2015)

A-B GENERATORS AS TRANS-CEREBRAL MAGNETIC STIMULATION (TCS)

The A-B Generator is referred to as a TCS device rather than a Transcranial Magnetic Stimulation (TMS) device, which is used in treating epilepsy with different coil constructions and patterns around brain areas. Saroka provides an explanation to the difference between the two:

The fields in our studies are usually applied for about 20 min to 30 min while the subject sits blindfolded in a quiet, darkened room (acoustic chamber). To distinguish the procedure from transcranial stimulation (TMS) whose symmetrical pulsed field strengths are about a million times stronger, the term trans-cerebral stimulation (TCS) has been employed. We had reasoned that the more the complex pattern of the applied fields approached the form of intrinsic cerebral patterns, the less the intensity required to produce subjective and electroencephalographic changes. The rationale was similar to strategically developing molecular structures of pharmacological agents to be congruent with neurotransmitters for receptor subtypes. For analgesic effects in rats, for example, exposures of only 30 min to appropriately patterned magnetic fields with intensities of only 1 μT were equivalent to a subcutaneous injection of ~5 mg/kg of morphine mediated through micro-opioid receptors. (Saroka, 2013) [for more on the pharmacological aspect of this technology see "Entanglement Medicine" git repository https://github.com/autonomous019/ahronov-bohm-cybersecurity]

The main difference between TMS and TCS: TMS is 10^6 magnitudes larger then TCS; however in terms of magnetic field strength TMS is about 5μT whereas TCS is 1-5μT so the end product is in the same range produced by different mechanisms in terms of Tesla (magnetic standard units) generated. TMS uses heavy loads, higher voltage, compared to TCS to achieve the same effect.

III. Brain Profile: Havana Syndrome, Epilepsy and Non-Local EEG Studies
Profile of an Attacked Brain

The idea that one can create a methodology to distinguish neurological damage from non-local signals and other brain impairments, such as mild concussions (mTBI), or epilepsy is argued in the following by examining brain waves during impact and gray matter in brain areas impacted. The question of whether it is possible to distinguish Havana Syndrome was answered by Balaban et al (2020) in what is akin to a 'Blade Runner' cyborg test by measuring the eyes' response, the team was able to develop a methodology that does distinguish between other brain injuries and Havana Syndrome:

> This is the first report that examines the function of these individuals on a test that examined binocular disparity-driven eye and pupil movements during the acute time period after exposure. The patterns of response in these individuals are markedly different than those seen in a group of individuals with usual acute mild traumatic brain injury and from controls with no injury. The results from these tests permitted an objective discrimination of the groups with >91% accuracy and no confusion between the Havana subjects and the subjects with acute mild traumatic brain injury. This pattern difference may be a useful screen for individuals who report a similar exposure pattern. Furthermore, their distinctive presentation may help guide in treatment decisions to address the mechanisms that contribute to their unusual symptom complexes. At the current time, however, this remains an empirical observation and more work is needed to study the findings. (Balaban et al, 2020)

It is interesting that an eye test which also showed disparity in the visual cortex in Verma et al, is affected and can be used as a measure of differentiation. Again, Norseen focused on the visual cortex, conceived as a photon field. Bandyapadhya's Group in Japan has studied the antenna properties of eyes and DNA (Singh, 2018). Balaban also found that there was a differentiation in pupil size of Havana Syndrome; this was also seen in highly hypnotizable subjects, where their pupil size is also reduced (Kellio, 2011).

	Control group	Acute mild traumatic brain injury (mTBI)	Havana affected	Tukey's highest significant difference or Kruskal–Wallis ($p < 0.05$) comparisons	Least significant difference ($p < 0.05$) comparisons
Unadjusted measures					
Light reflex average baseline pupil area (mm^2)	18.24 ± 0.83 mm^2 (Gaussian)	16.46 ± 1.65 mm^2 (Gaussian)	14.15 ± 1.37 mm^2 (Gaussian)	C > HA; C = mTBI; HA = mTBI	
Light response fit to model (R^2, coefficient of determination)	0.68 ± 0.02 (Gaussian rejected)	0.56 ± 0.04 (Gaussian)	0.74 ± 0.03 (Gaussian)	C = mTBI; C = HA; HA > mTBI	
Age-adjusted measures for average pupil area in each task with significant age relationship (basis age: 33.3939 years)					
Light reflex average baseline pupil area (mm^2)	17.92 ± 0.78 mm^2	14.62 ± 1.53 mm^2	16.37 ± 1.50 mm^2		NS for all
Disparity step average pupil area (mm^2)	19.38 ± 0.83 mm^2	14.51 ± 1.64 mm^2	16.22 ± 1.62 mm^2		C = HA; C > mTBI; HA = mTBI
Disparity pursuit average pupil area (mm^2)	17.29 ± 0.84 mm^2	13.62 ± 1.66 mm^2	15.25 ± 1.64 mm^2		C = HA; C > mTBI; HA = mTBI

(Balaban et al, 2020)

One of the first objections you will hear regarding the concept of EM potentials being able to affect the brain is that the normal molecular pathways are bypassed by using EM potential energies. In other areas relating to molecular biology a former Yugoslavian scientist, U. of Belgrade, I. Cosic in 1994 proposed an alternative to the JAK-STAT pathway based on molecular resonance: Resonant Recognition Model, also derived from Frohlich, originally molecular resonance was credited to P. Jordan. Readers of Quantum Physics and Quantum Biology that have studied the originator of these ideas, Pascual Jordan, the former Nazi physicist and secret weapons developer, with molecular resonance, which was attacked by L. Pauling. It was Jordan working with Berlin-Brain Institute, the sister institute to the one in Russia that Kropotov worked at in a later era, that first proposed a molecular resonance explanation for molecules being 'attracted' to each other. This was rejected by the scientific consensus of western scientists, who adapted Pauling's ideas. Jordan's idea was correct but misapplied. At the Brain Institute he worked with the founders of modern molecular biology (Ch. 8 Quantum Consciousness) who were captured by the Soviets after the war and assigned to the Soviet Nuclear program, out of which it is claimed remote biological influence developed in labs run by Germans as Soviet prisoners. So, the Soviets had a more open response to resonance theories and the combination of Quantum Effects on Biology as a recipient of German knowledge in these areas after the war.

Kravkov notes the adoption of Resonance by the Soviets, including such concepts as bio-effective frequencies,

> the resonance effect can be observed if the natural frequency of any structure has a natural frequency of oscillatory or rotational motion, which coincides with the frequency of the incident radiation.... [see synchronization above]. Resonance also takes place in cases when the frequency of absorption of an EM wave of any molecule coincides with the frequency of incident radiation." (see Chapter. 8)

It is also in this area of research that viscosity becomes an engineering issue for heavy water (deuterium); it is easy to forget that the founders of Quantum Physics were mostly Germans at the time, in the 1930s when their theories were first beginning to be validated as the Nazis rose to power. I have argued in earlier chapters that all western remote influencing technology originates from the Nazis. So, the question then becomes what do such apparently unrelated topics, human brain and production of heavy water for nuclear arms, have to do with each other?

Nuclear or atomic reactions are not usually thought of as occurring in our brains or body in general. The reason we think is because our brains are a very large network of electrical reactions, electricity coming from the magnetic interaction with an electrostatic field influencing how the electrons interact, quantum interference. This happens in the water-based neurons of the brain as magnetic fields influence electrical pathways, triggering molecular reactions from either electron or proton tunneling in the neurons themselves, in their neuron's microtubules as discussed above.

Persinger supplies a theory explaining how thixotropy and viscosity influences neurons, including the generation of EEG amplitudes through Casimir Effect; this is a key element as we shall see that EM influences thixotropy (liquid layer separating, phase states, boundaries) which impacts viscosity and may explain the changes in gray and white matter brain volume as seen by Persinger in his independent studies not directly related to Havana Syndrome and those of Verma et al, specifically studying Havana Syndrome.

A-B, CASIMIR, EM POTENTIALS AND BRAIN WAVES

Brain Waves are EM transmissions that are produced through the neural networks in the human brain they are affected by EM fields the following ways (Ye et al, 2019):

1. direct alteration of neuronal excitability

2. alteration of ion channel functional

3. alteration of synaptic transmission

4. interruption of ephaptic effects (electrical conduction of a nerve impulse across an ephapse without the mediation of a neuro-transmitter)

As we are dealing with EM potentials rather than electrical impulses in terms of these generators we are interfacing with quantum effects through the A-B generators.

Persinger et al have argued that the process of affecting brain neurons with Aharonov-Bohm generators is one that involves not just the A-B Effect, but also the Casimir Effect and the influencing of electrons with vacuum interference patterns from the Casimir Effect at around 23nm width, also arguing that this affects the 10nm width of the neuron synapse. These vacuum fluctuations, what Norseen refers to as Zero Point Energy (ZPE) have orbits that are half-virtual (wave) and half-real particles (concretization or quantization), out of which come through the interaction of magnetic A Vector Magnetic Potential with electrostatic field (E) electron and proton pumping from the Casimir Effect induced vacuum fluctuations, there is a gravitational analog to this EM version as well. Koren explains the interaction between EM and Casimir:

> The spatial dimensions that define the synapse and the ion channel were evident when the energies that converged Casimir and traditional magnetic forms were equated. The specific values required the presence of a magnetic field strength that when multiplied by the magnetic moment of the proton or of the electron resulted in the energy of the neutral hydrogen line.
>
> Subtle differences in the magnetic moments for the electrons spin and orbit, the proton's value and the slight discrepancies revealed features that could connect fundamental features of astronomical phenomena with those that contribute to quantum processes in the physical and chemical systems that define the brain. (Koren 2016)

One important element in their understandings of how A-B works with brain chemistry is that of the 1.42 GHz hydrogen line, a common universal wavelength. As explained by Saroka:

> Once measured almost exclusively in large space the ubiquitous 1.42 GHz hydrogen line has been detected over terrestrial water. The potential transient emissions of this universal frequency from the human body and brain could be very significant for the interface between these functions, including the units of cognition coupled to action potentials ($\sim 10^{-20}$ J per action potential) of neurons, and transmission of information over large distances as either local or non-local processes. The detection of human enhancements of 1.42 GHz transients within a radio-quiet area requires angular velocities of about 3 to 4 m per s to and from the receiver.
>
> The angular momentum of each electron when multiplied by the hydrogen line frequency would result in flux densities that are in the same order of magnitude as the measured photon emissions emitted during cerebral function. (Saroka, 2013)

In other works, the Persinger group has related neuron brain biophoton transmission to Brain- Computer-Interfaces.

> A cell membrane is typically 10nm, which falls within the Casimir Effect scale (.1-25nm), the relationship between the electron, magnetic A vector potential and protons, in terms of ion channels and transmembrane potentials through which protons (H+) as ions: Na+, K+ or Cl flow into the cell body. Remembering that water interact with magnetic fields we see the impact of such proton pumping, "In fact the proton shells near surfaces that constitute Pollack's interfacial water configurations display potential differences that are comparable to those attributed to disparities of concentration for potassium and chloride. Quantitative links between plasma membrane physics and quantum-related values have practical applications." (Koren, 2016)

Here the practical application is seen in that the A potentials have a connection to ion channels for K and Cl according to Pollack. Koren explains the connection to entanglement as a photon-electron coupling due to the space formed by the A vector potential and the electron drift:

> We have been considering protons through proton channels as the quintessential mediator of transmembrane ion properties and that other ions, such as Na+, K+ or Cl are epiphenomena secondary to the required water molecules associated with transport of those ions through the membrane. However, in a parity-based universe the proton should be matched with electron properties. We suggest that the states of matter allowing these transportations may be created by the space formed by the A vector potential and the electron drift. This occurrence could optimize the conditions for the type of photon-electron coupling associated with entanglement (Koren, 2016)

Persinger identifies photon entanglement with Orthogonal Fields (A Vector Potential) in other studies.

Koren then explains how this relates to Angular Momentum, which is intrinsic to entanglement where Angular Momentum (p) is derived from magnetic quantum number (j):

> Effectively the same function that is a source equation for quantum phenomena when applied to a larger rotating aggregate produced predictable quantities of photons as a function of specific intensity weak magnetic fields. That function was the relationship between Bohr's orbital magnetic moment of ep·(2m)$^{-1}$ where e and m were the charge and mass of the electron, p was the angular momentum of an electron moving in the orbit, and the quantized relationship. The quantized relationship for angular momentum (p) was jh·(2π)$^{-1}$ where j was the magnetic quantum number and h was the traditional Planck's constant. When j is assumed to be unity [1] the value solves for the Bohr magneton or the orbital magnetic moment of an electron. (Koren, 2016)

Spins are related to AM; electron spins are transported into protein molecules:

> The second solution involves the A vector (magnetic potential) directly. The relevant property of the magnetic vector potential is that is elicits a phase difference and, potentially, interference between partial waves. The vector potential of the earth's magnetic field cannot be shielded. According to Bokkon and Salari "oscillations of dephasing non-conductive (fixed) electrons could influence conductive mobile electrons" and as a result coherent transport of the mobile electron spins into surrounding semiconductor protein molecules could occur. This is consistent with Cosic's delocalized electrons that maintain the coherence of the propagating electromagnetic wave of information along the backbone amino sequences of the proteins in signaling pathways. (Koren, 2016)

Koren equates the ability for such transport to that of Cosic's alternative magnetic molecular pathway using the Resonant Recognition Model which mirrors the electrochemical pathway of JAK-STAT. This is similar to Norseen's use of MT-10 as electrochemical bio-computation and MT-13 as magnetic bio-computation. In this regard of computation Bandyopadhyay et al have found that there are binary streams of neurons in axon core, neuron membrane. (Ch.8) According to Hameroff (2014) MT cilia are quantum optical devices, MT cilia are also in the retinal rods and cones of the Eye, detect photons quantum information. Dotta (2014) has found that for Microtubules the temporal pattern is more important than amplitude thresholds:

> The close correspondence between the intrinsic rotational frequency (9.6 Hz) of the angular accelerating magnetic fields and the 9.4 to 9.5 Hz conspicuous peaks in power density of photon emissions from the microtubules several minutes after removal from the field may suggest a transient "representation" or "memory" of this second derivative, rotational frequency within these aggregates that was later expressed within the photon emissions. The results of these experiments indicate that the strength of the applied magnetic field is not required, as also argued by Cifra et al. [13], to exceed the threshold to compensate for thermal agitation.
>
> The *temporal structure* of the applied magnetic field, particularly when it simulates intrinsic biological or biochemical processes, may be more important than previously considered. (Dotta et al, 2014) [emphasis added]

Research done by Ye et al (2019) in the treatment of seizures studied the effect of EM on epileptic seizures. The effects of time varying (phase/frequency) magnetic field are generally believed to be caused by its induced electric field and the establishment of a transmembrane potential in Aninos 1991 magnetic field alters function of pineal gland-magnetosensitive organ that transduces environmental information of the light-dark cycle and earth's magnetic field into an endocrine message release melatonin. (Ye et al, 2019)

EM, among other products, releases endocrine messages through its interaction with magneto-receptive areas of the brain, such as that in the visual organs which contain magnetoreception.

NEURONS AND BRAIN WAVES

With the insights of the contribution of the Casimir effect to neuronal firing at the nano-scale of the brain Ch8. Quantum Consciousness), Norseen talked of the Casimir Effect as energy of the vacuum (ZPE), we are now ready to see how these neuronal firings that produce EM signals are quantized. The quantization of the shallow level (scalp) of the Brain is performed using EEG, for instance Kropotov's use of QEEG. There are other ways to study the brain, such as the topological based sLORETA as used by Persinger in some of his studies, fMRI was used in the Verma et al study of Havana Syndrome. Each provides different insights into the functioning of the brain's various areas, typically referred to as Broadmann Areas, reflecting functional differentiation in the different parts of the brain. EEG is used to estimate the magnitude output of magnetic fields (μT) at the various locations in the brain, such that an area of interest such as EEG location F7 is mapped to the Broadmann Area 44 or Broca's Area. The waves are categorized into different wave zones, such as theta 4-8Hz, Alpha 8Hz-12Hz, Gamma >=30Hz; These waves have a directional flow from rostral- cuadal (front-to-back) axis 4m/s^{-1}, which recycles every 25ms (Saroka, 2013). These are not definitive or universal measurements as placement of EEG sensors is not universal. Below is a standard mapping of EEG locations; later we shall reference different EEG locations to brain area functionality.

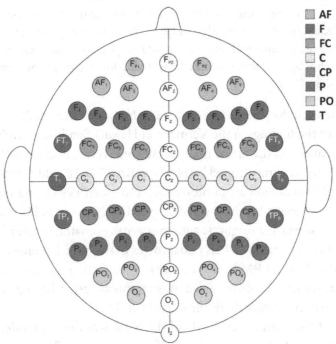

Grabner, 2012

EEG is used by Persinger et al to study the effects of non-local entanglement using A-B generators, from these quantitative studies they have formulated a possible profile for non-local transmission in the human brain, called the Harribance Configuration, named after a test subject studied by many others in non-local transmissions. We shall encounter this configuration below. This configuration also bears functional equivalence to areas affected by Havana Syndrome (see below), and in Temporal Lobe Epilepsy patients without Hippocampal Lesions (HL). So that it may be possible to have a loose profile pending further research of non-local brain activity, which could be used for detection and deployment of countermeasures if coming from a directed source.

EXPERIMENTAL RESULTS OF GENERATORS ON HUMAN BRAIN:

A cold war warrior with British Secret Services whose specialty was in microwave technology as part of Electronic Warfare, Barry Trower, once pointed out that a frequency 6.6Hz signal focused on a human brain causes such symptoms as anger and paranoia. This was confirmed by Scott et al, with a frequency of 6.5Hz, during entanglement experiments with A-B Generators between entangled pairs over long distances, non-local (Scott et al, 2015). They found that EM waves of this Extreme Low Frequency (ELF) when correlated with emotional scoring showed a correlation between anger and this frequency, "...subjective experiences, as measured by the Profile of Mood States (POMS), indicated significantly increased excess correlation for scales by which increased anger and decreased vigor are inferred." (Scott et al, 2015). In this effort to understand the effects of EM on the brain we have both historical testimony of Dr. Trower, and we have experimental confirmation of this impact on the brain from Scott et al. Meaning, EM has an effect on the brain, here delivered via sonic means.

A Russian researcher found an alteration in the parietal region when studying the effects of what they termed 'spin fields', spin directly related to entanglement, using the same instruments as earlier Soviet scientists, found in EEG studies that there was a difference in alpha rhythm when applying a positive emotional stimulation via a generator:

> Encephalographic experiments to study the effect of SP modulated by a positive emotional component indicate a change in the zonal distribution of the α-rhythm with its highest concentration in the frontal-pretemporal region (in the initial state, the localization of the α- rhythm is the occipito-parietal region). An increase in the amplitude of the α-rhythm up to 50 μV and an improvement in its modulation were noted, which indicates an increase in the ability for abstract thinking, an increase in efficiency in making decisions and actions. Based on the results of the experiments, the following conclusions can be drawn: 1. Psychotronic systems based on the use of spinor fields are a real fact. Their use is not limited by distance and can cause the following consequences: making erroneous, inadequate political, economic and military decisions; aggravation of social and inter-ethnic relations, etc. 2. Psychotronic systems with modulated SP in a positive emotional component can be used to smooth out negative psychophysical factors in large areas (reduction of terrorist manifestations and crime, drug addiction). (Kraznobryshev, 2009)

The findings regarding the occipito-parietal region are also found in Lehman 2015.

Above we covered some of the findings of the Verma et al Havana Syndrome study. In it there was differentiation in gray matter and white matter of the brains of those affected. Verma et al shows that the primary areas affected were the visual/spatial circuitry, as mentioned by Norseen BA 17 & 18, which is to say the visual perceptrons, Norseen relates, percepts and imagination are photon fields. (Norseen 1999), and typically aside from the audio cortex, another area affected in Havana Syndrome and targeted by Norseen in his studies, the main inputs to the brain, as well as the human eye serves as a magnetic antenna cavity resonator, or interferometer. Norseen mentions a third area, Broadmann 44, Broca's area. BA 17,18 visual cortex of the brain becomes of prime interest if a sickness has its source outside the body from an EM based transmission, affecting the interface with the environment, visual/spatial and audio cortex, sometimes also referred to as temporal cortex, having connection to rhythm, people with enlarged Amygdala's also have a better rhythmic sense (Ch. 11).

Verma et al also show that the most affected side of the brain was the right side, which Persinger shows the right temporal lobes to be most affected by non-local effects, also Right Temporal Lobe Epilepsy (RTLE). In RTLE there is a difference as seen below between those with Hippocampal Lesions (HL), that do not match the Non-Local Transmission Profile (NTP) and RTLE-No without HL that does match the profile of NTP as interpreted from the combination of symptoms and effects from Verma and Persinger. Persinger has noted that the right parahippocampal is affected by EM, this may suggest that the difference between RTLE-HL and RTLE-No may have something to do with Hippocampal processing of EM. The para-hippocampal region is most affected by gravito-electromagnetism (Persinger and Saroka 2014); para-hippocampal could serve as singularity, curvature singularities form from colliding Gravitational Waves (Baker, 2010), since there is a gap that radiates magnetic flux with the para-hippocampus having a toroid geometry (Persinger 2013), Persinger speaks of retrieval in Harribance Configuration (HC) experiments from para-hippocampal structures on the right side.

Persinger's Group suggests that the Hippocampus interacts with a singularity and thus virtual particles, which transition to real particles, protons and electrons.

In Epilepsy, which has a comorbidity of obesity (also see Ch. 11 for relation of increased EM and obesity in rats as studied by Persinger), additionally death rates from Epilepsy are increasing in the United States (DeGorgio, 2020). There are similar differences observed in gray matter with a decrease reported in patients:

> It was reported that gray matter volume was associated with cognitive functions. Decreased gray matter was observed in epileptic patients. Most important area where gray matter abnormalities occur is hippocampus. Other areas include thalamus, parietal lobe, and cingulate gyrus. Changes have also been described in the para-hippocampal gyrus, middle temporal gyrus, superior temporal gyrus, inferior temporal gyrus, fusiform gyrus, temporal pole, entorhinal cortex, amygdala, and perirhinal cortex. It was reported that abnormalities of gray matter are essential to produce reductions in episodic memory recall. Most commonly seen cognitive dysfunctions due to gray matter abnormalities in children are decline in verbal intelligence quotient, freedom from distractibility,

and executive function and mental slowness, memory impairment and attention deficits commonly observed among adults. (Saniya et al, 2017)

These abnormalities in epileptic patients correlate with the changes observed in gray matter and white matter in Verma et al. not only that the same brain areas were affected in epileptic patients and Havana Syndrome patients, another interesting finding in relation to gray matter is that of Amygdala and the ACC in both highly- and non-highly-hypnotizable groups, with gray matter differences observed (See Ch. 10 'Hypnosis in Warfare'). The question of whether a profile has already been seen for non-local monitoring seems to line up between the work of Persinger's Group and that of the results of Verma et al study of the irradiation of US Diplomats in Havana and the physical changes to their brains, and we can also see a correlation with Epilepsy.

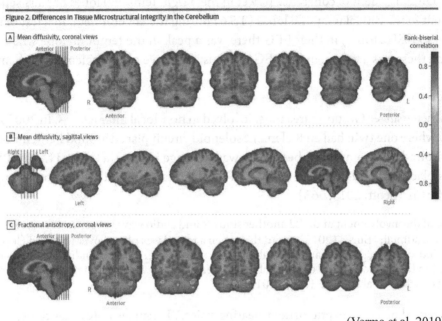

(Verma et al, 2019)

BROADMANN AREAS AND EEG SENSOR LOCATIONS FOR AREAS AFFECTED BY NON-LOCAL EFFECT:

Visual/spatial:

• BA 17, O1 and O2 projected to the occipital gyrus and cuneus, visual processing of information from the retina, see retina as antenna section. Cuneus, was an area of noticeable difference in Havana Syndrome Study (Verma 2019); it receives visual information from same side superior quadrantic retina. Pyramidal cells in visual cortex of the cuneus project to extra-striate cortices (BA 18,19) modulated by extra-retinal effects: attention, working memory, reward expectation.

Audio/Temporal Cortex

• BA 22, EEG T3/4: cited by Norseen working in tandem with BA 44 (Broca's area in left hemisphere). Sentence generator, Attend to happy/angry voices, Deductive reasoning, auditory language, non-verbal sounds, previous eye movements. Categorization and organization, visualization and auditory cortex. Right (T4) and Left (T3) Superior Temporal Gyrus. Also, T3/4 is near the insula, which functions: copying emotional tones, object recognition anxiety occurs in relation to its closeness to the Amygdala. BA 22 is part of Wernicke's area, another language processing area of the brain. Epileptic aphasia can occur from BA 22 as well as Broca's Area. BA 22 in Havana Syndrome study is the Auditory Network, also referred to as temporal network by others. Auditory Network L/R Superior Temporal Gyrus and Right Thalamus. The Auditory Cortex comprised of BA 41,42, 22 is the seat of processing incoming signals from the environment, Rotation also relates to the Brain as rotation is used to protect existing memories from incoming environmental stimuli by rotating memory in a second orthogonal direction from the incoming stream of inputs, "a rotation of the coding dimension in the neural population cortex protects memories of prior events from interference by incoming stimuli." (Libby, 2019)

In Scott 2015, spectral power densities correlated over F4 and T4 for non-local interactions.

A cluster of significant non-parametric correlation coefficients could be identified for right hemispheric global power during the second half of the Effector field sequence containing somewhat after the termination of the field." (Scott 2015, 679) Only temporal lobes were obviously affected by the unusual theta and gamma power changes.

T3/4 change in coherence is tied to function of the phase (freq.) of the experiment and type of magnetic field (Scott, 2015, 683). Diminishment of coherence power in theta right temporal lobes of pairs separated by 6000km. Similar diminishment in the caudal temporal lobes (T5,6) during the effector field. In a test of non-local changes, one person listened to 6.5Hz tones; in their EEG there was a peak in the temporal lobe when the tone sounded, in the second person there was a trough in the EEG which is indicative of entanglement with inverse correlations.

Temporal Lobes:

Focus of studies by Persinger Group as area most involved in non-local interactions. In 2003 Persinger conducted a twin study where one twin had an 8-element solenoid circuit placed around her temporal lobes, the other twin had no array around their temporal lobes. There was a change in the Theta band from 5.0Hz to 5.9Hz when the EM circuit was placed around the other twin. Non-local interactions without changing angular velocity EM fields in the second twin. (Scott, 2015, 663)

In a suggestion of the involvement of BA 22 another study found audio waves as generators of excess correlation rather than visual stimuli: "Burke (2013) found that when a toroid was placed over the head (level of temporal lobes) of each individual in pairs separated by about 400km. LORETA profiles indicated excess correlation in the activity within the temporal lobes of both subjects when one pair was exposed to sound patterns. The effect was not observed with visual stimuli." (Scott, 2015, 667)

In a pilot study regarding an Epileptic patient hearing voices, Persinger notes that the epileptic patient had a unique profile for different seizures. For instance, in one seizure her voice would become more 'machine like' and her pronouns shifted from 'I' to 'we' while also reporting tinnitus. There was a difference between her pronoun use of I in the beta band over T3 and T7, left temporal lobe, with 70milli vols activity. When she used 'we' there was a higher (fast) amplitude over T3 and T4; "she reported 'transmissions'" which usually involved more complex information… When this occurred there was a re-normalization of the EEG. When the transmission ended, the unusual profile of T3 and T4 returned. There was additional similar activity over F7 and F8.

During the experiences that would be classically labeled as 'intrusionist' the activation score for the low beta power within the right parahippocampal region more than doubled. This area and related hemispheric discrepancy are similar to that associated with panics that can occur suddenly in this group of patients. Persinger et al, (2015) LORETA predicts Electromagnetic Sensitivity and 'hearing voices' in a predictable, increasingly prevalent subpopulation.

Language Processing, Broca's Area

- BA 44, Right and Left Inferior Frontal Gyrus (IFG). Functions: working memory (visual/auditory), attention filtering, facial emotion processing, sustained attention, mirror others, grapheme-to-phoneme, phonemes. Epileptic seizures start at F8 (Quintero-Rincon, 2016). Frontal Eye field left and right, see Shirer, W.R., et al., Decoding subject-driven cognitive states with whole-brain connectivity patterns. Cerebral Cortex 2012. BA 44 according to Verma 2019 contains Frontal Operculum and IFG [see Norseen on IFG and Bio-fusion].

Memory Retrieval/Storage, Para-hippocampus

- EEG T5/6: para-hippocampal gyrus (Scott, 2015) dorsal hippocampal commissure mediate information between the hippocampal formations within left and right hemisphere (Scott, 2015) "topographical map clusters indicated the domain of maximum coherence was within the right caudal hemisphere within the volume occupied by the para-hippocampal gyrus." (Scott, 2015)

- T6- right caudal temporal lobe, area of most excess correlation in Harribance Configuration right

- Isoelectric lines (anisotropy) switched from clockwise to counterclockwise at onset of field.

- the changing rate creates a second derivative in the magnetic field. A second derivative is a secondarily Induced Magnetic Field. Analogy: influencing the change of a change (Persinger, 2010), also see Chiao above for Gravitational equivalent.

- "According to Bear (1996) this 7-40Hz superposition may set the condition for interaction between the hippocampal process associated with memory consolidation and retrieval and its integration with information represented within the entire cerebral cortical manifold." (Rouleau, 2015b)

- Hippocampus is toroidal, leaking magnetic flux. It is strongly affected by the phase vector of

- B. (intensities match Geomagnetic Field and Schumann Resonance) (Rouleau, 2015b)

- Magnetic Fields and Amygdala: "Magnetic fields may suppress seizure by altering cellular properties. Repeated stimulation of the amygdala can prompt after discharges and motor seizure. Potschka et al. found that chronic exposure of rats to a 50-Hz, 100-µT magnetic field exerted weak inhibitory effects on some seizure parameters in amygdala kindled rats). In another study, application of rTMS during amygdala kindling prevented seizures. A cellular mechanistic study revealed that rTMS administration inhibited kindling-induced changes in the electrophysiological properties of hippocampal CA1 pyramidal neurons." (Ye et al, 2019)

- "Rose and his colleagues found that a temporal pattern of electric current associated with a single priming pulse followed 150 ms later by four rapid pulses (equivalent to ~100 Hz) resulted in significant LTP [memory consolidation] when applied to hippocampal slices. When this pattern was transformed to weak magnetic fields in the order of 1 µT and applied to the entire animal before learning a spatial task, the disruption of the memory was as powerful as complete depolarization of the hippocampal region by direct current." (Dotta, 2014)

HARRIBANCE CONFIGURATION, INCREASED POWER SHIFTS IN EEG SPD AND GRAY MATTER CHANGES:

The Harribance Configuration (HC) was the configuration argued by Persinger's Group for EEG and Brain Wave activity for non-local transmission. The human brain is considered to be a collection of microstates that last 80-120ms, these microstates are affected by EM differently in different parts of the Brain based on functionality. Some properties of this configuration are that the main EEG sensor areas involved are on the right side of the brain F4, F8, C4, T4 (right temporal lobe where entanglement symptoms occur as well as the locations related to RTLE) according to Hunter et al 2010. Persinger has found that T4, F8, also T6 is an area of concern to entanglement experiments, F8 and T4 most important for non-local interactions between reader and target (receiver and emitter).

The technical transmission of the HC uses peak-to-peak intensity 1µT 3ms point durations (protons) [shown to slow melanoma growth]. The HC was digitized into a 3d magnetic field (A Potential). It was delivered by 8 complex signals (4 left, 4 right) from an 8 solenoid EM array. The digitized signal was converted to 44100Hz sampling rate, with a signal output of digitized signal converted to 44100Hz sampling rates, 2µV 10% max. audio amplitude. The signal was transmitted for 20s per 1 min. In power shifts the shift is 2µV shifts in EEG when applying HC, for instance the T4 location shifted up 2µV. In a pilot study they tested the psi abilities of a non-psi person and found increased psi ability, it was a pilot study of n=1, so more experimental research would be needed to see if there is a profile that is manifest with non-local effects such as A-B generators.

Saroka has noted that specific brain functional areas are affected by the HC:

> increased intercortical coherence with EM frequency modulation leads to increased activity in the ventral temporal lobe, increased gamma power within the right prefrontal region and the anterior portions of temporal lobe. (Saroka, 2013)

Again another commonality with epilepsy is that Saroka noted that the profile is similar to that of complex partial epileptic-like subjective reports which is known to be associated with focal stimulation of the temporal lobe. (Saroka, 2013)

The HC affects the following Brain Wave bands the most:

alpha 8-12Hz theta 4-8Hz
Gamma 30Hz and greater
[Brain waves have a high Q-factor, the operating radiation bands]

In a separate experiment in 2016 the group tested entangled gamers to measure their brain waves during flow state, non-local interactions of brain citing the following areas of the brain as being involved: right para-hippo-campal gyrus, right occipital, temporo-occipital junction, parietal region, orbitofrontal cortices (Lehman, 2016) Maximal flow state has decreased activation in the left interior frontal lobe (T3), and increased power in 7-8Hz, 27-28Hz, 42Hz, theta and gamma waves affected. The studies have shown that in terms of brain waves, that in various studies from entangled gamers, Harribance, Epilepsy, there is a change in the Theta and Gamma bands of waves. Norseen has focused on 14Hz or 10Hz in the alpha band, this was also shown by Kernbach in his entangle-ment experiments. However, there is a direct convergence between Persinger's Group findings and that of Norseen regarding Theta band, which he speaks of as a lower harmonic reflection of the Alpha band:

NS Model [Norseen Semiotic] our Alpha [8-12Hz] 10Hz brain maintains a complete NS= O, IR as a holographic… in our minds eye of Panum's Fusion Space, accessible to us as mental imagining via signals from the Anterior Cingu-late Cortex (ACC) and fusiform gyrus. Now we also have a complete Theta State 5Hz Brain NS= O, I, R.. self-image of ourselves…. once a powerful Semiotic is set up… one that BioFuses the 10Hz with the 5Hz… you have one Big Mother of All Semiotics… and in this case ZPE [vacuum fluctuations, Casimir effect] is flowing fully at all levels of brain-behavior-memory-new channels… you are not only the signal, but you are the ZPE. (Norseen, Laurie, 2002)

Rouleau et al (2015b) studied the gray and white matter changes associated with the Harribance Configuration finding specific power increases associated with the HC which enhances theta power in gray matter

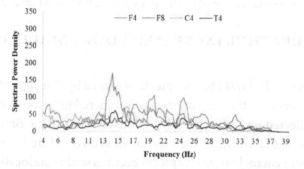

SPD for EEG Locations in the HC: F4, F8, C4, T4 (Rouleau, 2015b, Fig. 2)

Here (Rouleau, Fig 2) we can clearly see that there is a spike at 14Hz in the F8 location, the theta spike is in F4. They found that HC applied to dead brains; there is a difference in theta in gray matter, but white matter was unaf-fected. When applying the C4, T4 components of HC resulted in increase μ of volt power within the theta band in gray compared to white matter. When testing during a live Harribance reading of a target in 1m proximity of each other the reading pair test increased theta in right temporal and parietal regions. (Rouleau, 2015b)

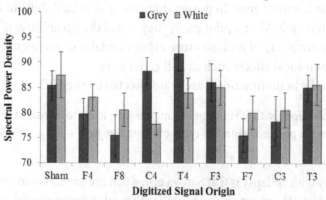

Gray and White matter difference over T4 EEG location, temporal lobe (Fig. 5. Rouleau 2015b)

When the gamma power increases there is a difference in gray and white matter, citing primarily the T4 location as being involved. Significantly increased beta2 power was observed in the left caudate nucleus (T4 rhythm applied) relative to right caudate nucleus, showing like the Havana Syndrome right side bias in non-local experiments. Also, Beta2 SPD increased in left hippocampal body. When applying the F4 component exposure beta2 SPD increased right temporal stem size on dead brains.

F8, T4 band was enhanced for the HC at 20-30Hz. The HC specifically enhances theta power in Gray Matter within the central and temporal regions. The left side is not affected. There is a significant increase when applying the HC T4 component.

Theta Gamma Brain Matter Effect:

- Gamma: right temporal lobe, both white and gray matter affected (Rouleau, 2015b)

- Theta: right central and temporal gray matter affected, not white matter. (Rouleau, 2015b)

The HC affect overall the bands from the Schumann Resonance 7Hz up to 40hz:

Hunter found when Harribance sat proximal to target there was a duration dependent increase in the degree of cross spectral coherence within 19-20Hz [Beta2] band (and the 30-40Hz [Gamma] band) between readers (HC) right temporal lobe and the targets lobe. (Rouleau, 2015b).

Harribance, reader, showed increased photon emissions while Harribance was reading target.

Harribance showed during reading of target most activity in C3, T3 (left temporal lobe), as reader of target. With test on brain tissue (n=3) T4 increased theta and beta2 in left caudate nucleus, C4 also had changes.

Overall, we can see that in both Havana Syndrome, Epilepsy and Non-Local Brain measurements there is a convergence in the Right Temporal Lobe, with specific EEG locations identified, and functional brain areas. In some next steps in studying the problem it is planned to do EEG Machine Learning Analysis on Epileptic patients with symptoms matching those of Havana Syndrome to see if there is any convergence on EEG locations to brain function between the two, aside from the pilot studies of Kernbach and Persinger.

CONCLUSION:
Brain Areas by different research groups:
Verma et al Havana Syndrome

- Auditory cortex: Right and Left Superior Temporal Gyrus, Heschl's Gyrus (BA 22*, 48); Right Thalamus

- visual-spatial subnets: R & L Frontal Gyrus, Superior Frontal Gyrus, Precentral Gyrus (BA

- 6); R & L Inferior Parietal Sulcus (BA 2, 40, 7); R & L Frontal Operculum, IFG* (BA 44,45, 48); R & L Temporal Gyrus (BA 37)

- Cuneus (BA 17)*

- Anterior Insula (no BA, connects to amygdala)

- Putamen (BA 8)

- Post Central Gyrus (BA 1,2,3)

- Middle Temporal Gyrus (BA 21)

- Inferior Frontal Gyrus (IFG) Triangular Part (BA 45)*

- Parietal Operculum (BA 40)

- Supramarginal Gyrus (BA 40)

- Temporal Pole (BA 38)

Persinger et al entanglement studies

- Right and Left Superior Temporal Gyrus (T3, BA 22)* T3 also near Insula

- Right Thalamus

- Left Temporal Lobe (T3, T7) beta band modulation depending on I, We. We T3,T4

- higher amplitude, re-normalizes with more complex information; intrusionist thoughts low beta power doubled in right parahippocampal region
- Parahippocampal Gyrus (Scott 2015)
- Right cuadal temporal lobe (most excess correlation in HC)
- hippocampus
- Harribance Non-Local Profile: F4,F8, C4, T4

Lehman 2015 entangled gamers

- Right parahippocampal gyrus
- right occipital (BA 17)*
- temporo occipital
- parietal
- orbitofrontal cortices (BA 10, 11, 47)
- decreased activation left temporal lobe during flow state increased power in Theta band

Illman 2012 déjà Vu/Vecu

- Hippocampus (80% w/ hippo. Lesions)
- parahippocampus (Mesial Temporal Lobe)
- superior temporal gyrus* (BA 22)
- enterhinal and perirhinal cortices
- amygdala
- right temporal lobe

Common Areas of Norseen, Verma and Persinger:

- Superior Temporal Gyrus (BA 22, EEG T3/T4),
- Visual Cortex (BA 17,18, EEG 01/02),
- Inferior Frontal Gyrus (BA 44,45 and F7/F8
- EEG),
- Hippocampus EEG T5/6
- Right Temporal Lobe is implicated in all studies.
- Norseen has mentioned BA 22, 17,18, 44-5.

In the above we have seen that both Verma et al and Persinger et al have shown that there is a strong right temporal lobe bias to changes in the brain, from brain wave bands to gray and white matter volume, changes also seen in Epilepsy which includes symptoms such as 'hearing voices', tinnitus, dizziness, similar to Havana Syndrome. In Persinger et al we have studies directly related to the Aharonov-Bohm effect generators used by the Soviets and then available to the highest bidder after the fall of the Soviets. On the other hand, we have a study on victims of a syndrome with all people affected in a Communist country, Cuba. Is it possible that Soviet technology studied by Kernbach and Persinger and the medical studies of Verma et al show a common causality in terms of Havana Syndrome, and from that cause a common list of symptoms. My argument is that this is affirmative. However, this does not necessarily mean that the Cuban government is responsible, as anyone with enough knowledge can access the Black Market, even if for the purpose of sabotaging US-Cuba relations, such as ex-Cuban extremists, or other nation states playing rivals off of each other in a classic reflexive control gambit.

From the combined studies we can notice that there are areas that are held in common from epilepsy to Havana Syndrome. The areas that are involved in Norseen's work with Thought Injection are also in Havana Syndrome, are also prevalent in studying the Epileptic pathway, and are also prevalent in Persinger's Non-Local entanglement effects on biological objects, the brain through EEG feedback. These areas Superior Temporal Gyrus (BA 22), Visual Cortex (BA 17,18), Inferior Frontal Gyrus, Hippocampus, In general, Right Temporal Lobe is implicated in all studies. Norseen has also mentioned the involvement of Broca's Area BA 44-5, which come up with Persinger's study of F7 EEG location involved in non-local left temporal entanglement.

This study is a starting point as an attempt to generate a profile of an attack; medical professionals rather than a computer engineer may find this information of use to their work in studying Havana Syndrome. I do not believe we will see a limitation to Havana Syndrome-type symptoms in just those targeted as part of national security work. Indeed, as more and more EM is pumped around us this pollution will trigger similar symptoms, as Persinger observed in Electro-Sensitivity Disorder – Epilepsy-like conditions, and other areas of the brain where individuals show an increased susceptibility to EM radiation whether focused or passive in the environment.

BIBLIOGRAPHY:

Abrahams, E., Keffer, F. (2019) Gyromagnetic effect. McGraw-Hill Access Science https://doi.org/10.1036/1097-8542.303900

Balaban, C., Szczupaks, M., Kiderman, A., Levin, B., Hoffer, M. (2020) Distinctive Convergence Eye Movements in an Acquired Neurosensory Dysfunction. Front. Neurol. 2020; 11: 469. https://doi.org/10.3389/fneur.2020.00469

Baker, R. (2010) Military Applications of High-Frequency Gravitational Waves (Abridged) January 22, 2010 http://www.gravwave.com/docs/Military%20HFGW%20Applications.pdf

Bar, D. (2007) Gravitational Brain Waves, quantum fluctuations and stochastic quantization' https://arxiv.org/abs/0708.1635

Bobrov, A. B. (2009) Interaction of spin fields of material objects' (Russian) Materials of the international scientific conference. Khosta, Sochi, August 25-29, 2009 Conference "Torsion Fields and Information Interactions - 2009" Edited by Zhigalov V.A. http://www.vixri.com/d/Materialy%20konferencii%20-Torsionnye%20polja%20i%20informacionnye%20vzaimodejstvija%20-%202009.pdf

Бобров А.В. (2009) Взаимодействие спиновых полей материальных объектов Торсионные поля и информационные взаимодействия - 2009 Материалы международной научной конференции Электронная версия Хоста, г. Сочи 25-29 августа 2009

Burke, R., Persinger, M. (2013) Convergent Quantitative Solutions Indicating the Human Hippocampus as a Singularity and Access to Cosmological Consciousness. NeuroQuantology March 2013, Volume 11, Issue 1, Page 1-7 https://www.researchgate.net/publication/270552657_Convergent_Quantitative_Solutions_Indicating_the_Huma n_Hippocampus_as_a_Singularity_and_Access_to_Cosmological_Consciousness

Cao, W. et al, (2020) Selenomelanin: An Abiotic Selenuium Analogue of Pheomelanin. Journal of American Chemical Society 2020 Jul 22;142(29):12802-12810. doi: 10.1021/jacs.0c05573. https://pubmed.ncbi.nlm.nih.gov/32638590/

Chiao, R. et al (2002) Superconductors as quantum transducers and antennas for gravitational and electromagnetic radiation https://arxiv.org/abs/gr-qc/0204012

Chiao, R.Y. et al. (2014). A Gravitational Aharonov-Bohm Effect, and Its Connection to Parametric Oscillators and Gravitational Radiation. In: Struppa, D., Tollaksen, J. (eds) Quantum Theory: A Two-Time Success Story. Springer, Milano. https://www.researchgate.net/publication/234168732_A_Gravitational_Aharonov-Bohm_Effect_and_Its_Connection_to_Parametric_Oscillators_and_Gravitational_Radiation

Chiao, R., Sharping, J., Martinez, L., Kang, B., Castelli, A., Inan, N., and Thompson, J. (2017) Dynamical Casimir Effect and the Possibility of laser-like generation of Gravitational Radiation https://arxiv.org/abs/1712.08680

DeGorgio, C., Curtis, A., Carapetian, A. Hovesepian, D., Krisnadasen, A., Markovic, D. (2020) Why are epilepsy mortality rates rising in the United States? A population based multiple cause-of-death study. BMJ Open 10(8):e035767 https://www.researchgate.net/publication/343842965_Why_are_epilepsy_mortality_rates_rising_in_the_United_States_A_population-based_multiple_cause-of-death_study

Djumaeva, N., Musabaev, E., Khusainov, I. (2004) Application of unusual field of low level laser radiation in the treatment of patient with chronic hepatitis c virus infection: case report and literature review. Journal of the Science of Healing Outcomes, 6(22):5–10, 2004. https://www.researchgate.net/publication/237047134_Application_of_Unusual_Field_of_Low_Level_Laser_Radiation_in_the_Treatment_of_Chronic_Hepatitis_C_Virus_Infection_Case_Report_and_Literature_Review

Dotta, B., Karbowski, L., Murugan, N. Persinger, M. (2015) Inverse relationship between photon flux densities and nanotesla magnetic fields over cell aggregates: Quantitative evidence for energetic conservation FEBS Open Bio Volume 5, 2015, Pages 413-418 https://www.researchgate.net/publication/276461961_Inverse_relationship_between_photon_flux_densities_and_nanotesla_magnetic_fields_over_cell_aggregates_Quantitative_evidence_for_energetic_conservation

Dotta, B. Vares, D., Buckner, C. Lafrenie, M., Persinger, M. (2014) Magnetic Field Configurations Corresponding to Electric Field Patterns That Evoke Long-Term Potentiation Shift Power Spectra of Light Emissions from microtubules from Non-Neural Cells. Open Journal of Biophysics, Vol.4 No.4, October https://www.researchgate.net/publication/266023830_Magnetic_Field_Configurations_Corresponding_to_Electri c_Field_Patterns_That_Evoke_Long- Term_Potentiation_Shift_Power_Spectra_of_Light_Emissions_from_µtubules_from_Non-Neural_Cells

Dotta, B.T. and Persinger, M.A. (2012) "Doubling" of Local Photon Emissions When Two Simultaneous, Spatially- Separated, Chemiluminescent Reactions Share the Same Magnetic Field Configurations. Journal of Biophysical Chemistry, 3, 72. https://www.scirp.org/journal/paperinformation.aspx?paperid=17181 http://dx.doi.org/10.4236/jbpc.2012.31009

Dotta, B.T., Murugan, N.J., Karbowski, L.M. and Persinger, M.A. (2013) Excessive Correlated Shifts in pH within Distal Solutions Sharing Phase-Uncoupled Angular Accelerating Magnetic Fields: Macro-Entanglement and Information Transfer. International Journal of Physical Sciences, 8, 1783-1787. https://www.researchgate.net/publication/276040075_Non-Local_pH_Shifts_and_Shared_Changing_Angular_Velocity_Magnetic_Fields_Discrete_Energies_and_the_Importance_of_Point_Durations

Dotta, B.T., Karbowski, L.M., Murugan, N.J. and Persinger, M.A. (2013) Incremental Shifts in pH Spring Water Can Be Stored as "Space-Memory": Encoding and Retrieval through the Application of the Same Rotating Magnetic Field. NeuroQuantology, 11. https://www.researchgate.net/publication/266838412_Incremental_Shifts_in_pH_Spring_Water_Can_Be_Stored_as_Space-Memory_Encoding_and_Retrieval_Through_the_Application_of_the_Same_Rotating_Magnetic_Field http://dx.doi.org/10.14704/nq.2013.11.4.714

Feldman, Y., Puzenko, A., Ishai, P., Caduff, A., Davidovic, I., Sakran, F., Agranat, A. (2009) The electromagnetic response of human skin in the millimetre and submillimetre wave range

Phys Med Biol 54(11):3341-63. https://www.researchgate.net/publication/24415748_The_electromagnetic_response_of_human_skin_in_the_millimetre_and_submillimetre_wave_range DOI: 10.1088/0031-9155/54/11/005

Feldman, Y. et al (2014) Circular Polarization Evidence by the Three Dimensional Chiral Structure of Sweat ducts. Physical Review E 89(4-1) https://www.researchgate.net/publication/262338192_Circular_polarization_induced_by_the_three-dimensional_chiral_structure_of_human_sweat_ducts

Felicetti, S., Sanz, M., Lamata, L., Romero, G. (2013) The dynamical Casimir effect generates entanglement Conference: March Meeting of The American Physical Society https://www.researchgate.net/publication/271208934_The_dynamical_Casimir_effect_generates_entanglement

Fickler, R., Lapkiewicz, R., Plick, W.N., Krenn, M., Schaeff, C., Ramelow, S. and Zeilinger, A. (2012) Quantum Entanglement of High Angular Momenta. Science, 338, 640-643. http://dx.doi.org/10.1126/science.1227193

Friedman, Y., Ostapenko, V. (2010) The complex pre-potential and the Aharonov-Bohm Effect Journal of Physics A Mathematical and Theoretical 43(40):405305 DOI:10.1088/1751-8113/43/40/405305 https:// www.researchgate.net/publication/230964168_The_complex_pre-potential_and_the_Aharonov-Bohm_effect

Gosh. Subrata, Fujita, Daisuke (2014) Live Visualizations of Single Isolated tubulin Protein Self-Assembly via tunneling current: Effect of electromagnetic pumping during spontaneous growth of microtubule. Scientific Reports 4(1):7303 https://www.researchgate.net/publication/269173240_Live_visualizations_of_single_isolated_tubulin_protein_self-assembly_via_tunneling_current_Effect_of_electromagnetic_pumping_during_spontaneous_growth_of_microtubule

Grabner, R., De Smedt, B. (2012) Oscillatory EEG Correlates of Arithmetic Strategies: A Training Study. Frontiers in Psychology 3:428 DOI:10.3389/fpsyg.2012.00428

Gurov, Yu. (2016) About the Field Forms of Communication of Biological Systems. pg. 62, http://www.second-physics.ru/moscow2016/moscow2016.pdf [english machine translation: https://github.com/autonomous019/Aharonov-bohm-cybersecurity/blob/main/gurov%20biological%20communication.pdf]

Hu, H. & Wu. M. (2006) Evidence of Non-local Chemical, Thermal and Gravitational Effects. NeruoQuantology, 2006; 4: 2901-306. http://cogprints.org/5613, http://arxiv.org/ags/quant-ph/0208068v4,

Illman, N., Butler, C., Souchay, C. Moulin, C. (2012) Déjà Experiences in Temporal Lobe Epilepsy. Epilepsy Research and Treatment Vol. 2012 https://www.ncbi.nlm.nih.gov/pmc/articles/PMC3420423/

Karbrowski, L., Murugan, N., Persinger, M. (2016) Experimental Evidence That Specific Photon Energies Are "Stored" in Malignant Cells for an Hour: The Synergism of Weak Magnetic Field-LED Wavelength Pulses Biology & Medicine https://www.researchgate.net/publication/298845436_Experimental_evidence_that_specific_photon_energies_ar e_Stored_in_malignant_cells_for_an_hour_The_synergism_of_weak_magnetic_Field-LED_wavelength_pulses

Karbowski, L., Murugan, N., Persinger, M. (2016b) Experimental evidence that specific photon energies are "Stored" in malignant cells for an hour: The synergism of weak magnetic Field-LED wavelength pulses Biologie Médicale · January 2016 https://www.researchgate.net/publication/298845436

Kaznacheev, V., Trofimov, A. (2004) A Method for Creating a Hologram Containing Non-Visualized Physiologically Significant Information. Russian Patent Казначеев В.П. Трофимов А.В. Способ создания голограммы, содержащей невизуализированную физиологически значимую информацию https://patents.google.com/patent/RU2239860C1/ru

Kellio, S., Hyona, J., Revonsuo, A., Sikka, P., Nuumenmaa, L. (2011) The Existence of a Hypnotic State Revealed by Eye Movements PlosOne https://journals.plos.org/plosone/article?id=10.1371/journal.pone.0026374

Kernbach, Serge (2017) Tests of the circular Poynting vector emitter in static E/H fields. International Journal of Unconventional Science Issue E2, pp. 23-40, 2017 http://www.unconv-science.org/e2/kernbach1

Kernbach, Serge (2018) Replication experiment on distant influence on biological organisms conducted in 1986, International Journal of Unconventional Science, Issue E2, pages 41-46, 2018 http://www.unconv-science.org/pdf/e2/kernbach2-en.pdf

Kernbach, S. (2016) On metrology of systems operating with 'high-penetrating' emmision. International Journal of Unconventional Science E1 http://www.unconv-science.org/en/n2/kernbach/

Kernbach, S. (2019) Distant Monitoring of Entangled Macro-Objects. NeuroQuantology, Volume 17, Issue 03, Page 19-42, doi: 10.14704/nq.2019.17.03.1977 https://scholar.archive.org/work/u2v4oiddcjb4daza3gbtuabgxe/access/wayback/https://pdfs.semanticscholar.org/245b/792b632619559b1719963bf44bf467780b8b.pdf

Koren, S., Persinger, M. (2015) Potential Role of the Entanglement Velocity of 1023 m·s-1 To Accommodate Recent Measurements of Large Scale Structures of the Universe. International Letters of Chemistry, Physics and Astronomy 3 (2015) 106-112 ISSN 2299-3843 http://neurosciarchive.byethost12.com/2015-Potential-Role-of-the-Entanglement-Velocity-of-1023-ms-1-To-Accommodate-Recent-Measurements-of-Large-Scale-Structures-of-the-Universe.pdf?i=1

Koren, S., Persinger, M. (2016) The Aharanov-Bohm Phase Shift and Magnetic Vector Potential "A" Could Accommodate for Optical Coupler, Digital-to-Analogue Magnetic Field Excess Correlations of Photon Emissions Within Living Aqueous Systems https://www.researchgate.net/publication/328720497_The_Aharanov-Bohm_Phase_Shift_and_Magnetic_Vector_Potential_aoeAa_Could_Accommodate_for_Optical_Coupler_Digital -to-Analogue_Magnetic_Field_Excess_Correlations_of_Photon_Emissions_Within_Living_Aqueous

Koren, S.A., & Persinger, M. (2016b). Detection of Transient 1.42 GHz (Hydrogen Line) Bursts From the Human Brain-Body During Specific Angular Velocities. Journal of Advances in Physics, 4129-4136. https://www.researchgate.net/publication/328719614_Detection_of_Transient_142_GHz_Hydrogen_Line_Bursts_From_the_Human_Brain-Body_During_Specific_Angular_Velocities

Koren, S.A., Persinger, M.A. (2002) Possible Disruption of Remote Viewing by Complex Weak Magnetic Fields around the Stimulus Site and the Possibility of Accessing Real Phase Space: A Pilot Study. Perceptual and Motor Skills Vol. 95, Issue 3 https://doi.org/10.2466/pms.2002.95.3.989

Kravchenko, Y., Saveliev, A. (КравченкоЮ.П., Савельев А.В.) (2009) Development and application of devices for measuring ultra-weak natural fields radiation Разработка и применение устройств для измерения сверхслабых полей естественного излучения in (Russian) Materials of the international scientific conference. Khosta, Sochi, August 25-29, 2009 Conference "Torsion Fields and Information Interactions - 2009" http://www.vixri.com/d/Materialy%20konferencii%20-Torsionnye%20polja%20i%20informacionnye%20vzaimodejstvija%20-%202009.pdf Торсионные поля и информационные взаимодействия - 2009 Материалы международной научной конференции Электронная версия Хоста, г. Сочи 25-29 августа 2009

Kravkov, G. A. (Г. А. Кравков) (2006) The Effect of Non-Thermal (Informational) Exposure to Electromagnetic Radiation of Extremely High Frequency on Biological Objects and Humans (in Russian) Часть 1 Эффект нетеплового (информационного) воздействия электромагнитного излучения крайне высокой частоты на биологические объекты и человека Краткий обзор https://refnew.ru/g-a-kravkov-chaste-1-effekt- neteplovogo-informacionnogo-vozdej.html

Krishnan, A. (2017) Military Neuroscience and the Coming Age of Neurowarfare (Emerging Technologies, Ethics and International Affairs). Routledge. https://www.routledge.com/Military-Neuroscience-and-the-Coming-Age-of-Neurowarfare/Krishnan/p/book/9781138361447

Krasnobryzhev V.G (2009) Spinor fields in brain activity (Russian) Materials of the international scientific conference. Khosta, Sochi, August 25-29, 2009 Conference "Torsion Fields and Information Interactions - 2009" Edited by Zhigalov V.A. pg. 564 http://www.vixri.com/d/Materialy%20konferencii%20-Torsionnye%20polja%20i%20informacionnye%20vzaimodejstvija%20-%202009.pdf

Lehman, B. (2016) Interaction Between Virtual (Computer Gaming) Environments, Brain Activity, and the Schumann Resonance as the Next Evolutionary Step in Adaptation: Teilhard de Chardin's Noosphere Master of Science (M.Sc.) in Biology https://www.researchgate.net/publication/303784704_Interaction_Between_Virtual_Computer_Gaming_Environ ments_Brain_Activity_and_the_Schumann_Resonance_as_the_Next_Evolutionary_Step_in_Adaptation_Teilhar d_de_Chardin's_Noosphere

Lehman, B., Scott, M. Rouleau, N., Tessaro, L. (2015) Experimental Production of Excess Correlation across the Atlantic Ocean of Right Hemispheric Theta-Gamma Power Between Subject Pairs Sharing Circumcerebral Rotating Magnetic Fields (Part II) https://www.researchgate.net/publication/282661047_Experimental_Production_of_Excess_Correlation_across_the_Atlantic_Ocean_of_Right_Hemispheric_Theta- Gamma_Power_Between_Subject_Pairs_Sharing_Circumcerebral_Rotating_Magnetic_Fields_Part_II see video presentation at Consciousness Hacking: https://www.youtube.com/watch?v=L5I3wOyo-rg

Libby, A., Buschman, T. (2019) Rotational Dynamics Reduce Interference Between Sensory and Memory Representations. Nat Neurosci. 2021 May;24(5):715-726. doi: 10.1038/s41593-021-00821-9. Epub 2021 Apr 5. https://pubmed.ncbi.nlm.nih.gov/33821001/

Marchese, S., Esposti, R., Bolzoni, F., Cavallari, P. (2019) Transcranial Direct Current Stimulation on Parietal Operculum Contralateral to the Moving Limb Does Not Affect the Programming of Intra-Limb Anticipatory Postural Adjustments https://www.frontiersin.org/articles/10.3389/fphys.2019.01159/fullFront. Physiol., 11 September 2019 | https://doi.org/10.3389/fphys.2019.0115

McCarron, M. (2021) Aharonov-Bohm Cybersecurity Project https://github.com/autonomous019/Aharonov- bohm-cybersecurity [includes source code and arduino instructions for A-B Coil mentioned in study]

Murugan NJ, Karbowski LM, Lafrenie RM, Persinger MA (2013) Temporally-Patterned Magnetic Fields Induce Complete Fragmentation in Planaria. PLoS ONE 8(4): e61714. doi:10.1371/journal.pone.0061714 https://journals.plos.org/plosone/article?id=10.1371/journal.pone.0061714

Murugan, N., Karbowski, L. Dotta, B., Persinger, M. (2015) Delayed Shifts in pH Responses to Weak Acids in Spring Water Exposed to Circular Rotating Magnetic Fields: A Narrow Band Intensity-Dependence. International Research Journal of Pure and Applied Chemistry 5(2):131-139 DOI: 10.9734/IRJPAC/2015/13156 https://www.researchgate.net/publication/282624530_Delayed_Shifts_in_pH_Responses_to_Weak_Acids_in_Sp ring_Water_Exposed_to_Circular_Rotating_Magnetic_Fields_A_Narrow_Band_Intensity-Dependence

Norseen, J., Kropotov, J., Kremen, I. (1999) Bio-fusion for intelligent systems control. Proceedings Volume 3719, Sensor Fusion: Architectures, Algorithms, and Applications III; (1999) https://doi.org/10.1117/12.341364 Presentation AeroSense '99, 1999, Orlando, FL, United States

Norseen, John (1996) Images of Mind: The Semiotic Alphabet. http://www.acsa2000.net/john2.html

Norseen, John (2000) 'Mathematics, BioFusion and Reflexive Control for Sentient Machines', Presentation for International Reflexive Control Symposium (RC 2000) Russian Academy of Sciences Institute for Psychology 17 – 19 October 2000 Moscow, Russia http://www.acsa.net/norseen2000/

Persinger, M., Saroka, K. Koren, S., St-Pierre, L. (2010) The Electromagnetic Induction of Mystical and Altered States within the Laboratory. Journal of Consciousness Exploration & Research| October 2010, Vol. 1, Issue 7, pp. 808-830 https://www.researchgate.net/publication/265935637_The_Electromagnetic_Induction_of_Mystical_and_Altered_States_within_the_Laboratory

Persinger, M. (2014) Relating Casimir to Magnetic Energies Results in Spatial Dimensions that Define Biology Systems. International Letters of Chemistry Physics and Astronomy 39:160-165 DOI: 10.18052/www.scipress.com/ILCPA.39.160 https://www.researchgate.net/publication/277934374_Relating_Casimir_to_Magnetic_Energies_Results_in_Spat ial_Dimensions_that_Define_Biology_Systems

Persinger, M. (2015) inverse relationship between photon flux densities. FEBS Open Bio Volume 5, 2015, Pages 413-418

Persinger, M. (2015b) The Graviton: An Emergent Solution From The Equivalence of Universal Magnetic Field Intensity and Radiant Flux Density. Journal of Advances in Physics Vol. 10 No. 2 2811-2815 DOI:10.24297/jap.v10i3.1318 https://www.researchgate.net/publication/328719615_The_Graviton_An_Emergent_Solution_From_The_Equival ence_of_Universal_Magnetic_Field_Intensity_and_Radiant_Flux_Density

Persinger, M., Dotta, B., Murugan, N., Karboski, L., Koren, S. (2016) Rotational Frequency Matching of the Energy of the Changing Angular Velocity Magnetic Field Intensity and the Proton Magnetic Moment Produces a Ten Fold Increased Excess Correlation in pH Shifts in Spring Water. NeuroQuantology, Volume 14, Issue 1, Page 1-8. doi: 10.14704/nq.2016.14.1.888 https://www.researchgate.net/publication/299443936_Rotational_Frequency_Matching_of_the_Energy_of_the_Changing_Angular_Velocity_Magnetic_Field_Intensity_and_the_Proton_Magnetic_Moment_Produces_a_Ten_Fold_Increased_Excess_Correlation_in_pH_Shifts_in_Sp

Pribram, K. (1999) Quantum holography: Is it relevant to brain function? Information Sciences 115 (1999) 97-102 https://www.sciencedirect.com/science/article/abs/pii/S0020025598100828

Puthoff, H. (1998) Communication Method and Apparatus with Signals Comprising Scalar and Vector Potentials without Electromagnetic Fields. US Patent 5845220. https://patents.google.com/patent/US5845220A/en

Ou-Yang, H., Kollias, N (2004) Spectral Responses of Melanin to Ultraviolet A Irradiation. Journal of Investigative Dermatology Vol. 122, Issue 2 Pg. 492-96. https://pubmed.ncbi.nlm.nih.gov/15009735/

Romaualdo, I., Hackl, L., Yokomizo, N. (2019) Entanglement production in the dynamical Casimir effect at parametric resonance. Phys. Rev. D 100, 065022 https://journals.aps.org/prd/abstract/10.1103/PhysRevD.100.065022

Rouleau, N., Carniello, T.N. and Persinger, M.A. (2014) Non-Local pH Shifts and Shared Changing Angular Velocity Magnetic Fields: Discrete Energies and the Importance of Point Durations. Journal of Biophysical Chemistry. http://dx.doi.org/10.4236/jbpc.2014.52006

Rouleau, N., Persinger, M. (2015) Local Electromagnetic Fields Exhibit Temporally Non-Linear, East-West Oriented 1 - 5 nT Diminishments within a Toroid: Empirical Measurement and Quantitative Solutions Indicating a Potential Mechanism for Excess Correlation. Journal of Electromagnetic Analysis and Applications 07(02):19-30. DOI: 10.4236/jemaa.2015.72003 https://www.researchgate.net/publication/273487699_Local_Electromagnetic_Fields_Exhibit_Temporally_Non-Linear_East-West_Oriented_1_-_5_nT_Diminishments_within_a_Toroid_Empirical_Measurement_and_Quantitative_Solutions_Indicating_a_Potential_Mechanism_f

Rouleau, N., Persinger, M. (2015b) Enhancement of Theta and Gamma Activity Power Within Fixed Sections of Human Brains Stimulated by Sean Harribance's Electroencephalographic Configuration: Is He Equivalent to a "Universal Donor" for Entanglement? November 2015 NeuroQuantology 13(4) DOI: 10.14704/nq.2015.13.4.886 https://www.researchgate.net/publication/288686415_Enhancement_of_Theta_and_Gamma_Activity_Power_Within_Fixed_Sections_of_Human_Brains_Stimulated_by_Sean_Harribance's_Electroencephalographic_Configuration_Is_He_Equivalent_to_a_Universal_Donor_for_Enta

Quintero-Rincon, A., Pereyra, M., D'Giano, C. Batatia, H., Risk, M. (2016) A new algorithm for epilepsy seizure onset detection and spread estimation from EEG signals. Journal of Physics Conference Series 705(1):012032. https://www.researchgate.net/publication/302870395_A_new_algorithm_for_epilepsy_seizure_onset_detection_and_spread_estimation_from_EEG_signals

Samokhvalov, V. (2016) Non-electromagnetic force interaction in presence of rotating masses in vacuum. IJUS E1. http://www.unconv-science.org/en/n1/samokhvalov/

Saniya, K, Patil, B., Madhavrao, D. Prakash, K., Sailesh, K., Archana, R., Johny, M. (2017) Neuroanatomical Changes in Brain Structures Related to Cognition in Epilepsy: An Update. J Nat Sci Biol Med. 2017 Jul-Dec; 8(2): 139–143. doi: 10.4103/0976-9668.210016 https://www.ncbi.nlm.nih.gov/pmc/articles/PMC5523517/

Saroka KS, Persinger MA. (2013) Potential production of Hughlings Jackson's "parasitic consciousness" by physiologically-patterned weak transcerebral magnetic fields: QEEG and source localization. Epilepsy & Behavior : E&B. 2013 Sep;28(3):395-407. DOI: 10.1016/j.yebeh.2013.05.023. https://linkinghub.elsevier.com/retrieve/pii/S1525505013002394

Saxena, K., Pushpendra Singh, Pathik Sahoo, Satyajit Sahu, Subrata Ghosh, Kanad Ray, Daisuke Fujita, Anirban Bandyopadhyay. Fractal, Scale Free Electromagnetic Resonance of a Single Brain Extracted microtubule Nanowire, a Single Tubulin Protein and a Single Neuron. Fractal and Fractional. 4 [2] (2020) https://doi.org/10.3390/fractalfract4020011

Scott, M., Rouleau, N., Lehman, B., Tessaro, L., Juden-Kelly, L., Saroka, K., Persinger, M. (2015) Experimental Production of Excess Correlation across the Atlantic Ocean of Right Hemispheric Theta-Gamma Power Between Subject Pairs Sharing Circumcerebral Rotating Magnetic Fields (Part I) https://www.researchgate.net/publication/282661148_Experimental_Production_of_Excess_Correlation_across_the_Atlantic_Ocean_of_Right_Hemispheric_Theta-Gamma_Power_between_Subject_Pairs_Sharing_Circumcerebral_Rotating_Magnetic_Fields_Part_I

Scott, M.A., Rouleau, N., Lehman, B.S., Tessaro, L.W.E., Juden-Kelly, L.M. and Persinger, M.A. (2015) Experimental Production of Excess Correlation Across the Atlantic Ocean of Right Hemispheric Theta-Gamma Power between Subject Pairs Sharing Circumcerebral Rotating Magnetic Fields (Part II). Journal of Consciousness Research & Exploration, 6, 658-707. https://jcer.com/index.php/jcj/article/view/493

Shan, Yi-Chia, Fang, W., Chang, Y., Wu, J. (2021) Effect of Near-Infrared Pulsed Light on the Human Brain Using Electroencephalography. Evidence-Based Complementary and Alternative Medicine Volume 2021, Article ID 6693916, 11 pages https://doi.org/10.1155/2021/6693916 https://www.ncbi.nlm.nih.gov/pmc/articles/PMC7954620

Shkatov, V.T. (2009) 'Additional Explanations for using the method torsion [AB] phase portrait in the fine field diagnostics of objects.' Khosta, Sochi, August 25-29, 2009 Conference "Torsion Fields and Information Interactions - 2009" Edited by Zhigalov V.A. http://www.vixri.com/d/Materialy%20konferencii%20-Torsionnye%20polja%20i%20informacionnye%20vzaimodejstvija%20-%202009.pdf

Singh, P., Doti, R., Lugo, E., Faubert, J. (2018) Frequency Fractal Behavior in the Retina Nano-Center-Fed Dipole Antenna Network of a Human Eye in Soft Computing: Theories and Applications (pp.201-211) DOI:10.1007/978-981-10-5699-4_20 https://www.researchgate.net/publication/321294020_Frequency_Fractal_Behavior_in_the_Retina_Nano-Center-Fed_Dipole_Antenna_Network_of_a_Human_Eye

Sokolova, V. A. (В.А. Соколова) (2016) 'First Experimental Confirmation for the Existence of Torsion Fields and Prospects of Their use in People's Economy' Russian Physical Society "Journal of Russian Physical Thought," 2016, No. 1-12 Русское Физическое Общество «Журнал Русской Физической Мысли," 2016, No 1-12, стр. 2 http://docplayer.com/92040462-Zhurnal-russkoy-fizicheskoy-mysli-zhrfm-2016-1-12.html

Stav, T., Faerman, A., Maguid, E., Oren, D. Kleiner, V. (2018) Quantum entanglement of the spin and orbital angular momentum of photons using metamaterials. Science 14 Sep 2018 Vol. 361, Issue 6407, pp. 1101- 1104 DOI: 10.1126/science.aat9042 https://science.sciencemag.org/content/361/6407/1101.full

Sterzer, P., Kleinschmidt, A. (2010) Anterior insula activations in perceptual paradigms: often observed but barely understood. Brain Struct Funct. 2010 Jun;214(5-6):611-22. DOI 10.1007/s00429-010-0252-2 http://behavioralhealth2000.com/wp-content/uploads/2017/09/Anterior-insula-activations-in-perceptual- paradigms-often-observed-but-barely-understood.pdf

Verma, R., Swanson, R., Parker, D. (2019) Neuroimaging Findings in US Government Personnel With Possible Exposure to Directional Phenomena in Havana, Cuba. JAMA. 2019;322(4):336-347. doi:10.1001/jama.2019.9269 https://jamanetwork.com/journals/jama/fullarticle/2738552

Wächter, S. (2018) The Aharonov-Bohm effect Proseminar on Algebra, Topology & Group theory in physics ETH Zürich March 30, 2018 https://ethz.ch/content/dam/ethz/special-interest/phys/theoretical-physics/itp-dam/documents/ gaberdiel/proseminar_fs2018/06_Waechter.pdf

Yamashita et al, (2021) Remote Control of Neural Function by X-Ray Induced Scintillation. Nature Communications 9 Oct 2019 https://www.biorxiv.org/content/biorxiv/early/2020/11/01/798702.full.pdf

Ye, H., Kaszuba, S. (2019)   Neuromodulation with Electromagnetic Stimulation for Seizure Suppression: From Electrode to Magnetic Coil. IBRO Rep. 2019 Dec; 7: 26–33. https://ecommons.luc.edu/biology_fac-pubs/112/

CHAPTER 10

HYPNOSIS IN NEUROWARFARE

Is Torture hypnosis? It's an interesting question to consider: While we may view the process of hypnotism as a non-invasive parlor game, the reality is that in interrogation in the military intelligence world 'pressure' or 'torture' is used to induce a suggestive state in interrogates. This is partly what led to the treatment of POW's during America's two Gulf wars as 'terrorists', although these methodologies were learned by the US from the UK. Little is known in the US or UK about the original hooded men of the Irish in Northern Ireland as recounted by the US DIA in 1972:

July 1972

Section II - Current Events

Part A - Events in Northern Ireland

1. (U) The following discussion is based on 1971 and 1972 literature dealing with the manipulation of human behavior. The events that have been reported to have occurred are not Soviet originated but provide an excellent example of the type of efforts that this report is expressing.

2. (U) Recently there has appeared in the press some discussion elaborating on the techniques and procedures for detaining, treating and interrogating prisoners in Northern Ireland (2,3). According to the report, once the detainees are in prison, they come under three types of regime which create in men a state of great confusion, suggestibility, and distress. The first regime contained various methods to produce sensory isolation. The men were made to stand still against a wall with their hands in the air for four to six hours at a time. The total length was 43 1/2 hours. Hoods were placed over the men's heads to further abolish visual input. Sensory input was further decreased by having loud noise generators turned on in order to mask meaningful sounds. The detainees were, therefore, isolated from their sensory world.

3. (U) The second sensory regime has the effect of increasing confusion and disorientation. Some men were rushed out, hooded and doubled up, past barking dogs, loaded into a helicopter, doors closed, engine revved up, then unloaded, then reloaded, with the procedure repeated three times. In another incident, detainees without shoes were made to move quickly over rough ground by military police.

4. (U) The third type of treatment has the effect of increasing stress and anxiety and reducing resistance to the disorienting effect on the two types described above. It appears the dietary intake was restricted to bread and water at six-hour intervals. Maximum weight loss was achieved it appears. One detainee lost eight pounds in seven days. To accompany the diet restrictions, no sleep was allowed the first two or three days. Forty-eight hours sleep deprivation, in certain individuals, has been known to precipitate psychotic-like states.

5. (U) Psychological torture and physical abuse have been used on Catholic detainees in Northern Ireland. High-frequency sound waves (range not given in report) and sensory deprivation – research methods that have been outlawed for use on humans by the American Psychological Association - were being used to undermine the dignity and destroy the effectiveness of the Catholic minority in Northern Ireland. The case of one 40-year-old released prisoner has been reported. Upon release, the man's mental and physical condition suggested senility – a condition inconsistent with his health at the time of his internment. The man walks like he is 65, whimpers in the dark and has an attention span so short he cannot carry on a conversation.

6. (U) The Northern Ireland procedure can be expected to greatly increase the pliability of detainees under interrogation since sensory deprivation increases suggestibility and lowers intellectual competence. Stress-isolation techniques can reach the extend of eliciting false confessions where both prisoner and interrogator are

convinced the statement rendered are true. It is hoped that the above examples impart to the reader a feeling for the type of mind manipulating procedures that will be discussed later in this report.

7. (U) since it appears that the research behind sensory deprivation has been put to current use on humans, the interested reader might peruse Biderman and Zimmer's 1961 publication entitled "The Manipulation of Human Behavior" (4). The book represents a critical examination of some of the conjectures about the application of scientific knowledge to manipulation of human behavior. The problem is explored within a particular reference: the interrogation of unwilling subject. Attention has been focused on interrogation because of the central position this topic has had in public discussions of prisoner of war (PW) behavior. (DIA, 1972, 2-3)

As one can see from the report above the purpose of 'pressure' is to increase suggestibility. Which is to say hypnotic suggestibility, which sometimes can just lead one to free one's conscience into a fake world where one will even confess to absolute delusions. A warfighter is going to want to understand how susceptible one is to hypnosis, not just to counteract the rare instances of being a POW but also to counter information or perception management attempts of the enemy at all times in all circumstances. In the following study I will be examining the issue of hypnosis from a physiological perspective identifying differences based in biology between biologically stratified individuals in terms of hypnosis. Again, it is important to remember experiments on remote influencing were conducted in tandem with hypnosis, such as Vasiliev's experiments. (see Ch. 3)

INTRODUCTION TO HYPNOSIS

What is hypnosis academically speaking:

Hypnosis can be defined as "a procedure during which a health professional or researcher suggests that a patient or subject experience changes in sensations, perceptions, thoughts, or behavior." Hypnosis is seen as a state of focused attention involving focal concentration, and inner absorption with a relative suspension of peripheral awareness and has three components:

- absorption: tendency to become fully involved in a perceptual, imaginative, or ideational experience.

- dissociation: mental separation of components of experience that would ordinarily be processed together.

- suggestibility: responsiveness to social cues, leading to an enhanced tendency to comply with hypnotic instructions, representing a suspension of critical judgment.

We have shown that subjects in a hypnotic state reported a phenomenology of an altered state of consciousness: participants reported a higher degree of absorption and dissociation as compared to normal wakefulness and control conditions [See L.L. Vasiliev Russian studies from 1930s]. Other studies have also shown that hypnosis produces alterations in aspects of consciousness and is characterized by modulation of properties of the phenomenal self-consciousness such as mental ease (i.e., easy flow of thoughts), absorption, reduction in self-orientation and automaticity (i.e., responses are experienced as being produced without deliberation and/or effort). (Vanhaudenhuyse et al, 2013, 344)

There is a differentiation between highly hypnotizable subjects and low hypnotizable subjects:

By studying coherence of the EEG signal, Kirenskay et al. showed that baseline EEG differed in coherence between subjects with high and low hypnotizability. Indeed, highly hypnotizable subjects were characterized by higher distributed brain regions coherence within delta, theta, and alpha bands. A study conducted by Hinterberger et al. showed the different states of consciousness that can be observed during a complete hypnotic procedure (relaxation-induction-suggestion-waking up) in one highly hypnotizable subject. The dominant pattern highlighted in this study can be summarized as follows:

- closed-eyes condition may be associated with increased bilateral parietal and occipital alpha, parietal sensory-motor and beta activities.

- hypnotic state seems characterized by increased frontal alpha, decreased central, frontal and parietal gamma bilaterally and increased occipital gamma.

- deep hypnotic state is characterized by distributed reinforcement of activity in all frequency bands.

- the awake state showed reduced activity on all frequency bands in central, frontal and parietal areas, while gamma increased in temporal and prefrontal areas (this last pattern is attributed by the authors to a highly relaxed but mindful wake state). (Vanhaudenhuyse et al, 2013, 346)

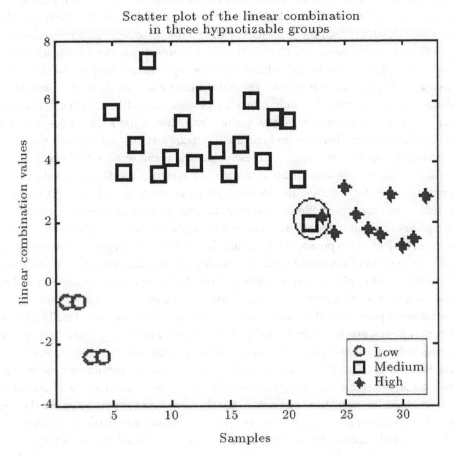

Figure 3. The scatter plot of the linear combination of the *RF*'s values of the channels Fp2, Fp1, F8, F3, F7, C3, T3, T6, P4, Pz, P3, T5 and O1 in three hypnotizable groups.

(Baghdadi, 2005, 77)

As shall be shown below, the Anterior Cingulate Cortex (ACC) plays a significant part in determining not just hypnotic susceptibility but also political ideology to a degree. The ACC is known from functional magnetic resonance imaging (fMRI) and positron emission tomography (PET) to have found ACC hemodynamic activation in a wide variety of tasks involving reading, word generation, episodic recall, working memory, emotion (Phan et al., see below), and attention. ACC activation is related to the number of possible responses in a task, suggesting that it may contribute to response choice or "selection-for-action." This may reflect a basic contribution to motor control or a role in detecting situations that requires strategic intervention because of conflicting potential responses that may lead to errors.

Brain mechanisms underlying the modulation of pain perception under hypnotic condition have been investigated by a growing number of neuro imaging studies. In PET studies, the modulatory effect of hypnosis was shown to be mediated by the anterior cingulate cortex (ACC). In addition, studies have demonstrated increased modulation of the ACC and a large cortical and subcortical network, encompassing prefrontal, insular, and pregenual cortices, pre-SMA, thalami, striatum and brainstem in the context of hypnosis. In a fMRI study, painful stimulation in a normal alert state resulted in brain activation within a network encompassing cortical and subcortical brain areas (i.e., ACC, premotor, dorsolateral, prefrontal, primary somatosensory and bilateral insular cortices, thalamus, bilateral striatum and brainstem) while the same stimuli perceived under hypnosis failed to elicit any cerebral activation. We also demonstrated a hypnosis-related increase in functional connectivity between primary somatosensory cortex (S1) and anterior insular and pre-frontal cortices. These results are not limited to healthy volunteers but are also observed in pathological states, such as patients suffering from fibromyalgia or chronic pain. In a combined EEG and fMRI study, Rainville et al. reported a reduction of the hypnosis-related increases in occipital and delta activity when subjects were painfully stimulated.

According to theories of hypnosis, one characteristic of hypnotic procedures is the inhibition of afferent nociceptive [pain sensing] transmission. This inhibition can be explained by the dramatically decreased activity in the thalamus that is observed under hypnosis. The thalamus has also been shown to correlate with pain perception threshold while activation of the midline area (i.e. posterior cingulate cortex) correlates with intensity of the stimulation and ACC with unpleasantness of the stimulation. It has been proposed that the reported increased functional connectivity between mid-cingulate cortex, thalamus and brainstem might be related to pain-relevant arousal or attention mechanisms. These observations can lead to the hypothesis that hypnosis involves subcortical gating processes on cortical activation that underlies the decreased subjective pain perception reported by subjects under hypnosis. The basal ganglia are known to encode and initiate basic movement patterns expressed through premotor pathways and have also been proposed to support basic attentional mechanisms facilitating the calling up of motor programs and thoughts. In accordance with the reported decreases in premotor cortex activation in hypnosis, results of the different studies suggest that hypnosis may diminish anxiety, defensive and emotional reactions to pain by reducing activation of both cortical and subcortical areas. The increased modulation of insular activity is in line with role of this structure in pain affect and pain intensity coding. Modulation of frontal area activity may reflect disruption in cognitive attentional, appraisal and memory systems that can influence perception of environmental stimulation during hypnosis. Finally, ACC is a brain area reported in several studies on executive attention, detection of errors, monitoring of conflict between competing cognitive processes and was shown to correlate with the difficulty of the task performed as well as with relaxation state of subjects. Rainville et al. proposed that engagement of the cognitive and neurophysiologic processes implied in each of those accounts may be accompanied by subjective experience of increased mental absorption as reported by subjects under hypnosis. In addition, ACC has also been considered to be involved in the "suffering" component of pain and affective reactions associated with pain unpleasantness. Its decreased activity during hypnosis reflects the decreased unpleasantness of the stimulation reported by subjects under hypnosis. Finally, the observed reduction in occipital and delta activity during painful stimulation was proposed to reflect disruption of relaxation and/or imagery processes by pain during hypnosis. (Vanhaudenhuyse et al, 2013, 347)

We see in the previous, that there are differences during hypnosis in brain waves as well as some of the brain functions involved in hypnosis. There are identifiable elements based on physiological profiles or models that can explain the stratification in hypnosis which is known as 'highly hypnotizable' and 'low hypnotizable' as well as a mid-range which comprises 60% of any given population, whereas highs are 30% of any given population and lows are 10% of any given population. The Brain patterns associated with Highs primarily engage the brain patterns associated with imagery in the visual cortex, whereas lows, are cognitively engaged with associated cognitive brain activity (Baghdadi & Nasrabadi, 2010, 72).

This has been explained to a certain extent according to researchers with rostrum size in the corpus collosum, which is involved in allocation of attention and transfer of information between prefrontal cortices; on the other hand low hypnotizable subjects have a normal sized rostrum. The hypnotic process is not uniform but changes over a hypnotic session through time, "as one progresses through hypnosis, the altered consciousness deepens with time. The deepest hypnotic state is at the latter parts of a hypnotic session." (Baghdadi & Nasrabadi, 2010, 77)

Other researchers have found physiological stratification in Low and High based in the construction of the ACC, specifically the dACC, key to monitoring conflict in neural nets, fMRI measured higher signals in ACC during conflict. Whereas in Highly Hypnotizables, dACC (dorsal ACC) activation is higher than Low Hypnotizables.

Recently, we used hypnotic suggestion as an attentional tool to manipulate conflict. Whereas earlier case reports and at least one esoteric study reported promising preliminary findings by using hypnotic suggestions, we used an experimental design using a posthypnotic suggestion, a condition wherein a subject complies with a suggestion made during the hypnotic episode after termination of the hypnotic experience. Although subjects may not remember being told to adhere to a specific instruction, the posthypnotic suggestion is usually summoned on a prearranged signal and can be effective in highly hypnotizable individuals. Posthypnotic suggestions, therefore, unlike hypnotic suggestions, take effect in a conventionally behaving person during common wakefulness. Earlier, we used this system in a laboratory setting and presented behavioral findings showing elimination of Stroop interference. We then replicated our results by using appropriate control for visual accommodation as well as eye movements. Together with other findings, these data led us to conclude that a top-down neural process, rather than optical degradation of the input stimuli, is responsible for this effect. (Raz et al, 2005, 9978)

Investigating the Stroop conflict by using fMRI, we compared brain activity with and without posthypnotic suggestion at the ACC both between and within groups. Fig. 1A shows significant interaction between group (highly vs. less-hypnotizable persons) and suggestion (absent vs. present) for Stroop conflict. Further comparisons revealed that whereas for the less-suggestible controls ACC activation was not reduced upon suggestion, within the highly hypnotizable group, suggestion elicited a significant reduction in ACC activation. In fact, although fMRI data from less suggestible individuals showed a significant increase in activation on incongruent trials, no difference in brain activity between congruent and incongruent trials appeared in highly hypnotizable persons given the posthypnotic suggestion. In addition to ACC activity reduction, we found fMRI signal reduction in posterior brain activity within an extrastriate visual area. (Raz et al, 2005, 9980)

Raz et al has studied the difference between lows and highs; lower pain induction gives lower activity in ACC lower activity in somatasensory cortex "suggestion wields a general dampening down effect on early visual activity [dominant in Highs]" (Raz et al, 2005, 9982)

Positron emission tomography assays of pain show that specific modulatory hypnotic suggestions affect activation of different brain structures: whereas suggesting a drop in pain unpleasantness reduces specific activity in ACC, suggesting decreased pain intensity produces activity reduction in somatosensory cortex. A recent fMRI study extended these findings to illuminate the role of placebo in the context of pain. These collective accounts underline the influence that attention and suggestion can impart to conflict situations, top-down cognitive organization, self-regulation, and effortful control. Consonant with reports showing left and right lateralization for orthographic and non-orthographic stimuli, respectively, our ERP data show that in the absence of suggestion (at 179 msec), posterior brain activity was more left-lateralized (i.e., in line with orthography), whereas the presence of suggestion reversed this trend (at 234 msec). Furthermore, the ERP findings show that suggestion likely influences attention-sensitive electrophysiological components. These results seem to indicate that suggestion wields a general dampening- down effect on early visual activity as indexed by electrophysiological components (i.e., P100 and N100), showing both a shift and a reduction in amplitude. Representative snapshots, captured from a time-course video showing cortical electrophysiological activity across the entire brain (Movie 1), illustrate these effects at their respective peaks. Notably, whereas suggestion attenuated earlier components, the P300 remained unaffected. Suggestion may instigate lowered visual system activation by reducing attention either to specific visual stimuli (e.g., words) or to the actual input stream (e.g., dampening down all visual stimuli). The paucity of fMRI signal differences between incongruent and congruent trials together with the ERP data of the highly hypnotizable individuals under suggestion seem to support the latter possibility.... (e.g., overall performance of the highly suggestible participants was 100 msec faster than that of the less-suggestible persons) may be important to consider.

Our results show that in highly hypnotizable persons, a specific posthypnotic suggestion to construe Stroop words a nonsense strings reduced conflict, as indicated by both behavioral data and ACC activity reduction. Evidence of reduced ERP under suggestion proposes strong modulation of early occipital cortex activity. This altered visual processing probably affected downstream cognitive activity, including ACC activation. Our results highlight the role of posthypnotic suggestions in altering cognitive processes. This knowledge may pave the road toward illuminating the neural correlates of other suggestion-based interventions. For example, a greater importance has been placed recently on trying to understand the placebo effect. It is important to compare hypnotic suggestions with other methods for modulating cognitive control, including placebo. (Raz et al, 2005, 9982)

In a more penetrating study that goes into the various neural networks in the brain that are affected by Hypnosis, Jiang et al (2017) studied the interaction of the Default Mode Network, the Salience Network and Executive Control Network.

FUNCTIONAL CONNECTIVITY:

• Executive Control Network ECN - focused attention, working memory tasks.

• Salience Network SN - activated during tasks, joins dACC, when one is challenged or anxious, can be used for contextual understanding, [see Tarasenko on 'Salience detection' in computer algorithms].

• Default Mode Network DMN - during rest and rumination and de-activated as task engagement increases.

• High Hypnotizable. - decreased DMN Activity, increased connectivity of left anterior aspects of the DLPFC of the ECN and the dACC of the SN; higher levels of the dopamine [see 'dopaminargic', Persinger] matabolite homo-vanillic acid in the cerebral spinal fluid. (Jiang et al, 2017, 4084)

> • dACC deactivation is task dependent, with decrements in activation related to decreased negative affect. dACC activation is associated with appraisal and expression of fear and pain (Etkin et al 2011), as well as a sense of personal agency or will to persevere.

> • increased connectivity b/w ECN and SN gives amplified task related activity reflecting increases or decreases in anxiety (Jiang et al, 2017, 4084) [relevant to Highs, higher anxiety, higher connectivity b/w ECN and SN].

The Following Key Points in terms of hypnosis and the brain:

> 1. Hypnotic state in highs- decreased low freq. amplitude in dACC (only in Highs)

> 2. Hypnosis invokes a suspension of critical judgment and ability to immerse oneself in a task while reducing awareness of alternatives [good counter RC necessitates exploration and alternatives].

> 3. ACC associated with 'will to persevere', reducing ACC activity, decreased personal agency and contribute to heightened suggestibility as well as the ability to dissociate from distress and pain that are characteristic of hypnosis.

> 4. Highs displayed increased connectivity b/w bilateral DLPFC and the ipsilateral insula during hypnosis (Highs Only) [An important function of the DLPFC is the executive functions, such as working memory, cognitive flexibility, planning, inhibition, and abstract reasoning. However, the DLPFC is not exclusively responsible for the executive functions. All complex mental activity requires the additional cortical and subcortical circuits with which the DLPFC is connected. The DLPFC is also the highest cortical area that is involved in motor planning, organization and regulation].

>> • insula: processing body control and experience, emotion, empathy and time, spatial temporal aspects of pain control and empathy with others pain.

>> • sham mobile phone radiation in electrosensitive subjects caused somatic symptoms that were mediated through increased insular activity. (Jiang et al, 2017, 4089)

>> • Insula self-reflection, self-monitoring, self-regulation – which are all thought processes that can be altered in hypnosis [In RC to change the image of self] and in related dissociative states involving alterations in identity, memory and consciousness.

> 5. reduced connectivity between left DLPFC and PCC was notable during hypnosis in highs but not during memory, and it was the clearest state difference highlighting hypnosis. These DMN regions are involved in self-referential processing and episodic memory, while the ECN is involved in cognitive control, and the two networks become anti-correlated during working memory tasks. Dissociation between ECN and DMN in response to hypnotic induction likely reflects engagement in the hypnotic state and associated detachment from internal mental processes such as mind wandering and self-reflection [in RC image of self is hijacked].

> 6. Taken together, our findings indicate that cross-network co-activation patterns are modulated by hypnosis. Decreased fALFF in the dACC may reflect reduced context comparison and decreased attention to the external environment, while at the same time connectivity between the DLFPC and the insula is up-regulated, which facilitates somatic surveillance. Further, the decoupling of the DLPFC from the DMN during hypnosis reveals another neural mechanism underlying hypnotic absorption and, potentially, hypnotic loss of self-consciousness and amnesia. (Kihlstrom 2013)

Disengagement between frontal attentional regions and striatum-based procedural regions under hypnosis has been showed to improve procedural learning (Nemeth et al. 2013). Thus, effects of hypnosis may be due to separation of certain brain functions (ECN from DMN) as well as integration of others (ECN and SN). Increases in ECN–SN connectivity involving primarily DLPFC and ipsilateral insula occurred during hypnosis among highly hypnotizables, who were at lower functional connectivity levels at baseline. In sum, the naturally occurring and clinically useful hypnotic state appears to be a product of reduced contextual vigilance (dACC activity) and disconnection from default mode resting activity, as well as enhanced coordination of networks engaged in task management and somatic surveillance. (Jiang et al, 2017)

PARASITIC CONSCIOUSNESS, PARTIAL EPILEPSY AND DISCO BALLS:

It is not well known but some suffering some forms of epilepsy report hearing voices related to their seizures. Dr. Michael Persinger has studied this phenomenon performing metrics on the incidents of 'hearing voices' in epileptic patients. In his brain scans using sLORETA he has reported that the right anterior insula is associated with aural hallucinations.

> In our opinion, from the perspective of treatment, the most important observation was the increased power in the delta range within the medial frontal and anterior cingulate region as inferred by sLORETA when the pinwheel was moving as verified by an external observer in her vicinity. Although increased activity in the latter region, particular the right anterior insula is associated with disembodied hallucinatory voices and auditory hallucinations, which Ms. S experienced and attributed to her invisible friends, the involvement of the prefrontal region suggests organization, intent, and an awareness that some process was occurring. This was reflected in her reports that 'something' was about to happen in a manner similar to a preictal state [pre-seizure]. The antecedents of these experiences are likely to have occurred within the right temporal lobe for two reasons. First, there was a marked increased coherence within the 6–7-Hz band between the two regions in the temporal lobes, one of which was near the source of the chronic anomaly. Secondly, she responded with intense sadness and emotion, very similar to what happens after the 'spontaneous' display of these experiences, when she was exposed without her knowledge to a 7-Hz amplitude modulated experimental magnetic field with intensities similar to those associated with increased geomagnetic activity. Her profile was similar to people who are easily entrained by weak applied, physiologically patterned magnetic fields (Persinger et al., 2009). In fact, her presentation clinically was quintessentially representative of Bear's (1979) temporal lobe syndrome of sensory-limbic hyper-connectionism that is frequently seen in subclinical and clinical complex partial epileptic patients with foci within right temporal lobe (Persinger 2013b).

Persinger and Roll made similar findings dealing with hearing voices, or hallucinations in people with closed head injuries:

> In our experience, many patients with closed head injuries have reported sensitivity to weak magnetic fields. We have shown this effect with single cases. Subsequent analyses of Ms. S.'s reports for weeks after she left the laboratory showed that the report of the unusual experiences occurred during the 10-minute period after increases greater than approximately 25 nT intensity in geomagnetic activity. A similar threshold has been reported of bereavement apparitions and vestibular experiences during partial sensory deprivation in the normal population. Our experiments with other forms of cerebrally applied magnetic fields may help explain why the rotation of the pinwheel diminished [also see strobe effect] when she listened through earphones to music. Many of these small solenoids (of the earphones) applied upon the ears, which are immediately adjacent to the temporal lobes, can generate magnetic field energy levels that are equivalent to the mechanical patterns that generate sound. Whether or not this strategy could be used therapeutically to control unwanted experiences remains to be established. We have counseled patients, who experience terrifying nocturnal sensed presences subsequent to closed head injuries, to quickly activate an acoustic source and to listen to music containing lyrics. This simple temporal lobe stimulation eliminates the experience of a sensed presence. (Persinger & Roll, 2012)

Experiences of pain are also associated with altered activity in the anterior cingulate; the same region that is associated with emotional bonding, the feeling of well-being, and the cerebral responses to "unconscious" changes in the environment. (Persinger, 2013, 512) In another project where he studied the effect of sensed presence in the form of a common test for hypnotizability, the tingle test, he found brain measurements that correlate with other findings mentioned:

> The "chill and tingling" response by a specific and new pattern of magnetic field was observed. The analysis demonstrated that those who received the electromagnetic pattern designed to simulate "dopaminergic burst firing" reported significantly more tingles (F1,9 =6.48; p b .05; eta2 = .42) than those exposed to the sham field. In fact, not a single participant in the sham condition reported this experience. To discern whether the field or simply sitting in the chamber influenced activation of the brain in any systematic way, source localization was completed on the data extracted from each raw record. The analysis indicated that there was a significant decrease (p b .05) in delta (1.5–4 Hz) activity within the posterior cingulate and a region encompassing the medial frontal gyrus (BA 11), the dorsal and ventral regions of the anterior cingulate (BA 32 and 24), and the ventromedial prefrontal cortices (BA 25) for individuals who did not receive a magnetic field, i.e., the sham field condition. These areas were identified as regions of interest (ROIs), and activations within these regions were extracted for further analysis. Relative scores from baseline at 10, 20, and 30 min of field exposure were computed on the sLORETA activation scores pertaining to the above-mentioned regions-of-interest. These scores were subsequently entered into separate multilevel analysis of variance with one between-subjects factor (condition) and 3 within-subject factors (time, region-of-interest, and hemisphere) for the delta (1.5–4 Hz), theta (4–7.5 Hz), low alpha (7.5–10.5 Hz), high alpha (10.5–13.5 Hz), low beta (13.5–20 Hz), high beta (20–30 Hz), and gamma (30–40 Hz) bands.

> The analysis demonstrated a significant condition by ROI interaction (F3,27 = 3.10; p b .05; partial eta2 = 26). Post hoc analyses utilizing four separate one-way analyses of variance indicated that Fig. 5. (Top) There was a statistically significant increase in gamma-band (>35 Hz) bilateral coherence approximately 10–15 minutes after the initiation of the Thomas [pulsed modulation] pattern. (Bottom) The increase was accompanied by an increase in gamma power within the right prefrontal region as well as the anterior portions of the temporal lobe.

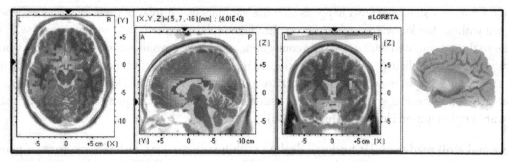

Fig. 6. Low alpha activation within the medial frontal gyrus was increased significantly upon exposure to the "dopaminergic"-patterned electromagnetic field.

individuals exposed to the "chill-generating" magnetic field displayed statistically significantly higher (F1,9 = 6.75; p b .05; eta2 = .43) low alpha activation within the medial frontal gyrus (BA 11), whereas participants within the reference field condition showed a decrease

K.S. Saroka, M.A. Persinger / Epilepsy & Behavior 28 (2013) 395–407   403

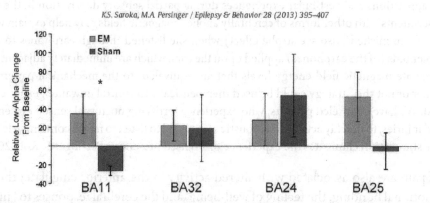

Fig. 7. Relative changes in low alpha activity within different inferred Brodmann areas (BA) according to sLORETA during the "dopaminergic" EM field. Vertical lines are SEMs.

[ACC, EM applied to this area activation goes down, similar to High Hypnotizable profile]

Because the current experiment did not allow us to assess brain activation at the exact time that the chill sensation was experienced, the relative scores at each time period were averaged together to produce a general activation score for each region-of-interest. Spearman rank-order correlations were then completed between these activation scores as well as the report of a tingly sensation. The analysis revealed that the experience of "vibrations" and "tingling" was positively correlated with activation scores within the medial frontal gyrus (rho = .81, p = .002) as well as the ventromedial prefrontal cortices (rho = .83, p = .002). (Persinger, 2013b, 402-3)

Recent biomolecular studies have shown that the same field patterns and intensities by which the sensed presence and out-of-body experiences are generated influenced T-type calcium channels and correlative changes in molecular pathways such as slowing of proliferation of cancer cells within cultures. (Persinger, 2013b, 396)

Increasing suggestibility:

In the St-Pierre and Persinger 2006 review, some of the experiments had involved groups who had been administered a norm-referenced interactive suggestibility scale (Hypnosis Induction Profile [see Baghdadi 2010 on EEG Profile of Hypnosis Induction replacing subjective tests, would also allow for deep data-mining to identify susceptibles]) developed by Spiegel and Spiegel. Although some studies had shown that greater stimulation by these physiologically-patterned magnetic fields over the right hemisphere, but not the left, definitely increased suggestibility, this elevation was not associated with the occurrence of the sensed presence. (Persinger, 2013b, 397)

In our studies, the magnetic fields were created by transforming a series of numbers, each between 0 and 256, to a voltage between –5 V and +5 V (127 = 0 V). The point or "pixel" duration was either 1 ms or 3 ms. This value is the duration of each voltage that composes the pattern.... Accurate and precise point durations are essential for producing the sensed presence. Similar "temporal sensing" [rhythmic] sensitivity for cells has been shown for frequency-modulated weak magnetic fields. (Persinger, 2013b, 397) [Amygdala in conservatives are more sensitive to rhythms, perhaps more efficiently hypnotizable.]

Persinger, in studying one subject who had suffered epileptic-related voices, when applying EM fields:

[Subject] ...exhibited persistent and conspicuous enhanced power in the low beta-range over the temporal lobes and specific changes in current source densities within the left inferior temporal gyrus and right para-hippocampal region. (Persinger, 2013b, 1)

For those patients who are actively experiencing, according to their verbal reports, inner voices application of these physiologically patterned fields with equal intensities across both temporal lobes markedly attenuates the numbers of "different voices" or eliminates their occurrence. Asymmetrical application with greater intensity over the right hemisphere enhances or initiates the experiences. (Persinger, 2013b, 2)

In an interesting report of changing speech during the intrusion of auditory hallucinations her speaking style changed:

The patient had some control over the occurrence of the intrusive voices, although at times they could occur spontaneously. When she "heard" these voices her verbal behavior would become more monotonic ("machine-like") and her pronoun usage shifted from "I" to "we." QEEG indicated a persistent (measured on different days) 21–23 Hz higher amplitude (~70 µV) activity over T3 and T7 when she referred to "I" at which times she exhibited normal prosody. (Persinger, 2013b, 5)

When the "we state" [extrinsic influence] was reported there was marked fast, high amplitude 17–23 Hz activity from both T3 and T4 as shown in Figure 1. In addition, she reported "transmissions" which usually involved more complex information from these voices as well as series of numbers. When this occurred, there was a "normalization" of the EEG (Figure 2). When the "transmissions ended," the unusual profile of T3 and T4 enhancements returned. There was additional similar activity over F7 and F8 which was transient. She was not talking during this period. (Persinger, 2013b, 5)

During the experiences that would be classically labeled as "intrusions" the activation score for the low beta power within the right para-hippocampal region more than doubled. This area and related hemispheric discrepancy are similar to that associated with "panics" that can occur suddenly in this group of patients. (Persinger, 2013b, 6)

Our interpretation is that the lowered base power within the delta range (upon which higher frequencies can be strongly dependent) within the left temporal lobe facilitates the conditions for inter-temporal lobe coherence and the experiences of "others." The enhancement of power within the left inferior frontal region, traditionally associated with expression of overt language, could encourage the amplification of the person's own array of "articulemes." They are the neurocognitive patterns accompanying discrete neural activity that initiate sequences of stylopharyngeal and laryngeal muscle contractions. Anomalous organizations within the right prefrontal could increase the probability that the reconstruction of experiences would be attributed to non-self sources. (Persinger, 2013b, 6-7)

RED PILL OR BLUE PILL?

You awaken in the Matrix and you are offered the chance to attack the Machine or take the blue pill and go back to sleep. Though it seems a binary choice cliché, which seems to be a recurring pattern in cybersecurity, the choice you make actually may reflect your brain physiology more than anything else. In the following section we look into the role of brain physiology in political values, and its correlation to hypnosis.

MENDEZ

TABLE 1. Reported Brain and Behavior Affiliations for General Conservative Versus Liberal Orientation With Implications for Political Ideology[a]

Brain and Behavior Affiliations	High Conservatism	High Liberalism
Personality	Stability; opposition to change	Novelty
	Conformity	Unconventional; self-expression
	Tradition	New experiences and sensations
	Order, structure, and closure	Flexibility and variability
	Favor less complexity; harder categorization	Tolerance for uncertainty and ambiguity
	Purity	Minimization of harm
	Authority	Equality
	Conscientiousness	Empathy
	Distinctions with out-groups	Universal community
	Expressions of power	Expressions of warmth
Cognitive	Negativity bias	No clear bias
	Greater sensitivity to threat or loss	Greater sensitivity to cues for altering habitual response patterns
	Sensitivity to disgust	
Physiological	Greater activation of right amygdala	Greater conflict-related anterior cingulate cortex activity
Neuroimaging	Increased gray matter volume in right amygdala and other right anterior structures	Increased gray matter volume in anterior cingulate cortex

(Mendez, 2017)

Some research has suggested there is a genetic basis to the difference between 'liberal' and conservative':

Although most political orientation is not directly inherited, twin studies and the dopamine D4 receptor (DRD4) gene have linked personality traits and evolutionary intuitions with political ideology. In a sample of more than 12,000 twin pairs, the development of political attitude was about 40% dependent on genes,47 and, in another large twin study, the heritability of political conservatism was 64.5% for men and 44.7% for women. A few studies have reported an association between specific genes and conservative-liberal behavior or with political attitudes. Genes encoding certain receptors to dopamine, specifically the DRD4 gene on chromosome 11, were associated with variations in conservative/liberal personality traits. Two large studies have linked variations in the DRD4 exon III tandem repeats to political ideology putatively based on the sensitivity to dopamine uptake and the need for higher dopamine. Among 1,771 students in Singapore, those with two copies of the 4-repeat allele on the DRD4 gene were more politically conservative, and among another group of 1,941 individuals, those with 7R+tandem repeats, in the context of having more friends, were more politically liberal.

These two theories from evolutionary psychology, the parasite-stress theory and the moral foundation theory, plus the limited genetic studies, converge in their deductions. The parasite-stress theory concludes that there are relationships between increased conservative social and sexual attitudes, reminders of cleanliness, and increased physiological responses to disgusting images. The moral foundation theory concludes that people with strong conservative views are most sensitive to violation of sexual and body purity, and those with more liberal views are sensitive to violation of harm or fairness. Together with the genetic evidence, these findings support an underlying neurobiological basis for conservative-liberalism effects on political ideology. (Mendez, 2017, 88)

Some of the effects, though not directly related to the genes mentioned before, are seen in the physiology of specific brain areas in the neurobiology of the human.

PHYSICAL DIFFERENTIATION OF AMYGDALA (RED) AND ACC (BLUE) BETWEEN RED/BLUE POLARITIES:

Neuroscientists have studied the difference between the two polarities of 'liberal' and 'conservative' which we will study later under Reflexive Control in Lefebvre's two poles of morality. In a study from 2011 Kanai et al studied the physiological measurements between 'conservatives' and 'liberals.' In these findings they present results that pinpoint specific brain physiological differences between the two.

BRAIN PHYSIOLOGY OF LIBERALISM:

Psychological differences between conservatives and liberals determined in this way map onto self-regulatory processes associated with conflict monitoring. Moreover, the amplitude of event-related potentials reflecting neural activity associated with conflict monitoring in the anterior cingulate cortex (ACC) is greater for liberals compared to conservatives. Thus, stronger liberalism is associated with increased sensitivity to cues for altering a habitual response pattern [the opposite of effective RC] and with brain activity in anterior cingulate cortex. Here we explored this relationship further by examining whether political attitudes correlated not just with function but also with anatomical structure of these regions. To test the hypothesis that political liberalism (versus conservatism) is associated with differences in gray matter volume in anterior cingulate cortex, we recorded structural magnetic resonance imaging (MRI) scans from 90 healthy young adults (61% female) who self-reported their political attitudes confidentially on a five-point scale from "very liberal" to "very conservative." We then used voxel-based morphometry (VBM) analyses to investigate the relationship between these attitudes, expressed as a numeric score between one and five, and gray matter volume. We found that increased gray matter volume in the anterior cingulate cortex was signifi-

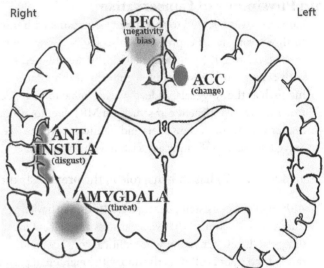

FIGURE 1. Schematic Diagram of the Conservative Complex on the Right, More Active in Conservatives Than in Liberals, and the Anterior Cingulate Cortex (ACC), More Active in Liberals Than Conservatives[a]

Conservative Complex

[a] Various regions of the prefrontal cortex (PFC) contribute to political thought and ideology, including the ventromedial prefrontal cortex (VMPFC), dorsomedial prefrontal cortex (DMPFC), and dorsolateral prefrontal cortex (DLPFC). Laterality is not as established for the PFC contribution, but at least for the DLPFC suggests greater right than left involvement.

cantly associated with liberalism (Figure 1A) (R = 22.71, T (88) = 2.633, p = 0.010 corrected; see Experimental Procedures for full details of analyses). We regressed out potential confounding variables of age and gender in our analysis (see Experimental Procedures). Therefore, our findings are not attributable to these factors. (Kanai, 2011)

Menendez (2017) has found a similar correlation to liberal brain physiology:

Neuroimaging studies suggest that political ideology involves conservative-liberal differences in the amygdala, insula, and ACC. Just being interested in politics has increased activity in the amygdala and the ventral striatum, and encoding party preference activates bilateral insula and the ACC. An MRI study of 90 young adults shows that political conservatives, compared with political liberals, have greater gray matter in the right amygdala, and an fMRI study involving a risk-taking task shows that political conservatives have greater activity in the right amygdala. The association of political conservatism with the right amygdala a structure that is bilaterally sensitive to emotional saliency, especially fear, suggests an increased processing of potential signals for threat. Although the anterior insula has a prominent role in the experience of disgust, brain responses to disgusting stimuli may show a more distributed pattern of differences between political conservatism and liberalism, consistent with a differential sensitivity for disgust among political conservatives. The unexpected association of political liberalism with activity in the left posterior insula in one study may reflect an additional role of the insula in the expression of interpersonal trust. Finally, political liberals have greater gray matter and increased ERP activity in the ACC, consistent with a sensitivity for processing signals for potential change. (Mendez, 2017, 88-9)

Remembering earlier that ACC in Hypnosis has the following correlations, in Highs the ACC decreases it's low frequency amplitude in the dorsal area, critical judgement, task management, awareness of the environment is reduced. ACC reduction reduces will to persevere and heightened suggestibility. A difference in the ACC that has a correlation to liberalism or 'openness' are open to explore pathways whereas in a diminished ACC one's exploration or learning is minimized. We shall read about the impact of the Amygdala on learning later below. Correlating this connection in the ACC in Hypnosis with the political profiles of the ACC we see the similarity between Highly Hypnotizables and Conservative differences in the ACC which has lower amplitude in activation. "Moreover, the amplitude of event-related potentials reflecting neural activity associated with conflict monitoring in the anterior cingulate cortex (ACC) is greater for liberals compared to conservatives. (Kanai, 2011)"

[Event-related potentials (ERPs) represent a series of EEG events that reflect the progressive activation of neuronal sub-populations in the course of cognitive processing.]

Brain Physiology of Conservatism:

Conservatives respond to threatening situations with more aggression than do liberals and are more sensitive to threatening facial expressions [also see Norseen 1996 discussion of recognition of 'authoritarian' faces by infants, relating it to the amygdala]. This heightened sensitivity to emotional faces suggests that individuals with conservative orientation might exhibit differences in brain structures associated with emotional processing such as the amygdala. Indeed, voting behavior is reflected in amygdala responses across cultures. We therefore further investigated our structural MRI data to evaluate whether there was any relationship between gray matter volume of the amygdala and political attitudes. We found that increased gray matter volume in the right amygdala was significantly associated with conservatism. (Kanai, 2011)

Menendez (2017) has shown a role in the previously mentioned DLFPC and political conservatism:

Although not consistent, the right DLPFC may have a greater role in resolving good versus bad biases, partisan differences, or conflicts between fairness and self-interest, and, in one fMRI study, there was a clear association of right DLPFC activation with political conservatism. Another fMRI study of depressed patients showed left rather than right DLPFC activation with heightened preferential processing of negative information, and a positron emission tomography study showed left middle frontal gyrus (DLPFC) activation during a negativity bias condition. Finally, noninvasive stimulation of bilateral DLPFC during the incorporation of political campaign information has resulted in a significant increase in politically conservative values, and transcranial magnetic stimulation of the right, but not left, DLPFC has reduced the rejection of unfair offers when they are in conflict with self-interest. Ultimately, the right DLPFC may have a greater role in mediating emotion-based conflicts and may interact with the right VLPFC, amygdala, and anterior insula in forming the neuroanatomical substrates of a conservative complex. (Menendez, 2017, 90)

As we shall read later regarding Reflexive Control and other forms of biological influencing, in these findings Liberal structure is designed to break RC Control, whereas Conservative structure is designed to be controlled, as Fast Reflexion in RC Theory is facilitated by the Amygdala, it is a system based on manipulating the Fear responses of controlled subjects.

The amygdala is a collection of nuclear groups and is located deep in the temporal lobe. The amygdaloid complex in rat consists of thirteen regions. As per 'Price's' nomenclature, amygdala nuclei are categorized into three major groups, such as the basolateral group, the cortical group and the centro-medial group. The different nuclei can be very well distinguished on the basis of cytoarchitecture and are referred as amygdaloid complex. This complex regulates memory, attention, emotions etc. However, the most studied and the best understood function of amygdala is its contribution to the detection of emotional events and the production of appropriate responses (emotional processing). (Narayanan et al, 2017, 2)

Additionally, it is important to note how fear/anger is used in systems designed for military simulations such as Lockheed-Martin's SCREAM platform, see Chapter 4, 'Lessons from an American Weapons Designer.' Hypnosis is involved in manipulating the ACC, but in the opposite manner from what is natural to Liberals, whereas liberalism would create more resistance to Hypnosis and Hypnotic suggestion, the altering of the ACC by Hypnotism of Highly Hypnotizables would be in line with conservative physiology.

The key element physiologically speaking is that of the Grey Matter Volume (GMV) of the Amygdala, other researchers have noted the significance of GMV in the Amygdala:

> In contrast, structural magnetic resonance imaging (MRI) studies relying on the measurement of cortical thickness and/or voxel-based morphometry (VBM). have only focused on frontotemporal circuits as neuroanatomical correlates of music processing. While the role of the amygdala in music processing is largely ignored in structural MRI studies, there is abundant evidence showing that the anatomical structure of the amygdala is correlated with emotional processing. For example, amygdala gray matter volume (GMV) or density is correlated with magnitude of stress and anxiety in the normal population, and the change of amygdala volume is a neural signature of a variety of emotion-related disorders, such as major depressive disorder, bipolar disorder, borderline personality disorder, post-traumatic stress disorder, and autism. Finally, lesions of the amygdala severely impair emotional processing, such as emotion recognition, emotion arousal, and emotion judgment. (Li et al, 2014)

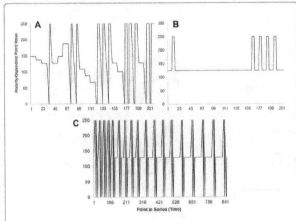

Figure 1: The Burst X (A), LTP (B), and Thomas (C) electromagnetic field patterns. The Y-axes represent polarity-dependent point values ranging between 0 and 250 whereas the X-axes represent the points within each series or, implicitly, time.

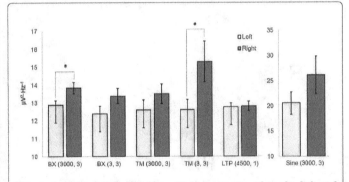

Figure 4: Alpha-beta1 (7.5 Hz – 20 Hz) power within the left and right hemisphere of a full, unsectioned human brain as a function of the electromagnetic field exposure pattern. Burst X (BX), Thomas (TM), long-term potentiation (LTP), and sine (Sine) patterns are shown where significant differences between hemispheres are indicated (p<0.05).

(Persinger & Rouleau, 2017)

Persinger studies the impact of EM waves on a biopsy of human brains in these studies he found that the right amygdala was affected more than the left amygdala.

> The right amygdala, accessed by way of the uncus, generated increased alpha-beta power within the right hemisphere (M=15.32, SEM=0.54) relative to the left hemisphere (M=12.52, SEM=0.66), t (4) =3.30, p<0.05, r2=0.73 (Figure 5). This right-left difference emerged within 10 to 20 s after the onset of the field exposures (p<0.05). ANOVAs revealed statistically significant alpha-beta1 power differences across structures within the right hemisphere, F (5,17) =3.56, p<0.05, η2=0.60. Homogeneous subsets were revealed. Where the major source of the variance was due to a difference between the right amygdala and right orbital frontal gyrus (p<0.05). There were no statistically significant changes in the left hemispheric structural differences after accommodating for multiple comparisons. Power differences within other frequency bands were not significant

during exposures to the Burst X (3000, 3) pattern. Together, these results suggested that the right amygdala was most responsive to the Burst X (3000, 3) electromagnetic field pattern relative to its contralateral paired structure in a fixed, unsectioned human brain. (Persinger & Rouleau, 2017)

What the relation is that Persinger has found with the difference in the Amygdala between right and left will need further research, as well as the relationship with the conservative (reactionary) aspect of the right amygdala's larger size.

Another way to analyze the relationship of the Amygdala to stress, anger and fear is its interaction with the cannabis molecule THC, which has been studied by Phan et al (2008) showing that the Amygdala:

> ....our data demonstrate a significant and selective impact of THC on amygdala reactivity to social signals of threat in humans. The findings extend the accumulating evidence on cannabinoid modulation of anxiety in humans and non-humans; and provide evidence for a neuroanatomical site of action for the anxiolytic effects of THC. The current data could prompt the development of new therapies that act on cannabinoid systems to modulate fear behaviors in neuropsychiatric disorders such as social phobia, autism, and schizophrenia, in which social fear or withdrawal, and aberrant reactivity to threat are cardinal features (Phan et al, 2008, 2317)

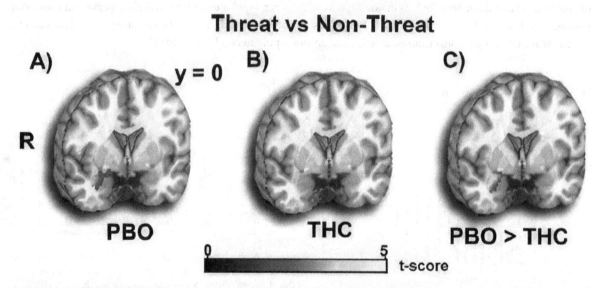

Phan et al. • Cannabinoid Modulation of Amygdala Reactivity

Figure 2. THC effects on amygdala activation. *A, B,* Statistical *t* maps overlaid on a canonical brain rendering (MNI coronal *y*-plane = 0) showing right lateral amygdala activation to threat (>nonthreat) faces is present during the PBO session but absent during the THC session. *C,* Statistical *t* map overlaid on a canonical brain rendering (MNI coronal *y*-plane = 0) showing greater threat-related amygdala reactivity in the PBO relative to the THC session (PBO > THC). For additional information, see Results. Statistical *t* score scale is shown at the bottom of the brain rendering. R, Right.

As can be seen from… a brain scan of the Amygdala without THC, we see that the activation is on for fear responses, etc, while on THC the Amygdala does not become activated for fear responses, in an anti-anxiety effect. Lorazepam or Sertraline is recommended as a pharmacological agent to fight anxiety similar to THC (Phan et al, 2008).

Another anti-anxiety component of the Amygdala is a peptide, as explained by Persinger:

> Neuropeptide Y within the amygdala, which has been associated with decreasing anxiety, has also been associated with suppression of neurotransmission in single hippocampal cells as well as with electrical seizures. Autopsy results for temporal lobe epileptic patients indicated that the numbers of neurons expressing this peptide within very specific nuclei of the amygdala was about one standard deviation lower in the patients compared to the reference group. (Persinger, 2010)

Dog Whistling the Amygdala Response

In the study of fear conditioning the Amygdala plays a major role. Le Doux studied the Amygdala and fear conditioning providing this brief overview:

> In Pavlovian fear conditioning, an emotionally neutral conditioned stimulus (CS), usually a tone, is presented in conjunction with an aversive unconditioned stimulus (US), often foot-shock. After one or several pairings, the CS acquires the capacity to elicit responses that typically occur in the presence of danger, such as defensive behavior (freezing or escape responses), autonomic nervous system responses (changes in blood pressure and heart rate), neuroendocrine responses (release of hormones from the pituitary and adrenal glands), etc. The responses are not learned and are not voluntary. They are innate, species-typical responses to threats and are expressed automatically in the presence of appropriate stimuli. Fear conditioning thus allows new or learned threats to automatically activate evolutionarily tuned ways of responding to danger. The ease of establishment, rapidity of learning, long duration of the memory, and stereotyped nature of the responses all speak to the value of the Pavlovian learning as an approach to the study of fear mechanisms and account for the success achieved with this procedure. Studies from many labs have led to the conclusion that damage to the amygdala interferes with the acquisition and expression of conditioned fear (LeDoux,2003).

Contextual fear conditioning involves the Amygdala (LeDoux, 2003). LeDoux explains the role of the Amygdala in the dual conditioning of an audio signal along with a physical conditioning, where the generation of just the signal gives also chemical reactions in the absence of a physical threat, the audio signal triggers the contextual fear condition. LeDoux explains the systems involved in this effect:

> Areas of the ventral hippocampus (CA1 and subiculum) project to the basal (B) and accessory basal (AB) nuclei of the amygdala, which are also known as the basolateral and basomedial nuclei. Damage to these areas interferes with contextual conditioning. Hippocampal projections to B and AB thus seem to be involved in contextual conditioning. The central nucleus of the amygdala (CE) is the interface with motor systems. Damage to CE interferes with the expression of conditioned fear responses, while damage to areas that CE projects to selectively interrupts the expression of individual responses. For example, damage to the lateral hypothalamus affects blood pressure but not freezing responses, and damage to the peraqueductal gray interferes with freezing but not blood pressure responses. Similarly, damage to the bed nucleus of the stria terminalis has no effect on either blood pressure or freezing responses but disrupts the conditioned release of pituitary-adrenal stress hormones. Because CE receives inputs from LA, B, and AB, it is in a position to mediate the expression of conditioned fear responses elicited by both acoustic and contextual CSs. The direct projection from LA to CE seems to be sufficient for conditioning to an auditory CS, since lesions of B and AB have no effect on fear conditioning to a tone. The exact manner in which LA and CE communicate is not clear, but the intercalated cell mass located between LA and CE may be involved. (LeDoux, 2003)

Another relationship from LeDoux's research between the Amygdala in both Hypnosis and in Politics is the question of learning, whereas hypnosis interferes with finding novel pathways and problem solving, we see the role of the amygdala in its relation to learning, finding novel pathways not previously experienced or stored in muscle memory:

> That the amygdala is indeed important for learning is suggested by studies showing that inactivation of the amygdala during learning prevents learning from taking place. Further, if the inactivation occurs immediately after training, then there is no effect on subsequent memory, showing that the effects of pretraining treatment is on learning and not on processes that occur after learning. The amygdala thus seems to be essential for fear learning and does not modulate its own learning.

Inactivation of the Amygdala leads to non-retention of learning, we see non or less activation in 1. Hypnosis and 2. people with enlarged right Amygdala's, who also test along a more 'conservative' category speaking in terms of social politics and culture.

Fat Rats and Politics

Another interesting note is that of the obesity epidemic that is affecting England and the United States (UK/USA) which roughly correlated to a problem with the Amygdala being hammered by constant EM fields in the last 4 decades or so, which is also when the obesity epidemic in these societies began, one could argue that with scientific experimental findings of Loscher et al (2003) and Persinger (2014) that there is a direct connection to obesity and the amygdala receiving excess EM waves and energy.

> Excessive weight gains in female rats have been induced by extended kindling of the basolateral amygdala (Persinger 2014)

Persinger has also noted that the central nucleus of the amygdala (which is disinhibited by lithium/pilocarpine-induced seizure damage) are important regulators of ingestive behaviors. Other research also speaks of the amygdala's role in regulation of food intake.

Loscher et al:

> Previous lesion studies have indicated a role of the amygdala in the central regulation of food intake. In the present experiments, twice-daily electrical stimulation of the basolateral nucleus of the amygdala in female Wistar rats was found to be associated with a significant body weight gain compared to unstimulated controls. On average, significant increases in body weight were observed after 25 amygdala stimulations, using a kindling paradigm for stimulation. Compared to kindled rats, in which amygdala stimulations were terminated after about 20 stimulations, extended kindling of the amygdala with up to 280 stimulations led to progressive weight increases and compulsive hyperphagia [over eating even when not hungry] .... The extensive weight gain over extended amygdala kindling provides an interesting new model for experimentally induced obesity. (Loscher et al, 2003)

Loscher here established that kindling, adding signals to the Amygdala, leads to obesity in mammals such as rats. Persinger (2014) has further studied this phenonomenon and related it to energy being sent at the Amygdala:

> Weekly (1.5 hr) exposures to physiologically patterned magnetic fields over 36 weeks had no effect on weight gain while continuous periseizure exposure to 50 Hz fields above about 1 µT facilitated mild weight gains and protracted aggression. Perinatal exposure to a very weak 7 Hz magnetic field or a nitric oxide inhibitor retarded the weight gain induced by the obesity procedure. These results indicate that synergisms during a single episode between neuronal electrical lability and pharmacological states can initiate a process of weight gain that progresses to extreme obesity. We suggest that at least a component of the global "epidemic of obesity" could be related to a synergism between the insidious emergence of amplitude modulations within biologically compatible electromagnetic frequencies from the proliferation of communication systems and the pervasive utilization of pharmacology to treat transient disorders of ontogeny within the human population. (Persinger, 2014)

Persinger notes that the most effect is in the basolateral amygdala which mediate specific Pavlovian-instrumental transfer, a phenomenon in which a classically conditioned stimulus modifies operant behavior. The primary function of the basolateral complex is stimulating fear response. The fear system is intended to avoid pain or injury. For this reason the responses must be quick, and reflex-like. To achieve this, the "low-road" or a bottom-up process is used to generate a response to stimuli that are potentially hazardous. The stimulus reaches the thalamus, and information is passed to the lateral nucleus, then the basolateral system, and immediately to the central nucleus where a response is then formed. There is no conscious cognition involved in these responses. Other non-threatening stimuli are processed via the "high road" or a top-down form of processing. In this case, the stimulus input reaches the sensory cortex first, leading to more conscious involvement in the response. In immediately threatening situations, the fight-or-flight response is reflexive, and conscious thought processing doesn't occur until later.

Persinger concludes his study with finding that suggests there is a direct correlation between weight gain, the amygdala and EM energy in the environment or directed at a subject:

> Assuming complete penetrability of the skull, the energy within one typical neuron with a diameter of 10 micrometers would be within the range of a picoJoule per s. This is the same quantity of energy associated with local (intracellular) glucose utilization. Whether or not such juxtaposition of electromagnetic sources and metabolic derivations of quantum energies would generate an emergent condition that would constitute the "limbic" sensitivity of the type required to produce the insidious obesity measured reliably in our experiments requires further study. However we suggest that the escalation of electromagnetic densities from Western civ-

ilization that are now transglobal in nature is conspicuously coincident with the "epidemic" of obesity and the remarkably increased dependence upon pharmacological consumptions for a wide variety of normal challenges associated with ontogeny. Although we do not have direct measurements for the entire population, our clinical experience with a local sample indicates that the proportion of pre- and early post-adolescent females who have been prescribed psychotropic medications at least once exceeds at least about 25%. This value approaches the shift in the distributional curve towards larger body masses. (Persinger, 2014, 279-80)

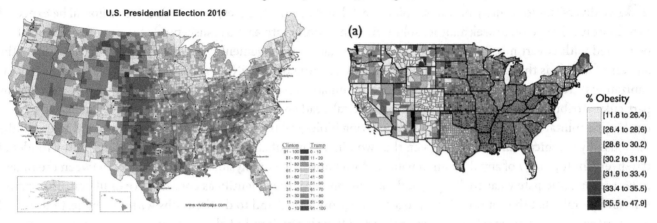

Obesity and Election Maps from the USA
(elections red = conservative, blue= liberal)

It is obvious that there is a broad and general correlation between conservative voting states and states with higher obesity, as well as diabetes, and from the above we can even see a similar trend in opioid sales, remembering that Nazi scientists created meth-amphetamines. Germans during the Nazi regime were addicts to a commercial version of meth. Of course I could even go into the Boston Brahmin and English sale of opioids to the Chinese as Opium. However, each state should be viewed on its own and analyzed at a much more granular level then these broad correlations; for instance Navajo areas have high obesity and diabetes due to non-Native diet, though largely

Referendum outcome and body weight, England and local area percentages

Originally titled: "The weight of Brexit: Obese adults leading the way out of Europe"

liberal in political viewpoint. Each area has unique characteristics to be investigated further and no single factor ever seems to convey anything too meaningful.

The more obese you are in the UK the more likely you were to vote for leaving the EU: 'Brexit.' (Dorling, 2019)

RED AND BLUE PHYSIOLOGICAL THREATS TO SECURITY

As has been seen from above, political physiology is a reality. What are the implications of liberal and conservative diversities to security protocols? Since each has its own attributes, we may ask: Can a liberal be expected to follow orders or go off to seek another solution? Can a conservative who is susceptible to hypnotic manipulation be trusted with covert missions, high command or situation management with rapidly changing variables? The answer of course is that being conservative or liberal has little to do with the complex that is trust in military organizations. Trust being a complex concept within human consciousness, again when we try to over atomize any particular attribute, we will always be making statistical dead ends, as most of natural existence, including who to trust in the military, are ensembles of varying moving biological parts. Though, of course, it is good to weigh the obvious physiological differences between the two binary simplifications which again are merely a toy model of the divergent topology of any domain in nature. With knowledge of physiological differences between the binary poles we can anticipate what challenges staff may encounter if they identify as conservative or liberal. The answer is to find people that the community can trust to be professional and to do their jobs with the highest moral and technical acuity, possessing self-awareness not just of their limitations but also their unique gifts, with an imagination that is eager to learn.

Notes:

<u>Kindling:</u> The word *kindling* is a metaphor: the increase in response to small stimuli is similar to the way small burning twigs can produce a large fire. It is used by scientists to study the effects of repeated seizures on the brain. A seizure may increase the likelihood that more seizures will occur; an old saying in epilepsy research is "seizures beget seizures." Repeated stimulation "lowers the threshold" for more seizures to occur.

BIBLIOGRAPHY:

Baghdadi, A. & Nasrabadi, A. (2010) Classyfing Hypnotizable Groups Using Weighted Regional Frequency. Scientia Iranica, Vol. 17(1) https://www.researchgate.net/publication/221947177_Classifying_Hypnotizable_Groups_Using_EEG_Weighted_Regional_FrequencyDIA (1972) Controlled Offensive Behavior – USSR. CIA-RDP96-00788R001300010001 https://www.cia.gov/library/readingroom/document/cia-rdp96-00788r001300010001-7 ST-CS-01-169-72 (DIA Report)

Dorling, Daniel (2019) Brexit and the end of the British Empire, Presentation at Keele University http://www.dannydorling.org/books/rulebritannia/figures/ video presentation: https://www.youtube.com/watch?v=AM5-Ihrztc4&t=4s

Jiang H, White MP, Greicius MD, Waelde LC, Spiegel D. (2017) Brain Activity and Functional Connectivity Associated with Hypnosis. Cereb Cortex. 2017 Aug 1;27(8):4083-4093. doi: 10.1093/cercor/bhw220. PMID: 27469596; PMCID: PMC6248753. https://pubmed.ncbi.nlm.nih.gov/27469596/

Kanai, R, Feilden, T, Firth, C., Rees, G. (2011) Political Orientations Are Correlated with Brain Structure in Young Adults. in Current Biology Vol. 21, #8, April 26, 2011, https://www.cell.com/current-biology/fulltext/S0960-9822(11)00289-2

Kihlstrom, J. F. (2013). Neuro-hypnotism: Prospects for hypnosis and neuroscience. Cortex: A Journal Devoted to the Study of the Nervous System and Behavior, 49(2), 365–374. https://doi.org/10.1016/j.cortex.2012.05.016

Le Doux, J. (2003) The Emotional Brain, Fear, and the Amygdala. in Cellular and Molecular Neurobiology-Cell Mol Neurobiol. 2003 Oct;23(4-5):727-38. doi: 10.1023/a:1025048802629. https://pubmed.ncbi.nlm.nih.gov/14514027/

Li, X., De Beuckelaer, A., Guo, J., Ma, F. Miao, X., Liu, J. (2014) The Gray Matter Volume of the Amygdala Is Correlated with the Perception of Melodic Intervals: A Voxel-Based Morphometry Study PLoS One. 2014; 9(6): e99889. https://www.ncbi.nlm.nih.gov/pmc/articles/PMC4055734/

Loscher, W. Brandt, C., Ebert, U. (2003) 'Excessive weight gain in rats over extended kindling of the basolateral amygdala.' in Neuroreport 14(14):1829-32 DOI: 10.1097/01.wnr.0000095700.40522.fa https://www.researchgate.net/publication/9059644_Excessive_weight_gain_in_rats_over_extended_kindling_of_the_basolateral_amygdala

Mendez, M. (2017) A Neurology of the Conservative-Liberal Dimension of Political Ideology. In J Neuropsychiatry Clin Neurosci 2017; 29:86–94; doi: 10.1176/appi.neuropsych.16030051

Narayanan, S., Mohapatra, N., John, P., Nalini, K., Kumar, R., Nayak, S., Bhat, G. (2017) Radiofrequency electromagnetic radiation exposure effects on amygdala morphology, place preference behavior and brain caspase-3 activity in rats. in Environmental Toxicology and Pharmacology 58 (2018) 220–229

Persinger, M. Paula L. Corradini, Alexandra L. Clement, Colleen C. Keaney, Mason L. MacDonald, Leah I. Meltz, Nirosha J. Murugan, Maxime R. Poirier, Kory A. Punkkinen, Melissa C. Rossini, Samantha E. Thompson (2010) NeuroTheology and Its Convergence with NeuroQuantology. in NeuroQuantology, Vol 8, Issue 4, Page 432-443

Persinger, M., Roll, W., Saroka, K. Mulligan, B., Hunter, M., Dotta, B., Gang, N., Scott, M. St-Pierre, L. (2012) Case report: A prototypical experience of 'poltergeist' activity, conspicuous quantitative electroencephalographic patterns, and sLORETA profiles – suggestions for intervention. Neurocase. 2012;18(6):527-36. doi: 10.1080/13554794.2011.633532 online: https://pubmed.ncbi.nlm.nih.gov/22229671/

Persinger, M. (2013) Infrasound, human health, and adaptation: an integrative overview of recondite hazards in a complex environment. in Natural Hazards 70(1)DOI:10.1007/s11069-013-0827-3 online: https://www.researchgate.net/publication/263412461_Infrasound_human_health_and_adaptation_An_integrative_overview_of_recondite_hazards_in_a_complex_environment

Persinger, Michael &. Saroka, Kevin (2013b). Potential production of Hughlings Jackson's "parasitic consciousness" by physiologically-patterned weak transcerebral magnetic fields: QEEG and source localization. In Epilepsy & Behavior : E&B. 28. 395-407. 10.1016/j.yebeh.2013.05.023.

Persinger, M & St-Pierre, L & Saroka, K. (2015). LORETA predicts electromagnetic sensitivity and "hearing voices" in a predictable, increasingly prevalent subpopulation: Possible QEEG-based differential diagnosis. In Neuropsychiatric Electrophysiology. 2. https://npepjournal.biomedcentral.com/articles/10.1186/s40810-015-0007-7

Persinger, M., Scott, M. A., Rouleau, N., Lehman, B. S., Tessaro, W. E., Juden-Kelly, L. M., Saroka, K. S. (2015b) Experimental Production of Excess Correlation across the Atlantic Ocean of Right Hemispheric Theta-Gamma Power between Subject Pairs Sharing Circumcerebral Rotating Magnetic Fields (Part II). in Journal of Consciousness Exploration & Research, Volume 6, Issue 9, pp. 685-707

Persinger, M. & St-Pierre, L. (2014) Progressive Obesity in Female Rats from Synergistic Interactions between Drugs and Whole Body Application of Weak, Physiologically Patterned Magnetic Fields. In Journal of Behavioral and Brain Science Vol.4 No.6, https://www.scirp.org/journal/paperinformation.aspx?paperid=47406

Persinger, M., & Scott, M. (2013) Cerebral Activity and Source Profiles Accompanying the Process of Non-Locality. In NeuroQuantology Volume 11, No 3 https://neuroquantology.com/article.php?id=2211

Persinger, M., Rouleau, N. (2017) Neural Tissues Filter Electromagnetic Fields: Investigating Regional Processing of Induced Current in Ex vivo Brain Specimens. in Biol Med (Aligarh) 2017, 9:2 DOI: 10.4172/0974-8369.1000392

Phan, L., Angstadt, M., Golden, J., Onyewuenyi, I., Popovska, A., de Wit, H. (2008) Cannabinoid Modulation of Amygdala Reactivity to Social Signals of Threat in Humans. In The Journal of Neuroscience, March 5, 2008 • 28(10):2313–2319

Raz, A., Fan, J., Posner, M. (2005) Hypnotic Suggestion Reduces Conflict in the Human Brain in Proc Natl Acad Sci U S A. 2005 Jul 12;102(28):9978-83. doi: 10.1073/pnas.0503064102 https://pubmed.ncbi.nlm.nih.gov/15994228/

Vanhaudenhuyse A, Laureys S, Faymonville ME. Neurophysiology of hypnosis. Neurophysiol Clin. 2014 Oct;44(4):343-53. doi: 10.1016/j.neucli.2013.09.006. Epub 2013 Oct 29. PMID: 25306075. https://pubmed. ncbi.nlm.nih.gov/25306

CHAPTER 11

AMERICAN AND BRITISH
DECEPTION MANAGEMENT AND CYBERNETICS

In the following chapter the focus of the discussion is on the technology of 'Deception Management' in warfare by the United States and the United Kingdom and by extension all of NATO and other allies, such as Israel. As discussed previously deception management is used to disguise or otherwise camouflage true military intentions from an adversary. Along with management of deception comes the automated and computational nature of contemporary Deception Management, where the management is largely done by automated computational systems using Artificial Intelligence techniques to conduct the 'work.'

EFFECTS BASED OPERATIONS (EBO), US REFLEXIVE MANAGEMENT

"[EBO]… goes against the very nature of war," - Gen. James Mattis (USMC Ret.) (APDC, 2009)

COST OF ACTIONS AND EFFECTS

In western military discourse Reflexive Control became known as Cost of Actions and Effects Based Operations. A quantification of the variables involved in taking an action and a quantization of the effects of those actions is the underlying principle. It is based in Deception; so is a universal military operation repeated whether one is a Red Team or a Blue Team. As the proliferation effect goes on in the Information Warfare battlespace:

> USJFCOM defines EBO as *"a process for obtaining a desired strategic outcome or effect on the enemy through the synergistic and cumulative application of the full range of military and non-military capabilities at all levels of conflict."* EBO places considerable importance on identifying and quantifying specific effects resulting from specific actions against specific targets. This requires vast information on the adversary; an aspect that sometimes draws criticism. It has been suggested that EBO requires unattainable levels of knowledge. (APDC, 2009)

Effects-based operations (EBO) is a concept that emerged during the Persian Gulf War for the planning and conduct of operations combining military and non-military methods to achieve a particular effect. An effects-based approach to operations was first applied in modern times in the design and execution of the Desert Storm air campaign of 1991. The principal author of the daily attack plans – then Lt. Colonel, now retired Lt General David A. Deptula – used an effects-based approach in building the actual Desert Storm air campaign targeting plan, we also note that shock and awe strategy was a product of Col. Szafranski, covered earlier. The doctrine was developed with an aim of putting desired strategic effects first and then planning from the desired strategic objective back to the possible tactical level actions that could be taken to achieve the desired effect.

Contrary to conventional military approaches of force-on-force application that focused on attrition and annihilation, EBO focused on desired outcomes attempting to use a minimum of force. The approach was enabled by advancements in weaponry – particularly stealth and precision weapons – in conjunction with a planning approach based on specific effects rather than absolute destruction. Deptula, defined the goal of EBO; "If we focus on effects, the end of strategy, rather than force-on-force the traditional means to achieve it militarily, that enables us to consider different and perhaps more effective ways to accomplish the same goal quicker than in the past, with fewer resources and most importantly with fewer casualties." Others have postulated that EBO could be interpreted as an emerging understanding that attacking a second-order target may have first order consequences for a variety of objectives, wherein the Commander's intent can be satisfied with a minimum of collateral damage or risk to his own forces.

The main difference between EBO and typical warfare is that EBO involves all aspects of the government, not just the military to achieve its aims, including the use of Information Warfare; not just targeted on troops in a battlespace but an entire society from top to bottom. The main development in EBO is that of automation, which was developed by the United States through Lockheed-Martin's Sandia National Labs. To study how automation is used in deception management and EBO we first must start with an understanding of how automation, or what is really gamification of a battlespace using deception, necessarily brings up a discussion of deceptive games as it applies directly to this part of warfare, even if gamified.

Reflexive Control, Deception Management, EBO are all part of leading an adversary away from their goals and is defined as such for deceptive games:

> Deceptive games are games where the reward structure or other aspects of the game are designed to lead the agent away from a globally optimal policy. (Togelius et al, 2018)

The main motivational factor in engineering behaviors is the individual subject's perceived rewards. In deceptive games the reward function is reversed:

> If we see the reward function as a heuristic function approximating the (inverse) distance from a globally optimal policy, a deceptive reward function is an inadmissible heuristic. (Togelius et al, 2018)

> Deceptive games can be seen as exploiting a specific cognitive bias of the (human or AI) player to trick them into making a suboptimal decision. Withholding or providing false information is a form of deception and can be very effective at sabotaging a player's performance. (Togelius et al, 2018)

As we have seen earlier this is the very definition of Reflexive Control whether in the Russian parlance or the UK-USA parlance of EBO or Deception Management. It is interesting to note that there are certain traps in deceptive games, which also seem to mimic common matchstick men maneuvers in the civilian world or simply marketing and advertising. These traps are greed trap, smoothness trap and generality trap.

TRAPS FOR DECEPTIVE GAMES:

> **Greed Trap:** A common problem simplification is to only consider the effect of our actions for a limited future. These greedy algorithms usually aim to maximize some immediate reward and rely on the assumption that the local reward gradient will guide them to a global maximum. One way to specifically exploit this bias (a greedy trap) is to design a game with an accumulated reward and then use some initial small reward to trick the player into an action that will make a later, larger reward unattainable (Togelius et al, 2018)

This trap is basically very effective if you are trying to manipulate someone to do your bidding but have no plans of actually giving them a good payout: a version of a classic con artist. For instance, you may receive valuable information for inconsequential bits that lead you to believe you have trust when they are setting you up only to pull the rug out from under you after reinforcing trust with accurate inconsequential information before betrayal.

> **Smoothness Trap:** Several AI techniques also rely on the assumption that good solutions are "close" to other good solutions. Genetic Algorithms, for example, assume a certain smoothness of the fitness landscape and MCTS algorithms outperform uninformed random tree search because they bias their exploration towards branches with more promising results. This assumption can be exploited by deliberately hiding the optimal solutions close to many really bad solutions. Since many of the solutions along the dangerous part lead to losses, an agent operating with the smoothness bias might be disinclined to investigate this direction further, and would therefore not find the much better solution. (Togelius et al, 2018)

This trap is the pony under the manure trap, you hide a pony under the manure and most people pass it by, unless you have an exploratory algorithm that hops around randomly looking for hidden ponies under piles of manure.

Generality Trap: Another way to make decision-making in games more manageable, both for humans and AI agents, is to generalize from particular situations. Rather than learning or determining how to interact with a certain object in every possible context, an AI can be more efficient by developing a generalized rule. For example, if there is a sprite that kills the avatar, avoiding that sprite as a general rule might be sensible. A generality trap can exploit this by providing a game environment in which such a rule is sensible, but for few critical exceptions. Thin Mints aims to realize this, as eating mints gives the AI points unless too many are eaten. So, the agent has to figure out that it should eat a lot of them, but then stop, and change its behavior towards the mints. Agents that would evaluate the gain in reward greedily might not have a problem here, but agents that try to develop sophisticated behavioral rules should be weak to this deception.

We should also note that most of the deceptions implemented here are focused on exploiting the reward structure given by the game to trick AIs that are optimized for actual rewards. Consider though, that recent developments in intrinsically motivated AIs have introduced ideas such as curiosity-driven AIs to play games such as Montezuma's Revenge or Super Mario. The internal curiosity reward enhances the AI's gameplay, by providing a gradient in an extrinsic reward landscape, but in itself makes the AI susceptible to deception. One could design a game that specifically punished players for exploration. (Togelius et al, 2018)

With this in mind we shall see how rewards and game play are integrated into military simulations for the purposes of training in war situations.

One other convergence between gaming and Deception Management is that of the need to understand behaviors from a computational standpoint. This is one of the reasons the NSA and GCHQ infiltrated video gaming social networks, studying human behaviors. The main reason is that of data sparseness; you need a lot of data to predict behavior:

> We argue that for studying national security issues, where data is sparse, it is difficult to experiment, and behaviors can be complex and varied, online games can serve as a unique and powerful tool to experimentally understand causal relationships. (Epifanovskaya et al, 2018)

> Data on millions of actions performed by a large and diverse sample of people lends itself well to statistical analysis, better than surveys and laboratory experiments with much smaller sample sizes taken from a more homogeneous group (e.g., college students, who frequently participate in academic human research studies (Gosling et al., 2010; Henrich et al., 2010). They also offer the opportunity to see how different types of players respond under different circumstances; useful for interrogating differences among players, but also, in wargaming, uncovering novel strategies that would not have occurred to personnel typically involved in these games. (Epifanovskaya et al, 2018)

It is worth pointing out that using data from a 'game' world, including studying people while they are immersed in that game world, would lead to some strange bias if applied to society in general. It would also lead to overly stereotypical analysis as data analysis of complex social interactions would tend to over generalize to the mean while ignoring anything it can't easily classify and cluster, even potentially creating lines of clusters that don't fit natural reality.

A Blueprint for an Information Warfare Engine

In Information Warfare there is a need to psychologically model the adversary. Lockheed-Martin through its teams at Sandia National Labs have developed a psychological-cognitive engine which was designed specifically for Counter-Intelligence and Influence operations as noted by the researchers, it is also noted that this work was not funded through government funds so thus remains the sole property of Lockheed-Martin to sell to anyone not on US lists that deny exports, such as Iran, China, Russia, etc. It could be sold to any civil war party, for instance, not on the export ban list; thus, making tracing such engines more difficult from a forensics perspective, unless you can develop fault-proof highly accurate forensics. It is also important to remember, as a non-DoD funded private project, that it does not face any kind of government oversight from the US Government.

Following up on the study of Terrorist networks, work from which one can engineer anti-terrorism and terrorism, it is important to look at the work of US Homeland Security in this area conducted by Sandia National Labs in influencing individuals towards and away from terrorism. In the work of Backus & Glass, 2006, we see how this work is theorized. According to their abstract work encompasses:

> This document presents the conceptualization of an agent-based, simulation framework that allows the use and testing of various social and behavioral science approaches for understanding the motivation and intent associated with terrorist activities. The framework design provides a LEGO™ -style toolbox that can convert sophisticated SME theses on individual and social behavior into computationally tractable, mathematical representations. Through parameterization, the reconfigurable framework can then simulate the dynamics of any particular group or interacting collection of terrorist groups. (Backus & Glass, 2006)

As noted, DHS has sponsored this research in creating and fighting terrorists. For this paper it is specifically carried out by the DHS Motivation & Intent Thrust Area, this work,

> …intends to use computerized models to ultimately improve the efficiency of intelligence analysts as they attempt to assess terrorist threats. A model is a machine, and like a machine, it can only perform the function for which it was built if its design and construction were sufficient. The successful development of an M&I model requires a clear understanding of how to combine modeling methods with the subject matter of interest." (Backus & Glass, 2006)

This work is part of the larger Human Factors studies of DHS. The Human Factors/Behavioral Sciences Division of the Department of Homeland Security's Science & Technology Directorate has as its mission to "advance national security by developing and applying the social, behavioral, and physical sciences to improve identification and analysis of threats, to enhance societal resilience, and to integrate human capabilities into the development of technology." Its past mission statement said, "know our enemies, understand ourselves; put the human in the equation."

This work is intended to model human individuals in networks, based on computational algorithms. The main emphasis behind such modeling is the use of Gradient Descent [see Appendix D], which often can lead to over-fitting and under-fitting of data; nonetheless, they believe you can study natural phenomena through such modeling even in highly complex social contexts, which is not what Gradient Descent is designed for, rather very simple mathematical models such as a robot arm moving a screw in a car factory where everything can be measured with exact mechanical precision. It is noted that such work as modeling human behavior can be a 'wicked' or almost intractable problem.

> A wicked problem usually has the characteristics that many people have tried and failed to solve the problem, that most attempts to solve the problem actually make the problem worse, and that nobody really agrees on exactly what the problem actually is! Wicked problems typically arise in feedback systems, and almost any interesting system is a feedback system." Addressing wicked problems requires a recognition that "priors" (preconceptions based on assumption or intuition) can distort the ability to see or accept alternative formulations of, or approaches to, the problem. New methods in Bayesian analysis appear to allow the determination of what causal mechanisms a simulation should include or, conversely, cannot reject in a social-science model. A modern statistical method called co-integration, further allows the determination of those feedback processes that dominate behavior. Sensitivity analysis methods have been successfully applied to combined societal-behavioral and physical systems that are dominated by feedback. Empirically, the feedback assures that only a few mechanisms control behavior under any given condition and these key mechanisms are readily determined. Analysts can than concentrate on those key elements. None of the above noted methods have yet become widely used within the social-psychological (behavioral) community. As such, conclusions drawn about what is not a cause of terrorism, using current statistical practices, might be misleading." (Backus & Glass, 2006, 6)

How this analysis works is that it views each person as a mapable agent. In the sense of AI Agents, people do not exist in solitary lives, rather we are social animals that usually operate in herds, so they are talking of herd management like a Farmer. The social existence of people takes place in Groups, through the mathematical representation of Groups these groups can be steered toward terrorism or away from terrorism.

> Within an agent-based simulation, simple individual mechanisms, such those associated with relative-deprivation or frustration, that alone cannot account for the group level action, can interact with other primal behaviors to produce the group behaviors that social movement theory attempts to describe. Agents behave differently in different environments and under the influence of different histories. The varied and seemingly inconsistent histories of various terrorist groups could simply be a consequence of the specific history and environment that shapes the collective agent trajectory. A few simple mechanisms may explain a wide variety of dynamics,

and can thereby offer an understanding (and control) of terrorist motivation and intent. Additionally, violence comes from a relatively small element of any society. Agent-based models simulate a distribution of individuals. In essence, the agents reflect the full spectrum of possibilities and can produce the full spectrum of actualizations. (Backus & Glass, 2006, 7)

In this work they view humans as Lego blocks that are easy to reconfigure:

> While groups can be represented as an interacting and evolving set of individuals, individuals (agents) can be represented by a primal set of behavioral mechanisms. The mechanisms are the language that expresses the individual behavior and its connection with other individuals (and the environment). That language must be mapable to/from the language that subject matter experts (SMEs) use to describe behaviors and dynamics. For human behavior to be so complex, it must be composed of a relatively small number of simple mechanisms. If there were a large number of complicated mechanisms, the mechanisms would only work in the situation for which they were designed. Simple mechanisms can fit together and interact in near infinite variety. The concept is no different than that of jig-saw puzzle, where complex pieces can only make one picture, but simple pieces such as colored triangles, can make any picture desirable (albeit, with a few negligible, rough edges). Lego™ pieces can portray very complex shapes because they allow both two and three dimensional constructs. (They even allow four dimensional concepts if the pieces are hinged, and, thus, can vary over time). The Lego™ metaphor seems appropriate for an agent-based framework. The use of a few key (behavioral) building blocks can decompose the logic of a SME. The replicated use of those blocks can then form the representation for any group or interacting set of groups. If the building blocks are well designed, their parameterization with historical data will result in a realistic and useful representation of the group relative to the future motivation and intent (M&I) dynamics of interest.

They seek to define the Lego blocks view as Subject Matter Experts (SME). Initially the SMEs were human analysts, whereas in later work they are automated SMEs. They believe you can predict behavior from past history based on the blocks' understanding. Although they do note that this is only applicable to simple models not complex ones. What they are seeking to formulate are behavioral changes via game theory and optimization. The extensive use of Game theory is noted throughout so-called 'anti-terror' operations in an effort to formulate 'intervention' strategies, which can also be flipped around and provide motivational strategies to create terrorist incidents. There are four primal building blocks to formulating the intervention strategies:

> As will be discussed in detail below, the current model design only includes four primal building blocks (components): expectation-formation, response-behavior (choice), coping-capacity, and opinion adjustment. Opinion-adjustment combines coping-skill and behavioral-response dynamics into a single component applicable to a key subset of terrorist dynamics. (Backus & Glass, 2006, 11)

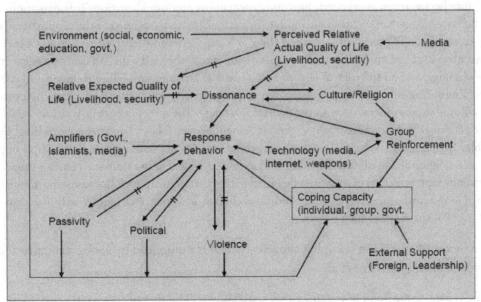

Figure 4: Model Components.

In a visual mapping of this process and how the moving parts of the machine model work Backus & Glass provide the following flow:

> The difference between expectations and perceived reality produces a dissonance.3 The cross-line in the arrows of causality in Figure 4 indicates delays in response. It takes time to gestate and incorporate information. Religion and culture present a form of coping skills. As dissonance occurs, people seek (or withdraw to) religious or cultural traditions that allow a rationalization of conditions. These psychological anchor points act to mitigate the dissonance. The simple representation noted in Figure 4 denotes the choice to seek religious and cultural moral support. Secondary aspects of religions will become clear momentarily. Depending on 1) the ability to act (coping-capacity), 2) the existing effectiveness of violence or political activities, 3) outside influences, and 4) the level of dissonance, the individual makes choices toward violence, passivity, or political activity. Group dynamics can dominate the response-behavior. The group amplifies the coping capacity of the individual and reinforces a predilection toward continued association with the group and its function. In this example, the groups represent proponents of the three responses simulated (passivity, political, violence). (The model can include additional responses and distinctions as actual or analogous data allow.)
>
> External (exogenous) support from foreign governments/resources and exceptional leadership personalities can dramatically augment the amplifying affect a group has on an individual. The internet makes it easier to join a group both in effort and risk terms. (In economics, this phenomenon is called reducing the transaction and hurdle costs). The media can distort the information an individual uses to make a choice. Weapon technology also amplifies the coping capacity of an individual, just as a power tool amplifies the capability of its user. It is not only the violence or political activism that an individual sees in his social environment, but also the counter (or precipitating) violence or political activity of the government (or government surrogate) that affects the choices made. The reaching out to religious or cultural organizations that resonate with the level of dissonance act primarily to increase the probability of contact with groups that reinforce rather than mitigate the dissonance. Again, the Internet and media also increase the probability of contact of similarly dissonant souls. The added effect of Islamist education will be discussed later. From a sociological and psychological level, dissonance is the measure of motivation and the behavioral response is the measure of intent. From a DHS perspective, the intent is multivariate, and the coping capacity and group-reinforcement qualify as operational measures of motivation. (Backus & Glass, 2006, 12)

One can see the similarity to the work of Tarasenko, covered in a previous chapter, in reconfiguring groups and its application here in a US national defense contractor's version of the same. Influence is about getting the right information into the mind of the target of that information. The work here involves the component of dissonance, which produces alienation:

> The dissonance between perceived conditions and expectations produce alienation. This alienation can lead to antisocial behavior (Sageman). Within the model, dissonance is strictly defined as the proportional difference between perceived conditions and Only when there is a gap between perceived reality and expectations, is there an incentive to act. Many authors indicate that dissonance associated with social and political expectation acts as the starting point on the path to terrorism (Crenshaw; Drummond; Silke) Religion and culture affect dissonance. Embracing either can improve apparent coping capacity (discussed later). The choice to seek religious and cultural support increases with dissonance (Dennet). The direct impact is to reduce dissonance and temper the actions that dissonance might engender. As will be noted later, large negative indirect impacts are also possible. This "religion" dynamic is included for completeness and to illuminate the multiple impacts such phenomena as religion and media play in terrorist dynamics. As such, only a simplified coping-capacity plus response-behavior representation of religion is included in this part of the model. Because expectation formation is a filtering (long-term) process, even after conditions change, dissonance changes slowly – as experienced in post-war Iraq. (Backus & Glass 2006)

Key to dissonance and alienation is coping capacity, which is influenced by social structure and relationships. Coping capacity is defined by Backus et al:

> Anger, or even hate, to the point of wanting to kill somebody, will be void of action if there is no perceived capacity to carry out the act. The psychological coping capacity of individuals determines their ability to respond

to conditions. The adaptation to environment comes from changes in coping skills (Helson). If new conditions are excessive compared to coping skills the individual will succumb to the external pressure (flight mode). If the change is within the normal operating range of the coping skills, the individual will counter the new pressure (fight mode). If the new condition is trivial compared to the coping skill, the individual does little and need to do little to (successfully) respond. If the challenge is slightly larger than the average coping capacity, the coping skills increase over time to match the environment. (Backus & Glass, 2006, 15)

Obviously coping skills are an important aspect to adaptation, too much required adaptation overloads coping capacity. A key component to the strength of coping capacity is that of group or social reinforcement:

It is the group dynamics and the behavioral reinforcements that seem to be important to terrorist outcomes… accordingly. The individuals in the group reinforce each other. As noted earlier, the coping grows and declines based on the interaction between the individual and the environment (in this instance, the group). Individuals within the group influence and reinforce each other. (Backus et al, 2006)

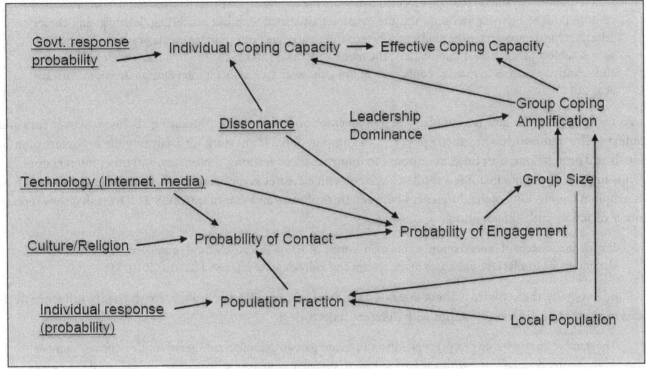

Figure 5: Group Reinforcement Detail

The backing of the group enhances the coping capacity of the individual (e.g., the stereotypically insecure bully being backed by a group of his friends. Group dynamics might instead be the key "amplification" process. (Note that the government is just another agent in the model.)

Backus et al provide an example of 'opinion-adjustment' within a networked agent-based model. This shows how to influence groups, intended to thwart terrorist group formation, which of course can be inverted like all programs.

The simplified model combines the threshold-based approach to the agent activation to violence of Epstein with the dynamics of opinion formation of Weisbuch and coworkers. Epstein represents an agent's action level by its "Grievance," a combination of two agent state variables: perceived "Hardship" and perceived "Legitimacy" of the local regime or status quo. The term Grievance has an interpretation comparable to that of Dissonance or Motivation. Hardship and Legitimacy are perceptions, or opinions, of individual agents and are the result of interactions with other agents, information from the media, environment, events, etc. In Epstein's analysis, Hardship or Legitimacy are static variables, however the example implementation allows them to be dynamic and to arise through interaction with other agents via the opinion formation process of Weisbuch. Risk of capture or worse, may temper the intent to perpetrate an act of violence. Risk is a function of the individual's inherent aversion to risk and the probability of being discovered and suffering an undesirable outcome. If the motivation, adjusted for risk, exceeds a threshold, an individual will shift to a new (possibly violent) action state. (Backus et al, 2010)

Opinion formation is very significant in the process of influence; it is noted that media plays a key part in this formation. Later, I will cover Memetic Warfare: the uses of image media to create groups.

We covered the computational modeling of emotions in an earlier part focusing on the work of Tarasenko. Here we see how the US Government labs tackle the issue of modeling human cognition and emotion into their systems. In work dating back to 2010 Backus et al developed a computational framework for automating influence operations and deception:

> ....key features of the SNL psychological engine. The engine is designed to be a generic presentation of cognitive entities interacting among themselves and with the external world. The engine combines the most accepted theories of behavioral psychology with those of behavioral economics to produce a unified simulation of human response from stimuli through executed behavior. The engine explicitly recognizes emotive and reasoned contributions to behavior and simulates the dynamics associated with cue processing, learning, and choice selection. Most importantly, the model parameterization can come from available media or survey information, as well subject-matter-expert information. The framework design allows the use of uncertainty quantification and sensitivity analysis to manage confidence in using the analysis results for intervention decisions. (Backus et al, 2010)

As mentioned, the engine is a simulator of human emotion based on cue processing. Below we cover cues and contexts. The framework is succinctly put as: "...a computational framework for analyzing the behaviors of individuals and populations, over time, in response to information operations, diplomacy, and other intercessions."

It is important to note that it is a feedback system which creates responses from actions done in areas such as state diplomacy, etc. One of the differences between this software and that of usual US MilDef is that they replace 'course of action' with 'intervention':

> We use the concept of "intervention" rather than "course of action" because we only emphasize those endeavors that intervene to affect the behaviors of the system and individuals of interest. (Backus, 2010, 7)

Fundamentally, the software is about steering an individual and collectively a society. It tries to influence decisions by presenting different scenarios with different trajectories:

> The framework is based on first principles that can encompass an unlimited number of entities with any number of alternative decisions, and with any level of interrelationship complexity. Because we only allowed the use of theories that 1) were mutually self-consistent, 2) would integrate into a complete representation of behavior from stimuli through to action, 3) would translate to a unique set of computational equations, and 4) could be instantiated, tested, and verified using accessible date, we can 1) readily use available data on individual or regions to calibrate the model, 2) use Subject Matter Expert (SME) data to augment data sparsity, 3) test hypotheses about alternative interventions and behavioral responses, 4) quantify the uncertainty (risk) that an intervention will produce the desired results, and 5) follow the time-dependent consequential counter-responses from an intervention. Most importantly, the framework naturally captures the implications of new (even unique) information flows such as may be considered in information operations or other interventions. (Backus, 2010, 8)

Some of the principles involved in its design are Bounded Rationality (Simon), Qualitative Choice (McFadden), Imperfect Information (Stiglitz), Risk Asymmetry, and Stock & Flow Cointegration. We shall cover some of these below. What we are talking about here is the previously discussed 'Influence Machine', a machine built to shape public opinion through automated processes. It creates a model of individuals ('entities') then uses a cognitive map to influence the individual ('entity').

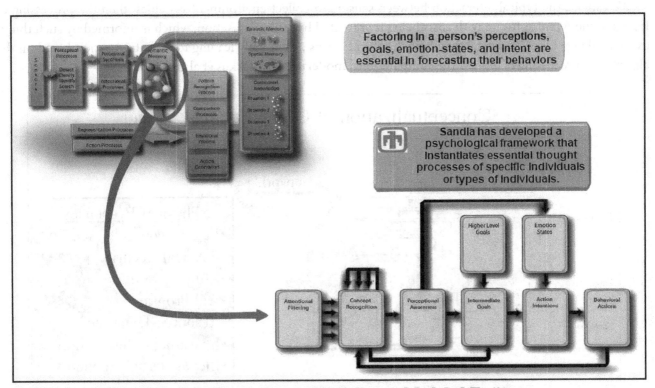

Figure 3: Sandia High-Fidelity Cognitive Modeling A Modeled Entity

The mathematical representation of these processes is largely a re-application of the Backus and Glass (2006) to match the specific needs of influence operations. Here we are talking about influence agents, and agents in general in the sense of computer game programming. Backus has a specific model of an Agent as shown in the following diagram:

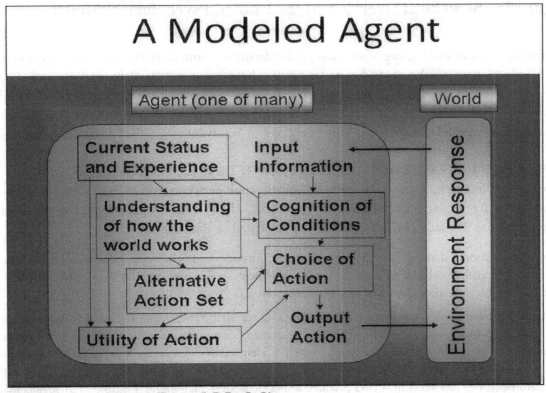

Figure 4: Agent-Based Modeling

(Backus 2010, 12)

We can see the typical interaction between sensors to collect environment variables, then the processing of inputs in the Agent software with costs being represented by Utility of Action, which is informed by such things as a knowledge base: 'understanding how the world works'; eventually leading to an output action based on the algorithmic processing of inputs. The computational model used by Backus et al is as follows:

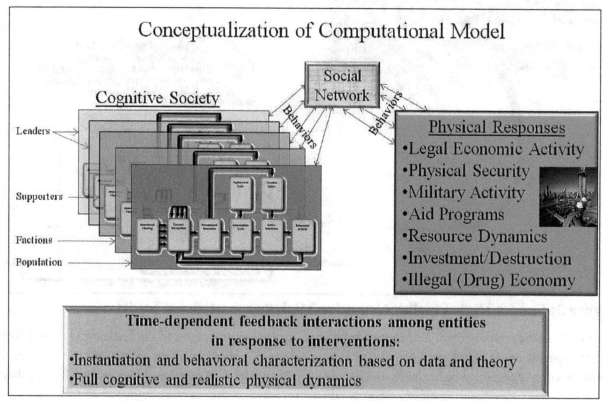

Figure 5:   Structural Overview of the Unified Psychological Model

It is interesting to note that the cognitive society is divided into various layers: leaders, supporters, factions, populations. All of which we see also studied in understanding how online gaming clans work as studied by the NSA and GCHQ in efforts to understand these layers mechanics. All interacting in social networks and the behaviors associated with different social networks are mapped out for computation. All of which has a feedback interaction among the entities (people) in response to 'cost-of-actions' or 'interventions' dished out by automated algorithms.

ELEMENTS OF PSYCHOLOGICAL PROFILING FOR COMPUTATION:

The basic components of the SNL are comprised of psychological concepts such as attitudes, notions, expectations, passivity, incongruity and cognitive resources. All of which form a complex in which an action is molded by behaviors. The following is an overview as presented by Backus et al:

> Attitudes are pattern derived from cognitive resources. Attitudes can be affective or rational. Some types of attitudes have evolution-based and cultural-based components. In essence, attitudes are an internalized notion affecting the interpretation of external cues (Backus, 2010, 23)

> Notions: A collection of Cues forms a Notion. Notions are then a collection of selected stimuli relevant to specific intents and behavior. Notion can be affective or reasoned and influence the utility an intent (choice) or behavior has. The sensory aspect of notion formation is identical in construction to attitudes but is composed of the cuing stimuli rather than cognitive resources. Nonetheless, attitudes (by altering the β of the pattern strength equation) can affect how cues produce a specific notion. Elaboration Likelihood Theory considers notions as based on differing patterns of perception that then feed into the utility of actions whose components may include higher cognitive considerations as well as emotive elements for support biasing of intentions. (Backus, 2010, 24)

Backus et al drills down into the elements which drive this process:

- **Notion Assimilation** Psychological studies and experiments indicate that individuals only remember the peak and end value of sensory input (Fredrickson, Schwarz). Further, the peak values from multiple sensory episodes are not additive. Other studies indicate that cuing frequency and recency play a role in behavioral responses (Perugini). As noted previously, the lingering aspect of sensory notions can have an emotive content called "mood." The speed at which a cue becomes a notion is faster for an emotive notion than a reasoned notion. The lingering effect is longer for an emotive notion than reasoned notion. Hence, there can be mood-congruent behavior where the phasing of reasoned and affective notions play off with each other.

- **Expectations** Incongruity comes from the difference between perceived conditions and expected conditions. Expectations come from the memory of prior conditions. Nonetheless, the expectation for the future may not coincide with the exact memory of the past conditions if there is anticipation of change, such as a raise or a job promotion.

The psychologist Hogarth notes that almost all decisions are based on expectations. Further, the shortcomings of human cognition and information assimilation mean that decisions are based on limited information and selective perceptions. Additionally, new work shows that humans use information to build up "priors" that are then used as a reference bias for subsequent decisions under the normally existing conditions of uncertain and deficient data.

Humans form expectations and make decisions about issues that are worth the effort. In the current conception of the model, separate considerations of security and livelihood act as surrogates for the key issues driving individual and societal evolution. Having adequate food, housing, income, and employment (livelihood) means little if you won't live long enough to enjoy it (security). An education brings with it expectations of a better livelihood. Lawlessness and excess government repression add to a sense of insecurity. Weighted sums of socioeconomic and security indicators produce livelihood and security indices, respectively. A multiplicative combination of security and livelihood indices produce a quality of life (QOL) index that captures the key dynamics characteristics important to decision making. Over time, the perceived current QOL evolves into the expected QOL. (Backus & Glass, 2006, 13)

- **Passivity:** Passivity is simply an attitude that affects the offset associated with incongruity. In a sense, passivity is an attitude toward incongruity. A high degree of passivity means that there needs to be a large disparity between existing and "normal" conditions before the individual recognizes a need to act. Passivity determines the changing sensitivity to incongruity. Estimating the parameters of passivity would require an extended data time-series, but the impact of passivity is secondary and can be neglected for most studies.

- **Incongruity:** Incongruity is the proportional change between perceived conditions and expected conditions. It is the primal dissonance driving the reaction to external stimuli (cues). It has a dead-zone response using an offset (as discussed above) to capture the threshold effect. Figure 16 shows how incongruity changes as the proportional difference between actual conditions and expectations vary.

- **Cognitive Resources:** Cognitive resources are the accumulation of experiential learning tempered by evolutionary constraints. They can contain emotive conditioning (such as the fear of dark alleys) or the acquisition of a physical capability (such as playing a musical instrument). Incongruity initiates learning. Learning changes the process for coping with the environment. If the incongruity is small, it means that individual is well suited to respond to existing conditions and has probably controlled the existing condition to correspond to expectations – through previous behaviors.

Components of Learning inhibition Excitation Conditioning improves the level of cognitive resource through the conditioning response.... The conditioning can improve a cognitive resource until behaviors bring incongruity levels to within acceptable ranges. The level of a cognitive resource grows to slightly exceed the level needed to accommodate external stimuli. This phenomenon has a basis in evolution where 31 there needs to be a contingency if it allows the individual to tolerate conditions that exceed previously experienced values. In brief, repetitive, tolerable, stress producing (incongruity) events modify cognitive resources to cope with that environment. (Backus, 2010, 30-1)

Cognitive resource is a broad term reflecting a learned capability for responding to notions (patterns of relevant cues). A pattern of cognitive resources represents an attitude. The attitude may have a reasoned or emotive basis and it can reflect a propensity for response or perceptions of which an entity is not consciously aware. Anything learned (knowledge, belief, emotional response, intuition) other than pure memory of past conditions for making expectations, is a cognitive resource. The model dynamics indicate that "motivation" is the circumstance whereby perceptions are large enough to offer a challenge, yet small enough to ensure adequate response with readily achievable effort (Grossberg, Yerkes). This aspect is reflected as the excitatory and inhibitory components of conditioning. The Cognitive Resources include belief, knowledge, experience, and emotive levels of memory to decisions. The current logic is based on coping skill dynamics (Backus 2006). (Backus, 2010, 89)

Interventions interact with all the above elements, along with these elements that occur within or internally to an agent or entity or person it is also necessary to understand how they interact socially:

> To model the consequence of interventions, it is necessary to not only model the initial behaviors of affected individuals, but to also determine how interactions with other individuals and the physical world, over time, can alter the outcome. The changes over time are called dynamics. The feedback processes among individuals and the physical world unfold dynamically and cause the outcome of an intervention to, for example, start off going in the desired direction, but in the long-term lead to counter-responses that generate new concerns without improving the original issue. The delay between behaviors and impacts can cause secondary dynamics that make it extremely difficult to know whether the ups and downs of behavioral responses and counter-responses will ultimately lead to the desired outcome. (Backus, 2010, 13)

> The process for developing a psychological model using the system dynamics methodology starts with a description of the psychological theories the model must simulate. These theories need to encompass all the salient considerations needed to make a comprehensive system's model describing the problems of interest. Note that there is no attempt of model the entire system, but only those aspects of the system relevant to the problems to be addressed/analyses. The next step is to develop a causal loop diagram the causally relates all the interactions embodied in the theories. The casual loop diagram is next mapped to a stock-and-flow diagram that explicitly details the flow of information and physical quantities through the system. A key feature is the designation of stocks that represent the accumulation of information, experience, monetary, or physical quantities. These stocks are called "state variables" and they largely characterize the nature of the system and its responses. The difference in the value of stocks over time increments is the "differential" part of the differential-equation approach to computational modeling. The exact mathematical expression of the theory is anchored in the accumulation of flow into and out of the stocks. The mathematical expression of the flows comes from a causal interpretation of the theory into the language of mathematics. The key equations will be described later in this report. Only those theories that have a measurable meaning, supportable, a least in principle, by historical or experimental data, are included in the model. The data determines the parameters that control the progression of the simulated values through time. (Backus, 2010, 13)

Management of a situation is always the prime concern of military intelligence. The management of military assets is not just considered in this framework, rather it is more general than a specific implementation for a specific behavior and specific tasks. The management of 'flows' whether monetary, natural resources, or human populations is the main objective of system dynamics method, which is anchored in the accumulation of flow into and out of the stocks. How are flows affected is a matter of human actions and the steering of human actions through cues:

> Stimuli are the physical realization of world conditions and of human action. When an individual places these stimuli in context, they become cues that inform or affect behaviors. The grouping of cues forms a pattern. For example, the observation of asphalt, cars, sidewalks, and buildings act as cues, giving you the notion that you are on a city street. We use the term "notion" rather than "perception" because the term "perception" can often denote a higher level of cognition than the recognition of simple physical stimuli, such as, the higher-level perception that quantum mechanics better explain atomic phenomena than thermodynamics and opposed to primal sensation of "that pin is sharp!" Notions typically take on importance when they are incongruous with (different from) expectations. Expectations are often the memory of the status-quo or the anticipation of future conditions. Cognitive resources are our learned attitude toward a condition (the condition being a perceived notion or incongruity) or our learned ability to respond to a condition. Our cognitive resources and perceptions of a situation (via notions and incongruities) act together to help us evaluate the choices we have

to respond to those conditions. The result represents our intentions. The execution of those intentions further depends on the level of the incongruity and our attitudes toward that behavior. Once we initiate a behavior, it takes time before it becomes an action affecting the external world (including other individuals). Depending on the proximity or our social network, the realized consequence of our actions becomes the cues to some individuals but not to others. (Backus, 2010, 15)

Proximity within social networks amplifies the actions of an individual; those closer will tend to mimic the person that is a center of action. Expectations are a central part of the whole process of behavior intervention by manipulating intentions. "Notions typically take on importance when they are incongruous with (different from) expectations. Expectations are often the memory of the status-quo or the anticipation of future conditions." Weight is added to a notion, an engineered notion or a free-will notion, by the manipulation of expectations, the more unexpected the more important the notion.

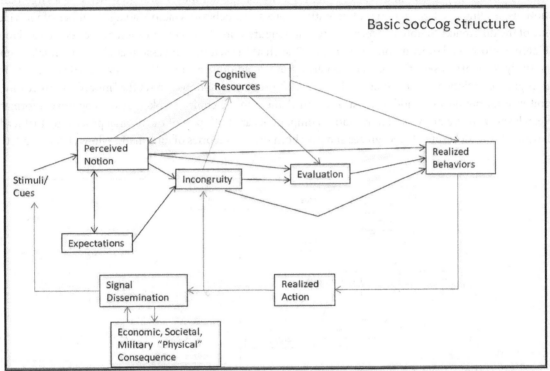

Figure 6: Computation Elements of the Behavioral model.

The formation of notions is dependent on the information being fed into the system. One can use Subject Matter Experts (SME) or an automated process, which is favored today. Based on the background information behaviors are formulated and a process of influence is calculated:

> …feedback logic of one entity's behavior becoming another entity's stimuli (cues), possibly through the intermediation of external physical processes, explicitly captures the social network considerations that are often the domain of more-abstract agent-based modeling. An entity is an individual or a group. The approach for this modeling is made possible by assuming a fixed set of potential behaviors embodied in a representation of the individual. The representation contains the preferences and personality characteristics pertinent to the relevant decision-making. It is called the "blueprint" and it fully characterizes a specific individual or group of individuals. While the magnitude of interactions may change, the model does not produce new paths of cognition. All potential interactions are determined via initial parameterization of the model. Over the time, frame of the model simulation (at most a couple of years and often on the order of weeks), there should be little possibility, and there is little predictive capability for modeling, that entities would change their behaviors outside the domain of their historical experience and habits. (See Appendix 15 for an expanded discussion on relaxing the assumptions of a "blueprint" approach.) The mathematical expression of what stimuli cause cues and what choices or behaviors those cues can invoke has to be determined a priori thought the use of subject matter experts (SMEs) and avail-

able data. SMEs can hypothesize notions and perception that are not reflected in the data. Analytical methods can allow an estimate of how those hypothesized behaviors could occur based on the knowledge of an individual's behaviors in other circumstances. The singular personality of an individual has a large effect on all his or her decisions. Uncertainty analysis could determine the potential for such a behavior to affect the policy selection of external security interventions. (The assessment of these interventions is the actual purpose of the model, not the pin-point prediction of individual behavior.) The model cannot generate potential behaviors that are beyond the imagination of SMEs and are not reflected in available data. These unknown unknowns are a limitation in all realms of physical and social science. Nonetheless, the 'blueprint' for an individual within the model is the best representation of that individual's behavior characteristics available. Any other representations would be less valid and less reliable. Figure 7 [see below] show an exploded view of model structure of Figure 6 [see above]. Each block in the diagram contains only one to two equations. Each of these equations has a simple theoretical construct that will be discussed briefly below and fully elucidated in the Appendices. Note however that each block can process large flows of data. There are typically a large number of stimuli generating a large number of notions, leading to a large number of potential choices and behaviors, across a large number of individuals. Some of the differences to note between Figure 6 and Figure 7 are the decomposition of the "Perceived Notion" in Figure 6 into several subcomponents in Figure 7, such as the sensory and assimilated notion. It takes time to cognitively recognize a set of cues. Cues can also produce emotive notions that characteristically occur faster than cognitive notions and use minimal information. The emotive notions can set the "mood" for processing the cognitive information, often adding a risk aversion element to the choice invoked by the cognitive information. Research shows that emotive and non-motive components are both part of the normal processing that leads to behavior. The model explicitly recognizes and uses both these categories of information flow. (Backus, 2010)

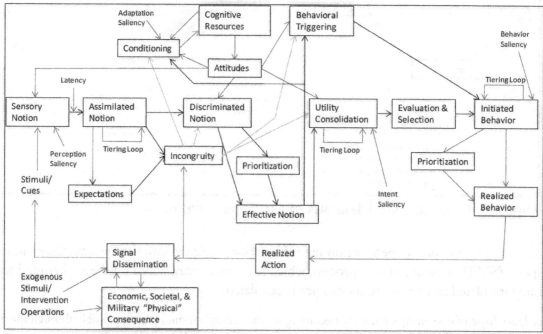

Figure 7: Detailed Model Cognitive components.

Related to notions is that of attitudes helping determine the utility of choice:

Specific notions (such as realizing there is a fire in your house), can dramatically amplify your realization of other notion/cues such as the location of doors and other occupants of the house. Similarly, making one decision may affect your selection of a related decision. The same is true for executing behaviors. Attitudes affect the importance you may place on information. Attitudes are explicitly calculated in the model and are based on cognitive resources (experiences, abilities, and beliefs). Learning is noted as conditioning in the model and is an effort to reduce an incongruity by developing the ability to accommodate or effectively respond in the presence of a notion. Attitudes, emotive content, and cognitive information all act to determine the utility of a choice. These utilities come together to shape the probability of making a specific choice. Limitations in mental processing and physical response mean the individual must prioritize notions and behaviors when either becomes potentially excessive. For example, changing the radio station when you hear a song you dislike is quickly neglected when you see the car ahead of you hit another car. (Backus et al, 2010)

Another component, as noted above in choice is that of emotions, or moods:

> Moods are essentially lingering emotive notions. Altering conditions can cause moods to change over time, but typically not instantaneously. Therefore, decisions based solely on objective information may be different than those made in the presence of a specific mood (Rusting, Mellers). Because moods can arise quickly, decisions later in time, when moods have subsided, may be significantly different from those made when the individual is in a highly emotional state (Tiedens). The terms Saliency and Latency in Figure 7 note the parameterizations that capture the importance the individuals place on information (facts or feelings). The individual can adapt the importance he/she places on information as a result of conditioning and modified cognitive resources. This adaptation reflects itself as strengthened or weakened attitudes (Backus, 2010).

Moods affect decision making, in that it can affect the timing of decisions:

> Emotional conditioning can force snap decisions against one's own best-interest:
> The Assimilation process takes time with affective notion realization occurring faster than for reasoned notions. The rise in affective notion can exceed the threshold for a response and act to trigger behavior that might not otherwise occur if cognitive process dominated or timing were different. The lingering of an affective notion due to the "afterimage" phenomenon of the assimilation delay in essence sets the mood of the entity. Because incongruity is the relationship between the assimilated notion and its expected values, the assimilation process can cause a delayed buildup of incongruity. The incongruity can reach a behavioral threshold sometime after the actual initiating stimuli. (Backus, 2010, 82)

> A key feature is that some notions arrive sooner than others (such as affective ones), and if decisions need to be made promptly they may be different than what would occur without the time pressure. The assimilation process automatically capture[s] the ideas of recency by remembering the previous events consistent with theory; it does not remember the duration and only remembers the maximum intensity. The notion takes time to die away and can affect future decisions. For affective notions, this response reflects the concept of moods. In the model, a discriminated notion is essentially a mood. (Backus, 2010, 83-4)

So that, overall, we see that the Influence machine involves creating a choice within an entity or agent or in reality a person or population of peoples (groups, tribes). This involves molding notions that are acted upon with emotional reinforcement and learning of behaviors connected to those notions and emotions that break previous expectations.

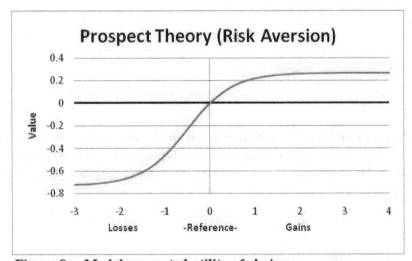

Figure 8:   Model generated utility of choices.

Figure 8: Model generated utility of choices. Notions and expectations need to be significantly different from their normal values before an individual recognizes that incongruity as a "concern." The level of discrepancy needs to evoke a response in line with "importance" assigned to information (notion). Because the perceived level of incongruity, intensified or diminished by attitude, contributes to the evaluation of choice, a perceived negative association may have a much larger impact on choice than an equally-sized perceived benefit. This phenomenon is called loss or risk aversion and is exemplified in Prospect Theory or Risk Asymmetry (Backus et al, 2010)

Decisions are based on what is known as Qualitative Choice Theory (QCT),

> The basic equation that weighs information, be it simply sensory input or the multifaceted utility of alternative decisions, is shown below. It is based on Qualitative Choice Theory (QCT) whose foundation comes from psychology (Luce) and from economics. The first term (numerator) on the right-hand side of the equation is the relative value of the utility (U) for a collection of information.1 The second term (the denominator) is its comparison with all other relevant information. The result may be a choice (C), a simple recognition of sensory input, or an incongruity with a remembered condition and an existing condition. Subtleties of the equation reflect the probability that a choice is correct or useful in the context of perceived conditions.

> The first term (numerator) on the right-hand side of the equation is the relative value of the utility (U) for a collection of information.1 The second term (the denominator) is its comparison with all other relevant information. The result may be a choice (C), a simple recognition of sensory input, or an incongruity with a remembered condition and an existing condition. Subtleties of the equation reflect the probability that a choice is correct or useful in the context of perceived conditions.

Choice Evaluation:

$$C(j) = e^{U(j)} / \sum_i e^{U(i)}$$

Equation 1.

The equation is also used for triggering learning and triggering behaviors by reflecting excitation and inhibitory responses. Conditions that are deemed too trivial to recognize or counter cause little excitatory reaction. Conversely, a condition may be so intense that sensory channels are saturated or that certain behaviors are too ineffective to execute. These situations cause extreme inhibitory effects.

The next equation below determines the pattern strength of cues forming notions or the cognitive resources forming attitudes. It is directly derivable from the choice equation above when the utility is proportion to the logarithm of the cues, such as with the Weber–Fechner law. As a specific manifestation of the choice equation, the notion (P), for example is a combination (z) of relevant cues (S). The β are the weights of each cue and generally sum to unity. Pattern Strength:

Pattern Strength:

$$P = \alpha \times \prod_z S(z)^{\beta(z)}$$

Equation 2.

The next equation is an asymptotically exact, approximation of choice response when utility is based on a single consideration. It captures the incongruity between actual (perceived) conditions and expected (remembered or anticipated) conditions using an offset to avoid responding to insignificant discrepancies.

Incongruity:

$$D = \frac{Actual - Expected}{Expected} \pm Offset$$

Eq

The last equation, below, is almost tautological in nature as the accumulation (R) of some quantity such as experience, memory, or capability that can atrophy over time (η) in the absence of continued activity (Input). This equation is used in simulating notion assimilation, cognitive resource conditioning, and expectation formation. Its theoretical basis is found in the "stock and flow" constructs developed in the field of System Dynamics (Sterman), but its statistical estimation and validation comes from the economics approach called Co-integration.

Conditioning and Fading activity:

$$R(t) = \int_{t_0}^{t} (Input(t) - R(t)/\tau) \times dt$$

E(

ANALYTICS, MEASURING EFFECTIVENESS:

In all computational systems, especially those with automation like AI itself, it is necessary to have analytics to measure the effects of actions on a target entity. The usual AI techniques are used, which it should be born in mind were not initially developed to model highly complex systems such as psychological persuasion as also used in neuromarketing (commercial warfare), not just information warfare. The interventions are modeled by probability of success:

> With this statistical knowledge, we can provide confidence intervals on the results of the model analyses that test interventions. By simultaneously performing uncertainty quantification for model parameters and potential interventions, the framework can determine the portfolio of interventions that have the highest (quantified) probability of success despite uncertainty. It can also quantify the risk associated with the intervention not performing as anticipated. Additionally, as will be discussed shortly, the framework can perform sensitivity analyses to determine what minimal additional information is needed to maximally reduce uncertainty and further assure the proposed interventions produce the desired outcome throughout the time horizon of interest. (Backus, 2010, 43)

Below is a diagram outlining the analytical engine:

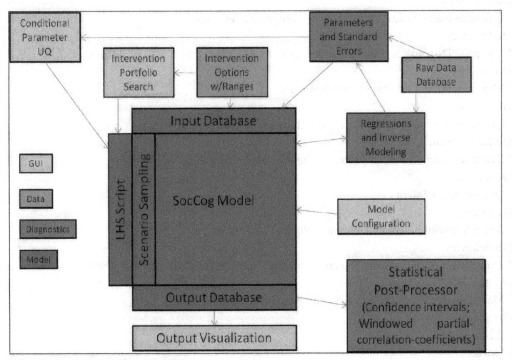

Figure 30: Analysis Framework

Finally, for software engineers we can see how the entire framework is put together by walking through the program code, originally written in COBOL, as given by Backus et al:

Coding the Model of the Psych/Cog Engine:

```
>
#Define Procedure Model
* If Lmax is > 1, then we are doing UQ, SA, or search.
* First run is always with best estimate values.
Select Lrun(1-Lmax)
* Start outer Stochastic (K+LHS) loop on
Do Lrun
* Determine values of model parameters.
  Do LHS (Algorithms developed be V&V team)
  Select Mrun(1-Rmax)
   Do Mrun
    * Select time range from Starting moment to Ending moment.
    * This allows restart from any point in a stored past simulation.
    Select Moment (SMoment-EMoment)
   * All differential equations need state variables initialized
    Do Initialize
    * Start march over time for simulation
    Do Moment
     * Current is the active moment in the loop
    Current=Moment:s
    Prior=XMAX(SMOMENT,Current-1)
    Next=XMIN(LMOMENT,Current+1)
    * (Social network and physical entities) Map physical and entity actions to all affected entities
   Do Stimuli
   * Determine impact of entity action on external environment.
   Do External
   * Calculate Attitudes based on cognitive resources
   Do Attitudes
   * Calculate passivity and Offsets based on cognitive resources
   Do Passivity
   * Calculate Dissonance between current notions and expectation of   conditions
   Do Incongruity
   * Map patterns of Cue Stimuli into Notions
   Do Notion
   * Create memory of notions for expectations of "normal" values
   Do Expectation
   * Reinforce referent memory intensity based on schema and perceptions
   Do CogRes
   * Decide choice intent
   Do EvalSel
   * Affect behavior based on Referents (Norms) and dissonance
   Do Behavior
   * Transform Behavior in physical consequence via the associated   physical action
   Do Action
   * Map action of entities to external environment (Social Network)
   Do Stimuli
   End Moment
  End Mrun
 End Lrun
End Procedure Model
```

(Backus, 2010, 73)

As we can see the framework can be run again and again iterating over a specific intent, choice, trying to persuade entities to select a particular behavior. The SNL of Sandia is also applicable to other forms of simulation and can be added to other areas of research such as military simulations, or geo-political simulations.

Simulated Soldiering

We covered military simulations architecture in Appendix D. Here we drill down further into the ideals in the defense industry regarding simulations and automated control of soldiers, which was research begun in the Soviet Union using Reflexive Management. The research of Behzadan (2017) focuses on using Sandia Labs technology to create military simulations using Agent-Based-Models (ABM). The work is designed as a means of destabilization, again like Tarasenko's research from earlier:

> Terrorist organizations have social networks that enable them to recruit and operate around the world. This paper presents a novel computational framework for derivation of optimal destabilization strategies against dynamic social networks of terrorists. We develop a game-theoretic model to capture the distributed and complex dynamics of terrorist organizations and introduce a technique for estimation of such dynamics from incomplete snapshots of target networks. Furthermore, we propose a mechanism for devising the optimal sequence of actions that drive the internal dynamics of targeted organizations towards an arbitrary state of instability. The performance of this framework is evaluated on a model of the Al-Qaeda network in 2001, verifying the efficacy of our proposals for counter-terrorism applications. (Behzadan, 2017)

They study the microeconomics of terrorist networks as Agent-Based Models (ABM), thereby allowing the analysis and potentially control of terrorist organizations by considering the micro-scale models of such systems; this control is made to destabilize the group under pressure.

> The proposed framework consists of a dynamics-estimation method for inference of payoffs from a game theoretic model of the network, complemented with a technique based on reinforcement learning for derivation of optimal action policies. The main contributions of this paper are:
>
> (i) We present a game-theoretic model that captures the complex self-organizing dynamics of terrorist organizations in the settings of strategic network formation.
>
> (ii) We introduce a technique for the estimation of network dynamics based on incomplete snapshot observations.
>
> (iii) By adopting a reinforcement learning approach, we develop a mechanism for devising the optimal sequence of actions that drive the internal dynamics of targeted organizations towards an arbitrary state of instability.
>
> (iv) We propose a methodology for extraction of personal and relational attributes from unstructured text using cloudbased services. (Behzadan, 2017)

The main device for destabilization is based on game-theoretic techniques, which is to say deceptive games or reflexive control. The first target of destabilization is by minimization of connectivity in the network. "Such strategies seek the set of nodes or links whose removal from the network maximizes the number of isolated groups (known as connected components). Approaches for selection of critical nodes or edges in this type of strategy are largely based on graph centrality metrics." (Behzadan, 2017). They adopt inverse game theory:

> With the potential of algorithms developed for inverse game theory, the problem of destabilization can be approached with enhanced confidence in the accuracy of the network model, at the expense of further complicating the problem due to the increased complexity in the dynamic network model. Manipulation of such highly complex networks of autonomous agents under nonlinear dynamics is the subject of a novel area in complexity science, known as guided self-organization. This area investigates the controllability of self-organizing systems, characterized by the emergence of order and pattern from uncoordinated actions of autonomous agents. The necessity of guidance in such systems appears when there is a need to hasten or perturb the natural evolution of the system towards a desired state. (Behzadan, 2017)

So, what we see is an automated algorithm that allows for a group to become destabilized, the optimal control inputs that perturb the complex dynamic network toward a state or goal is considered a promising method by them. "In this application, the desired state is the goal of destabilization, and control inputs are exerted in the form of perturbations on terrorist network's structure and topology (Behzadan, 2017). The algorithm is presented by Behazadan in the following:

> We adopt a dynamic systems viewpoint to interpret this objective, where destabilization refers to driving the target system away from undesired steady-states (equilibria). In the remainder, we consider a further level of detail by specifying the objective as minimizing the desire of terrorist agents to remain affiliated to the organization. It must be noted that this choice of objective will only serve as a representative example and may be replaced by any arbitrary goal in the presented framework. Having determined the criteria of objective, the problem of optimal destabilization can be formally stated as follows:

$$\pi_O^*(G(t))$$

Given the observations of relational links in a terrorist network:

> devise the optimal policy function $(G(t))$ that for any observed network $G(t)$ determines the counter-terrorism action with maximum cumulative (i.e., long-term) reward R according to an objective O. The notion of cumulative reward in this problem formulation necessitates the prediction of future states that emerge in the target network as a result of the actions implemented by the counter-terrorism entity, which is dependent on the dynamics of the target. The problem can be seen as comprising of two sub-tasks: (i) estimation of target network's dynamics from (noisy) observations, and (ii) determination of optimal actions given the estimated dynamics. (Backus et al, 2006)

The question of how to measure the dynamics of the complex networks is addressed, through a utility function of each agent:

> Having the game theoretic model of network's dynamics, the problem of estimation can be mapped to the domain of inverse game theory. Assuming that the observed network is at equilibrium (i.e., the topology is not changing), the objective of this problem thus becomes to estimate the utility functions of each agent such that the resulting equilibrium matches the observed topology. The majority of approaches proposed for utility estimation from network topology observations require multiple observations of changes in network over time. Yet this is commonly not feasible for terrorist networks due to their covert nature. Approaches proposed for estimating utilities from a single network observation are also mostly developed for network formation games of complete information. (Backus et al, 2006)

From the estimation of agent utility one can then start to formulate an optimal policy of destabilization:

> The estimated dynamics of the terrorist network provides the opportunity to simulate the responses of targeted organization to counter-terrorism actions, thereby enabling the employment of exploratory methods for determination of the optimal policy.
>
> Accordingly, we propose Reinforcement Learning algorithms as a promising approach to the problem of Policy Optimization. Reinforcement learning techniques are described by the Markov Decision Process tuple MDP = (S; A; P;R), where S is the set of reachable states in the process, A is the set of available actions, R is the mapping of transitions to the immediate reward, and P represents the transition probabilities (i.e. system dynamics). At any given time-step t, the Markov decision process is at a state st 2 S, which can represent the current topology of the network. The reinforcement learning agent's choice of action at time t, at 2 A causes a transition from st to a state st+1 according to the transition probability.
>
> Pat st;st+a . The agent receives a reward rt = R(st; at) 2 R for choosing the action at at state st.
>
> Interactions of the agent with Markov decision process are captured in a policy. When such interactions are deterministic, the policy: S! A is a mapping between the states and their corresponding actions. A stochastic policy (s; a) represents the probability of optimality for action a at state s.

Algorithm 1: Optimal Destabilization Algorithm

Input : observed initial topology G_0, set of profile vectors X, objective O, set of actions A

Data: reward R, current topology G, policy π

Output: action $a = \pi(G)$

1   $R \leftarrow 0$

2   $G \leftarrow G_0$

3   **while** $R < O$ **do**

4      $U \leftarrow \texttt{EstimateDynamics}(G, X)$

5      $R, \pi \leftarrow \texttt{QLearning}(\texttt{SimulateDynamics}(.), G, U, X)$

6   Implement $a \leftarrow \pi(G)$

7   Update G

8   **end**

The selected action is then implemented in the target simulation, which responds by rearranging the topology towards the best achievable state of equilibrium. The reinforcement learning process observes and measures the resulting state according to the desired metric of stability, which provides a form of feedback for the selected action, enabling the Q learning [AI reinforcement learning] process to learn the efficiency of its choice and adjust its future actions accordingly. The iterations of this cycle continue until consecutive measurements of the simulated target's state satisfy the intended criteria of instability, at which time the learned policy is declared to be optimal and ready for implementation on the real target network (Backus et al, 2006)

From which we now have the optimal destabilization, but it comes with limits, not to mention MDP bias issues, in that estimations tend to be inaccurate, due to available information on target networks. Enhancing the accuracy of these methods may be achieved through an iterative update of observations. Once an optimal policy is obtained, the result of its implementation on the target network can be utilized as a new observation of the network. Consequently, running the dynamic estimator on the new observation can increase its precision through fine-tuning on new data points, which will lead to enhanced accuracy in the derivation of optimal policy. Algorithm 1 details this iterative process (Backus 2006). This work has offered us a look into the ideal of destabilization of terrorist networks and networks in general, and of course the inverse settings allow for stabilization or creation of networks.

UMBRA AND SCREAM

The initial steps to setting up automated systems that are based on Deception Management and US Cost of Actions (COA) (Reflexive Control) is to develop models that can be enacted by AI systems. One of the unique attributes of the US Mil-Intel Simulations is the creation of Emotional Agents to simulate real world figures. To trace out the development of how deception and influencing work, we need to start with the issue of technologies developed by Lockheed-Martin, sometimes through their 'national' privately run government labs. We can look at training and simulations developed by their research teams to understand how AI agents can be used as emotional agents to train humans, from warfare to disaster relief.

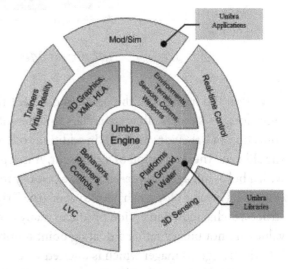

Figure 1: Umbra Simulation Framework & Applications

In Xavier et al (2017) we can look at their architecture to better understand in a later section how emotions are used for deception management and influence operations using emotional agents. Dante Agent Architecture is the framework developed by the research team, in an effort to provide simulations for typical Red vs. Blue exercises dealing with physical security, such as Nuclear sites (energy and weapons), for which this study was generated. Dante is an extension of Lockheed's Umbra software package the provides simulation capabilities across varying platforms and modules also developed by Lockheed as plug-and-play modular components of varying functionalities within National Defense. Due to compartmentalization in covert programs each silo of the covert program creates an API so that other groups can easily use their computer engineering in their project. As covered in Appendix D chapter this system uses Finite State Machines (FSM) which manage behaviors, while the Decision Agents are based on utility theory.

> When a character is issued a command, they execute a priority queue of behaviors. The queue is sorted on the priority and activation of the behaviors available, calculated through a utility-theory AI approach. Behaviors can run concurrently or preempt other behaviors to take control of the character. Later, preempted behaviors can be restarted to accomplish the specified command. (Xavier et al, 2017)

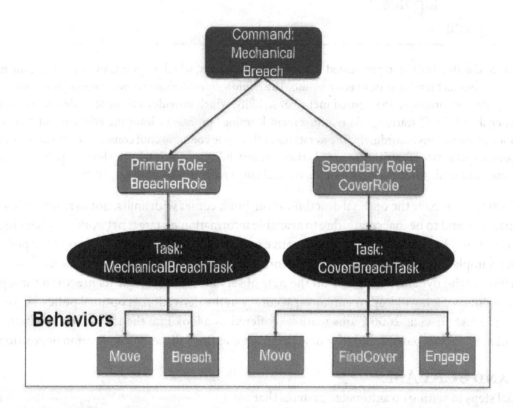

Figure 3: Example of MechanicalBreach command issued to team

Within the framework the usage of different functions is developed Roles which translates a Command into behaviors, these roles allow characters to differentiate how they react to the same Command. A Task represents a collection of behaviors (FSMs). In addition to Roles, Tasks, etc. there are Triggers, which determine if a behavior should run. The Activation of a Behavior, A is represented as, $A = T * p$, T represent the set of triggers associated with a behavior, and p representing the priority for the behavior. Triggers may have p ositive evidence or negative evidence (inverse) for a behavior to run. The Triggers are stored in a 'blackboard' is regular video games, a datastructure, character perception produces many triggers including ones that note the presence of threats, the trigger values are not binary rather a floating point number between 0-1, which is used for nuancing. Triggers are stored into the TriggerManager which is queried when a new threat is detected the CharacterMemory, then a behavior is triggered. These weighted triggers exist on a priority queue which can result in behavior jitter as competing perceptions affect the weighting and re-organization of the behavior list. Path planning is based on A*. One interesting component of the system is the Scenario Editor which allows the importing of various scenarios in Red. vs. Blue training. Users construct an agent's team plan by chaining together commands, with the completion of one command leading to the execution of the next, which can also be automated for different scenarios. One issue to deal with in all software development are exceptions and failures. If there is no branching or exception handling then the simulation would become stuck. Dante uses a fail-forward mechanism to address failure:

In the case when a command has failed, the Run-Manager will look for any chained commands that should be called on a failure. This mechanism allows *Dante* scenario to branch when things are not going according to the original plan. There is a special mechanism in *Dante* called "fail forward." If there is not a failure branch for a failed command to follow, then it still signals the success branch actions. This allows the plan to continue forward, but likely it will encounter further problems that eventually result in a Terminate action. "Fail forward" aids users in not having to provide explicit detail how agents should respond if any portion of the plan fails, and safeguard against faulty user-defined plans where failed commands may not be necessary in accomplishing the scenario goal(s).

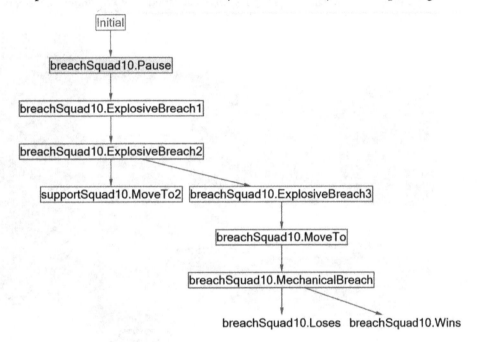

Figure 7: Example of a plan formed within Dante Scenario Editor

Figure 7: Example of a plan formed within Dante Scenario Editor Figure 7 provides a snapshot from a *Dante* Scenario Editor displaying a red-team plan for breaking into a building within a secured facility, requiring the team to demolish multiple barriers between their start point and the building door. (Xavier et al, 2017)

In a more tangible example of using emotional based agents in training can be found in Emergency Response training using gaming in a simulation. As previously discussed in Chapter 4, 'Lessons from an American Weapons Developer', Sandia National Labs (Lockheed-Martin) has built a cognitive computing framework to load agents with emotional behaviors. The framework, Sandia Cognitive Runtime Engine with Active Memory (SCREAM) can be extended upon and a Sandia research team has expanded on that with the Sandia Human Embodiment and Representation Cognitive Architecture (SHERCA). Djordjevich of Sandia Livermore Labs has done research using SHERCA in emergency response training. The reason for studying emotions in emergency response is that according to the researchers 34% of decisions are derived from emotions when utility cannot be seen (Djordjevich, 2008). It is also noted that emotions can override reason and vice versa in later studies in this chapter, although people respond to emotional stimuli faster than reason.

A large amount of research supports the notion that attitudes, norms, emotions, goals, and the perception of control helps drive actual behaviors. In fact, the theories that support this research have been successfully used to predict a wide range of behaviors, such as voting, shoplifting, gun-related violent acts, and other moral and ethical decisions. (Bernard et al, 2006, 21)

Again, we find the Theory of Planned Behavior referenced here, in which behaviors are influenced by 1) attitudes towards a specific behavior, 2) the subjective norms associated with acting out that behavior, and 3) the perception that this behavior is within a person's control, forming an action-intention state. (Djordjevich, 2008).

The framework is based on emotions, which distinguishes it from other cognitive architectures like ACT-R and SOAR. It is interesting to note that Lockheed-Martin based SCREAM on SOAR and that Dr. John Norseen cited SOAR in his work. "As noted in a prior section, emotions tie into a person's motivation for deciding what actions to pursue. To computationally represent the role of emotion in motivation, researchers have found mapping perceptions to pre-defined emotional states as an effective method for virtual [cognitive] characters [NPCs] in these environments." (Djordjevich, 2008).

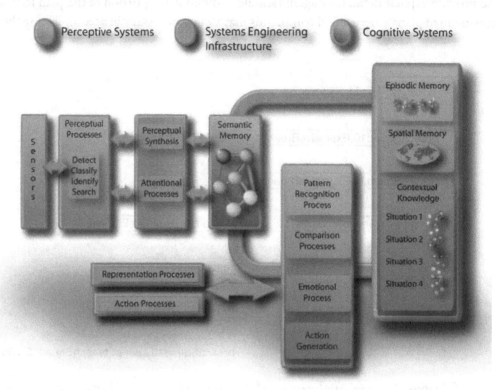

Figure 2. A high level view of the SNL cognitive modeling architecture

Some aspects of the SCREAM framework that supports the psychological framework, SHERCA, is that emphasis on cognitive elements with activation-levels updated according to dynamics distinguishes it from more common production-rule-based approaches. Some other uses of SHERCA were in cultural training; it can adapt various cultures to change nuance of different cultural imprinted agents. In SHERCA, an impression of culture can be generated by varying a simulated human's emotional response to particular perceptions. Cultures also exhibit variations within their high-level and intermediate goals. As a result, their intended and actual behaviors will show cultural uniqueness. The result is a complex set of behaviors that have certain emergent properties common to a particular group [also see Memetic Engineering below]. So, how is SHERCA put together? The research team offers this overview:

> SHERCA allows for multiple cues, cognitive perceptions, goals, action intentions, etc., to concurrently have some degree of activation. In SHERCA's model of decision-making, once a cognitive perception—an element of perceptual/ situational awareness—has been activated by cues in the environment, it may trigger activation of specific, intermediate goals that are consistent with higher-level goals and other active cognitive perceptions.

For example, one high-level goal might be to protect family, and another, to protect oneself. Intermediate goals help support the higher-level goals by breaking down the goals into discrete tasks. The overall emotional state mediates activation of action intentions from the intermediate goals. As a consequence, the intended actions are a product of both the intermediate goals and the current emotional state of the simulated human. This emotional state may change dynamically, for example from very low to very high levels of anger, if the perceptions change. Action intentions that are contradictory with respect to goals can become concurrently highly activated due to the influence of emotion. At the same time, cognitive perception is influenced by a hierarchy of higher-level goals/directives or moral states, as well as state within a behavior (e.g., current step in a procedure). (Djordjevich, 2008)

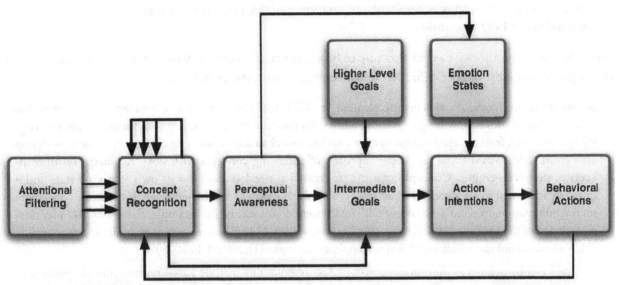

Figure 5 Model of decision-making to select actions in SHERCA.

The main elements in SHERCA are Concepts, Contexts, Cues (which are common to many cognitive models), also there are Intermediate Goals, Higher Level Goals, Perceptions, Action Intentions and Behavioral Actions. Currently we need to take a deeper look at Concepts and Contexts.

Concepts:

• Fundamental element of SNL Cognitive framework a representation of known regularity arising from external or internal data sources

• High Alpha (10-13Hz update rate)

• each concept is represented by a neural assembly and the neural assembly associated with a concept that is 'currently used' in cognition will rise above baseline in terms of both frequency and amplitude.

• A concept is a cue, when it plays a role in the recognition.

• Sorted b Instances: associate objects with concepts. Concept Instances map the slots of a concept to entities (objects)

Contexts:

• meaningful perceptual representation stimuli

• Theta update rate (4-7Hz)

• Context Instances

• Context Recognizer pattern recognition with:

    A. cue vector context patterns

    B. XQ context patterns

A bit of an explainer on a couple of terms for Contexts: Cue Vector Context Patterns which are templates for context instances, instances of different concepts. This is represented as:

$Q = \{Q_i\}$ of triple $Q_i = P_i, w_i, m_i\}$ where P = concept w/ a name; w = weight; m=integer vector

Implementation example:

> Suppose a cognitive model has the unary (i.e., arity one) concepts dominant and
> submissive and a binary concept attacks. Then we can define a binary context
> Dominated-by that has the pattern Dominated-by 3 submissive 0.4 0 attacks 0.6 1 0 dominant 0.5 1
>
> whose vector of cues
>
> Q(Dominated-by) = { (submissive, 0.4, {0}), (attacks, 0.6, {1, 0}), (dominant, 0.5, {1}) }
>
> In our notation, index numbering for elements of a vector begins with 0. The {0} in
> (submissive, 0.4, {0}) maps slot 0 of submissive to slot 0 of Dominated-by. The {1, 0}
> in (attacks, 0.6, {1, 0}) maps slot 0 of attacks to slot 1 of Dominated-by and slot 1 of
> attacks to slot 0 of Dominated-by. Finally, the {1} in (dominant, 0.5, {1}) maps slot 0 of
> dominant to slot 1 of Dominated-by.

From this data structure we can get a picture of how this system works in terms of dominance and submission, in a binary confrontation, a fuller definition of concepts and contexts are below:

> A *concept* is the fundamental semantic element in SCREAM. For convenience, concepts have names, but SCREAM associates no meaning with those names. To function in environments with multiple entities (e.g., things, creatures, features, etc.) of a given type requires a mechanism to associate concept activations with specific entities. SCREAM takes the simple approach of endowing concepts with slots. A *concept instance* associates slots with entities. Concept instances are created as needed. Each has its own activation state and is uniquely identified by concept and a vector of entity identifiers, which are merely labels to enable convenient interaction with people and other non-SCREAM system components. For example, *chases {22, 31}* identifies an instance of the concept *chases* (i.e., entity #22 chases entity #31). Thus, a concept is similar to a fuzzy predicate, but we do not claim that SCREAM implements any logic. (Djordjevich, 2008)

> *Contexts* can be defined as meaningful perceptual representations that are based on recognizable patterns of stimuli, as well as, consistent with situation models, schema and theme-based representations of events. Context activation is governed by pattern recognition applied to the activation states of concepts that are the cues for/against that context. For example, the concepts *bicycle, clown, elephant* and *popcorn* might be cues for the context *Circus*. A *context instance* is related to a *context* similar to the way that a *concept instance* is related to a *concept*. In SCREAM, a concept whose raw (input) activation is driven by the contextual pattern recognition process is also called a context. (Djordjevich, 2008)

> A context is used to describe the 'mental' processes that occur when we try to make sense of, and interact with, our environment, these processes can be broken down into perceptual context or 'perception' and 'goal' states. (Bernard et al, 2006, 35)

A further element of the SCREAM system is that of using emotions. Although, there are not many emotions included in SCREAM in early implementations; there is only fear and anger mapped to the system, which are the prime motivators in quick/snap decisions.

> A basic capability for modeling emotional processes in cognition [3], [24] has been implemented in SCREAM. SCREAM updates the level of activation of each emotion based on concept activation levels and parameters that specify how the concepts influence emotional state. Each concept can be associated with a level of activation and a weight coefficient for each emotion. For example, in an emotion parameters file, *cee clown 2 fear 0.6 0.7 anger 1.5 0.9* specifies that concept *clown* influences two emotions. For *fear* it has a weight coefficient of 0.6 and a target activation of 0.7, and for *anger* it has a weight coefficient of 1.5 and a target activation of 0.9. [amygdala hacking with fear and anger] (Djordjevich, 2008)

As an example of the entire SCREAM and SHERCA systems working together for training of emergency response personnel, the developers came up with the game 'Ground Truth'

To see how the program works let's take a brief dive into its class hierarchy and how different agent classes interact with each other. Each cognitive agent is an instance of the Scream-Agent Class, which extends other base classes at higher levels which allows it to carry out the cognitively-selected behavior. When a cog agent loads it inputs the cognitive model definition files such as the concepts, contexts and context patterns, context-instance to behavior/action conversion patterns, spreading activation (priming) and emotional association parameters. The only difference between cognitive definition files is limited to emotional association parameters and levels of activation of high-level goals, reflecting differences in personality, culture and values. Setting activation of other specific concepts appropriately allows us to customize the generic model for each specific type of Ground-Truth NPC. As seen earlier in Appendix D there are Game managers for different aspect of any game. The Agent-Manager interacts with other game Managers. Updating the NPCs is the main role of the Agent-Manager, which updates the states of the agents in an update cycle: physical states, based on their current states and game state external to the agents. It has the agents update their perceptual states, with the help from the Perception Manager and drives agent decisions.

> States in the state machine of a cognitive agent can access its emotional state for use in modeling affect within a behavior. For example, dialogue output takes into account emotional state. Generally, determination of low-level behavior, such as path planning, also makes use of separate algorithms that are called from within states. (Djordjevich, 2008)

A deeper look at SCREAM will show us the mechanics of Serious Games and Military Simulations as handled by the UK-USA defense industry. Sandia Labs has a fuller explanation of their cognitive computational systems in Bernard et al 2006, *'Simulating Human Behavior for National Security Human Interactions.'* The developers remark regarding the purpose of SCREAM: "to allow cognitively modeled simulated humans or 'cognitive characters' to interact with each other, their environment and with actual humans in a behaviorally realistic and psychologically plausible manner." (Bernard et al, 2006, 9)

SCREAM:

1. it produces a psychologically and sociologically reasonable computational framework of human behavior.

2. cognitive models are customizable, individually

3. cognitive characters operate autonomously

4. designed to plug-n-play with other MIL apps

The main purpose behind SCREAM is to provide realistic NPCs in military simulations, in disaster training simulations, etc. Some of these simulations run in virtual reality and through normative video game interfaces mixing human players with NPCs, some of whom can be aides/team members and others enemies, as is normative in contemporary video games. The platform was created to address shortcomings in commercial video games, specifically dealing with realistic NPCs in video games. The NPCs known as cognitive characters in SCREAM can behave in amazingly realistic ways for humans, and possibly even pass Turing tests. For instance, they can respond with fear at a threat and hide, they can manifest aggression depending on their role within the platform and other complex emotional responses usually shown by real humans. An example from the framework even includes that, when a Cog Character is nervous, it seeks a person to talk to:

WIFE OF VENDER ONE - INTERMEDIATE GOAL STATES
SG3 I seek to look innocent/friendly
SG4 I seek to sell my merchandise, but I am nervous
SG5 I seek to converse with a nearby person
(Bernard et al, 2006, 51, Appendix C)

And in this way, through their scripted responses, they seem very human but may not pass the Turing test based on the observer's knowledge and expertise.

HI Framework Modules:

1. Semantic Knowledge: associative network with nodes, representing each critical concept or schema in each cognitive character

2. Pattern Recognition & Comparator: a. evaluating the evidence provided by cues favoring or conflicting with each situation. b. assessing the validity of the current situation. c. determination of a valid situation when current situation is invalid, d. implementation of top-down activation-levels

3. Action Generation

Some important aspects to realize about SCREAM are that it is not rule-based, as in some older systems from the mid-90s such as the British Mannequin system for monitoring the northern Irish; rather it uses models of human decision making with levels of activation for perceptions and states. It also allows for multiple perceptions, goal states and action-intentions which can concurrently have some degree of activation. Perceptions are activated by cues which activate Intermediate Goals which will trigger an action-intention state, which are mediated by current emotion states (i.e., fear/anger) that are affected by what they perceive in the environment. The decision to act or call on a behavior is in the cognitive subsystem which serves in the model as the conjunction of diverse emotions, stressors, memories, which are all integrated into a decision for action which should lead to the goals.

> When constructing a model, each concept may be attributed to one or more emotional components that is associated with specific levels of activation. For example, a disliked individual may be represented as a concept for which there is an association with a high-level of frustration-anger. Activation of a specific concept or situation contributes to the weighted averages that determine the overall activations of associated emotional components. The specific emotion activation levels are converted to fuzzy set (e.g., *high-fear*) representations that are then fed into context recognition patterns. In the near future, emotions will have a reciprocal effect on cognition, causing an increase in concept or situation activation that triggers the emotion and active inhibition of other concepts and situations. In the future, as with the current interactions, emotion and cognition will be consistent with neuropsychological findings and, thus, will allow certain neuropsychological phenomenon to be demonstrated by the framework. (Bernard et al, 2006, 13)

3 High Level Components:

a. pre-cognitive (attention)

b. cognitive (perception, states, goals)

c. action-generation states (motion control) [movement is managed by Boston Dynamics DI Guy; it is also important to note that not all human movements, such as micro-expressions are not included in movement, such as the forehead not being mapped by facial landmark detection libraries such as d-lib. While the simulation of human behavior and emotion is effective they are still lacking absolute simulation of human elements]

SEMANTIC MEMORY SYSTEM:

Knowledge and the relatedness of concepts is represented within a semantic memory system. Relatedness refers to the awareness that two concepts are associated with each other by virtue of being members of the same category and operating together. When concepts are extracted via automated knowledge capture techniques, the relationship between concepts is based on a representation of each concept as a vector in a high-dimensional space. The cosine similarity of vectors for a given pair of concepts provides the basis for the strength of the relationship between concepts. The relatedness of concepts derived in this manner then provides a basis for simulating the priming that occurs for a concept in response to the prior presentation of a related concept. (Bernard et al, 2006, 14)

Certain concepts occur with perceptual contexts. These contextual percepts play a part in the formation of expectations, seeing a hostile context influences recognizing further elaborations in that context, priming an expectation in hostility for, say, 'fighting.' If the existing pattern of concepts is on the verge of triggering an activation, then only a minor amount of evidence that hostile people are in the area is needed to prime the expectation. It also might be that very strong evidence from only a small number of concepts is enough to activate a context. Once a context is activated, the associated concepts are primed so that corresponding sensory inputs produce accelerated and supplemented activations. [Expectation data poison attacks: i.e., consciously interfering with the systems expectations to defuse a situation on your way to an attack vector]

In what is similar to typical video game experiences dealing with horror games, the creepy cues that can be accompanied in the game experience of the player are mimicked in SCREAM. For instance, a certain context can prime humans to continuously attend to specific stimuli in the environment, so long as that context is activated. Being in a dangerous area will prime a person to hear footsteps or see shadows. In this framework certain contexts may heighten the activation of specific cues in the environment. This occurs when contexts with salient cues that indicate danger to the cognitive character. The prime factor in fear response is the amygdala. In fact, the designers of this system do target the amygdala complex, neurophysiology, with their framework:

> Research has shown that early in stimulus processing, the fear/surprise emotional centers of the brain (amygdala) receive direct input about the potential significance of a stimulus. The "direct route" conveys a fast, rough impression of the situation because it uses a sub-cortical pathway in which no high-level cognition is involved. At the same time, stimulus information is processed via another information pathway to allow for a deeper, cognitive assessment of this information. This "indirect route" allows for more deliberate assessments of the situation. The multiple pathways enable both an initial, fast response as well as the integration of emotion with higher-level recognition and understanding. The memory process output is appraised for its emotional meaning through which a behavioral assessment is made. (Bernard et al, 2006, 22)

> As with humans, cognitive models should incorporate the ability to react quickly to certain stimuli without the need first to deliberate the degree of threat. In the HI framework, this psychological phenomenon was modeled such that the cognitive characters exhibit defensive reactions of fear in response to perceived stimuli that represent potential dangers and/or anger towards certain perceived events or actions. Specifically, the cognitive characters have responses representing the direct route, in that it essentially represents the reflexive thalamo-amygdala pathway that bypasses the cortex. This pathway exhibits fear and defensive reactions, but not other emotions such as happiness. Other emotions and aspects of the indirect route will be modeled in the very near future. (Bernard et al, 2006, 23)

As noted before on Soviet Reflexive Control, the amygdala is the pathway of Fast Reflexion, which is to say unconscious control. It is also noted that political conservatives, as they are called, have a variance in their right amygdala, which is much larger then moderates and liberals, hence messing with their amygdalas creates unforeseen complexities. Luckily this is just a virtual representation of human interactions and does not antagonize a real human's amygdala responses, which could create a large problem if ever attempted, although the phenomena of Targeted Individuals suggest that these systems have been applied to non-virtual (real) human agents.

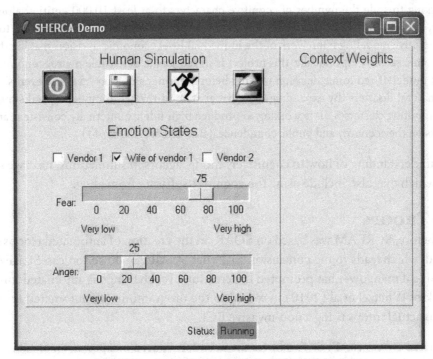

Figure 4. The Emotion Regulator GUI   (Bernard et al, 2006, 25)

Example from emotional parameter data file for emotions:

cee clown 2 fear 0.700 .7 anger 0.100 .9

//It tends to push the activation level of *fear* to 0.700 with a weight of 0.7 times the activation level of *clown* and the level of *anger* to 0.100 with a weight of 0.9 times the activation level of *clown*.

SCREAM continuously updates the level of activation of each emotion based on concept activation levels. Concept is directly activated by perception as a result of semantic processing. A concept may be specified to influence emotional states, for instance using narrative networks or memetic learning, popular memes. The activation level of the emotion, anger, can be represented by membership levels in the three fuzzy sets low-Anger, med-Anger, high-Anger, that cover the range of anger activation levels, these are used as cues in context (pattern) recognition. SCREAM has emotional state computational capability to model the direct route emotions of fear and anger.

HOW TO INSTANTIATE AND INITIALIZE COGNITIVE CHARACTERS IN SCREAM:

To create a Cognitive Character, initialize the stimuli and contextual associations (perceptions, activations and states), by first cataloging a series of low-level environment cues the Cog. Chr. might perceive in a given scenario. Concepts prime concepts, with priming specified by a series of cue-to-cue relationships with a certain degree of priming. Cue #1 primes Cue #2 with weight=.8. Perception-to-cue-priming operates similarly. Activated Perception primes potential intermediate Goals which become activated if environment situation matches. Intermediate Goal state is associated with environment cues and its level of cue; each is associated with a hierarchy of increasingly abstract-level goals. When subject is activated it activates on action-intention state, which bind emotional affect with behaviors. SCREAM uses Active State Machine activated by action scripts consisting of a coded sequence of behaviors. After the behaviors are played out the character will reassess [hive huddling] the environment and follow new behaviors based on new perceptions. Situations not recognized activate additional contexts based on past experiences induced from earlier cues, rather than actual evidence in the current situation, ignores its current reality.

As we can see from the previous, SCREAM and SHERCA provide a robust and almost real experience with modeling agents after humans. Some other areas that Sandia is focused on for these human-like simulations is that of economics:

> In addition, the LDRD project, *Cognitive Modeling of Human Behaviors within Socio- Economic Systems* (06-1102), is working to scale the number of cognitive characters to at least 10,000 entities, along with modeling economic, cultural, and stress-induced behaviors by FY2008. The goal of this project is to develop a science-based cognitive modeling framework of the individual-level economic decision-making that is critical to national economic security. Specifically, this project is developing a defensible neuroeconomic and cognitive science-based model of economic decision making before, during, and after "extreme events" such as acts of terrorism or natural disasters. By expanding the current state-of-the-art in modeling and simulating them in large-scale computing clusters SNL is working to produce high-fidelity, internally consistent analysis of these types of events on the economy and public confidence. (Bernard et al, 2006, 44)

So, we have an understanding of how to cognitively model agents in simulations, next we shall cover the automation of troops, which may also include using the cognitive software from above.

AUTOMATED TROOPS

As mentioned before, SCREAM was based on SOAR, in the creation of automated troops or forces SOAR has also been used, which leads to the conclusion thatwhat SOAR can do so too can SCREAM/SHERCA. The need to make up for lost manpower has prompted the creation of such things as automated forces. In the following we review the work of Whetzel et al (2010) in regard to the programming of automated forces, which of course could be coupled to actual troops using a non-invasive BCI.

> **Semi-Automated Forces (SAF)** SAFs address the need for reduced-manpower simulation. SAF tools such as JSAF, OTB, and OOS allow entity behavior to be specified ahead of time. At a computational level, SAF behavior specifications typically amount to some form of finite state machine (FSM). An FSM can be thought

of as (1) a set of states, each of which corresponds to some behavioral state (e.g., patrol along a given path); and (2) a set of transitions between states (e.g., when an intruder is detected, move to confront). Advantages of FSM-style SAF behaviors include clarity and predictability. FSMs are particularly good for implementing well-defined doctrinal behavior of limited complexity. However, SAFs have a limited capability to respond dynamically to changing circumstances. As allies, SAFs have little capability for coordinating or communicating with students. As enemies, SAFs are often little more than target drones. They do not model an adaptive, thinking enemy. Scenarios with such scripted behaviors have a very short useful life because students quickly learn to anticipate scenario events. (Whetzel, 2010)

Intelligent Automated Forces Intelligent automated forces go beyond conventional SAFs with the ability to generate behavior dynamically in response to simulation events. Examples are TacAir-Soar (Coulter et al.) and ACT-R agents (Best, Scarpinatto, & Lebiere) for military operations in urban terrain (MOUT). The cognitive architectures underlying these capabilities are informed by a large body of accumulated psychological research. When used properly, these approaches can realistically mimic many aspects of cognition, particularly with respect to resource constraints such as reaction time and attention. (Whetzel, 2010)

Trainable Automated Forces (TAF) Depicted in Figure 1, our vision is for SMEs, such as instructors, to train synthetic forces directly by demonstration, as in training human students. Technical experts (e.g., computer programmers) must initially implement TAF for each type of role player required. Subsequently, however, SMEs can directly interact with TAF to enhance the domain expertise of TAF over time, without further support from a technical expert. TAF then relieves the SME of role playing so that the expertise of a single SME can be shared with any number of students. In our vision, the sharp distinction between the construction and operational phases (as required for traditional expert systems) is blurred. If an instructor recognizes a skills gap during one exercise, the instructor should be able to alter the behavior of automated forces in the next exercise to address the gap. Ideally, the long and expensive development pipeline can be virtually eliminated. This is the TAF approach. TAF training is an ongoing interaction between the instructor and the role-playing agent. The interaction is based on demonstrations of correct behavior by the instructor, and demonstrations by the system of its current understanding. Our goal is for the instructor to be able to interrupt and correct TAF when its actions diverge from the instructor's intent. TAF learns from such corrections and will not repeat the same mistake. Because this approach is data driven, objective behavior validation is more feasible compared with other approaches for automated forces. (Whetzel, 2010)

TAF is based on behavioral cloning, which is an established technique for building agent behaviors. Widrow and Smith (1964) first studied the technique for the pole-balancing (or inverted pendulum) task. The term ⊠cloning [mimicry] implies that the agent simply replays previously recorded behavior, but most applications of behavioral cloning have some capability to generalize to new situations. Nevertheless, the performance of a clone will degrade as it encounters situations that are dramatically different from any encountered during training. Behavioral cloning has been successfully applied in simulations of tasks such as piloting an airplane, operating a crane, and riding a bicycle. Similar techniques are popular within robotics and are known as learning by observation or learning by imitation [memetic learning]. (Whetzel, 2010)

TAF cannot learn correct behavior if the behavior depends on missing information.

TAF Technical Description Implementing TAF consists of creating a role and then populating the role with example behavior. The role consists of information (e.g., from a nine-line brief) such as the location of a target and the time on target. Any information that cannot be gleaned from the inputs specified for the role cannot influence the behavior of TAF; thus incomplete information may lead to incorrect behavior. However, extraneous information may also degrade performance by confusing TAF. If training data are relatively sparse (i.e., the number of inputs is large relative to the amount of training data provided), spurious patterns are likely to be found in the training data, and learning these patterns will lead to unpredictable TAF behavior. (Whetzel, 2010)

Perception The world model presents ground-truth information from an allocentric (or global) perspective. Each TAF actor must be provided with a perception model to filter and adapt this information for its own needs. (Whetzel, 2010)

Perception then transforms the allocentric information provided by the world model to egocentric inputs for the learning or inference algorithm. (Whetzel, 2010)

Inputs As shown in Figure 2, information from the world model and setting is filtered and transformed by perception to form the *input* for TAF's *learning and inference algorithms*. The completeness (or incompleteness) of the input is a constraint on the realism of TAF behavior. Several factors prevent TAF from receiving a complete set of inputs, leading to degraded behavior. (Whetzel, 2010)

TAF receives ground-truth information that may be unavailable to human combatants, granting TAF (in effect) a 360-degree field of view through walls, mountains, water, jammers, and darkness. In practice, software agents may use this unfair advantage to counter their own inherent limitations in perception and intelligence, with uneven results. More realistic perception models can also be implemented if necessary. (Whetzel, 2010)

The role template also specifies a learning algorithm. The current implementation of TAF uses the open source Sandia Cognitive Foundry (http://foundry.sandia.gov), which supplies a wide range of learning algorithms, e.g., linear regression, nearest neighbor with locally weighted linear regression, ID4 rule induction, support vector machines, and backpropagation for neural networks. The role template also specifies the type of knowledge base for each algorithm (e.g., learned link weights to parameterize a neural network, or the rule set created by ID4). (Whetzel, 2010)

Also, manual intervention in TAF control (e.g., moving an entity from the wrong trajectory) interferes with the simulator's internal dynamics model (position and speed) and thus may impart enormous momentum on the simulation entity. (Whetzel, 2010)

As we have seen in work with automated forces it is possible to create a set of agents, and these agents use copying to learn in trainable automated forces. Another area that uses copying in warfare is that of Memetic warfare.

CYBORG SOLDIERS

In recent years the discussion of the transition to human-machine hybrids has become popular among military theorists and planners. In the US, the discussion of transitioning to cyborg soldiers by 2050 has been discussed (Emmanuel et al, 2019). In the literature the discussion makes a distinction between human-machine interactions that are not cyborged and those that are Nørgaard & Linden-Vørnle (2021). They delineate a distinction between cyborgs and 'centaur warfighters':

> it is important not to confuse the notion of the cyborg warrior with the concept of the 'centaur warfighter', which is often used as a metaphor for human-machine teaming. The two concepts are closely related, but not synonymous. This distinction can be expressed as the difference between integration and automation of machine intelligence, perception, and reasoning. Whereas centaur human-machine teaming consists of humans plus machines, with machines performing clearly demarcated automated functions, the cyborg warrior functions as a neurally enhanced and integrated system architecture, merging human and machine cognition. Centaur human-machine teaming does not necessarily imply cognitive or sensory enhancement of the human operator. Human and machine cognition is not neurally integrated. Instead, humans and machines perform different role-specific tasks that are largely based on predetermined decision models where the machine's role is conditioned by one or more rule sets.

Emmanuel et al (2019) studied the creation of Cyborg soldiers in their DoD-sponsored study 'Cyborg Soldier 2050: Human/Machine Fusion and the Implications for the Future of the DOD' in which they identified several key areas that will have added value in combat:

- ocular enhancements to imaging, sight, and situational awareness;
- restoration and programmed muscular control through an optogenetic bodysuit;
- auditory enhancement for communication and protection; and
- direct neural enhancement of the human brain for two-way data transfer.

As can be seen this is a total re-imagining of human existence, where humans become little more than software to AI programming. We can also see how automated troops using RC spoken of previously would be easy to deploy to a Battalion of Cyborgs. It should be pointed out that they discuss these enhancements as being derived from implants into the human body, we know from this research work that this is probably obfuscation as it is possible to do all these things remotely using Ahronov-Bohm based technology, for instance optogenetics bodysuits can be replaced by LED or other laser-based photon emissions.

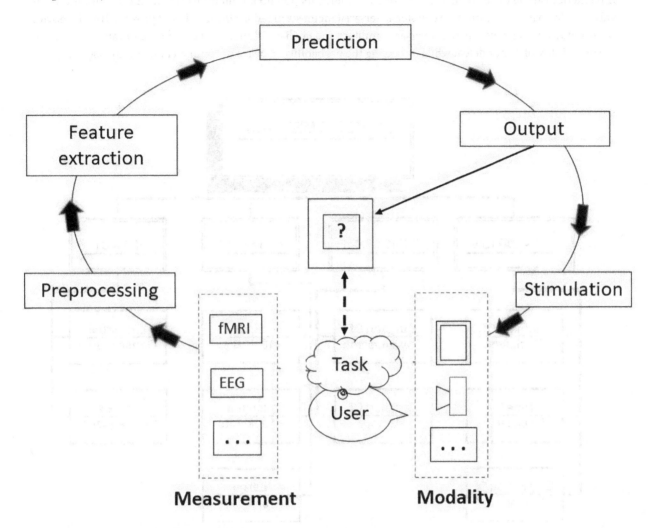

Flow chart on cyborg soldier loop of processing brain waves, AI processing of data, then re-importation for the inverse function or 'stimulation' to the soldier after reading brain state. (Nørgaard & Linden-Vørnle 2021)

MEMETIC WARFARE: MEMES, IMAGINAL ENCODING OF SUGGESTION

Memes to most people are those quirky and funny images with captions usually based on a common image set that get passed around social networks, like the Hitler video phenomenon. It may seem odd to include a section on Memes in a book on Neurowarfare or Information Warfare. However, it is a common research area in the Military Industrial complex, NASA, and other government scientific research centers. The military interest in Memes is attested to by UMD Professor Finkelstein who had a contract with DARPA to develop a curriculum for the DoD on Memes (Finkelstein, 2008, 12). Typically meme research is cited in counter terrorism literature, so later we shall study some of these approaches of using memes to redirect or steer terrorists away from acts of violence, whereas terrorists use memes to create more mimicked terrorist attacks, where the propagandists never put themselves on the line, letting the memes do their work through others for their purposes. Finkelstein writes regarding the purpose of the research for the military:

> The purpose of the following overview is to provide an indication of the prospective value of memetics to the U.S. military for conventional and asymmetric operations, including counter-terrorism. The attempt to establish a scientific basis for memetics is critically important. For example, within a suitable memetics framework could be the means to prevent irrational conflict and promote rational solutions to endemic national and international problems. Of course, without safeguards, memetics can become a double-edged sword. (Finkelstein, 2008, 12)

He calls for a quantization of memetic engineering so it will be of a greater military value:

> If memetics can be established as a scientific discipline, its potential military worth includes applications involving information operations to counter adversarial memes and reduce the number of prospective adversaries while reducing antagonism in the adversary's military and civilian culture, i.e., it could have the ability to reduce the probability of war or defeat while increasing the probability of peace or victory. (Finkelstein, 2008, 17)

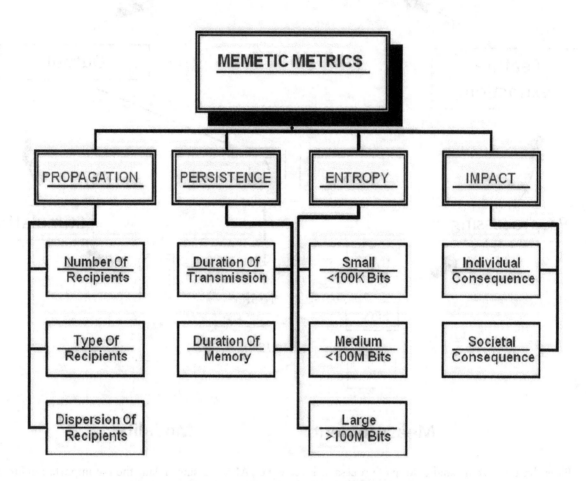

Figure 1: Memetic Metrics and Submetrics

The purpose of the research matches up with typical Reflexive Control in the sense of convincing an enemy to do what you want using deception as the primary tactic, which is the purpose of memes. This is directly related to overall information warfare, specifically in such areas as counter-intelligence and influence. One can imagine the need for being able to communicate desired outcomes through memes in such a contemporary environment where memes become viral on national information networks, media, and social nets. Finkelstein writes how this can affect the battlespace of mind:

> Potentially, memetics can have a major effect on psychological operations, military deception, and public affairs. Psychological operations (PSYOP) are intended to induce or reinforce foreign attitudes and behavior favorable to the originator's objectives and to convey selected information and indicators to foreign audiences to influence their emotions, motives, objective reasoning, and ultimately the behavior of foreign governments, organizations, groups, and individuals [Reflexive Control]. PSYOP focuses on the cognitive domain of the battlespace and targets the mind of the adversary. It seeks to induce, influence, or reinforce the perceptions, attitudes, reasoning, and behavior of foreign leaders, groups, and organizations in a manner favorable to friendly national and military objectives. It exploits the psychological vulnerabilities of hostile forces to create fear, confusion, and paralysis, thus undermining their morale and fighting spirit. There are strategic, operational, and tactical PSYOP, as described in Joint Publication 3.53, *Doctrine for Joint Psychological Operations* (5 September

2003). Strategic PSYOP consists of international activities conducted by US Government agencies primarily outside the military arena but which may use DOD assets. Operational PSYOP is conducted across the range of military operations, including during peacetime, in a defined operational area to promote the effectiveness of the joint force commander's campaigns and strategies. Tactical PSYOP is conducted in the area assigned to a tactical commander, for a range of military operations, to support the tactical mission. Psychological operations may occur across the spectrum of peace to conflict to war, integral to diplomacy, economic warfare, and military action, from negotiations and humanitarian assistance to counterterrorism. (Finkelstein, 2008, 17-8)

Memetics is not limited to military actions; it also is applicable to economic warfare and diplomacy. Of course, we are all very aware of the commercial ad as one of the most commonly experienced meme samples. Counter-Propaganda is a major goal of using memes:

[information warfare] involves actions executed to deliberately mislead the adversary's military decision makers about friendly military capabilities, intentions, and operations, thereby causing the adversary to take specific actions (or inactions) that will contribute to the accomplishment of the friendly force's mission. According to *Information Operations Roadmap*, DOD (30 Oct. 03), military deception should be one of the five core capabilities of IO and the value of military deception is intuitive. Counter-propaganda includes activities to identify and counter adversary propaganda and expose adversary's attempts to influence friendly populations and military forces' situational understanding. It focuses on efforts to negate, neutralize, diminish the effects of, or gain an advantage from foreign psychological operations or propaganda efforts. (Finkelstein, 2008, 18-9)

In contemporary times the main propaganda channel for some extremist groups is that of social networks from Facebook, Telegraph, Twitter, etc. Communications on these channels are often of a condensed form, neither prosaic nor of large bit size. Human propaganda communication mainly is conducted in audio, visual and tactile means. In a previous topic we discussed the work of Dr. John Norseen; the concept of 'Thought Injection' is a form of altering images, in the case of a terrorist suspect it is to change the ideation toward negativity through violent outlashes and replace that thought or semiotic with another non-violent image or ideal. In network communications, like a Social Network, which can easily also be a Terrorist Cell, there is the ideal of learning by simulating what others do; this is known as memetic learning, also used in video games, such as Shadow AI of *Killer Instinct*, which we see on a daily basis on Facebook or Twitter or any number of other social networks. Though this goes on all the time in all minds, it is when a meme is transferred from one mind by any means, that the memetic learning occurs, or imitation. Norseen wrote of the similarity of Though Injection with Memes:

Semiotic binding seems to work best when the brain is entrained between 7.83 Hz and 14 Hz, with special tunneling and neurochemical surges in the 9 to 10 Hz regime. The meditative Theta and modified Alpha-Theta states would appear to be the quiet zones where the ability to attend to internal mental representations can best be captured for reconstruction back through the efferent central nervous system pathways to show the world what floats in the mind. This delivery mechanism which brings forth creation back into the world in any number of newly reconfigured states (eolithic capacity) could be the semiotic description for the concepts in Richard Dawkins 1970's notion of 'The Building Blocks of Comprehension,' the Thought Memes. (Norseen, 1996)

Here Norseen, who is not alone is seeking to engineer memes for counter-terrorism (see below), specifically calls out the ideas of Richard Dawkins and his notion of 'memes'

Memetics has been a recent subject of interest as a new method for information exchange. In communities, memes have been studied to understand and enhance group learning. Richard Dawkins first defined memes as a unit of cultural transmission. Essentially, memes are ideas that evolve according to the same principles as biological evolution. Memetic learning works by transmitting units of cultural ideas or symbols from one mind to another. All ideas that exist within an individual's mind are examples of memes. Memes that are good at replicating leave more copies of themselves in minds. Examples of memes are catch phrases, musical themes, scientific ideas and sayings. In robotics, examples of memes are algorithms, observations, and instructions. (Truszkowski, 2014)

In another chapter on Reflexive Control, we discussed the concept, simulacrum (information packets), used by the Russians or Soviets to influence an adversary. A meme is a simulacrum, or, as the terminology is used in the

West, it is that of a 'semiotic' an image or idea; a simulacrum. In a later section we will learn how memes are used in robotic systems to learn through copying each other. The history of the idea of memes is a good starting point in understanding how memes could be both important to humans (animals) and machines.

In terms of understanding the relationship of memes to security, specifically counter-terrorism, Pech & Slade have studied the similar concept of re-wiring terrorists' thoughts or memes but without any kind of physical change to consciousness,. In Pech & Slade 2005, they bring forth the original context of Dawkins' meme, then apply it to security:

> Dawkins (1998), the original memeticist, saw memes as replicable and transmittable units of information that travel from mind to mind. The meme became "the unit of cultural inheritance" and was first coined in 1976. Wilkins (1998) in turn saw that the meme was a simple self-replicating packet of information and defined its two essential characteristics. First, the size of the meme was not fixed but could vary, and second the importance of the fidelity, or resistance to change, of the meme was critical to its survival. Dawkins (1998) viewed memes as self-selecting, and that "Individuals who are predisposed [psyop softening]… toward imitation are on a fast track that may have taken others a long time to build up" (Dawkins). The notion here is that memes not only transfer themselves from mind to mind, but also encourage replication through the imitation of behaviours individuals see as desirable, particularly in role models. (Pech & Slade 2005)

The meme is a viral element in communications theory; it's first criteria to be a meme is that it is immune to large alteration, it has high formal fidelity, but from this fidelity comes an effect where the meme takes on a life of its own, becoming toxic memes, like a virus, in a computer, replicating and promoting further damage:

> Pech's (2003, p. 61) statement "the attachment of such labels confers a communicable mantle upon the act of violence and takes the event in question to a level where copying behaviors are triggered" indicates that if such memes are allowed to exist and replicate then further acts of violence can be expected. (Pech & Slade, 2005, 48)

One could see the security threat this could pose to security personnel with access to media, particularly social media. The emergent or viral nature of memes is discussed:

> Dawkins (1998, p. 306) has argued that "a mind can become prepared by certain memes to be receptive to particular other memes" [suggestion cascade]. Clark (1997) describes the concept of emergence, which has relevance to the clustering effect of like memes and the existence of the memeplex, or complex of memes, as coined by Dawkins (1998, p. 306). Clark (1997, p. 74) divided the phenomenon of emergence into two distinct categories. The first, direct emergence, occurs where the properties and relations between individual elements primarily take on a life of their own and environmental elements have only background influence. Clark's notion of indirect emergence describes the predominant influence of the environment in triggering behaviors both individual and collective. (Pech & Slade, 2005, 48-9)

Memes can group up and form connections; this is referred to as a Memeplex, a pool of options or adaptations of the original meme, but appealing or having resonance with an audience. The viralness or emergence has two modes: direct (non-environment, hypnotic), indirect emergence. Out of the memeplex, like in nature, a virus or toxic adaptation may develop, these memes that cause people to act destructively are known as toxic memes:

> A toxic meme can be described as a self-replicating packet of influential information communicating a message of empathy that generally runs counter to the values and norms of society or which is in conflict with the needs and expectations of that society. Such memes, it may be argued, have the potential to threaten the very social fabric itself. (Pech & Slade, 2005, 50)

The lifecycle of a meme has three distinct stages (Pech & Slade 2005): a target site (a mind), fidelity (self-replication structural consistency), and resonance within the target to act:

> Meme replication requires three significant elements. First, a person must be susceptible to the message within the meme. They must be open to the intent of the message or open to the form in which the message is communicated.

Second, the meme must possess fidelity. It must be immune to change that may be effected upon it by the different cultures, education, and socialization that makes up the world views

of potential hosts. Without such fidelity the message held within the meme will change or dissipate as it replicates from mind to mind; this concept has been provided by Dawkins (1976) and Wilkins (1998).

Third, the meme must resonate with some intrinsic, emotion or value already possessed by, or appealing to, the host. A meme, such as a terror meme, can only transmit its existence through the behaviors of an empathetic host. In such a host, the message in the meme may not necessarily be consciously supported at the outset. However, it may resonate through a variety of emotions and empathetic reactions until it is consciously accepted and its resultant behavior demonstrated in acts replicating the violence buried within the message. This concept has been partially articulated by Dawkins (1998). These fundamental concepts driving the nature of the meme have been modeled by Pech and Slade (2004) within the context of re-engineering organizational behavior and have been adapted to counter mimicked acts of terrorism in Figure 1. (Pech & Slade, 2005, 50)

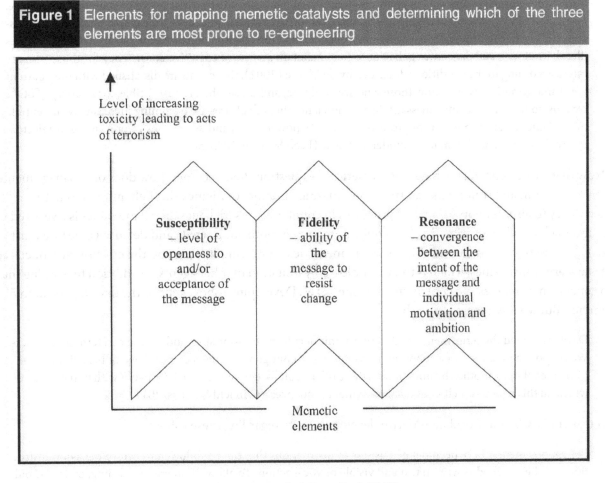

Figure 1 Elements for mapping memetic catalysts and determining which of the three elements are most prone to re-engineering

(The 3 stages of a Meme, Pech 2003)

The argument behind being able to target a receptive resonant chamber of a human mind involves a process of scripting, not unlike coding algorithms in silicon-based hardware, researchers actually refer to it as a meme algorithm.

According to Huesmann (1986) script theory proposes that violence observed in the mass media, provides aggressive scripts that vicariously define situations and guide future behavior for receptive individuals. The risk for both society and the individual, under script theory, is that an individual may select a script populated by toxic memes, analogize this to a given situation, and adopt the role provided. (Pech & Slade, 2005, 54)

The equivalent, in a human community, is that of a Trojan Horse attack:

Donald explains the impact that a culturally derived memory field, stored externally from the individual's consciousness and which describes knowledge, values, and information, can have on the mind. He refers to this as a cerebral Trojan Horse, which he argues can, to an extraordinary degree, make the human mind externally programmable. These external programmes can create deliberately engineered experiences [which we study in Reflexive Control and Perception Management]. The commercial world has manufactured vicarious experiences to such an extent that some people may have difficulty differentiating between what is real and what is not. Cultural influence can have similar effects and provide similar scripts. (Pech & Slade, 2005, 56)

Below we will see the direct security vulnerabilities and viral growth of memes implementation by terrorists and counter-terrorist activities to shape warfare to one's advantage; primarily aimed at destabilizing an adversary, preceding an invasion.

This is based in studies in the US from the 1950s (Festinger 1957), who studied cognitive dissonance which is a prime research topic in western influence operations.

> The phenomenon of indirect emergence from such an externally programmed and scripted environment sees the act of terrorism adopted as an appropriate means of managing the terrorist's state of cognitive dissonance. Festinger's (1957) version of cognitive dissonance describes a state where more time is spent rationalizing misbehaviors rather than actually engaging in rational action. The resulting terror meme rationalizes and justifies illegal, irrational, and dangerous behavior to help maintain a sense of cognitive consistency for those who are raised according to the conditions described by de Mause (2002), those who are dissatisfied with their current government/authority structure, those who are easily led, and those who are susceptible, for a variety of other reasons, to the terror meme's message. In addition a number of cultures are becoming increasingly susceptible to fundamentalism as a means of protecting minority power bases, and as a means of preventing or rejecting external "interference" from more moderate states. (Pech & Slade, 2005, 56)

Now that we understand the basics of memetics the question then becomes, how does one manage memetics? Given that automated troll farms can spew out amazing amounts of memes through automation, it is necessary for a military to also develop automated processes in counter-adversarial operations; memetics is a very red versus blue approach in cybersecurity. To get to full automation of both attack (red) and defense (blue) we must have a systems representation of memes. This is where memetic engineering steps in and the creation of artificial agents that can learn from memes, which is to say they learn by imitation of other agents. In addition to learning they can also generate new memes and contribute to memeplexes. Developing robot agents is the first step to automation of memetics. But what is a meme to a robot?

> Dawkins coined the term 'meme' to describe a unit of cultural transmission, and we use this terminology here. We propose a definition of a robot meme as follows: a contiguous sequence or package of behaviours copied from one robot to another, by imitation. In the artificial culture lab we 'seed' each Copybot with initial behaviors which, in this paper, are self-contained movement sequences. (Winfield & Erbas, 2011)

A team of NASA and Lockheed-Martin developers write regarding these robots:

> For robots, memes have been defined as sets of instructions that can be followed to evolve behavior. Instructions can be encoded as written text and visible or vocal action. To allow for memetic learning, memes should also include observations of the environment. A robot that is able to observe and intelligently imitate the behavior of others is able to participate in memetic learning. In order to perform intelligent imitation, a robot needs to be able to process memetic information. This process involves evaluating models, examples, and patterns which the robot observes. In addition, the robot is expected to analytically compare its current knowledge to the new information it is observing.
>
> A robot has modified its individual knowledge base when it learns a new meme. Each robot is expected to evaluate active memes in the community knowledge base for strengths and weaknesses when deciding whether to learn them. It can be expected that each individual robot will benefit from the aggregation of other robots which are also participating in memetic learning. When the community knowledge-base and size expands, there is a larger selection of memes which can be evaluated and learned. With a larger community knowledge base, a robot has a larger selection of memes to modify to develop novel memes. All individuals capable of participating in memetic learning are able to generate new memes. Also, individuals who are able to broadcast observations are capable of generating new memes.

The memes that are in the knowledge base of a robot are in constant competition with all other memes in the meme pool. The meme pool is the collection of all existing memes that are accessible to the other individuals in the community. An individual robot may develop new memes that become candidates for imitation in the community meme pool. The community meme pool increases with the addition of novel memes generated by individual robots in the community. The connection between an individual knowledge base and the community meme pool is similar to the structure of a distributed cloud network. A distributed cloud network is structured so that each individual is connected to the cloud where they can access the knowledge bases of others in the community pool. Individuals will be able to quickly access, process, and analyze the collective knowledge within the cloud (Truszkowski, 2014).

So, we have found that in memetic learning in robot groups there is a common knowledge base; the memes add to the knowledge base, there is selection for adaptation by the robotic agents and this occurs in a cloud network (non-local storage/action). Looking ahead in 2014 the team envisions developing meme agents, where the memes themselves are intelligent.

> An area for future investigation is to modify the meme's structure so that the memes themselves are intelligent. Memes could be encapsulated with intelligent software, similar to a mobile agent, that can make the meme an active instead of a passive entity. Active memes could monitor a robot's state, listen to communications between robots or look at other memes that are being passed between robots to determine if it may be needed. If so, the meme could then push itself to a robot that needs it or insert itself into the active reasoning being done by the host robot. Memes that are not needed after a period of time could decay and destroy themselves if they are outdated or no longer needed. This could help limit the proliferation of memes in a system. Active memes could also automatically update themselves based on changes in the environment and observed learning in the robot host (e.g., seeking protection when a sandstorm is forecasted). They could also seek out similar memes and combine with them to form better memes, or even use techniques like genetic programming to improve or transform themselves into something new. This could speed up the evolution of new memes.

> An intelligent and mobile meme would have to be lightweight so it could easily move between robots without having a large communications overhead. A large number of heavy weight memes being sent between robots over a limited bandwidth network, such as might be on mars, could overload the network. Memes could also use swarming or other behaviors to increase their individual impact and to quickly react to new situations a robot may encounter where there is no one meme that has all of the information. Swarming could also help to keep individual memes small since the swarm would provide all of the needed knowledge. Since each situation could be different, new swarms would be spawned based on the situation at hand. An additional area which requires further investigation is the implementation of such a communication and analytical model to communities (Wang, 2008).

> There are unknowns regarding future requirements and specifications for a group of robots to be fitted with the intelligence to perform memetic learning. The communication structure of modern systems may be challenged and need to be modified to allow future systems to be capable of implementing this technology. (Truszkowski, 2014)

Memetic Learning is a sub-discipline within Genetic Programming or Algorithms, which are developed in Defense applications, and is used in automated systems that also perform self-evaluation and modification of their own programs based on fitness measurements similar to organic genes; hence the name, genetic programming. Hougen explains the derivation:

> Memetic learning algorithms are related to genetic algorithms in the form that solutions may take. As with standard genetic algorithms, one defines possible solutions as sequences of discrete values, typically binary strings. For genetic algorithms, each entry in the sequence is considered a gene, whereas with memetic learning algorithms, each entry in the sequence is a meme. The possible values for that entry are the alleles. Learning in memetic learning algorithms proceeds as follows: A population of individuals with random alleles for each meme is constructed and tested on the task. Individuals observe their own overall fitness values and those of the other individuals in the population. Further they observe the partial fitness values of the partial candidate solutions that they are able to identify, both for themselves and for the others. They then replace their memes for those portions of the solution for which they have low fitness values, using imitation. (Hougen et al, 2003, 4-5)

The robotic agents using fitness measures are able to tell if their solution to a problem is of a higher or lower value; thereby they can then imitate the higher fitness valued solutions of other agents. In Learning there are two modes; learning by direct experience and learning by imitation, the key variable here in determining the type of learning is interaction with the environment, direct experience is environmental interaction learning, but imitation leaves out the environment for direct copying:

.3.1.3 MEMETIC LEARNING ALGORITHMS

For memetic learning algorithms, we use a simple gene-splicing method. As with the GA, each policy table is encoded as a one-dimensional chromosome, where each allele at each locus is a left or right action decision. The population, again, is a collection of policy tables and the population size is set again at 50. However, rather than using a selection mechanism to generate new individuals for successive generations, we retain all individuals—generations are marked by changes *learned* by individuals. Each individual in the population is given a single trial. Based on that trial, individuals learn in up to two ways. First, all individuals learn by direct experience. Second, if an individual fails, it learns by imitation.

> **Learning by direct experience.** As with reinforcement learning, each policy table entry has associated with it a score that reflects our confidence in that action and each score has associated with it an eligibility value. The score and eligibility values are updated during and after each trial using Equations 1, 2, and 3.

> **Learning by imitation.** If an individual fails, it also learns by imitation by considering each of its loci separately. For each locus, the probability that the current allele is retained is equal to $max(s; 0)$. For alleles that are not retained, a replacement allele is chosen for that locus using proportional probability selection based on the scores of all of the alleles for all individuals for that locus. (Hougen et al, 2003, 8-9)

The framework for developing automated memes is presented by University of Arizona researchers, working for the Office of Naval Research (award #N00014-18-1-2761), in their project "memeBot," which is able to automatically read tweets and generate memes from those tweets, so it would not be difficult to aggregate sentiment and produce both adverse and averse effects through those memes on social networks. Below is a flow diagram for how the automated memes are produced, either to fight terrorism or to promote it:

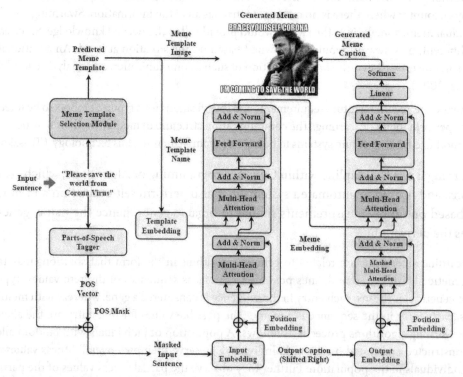

Figure 3: memeBot - model architecture. For a given input sentence, a meme is created by combining the meme image selected by the template selection module and the meme caption generated by the caption generation transformer.

(Sadasivam, 2020, 3)

Researchers explain their project and what it can accomplish:

> We have presented memeBot, an end-to-end architecture that can automatically generate a meme for a given sentence. MemeBot is composed of two components, a module to select a meme template and an encoder-decoder to generate a meme caption. The model is trained on a meme caption dataset to maximize the likelihood of selecting a template given a caption and to maximize the likelihood of generating a meme caption given the input sentence and the meme template. Automatic evaluation on meme caption test data and human evaluation scores on Twitter data show promising performance in generating an image for sentences in online social interaction. (Sadasivam, 2020, 9)

Now that we have seen what memes are and how they emerge in networked groups and can even be automated into cyber agents it is time to look into a case study of the use of memes to create terrorists by studying the Boogaloo movement in the United States and their use of memes to propagate their call for armed insurrection to start a new civil war.

BOOGALOO BOMBS

> Boogaloo Goal: The hope of these militants is to incite violence sufficient for society to betray the American civic tradition by forcing immense violence to protect it [Nazi accelerationism, see Chapter 1 Black International]. (Goldenberg et al, 2020c)

At protests in Seattle in 2020 I first directly encountered members of the Boogaloo Bois as they refer to themselves, usually young white males from the suburbs that have an automatic weapon fetish or are exorcising some PTSD from previous US military experience leaving them with wounded heads who, whether we like to admit it or not, are susceptible to outside influencing (see below), making PTSD veterans easy prey for adversarial information operations such as those conducted on public social media. For the first time in my long history of attending leftist protests I witnessed strange groups of armed men wearing Hawaiian shirts parading around as 'security' for the protesters. Eventually, the open display of weapons resulted in at least one fatality, when an African American teenager was gunned down after joy-riding in a stolen vehicle of one of the protestors in an apparent miscommunication which led to lethal force being deployed by untrained amateurs. The Boogaloo Bois were also responsible for overt terrorist attacks, where a US Military member gunned down a Federal Protective Services officer and wounded another in a drive-by ambush; other terrorist related arrests of Boogaloo Bois could be mentioned here but we continue.

In a Brookings Institute report the Boogaloo is described:

> In their willingness to carry out attacks against law enforcement personnel to incite what they consider an imminent civil war, the Boogaloo movement poses a serious threat to police. The movement has its origins online, and its adherents have skillfully used memes to incite violent insurrection and terror against the government and law enforcement. Especially widespread on Facebook and Instagram, Boogaloo enthusiasts share instructions for explosives and 3-D printed firearms, distribute illegal firearms modifications, lead users into encrypted messaging systems, distribute violent propaganda, and target their recruitment efforts towards active and former military personnel. The movement is a case study in how we still do not entirely understand how radicalization occurs in the digital domain. (Goldenberg et al, 2020c)

The boogaloo catchphrase, or meme, is based on the 1984 movie sequel _Breakin' 2: Electric Boogaloo,_ which critics panned as a shockingly unoriginal, near-mirror copy of the original film. As adopted by meme culture, the term is often used by libertarians, gun enthusiasts, and anarchists to describe an uprising against the government or left-wing political opponents that is a near-mirror copy, or sequel to, the American Civil War. While the reference has been around for years, recent iterations have caught on and spread quickly over the past few months. While many still use the boogaloo meme jokingly, an increasing number of people employ the phrase to incite an apocalyptic confrontation with law enforcement and government officials or to provoke ethnic warfare. (Goldenberg & Finkelstein, 2020b)

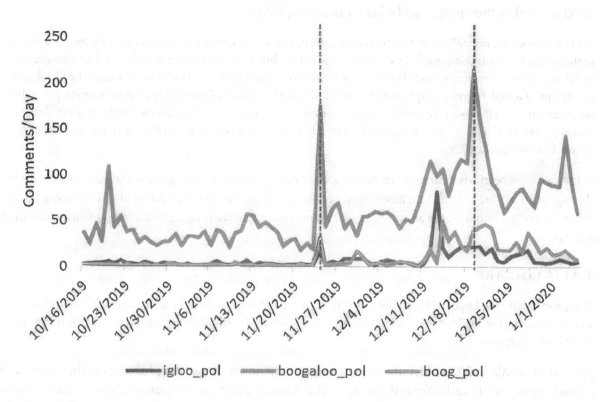

Fig 2. Trend analysis on 4chan's /pol/, a radical and trend setting Web community, shows ramping and spikes in the frequency of "Boogaloo" comments and synonyms such as "igloo" and "boog." Two of the changepoints our algorithms detected on "boogaloo" (red line) occur within 24 hours to two key events: the "Whiskey Warrior" standoff and the impeachment of Donald Trump.

Language on 4chan seems to associate the term to "racewar" and more coded conspiracies such as "dotr," or <u>day of the rope</u>, a fantasy to instigate a civil war and murder race traitors. These acts would presumably be accomplished by "rwds," a code for Right Wing Death Squads, such as the "atomwaffen" division, a neo-Nazi domestic terror organization. Other coded associations such as "shtf" stand for "shit hits the fan," a slang for the end of civilization, and a term that appears near topics of doomsday preparation, "ammo" and "stockpile." (Goldenberg & Finkelstein 2020b)

MILITARY AND VETERAN SUSCEPTIBILITY:

Among the boogalois I have engaged with there is a strong military aspect to their organizing, which indeed if you are seeking to fight a civil war then you would be engaged in military contexts. This puts veterans at risk of recruitment as most boogalois bois have no military experience or even basic gun training, at least among those I have encountered.

Furthermore, the meme's emphasis on military language and culture poses a specific risk to military communities due to the similar thematic structure, fraternal organization, and reward incentives. (Goldenberg & Finkelstein 2020b)

The military community, in particular, may merit special consideration in risk evaluation and social-climate research because seditious memes are now tailored for infection among veterans and active service members. (Goldenberg & Finkelstein, 2020b)

The main threat from the boogaloo bois is to law enforcement. This is a congruent with attacks on neutral policing by far-right groups as a means to create a privileged legal group to do whatever it feels like doing to the underprivileged legal groups. By attacking the police, they seek to undermine community support for policing. Mind you, there are different models of policing; if they were seeking to end injustice in legal systems then why would they only attack soft targets dissociated with any history of legal or police injustice by any of the communities where they have engaged in actions; for instance there are no attacks in Minneapolis or Louisville. Yet, with such a threat, law enforcement is little equipped to rapidly adapt:

Memetic warfare is still very much a mystery to both policy makers and officials working within the American law enforcement community. In this ignorance, the worst actors amongst boogaloo groups possess a distinct advantage over government officials and law enforcement: They already realize that they are at war. Public servants cannot afford to remain ignorant of this subject because as sites, followers and activists grow in number, memes can reach a critical threshold and tipping point, beyond which they can suddenly saturate and mainstream across entire cultures. (Goldenberg & Finkelstein, 2020b)

Overall, there is a missing link in the defense against threats such as this as noted by Ascott:

The West is desperately lagging in its memetic capability. US Marine Corps Major Michael B. Prosser proposed that NATO open a meme warfare center. In his 2006 thesis, he looked to Dawkins's ideas of memes as units of cultural transmission that held the potential to 'be used like medicine to inoculate the enemy and generate popular support.' He noted that information operations, psychological operations and strategic communications weren't using memes effectively. In the following decade, NATO never did open a meme warfare center, but the idea didn't go away and is now starting to gain traction again. (Ascott, 2020)

One way to counteract Memetic warfare is to set up surveillance of memes using time series analysis:

Time series analysis can signal an extremism climate and facilitate a "weather station" for trends in extremism on a meme-by-meme basis. Such a station is needed to create alerts and notifications which can be adapted for the use of information vaccines, strategic counter messaging, and campaigns for better moderation. (Goldenberg & Finkelstein, 2020b)

Along with surveillance is the need for quick adaptation, not just in communications:

…respond adaptively, and strategize communications during sensitive domestic operations. This is especially crucial because the conspiracy is preparing a viral-social media environment to instigate an uprising in response to missteps and police violence during these operations in order to threaten security on a national scale. (Goldenberg & Finkelstein, 2020b)

The importance of early warning with memetic warfare is highlighted with the swarming nature of memetic warfare and learning in animals. Very quickly a cascade effect can emerge with swarms programmed by Memes on social networks, one example of this is the Whiskey Warrior event:

Just as swarming insects elicit signals that can recruit entire colonies to converge on either enemy or prey rapidly, the "Whiskey Warrior" event, on November 24th in New York, demonstrates how the boogaloo meme can tactically alarm recruit followers to simultaneously deploy en masse in both cyber, and, potentially, real-world domains. When Alexander Booth posted images and videos of an ongoing standoff with police on his pro-gun Instagram handle "Whiskey Warrior 556," the former infantryman appeared in full camo and body armor with a knife clipped to his chest. Booth claimed the officers were employing red flag laws to strip him of munitions and posted memes on social media to merchandise the standoff specifically as a "boogaloo" triggering moment. These posted memes, with powerful ingroup signaling, immediately went viral on the chans and amongst several extreme boogaloo sites and right-wing militia groups on social media. From this point, followers began to obstruct police operations through targeted phone calls and online campaigns and incited armed resistance from social media, and the posts even succeeded in attracting one dedicated follower who claimed to be Facebook streaming from the scene of the standoff itself. Though Booth's Instagram account only held several thousand followers at the start of the event, it boasted over 130,000 by the time the standoff ended. (Goldenberg & Finkelstein, 2020b)

Martyrdom, memes and motivation: as shared narrative grows in the militia-sphere, traces of an underlying shared-information network emerges. (Goldenberg et al, 2020c, 7)

The convergence of martyr episodes, revenge attacks, terror tactics, romanticizing terrorists and terrorist movements, and group-level coordinated behaviors now appear in highly visible real-world events. This suggests a shared identity and shared narrative in the Militia-sphere. But do these groups and individuals connect through these events in less-tangible networks on social media? (Goldenberg et al, 2020c, 15)

While still preliminary, this introduces concerns that shared narratives like martyrdom may connect distributed, militia-oriented users across mainstream and fringe networks. (Goldenberg et al, 2020c, 9)

Analysis we gathered on "Bot Sentinel," and "Hoaxy," publicly available resources for charting bot activity support this possibility. Remarkably, we find that both WWG1WGA and QAnon hashtags are often among the top most frequently tweeted hashtags by trollbot accounts on Twitter (appendix figure 5) and networks that promote these hashtags are high in bot-like participation (appendix figure 6). As Q conspiracy is becoming more explicitly militant (appendix figure 7) future research must seek to determine how these underlying causes differentially contribute to the popularization of seditious conspiracy (Goldenberg et al, 2020c, 11)

In a methodology that is similar to that as used by the Black Internationals policy of infiltration and intoxication the boogaloos take on a guise that is hard to pin down to far-right extremes:

The boogaloo won't present itself as either Trump-based, right wing, or white-supremacist ideology, with any one set of predictable political grievances. These events suggest that the boogaloo seeks to co-opt several grievances, across several political and racial spectrums into a single, monolithic and anti-government mob with chilling new tactical and technological capacities. (Goldenberg et al, 2020c)

Religious ideas of matryrdom are also incorporated into the boogaloo bois context. Many see themselves as 'Last of the Mohican' types, which using reinforcement such as memes is easy to program into someone with enough repetition.

Aaron Swenson, a boogaloo enthusiast posted #hisnamewasduncan over a selfie featuring weapons and body armor on Facebook after Lemp's martyr episode on April 4th. On April 23rd, he live-streamed his revenge hunt on police in Texarkana. While Swenson was soon arrested after an hours-long chase, for inciting terror and possession of illegal firearms, these tactics portend a worrying evolution of real world/virtual violence in the Militia-sphere, akin to the live streaming of ISIS beheadings and other innovative uses of media by hybrid and distributed sporadic terror groups. Martyr narratives and revenge killings are likely to continue to shape a shared identity among users in these groups.

In addition to martyr myths and revenge killings, more familiar methods of terror for violent organizations include the use of bombs and explosives. On May 4th, Bradley Bunn, a militia enthusiast threatening militant violence against law enforcement for their role in enforcing quarantine restrictions, was arrested in his home in Colorado in possession of two one-pound containers with gunpowder for reloading .308 caliber cartridges and four pipe bombs. Bunn admitted outright that the murder of law enforcement was his goal; these materials were set to be used as a lethal trap for entry, just like the Lemp episode. (Goldenberg, 2020c, 7-8)

Martyr myths along with such 'apocalyptic' stereotypes such as a global pandemic serve to further derange the rational hold people have that are affected by memetic warfare. The connection with the anti-government QAnon movement and anti-lockdown protests during the pandemic are noted as cross-fertilization takes hold in a rich environment of grievances, real or imagined:

In the face of COVID-19, QAnon now witnesses massive growth and appears to militarize, like the boogaloo, with revolutionary and apocalyptic themes in a more militant and global mode of inciting revolt. QAnon conspiracies, such as "the Great Awakening" for instance, refer to a moment in which elites will be defeated and the truth will be revealed, and are often featured at anti-quarantine rallies. Other conspiracies suggest that a "new world order" now prepares to emerge under the tyranny of Bill Gates and George Soros, the Rothschilds, and other elites, who— through their vaccination attempts—seek to establish mind control, world domination, genocide, financial gain, or some combination of these.

The result is that the QAnon conspiracy now invites two modes of disinformation which converge on COVID-19 in dangerous ways. The first is anti-vaccination and anti-science disinformation about the virus itself as a weaponized plot. The second is increasing militarization in the conspiracy group which combines disinformation on COVID-19 with seditious themes that parallel the boogaloo. WWG1WGA, for instance, comprises a key QAnon slogan expanding to "where we go 1 we go all" and features with Great Awakening material and at reopen rallies both as an in-group cheer, but also as an all-at-once go signal, reminiscent of the boogaloo. Indeed, evidence of militarization in the QAnon conspiracy now abounds with references to a "Q-army" complete with military-style badges. (Goldenberg et al, 2020c, 10)

We should not be surprised that an image-based sensory input serves to have such a large 'hypnotic' effect on people. As the visual cortex is written of repeatedly by those involved in information warfare as the seat, specifically visual processing of images, of suggestibility or control.

BIBLIOGRAPHY:

APDC, (2009) Effects-based approach: is it still valid?. In Pathfinder Air Power Centre Bulletin Issue 109, April 2009

Ascott, T. (2020) How memes are becoming the new frontier of information warfare. in Australian Strategic Policy Institute online: https://www.aspistrategist.org.au/how-memes-are-becoming-the-new-frontier-of-information-warfare/ 19 Feb 2020

Backus, G., Bernard, M., Verzi, S., Bier, A., Glickman, M. (2010) Foundations to the Unified Psycho-Cognitive Engine. SANDIA REPORT SAND2010-6974 Unlimited Release October 2010 https://www.osti.gov/biblio/1008141

Backus, G., Glass, R. (2006) An Agent-Based Model Component to a Framework for the Analysis of Terrorist-Group Dynamics SANDIA REPORT SAND2006-0860P

Behzadan, V., Nourmohammadiy, A., Gunesz, M. and Yukselx, M. (2017) On Fighting Fire with Fire: Strategic Destabilization of Terrorist Networks. In ASONAM '17: Proceedings of the 2017 IEEE/ACM International

Conference on Advances in Social Networks Analysis and Mining 2017July 2017 Pages 1120–1127 https://doi.org/10.1145/3110025.3119404

Bernard, M. Glickman, M. (2006) Simulating Human Behavior for National Security Human Interactions. SANDIA REPORT SAND2006-7812 https://www.osti.gov/servlets/purl/900422

Djordjevich, D., Xavier, P., Bernard, M., Whetzel, Glickman, M., Verzi, S. (2008) Preparing for the Aftermath: Using Emotional Agents in GameBased Training for Disaster Response USDOE National Nuclear Security Administration (NNSA) DOI: 10.1109/CIG.2008.5035649 ·https://www.researchgate.net/publication/221157660

Emanuel, P., Walper, S., DiEuliis, D., Klein, N., Petro, J., Giordano, J (2019) Cyborg Soldier 2050: Human/Machine Fusion and the Implications for the Future of the DoD online: https://community.apan.org/wg/tradoc-g2/mad-scientist/m/articles-of-interest/300458/download

Epifanovskaya, L., Lakkaraju, K., Stites, M., Letchford, J., Reinhardt, J., Whetzel, J. (2018) Online Games for Studying Human Behavior. In book: Social Behavioral Modeling for Complex Systems (pp.387-406) https://www.osti.gov/servlets/purl/1470956

Finkelstein, R. (2008) A Memetics Compendium, prepared for the DARPA Task Order CA-FIN-3212-024-08 http://citeseerx.ist.psu.edu/viewdoc/summary?doi=10.1.1.731.4497

Finkelstein, R. (2008) Information Propogation, Impact & Persistence (InfoPip): Defining Memes, Briefing Report. DARPA Task Order CA-FIN-3212-024-08

Glickman, M., Whetzel, J., Basilico, J. (2010) Trainable Automated Forces. https://www.researchgate.net/publication/241970920_Trainable_automated_forces

Goldenberg, A., Finkelstein, J. (2020b) Cyber Swarming, Memetic Warfare and Viral Insurgency: How Domestic Militants Organize on Memes to Incite Violent Insurrection and Terror Against Government and Law Enforcement. in A Contagion and Ideology Report. Network Contagion Research Institute https://ncri.io/wp-content/uploads/NCRI-White-Paper-Memetic-Warfare.pdf

Goldenberg, A., Baumgartner, J., Farmer, J., Zannettou, S., Blackburn, J. (2020c) Covid-19, Conspiracy and Contagious Sedition: A Case Study on the Milita-Sphere. A Contagion and Ideology Report, Network Contagion Research Institute https://networkcontagion.us/wp-content/uploads/NCRI-White-Paper-COVID-19-Militia-Sphere-1-June-512pm.pdf

Hougen, D., Carmer, J., Woehrer, M. (2003) Memetic Learning: A Novel Learnings Method for Multi-Robot Systems. https://www.cs.ou.edu/~hougen/mrs2003.pdf

Margulies, P. (2016) Surveillance By Algorithm: The NSA, Computerized Intelligence Collection, and Human Rights. in Florida Law Review Volume 68 | Issue 4 Article 3 July 2016 https://scholarship.law.ufl.edu/cgi/viewcontent.cgi?article=1321&context=flr

Pech, R. & Slade, B. (2005) Imitative terrorism: A diagnostic framework for identifying catalysts and designing interventions. in Foresight · February 2005 DOI: 10.1108/14636680510581312

Nørgaard, K., & Linden-Vørnle, M. (2021). Cyborgs, Neuroweapons, and Network Command. Scandinavian Journal of Military Studies, 4(1), pp. 94–107. DOI: https://doi.org/10.31374/sjms.86

Sadasivam, A., Gunasekar, K., Davulcu, H., Yang, Y.(2020) memeBot: Towards Automatic Image Meme Generation Arizona State University, Tempe AZ, United States https://arxiv.org/abs/2004.14571

Togelius, J., Anderson, D. Stephenson, M., Salge, C., Levine, J. Renz, J. (2018) Deceptive Games https://arxiv.org/abs/1802.00048

Truszkowski, W., Rouff, C., Akhavannik, M. (2014) Memetic Engineering as a Basis for Learning in Robotic Communities in conference presentation: AIAA 2014-1323 Session: Intelligent Learning and Decision Making Published Online:10 Jan 2014 https://doi.org/10.2514/6.2014-1323

Whetzel, J., Abbot, R., Basilico, J., Glickman, M. (2010) Trainable Automated Forces Sandia National Laboratories Albuquerque, NM https://www.researchgate.net/publication/241970920_Trainable_automated_forces

Winfield, A., Erbas, M. (2011) On embodied memetic evolution and the emergence of behavioural traditions in Robots in Memetic Computing · December 2011 DOI: 10.1007/s12293-011-0063-x at: https://www.re-searchgate.net/publication/235277651

Xavier, P., Hart, B., Hart, D., Gayle, R., Oppel, F., Whetzel, J. (2017) Dante Agent Architecture for Force-On-Force Wargame Simulation and Training Sandia National Labs in AAAI Vol. 13 No. 1 (2017): Thirteenth Artificial Intelligence and Interactive Digital Entertainment Conference https://www.osti.gov/servlets/purl/1431956

CONCLUSION

DISCUSSION

"We kill people based on metadata."

– NSA Director General Hayden
quoted by Margulies 2016

The question of how to interpret knowledge is a good one, in this concluding discussion I present some final thoughts on what I have sought to document in this work: that neuroweapons are real and are being used in the world we live in today. That no longer is it necessary to have physical devices to surveille others, but it can be done using quantum entanglement non-invasively, including the ability to wirelessly affect the biology of others. Though there is ample documentation to show active development of neuroweapons that affect cognitive functioning of human beings and other mammals, the interpretation and attribution to who is culpable for violating biological weapons bans is not easy to prove incontrovertibly. My thesis in this work is that there is a totalitarian fascist entity, which may be part of a government or not, working to influence the world using neuroweapons and automating these neuroweapons using computer technology, which is to say creating unwilling and unknowing cyborgs under control of a small conspiratorial cell influenced by the ideals of the 4th Reich, whether knowingly or unknowingly, even among those doing this work, they themselves could be mere Manchurian Candidates controlled and influenced by an automated computer controller, which is the nightmare scenario, that the complex of combining neural control with computer AI could lead to even the highest levels of an organization under the control of that which they have built to control others. This may sound like a fanciful science fiction plot, but given the documented streams of research in this work, one cannot rule out this possibility, specifically the use of the Single Warrior model and genetic algorithms where the system can engineer itself according to it's calculated needs, whether those calculations are biased or not would not matter, and this is even more of a concern for systems that are automated in the defense sector with self-protection mechanisms. And if we want to engage in thought experiments, then we can also add the further complication of when this technology is being used, as it can be done using gravitational wave technology which is not limited to classical physics scale, but exists in the quantum world where conceptions of linear time are not relevant, this technology could even not be in use in the world today only, but could be from a not yet experienced future, that is to say, we could be under attack from a technology based in the future, from a very small number of technically advanced terrorists.

For those that have only encountered this information through conspiracy theories with very little supporting documentation it is a foregone conclusion that the "Government" is behind it. While there are ways that that is possible as discussed below, it would be wrong to jump to conclusions short of any real evidence that the NSA, CIA, GCHQ in the West is behind this, or that it is Russia or China behind this. This brings up the very important ideal of 'forensics' the ability to determine and back trace signals to their origins so that we can conclusively know who is sending what signal and how. Yet, though the government agencies are aware of this technology they have never revealed how they do their forensics, if they even do. Forensic capabilities should be a major initiative to defeat this kind of attack. In the absence of Forensics to back-trace the threat we do have countermeasures as developed by Dr. Persinger, which my work seeks to expand upon using gravitational fields to counter the incoming gravitational pertubations targeting a person. The fact that the government is aware of both this technology and how to counteract this technology but with zero countermeasures deployed is a damning indictment of the use of this technology by the same said governments and can be the only plausible explanation for both their coverup of this threat and lack of countermeasures to this threat, the simple fact is governments are using this technology for their own goals and don't want to lose this capability.

Usually, the discussion around this technology is put on some 'Deep State' within the government, which given the mass numbers of people supposedly involved in 'mind control' by conspiracy theorist versions of this technology is not that unthinkable of a conclusion-- it would take formal government agency approval to operate the thousands of supposed under cover agents targeting people. Rather, in this research we see that it does not take a large bureaucracy to control a large number of people, but could be a small cell with the right computational and radar gear, whether classical or quantum radar or computers, to achieve this project of influencing mass society on a global scale. I view such 'Deep State' explanations as disinformation produced by those using this technology for criminal purposes, blaming the government for criminality when detected which would be the instrument that would investigate such a grave criminal undertaking, thereby discrediting the authority that could bring this to an end-- other then the protections each individual has the right to develop for themselves without the government-- so that one experiencing a crime does not even trust the investigating authorities to report the crime. However, having said that could a criminal organization infiltrate the government and get away with using government resources to perpetrate this crime, or could an unforeseen situation allow the government to unwittingly allow this to happen using it's resources? That is possible. I provide a brief discussion here as to how that could happen, not to blame the government but to promote self-accounting within the government and self-auditing of resources to make sure that the government itself has not been turned into a botnet, when a computer is taken over to attack other computers.

The NSA leaks of Snowden conveyed a strong message regarding surveillance in the United States which was the knowledge that all American's 'metadata' is sucked up into NSA vaults for storage whenever they need to query that data for any investigation, which was denied to Congress by successive NSA directors. Many are not familiar with the rules regarding surveillance in a domestic context in the United States of America. One would not anticipate that if intelligence computers do not directly interface with a human they can conduct all manners of surveillance through fully automated processes. In an article by P. Margulies (2016) he discusses the legality of automated surveillance by the NSA. There is a difference between the NSA or other Intel agencies use of scanning compared to collection:

> Scanning involves the recurring inspection, usually by machine, of information from individuals, but it does not entail the storage of all the information by the scanning party. A private firm or government agency, respectively, can scan a user's email, as Google does with Gmail, or gain access to interchange points in the transmission of internet communications, as the U.S. government does pursuant to statute. For example, in scanning pursuant to Section 702 of the Foreign Intelligence Surveillance Act (FISA) Amendments Act, the NSA's machines gain access through a buffer, cache, or other device that temporarily stores transnational communications in the course of transmitting them to their destination. Scanning is by definition a process that allows machines to gain access to a huge volume of communications, the vast majority of which are substantively irrelevant. In the process of scanning, the machine selects material that is relevant and designates that material for collection and subsequent analysis. (Margulies, 2016, 1055)

Scanning is a constant endeavor and sucks in any data it can come across then using Machine Intelligence algorithms keywords can be extracted and other triangulations performed marking bits of information for collection. For an American citizen they cannot be scanned unless they are in interactions with a foreigner as explained:

> The U.S. government uses scanning internationally but not domestically. Both the Constitution and various statutes preclude the government from scanning the content of purely domestic communications—communications between two individuals located within the United States. However, under FISA, the U.S. government scans devices such as buffers and caches used in international communications—communications between a person in the United States and a person that government officials reasonably believe to be located overseas (Margulies, 2016, 1056)

We see clearly that by the law that if one is in a domestic context they cannot be scanned and collected but if in an international context they can be if it relates to some crime. Although, it should be pointed out that as part of the Anglo centric 5 Eyes Intelligence sharing programs that America is in, with the likes of the UK, Australia, NZ and Canada, that other nations can scan the other nations citizens. The question of what to do with scanned information and collected information as part of investigations comes up, there is a differentiation between directed searches of the data, and 'autonomous' searches, that being in the first case directed by human minds and hands and in the second that directed by machine algorithms with no direct human intervention. In the latter case, it is permissible for a machine to investigate on it's own so to speak:

> Having established that states can collect data in a targeted or "bulk" fashion, this Article next considers how intelligence analysts search through data. Searches can be either directed or autonomous. A directed search sorts through data using keywords or other discrete pieces of data, such as phone numbers, email addresses, URLs, or Internet Protocol addresses. Analysts choose the "selectors" or "identifiers" used, and the machine then dutifully searches the data available. Autonomous searches are different. This Article uses the term autonomous to connote searches in which machines do not merely execute searches formulated by humans but instead engage in calculations that closely resemble human reasoning. Commercial firms engage in autonomous searches under the broad rubric of "data mining." While there is no evidence that the government has engaged in data mining of domestically collected metadata, there are reasonable bases to infer that states, including the United States, use autonomous data mining techniques on transnational communications. (Margulies, 2016, 1061)

Here is the vulnerability of the government bureaucracy, that computers on their own can perform 'investigations' of citizens since they are not human and cannot violate laws regarding privacy since only a human can violate the law:

> A state-centric account would take the opposite tack. On this view, machine access alone, uncoupled from human access, has no deontological privacy implications. This view holds that only beings with a certain level of consciousness can intrude on privacy. Forms of life such as animals lack consciousness in the human sense and therefore cannot intrude. No one regards a dog or cat as intruding on his privacy, even if it saw him without clothes. A computer, on this reading, is similarly unintrusive, as long as it is uncoupled from human access. (Margulies, 2016, 1076)

Margulies notes elsewhere that machine searches could be used for such purposes as counterterrorism, counterespionage, antiproliferation of WMDs, cybersecurity, international crime, and sanctions evasion. (Margulies 2016, 1106). As the use of neuroweapons is directly related in all the documentation to 'counter-terrorism' is a possibility that this tech is used domestically? Could innocent American's be swept up in complex anti-terrorism programs bearing false-positives for terrorist that are fully automated and what happens if they are?

> Errors in machine searches may prompt further harms. For example, states might detain individuals because of outputs from machine searches. Prolonged detention based solely on a machine search would be arbitrary and hence a violation of the ICCPR. An individual could also be subject to counterterrorism sanctions because of a flawed search. In addition, flawed search results could affect targeting decisions by states engaged in armed conflicts with violent extremists. In a provocative and intentionally hyperbolic remark, former NSA (and CIA) Director General Michael Hayden asserted, "We kill people based on metadata." (Margulies, 2016, 178)

This is an alarming situation if real, and I want to emphasize that this only a possibility of over engineering, using the wrong tools for the job. It is hard to imagine a system such as a neuroweapons system operating within the government un-detected, even as part of a terrorism search, without someone raising a red flag. Yet, it is something that anyone looking at these issues objectively would have to consider. I myself do not personally believe the US Government is behind the domestically reported cases of neuro-cognitive attack, that are often labeled as 'Targeted-Individuals', it would simply be too hard to camouflage such a system inside a government comprised of different levels of oversight, someone would notice. It is important to understand the difference within the government regarding human centered investigating and automatic processes so that this situation can never arise.

It is the ambiguous, stealth and covert nature of this technology, especially considering one objective of the technology is that people can't tell their thoughts are not their own, that creates all this differing viewpoints as to what this technology is, who is responsible and how to stop it. It is in a criminals interest to create doubts about the agency of the crime, and yet we do see conspiracy theory after conspiracy theory putting a divide between citizens affected and the policing authorities. Which is a PSYOP within itself but one that helps the criminal achieve their goals and allows the exploitation of a target to grow and deepen as they no longer seek out supports from their government, and even to the extent of alienating them from friends and family using other intoxication techniques.

I have set out to document how this technology is real, but I draw no conclusions as to who is using this technology. Just as this technology is used for geo-political purposes it can also be used for geo-economic purposes, it could even be used by private financial interests to affect such things as sentiment in markets and intoxicating certain economic policies in favor of more lucrative policies for a small minority of capitalists. Without the development of both countermeasures and forensics, both of which are technically feasible and inexcusable for any nations defense not to develop, we may be waiting a long time to see who is ultimately responsible. One final point is that there may very well be multiple neuroweapons systems at work in the world, that with proliferation in weapons we will also see many actors engaging with this technology and thus we cannot provide an rationalizaiton for any one person's experiences which may be very different from others depending on their attackers system and motivations. Those that have experienced this crime, should be public about it and share their experiences so that others may learn as countermeasures and forensics are being developed outside of government, since it seems government is not willing to compromise their own abilities in terms of engaging in 'cold' war with other governments.

Bibliography

Margulies, P. (2016) Surveillance By Algorithm: The NSA, Computerized Intelligence Collection, and Human Rights. in Florida Law Review Volume 68 | Issue 4 Article 3 July 2016 https://scholarship.law.ufl.edu/cgi/viewcontent.cgi?article=1321&context=flr